Commercial Banking

THE MANAGEMENT OF RISK

4th Edition

JAMES W. KOLARI

Chase Professor of Finance

Texas A&M University

BENTON E. GUP

Professor Emeritus

University of Alabama

Textbook Media Press

The Quality Instructors Expect
At Prices Students Can Afford

Replacing Oligarch Textbooks Since 2004

For more information, contact

Textbook Media Press
1808 Dayton Avenue
Saint Paul, MN 55104

Or you can visit our Internet site at

http://www.textbookmedia.com

or write

info@textbookmedia.com

For permission to use material from this text or product, submit a request online at info@textbookmedia.com

Commercial Banking: The Management of Risk 4e

Kolari-Gup

13 Digit ISBN: 978-0-9969962-4-2

10 Digit ISBN: 0-9969962-4-9

Textbook Media Press is a Minnesota-based educational publisher.

We deliver textbooks and supplements with the quality instructors expect, while providing students with media options at uniquely affordable prices.

All our publications are made in the U.S.A.

Dedication

Kolari—To Karie and Wes

Gup—To Jean, Lincoln, Andrew and Carol, Jeremy and Elise

Brief Table of Contents

Detailed Table of Contents

PREFACE

Charles Darwin is best known for the concept of survival of the fittest. Although Darwin wrote about animals, the same concept can be applied to business corporations, including banks. The environment in which banks operate changes continuously. Three major changes are new laws, new technology, and globalization. In this regard, the Dodd-Frank Act, Basel capital rules, Financial Services Modernization Act, growth of derivatives, unbundling of financial services, cybersecurity, and large number of foreign-owned financial holding companies in the United States are a few examples of changes. Some obvious consequences of these changes are the consolidation and convergence of financial services. Another consequence is that an increasing number of financial services are being offered on the Internet. And internationally, we see more emphasis on harmonizing bank regulations in an attempt to regulate large complex financial organizations, prevent system-wide banking collapses, and manage other issues. The fourth edition of this book reflects these and other changes that have occurred in banking in recent years. Our goal is to equip students with the knowledge and skills needed to apply for good jobs in the banking industry.

A central theme of this book focuses on bank management as the management of risk. Bankers take risks in order to make a profit. Due to dynamic changes in the banking environment, the risks in banking require competent management to attain opportunities for growth and profits. For this reason, the management of risk is the central theme of our book, including credit risk, liquidity risk, investment risk, capital risk, derivatives risk, and more. This fourth edition is updated to cover the 2008-2009 financial crisis that severely challenged the banking industry, especially large money center banks. A number of legal and regulatory changes emerged from the crisis that we cover in this new edition. Many changes have occurred in banking over the past decade, and the pace of change seems to be accelerating. Banks are innovating new electronic financial services and developing customized services to meet the convenience and needs of their customers. More than ever before, it is essential that the industry attract well-educated employees that are able to learn and grow with the future.

Organization of the Text

The book is divided into five parts.

Part 1: Introduction explains what banks are and the functions they perform. It also delves into the major laws that have shaped our financial structure in the past and in the future. Finally, it explains how to evaluate the financial performance of a bank.

Part 2: Asset/Liability Management examines the factors that affect the value of a bank and techniques for managing that value, including the use of financial derivatives.

Part 3: Investment, Lending, and Liquidity Management is concerned with the asset side of the balance sheet, which involves lending, investment, and liquidity management. Because banks make most of their profit from lending, we examine their principal lending activities to businesses and individuals. Also, banks invest a sizeable portion of their assets in various investment securities, which we discuss. Both lending and investment activities have liquidity implications to the bank that must be effectively managed.

Part 4: Capital, Liabilities, and Off-Balance-Sheet Management focuses on the right side of the balance sheet, which consists of bank capital and bank liabilities. These are the sources of funds that banks use to finance loans and investments. Banks also make extensive use of off-balance-sheet activities to service customer needs.

Part 5: Domestic and International Financial Services overviews the wide array of financial services offered by commercial banks nowadays. Under laws passed in 1999, banks can do anything financial, including various securities and insurance services. These chapters help students to better grasp the many different careers that exist in the banking industry both domestically and internationally.

Acknowledgements

We want to express our gratitude to a number of individuals who, through their comments and suggestions, helped us improve the quality of previous editions.

James Barth *Auburn University*
M. E. Bond *University of Memphis*
Ben Branch *University of Massachusetts–Amherst*
Conrad Ciccotello *Georgia Institute of Technology*
Steven Dennis *Ball State University*
David Ely *San Diego State University*
Joseph Finnerty *University of Illinois at Champaign –Urbana*
Donald Fraser *Texas A&M University*
Anne Gleason *University of Central Oklahoma*
Jack Griggs *Abilene Christian University*
Alan Grunewald *Michigan State University*
Donald Hunkins *Northwood University*
William Jackson *University of North Carolina*
James Kehr *Miami University*
Kenneth Kopecky *Temple University*
Gary Koppenhaver *University of Iowa*
Laureano J.Martinez *Florida International University*
Donald Mullineaux *University of Kentucky*
Manferd Peterson *University of Nebraska–Lincoln*
Rose Prasad *Central Michigan University*
James Ross *Radford University*
Robert Schweitzer *University of Delaware*
David Schauer *University of Texas–El Paso*
Sherrill Shaffer *University of Wyoming*
Suresh Srivastava *University of Alaska*
Harold Thiewes *Minnesota State University–Mankato*
Edward Waller *University of Houston–Clear Lake*
Larry White East Tennessee State University
Bob Wood, Jr. *Tennessee Tech University*

James W. Kolari

Professor Kolari is the Director of the Commercial Banking Program in the Department of Finance at Texas A&M University. He has taught financial institutions and markets classes there since 1980 and been active in international education, consulting, and executive education. Receiving a PhD in Finance from Arizona Station University in 1980, he today holds the JP Morgan Chase Professorship in Finance in the Mays Business School. In 1986 he was a Fulbright Scholar at the University of Helsinki and he Bank of Finland. He has served as a Visiting Scholar at the Federal Reserve Bank of Chicago in 1982-1983, Senior Research Fellow at the Swedish School of Business and Economics (Hanken), Finland, and Faculty Fellow with the Mortgage Bankers Association of America, in addition to being a consultant to the U.S. Small Business Administration, American Bankers Association, Independent Bankers Association of America, and numerous banks and other organizations. He has worked as an advisor on the North American Free Trade Agreement for the State of Texas, consultant for the Mexican government in financing technology, and member of the Academy of Sciences for Higher Education in Russia. With over 100 articles published in refereed journals, numerous other papers and monographs, 15 co-authored books, and over 100 competitive papers presented at academic conferences, he ranks in the top 1-2 percent of finance scholars in the United States, according to recently published guides of research productivity among finance professors. His papers have appeared in such domestic and international journals as the *Journal of Finance, Journal of Business, Review of Financial Studies, Review of Economics and Statistics, Journal of Money, Credit and Banking, Journal of Banking and Finance, Journal of Financial Research, Real Estate Economics, Journal of International Money and Finance, and the Scandinavian Journal of Economics.* Papers in Russian, Finnish, Dutch, Italian, and Spanish have appeared outside of the United States. He is a co-author of leading college textbooks in introductory business and commercial banking courses.

Benton E. Gup

Dr. Benton E. Gup has a broad background in finance. His undergraduate and graduate degrees are from the University of Cincinnati. After receiving his Ph.D. in economics, he served as a staff economist for the Federal Reserve Bank of Cleveland. He recently retired from the University of Alabama where he held the Robert Hunt Cochrane/Alabama Bankers Association Chair of Banking at the University of Alabama, Tuscaloosa, Alabama, U.S.A. He also held banking chairs at the University of Virginia and the University of Tulsa. He worked in bank research for the Office of the Comptroller of the Currency while on sabbatical.

He is an internationally known lecturer in executive development and graduate programs in Australia (University of Melbourne, University of Technology, Sydney, Monash University, Melbourne), New Zealand (University of Auckland), Peru (University of Lima), and South Africa (Graduate School of Business Leadership). He has been a visiting researcher at the Bank of Japan, and at Macquarie University, Sydney, Australia. Finally, he lectured in South America, Europe, and North Africa for the U.S. Department of State, and served as a consultant to the IMF in Uruguay.

Dr. Gup is the author or editor of the following books: *Banking and Financial Institutions: A Guide for Directors, Investors, and Counterparties (2011), The Valuation Handbook: Valuation Techniques from Today's Top Practitioners* (with Rawley Thomas, (2010), *Handbook for Directors of Financial Institutions (2008); Corporate Governance in Banking: A Global Perspective; Money Laundering, Financing Terrorism, and Suspicious Activity (2007), Capital Market, Globalization, and Economic Development (2005); Commercial Banking: The Management of Risk, 3rd. ed.*, (with J. Kolari, 2005);*The New Basel Capital Accord (2004); Too-Big-To-Fail: Policies and Practices in Government Bailouts (2004); Investing Online (2003); The Future of Banking (2003); Megamergers in a Global Economy - Causes and Consequences (2002); The New Financial Architecture: Banking Regulation in the 21st Century (2000); Commercial Bank Management, 2nd ed.* (with D. Fraser and J. Kolari); *International Banking Crises; Bank Failures in the Major Trading Countries of the World; The Bank Director's Handbook; Targeting Fraud; Interest Rate Risk Management* (with R. Brooks); *The Basics of Investing, 5th ed.; Bank Fraud: Exposing the Hidden Threat to Financial Institutions; Bank Mergers; Cases in Bank Management* (with C. Meiburg); *Principles of Financial Management; Financial Institutions; Financial Intermediaries; Personal Investing: A Complete Guide; Guide to Strategic Planning; and How to Ask for a Business Loan.*

Dr. Gup's articles on financial subjects have appeared in *The Journal of Finance, The Journal of Financial and Quantitative Analysis, The Journal of Money, Credit, and Banking, Financial Management, The Journal of Banking and Finance, Financial Analysts Journal,* and elsewhere.

PART 1

INTRODUCTION

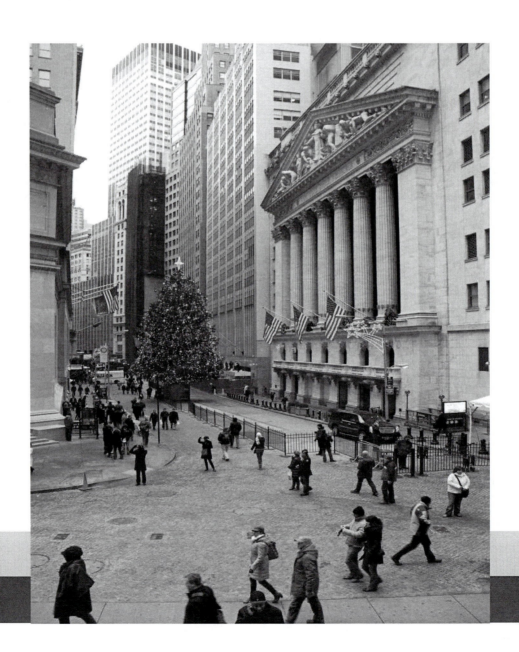

Chapter 1

Functions and Forms of Banking

After reading this chapter, you will be able to:

- Understand what a bank is and how they differ from other financial service organizations such as savings and loans, credit unions, on-line lenders, and mutual funds.
- Explain types of services that banks offer to their deposit and loan customers.
- Understand the motivation behind bank behavior such as pricing deposits and loan rates.
- Understand how banks get their funds and what they do with them.
- Describe the economic and financial forces that have changed the way banks operate and that have also changed the basic management strategies of individual banking organizations.

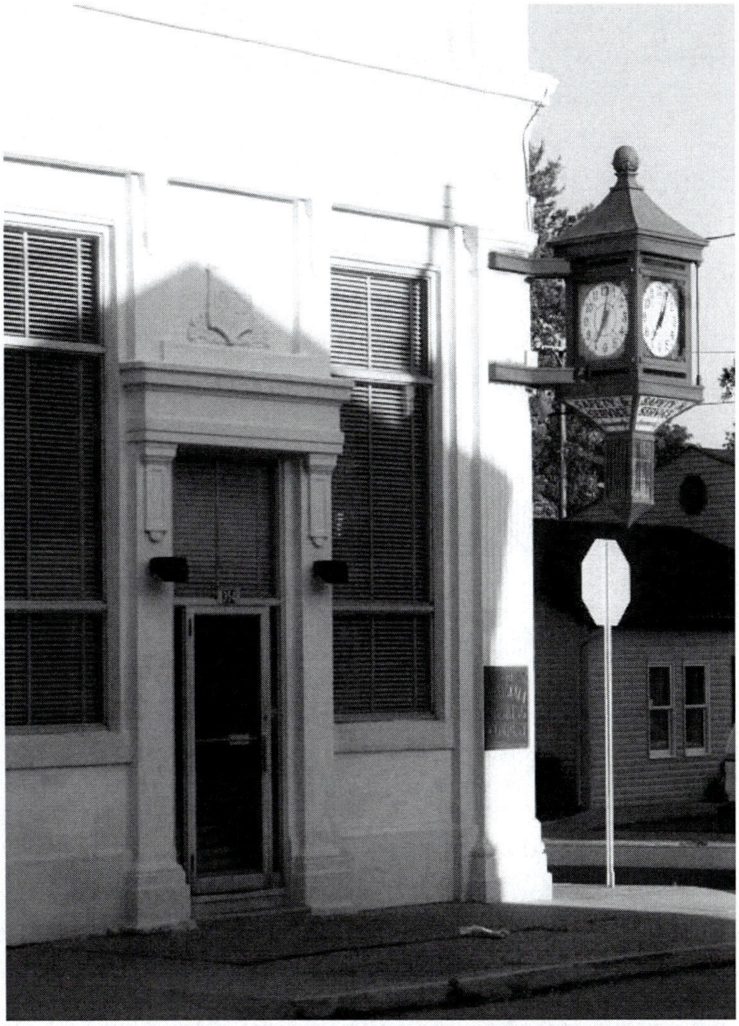

For many centuries banks have played a vital role in the financial system. That vital role continues today, although the forms of banking have changed as the needs of the economy have changed. This chapter provides an overview of the role of commercial banks by concentrating on six topics.

- What is a bank?
- What do banks do?
- Why do they perform those services?
- How do banks compare with other financial service organizations?
- What factors have affected the operations of commercial banks and other financial service organizations?
- What are the principal sources and uses of funds for banks?

Our discussion focuses on the manager of the bank; that is, the focus is from inside the banking institution looking outward at the environment within which banks operate. In examining each of these questions, the basic aim is to acquaint the existing or potential manager of the bank with the information and techniques necessary to succeed in managing the organization.

WHAT IS A BANK?

DEFINITIONS

The answer to the question "What is a bank?" might seem quite simple. In reality, however, the answer is complicated. One reason why it is complicated is that there is a distinction between the legal definitions of ***commercial bank*** and the functional definition of what banks do. As will be explained below, nonbank competitors perform many of the functions of banks. Another reason why defining a commercial bank is complicated is that the legal definition and regulators' definitions change over time, and different countries have different legal definitions. Likewise, the functions of banks have changed over the years.

In the United States, a "bank" is defined by federal and state laws and by the bank regulators. Let's consider the definition of a bank in an historical context.

1781

The Bank of North America, the first commercial bank in the United States, was founded in Philadelphia in 1781.[1] It was chartered by the Continental Congress. Subsequently, it acquired a Pennsylvania state charter.

By 1800, every state except for Georgia, New Jersey, North Carolina, and Vermont had chartered one or more banks.[2] The banks chartered by states were referred to as ***state banks***. In 1811, there were 88 state banks. That number grew to 1,462 by 1862.[3]

Each state bank issued its own notes that served as currency. However, the bank notes were not backed by adequate assets, and they were not universally acceptable at all banks. In some states, banks could be organized without any capital and with little or no supervision. A few "shady bank operators became experts at evasion, moving their hole-in-the-wall offices to frontier backwaters 'where only wildcats roamed.'" This is the origin of the term ***wildcat banking***.[4]

Banks in the latter part of seventeenth and the eighteenth century believed that the ***real bills doctrine*** was the cornerstone of banking. The real bills doctrine held that banks should make short-term, self-liquidating, productive loans for goods of real value, such as inventory. They should not make long-term loans for real estate and securities. The fact that banks concentrated on short-term loans and commercial paper (promissory notes, bills of exchange [5], etc.), gave rise to the term ***commercial bank***.

1863

Before and during the Civil War, there was a need for a sound national currency and national banking supervision. These needs were met by the enactment of The National Currency Act of 1863, which was rewritten as the National Bank Act of 1864. It created the Office of the Comptroller of Currency (OCC), and national banks – banks with a national charter issued by the OCC. The National Bank Act gave the OCC the power to 1) charter, 2) regulate, and 3) supervise ***national banks***. National banks have the word national or national association (NA) in their names.

The National Bank Act said that a national banking association shall have the power to carry out the "... business of banking..." It defined the business of banking as "....discounting and negotiating promissory notes, drafts, bills of exchange, and other evidences of debt; by receiving deposits; by buying and selling exchange, coin and bullion, by loaning money on personal security; and by obtaining, issuing, and circulating notes .... " [6]

The National Bank Act also preempted state laws that tried to direct or control the activities of national banks that were authorized under Federal Law.

"It is a matter of constitutional law and federal statute that the powers of national banks cannot be obstructed by state laws or regulation," said Comptroller Hawke. "***Preemption*** is a principle that is almost as old as our nation itself and the Supreme Court has repeatedly ruled against the states when they have sought to limit the activities national banks are authorized to conduct under federal law." Specifically, the Supreme Court ruled in M'Culloch v. Maryland (1819) that states cannot constitutionally restrict the powers of entities created under federal law.

1956

The Bank Holding Company Act of 1956 changed the definition of a bank. Under this Act, banks accepted deposits that could be withdrawn on demand, and they made commercial loans.[7] ***Commercial loans*** are loans to a business customer for the purpose of providing funds for that business.[8] This definition contained several loopholes for banks that accepted deposits and made loans to individuals – consumer loans -- but did not make commercial loans. Also, industrial loan companies made commercial loans and offered deposits, but did not accept demand deposits.[9] These institutions were defined as a nonbank bank, and they were not subject to the same federal regulations as a bank. This loophole allowed nonbank banks to conduct interest operations that were not available to banks at that time. More will be said about this in the next chapter.

1987

The nonbank bank loophole was closed by the Competitive Equality Banking Act of 1987 (CEBA) and no new nonbank banks were chartered.[10] The new definition of a bank became a financial institution that accepts deposits and makes loans. CEBA further modified the definition of a bank to include only those institutions that had their deposits insured by the Federal Deposit Insurance Corporation.

2015

The working definition of a ***commercial bank*** used in this text is "A financial Institution that is owned by stockholders, operates for a profit, and engages in lending activities." This definition of a commercial bank appears in the Federal Reserve System's National Information Center's Glossary.[11] We use the terms "bank" and "commercial bank" interchangeably.

The legal definition depends on whose rules or laws are being used. For example, the terms "bank" and "state bank" are defined in Section 3 of the Federal Deposit Insurance Act. SEC. 3, as used in this Act, has the following definitions: [12]

(a) DEFINITION OF BANK AND RELATED TERMS.--

(1) BANK.--The term "bank"--

(A) means any national bank, State bank, and District bank, and any Federal branch and insured branch;

(B) includes any former savings association that--

(i) has converted from a savings association charter; and

(ii) is a Savings Association Insurance Fund member.

(2) STATE BANK.--The term "State bank" means any bank, banking association, trust company, savings bank, industrial bank (or similar depository institution which the Board of Directors finds to be operating substantially in the same manner as an industrial bank), or other banking institution which--

(A) is engaged in the business of receiving deposits, other than trust funds (as defined in this section); and

(B) is incorporated under the laws of any State or which is operating under the Code of Law for the District of Columbia (except a national bank),
including any cooperative bank or other unincorporated bank the deposits of which were insured by the Corporation on the day before the date of the enactment of the Financial Institutions Reform, Recovery, and Enforcement Act of 1989.

(3) STATE.--The term "State" means any State of the United States, the District of Columbia, any territory of the United States, Puerto Rico, Guam, American Samoa, the Trust Territory of the Pacific Islands, the Virgin Islands, and the Northern Mariana Islands.

(4) DISTRICT BANK.--The term "District bank" means any State bank operating under the Code of Law of the District of Columbia."

The legal definition of a commercial bank is important because other types of financial institutions offer the same or similar services, but they are not subjected to the same regulations as banks. For example, credit unions accept deposits and make loans. Their deposits, however, are not insured by the FDIC; and they are not subject to the same regulations or taxes as banks. Similarly, finance companies make loans, and money market mutual funds are a substitute for deposits. Accordingly, G E Capital Corporation, Fidelity Funds, and The Principal Group are firms that provide "financial products and services," although they are not banks in the legal sense of the word.[13] For example, The Principal Group advertises on its web page "The Principal Financial Group® is a leading global financial institution offering businesses, individuals and institutional clients a wide range of financial products and services… "[14] Google the term "online lenders" and you will get more than 69 million hits showing that they make personal loans, real estate loans, business loans, etc.

Bankers argue that the legal distinction gives the nonbank financial institutions and other lenders unfair competitive advantage because they are not regulated to the same degree and thus operate with greater freedom than banks. And, in fact, banks' share of total loans and deposits has declined over the years.

(5) S Corporation Banks – An S Corporation is a special type of domestic corporation that is created through an Internal Revenue Service (IRS) application. According to the Small Business Administration, the advantages of S Corporations are:

Advantages of an S Corporation

- **Tax Savings.** One of the best features of the S Corp is the tax savings for you and your business. While members of an LLC are subject to employment tax on the entire net income of the business, only the wages of the S Corp shareholder who is an employee are subject to employment tax. The remaining income is paid to the owner as a "distribution," which is taxed at a lower rate, if at all.

- **Business Expense Tax Credits.** Some expenses that shareholder/employees incur can be written off as business expenses. Nevertheless, if such an employee owns two percent or more shares, then benefits like health and life insurance are deemed taxable income.

- **Independent Life.** An S corp designation also allows a business to have an independent life, separate from its shareholders. If a shareholder leaves the company, or sells his or her shares, the S corp can continue doing business relatively undisturbed. Maintaining the business as a distinct corporate entity defines clear lines between the shareholders and the business that improve the protection of the shareholders.

Disadvantages of an S Corporation

- **Stricter Operational Processes.** As a separate structure, S corps require scheduled director and shareholder meetings, minutes from those meetings, adoption and updates to by-laws, stock transfers and records maintenance.

- **Shareholder Compensation Requirements.** A shareholder must receive reasonable compensation. The IRS takes notice of shareholder red flags like low salary with high distribution combinations, and may reclassify those distributions as wages. The shareholder could pay a higher employment tax because of an audit with such results."[15]

In addition to taking deposits and making loans, banks have been granted legal "powers" to provide other financial services. The financial services that they offer have changed over the years as new technologies have emerged. The services listed in Table 1-1 give an indication of the range of expanded services offered by banks. Before these services became available in the last half of the twentieth century, banks offered only a small number of basic services.

Table 1-1: SELECTED BANKING SERVICES

EXPANDED SERVICES	BASIC SERVICES
Cash management services	Non-interest-bearing transaction accounts
Consumer loans	Commercial loans
Credit and debit cards	Savings accounts
Derivatives	
Digital/mobile/internet banking services	
Federal preemption	
Fixed- and floating-rate certificates of deposit	
Foreign exchange	
Insurance, annuities	
Interest-bearing transaction accounts	
Investment banking	
Leases	
Mutual Funds	
Real estate loans	
Stock brokerage/investment services	
Trust services	
Trade finance for international transactions	
Websites	

NUMBER OF BANKS

The number of commercial banks in the United States peaked at 14,451 in the United States in 1982. Subsequently, the number of banks declined to 5,570 in 2015, due to mergers and failures. The decline in the number of banks and increased concentration of bank assets being held by a relatively small number of large banks is referred to as ***consolidation*** in the banking literature.

As shown in Table 1.2, the system is dominated by a 94 large banks with assets greater than $10 billion that control 83 percent of the total assets. Some large banks are considered to be Systematically Important Financial Institutions or SIFIs. The SIFIs are banks that are considered "***Too-Big-To-Fail***," and are eligible for government support if they fail. Regulations under the 2010 Dodd-Frank Act require SIFIs to

Table 1-2: ASSET SIZE DISTRIBUTION OF ALL FDIC INSURED COMMERCIAL BANKS

First Quarter, 2015

		Assets less than $100 million	Assets $100 million to $1 billion	Assets $1 - $10 billion	Assets greater than $10 billion
Number of banks	5,570	1,607	3,389	480	94
Total assets	$1,736.6	$94.7	$1,038.3	$1,319.4	$12,284.3
Assets as % of total	100%	0.64%	7.05%	8.95%	83.36%

Source: FDIC Quarterly Financial Profile, First Quarter 2015, Table III-A. www.fdic.gov

meet higher capital standards and to develop contingency plans for potential future failures.

At the other end of the asset size spectrum are community banks. Many bankers think of them as small- to medium-sized banks that serve their local community in terms of basic financial services for citizens, small businesses, and local government and charitable organizations. Community banks are relationship oriented with an emphasis on personal connections to their clients. Some consider banks in the $100 million to $10 billion range community banks. [16]

The technical definition of community banks used by bank regulators is complex and confusing. It is based on the size and composition of their assets and liabilities. Community banks are defined by the FDIC to:[17]

Exclude: Any organization with:

- No loans or core deposits
- Foreign Assets ≥ 10% of total assets
- More than 50 percent of assets in certain specialty banks,
  - Including:
    - . credit card specialists
    - . consumer nonbank specialist
    - . industrial loan companies
    - . trust companies
    - . bankers' banks

Include: All remaining banking organizations with:

- Total assets < indexed size threshold ($1 billion in 2010)
- Total assets ≥ indexed size threshold, where:
  - . Loans to assets > 33 percent
  - . Core deposits to assets > 50 percent
  - . More than one office, but no more than 75 in 2010.

. Number of large MSA with offices ≤ 2
. Number of states with offices ≤ 3
. No single office with deposits > indexed in 2010.

TYPES OF BANKS

It is common practice to classify banks by the markets they serve, such as community banks.

Some of the largest banks (assets greater than $10 billion) are internationally active and serve markets throughout the world. They are referred to as ***global banks***, ***international banks***, or ***money center banks*** (e.g., Citibank, NA; JPMorgan Chase Bank). These and other large banks (e.g., Wells Fargo Bank, NA) are ***full service banks***, providing a wide range financial services. JPMorgan Chase Bank is the name of the bank that is owned by J. P. Morgan Chase & Co. which is a bank holding company – a company that owns multiple banks and related firms. Table 1-3 lists the top fifteen bank holding companies in June of 2015. Some of our large bank holding companies are foreign owned, such as HSBC North America Holdings and TD Bank US Holding Company. Selected other large foreign-owned banks include Santander Holdings USA, MUFG Americas Holdings Corporation, and BBVA Compass Bancshares. [18]

Table 1-3: TOP FIFTEEN BANK HOLDING COMPANIES, 6/30/15

Rank/ Name	Location	Total Assets (000)
1. JP Morgan Chase & Co.	New York, NY	$2,447,994,000
2. Bank of America Corporation	Charlotte, NC	$2,152,082,000
3. Citigroup Inc.	New York, NY	$1,829,370,000
4. Wells Fargo & Co.	San Francisco, CA	$1,720,617,000
5. Goldman Sachs Group, Inc., The	New York, NY	$859,932,000
6. Morgan Stanley	New York, NY	$825,755,000
7. General Electric Capital Corporation	Norwalk, CT	$466,871,489
8. U.S. Bancorp	Minneapolis, MN	$419,075,000
9. Bank of New York Mellon Corporation, The	New York, NY	$395,254,000
10. PNC Financial Services Group, The	Pittsburgh, PA	$354,201,925
11. Capital One Financial Corporation	Mclean, VA	$310,636,497
12. State Street Corporation	Boston, MA	$294,570,652
13. HSBC North America Holdings	New York, NY	$277,249,331
14. Teachers' Insurance Annuity Assoc. of America	New York, NY	$266,931,428
15. TD Bank US Holding Company	Cherry Hill, NJ	$253,195,880

Source: "Holding Companies with Assets Greater Than $10 Billion," National Information Center, Federal Financial Institutions Examination Council,

http://www.ffiec.gov/nicpubweb/nicweb/HCSGreaterThan10B.aspx

Although large banks and bank holding companies control most of the assets, the majority the banks in the United States are small- and medium-size ***retail*** or ***consumer banks*** that serve the credit needs of their local communities (see Table 1-2). These banks also offer a wide range of financial services by using ***correspondent banks*** – larger banks that provide financial services to them, and by outsourcing. Outsourcing refers to acquiring services from specialized vendors such as insurance companies, mutual funds, information technology companies, etc.

A few banks concentrate on dealing almost exclusively with medium- and large-size businesses. These specialized banks are known as wholesale banks (e.g. Bank of America Rhode Island, National Association, Bank of China, Morgan Stanley Bank, N.A.).[19] They do not extend home mortgage credit, consumer loans to retail customers, or loans to small businesses or small farms. Wholesale banks make loans to corporations, interbank loans, and sovereign loans (loans to central banks and other public-sector entities).[20] They also make commercial real estate loans. A few large banks specialize in a narrow product line, such as credit cards or motor vehicle loans. They are called ***limited purpose banks*** or ***monoline banks*** because of their focus primarily on one line of business (e.g., American Express Bank, Capital One Bank (USA), National Association, and others).[21] Next, there are ***internet banks***, banks that operate exclusively or predominantly on the Internet. Some internet banks may have branches, kiosks, or Automated Teller Machines (ATMs). Internet banks can have state or national charters.

WHAT DO BANKS DO FOR THEIR CUSTOMERS?

Most of the functions performed by commercial banks for their customers can be divided into three broad areas:

1. Payments
2. Intermediation
3. Other financial services.

PAYMENTS

Banks are the core of the ***payments system***. Payment refers to the means by which financial transactions are settled. Banks also dispense of coin and currency.

Financial transactions in the United States have become increasingly based on credit and debit cards, while the number of check payments has declined in recent years.[22] The number of checks processed by the Federal Reserve declined from 541 million in 1989 to 63 million in 2014.[23] In addition, the use of mobile phones and the Internet is changing the way that consumers access financial services, transfer funds, and make payments. Nevertheless, bank branches and automated teller machines (ATMs) were still the primary means of accessing banking services.[24]

Therefore, the means by with such payments are settled is an integral part of the payments system. The payments system also involves the settlement of credit card transactions, electronic banking, wire transfers, and other aspects in the movement of funds. Increasingly, the focus is on real-time payments "as an immediate, irrevocable, interbank account-to-account transfer that utilizes a real-time messaging system connected to every end-user through a financial institution, third party, or another real-time system."[25]

The role of banks in the payments system takes on an important social dimension because an efficient payments system is vital to economic stability and growth. At one time, commercial banks had a monopoly on transactions accounts, but that is no longer the case. Savings and loans, savings banks, and credit unions (known collectively along with commercial banks as depository institutions), as well as money market mutual funds and brokerage firms also offer transactions accounts.

Commercial banks, along with the Federal Reserve System, are the heart of the payments system. The payment system can be divided into two parts, the retail payments system that is used by individuals to pay their bills or receive funds, and the large-dollar payments system that is used by business concerns and governments to handle large-dollar domestic and international payments and receipts.

The retail payments system in the United States makes extensive use of paper checks, but as previously noted, the number of paper checks is declining, and various electronic payments and credit and debit cards are becoming increasing important means of retail payments. Banks also provide coin and currency to businesses and individuals for cash transactions.

Large-dollar payments in the US are electronic payments between commercial banks that are using the Fedwire -- a wholesale wire transfer system operated by the Federal Reserve System, with more than 538,000 transfers per day with an average daily value of $3.5 trillion or more in 2014.[26]

In addition, ***CHIPS (The Clearing House Interbank Payments System)*** is a private electronic transfer system operated by large banks in New York that transfers another $1.5 trillion per day, principally involving international movements of funds. Further, ***SWIFT (the Society for Worldwide Interbank Financial Telecommunication)*** is operated by banks throughout the world to facilitate international payments. More is said about the payments system in Chapter 17, "Electronic Banking."

FINANCIAL INTERMEDIATION

Deposit type financial intermediaries are economic units whose principal function is obtaining funds from depositors and others, and then lending those funds to borrowers. As listed in Table 1-1, they also provide other financial services. Banks are one type of financial intermediary. In financial terms, the deposits represent bank liabilities and the loans are assets. Most of their profit is the difference between the rates at which they borrow and lend, after taking into account all of their expenses. Banks also invest in securities, and provide other services, such as automated teller machines, trust accounts, safety deposit boxes, and other activities where they earn noninterest income.

Bank Balance Sheet

Assets	Liabilities and Equity
Loans	Deposits
Other assets	Equity

Deposit Function

Commercial banks act as intermediaries between those who have money (savers or depositors) and those who need money (borrowers). As financial intermediaries, banks enhance economic efficiency and economic growth by allocating capital to its best possible uses. Banks obtain deposits from savers by offering deposit instruments with:

a. a wide variety of denominations, interest rates, and maturities,

b. risk-free (FDIC insured) benefits, for deposits up to $250,000.

c. a high degree of liquidity

These are characteristics that meet the needs of most savers better than bonds and stocks that may have high denominations, high risk, less liquidity, and higher transaction costs. Nonbank financial institutions may offer similar services, such as money market mutual funds, but mutual fund shares are not FDIC insured.

Loan Function

Commercial banks use the deposits, other sources of borrowed funds, and equity to make loans to borrowers. Historically the short-term deposits were used to finance short-term commercial lending. This explains the origin of the term commercial bank. Today, however, banks make every type of loan that is legally permissible and for periods up to 30 years (such as home mortgage loans). By doing so, they gain expertise in evaluating and monitoring the risks associated with lending. Thus, the intermediation allows for the shifting of risk from individuals, who are not equipped to deal with the risk, to banks that specialize in risk management.

Financial intermediation between depositors and borrowers is crucial to the growth and stability of the economy. Economic growth depends on a large volume of savings and the effective allocation of the savings to productive and profitable uses. By offering depositors financial instruments that have desirable risk/return characteristics, commercial banks encourage savings and, by effectively screening credit requests, they channel funds into socially productive and profitable uses.

OTHER FINANCIAL SERVICES

In addition to their traditional role of providing financial intermediation between depositors and borrowers, commercial banks provide a variety of other financial services that are discussed further in Chapters 14 -18. Some of these services a briefly described below.

Off-Balance Sheet Activities. Banks use financial derivatives - interest rate swaps, financial futures, and options - to hedge interest rate, foreign exchange, and credit default risks. In addition, banks may earn fee income by guaranteeing the payment of another party. This type of guarantee is a contingent claim (the bank must pay only if the party defaults) and does not appear on the bank's balance sheet. The ***standby letter of credit*** is the best known of those contingent claims and involves the agreement by a bank to pay an agreed-upon amount on presentation of evidence of default or nonperformance of the party whose obligation is guaranteed. Commercial letters of credit, that are widely used in trade finance, are also supplied by banks but do not appear on their balance sheets.

Insurance and Securities-Related Activities. Commercial banks and their affiliates are able to offer various types of life insurance policies, annuities, and other related products. In addition, they can provide brokerage services - buying and selling securities for their customers. In addition, they may act as securities dealers – buying and selling for their own accounts. Finally, they may offer investment banking services such as underwriting securities.

Trust Services. Commercial banks may operate "trust" departments in which they manage the funds of others for a fee, under the terms of a trust agreement. Because the bank does not "own" the assets held in trust, they do not show up on the bank's balance sheet. In their fiduciary role, the trusts manage estates, employee pension and profit-sharing programs, and a variety of securities-related activities for corporate businesses. Trust departments provide fee income for the banks.

BANKS ARE PRIVATE FIRMS WITH A PUBLIC PURPOSE

Commercial banks in the United States are private corporations that provide payments services, financial intermediation, and other financial services in anticipation of earning profits from those activities. The payments system and intermediation are required for economic growth. Like any other "for profit" corporation, their principal goal is to maximize shareholder wealth. Thus, decisions on lending, investing, borrowing, pricing, adding new services, dropping old services, and other activities depend on the impact on shareholder wealth.

Shareholder wealth is measured by the market value of a bank's stock, and amount of cash dividends paid. Market value depends on three factors: (1) the amount of cash flows that accrue to bank shareholders, (2) the timing of the cash flows, and (3) the risk involved in those cash flows. Management decisions involve evaluating the impact of various strategies on the return (the amount and timing of the cash flows) and the risk of those cash flows (Figure 1.1 on next page).

BANK RISK MANAGEMENT

Banking is the management of risk. Banks accept risk in order to earn profits. They must balance alternative strategies in terms of their risk/return characteristics with the goal of maximizing shareholder wealth. In doing so, banks recognize that

FIGURE 1-1 BANK GOALS AND CONSTRAINTS

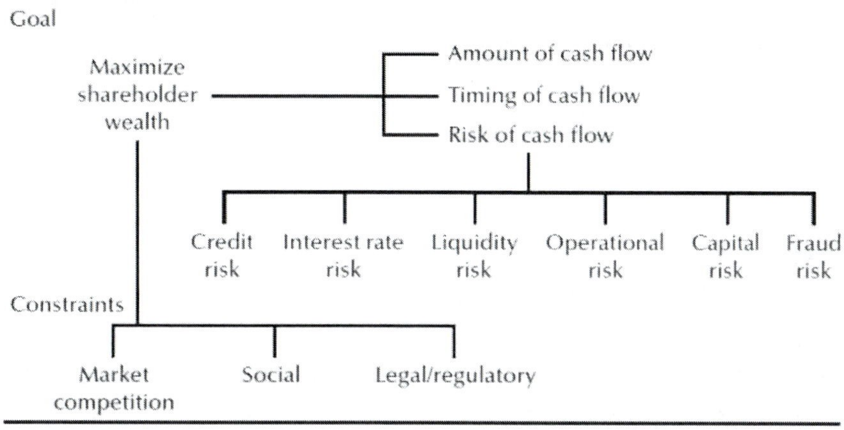

there are different types of risk and that the impact of a particular investment strategy on shareholders depends on the impact on the total risk of the organization. The Office of the Comptroller of the Currency (OCC) lists eight risks for purposes of bank supervision.[27]

Credit Risk

Credit risk is the risk to earnings and capital that an obligor will fail to meet the terms of any contract with the bank, or otherwise fail to perform as agreed. It is usually associated with loans and investments, but it can also arise in connection with derivatives, foreign exchange, and other extensions of bank credit. Although banks fail for many reasons, the single most important reason is bad loans. Banks, of course, don't make "bad" loans. They make loans that go bad. At the time the loans were made the decisions seemed correct. However, unforeseen changes in economic conditions, and other factors such as interest rate shocks, changes in tax laws, and so on, have resulted in credit problems. Credit risk is the primary cause of bank failures, and it is the most visible risk facing bank managers.

Interest Rate Risk

Interest rate risk is the risk to earnings and capital associated with changes in market rates of interest. This risk arises from differences in timing of rate changes and the timing of cash flows (repricing risk), from changes in the shape of the yield curve (yield curve risk), and from option values embedded in bank products (options risk). In essence, the market value of a bank's assets (loans and securities) will fall with increases in interest rates. In addition, earnings from assets, fees, and the cost of borrowed funds are affected by changes in interest rates. Banks can reduce their interest rate risk by hedging with derivative securities and by using other asset/liability management techniques described in other chapters of this book.

Operational Risk

Operational risk (also referred to as transaction risk) is the risk to earnings or capital arising from problems associated with the delivery or service of a product. Operational risks encompass the efficiency and effectiveness of all back-office operations including management information systems, personnel, compliance, external and internal frauds, lawsuits, and so on. The increased use of mobile phones, computers, the internet, and other electronic means for accessing banking services are examples of operational risk.[28] In addition, they have exposed banks and their customers to the increased risk of cybercrimes – i.e., criminal offenses involving the internet and computer technology.[29]

The Office of the Comptroller of the Currency (OCC) had the following to say about cybersecurity: "Efforts to safeguard the security of bank information systems and data remained one of the OCC's areas of highest concern in 2014. Banks have long been a target for electronic attacks. Hackers may have a number of motivations for breaching bank systems, including fraud, political activism, and intent to undermine public confidence in the U.S. financial system. New and more sophisticated threats surface almost daily and have affected a number of organizations in various industries. For example, attacks involving retailers cost merchants and credit card issuers tens of millions of dollars in lost business and remediation costs, and raised concerns among consumers about the safety of Internet commerce and electronic banking."[30]

Liquidity Risk

Liquidity risk is the risk to earnings or capital arising from a bank's ability to meet its obligations to depositors and the needs of borrowers by turning assets into cash quickly with minimal loss, being unable to borrow funds when needed, or falling short of funds to execute profitable securities trading activities. Given the large amount of bank deposits that must be paid on demand or within a very short period, liquidity risk is of crucial importance in banking.

Price Risk

Price risk is the risk to earnings or capital arising from market-making, dealing, or taking positions in securities, derivatives, foreign exchange, or other financial instruments. For example, as a result of the financial crises in Russia in 1998, several large banks (i.e., Bankers Trust, BankAmerica, Citicorp, and others) suffered losses in their foreign exchange and derivatives positions.

Compliance Risk

Compliance risk is the risk to earnings or capital arising from violations of laws, rules, regulations, and so on. For example, banks failing to meet minimum capital requirements must raise new capital, or they may be closed, forced to merge, or take some other corrective action.

Strategic Risk

Strategic risk is the risk to earnings or capital arising from making bad business decisions that adversely affect the value of the bank.

Reputation Risk

Reputation risk is the risk to earnings or capital arising from negative public opinion of the bank. Negative public opinion can arise from poor service, failure to serve the credit needs of their respective communities, and for other reasons. Regulators feared that negative public opinion would contribute of a loss of market share and be a potential source of litigation.

"Examiners also should be alert to concentrations that can significantly elevate risk. Concentrations can accumulate within and across products, business lines, geographic areas, countries, and legal entities."... "When examiners assess risk management systems, they consider the bank's policies, processes, personnel, and control systems. If any of these areas is deficient, so is the bank's risk management."[31]

CONSTRAINTS

Bank management must balance risk and return in seeking to maximize shareholder wealth. However, such decisions are constrained by a number of factors. These constraints may be classified into three separate, though overlapping, areas:

Market Constraints

A bank's growth and profitability is limited by the growth rate of the economy and the markets that it serves. If the economy is growing and prosperous, a soundly managed bank should grow and be profitable. However, if the economy is faltering, or there are natural disasters such as floods and tornadoes, banks will suffer too. Most bank failures occur during periods of economic distress.

Second, there is competition from other providers of financial services, and from the capital market. For example, if a bank's management believes that it must charge 8 percent on a loan in order to be fully compensated for credit risk, but other lenders will provide credit to the borrower at 6 percent, this is a market constraint that has a potentially serious impact on the bank.

Third, there is an increased completion from online nonbank lenders, such as Quicken Loans and Lending Club. Google the term "nonbank lenders", and you will get more than three million hits – offering personal loans, mortgage loans, business loans, and the like.

Social Constraints

Social constraints stem from the historical position of the commercial bank at the core of the financial system. They are expected to provide deposit and credit services to the communities they serve.

Because the financial performance of a bank is inextricably linked with the economic health of the community it serves, bankers perform numerous social functions (and they are expected to do so). They are active in local Chambers of Commerce, charities, and other activities that promote the economic development and quality of life.

Legal and Regulatory Constraints

There are legal and regulatory constraints on commercial banks. The legal and regulatory constraints are discussed in considerable detail in other parts of the book. It is sufficient at this point to mention the following constraints on bank operations:

• Constraints on balance sheet composition, including the prohibition on holding equity securities, and capital requirements.

• Constraints on customer relationships, including a large number of consumer protection laws.

Most legal and regulatory constraints on bank behavior are designed either to reduce the risk of failure or the allocation of bank credit. The risk reduction constraints stem primarily from the banking collapses of the 1930s and 1980s. The constraints designed to restrict the relationship of banks with their customers stem from the consumerism movement of the 1960s and 1970s. These subjects and recent legal changes are examined in Chapter 2.

MAJOR FACTORS AFFECTING BANKING AND MARKET SHARES

Shifts in the market shares of commercial banks and for other financial service organizations reflect the confluence of a number of economic, technological, and regulatory factors. The principal factors at work are: inflation, volatile interest rates, securitization, technological advances, consumers, capital markets, deregulation, despecialization and competition, and globalization.

INFLATION AND VOLATILE INTEREST RATES

As shown in Figure 1-2 (next page), interest rates were relatively low and stable throughout the 1950s and early 1960s, averaging about four to five percent. Beginning in the mid-1960s, the inflation rate began to rise, and interest rates soared. Interest rates on the 10-year Treasury Constant Maturity peaked at 18.45% in 1981.[32]

The sharp increase and high level of interest rates placed intense pressure on the financial system and contributed to the failure of a large number of institutions. Many institutions had borrowed short-term funds and made long-term real estate loans at fixed rates of interest. When interest rates soared, their cost of borrowing increased, and exceeded the low fixed returns on their assets. In addition, the market value of their assets declined. Equally important, large numbers of borrowers defaulted on their loans. Between 1980 and 1994, more than 1,600 FDIC banks failed or needed assistance. Stated otherwise, 9.14 percent of the total number of banks in the U.S. failed during this period.[33] Savings and loan associations – that specialized in real estate loans - were also affected adversely by the changes in economic conditions. The number of savings and loan associations declined from 4,613 in 1980 to 1,345 in 1990 due to failures and mergers.[34]

Interest rates continued to decline in the late 1990s through 2016.[35] In September 2015, the 30-year conventional home mortgage interest rate was 3.89%, a 45-year low. The declining interest rates encouraged borrowers to refinance their loans and others to borrow. As savings and loans exited the market, commercial banks became the largest real estate lenders.

FIGURE I-2 **INTEREST RATES: 1953 -2015**

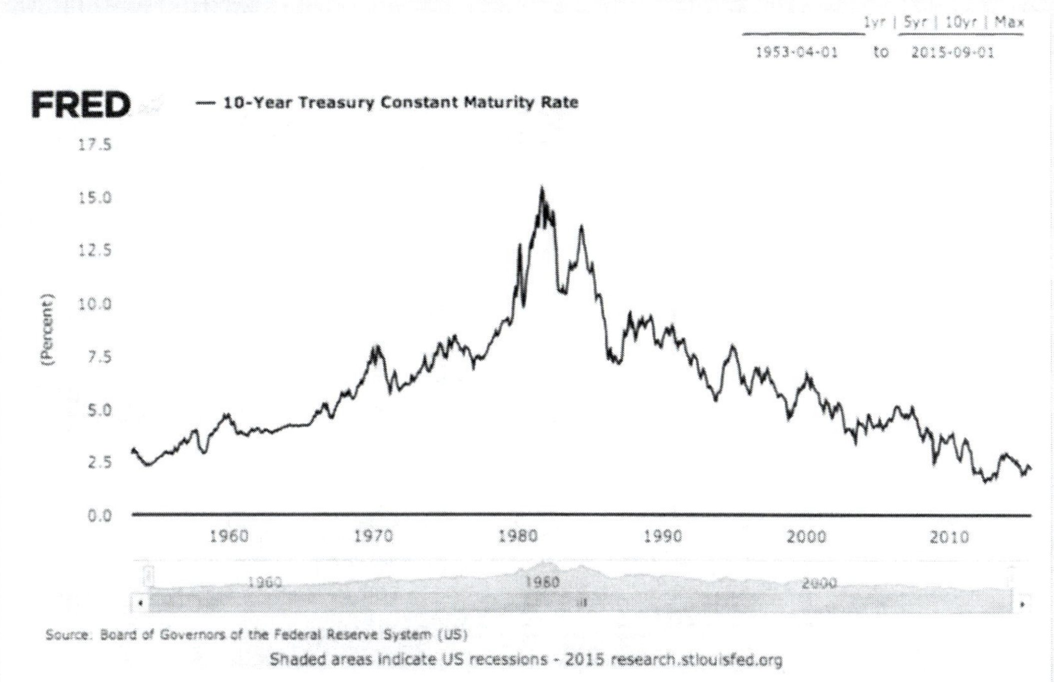

SECURITIZATION

Securitization has had a major impact on the structure of the financial services industry. Securitization is the issuance of a debt instrument in which the promised payments are derived from revenues generated by a defined pool of loans. The pools include mortgage loans, credit card loans, car loans, and loans to businesses. Prior to the development of securitization, such small loans were considered unmarketable, and they remained on the balance sheets of the banks. However, securitization allows banks to package and sell the loans, thereby improving the banks' liquidity and increasing their access to the capital markets.

In addition, securitization has allowed the traditional lending process to be decomposed into various parts – originating loans, packaging them for the sale to others, servicing of loans, and funding them. The decomposition, or the "unbundling" of the lending process, has opened the door for nonbank firms to compete in bank loan markets.

TECHNOLOGICAL ISSUES

Advances in technology have affected the competitive position of financial service providers. The changes in computer and communications technology have lowered the costs for processing financial transactions. Accordingly, we have seen the development of large institutions that specialize in credit cards, investment services, and servicing securitized loans. These institutions have economies of scale –

high volume, low costs. Other institutions have developed or expanded their activities to provide banking services over the Internet because of the declining entry barriers. The firms that have been most effective in implementing the new financial technology have achieved an edge through automation and lower personnel costs.

Computer technology has also reduced the cost of screening and monitoring loan portfolios. Prospective loans are increasingly being evaluated with credit scoring models. These are models that evaluate a prospective borrower's financial history and other data to generate a numerical score that is used by lenders to determine their willingness to make loans.

Perhaps more important, the advances in technology have made the production of diverse financial services within one firm more feasible through increasing the prospects for realizing economies of scope (economies of scope exist when two different products can be produced more cheaply at one firm than at two separate firms). For example, banks can offer a variety of services to distant customers over the Internet that might be too costly to offer from traditional brick and mortar facilities.

Finally, communications technology, such as the use of cell phones and other digital devices, has greatly increased the geographical boundaries over which financial services could be produced, thereby substantially intensifying the extent of competition in the industry. For example, Apple Pay, Android Pay, and Samsung Pay can be used as alternatives to credit cards where the technology is available. And Square credit card readers can be used for processing credit card transactions.

CONSUMERS

More sophisticated consumers have played a major role in the changing structure of the financial services industry. Greater education in personal money management, as well as high returns on financial assets in some periods and losses in others, have made fund flows more volatile. Access to the Internet and on-line banking and investment services gives consumers of financial services the means to move funds around for very small cost.

It also gives them access to other sources of loans, such as on-line nonbank payday lenders. These are generally short-term loans for $500 or less that are due on the borrower's next payday.[36] The finance charge may range from $10 to $30 for every $100 borrowed. A $15 charge for a $100 two-week loan equates to an Annual Percentage Rate (APR) of almost 400 percent.

DEREGULATION

Deregulation has affected the operations of commercial banks and other depository financial institutions. Deregulation of banks refers to the reduction or elimination of laws that placed geographic limits on banks, the products and services they could offer, and the interest rates they could pay. In the past, banks were limited as to the interest rates that they could pay on deposits. In 1980, the Monetary Control Act eliminated that constraint for time and savings deposits, but not for demand deposits.[37] Similarly, banks located in one state could not have branches in other states. The elimination of geographic barriers to entry in the 1990s contributed to the large number of bank mergers and the increased consolidation in the industry. As previously noted, the number of banks declined from 14,451 commercial banks in the United States in 1982 to 5,570 banks in 2015 as a result of mergers and failures.[38]

Further deregulation in 1999 under the Gramm-Leach-Bliley Act allowed banks and investment banks and insurance companies to come together. For example, the Gramm-Leach Bliley Act sanctified the 1998 merger between Travelers Insurance Group and Citibank to form Citigroup. Travelers Group also owned Salomon Smith Barney Inc. - a brokerage, investment banking, and asset management firm. Citibank is one of the largest banks in the U.S.

DESPECIALAZATION AND COMPETITION

The despecialization of financial institutions has been an important force in changing the structure of the financial service industry. The trend is for banks to become a one-stop shopping center for all financial services, offering broker investment services, insurance products, mutual funds, trust services, and other financial services. Equally important, the financial service offerings by banks' competitors -- Merrill Lynch, Fidelity Funds, General Electric's GE Capital Corporation, and others -- have expanded greatly. They have a significant competitive advantage in that they are not limited by the same legal and regulatory constraints as banks. One consequence of the expanded services offered by banks and their competitors is the increasing overlap of financial services offered by banks and nonbanking firms.

There is also competition from business concerns that provide trade credit for their customers. ***Trade credit*** is credit granted by a selling firm to finance another firm's purchase of the seller's goods and services.[39] It is a large source of short-term borrowed funds for business concerns in the U.S. and elsewhere.[40]

GLOBALIZATION

Globalization refers to the extent to which each country's economy and financial markets becomes increasingly integrated, resulting in development toward a single world market.[41] Globalization differs from "internationalization," which only refers to the extent to which certain international transactions increase.

Globalization of financial service organizations has affected the operations and structure of many financial service organizations. An increasing amount of funds are flowing across national borders both for long-run investment purposes and for short-run liquidity management. Foreign financial service organizations have entered the U.S. market, and many U.S. financial service firms have expanded abroad. For example, GE Capital bought Japan Leasing Corp, and T. Rowe Price Associates (a Baltimore asset-management company) entered into a joint venture with Daiwa Securities Company and Sumitomo Bank. The result of this global integration of financial markets is growing competition among financial service firms.

As shown in Figure 1-3, the growth of globalization and world trade activities over the years has contributed to the increased asset size of large banks with international operations.

FIGURE I-3 **GLOBILIZATION OF BANK ASSETS**

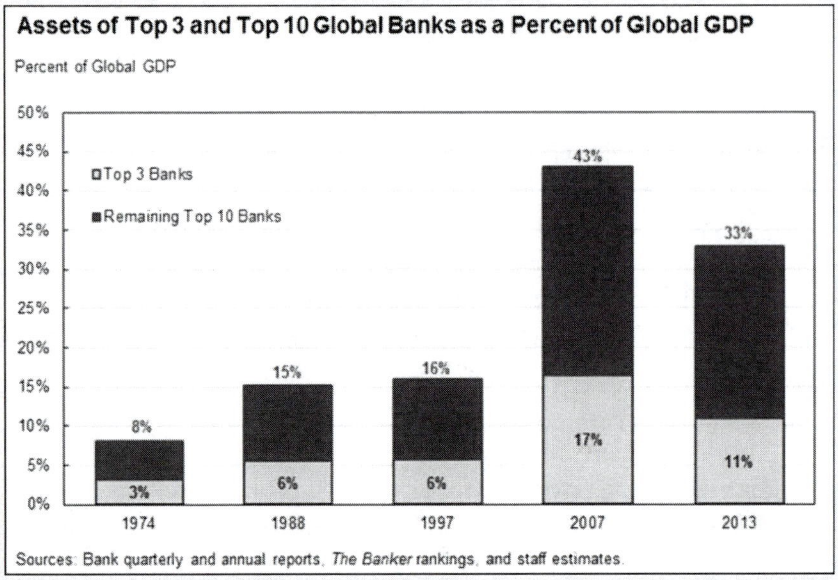

Federal Reserve Governor Daniel K. Tarullo, "Regulating Large Foreign Banking Organizations," Slide Show, March 27, 2014.
http://www.federalreserve.gov/newsevents/speech/tarullo20140327a.htm

MONEY AND CAPITAL MARKETS

Increased competition from the money markets (short-term funds) and capital markets (long-term funds) has played a role in the decline of banks' market share of financial assets. Large, high-quality corporations have found that they can access funds more cheaply through direct borrowing in the capital market (through selling commercial paper, or other securities) than by borrowing from banks. For example, in October, 2015, the prime rate (the base rate on corporate loans) was 3.25 percent, while the 60-day commercial paper rate was 0.14 percent.

ASSETS AND LIABILITIES OF COMMERCIAL BANKS

Table 1-4 (next page) presents the major assets and liabilities of the commercial banking industry. This table, in conjunction with attention to the various functions performed by commercial banks, serves as a vehicle for our discussion of the general sources and uses of bank funds. An analysis of individual bank balance sheets is contained in Chapter 3.

Table 1-4: ASSETS AND LIABILITIES OF COMMERCIAL BANKS September, 2015

ASSETS	AMOUNT (BILLIONS OF DOLLARS)
Bank Credit	$11,410.7
Securities	3,017.9
Loans and Leases in Bank Credit	8,392.9
Commercial and Industrial Loans	1,912.9
Real Estate loans	3,784.5
Consumer Loans	1,244.6
Other loans and leases	1,450.8
Less allowance for loan losses	106.1
Interbank loans	59.4
Cash assets	2,623.8
Trading assets	213.9
Other assets	1,194.1
TOTAL ASSETS	**$15,380.8**
LIABILITIES	$13,689.8
Total deposits	10,863.3
Large time deposits	1,684.1
Other deposits	9,179.2
Borrowings	1,798.7
Trading liabilities	213.4
Net due to related foreign offices	412.4
Other liabilities	402.1
RESIDUAL ASSETS*	$1,660.9
TOTAL LIABILITIES AND EQUITY CAPITAL	**$15,380.8**

Source: Federal Reserve Statistical Release H.8, October 9, 2015. Page 2-3, Data are seasonally adjusted.

*Residual Assets are a balancing item that is not intended as a measure of equity capital for use in capital adequacy analysis. On a seasonally adjusted basis this item reflects any differences in the seasonal patterns estimated for total assets and total liabilities.

ASSETS

Loans

The credit-creation function of commercial banks is reflected in the asset side of their balance sheet. As shown in Table 1-4 (next page), total loans were $8,392.9 billion, making them the banks' largest asset. The three major categories of loans are commercial and industrial loans (C&I loans), real estate loans, and consumer loans. The relative shares of these loans are shown in Table 1-5. The two principal categories of loans are real estate loans and commercial and industrial (C&I) loans.

Real estate loans are the largest component of bank loans, accounting for 44.8 percent of the total. Real estate loans are used for the purchase of homes, income-producing properties (such as apartments and office buildings), and commercial properties. Real estate loans also include home equity loans, where a borrower's home is used as collateral for a personal loan. As a result of securitization, some real estate loans are liquid. Nevertheless, history tells us that long-term real estate loans, especially those for commercial properties, are more risky than short-term C&I loans. [44]

Table 1-5: COMPOSITION OF BANK LOANS, September 2015

Type of Loans	$ Billions	%
Commercial and Industrial	1,912.9	22.6
Real Estate	3,784.5	44.8
Consumer	1,244.6	14.7
Other including interbank loans	1,510.2	17.9
Total	$8,452.2	100%

C&I loans are the next largest component, and they are used by businesses for acquiring inventory, carrying accounts receivable, and purchasing new equipment and real estate. In addition, substantial amounts of credit are extended by commercial banks to other financial institutions, principally to securities firms and to finance companies. Indeed, most small finance companies obtain the bulk of their funds from commercial banks.

The third major type of credit at commercial banks is "Other" loans including interbank loans. In this case, there is no clearly identified type of credit being extended.

Finally, there are loans to individuals -- consumer loans for the purchase of consumer durable goods, consolidation of debts, vacations, and for other purposes. This category includes credit card debt, auto loans, and other forms of consumer credit.

The allocation of loans varies widely among banks of different sizes, different strategies, and different locations. Community banks focus on the local needs of the communities that they serve. Nearly one in five U.S. counties --including small towns, rural communities, and urban neighborhoods -- would have no physical banking presence if not for the community banks operating locally. They account for approximately 45 percent of all the small loans to businesses and farms made by all banks.[45] Thus, agricultural, consumer, and real estate loans often account for a larger fraction of their total loan portfolio than at large and global banks that serve a broader group of borrowers. Some large banks offer a full range of loans, while others specialize in credit cards, investment banking, and so on.

Investments

Commercial banks hold substantial amounts of liquid assets. A large fraction of the investment portfolio of commercial banks is held in the form of short-term securities, especially the holdings of U.S. Treasury securities. Their holdings of liquid assets are attributable to the large volume of volatile transactions deposits, the role played by commercial banks in administering the nation's payments system, and the demand for loans. In addition, commercial banks play an important role in assisting the U.S. government in financing its own activities. Banks serve as a depository of the U.S. government (tax and loan accounts) as well as for state and local government securities. Tax collections of the U.S. government are deposited at commercial banks, which play an important role in the sale of U.S. savings bonds.

Cash

Commercial banks are the core of the payments system and they provide individuals and businesses with currency and coins. This function is reflected on the balance sheet of commercial banks as a $2,623.8 billion holding of cash assets. While we tend to associate banks with cash, as shown in Table1-4, it accounted for 17 percent of total assets. Since cash is a non-earning asset, banks hold the minimum amount they need to operate efficiently.

Other Assets

Other assets include buildings, equipment, and some other odds and ends that account for about one percent of total assets. To put this in context, the overwhelming majority of bank assets are earning assets.

DEPOSITS

Two closely related functions of the commercial banking industry are to offer transaction accounts to the public and to administer the payments system. These basic functions have been historically reflected in the large amount of transactions deposits at commercial banks – deposits that can be withdrawn on demand. To offer these services, individual banks must cooperate with other banks on the clearing and processing of checks. This cooperation among banks leads to a large volume of interbank deposits (deposits from one bank held at another bank). They also must maintain an adequate amount of cash on hand to meet withdrawals.

Transaction accounts include all deposits against which the account holder is permitted to make withdrawals by negotiable or transferable instruments, payment orders of withdrawal, or telephone or preauthorized transfers for the purposes of making payments to third parties and others. Checking accounts and money market accounts are examples of transaction accounts. Accounts that limit the number of withdrawals to six or less are considered savings accounts. The role of passbook savings accounts has diminished sharply in recent years as banks and consumers rely more on money market deposits and money market mutual funds.

EQUITY

Equity represents a small but vitally important part of the balance sheet of commercial banks. In a market-based economy in which banks seek to maximize shareholder wealth, equity is the tangible representation of this private ownership. It is the owner's capital investment. Note, however, that equity capital finances a very small portion of total bank assets. The minimum risk-based capital requirement in 2015 was 8 percent. But banks are required to add a conservation buffer that will increased bank capital to 10.5 percent in 2019.[46] Fundamentally, banks are highly leveraged business organizations, and depositors and other creditors provide 92 percent of the funds that banks need to operate. Because of leverage, bank earnings increase dramatically during periods of prosperity. In contrast, economic declines are magnified into dramatic reductions in bank earnings, erosion in the capital account, and the failure of a large number of banks. The role of bank capital is discussed in detail in Chapter 12.

BANK PROFITABILITY

This section examines the growth in bank profitability, including the reasons for this trend -- economic growth, banks taking on increased risks, earning more fee income, and operating more efficiently.

ECONOMIC GROWTH

The primary determinant of bank profitability is the state of the economy – including economic growth, the level interest rates, and other factors. If the economy is doing well, banks will prosper. If the economy falters, banks will suffer. Recall that credit risk – the risk that borrowers will default on credit obligations – is the greatest risk facing banks. The ability of borrowers to repay their loans is directly related to economic activity at both the national and regional levels.

Regional differences in economic activity are also important because not all geographic regions of the economy grow or contract at the same rate. For example, population and economic growth are greater in the South and Southwest than in Northern states.

The level of market rates of interest that was shown in Figure 1-2 is also important. Recall that interest rates were near record low levels in 2015. Collectively, the level of economic activity, interest rates, and other factors affect bank profits as measured by the return on assets (ROA).

As shown in Table 1-7, the ROA for all FDIC-insured institutions, which includes commercial banks and savings institutions, increased from the recession low of 0.48 percent in 1990 to 1.28 percent in 2005. As a rule of thumb, a one percent ROA is considered good.

Table 1-7: RETURN ON ASSETS OF ALL FDIC-INSURED INSTITUTIONS

1990	0.48%
1995	1.17%
2000	1.14%
2005	1.28%
2010	0.65%
2015 (1st Qtr.)	1.02%

Source: Various *FDIC Quarterly Banking Profiles*

INCREASED RISK

Over the years, bank loan portfolios have shifted from short-term C&I loans to longer-term real estate loans. The interest rate charged on loans reflects their risk, maturity, and collateral values. The higher the risk and longer the maturity, the higher the interest rate charged. However, with interest rates near record low levels in October, 2015, there wasn't much difference in the rates charged on loans. A 48-month new car loan was 3.17 percent, a 15-year mortgage was 2.97 percent, and a 30 -year mortgage was 3.75 percent.[47]

FEE INCOME

Fee income (noninterest income) is becoming increasingly important to banks as more liberal banking powers allow them to provide a wider range of financial services. Currently, some banks charge fees for the services they provide consumers, such as those listed below for business accounts:

- Cash deposits per $100, $0.05
- Check paid or other debit posted, $0.14
- Deposit or other credit posted, $0.25
- Inactive checking account fee (no activity for one year), $3 per month
- Insufficient funds, $24
- Night depository, $15 per bag, $20 per year
- Stop payment charge, $24
- Telephone transfers, $3

In addition, they earn fees from their other financial service activities including brokerage, derivatives, mutual funds, trade finance, trust accounts, and so on. In 2014, total interest income for all FDIC-insured institutions was $469,780 million, and total noninterest income was $247,899 million.

EFFICIENCY

Banks are operating more efficiently than they have in the past. The efficiency ratio measures the proportion of net operating revenues absorbed by overhead expenses. It is calculated by dividing noninterest expense less amortization of intangibles by total revenues. A lower value indicates greater efficiency. The ratio was about 66 percent in 1980 and moved to 60 percent in the first quarter 2015.[48] Personnel expenses account for the largest part of overhead expense. Therefore, the decline in the ratio tells us that banks lowered their personnel expenses by operating with fewer people.

SUMMARY

The basic theme of this chapter is that the functions of banking are constant, but the forms of banking are changing. A basic law of structural design is that form follows function. That concept applies to banking as well.

In general terms, a bank is an organization that engages in the business of banking -- it accepts FDIC-insured deposits and makes loans. Banks perform three basic functions: (1) they provide a leading role in the payments system, (2) they intermediate between depositors and borrowers by offering deposit and loan products; and (3) they provide a variety of financial services, encompassing fiduciary services, investment banking, and off-balance sheet risk taking.

Commercial banks are private, profit-seeking enterprises, balancing risk and return in their portfolio management with the goal of maximizing shareholder wealth. Shareholder wealth depends on three factors: (1) the volume of cash flows resulting from portfolio decisions, (2) the timing of those cash flows, and (3) the risk or volatility of the cash flows. Risks include credit risk, interest rate risk, operational risk, liquidity risk, price risk, foreign exchange risk, compliance, strategic, and reputation risks. The maximization of shareholder wealth is constrained by certain social responsibilities of banks as well as extensive legal and regulatory restrictions, including balance sheet, pricing, geographical, entry, and consumer protection constraints.

The environment within which bank managers operate is changing dramatically. The principal regulatory and competitive changes are (1) inflation and volatile interest rates, (2) securitization (3) technological advances such as digitalization, (4) more sophisticated consumers, (4) deregulation, (5) despecialization and competition, (6) globalization, and. (7) competition from the money and capital markets. The net result of these changes is to increase the risk involved in bank management and the complexity of bank decision making.

Next we examined the balance sheets and profitability of commercial banks. The data revealed that loans account for the largest share of bank assets followed by investments. The loans and investments are funded by deposits and other borrowed funds, and to a lesser extent, equity. Bank profitability depends on the state of the economy, the markets that the banks serve, the bank's efficiency, and other factors.

KEY TERMS AND CONCEPTS

Bank (definition, functions, and types)
Bank risk management
CHIPS (The Clearing House Interbank Payments System)
Commercial bank
Commercial loans
Community banks
Compliance risk
Consolidation
Consumer banks
Correspondent banks
Credit risk
Deregulation
Efficiency ratio
Foreign exchange risk
Global banks
Globalization
Economies of scale and scope
Fedwire
Fee income
Full service banks
Insurance services
Intermediation (financial)
International banks
Internet banks
Interest rate risk
Limited purpose banks
Liquidity risk
Money center banks
Monoline banks
National banks
Operational risk
Payments systems (retail and large dollar)
Preemption
Price risk
Real bills doctrine
Reputation risk
Retail banks
Securitization
Securities services
Standby letter of credit
State bank
Strategic risk
SWIFT (the Society for Worldwide Interbank Financial Telecommunication)
Too-Big-To-Fail doctrine
Trade credit
Transaction accounts
Trust services
Wholesale banks
Wildcat banking

QUESTIONS

1.1 It is sometimes argued that bank managers are fundamentally involved In risk management. In what sense are they risk managers? Is there risk management similar to or different from that of managers of manufacturers and other nonfinancial firms?
1.2 How do commercial banks differ from other types of depository institutions such as credit unions?
1.3. List three broad functions of commercial banks. What other financial institutions compete with

banks in providing these services to the public?
1.4. What is the principal goal of a commercial bank? How does profitability of a bank and the risks it faces affect this goal?
1.5 What are the principal factors that have affected the operations of commercial banks in recent years? Which (if any) of these are under the control of bank management?
1.6. What risk historically accounts for most bank failures?
1.7. What constraints do banks face in achieving their goals?
1.8. Discuss market share trends over time among commercial banks. Why has the market share of banks fallen?
1.9 What is meant by securitization?
1.10. What are the principal assets and liabilities of commercial banks? How have they changed over time?
1.11 What are some of the major external and internal factors that affect bank profits?

CASE: THE POLICY CONSULTANT (Part 1)

Jack Anderson is a policy consultant for North Information Services (NIS), a firm that specializes in lobbying Congress for banks and financial institutions that want to protect their economic interests. Mr. North, President and C.E.O. of NIS asked Jack to prepare a brief for one of their major clients, an international bank, on the major issues that Congress will address this next term. For the first part of his brief, Jack is going to begin his research by reviewing the following sources of information concerning banking issues that are available on the Internet:

- Speeches and testimony by members of the Board of Governors of the Federal Reserve System: (http://www.federalreserve.gov)
- Current Federal legislation in the U.S. House Committee on Financial Services: (http://www.house.gov)
- The Bank for International Settlements deals with international issues (http://www.bis.org)

Based on these and other sources that he finds, Jack wants to determine:

1. What are the current major issues facing domestic banks and their regulators?
2. Because the client is an international bank, what are the current major issues facing international banks and their regulators?
3. How might these issues affect the client?

ENDNOTES

1. Herman E. Kroos, and Martin R. Blyn, *A History of Financial Intermediaries*, New York, Random House, Inc., 1971.
2. Ibid.
3. Ross M. Robertson, *The Comptroller and Bank Supervision: A Historical Perspective*, Washington, D.C., Office of the Comptroller of The Currency, 1995, p. 16.
4. Julie I. Williams, First Senior Deputy Comptroller and Chief Counsel, Office of the Comptroller of the Currency, "The OCC, The National Bank Charter, & Current Issues Facing the National Banking System," Prepared for the Financial Services Regulatory Conference, Washington, D.C., March 17, 2003. www.occ.treas.gov
5. A bill of exchange is a written order issued by the drawer instructing a second party – the drawee -- to pay a stated amount of money on some future date. Bills of exchange were used by merchants in connection with goods and inventory that were shipped.
6. National Bank Act, 12 U.S.C.A. 24 (7).
7. A bank holding company is defined as a company that controls one or more banks. The term "control" means owning 25 percent or more of the voting shares in two or more banks, but in some cases control can occur at lower levels of ownership. The control level for a financial holding compa-

ny is 15 percent. For additional details, see the Federal Reserve, Commercial Bank Examination Manual, http://www.federalreserve.gov/boarddocs/supmanual/supervision_cbem.htm
8. Board of Governors v. Dimension Financial Corporation, 474 U.S. 361 (1986).
9. John R. Walter, "Banking and Commerce: Tear Down the Wall," *Economic Quarterly*, Federal Reserve Bank of Richmond, Spring 2003, 7-31.
10. Although the nonbank bank loophole was closed, about 160 enterprises were allowed to continue to operate at nonbank banks, subject to certain limitations.
11. www.ffec.gov/nic. The "Glossary" is found under FAQ (Frequently Asked Questions).
12. 12 USC 1813(a)
13. See http://www.fidelity.com/.; http://www.gecapital.com
14. See: http://www.principal.com/
15. U.S. Small Business Administration, "S Corporation," https://www.sba.gov/content/s-corporation
16. "Community Banks Remain Resilient Amid Industry Consolidation," *FDIC Quarterly*, Volume 8, No. 2, 2014, p. 33. Also see: Statement by Maryann F. Hunter, Deputy Director, Division of Banking Supervision and Regulation Community, Federal Reserve Board, Before the Subcommittee on Financial Institutions and Consumer Protection, Committee on Banking, Housing, and Urban Affairs, U.S. Senate, Washington, DC, April 6, 2011, http://www.federalreserve.gov/newsevents/testimony/hunter20110406a.htm.
17. "Summary of FDIC Research Definition of Community Banking Organization," *FDIC Quarterly*, First Quarter, 2015, Volume 9, No. 2, p. 29; FDIC Community Banking Study, Chapter 1 - Defining the Community Bank, December 2012, p. 1-1.
18. See the National Information Center, Holding Companies greater than $10 billion (HC>B). https://www.ffiec.gov/nicpubweb/nicweb/HCSGreaterThan10B.aspx
19. The definitions banks used above reflect the general use of those terms, not the legal definitions, or those used by bank regulators. The OCC's Comptroller's Corporate Manual – Charters, is available on their web page (www.occ.treas.gov), and it provides their current definitions of various types of banks. Office of the Comptroller of the Currency, "Wholesale and Limited Purpose Banks under the Community Reinvestment Act," As of January 11, 2012, recovered10/13/15.
20. "Risk-Based Capital Guidelines," Federal Register, National Archives and Records Administration, August 4, 2003, 45902-45903.
21. http://www.occ.treas.gov/cra/limited.htm See this website for a further discussion of limited purpose banks.
22. "The 2013 Federal Reserve Payments Study," Board of Governors of the Federal Reserve System, December 19, 2013.
23. "Government Checks Processed by the Federal Reserve –Annual Data," Check Services, Board of Governors of the Federal Reserve System, February 27, 2015.
24. "Consumer and Mobile Financial Services 2015," Board of Governors of the Federal Reserve System, March 2015.
25. "Real Time in Real Life: The Impact of a Real-Time Payments System on its Users." NACHA, The Electronic Payments Association, 2015.
26. Fedwire Funds Services Annual, Board of Governors of the Federal Reserve System, http://www.federalreserve.gov/paymentsystems/fedfunds_ann.htm
27. Office of the Comptroller of the Currency, Large Bank Supervision, Comptroller's Handbook, January 2010. The risks listed by the OCC may appear to differ from those listed by different bank supervisory agencies.
28. Robert Barba, "How B of A Plans to Personalize Mobile Banking," *American Banker*, October 8, 2015. http://www.americanbanker.com/news/bank-technology/how-b-of-a-plans-to-personalize-mobile-banking-1077151-1.html?zkPrintable=true.
29. For current information/daily updates about cyber security, see "The CyberWire," http://www.thecyberwire.com/. Also see the FBI's website on Cyber Crime; https://www.fbi.gov/about-us/investigate/cyber. And the Federal Financial Institutions Examination Council's website: www.FFIEC.gov/cybersecurity.htm and through the FFIEC IT Handbook InfoBase at ithandbook.ffiec.gov.

30. Office of the Comptroller of the Currency, "Annual Report: Fiscal Year 2014," p. 13.
31. The OCC Comptroller's Handbook, Large Bank Supervision, (January, 2010, updated May, 2013 for risk definitions).
32. Federal Reserve Bank of St. Louis, FRED, Graph: 10-Year Treasury Constant Maturity Rate, https://research.stlouisfed.org/fred2/graph/?id=GS10.
33. History of the Eighties: Lessons for the Future, Vol. 1, Washington, D.C., Federal Deposit Insurance Corporation, 1997, Chapter 1.
34. Statistical Abstract of the United States, 1992, Washington, D.C., U.S. Department of Commerce, 1992, Table 794.
35. Federal Reserve Bank of St. Louis, FRED, Graph: 10-Year Treasury Constant Maturity Rate, https://research.stlouisfed.org/fred2/graph/?id=GS10
36. Consumer Financial Protection Bureau, "What Is A Payday Loan?" www.consumerfinance.gov/askcfpb/1567/what-payday-loan.html
37. Federal Reserve Regulation Q; 12 CFR. 217.
38. FDIC Quarterly Financial Profile, First Quarter 2015, Table III-A. For recent information on bank acquisitions, see Federal Reserve Release H.2A -"Notice of Formation and Mergers of, and Acquisitions by, Bank Holding Companies or Savings and Loan Holding Companies; Change in Bank Control."
39. Mitchell Berlin, "Trade Credit: Why Do Production Firms Act as Financial Intermediaries," *Business Review,* Federal Reserve Bank of Philadelphia, Third Quarter, 2003, 21-28.
40. Annalisa Ferrando, Klaas Mulier, "Do Firms Use The Trade Credit Channel to Manage Growth?" *Journal of Banking & Finance,* Volume 37, Issue 8, August 2013, 3035-3046
41. Shirakawa, Masaaki, Kunio Okina, and Shigenori Shiratsuka, "Financial Market Globalization: Present and Future," Institute for Monetary and Economic Studies, Bank of Japan, Discussion Paper No. 97-E-11, 1997.
42. Sapsford, J., "U. S. Financial Firms Delve Deeper in Japan," *Wall Street Journal*, January 26, 1999, a13.
43. Federal Reserve statistical release H.15 Selected Interest Rates, October 13, 2015
44. See: "*International Banking Crises: The Real Estate Connection,*" appears in Benton E. Gup, International Bank Crises: Large-scale Failures, Massive Government Interventions, Westport, CT: Quorum Books 1999.
45. Remarks by FDIC Chairman Martin Gruenberg to the Economic Growth and Regulatory Paperwork Reduction Act (EGRPRA) Outreach Event; Federal Reserve Bank of Chicago, Chicago, IL, October 19, 2015.
46. FDIC, Regulatory Capital Interim Final Rule, https://fdic.gov/regulations/resources/director/RegCapIntFinalRule.pdf
47. "Consumer Rates and Returns to Investor," *The Wall Street Journal*, October 19, 2015, C4.
48. FDIC Quarterly Banking Profile, Table IIIA, First Quarter 2015, All FDIC-Insured Institutions.

Chapter 2

The Bank Regulatory Environment

After reading this chapter, you will be able to:

- Understand the rationale for bank regulation.
- Explain why banking regulations changed during the 1980s, 1990s and 2000s.
- Describe the principal legislative changes in banking and the effects of those changes on banking operations.
- Evaluate the principal issues facing the banks and bank regulators today.

Alan Greenspan, former chairman of the Board of Governors of the Federal Reserve System, had the following to say about the purpose of bank regulation: "If risk-taking is a precondition of a growing economy, and if banks themselves exist because they are willing to take on and manage risk, what should be the objectives of bank regulation? The answer clearly should begin with the goal of circumscribing the incentive of banks to take excessive risks owing to the moral hazard in the safety net designed to protect the financial system and individual depositors. But the full answer must involve some benefit-costs tradeoffs between, on the one hand, protecting the financial system, and on the other hand allowing banks to perform their essential risk-tanking function. Herein lays the basic problem with much of U.S. banking law and regulation.

If banking were not regulated to any greater extent than, say, restaurants, our banking system would operate a great deal differently than it does. Banks could be formed and liquidated with minimal limitations on their entry and exit from the banking market. Inefficient banks would go out of business. Competition would determine the prices and availability of banking services. Banks would also operate anywhere in the world without geographic or portfolio restrictions. Capital structure would be the prerogative of management. The cost of a bank's funds would be determined by its business and financial risk profile. And, of course, the penalty for either excessive or inadequate expansion of risk-taking would be failure.

But banks (and other depository institutions) are not allowed to operate with such freedom. Both entry and exit are controlled and limited, as are mergers with other institutions and nonbanking firms. The scope and nature of banking activities are regulated." [1]

WHY ARE BANKS REGULATED?

PREVENT DISRUPTION OF THE ECONOMY

Domestic Economy

Banks are regulated for three different reasons. The first two reasons involve prudential regulation of banks, dealing with their safety and soundness. The third reason concerns social goals.

First, banks are regulated to reduce the risk of large-scale failures that would adversely affect the level of economic activity. This does not mean the individual bank that is poorly run should not be allowed to fail. It does mean that the government and bank regulators are concerned that if one or more of the largest banks fails, or if there are a large number of bank failures, it would adversely affect the financial markets and the economy.

In this regard, the smooth functioning of the economy is dependent on the money supply, the payments system, and on an uninterrupted flow of credit. Bank demand deposits, other fully checkable deposits, savings deposits, and time deposits in amounts less than $100,000 are components of the money supply.[2] Such accounts offered by banks and other depository institutions offer the liquidity, mobility, and acceptability necessary for our economy's payments system to function with ease and efficiency. Further, banks are the primary source of liquidity for other financial institutions and are the "transmission belt" for the implementation of monetary policy. A safe, sound banking system is thus viewed as essential to a nation's monetary system and financial marketplace because large-scale bank failures could disrupt the U.S. economy.

Federal Deposit Insurance Corporation (FDIC) deposit insurance at FDIC insured banks also contributes to a smooth-functioning economy. As shown below, certain deposits are insured up to $250,000.[3]

The FDIC covers:

- Checking accounts
- Negotiable Order of Withdrawal (NOW) accounts
- Savings accounts
- Money Market Deposit Accounts (MMDAs)
- Time deposits such as certificates of deposit (CDs)
- Cashier's checks, money orders, and other official items issued by a bank

The FDIC does not cover

- Stock investments
- Bond investments
- Mutual funds
- Life insurance policies
- Annuities
- Municipal securities
- Safe deposit boxes or their contents
- U.S. Treasury bills, bonds or notes

Global Markets

There is also concern of systemic risk. ***Systemic risk*** occurs when bank failures are potentially contagious, and only then if the losses in one bank cascade into other banks, or to other economies throughout the world. All of the world's major economies are linked together through the financial markets and other business relationships. A major shock in the U.S. economy will have world-wide repercussions. Likewise, economic disruptions in Asia, Europe, and elsewhere can and do impact the U.S. economy. Because such economic disruptions might result in large-scale failures in the banking system, and in view of the moral hazard incentives created by the safety net that is designed to contain systemic risk, some government supervision of banks is essential for economic stability. In this case, ***moral hazard*** means that banks may take on more risk than is desirable from the deposit insurers' (safety net) point of view that is described below. If the banks taking on the higher degree of risk are profitable, the shareholders gain. If, on the other hand, the banks fail, the FDIC loses. Therefore, some regulation is needed.

GUARD AGAINST DEPOSIT INSURANCE LOSSES

Second, in any debtor – creditor relationship, the creditor limits the debtor's actions and monitors their behavior to ensure repayment of the loan. In the case of banks, the largest numbers of creditors are small depositors, most of whom are not capable of evaluating the financial condition of banks or monitoring their actions. Therefore, it is in public interest to protect small depositors by having their deposits insured by a government agency -- the Federal Deposit Insurance Corporation (FDIC). Thus, the FDIC represents the depositors and the public's interests to ensure that banks operate in a safe and sound fashion. This helps to protect the deposit insurance fund. If bank failures are large enough to exhaust the deposit insurance fund, the taxpayers will be called on to repay depositors. This is what happened when more than 550 savings and loan associations (S&Ls) failed in the 1980s, and exhausted the Federal Savings and Loan Insurance Corporation's (FSLIC) insurance fund. The General Accounting Office estimated that the S&L debacle cost federal taxpayers $132 billion.[4] In contrast to FSLIC, the FDIC had sufficient funds to cover the costs of the 1,617 bank failures during the 1980-1994 period.[5]

SOCIAL GOALS

Third, banks are regulated to achieve desired social goals. This public choice approach to regulation serves to reallocate resources from one group to another.[6] According to Federal Reserve Governor Edward Kelley, Jr., banks are regulated "to promote an efficient and effective banking system that finances economic growth, impartially allocates credit, and meets the needs of the customers and communities that banks serve."[7] Thus, banks cannot discriminate against borrowers on the basis of race, sex, age, and other factors. Borrowers must be judged on the basis of their creditworthiness. In addition, banks must supply borrowers with accurate information about the cost of borrowing.

Another social goal is fighting crime. The Bank Secrecy Act of 1970 (BSA) was the first federal legislation targeting money laundering and other white collar crimes.[8] It is called the Bank Secrecy Act because it helps provide information to law enforcement agencies by creating a "paper trail," since banks are required to file ***Currency Transaction Reports (CTRs)*** for domestic currency transactions (deposits, withdrawals, exchanges) in excess of $10,000, and ***Currency or Monetary Instrument Reports (CIMRs)*** for international currency transactions in excess of $10,000. All of the reports are filed with the Treasury's Financial Crimes Enforcement Network, which is known as FinCen.[9]

WHY BANKS FAIL

The focus in this section is on the failure motive for bank regulation, and why banks fail. Individual banks fail for three major reasons: credit risk, interest rate risk, and foreign exchange risk. Two other potential sources of failure are bank runs and fraud. Bank runs will be explained shortly. Fraud is a legal concept, and what constitutes fraud in one country may be standard business practice in another. What was called “crony capitalism” in Indonesia (giving preferential treatment in terms of loans and grants to relatives and friends) is called fraud in the United States. Therefore, fraud is not addressed here.[10] We are going to examine credit risk as a cause for failure in this chapter. Interest rate risk and foreign exchange risk are addressed in later chapters.

CREDIT RISK

Banks’ primary source of revenue is interest income from their loan portfolios, and their primary risk is credit risk. Credit risk was defined in Chapter 1 as the risk to earnings and capital that an obligor will fail to meet the terms of any contract with the bank, or otherwise fail to perform as agreed. It is usually associated with loans and investments.

Bankers know that lending is a risky business and that some of the loans will not be repaid. Therefore they set aside a reserve for expected losses, usually one to two percent of total loans and leases. If the losses exceed the amount set aside, the excess amount of losses are deduced from bank capital. If the losses are large enough to eliminate most of the bank's capital, the bank will fail unless additional capital is added.

The amount of financial leverage (bank capital relative to the assets) is important. Banks' ratio of capital to assets declined from over 50 percent in the 1840s to about 7.5% during the financial crises 2008-09, but then the ratio increased to 9.5 percent in the 2015. A small capital base puts banks at a greater risk of failure if there are large losses. However, banks are required to increase their capital requirements over time. This will be explained in greater detail in Chapter 12.

In order to examine the process of bank growth and failure, we make five simplifying assumptions. First, the stakeholders in a bank include shareholders, managers, employees, customers, and the communities they serve. Each of these stakeholders wants to maximize their own utility. They see higher growth of assets, loans, and profits as a means to an end. Simply stated, everyone wants the bank to grow in order to be better off.

Second, some bank loans can go bad over time because of factors that are unique to a borrower, or that are beyond the borrower’s control. Changes in macroeconomic or international conditions might adversely affect a large number of borrowers, which can cause them to default. Such macroeconomic and international factors include, but are not limited to, shocks in interest rates and exchange rates, widespread asset price deflation, and global contagion.

Third, we assume that banks have an excess concentration of loans to a group of borrowers, and they are not adequately diversified. In countries with developed capital market like the U.S., this is considered poor management. In a developing country with repressed financial markets, there may not be any alternatives.

Fourth, the loans are not backed by collateral.

Fifth, the loan-to-value ratio is 100 percent. That is, the bank lends 100 percent of the amount of the value of the underlying asset.

BANK GROWTH AND FAILURE

Consider the hypothetical bank that is shown in Table 2-1 (next page), Panel A. It has a single loan as its sole asset, and it is funded by deposits and stockholders' equity. The ratio of equity capital to risk-assets (E/A) is sufficiently large so that the bank is "well-capitalized"[12] at 10 percent, and it has an ample loan loss reserve. In addition, the bank is very profitable. It has a return on assets (ROA) of 2.88 percent, more than twice the 1.06 percent ROA for all FDIC-insured commercial banks in the United States in 2015.[13] As previously noted, the stakeholders of the bank want it to grow so that they get higher returns on their investment, higher salaries, and other gains.

In order to grow, the bank raises an additional $20 million in deposits, and it invests those funds in two loans of $10 million each (Table 2-1, Panel B). No additional loan loss reserves are required. In this period, the ROA is 2.73%, and the ratio of equity/assets is 8.33 percent, meaning that the bank is "adequately capitalized."
The terms "well capitalized," "adequately capitalized," and so on, for total risk-based capital are defined in Table 2-2. The discussion of Table 2-1 does not make the distinction between E/A and risk-based capital. Capital requirements are examined in Chapter 12.

In the next period, which is shown in Table 2 -1, Panel C, one of the $10 million loans goes into default. The reason for the default in this example resides exclusively with the borrower.

The $10 million default exceeds the loan loss reserve by $8 million. That difference is deducted from stockholders' equity, leaving only $2 million in equity. After the deduction, the bank has tangible equity/risk assets of 1.79 percent. Now the bank is "critically undercapitalized," and it fails unless additional capital is injected. [14]

What could the bank have done to reduce its credit risk? First, there was undue loan concentration - it lent too much of its capital to a single borrower. Excess concentration can also occur with a particular type of loans. For example, a large number of bank failures are associated with real estate loans. Therefore, a bank that has a large number of real estate loans may be riskier than one with a well diversified portfolio. As previously noted, banks in repressed financial markets may not have a choice about loan concentration. Banks in developed capital markets, however, have better loan opportunities and can avoid undue concentration.

Second, the loan-to-value ratio and collateral are important determinants of a borrower's vested interest in a loan. From the borrowers' point of view, a high loan-to-value ratio (i.e., 100 percent) is desirable. From the bank's point of view, a lower loan-to-value ratio, say 70-80 percent, is desirable to reduce risk. In a competitive environment, some banks will compete on the terms of the loan as well as interest rate and forgo safety in order to grow. Borrowers that have 20-30 percent of their own funds invested in an asset are less likely to default than those that have smaller amounts of their own funds at risk.

Third, the bank could have reduced its risk by requiring collateral that could be sold in the event of default. Borrowers have a positive incentive not to lose valuable collateral.

Table 2-1: BANK GROWTH AND LOSSES (CREDIT RISK)

Panel A

Assets ($ millions)		Liabilities	
Loan	$102 @ 9%	Deposits	$90 @ 7%
Loan loss reserve	−2		
Net loans	$100		
		Stockholders' equity	$10
Totals	$100		$100

Net income: $9.18 – $6.30 = $2.88
Return on assets (ROA): $2.88/$100 = 2.88%
Equity/Assets (E/A): $10/$100 = 10%
With an E/A of 10%, the bank is *well-capitalized.*

Panel B

Assets ($ millions)		Liabilities	
Loan	$102 @ 9%	Deposits	$110 @ 7%
Loan	10 @ 9%		
Loan	10 @ 9%		
Loan loss reserve	−2		
Net loans	$120		
		Stockholders' equity	$10
Totals	$120		$120

Net income: $10.98 – $7.70 = $3.28
Return on assets (ROA): $3.28/$120 = 2.73%
Equity/Assets (E/A): $10/$120 = 8.33%
With an E/A of 8.33%, the bank is *adequately capitalized.*

Panel C

Assets ($ millions)		Liabilities	
Loan	$102 @ 9%	Deposits	$110 @ 7%
Loan	10 @ 9%		
Loan default	−10		
Loan loss reserve	2		
Net loans	$112		
		Stockholders' equity	$2
Totals	$112		$112

The defaulted loan of $10 exceeds loan loss reserve by $8, which is deducted from stockholders' equity.
Net income: $10.08 – $7.70 = $2.38
Return on assets (ROA): $2.38/$112 = 2.13%
Equity/Assets (E/A): $2/$112 = 1.79%
The bank is *critically undercapitalized,* and it fails.

Fourth, the creditworthiness of the borrower was not an issue at the time the loan was made. Nevertheless, over time, the creditworthiness of the borrower deteriorated to the extent that the loan went into default. Regular monitoring of the loan may give the bank sufficient early warning to deal with the borrower's problems and avoid the default.

Fifth, the bank could have hedged some of its credit risk with credit derivatives. Credit derivatives include credit default contracts, total return swaps, credit spread contracts, and credit linked notes. These products are explained in a later chapter.

BANK RUNS

Bank runs occur when depositors or other creditors fear for the safety or availability of their funds, and large numbers of depositors try to withdraw their funds at the same time. Banks do not keep enough cash on hand to meet large-scale unexpected withdrawals of deposits. Deposits can be withdrawn on a first come, first serve basis. Therefore, a run reflects the herd behavior of depositors to obtain the limited amount of cash that is available. In August 1998, CNN and other television stations showed long lines of Russians citizens trying to withdraw their funds from local banks during the financial debacle in Russia. The Russian government defaulted on the payment of some of its securities, and the citizens thought that the banks were unsound. The banks were not able to pay off all depositors, and they were closed.

Similarly, a "silent run" occurs when large creditors, such as banks and investment companies, withdraw their funds in order to protect themselves. This happened to Continental Illinois Bank in 1974. International banks had uninsured deposits of tens and hundreds of millions of dollars in Continental. Subsequently, Continental Illinois Bank failed.

Bank runs on one bank may spark bank runs on other banks and create a domino or contagion effect. If that occurs, solvent banks that lack liquidity may be able to borrow from the Federal Reserve – the lender-of-last resort.

Finally, it should be noted that bank runs are not limited to uninsured deposits. On Friday, January 4, 1991, the Bank of New England announced that it expected a loss that would render it technically insolvent.[15] Depositors had a "run" on the bank, and they withdrew more than $1 billion. Although their deposits were insured, they did not want to be inconvenienced, and they wanted liquidity. On Sunday, January 6, 1991, the bank failed, due in part to the run -- it was declared insolvent by the Office of the Comptroller of the Currency (OCC), and the FDIC was appointed as receiver.

THE FOUNDATION OF THE REGULATORY FRAMEWORK

As explained in Chapter 1, state banks were the first commercial banks chartered in the United States. Then the National Currency Act of 1863 and the ***National Bank Act of 1864*** established a national banking system, and gave the Office of the Comptroller of the Currency (OCC) the authority to charter, regulate, and, supervise national banks. The notes issued by national banks were to be the circulating currency, and the Comptroller exercised some monetary control functions. Today the OCC plays a minor role in the administration of currency.[16]

In this chapter the focus is on laws that affected banking structure. Real estate and consumer credit legislation is examined in Chapter 10.

The ***Federal Reserve Act of 1913*** created the Federal Reserve System as the central banking system of the United States. In 1913, the United States was a developing country, and the Federal Reserve was created to facilitate economic development. The Federal Reserves functions were to provide an elastic currency, to provide facilities for discounting commercial paper, and to improve banking supervision.

Over time, these functions evolved into controlling inflation and deflation and creating conditions for stable prices, economic growth, employment, and consumption.

THE 1930s

More than 14,000 banks failed between 1921 and 1929. Most of these were small banks in rural, agricultural communities. Failures and mergers (many of the latter serving to forestall failure) had reduced the number of commercial banks to about 25,000 in 1929. The economic collapse known as the Great Depression began that year. Legislation stemming from the economic crisis of the 1930s is responsible for our present banking structure. In the following sections, we are going to examine the principal laws that shaped our banking structure.

THE MCFADDEN ACT OF 1927

The Federal Reserve Act of 1913 was amended into what is commonly called The McFadden Act of 1927. This federal law prohibited interstate banking. Some state laws allowed unlimited branch banking within their states, while others only allowed branching in limited geographic areas. In general terms, a branch is a non-main office facility that is capable of offering services similar to those of the main office. An auxiliary teller window was not considered a branch. Automated teller machines (ATMs) did not exist then. Still other states prohibited any branch banking, called unit banking. In 1990, Texas and Illinois, both unit banking states, had 1,184 banks and 1,087 banks, respectively, out of a total of 12,327 banks in the U.S.[17]

THE BANKING ACT OF 1933 (GLASS-STEAGALL ACT)

The Banking Act of 1933, also known as the Glass-Steagall Act, did the following:

1) separated commercial banking from investment banking (underwriting stocks and bonds),

2) established the Federal Deposit Insurance Corporation (FDIC) as a temporary agency,

3) permitted the Federal Reserve to regulate the interest paid on time deposits, and prohibited the payment of interest on demand deposits,

4) raised the minimum capital requirements for national banks.

Securities Power

The Glass-Steagall Act prohibited commercial banks from engaging in investment banking – underwriting issues of corporate securities and nonguaranteed revenue bonds of state and local governments. The separation of commercial and investment banking was regarded as a means of reducing bank risk, and it was intended to help restore public confidence in commercial banks. Further, some legislators were swayed by alleged abuses (of the conflict-of-interest variety) stemming from mixture of the two functions. And, as always, there was concern about the concentration of financial power in institutions exercising commercial banking, investment banking, and trust powers. In the early 1930s, commercial and investment banking were almost totally integrated. The new law thus obliged the numerous institutions performing both functions to choose either commercial or investment banking as their line of business and divest themselves of the other.

Deposit Insurance

The Glass-Steagall Act established federal deposit insurance to protect small depositors to reduce the incidence of bank runs. Insured depositors have less incentive than uninsured depositors to join in "runs" on institutions in which they have deposits. The creation of deposit insurance is credited with having stabilized the U.S. banking system in the wake of crises in the 1930s. At that time the deposits were insured for a maximum of $2,500, and the Federal Deposit Insurance Corporation (FDIC) was funded by premiums of one-twelfth of one percent of the domestic deposits (less certain adjustments) of insured banks.

THE BANKING ACT OF 1935

This act was primarily intended to strengthen the Federal Reserve System and its monetary management power. The act gave the Federal Reserve Board expanded reserve requirement authority, allowed it to regulate discount rates of the District Banks, and gave it the power to regulate the rate of interest paid by member banks on time and savings deposits. The discount rate is the rate at which member banks can borrow from the Federal Reserve.

The 1935 act also marked the end of easy entry into banking. Congress, seeking to curb the high rate of bank failure that had long characterized the U.S. banking system, gave the Comptroller of the Currency greater authority to exercise discretion in the granting of national bank charters. Applicants for a charter henceforth had to demonstrate the need for the proposed bank and make the case that the new bank would be successful without significantly injuring existing banks. If the applicant's case were not convincing to the Comptroller, or if the Comptroller's own investigation of these issues raised reasons for denial, the charter would not be issued.

The effect of greater restrictions on bank entry is evident in the record of new bank charters. During the 1920s, new bank charters granted averaged about 360 per year. From 1935 until the U.S. entry into World War II an average of only about 50 new banks were chartered each year. Although this sharp reduction in the rate of new bank chartering largely reflected depressed economic conditions (and thus a decline in requests for charters), it also reflected the fact that charters were more difficult to obtain. In the postwar expansion (1945-1960) the annual average of new bank charters remained below 100.

Finally, the Banking Act of 1935 established the FDIC as a permanent government agency.

BANK REFORMS OF THE 1980S AND 1990S

The structure and nature of U. S. banking changed dramatically in the 1930s as a result of the wave of bank failures and the reform legislation it evoked. The reduction in the number of banks proved to be enduring, partly as a result of increased entry restrictions. Deposit insurance became a salient feature of the U.S. banking system. Bank failures became rare until the 1980s. The 1933 and 1935 banking acts, in conjunction with previously existing regulations, set in place a regulatory structure that placed the following constraints on banks:

- Pricing - restrictions on pricing of deposits
- Geography - restrictions on entry and geographic expansion
- Products - restrictions on scope and nature of activities, especially limitations of the securities activities of commercial banks
- Capital - minimum capital requirements and restrictions on other balance sheet elements.

After the reforms of the 1930s, banking entered a relatively tranquil period. Banks, like the rest of the U. S. economy, remained generally depressed until World War II. Not until the late 1940s did banking regain its pre-Depression vitality. The ratio of bank loans to assets (only 16 percent in 1945 compared to 63 percent in 1925 ratio) began to rise steadily throughout the 1950s. This resurgence of bank lending continued in the vigorous economic expansion of the 1960s, with banks becoming more aggressive, competitive, and less averse to risk. Dramatic expansion of foreign banking activities by U. S. banks occurred, and banks sought new avenues of profitable growth outside traditional banking.

DEREGULATION

By the late 1970s, it was apparent that the severe set of restrictions imposed on commercial banks in the 1930s was inconsistent with the innovations that were taking place in the financial world. In particular, the limitations on the maximum rates that banks could pay on time and savings deposits (Regulation Q ceilings) had caused banks to lose substantial amounts of funds to nonbank institutions, particularly money market mutual funds. Recall that in the late 1970s, interest rates soared from about five percent to about 18 percent, and banks and thrifts suffered.

Concern also existed about the limitations on the geographic area over which banks could offer their services to an increasingly mobile customer base and whether the limits placed on bank activities were really achieving their objectives. As a result, a number of proposals were advanced to "deregulate" banking.

Deregulation in banking has three separate but closely related dimensions: price (e.g., deposit rate) deregulation, product deregulation, and geographic deregulation. Price deregulation refers to the lifting of legal restrictions on the interest rates that depository institutions may pay to obtain funds (and to a lesser extent, in terms of the importance of the restrictions, on the rates that may be charged for loans, commonly referred to as usury laws). Product deregulation refers to the removal of the restrictions placed on banks and other depository institutions regarding the types of services offered, such as investment banking services or insurance underwriting. Geographic deregulation, of course, refers to the removal of limitations on the geographic extent over which banks (and other depository institutions) may operate deposit-taking facilities.

DEPOSITARY INSTITUTIONS DEREGULATION AND MONETARY CONTROL ACT (DIDMCA)

The Depository Institutions Deregulation and Monetary Control Act (DIDMCA) was passed in 1980 and provided, among other things, for the following:

1. Uniform reserve requirements: Reserve requirements were extended to all depository institutions, commercial banks, mutual savings banks, savings and loan associations, credit unions, agencies and branches of foreign banks, and Edge Act corporations. Only size and type of deposit are relevant in determining reserve requirements.

2. Federal Reserve services: Services provided by the Federal Reserve, such as check clearing and providing vault cash, must be offered to all depository institutions and must be priced on the basis of the Fed's production costs plus a "normal" profit margin. Before this legislation was passed, the Fed provided its services only to member banks and then generally without explicit cost.

3. Regulation Q: The legislation began the process of eliminating interest rate ceilings on time and savings deposit accounts at all depository institutions.

4. Deposit Insurance: It also raised the deposit insurance from the $40,000 ceiling at that time to $100,000.

5. Negotiable order of withdrawal (NOW) accounts: The legislation authorized all depository institutions to offer interest-bearing transactions accounts, generally in the form of NOW accounts. For the first time on a nationwide basis the traditional monopoly by commercial banks of transaction (checking) accounts was broken. Also, for the first time in almost 50 years, explicit interest payments on transactions accounts were allowed.

6. Savings and loans: The lending powers of savings and loans were broadened with passage of the 1980 legislation. In particular, savings and loans were allowed to commit a substantial fraction of their assets to consumer loans. They were also given trust powers. The reforms of the powers of savings and loans contained in this legislation went a long way toward the creation of a "department store of family finance" in the form of savings and loan associations.

THE GARN-ST. GERMAIN ACT OF 1982

The provisions of The Depository Institutions Act of 1982, popularly called the ***Garn-St Germain Act***, can be viewed in some respects as dealing with the problems that had not been resolved by the 1980 legislation. The DIDMCA of 1980 attempted to deal with the interest rate ceilings. By 1982 the thrift institutions problem had become a thrift institutions crisis, and it was reflecting the extraordinarily high interest rate environment of 1981-1982. As a result, the bill provided for the following:

1. FDIC/FSLIC assistance for floundering and failing institutions: In past years the regulatory agencies had been constrained in arrangements to purchase floundering or failing institutions by restrictive laws on interstate acquisition of failing institutions. The new law allowed for acquisition according to the follow-

ing priority schedule: (a) same type of institution, same state; (b) same type of institution, different state; (c) different type of institution, same state; (d) different type of institution, different state. For example, if the failing institution was a commercial bank in Texas, the first potential acquirer would be another bank in Texas; the second potential acquirer would be a commercial bank located outside Texas; the third potential acquirer would be another type of financial institution in Texas; and the fourth potential group of acquiring institutions would be another type of financial institution located outside Texas.

2. Net worth certificates: The 1982 legislation provided for an exchange of debt (called net worth certificates) between depository institutions and the regulatory agencies. Although of substantial legal significance in maintaining an adequate capital position for floundering and failing depository institutions, the economic importance of this portion of the 1982 legislation was relatively minor.
3. Additional thrift institution restructuring: Savings and loans and other thrifts were given even greater powers to offer deposit-taking and lending services. Savings and loans were permitted to offer demand deposit services to qualified commercial, corporate, and agricultural customers, and expand consumer lending and engage in a limited amount of commercial lending.
4. Money market deposit accounts: Perhaps the most significant feature of the 1982 legislation was the provision instructing the Deregulation Committee to create (within 60 days) a money market deposit account MMDA equivalent to and competitive with money market mutual funds. The Deregulation Committee created such an instrument effective in January 1983.

FINANCIAL INSTITUTIONS REFORN< RECOVERY AND ENFORCEMENT ACT (FIRREA) 1989

Unfortunately, neither DIDMICA nor the Garn-St. Germain Act solved all of the serious problems confronting thrift institutions, especially the savings and loan industry. By early 1989 almost 500 savings and loan associations (S&Ls) were insolvent or close to failure. These failures resulted principally from credit risk problems associated with the new power given to S&Ls in the early 1980s. The growing crisis in the thrift industry led to the passage of the ***Financial Institutions Reform, Recovery, and Enforcement Act*** (FIRREA), signed into law on August 9, 1989. The law sought to stem the rising tide of red ink in the thrift industry that the General Accounting Office claims cost the taxpayers $132 billion. Other estimates of losses ranged up to $200 billion. Although the thrift crisis was much smaller in magnitude than bank losses during the Great Depression of the 1930s, thrift losses in the 1980s and 1990s exceeded those suffered by depositors in the Great Depression. Importantly, the thrift crisis illustrated problems in the financial system that FIRREA attempted to overcome.

Regulatory Structure

FIRREA made changes in the structure of the regulatory agencies and the deposit insurance system. First, the Federal Home Loan Bank Board was closed and ceased to be the regulator for thrifts.

Second, the ***Office of Thrift Supervision (OTS),*** a bureau of the U.S. Treasury, was established to replace the Federal Home Loan Bank Board as a regulator of thrifts. OTS is responsible for chartering federal savings institutions and examining and supervising federally insured thrifts and their holding companies. Second, the Federal Housing Finance Board was established to coordinate the activities of the 12 ***Federal Home Loan Banks (FHLBs)*** which provide loans to member institutions for housing finance. OTS took over the previous supervisory powers held by the FHLBs. The FHLB's federal charter allows them to borrow at a relatively low cost, and then lend the money to banks and others to finance housing. The FHLBs are owned by the banks that join the FHLB System.

Third, the FSLIC was dissolved and replaced with the Savings Associations Insurance Funds (SAIF), and The Bank Insurance Fund (BIF), both of which are under FDIC control.

Fourth, FIRREA established the Resolution Trust Corporation (RTC) to manage and dispose of the assets of the failed S&Ls.

Thrift Regulation

FIRREA reversed some of the asset powers given to thrifts under the Garn-St Germain Act of 1982 and increased their capital requirements. To avoid being regulated as banks, thrifts had to conform to qualified thrift-lender (QTL) standards. QTLs have at least 70% of their assets in real estate-related assets (e.g., home loans and securities backed by mortgages). Junk bonds are prohibited, and commercial real estate is limited considerably, as is the amount that can be loaned to a single customer. Further, state-chartered S&Ls are generally prohibited from engaging in activities not allowed federally chartered S&Ls.

New capital requirements for thrifts were intended to increase the stake the shareholders (owners) have invested in each thrift and, thereby, reduce insurance losses and encourage more prudent management. The ratio of core capital to total assets must be at least three percent (core capital is composed of stockholders' equity plus a certain amount of goodwill). At least 50 percent of core capital must represent tangible capital, calculated as tangible assets minus liabilities. Moreover, S&Ls are required to meet capital standards imposed on national banks. Under an international agreement (known as the Basle Agreement), national banks must have capital, defined as stockholders' equity plus some types of debt and other items, equal to at least eight percent of risk-adjusted assets and off-balance-sheet items, and at least four percent of this capital ratio has to be in the form of stockholders' equity. Failure to comply with these guidelines will cause an S&L to be put on a problem list, with subsequent possibility of limits on its deposit rates, asset growth, and dividend payments to stockholders. These higher capital requirements attempt to blunt the incentives for insured thrifts to take excessive risks.

Enforcement Powers

Last, FIRREA enhanced the enforcement powers of bank and thrift regulators. Regulators were given new expanded "cease-and-desist" authority and can impose civil money penalties for violations of regulatory and statutory procedures.

It also established judicial civil penalties and more stringent criminal penalties for financial institution offenses. These enforcement powers are intended to reduce risks from fraud, which played a significant role in the thrift crisis.

Another important provision of FIRREA is cross-bank guarantees. Congress added a statute in FIRREA that makes healthy banks in a multibank holding company (MBHC) liable to the FDIC for the losses of failed member banks. This ***source of strength doctrine*** means that bank holding companies act of a source of financial strength for their affiliates. Unlike the past, if a failed bank in a MBHC incurs losses for the FDIC in its closure and assistance activities, the FDIC can charge the losses against the net worth of profitable banks affiliated with the MBHC. This change in insurance liability for MBHCs should help reduce the risk of bank failures.

FIRREA also allowed bank holding companies to acquire savings and loan associations. The S&L failures plus acquisitions led to further consolidation in the S&L industry. During the 1980s the number of thrifts declined from about 4000 to about 2200. By restricting their activities and raising capital requirements, bank holding company (BHC) acquisitions of thrifts continued throughout the 1990s.

FIRREA represents a dramatic shift in the regulatory reform of the early 1980s. It not only completely restructured the regulatory system for savings and loans but also brought a temporary halt in the trend toward financial deregulation.

FEDERAL DEPOSIT INSURANCE CORPORATION INPROVEMENT ACT OF 1991 (FDICIA)

The FDIC Improvement Act of 1991 (FDICIA) focused primarily on interrelated capital requirements and deposit insurance issues in depository institutions.

Federal banking agencies are empowered to apply ***prompt corrective action*** (PCA) to undercapitalized institutions that are increasingly restrictive as an institution's capital declines. The regulatory capital requirements expressed as a percentage of risk-weighted assets are shown in Table 2-2 (next page). Some examples of these restrictive measures that may be required are the addition of more capital, the denial of an acquisition or merger, the termination of activities posing excessive risk, replacement of directors or officers, divestiture of a subsidiary or affiliate company, or disapproval of bonuses and salary increases. Restrictions on asset growth, deposit interest rates, and dividends could be imposed under certain capital conditions. The Act requires the FDIC to close an institution in the least costly manner when it reaches a critically undercapitalized position – having less than two percent tangible equity.

Also, the Act severely restricted the ability of the FDIC to protect uninsured depositors in bank failures, an issue that is particularly relevant for the failure of systemically important large banks (known as the "too big to fail" doctrine).

It should be clear from the design of the act that capital and deposit insurance are viewed as linked to one another. The thrust of the changes is to shift more of the burden of losses from the public to depository institutions Capital is needed to absorb initial losses, and deposit insurance is necessary to cover more serious losses that exhaust capital reserves. To the extent that more capital is required and penalties are imposed for capital shortfalls, less deposit insurance should be needed in the long run.

The FDICIA also made numerous changes in the ***deposit insurance system***. The FDIC can borrow $30 billion from the U.S. Treasury (raised from $5 billion previously), and the FDIC can impose special assessments on insured institutions to repay FDIC borrowings. In a related measure the FDIC increased the deposit insurance fees to bring federal insurance reserves up to 1.25 percent of all insured deposits. It also developed a risk-based deposit insurance scheme. These changes have the force of shifting the burden of failed institution losses from taxpayers to banks. Theory and practice suggest that these higher insurance costs will be shared by different parties benefiting from depository institutions' services, namely, depositors, borrowers, and shareholders.

Table 2-2: CAPITAL ADEQUACY

Capital Adequacy	Total Risk-Based Capital %*
Well-capitalized	$\geq$ 10%
Adequately capitalized	$\geq$ 8%
Undercapitalized	$\geq$ 6
Significantly undercapitalized	< 6
Critically capitalized	–

* As a percentage of risk-weighted assets.

THE OMNIBUS BUDGET RECONCILLATION ACT OF 1993

This Act provided that insured depositors of failed banks have a priority of claims over noninsured depositors' and creditors' claims. Large deposits of businesses and state and local governments are not covered by FDIC insurance. It was hoped that this would encourage creditors to monitor bank risk behavior thereby instilling ***market discipline*** on the banks. Creditors can impose market discipline on risky institutions by not making deposits, withdrawing their funds, requiring collateral against deposits, requiring guarantees, or requiring interest rates that are commensurate with the risks they are taking.

RIEGLE-NEAL INTERSTATE BANKING AND BRANCHING EFFICIENY ACT OF 1994

The Riegle-Neal Act opened the door for interstate banking by allowing bank holding companies to acquire banks in any state, subject to certain conditions. Beginning in 1997, the Act eased most restrictions on interstate branching. The Riegle-Neal Act was one of the factors contributing to bank mergers and increased banking concentration that was mentioned in Chapter 1. Another catalyst for change and mergers is the Gramm-Leach-Bliley Act of 1999.

GRAMM-LEACH-BILLEY ACT OF 1999

The Gramm-Leach-Bliley Act of 1999 (GLBA), also known as the Financial Services Modernization Act of 1999, marked the end of the 1933 Glass-Steagall prohibitions concerning the separation of banks from investment banking, and the 1956 Bank Holding Company Act's prohibitions on insurance underwriting. ***Financial holding companies,*** organized under the GLBA, may engage in a wide range of financial activities including underwriting and selling insurance and securities, commercial and merchant banking, investing in and developing real estate, and "complementary activities." The states still regulate insurance, but the GLBA prohibits states from making laws that would prevent bank-affiliated firms from selling insurance-related products on an equal basis with other insurance agents. GLBA also allows national banks to underwrite municipal securities.

The GLBA opened the door for further consolidation in the financial services industry. Under the act, banks can buy insurers, brokerage firms can buy banks, and so on. Thus, the Act paved the way for the development of financial supermarkets to serve the needs of consumers. One expected benefit of consolidation is that diversification of services and geography will serve to strengthen financial institutions that heretofore served limited geographic markets with limited products.

The GLBA also permitted the Federal Home Loan Banks to extend credit to community banks (those with assets of $500 million or less) to fund small business and agricultural loans. About 70 percent of the commercial banks are members of the Federal Home Loan Bank system, and about half of all banks have borrowed from the FHLBs.[18] Recall that FHLBs are regulated by the Office of Thrift Supervision (OTS).

Despite the liberalization offered by the GLBA, there are still barriers between commerce and banking that prevent firms, such as Wal-Mart, from offering financial services by acquiring or establishing unitary thrifts.[19] Before GLBA, any financial or nonfinancial corporation could own a unitary thrift. ***Unitary thrift*** holding companies are corporations that own all or part of a single savings bank or savings association. Unitary thrifts can invest in activities that are denied to banks, such as owning and operating hotels, manufacturing, and auto sales and rentals. Thus, unitary thrifts could merge banking with commerce. Commercial firms, such as AllState Insurance Co., American Express, Ford Motor, General Electric, and Merrill Lynch & Co., owned unitary thrifts prior to the enactment of GLBA and were allowed to continue their ownership.

In 2002, Wal-Mart tried to acquire Franklin Bank of California, in Orange California.[20] Their request was denied. Nevertheless, Wal-Mart has an agreement with Chase Manhattan, a J.P. Morgan Chase subsidiary, to provide credit cards with the Wal-Mart name.

DODD-FRANK WALL STREET REFORM AND CONSUMER PROTECTION ACT[21]

The Dodd-Frank Act was signed into law in 2010 following the 2008-09 financial crisis. It is the largest overhaul of financial regulations since the Banking Acts in the 1930s at the time of the Great Depression. The law spans almost the entire financial services industry with major reforms that affect all regulatory agencies. Some argue that the reforms go too far and create regulatory costs that are burdensome to financial firms. Others believe that they did not go far enough to prevent another national financial crisis.

The Act seeks to foster U.S. financial system stability by increasing accountability and transparency in financial institutions and markets. Concerning stability, the Financial Stability Oversight Council was created to oversee financial institutions to identify and respond to emerging risks and systemic risks in the financial system. The Council is chaired by the Secretary of the Treasury and includes appointees from the Federal Reserve, Securities and Exchange Commission (SEC), Commodity Futures Trading Commission (CFTC), Office of the Comptroller of the Currency (OCC), Federal Deposit Insurance Corporation (FDIC), Federal Housing Finance Authority (FHFA), National Credit Union Administration (NCUA), a newly created Consumer Financial Protection Bureau (CFPB), and an independent appointee with insurance expertise. The CFPB oversees credit-reporting agencies, credit and debit cards, payday and consumer loans (but not auto loans from dealers). It also regulates credit fees.

The law also aims to end too-big-to-fail bailouts by putting certain limits on large, complex financial companies. It requires systemically important financial institutions (SIFIs) to periodically submit "funeral plans" to the Federal Reserve for their orderly liquidation if they get into financial trouble.

The so-called "Volcker Rule" limits proprietary trading. (Paul Volcker was a former Chairman of the Federal Reserve). Banks can own at most three percent of the total equity of a hedge fund or private equity firm. Such ownership cannot exceed three percent of Tier 1 capital (see Chapter 12).

Regarding bailouts, the law reformed the Federal Reserve's emergency lending authority by requiring the Secretary of the Treasury's approval.

The comprehensive law also has new rules dealing with derivatives, mortgage reforms, hedge funds, credit rating agencies, executive compensation and corporate governance, and thrift regulation. It created a new Office of Minority and Women Inclusion, improving investor protection, monitoring the insurance industry, and other issues. A truly sweeping set of regulations contained under 16 titles, it has transformed our financial system and promises to be the subject of continued debate and amendments in the future.

HARMONIZATION

As noted in Chapter 1, major U.S. banks, such as JPMorgan Chase and Citibank, have a large part of their assets invested overseas. The other side of the coin is that large foreign-owned banks, such as Deutsche Bank, ABN Amro, Credit Lyonnais, BBVA, and the Royal Bank of Scotland (RBS) have large investments in the U.S. and elsewhere.[22]

In 2014, the total assets of the world's largest banking organizations equaled about eight percent of the global Gross Domestic Product (GDP).[23]

Because of globalization, international banking regulators have undertaken major efforts to harmonize prudential standards. ***Harmonization*** refers to uniform international banking regulations. It also refers to stemming the divergent standards that are applied to similar activities of different financial institutions.

The Bank for International Settlements (BIS) was established in 1930, and it is located in Basel, Switzerland. It is the principal center for international central bank cooperation dealing with bank regulatory issues. More than 50 central banks (including the U.S.) from around the world are members of the BIS. ***The Basel Committee on Banking Supervision***, a committee of BIS, has led the efforts for uniform international regulatory standards. In 1988, the Basel Committee established uniform risk-based capital standards for banks, and later methods for dealing with trading risks. A new set of capital standards (Basel II) went into effect in 2007, and "Basel III: A global regulatory framework for more resilient banks and banking systems" is being phased in over the 2013-2019 period.[24] The new capital standards in the U.S. will apply to large internationally active banks and thrifts (assets of $250 billion or more, or off-balance sheet foreign exposure of $10 billion or more), bank holding companies, and the parent companies of internationally active "banking groups." Basel III is discussed in Chapter 12.

In the European Union (EU), harmonization is reflected in a number of Directives and Recommendations. For example, the EU's Second Banking Directive, adopted in 1989, establishes home country control and mutual recognition of national supervisory regimes. The Second Banking Directive also established a listing of banking activities subject to mutual recognition, such as leasing, lending, guarantees, investment banks, and money brokering. Although the focus here is on the Basel Committee, one should recognize that other international supervisory groups coordinate some of their activities with the Basel Committee.[25] Accordingly, the EU's own Funds Directive and Solvency Ratio Directive are generally consistent with the recommendations of the Basel Committee.

With respect to services offered by different types of financial institutions, some countries have eliminated the distinctions between banks and nonbank financial institutions for purposes of regulation. For example, in France, the 1984 Bank Law eliminated the distinction between commercial banks, savings banks, and medium and long-term credit banks. In 1990, the Banking Act in Switzerland was amended to put nonbank financial institutions and underwriters under the same regulations as banks.[26]

Finally, the International Monetary Fund (IMF) becomes involved in bank regulation during banking crises. In the crises in Southeast Asia that began in 1997, for example, the IMF programs included closure of financial institutions that were not viable, recapitalization of undercapitalized institutions, close supervision of weak institutions, and more.[27]

"The IMF promotes financial system soundness in member countries through its ongoing bilateral and multilateral surveillance, the design of its lending programs, and the provision of technical assistance." Special attention was paid to 29 countries whose financial sectors are considered "systemically important." The countries are: Australia, Austria, Belgium, Brazil, Canada, China, Denmark, Finland, France, Germany, Hong Kong SAR, India, Ireland, Italy, Japan, Korea, Luxembourg, Mexico, Netherlands, Norway, Poland, Russia, Singapore, Spain, Sweden, Switzerland, Turkey, the United Kingdom, and the United States.

THE DUAL BANKING SYSTEM

BANK CHARTER TYPE

Congress gave the Office of the Comptroller of the Currency (OCC) the authority to charter national banks. National banks have the word "National," or the letters "N.A." standing for "national association" in their names. However, banks can also be chartered by the fifty state bank commissions. Thus, we have what is called a dual banking system, whereby banks can choose to have a national or a state charter.

Banks that have national charter are required to be members of the Federal Reserve System. Banks that have state charters may elect to be members of the Federal Reserve if they choose. Out of the nation's 5,472 commercial banks, 1,152 are national banks.[29] The national banks include some of the largest banks in the country, and they accounted for 71 percent of total U.S. banking assets in 2014. The remaining 4,320 banks have state charters.

BANK AND FINANCIAL HOLDING COMPANIES

The process of regulation becomes more involved when bank holding companies are involved. Bank holding companies are authorized under ***the Bank Holding Company Act of 1956.*** A bank holding company is a corporation that holds stock in one or more banks and other financial service organizations. Bank holding companies can expand their financial services into permissible nonbanking activities that are closely related and incident to banking. Credit-related insurance, leasing, and mortgage banking are three examples of such activities. Under the 1956 Act, bank holding companies headquartered in one state could not acquire banks in other states. That restriction was removed under the Riegle-Neal Interstate Banking and Branching Efficiency Act of 1994.

Bank holding companies are authorized by law or by permission of the Federal Reserve to engage in a wide variety of nonbanking activities that are closely related to banking. These include, but are not limited to: making and servicing loans, trust company functions, certain leasing activities, providing investment and financial advice, operating savings associations, securities brokerage, and other activities.[30] For example, in 2009, Bank of America acquired Merrill Lynch, which had more than 15,000 financial advisors and managed more than $2.2 trillion in client assets.[31]

Bank holding companies are regulated by the Federal Reserve, and the holding companies may include both national and state-chartered banks. The overlapping responsibilities led to turf battles between the Federal Reserve, the OCC, and state banks over which agency regulates certain banking activities under Section 20 of the

Glass-Steagall Act.[32] Section 20 of the Glass-Steagall Act deals with the separation of commercial banking from certain investment banking activities. The issue was resolved with the passage of the Gramm-Leach-Bliley Act 1999 that gave most of the regulatory power to supervise securities and insurance in financial holding companies to the Federal Reserve. Bank holding companies and foreign banks with U.S. offices may elect to be treated as financial holding companies.[33] Under the GLBA, and subject to the approval of the Federal Reserve, ***financial holding companies*** can engage in:

- "General insurance agency activities in any location and travel agency activities;
- Underwriting, dealing in, and making a market in all types of securities;
- Any activity that the Federal Reserve determined by regulation or order to be closely related to banking or managing or controlling banks so as to be a proper incident thereto and that was in effect on the effective date of the Gramm Leach Bliley Act....
- Activities that the Secretary of the Treasury, in consultation with the Board, determines to be financial in nature or incidental to financial activities and permissible for financial subsidiaries of national banks,..
- Activities that the state member bank is permitted to engage in directly under state law..." [34]

WHAT BANK REGULATORS DO

Commercial banks are private business corporations with a public role. Their public role includes their role in the money supply, payments system, insured deposits, and more. It is because of this public side of banking that they are regulated. Bank regulators have four primary responsibilities: chartering, regulating, supervising, and examining, which are discussed here. There are additional duties that are not covered here. For example, the Federal Reserve must approve bank mergers, it is specifically charged with the regulation of bank holding companies, it can lend money to banks at the "discount window," and it acts as a lender of last resort.[35] Thus, not all bank regulators have the same responsibilities.

Chartering

As previously noted, the OCC and state banking commissions have the authority to charter banks. In doing so, they have to determine if the proposed bank will have adequate capital and management for its respective market area. The OCC and state banking commissions also have to take into account the needs and convenience of the community, competition, and other factors.

Regulating

The terms "regulation" and "supervision" are sometimes used interchangeably. However, there is a technical difference. Bank regulation refers to "the formulation and issuance by authorized agencies of specific rules or regulations, under governing law for the structure and conduct of banking....Bank supervision is concerned primarily with the safety and soundness of individual banks, and involves general and continuous oversight to assure that banks are operated prudently in accordance with applicable statutes and regulations."[36] Today regulations involve the types of products that banks can offer, such as investment banking, insurance, and brokerage services, enforcement of laws such as the Truth in Lending Act, and rules involving safety and soundness.

Supervising

Supervision is exercised by regulators to ensure that bankers are complying with banking regulations. Bank examinations are one means of determining compliance with regulations.

Bank supervisors have a variety of techniques at their disposal to deal with problem banks – banks that are not in compliance with rules and regulations. The least intrusive technique is a memorandum of understanding (MOU) issued by the regulator to the bank detailing the changes that must occur to put the bank back in good standing. Other techniques include cease and desist orders that prohibit the bank or a person from continuing a particular course of conduct. Finally, the regulators can close the bank.

Examining

As noted above, bank examinations are part of the supervisory process. Banks face two types of examinations. The first is to determine the safety and soundness of the bank. In this connection, bank examiners from the OCC, the Federal Reserve, the FDIC, and the Office of Thrift Supervision are required to use the Uniform Financial Institutions Rating System that is commonly referred to as ***CAMELS.*** This acronym stands for:

Capital adequacy – referring to the amount of regulatory capital that banks are required to maintain.

Asset quality – reflects the risk associated with managing assets including the quality of loans and investments. Assets are rated by federal bank examiners as "Pass" or they are problem assets because they represent potential losses. Table 2-3 (next page) lists the problem asset categories and brief explanations of each. However, delinquent loans are not mentioned. Delinquent loans are those past due thirty days or more and still accruing interest as well as those in nonaccrual status. The worst thing that can happen to a loan is that it is classified as a loss, and it must be charged off. Charge-offs are the value of loans removed from the books and charged against loss reserves, and are measured net of recoveries. Lenders must charge-off open-end loans (e.g., credit card loans) when they are 180 days past due, and closed-end loans (e.g., mortgage loans) when they are 120 days past due.[37]

Management – referring to the capability of the board of directors and management's ability to measure, monitor, and control and risk. Earnings – the profitability of the bank and sources of those earnings taking risk into account.

Liquidity – the bank's ability to meet its financial obligations when they come due, and the needs of their customers (deposit withdrawals and loans).

Sensitivity to market risk (interest rates, foreign exchange) and the ability of the bank to manage that risk.

Composite ratings of institutions range from a score of 1 to 5. A composite score of 1 is the highest rating given, and it means that the administration of the institution is sound in every respect - there is no cause for supervisory concern. At the other extreme, a composite score of 5 means that the institution's "fiduciary activi-

Table 2-3: PROBLEM ASSET CATEGORIES

Category	Explanation
"Criticized and Classified Assets"	Has potential for weakness and needs close attention. If uncorrected, it may deteriorate further.
Substandard	Inadequately protected by current worth/paying capacity of obligor, or collateral. There is the distinct possibility of a loss.
Doubtful	Doubtful assets have all the weaknesses of assets classified as substandard and when the weaknesses make collection or liquidation in full, on the basis of available current information, highly questionable or improbable.
Loss	Assets classified as loss are considered uncollectible and of so little value that their continuance as bankable assets is not warranted. Amounts classified as loss should be promptly charged off. This classification does not mean that there is no recovery or salvage value, but rather that it is not practical or desirable to defer writing off these assets, even though some value may be recovered in the future.
	Nonaccrual—Nonaccrual loans are defined for regulatory reporting purposes as loans and lease financing receivables that are required to be reported on a nonaccrual basis because (a) they are maintained on a cash basis owing to a deterioration in the financial position of the borrower, (b) payment in full of interest or principal is not expected, or (c) principal or interest has been in default for 90 days or longer, unless the obligation is both well secured and in the process of collection.

Board of Governors of the Federal Reserve System, Federal Deposit Insurance Corporation, Office of the Comptroller of the Currency. Shared National Credits Program, 2013 Review, September 2013.

ties are conducted in an extremely unsafe and unsound manner.....Continuous close supervision is warranted and may include termination of the institutions fiduciary activities."[38] The composite ratings are not publicly available information, although many economists argue that such information would aid in the "market discipline" of banks.

Megabank mergers (such as Citibank and Travelers), global banking, and the expanded used of derivative securities (such as interest rate swaps) have resulted in the increased size and complexity of the largest banking organizations. Bank regulators recognize that they can no longer rely on periodic examinations alone to ensure that the banks remain sound. Consequently, they are placing greater emphasis on those banks' risk management practices and internal controls.[39]

The second type of examination is to determine if the bank is in compliance with all of the relevant regulations and laws. Banks can do only those activities as permitted by laws, and how they do them is regulated too. Table 2-4 (end of chapter) lists the very extensive Code of Federal Regulations (CFR) that banks must adhere to. Banks must comply with other laws and regulations as well. Thus, "compliance" is a significant part of bank operations.

IS PRUDENTIAL REGULATION EFFECTIVE?

The answer to whether prudential bank regulation is effective depends on what one thinks prudential regulation is supposed to do. Prudential regulation ranges from safety and soundness to consumer protection. In this context, it may be successful in accomplishing some goals and less successful in other areas. One thing is clear, however. Safety and soundness of the banking system is the primary objective of prudential regulation. If banks fail in large numbers, the other objectives of prudential regulation cannot be met.

Another view is the facts speak for themselves. During the 1980 -1996 period, more than 130 IMF member countries, including the United States, had significant banking sector problems or crises.[40] During the 1997 – 1999 period there were banking crises in several Southeast Asian countries, Russia, and Brazil. The large numbers of bank failures and crises suggests that prudential regulation, at least in its present form, has limits, and that it works better in some countries than in others. Systemic causes of bank failures are one of those limits. An FDIC study of banking crises in the 1980s and early 1990s concluded by saying that "bank regulation can limit the scope and cost of bank failures, but it is unlikely to prevent bank failures that have systemic causes."[41] More recently, the 2008-09 financial crises in the U.S. and Europe was triggered by the mortgage market problems that led to the near collapse of many large banks and financial institutions. Government intervention by regulators was needed to correct severe imbalances in the financial system.

Prudential regulation works best in a stable economic environment. The Basle Committee on Banking Supervision's Core Principles[42] states that "In the absence of sound macroeconomic policies, banking supervisors will be faced with a virtually impossible task." Most banking crises are associated with unstable economic conditions, such as asset price deflation, interest rate shocks, foreign exchange rate shocks, and so on. The flip side of that coin is that prolonged stability and strong economic growth may lead to complacency with respect to risky lending. That, in part, is what happened in Asian countries when their stability and rapid economic growth encouraged banks to lend injudiciously, resulting in overspending in the government sector. In 2015, economic growth in China declined, which affected global exports and imports.

Beyond banking crises, the growth of heterogeneous financial conglomerates that cross regulatory and national boundaries, as well as changes in information technology, are testing the limits of prudential banking regulation.

Table 2-4: Federal Reserve Regulations and Code of Federal Regulations (CFR)

Regulation	Subject
A 12 CFR 201	Extensions of Credit by Federal Reserve Banks
B 12 CFR 202	Equal Credit Opportunity
C 12 CFR 203	Home Mortgage Disclosure
D 12 CFR 204	Reserve Requirements of Depository Institutions
E 12 CFR 205	Electronic Funds Transfer
F 12 CFR 206	Limitations on Interbank Liabilities
G 12 CFR 207	Disclosure and Reporting of CRA-Related Agreements
H 12 CFR 208	Membership of State Banking Institutions in the Federal Reserve System
I 12 CFR 209	Issue and Cancellation of Federal Reserve Bank Capital Stock
J 12 CFR 210	Collection of Checks and Other Items by Federal Reserve Banks and Funds Transfers through Fedwire
K 12 CFR 211	International Banking Operations
L 12 CFR 212	Management Official Interlocks
M 12 CFR 213	Consumer Leasing
N 12 CFR 214	Relations with Foreign Banks and Bankers
O 12 CFR 215	Loans to Executive Officers, Directors, and Principal Shareholders of Member Banks
P 12 CFR 216	Member Bank Protection Standards (Repealed, June 30, 2014)
Q 12 CFR 217	Capital Adequacy of Bank Holding Companies, Savings and Loan Holding Companies, and State Member Banks
R 12 CFR 218	Exceptions for Banks from the Definition of Broker in the Securities Exchange Act of 1934
S 12 CFR 219	Reimbursement to Financial Institutions for Providing Financial Records; Recordkeeping Requirements for Certain Financial Records
T 12 CFR 220	Credit by Brokers and Dealers
U 12 CFR 221	Credit by Banks and Persons other than Brokers or Dealers for the Purpose of Purchasing or Carrying Margin Stock
V 12 CFR 222	Fair Credit Reporting
W 12 CFR 223	Transactions between Member Banks and Their Affiliates
X 12 CFR 224	Borrowers of Securities Credit
Y 12 CFR 225	Bank Holding Companies and Change in Bank Control
Z 12 CFR 226	Truth in Lending
AA 12 CFR 227	Unfair or Deceptive Acts or Practices
BB 12 CFR 228	Community Reinvestment (Table 2-3 continued on next page)

Table 2-4: Federal Reserve Regulations and Code of Federal Regulations (cont.)

CC 12 CFR 229	Availability of Funds and Collection of Checks
DD 12 CFR 230	Truth in Savings (Repealed June 30, 2014)
EE 12 CFR 231	Netting Eligibility for Financial Institutions
FF 12 CFR 232	Obtaining and Using Medical Information in Connection with Credit
GG 12 CFR 233	Prohibition on Funding of Unlawful Internet Gambling
HH 12 CFR 234	Designated Financial Market Utilities
II 12 CFR 235	Debit Card Interchange Fees and Routing
JJ 12 CFR 236	Incentive-Based Compensation Arrangements
KK 12 CFR 237	Margin and Capital Requirements for Covered Swap Entities
LL 12 CFR 238	Savings and Loan Holding Companies
MM 12 CFR 239	Mutual Holding Companies
NN 12 CFR 240	Retail Foreign Exchange Transactions
OO 12 CFR 241	Securities Holding Companies
PP 12 CFR 242	Definitions Relating to Title I of the Dodd-Frank Act
QQ 12 CFR 243	Resolution Plans
RR 12 CFR 244	Credit Risk Retention
TT 12 CFR 245	Supervision and Regulation Assessments of Fees
VV 12 CFR 248	Proprietary Trading and Relationships with Covered Funds
WW 12 CFR 249	Liquidity Risk Measurement Standards
XX 12 CFR 251	Concentration Limit
YY 12 CFR 252	Enhanced Prudential Standards

Source: Board of Governors of the Federal Reserve System, Regulations, All Regulations, http://www.federalreserve.gov/bankinforeg/reglisting.htm

SUMMARY

Banks are regulated to limit their incentives to take risks in order to protect the financial system and individual depositors. However, we don't know how much risk is optimal. We do know that the primary reason for bank failures is credit risk, and that the failure of very large banks, or large numbers of banks can disrupt the economy. With the collapse of the banking system in the early 1930s, legislation (Banking Acts of 1933 and 1935) was put into place that dramatically circumscribed the ability of banks to take risk. However, after years with few bank failures in the post-WWII era, legislation was passed in the early 1980s: DIDMCA in 1980 and the Garn-St. Germain Act in 1982 that allowed banks and thrifts to have greater flexibility in their activities. In the late 1980s and early 1990s, legislation was passed (FIRREA and FDICIA) that responded to the upsurge of failures in the 1980s and again restricted the ability of banks to take risk. The GLBA was enacted in response to market dynamics, and it is contributing to a major change on the structure of banking. Finally, in the wake of the 2008-09 financial crisis, the Frank-Dodd Act of 2010 made sweeping regulatory changes that affect all U.S. financial institutions and regulatory agencies.

Banking legislation is ever changing, as are perceptions about the proper amount of risk-taking at commercial banks. The expansion of banking powers and global banking became important issues in the late 1990s. Increased competition from nonbank financial institutions contributed to demand from bankers to "level the playing field."

We have a dual banking system in the United States whereby banks can have national charters issued by the OCC or state bank charters. In addition, the Federal Reserve regulates bank holding companies that may have banks with both national and state charters. The overlapping authority has led to turf battles over who should regulate what when it comes to banking. Finally, as globalization increases, the role of harmonization becomes increasingly important. The Basel III capital standards are one example of harmonization.

Table 2-5 shows the influence of various bank regulators and agencies on commercial banks, bank holding companies and financial holding companies. The table also lists some key dates. For example, the first commercial bank (Bank of North America) was created in 1781, the OCC was created in 1863, and so on. By looking at the dates and the various agencies, you can see how our regulatory structure evolved over time.

The tasks of the bank regulators were examined. These include chartering, regulating, examining, supervising, and other tasks. Finally, the effectiveness of prudential regulation was questioned. It is clear that banking regulation must change to keep up with the ever-changing world in which it operates. Changes in technology and globalization are two of the major drivers of the changes that are occurring.

Table 2-5: BANKING REGULATIONS

	Commercial Banks 1781	*Bank Holding Companies* 1956	*Financial Holding Companies* 1999
State bank charters 1700s	x		
OCC 1863	x		
Federal Reserve 1913	x	x	x
FDIC 1933	x		
OTS/FHLBs 1999	x		
BIS/Basel Committee 1988	x	x	x

KEY TERMS AND CONCEPTS

Bank holding companies
Bank runs
Banking Act of 1933 (Glass-Steagall Act)
Banking Act of 1935
Bank Holding Company Act of 1956
Basle Committee on Banking Supervision
CAMELS score
Deposit insurance
Deregulation (price, product, geographic)
Depository Institutions Deregulation and Monetary Control Act, DIDMCA (1980)
Dual banking system
Federal Deposit Insurance Corporation Improvement Act of 1991 (FDICIA)(1991)
Federal Home Loan Banks
Federal Reserve Act of 1913
Financial holding companies
Financial Institutions Reform, Recovery, and Enforcement Act (FIRREA) (1989)
Financial repression
Garn-St Germain Act (1982)
Gramm-Leach-Bliley Act of 1999
Harmonization
Investment banking
McFadden Act of 1927
Market discipline
National Bank Act of 1864
National bank charter
Office of Thrift Supervision (OTS)
Omnibus Budget Reconciliation Act of 1993
Prompt Corrective Action (PCA)
Prudential regulation
Riegle-Neal Interstate Banking and Branching Efficiency Act of 1994
Source of strength doctrine
Unitary thrifts

QUESTIONS

2.1 Why are banks regulated? Is the regulation justified?
2.2 What is a bank run? Why is it important?
2.3 How can banks reduce their risk of failing due to credit risk?
2.4 How did the banking crisis of the 1930s change the nature of banking regulations?
2.5 What are the principal features of the Banking Acts of 1933 and 1935?
2.6 What was the DIDMCA? What were its principal provisions? Why was it enacted?
2.7 What was the principal feature of the Garn-St. Germain Depository Institutions Act?
2.8 How did the goals of FIRREA differ from those of DIDMCA and Garn-St. Germain? Why did the goals differ? Be specific.
2.9 What were the principal features of FDICIA? Why was it created?
2.10 What are the major benefits of the Riegle-Neal Act and the Gramm-Leach-Bliley Act (GLBA) of 1999?
2.11 What is the significance of the GLBA? The Dodd-Frank Act?
2.12 How does bank regulation differ from bank supervision?
2.13 Should prudential bank regulations be harmonized? Explain your position.

CASE: THE POLICY CONSULTANT (Part 2)

Jack Anderson is a policy consultant for North Information Services (NIS), a firm that specializes in lobbying Congress for banks and financial institutions that want to protect their economic interests. Mr. North, President and C.E.O. of NIS, asked Jack to prepare a brief for one of their major clients, an international bank, on the legislative issues that Congress will address this next term, including legislation that might affect this bank. The client bank is headquartered in Zurich Switzerland, but has global operations. To deal with the legislative part of his brief, Jack is going to examine information available from the Library of Congress (http://www.loc.gov) concerning all of the bills under consideration by the Senate and House. Details of the bills can be founds at http://lcweb.loc.gov/global/legislative/bill.html. Information about current legislation is also available from the Conference of State Bank Supervisors at http://www.csbsdal.org/legreg/legregndx.html, and from the Committee on Banking and Financial Services: (See http://house/gov/banking) and the Senate Banking Committee (See http://www.senate.gov/~banking/.

1. Using this or other internet sources, list the major banking legislative issues facing Congress.
2. Write a position paper concerning the pros and cons of the major issue.
3. If the law is passed, what impact will it have on international bank customer?

ENDNOTES

1. Alan Greenspan, chairman, Board of Governors of the Federal Reserve System, before the 29th Conference on Bank Structure and Competition, Federal Reserve Bank of Chicago, May 6, 1993.
2. The money stock is defined by the Federal Reserve, and there are various measures of it, such as M1 and M2. See the Board of Governors of the Federal Reserve System ... Money Stock Measures - H.6. http://www.federalreserve.gov/releases/h6/current/
3. FDIC (US), "Deposit Insurance At A Glance," https://www.fdic.gov/deposit/deposits/brochures/deposit_insurance_at_a_glance-english.html
4. For an excellent discussion of the S&L debacle, see History of the Eighties: Lessons for the Future, Volume 1, Federal Deposit Insurance Corporation, 1997, Chapter 4 (The Savings and Loan Crises and its Relationship to Banking). The $132 billion cost to taxpayers is from U.S. General Accounting Office, Financial Audit: Resolution Trust Corporation's 1995 and 1994 Financial Statement, GAO/AIMD-96-123, July 1996.
5. History of the Eighties: Lessons for the Future, Volume 1, Federal Deposit Insurance Corporation, 1997, Table 1.1.
6. George Stigler, "The Theory of Economic Regulation," *Bell Journal of Economics and Management Science*, and Sam Peltzman, "Toward a More General Theory of Regulation," *Journal of Law and Economics*, Volume 19, 1976.
7. Kelley, E. W., Jr., "The Why, What, and How of Bank Regulation," appears in Federal Reserve Bank of Chicago, Proceedings; Rethinking Bank Regulation: What Should Bank Regulators Do?, 32nd Bank Structure Conference, May 1996, 24-28.
8. Benton E. Gup, *Money Laundering, Financing Terrorism, and Suspicious Activities*, New York, Nova Science Publishers, Inc., 2007.
9. For additional information, see www.fincen.gov
10. See Gup (1995, 1998) for a discussion of frauds that led to bank failures. Benton E. Gup, *Targeting Fraud: Uncovering and Deterring Fraud in Financial Institutions*, New York, McGraw-Hill, 1995; Benton E. Gup, *Bank Failures in the Major Trading Countries of the World: Causes and Remedies*, Westport CT.: Quorum Books, 1998.
11. FDIC Quarterly Banking Profile, First Quarter 2010, Table1-A, "Selected Indicators, All FDIC-Insured Institutions." FDIC Quarterly Banking Profile, Second Quarter, 2015, Table1-A, "Selected Indicators, All FDIC-Insured Institutions."
12. The terms "well capitalized," "adequately capitalized," and so on, for total risk- based capital are defined in Table 2-2. The discussion of Table 2-1 does not make the distinction between E/A and risk-based capital. Capital requirements are examined in Chapter 12.
13. FDIC Quarterly Banking Profile, Second Quarter, 2015, Table1-A, "Selected Indicators, All FDIC-Insured Institutions."
14. A bank is "critically undercapitalized" when its tangible equity is 2 percent or less.
15. History of the Eighties: Lessons for the Future, Vol. 1., Washington, D.C., Federal Deposit Insurance Corporation, 1997, 375.
16. For more details on the history and current operations of the OCC, see their web page: http://www.occ.treas.gov.
17. U.S. Department of Commerce, Statistical Abstract of the United States 1992, Bureau of the Census, Washington, D.C., 1992, Table 779.
18. James B. Thomson, "Commercial Banks' Borrowing from the Federal Home Loan Banks," Economic Commentary, Federal Reserve Bank of Cleveland, July 2003.
19. See John R. Walter, "Banking and Commerce: Tear Down This Wall?" Federal Reserve Bank of Richmond Economic Quarterly, Spring 2003, 7-31; Joseph G. Haubrich and "João A. C. Santos, "Alternative Forms of Mixing Banking with Commerce: Evidence from American History," *Financial Markets, Institutions & Instruments* 12 (2), February, 2003, 121-164/
20. Riva D. Atas, "Wal-Mart Seeks Approval to Buy California Bank," New York Times, May 16, 2002. www.nytimes.com (visited 5/16/02).

21. "BRIEF SUMMARY OF THE DODD-FRANK WALL STREET REFORM AND CONSUMER PROTECTION ACT," http://www.banking.senate.gov/public/_files/070110_Dodd_Frank_Wall_Street_Reform_comprehensive_summary_Final.pdf
22. For a listing of foreign banks in the U.S., see the Board of Governors of the Federal Reserve's "Structure Data for the U.S. Offices of Foreign Banking Organizations," http://www.federalreserve.gov/releases/iba/201506/bycntry.htm
23. Daniel K. Tarullo, (Governor), "Regulating Large Foreign Banking Organizations," Speech at Harvard Law School Symposium, Board of Governors of the Federal Reserve System, March 27, 2014.
24. Basel Committee on Banking Supervision, http://www.bis.org/; The new capital rules are explained in http://www.bis.org/publ/bcbs189.pdf
25. For current information about the EU's Directives, see European Commission, Banking and Finance, http://ec.europa.eu/finance/bank/guarantee/index_en.htm
26. United States Department of Treasury, National Treatment Study, 1994, Washington, D.C., December 1994.
27. "The IMF's Response to the Asian Crisis," Washington, D.C., International Monetary Fund, April 16, 1998.
28. International Monetary Fund, FACTSHEET, "Financial System Soundness," September 21, 2015, http://www.imf.org/external/np/exr/facts/banking.htm
29. FDIC Quarterly, Second Quarter 2015, Table IV-A
30. 12 CFR 225, Federal Reserve Regulation "Y."
31. Merrill Lynch, https://en.wikipedia.org/wiki/Merril_Lynch
32. The regulation of Section 20 Securities Affiliates of bank holding companies was a source of dispute between the Federal Reserve and the OCC that was resolved by the passage of the GLBA in 1999 that made the Federal Reserve the top regulator.
33. Federal Reserve Press Release, Federal Reserve Board, January 19, 2000. 12 CFR 225.81 Because a bank holding company can elect to be treated as a financial holding company, an institution such as Bank One Corporation can be can be classified as both types of holding companies.
34. For additional details, see the Federal Reserve, Commercial Bank Examination Manual, April 2010, Section 4052.1
35. For an overview of the Federal Reserve System, see: The Federal Reserve System: Purposes and Functions, 8th ed., Washington, D.C., Board of Governors of the Federal Reserve System, 1994.
36. The Federal Reserve System: Purposes & Functions, Washington, D.C., Board of Governors of the Federal Reserve, 1984, p. 88).
37. Seiberg, J., "Scrapped: Uniform 150-Day Rule for Writing Off Past-Due Loans," *American Banker,* February 11, 1999, 3.
38. Federal Register, Vol. 63, No. 197, October 13, 1998, 54707.
39. "Remarks by Governor Laurence H. Meyer, At the Conference Boar's 1999 Financial Services Outlook Conference, New York, NY, January 11, 1999," Board of Governors of the Federal Reserve System, January 11, 1999.
40. Lindgren, C.J., G. Garcia, M.I. Saal, *Bank Soundness and Macroeconomic Policy*, Washington, D.C., International Monetary Fund, 1996.
41. Hanc, G. "The Banking Crises of the 1980s and Early 1990s: Summary and Implications," *FDIC Banking Review*. Vol. 11. No. 1, 1998, 1-55.
42. "Core Principles for Effective Banking Supervision," Basle, Switzerland: Bank for International Settlement, Basle Committee on Banking Supervision, April 1997.

Chapter 3

Evaluating Bank Performance

After reading this chapter, you will be able to:

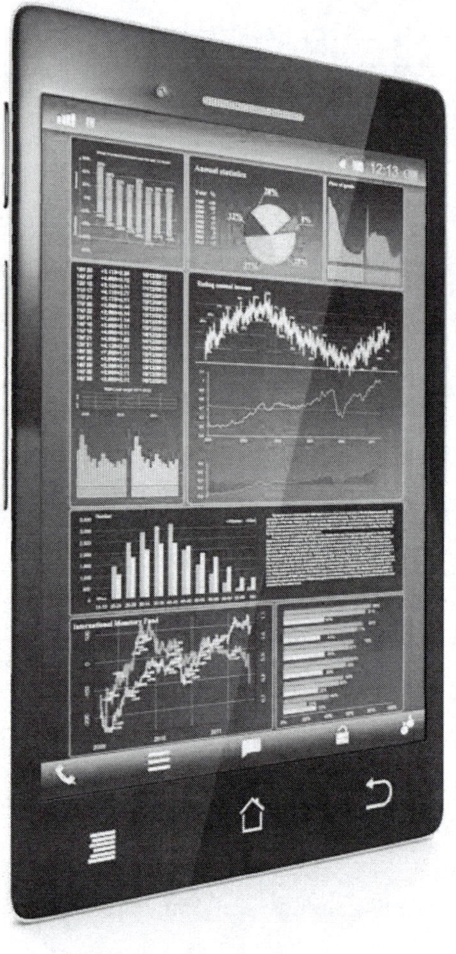

- Define the principal balance sheet and income statement items for a commercial bank.
- Evaluate the profitability of a commercial bank in order to determine whether its profitability is low or high and the reasons for such difference with other banks.
- Evaluate the risk profile of a commercial bank, including the potential for failure.
- Describe the procedure used by the bank regulatory agencies to evaluate the quality of commercial banks.

Deregulation of financial services, competition and consolidation among banks and nonbanks, changing economic and financial environments, and the development of new, innovative financial services are all reasons for continued interest in evaluating bank performance. Unlike in the past, banks can no longer earn legally mandated yield spreads between the average interest rates earned on sources and uses of funds. Nor can banks continue to reap monopoly rents from bank charters that naturally endowed them with a considerable degree of market power. Instead, today's more competitive banking environment is causing banking institutions to evaluate carefully the risks and returns involved in serving the needs of the public.

Various groups of individuals are particularly interested in evaluating bank performance. First and foremost, ***bank shareholders*** are directly affected by bank performance. Investors take advantage of bank information to develop expectations concerning future performance that can be used to help price common shares (in addition to capital notes and debentures that may be issued by the bank). Second, ***bank management*** traditionally is evaluated on the basis of how well the bank performs relative to previous years and compared with similar (or peer group) banks. Hence, employees' salaries, bonuses, and promotions are frequently tied to the performance of the bank. Bankers also need to be informed about the condition of other banks with which they have business dealings. Loan purchases and participations from poorly managed institutions may be suspect; moreover, federal funds sold and repurchase agreements with other banks require that some knowledge of their performance be obtained to prevent loss of funds in the event of their failure and subsequent closure by regulatory authorities. Third, ***regulators*** concerned about the safety and soundness of the banking system and the preservation of public confidence, monitor banks using on-site examinations and computer-based "early warning systems" to keep track of bank performance. Fourth, ***depositors*** may be interested in how well the bank is doing, especially if (such as business firms) they hold deposits in excess of the insured amount (each depositor is allowed federal insurance up to $250,000) and must depend on bank funds for their continued operations. Fifth, and last, the ***business community*** and general public should be concerned about their bank's performance to the extent that their access to credit and other financial services is linked to the success or failure of their bank.

The present chapter is organized into two parts. The first part provides a general framework for evaluating bank performance. This framework helps to conceptualize the nature of bank behavior, in addition to pointing out possible interactions between various aspects of performance. In this section we discuss both internal and external performance factors that need to be evaluated.

The second part of the chapter discusses a variety of key financial characteristics that can be calculated from bank accounting statements known as *Call Reports of Income and Condition*, including profitability, capitalization, asset quality, operating efficiency, liquidity, taxes, and more. [1]

A FRAMEWORK FOR EVALUATING BANK PERFORMANCE

Like any corporation, the ultimate measure of a bank's performance is the value of its common shares. Maximization of shareholder wealth is a complex issue that involves both internal and external management factors. Internal factors are areas of bank management that the officers and staff of the bank have under their immediate control. By contrast, external factors are environmental aspects of the bank's market over which management has no direct control. Figure 3-1 shows the interrelationship between these two performance factors. The problem that bank management faces is allocating scarce resources to the different performance dimensions shown there in order to maximize the total value of the bank. In this regard, interactions between different performance areas must be carefully considered. For example, increasing the bank's market share and competitiveness requires higher operating expenses, which may compromise the bank's financial condition if revenues do not keep pace with expenses. In turn, regulatory compliance and public confidence may be affected. Of course, changes in the bank's environment can alter the investment decisions of management with regard to the internal and external performance areas shown in Figure 3-1.

FIGURE 3-1 A FRAMEWORK FOR EVALUATING BANK PERFORMANCE

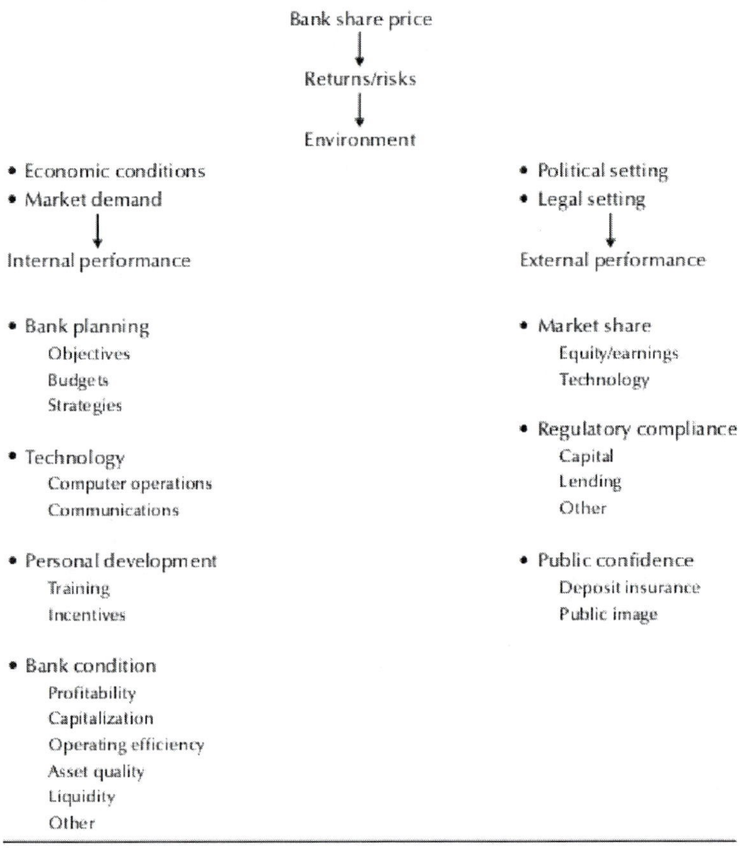

INTERNAL PERFORMANCE

In this section we discuss three aspects of internal performance: ***bank planning, technology,*** and ***personnel development.*** Bank condition is another dimension of internal performance, which is discussed in more detail in the second part of this chapter.

Bank Planning

As a first step in planning, bank objectives should be stated. Obviously, the ultimate objective of the bank (as mentioned earlier) is the maximization of owners' equity. Other bank objectives facilitate this result. Some examples of bank objectives are the following:

- Improve the market share of prime grade loans
- Upgrade the quality of management expertise in the area of high-technology lending
- Expand the financial services being offered to retail customers to increase the size and diversification of the deposit base
- Implement an automated delivery system for payment services
- Help the community grow to organically increase bank assets
- Facilitate employee training
- Diversify the loan portfolio to a greater extent in terms of both different assets and the geographic distribution of these assets
- Cross sell a wide variety of financial services, including banking, securities, and insurance activities

Once the objectives of the bank are developed, they can be translated into specific, quantifiable goals. These goals should clearly communicate the results that management seeks on both the short- and long-term planning horizon. For example, with reference to the market share objective given earlier, the following goals could be adopted:

- Expand prime grade loans to manufacturing companies by 15 percent the first year and 10 percent thereafter annually for a period of four years
- Maintain retail business lending at the same pace as in the past year
- Trim lending in other areas of the bank by five percent per year across the board for the next five years
- Purchase a small bank and convert it to a branch office of your organization to gain a foothold in a new geographical market.

By quantifying goals, management formalizes the planning process. This step in bank planning should involve all levels of management in order to ensure that reasonable goals are established and understood by everyone. Also, personal involvement in the process of setting goals may improve morale, increase communication between departments, and help to coordinate bank operations.

Budgets, or profit plans, are in-depth statements that are intended to bring these objectives down to the departmental level of the bank. Budgets allocate estimated labor and capital resources to various departments with the goals of the bank in mind. Typically, budgets are for a one-year period and contain monthly and quarterly refinements. The specific results expected of each department are defined in the budget, which enables periodic reviews to monitor progress toward goals. Budgets are used to improve internal control over the bank's operations.

By contrast, strategic planning seeks to anticipate emerging internal and external conditions that could affect the bank's achievement of goals in the long run. Rather than being mechanical, strategic planning is creative in nature. It is more concerned with effectiveness in achieving goals, whereas budgeting focuses on cost efficiency. Also, strategic planning is more general than a budget plan in its content, and thus provides guidance for the future as well as a blueprint for managing the bank's environment. However, this planning must be compatible with the bank's annual budget.

The way in which the planning process is managed by officers and staff will have a major influence on the performance of the bank. Increasing competition has tended to accentuate the importance of careful planning. Institutions that do not implement comprehensive planning procedures will have lower share prices on average and be at greater risk of failure than other banks. Many banks work with outside consultants to help refine their strategic and budgeting plans.

Technology

Automation of operations can improve internal performance in a number of ways. For example, more up-to-date and accurate information can be supplied to customers and managers alike. Automated financial services, such as direct deposit, automatic bill paying, smart phone access, and Internet services, can be offered to the public. Also, at least in the long run, the operating costs of the bank may be reduced, as capital investment in computer and communications equipment is substituted for labor. Especially for small banks, automation may not be feasible because of low public demand for electronically produced financial services or lack of internal information needs. In this case cooperative relationships with correspondent banks, and joint ventures among banks (including franchising relationships, network sharing, and other third-party business arrangements), can be employed. Large banks typically lease or purchase equipment and spread the cost among subscribing smaller banks (also known as correspondent banks). However, large banks may benefit from cooperative relationships also. For example, large banks syndicate multi-million dollar loans to large corporations to pool loanable funds and spread credit risk.

Personnel Development

Because commercial banks require a highly skilled labor force, it is essential that attention be focused on personnel development. Human resources play a critical role in the achievement of bank goals and objectives. Indeed, the most important asset in any company is their employees. Without talented, experienced, and up-to-date managers, even firms with excellent products and services may well fail. Banks must provide opportunities for the continuous training of their employees in the latest banking operations and techniques and must provide the means for their employees to keep up with the changes in bank regulations.

Challenges

Two major challenges that face today's banks are the greater emphasis on personal selling of financial services and the trend toward **geographic expansion** in banking. The wide variety and complexity of today's banking services require interpersonal skills to communicate with and sell to customers. Thus, existing officers and staff need to be involved in sales training and marketing techniques. Moreover, geographic expansion in banking has gained considerable momentum during the past decade. As a bank expands throughout its state, across state lines, and into international markets, employees need additional training to develop the skills necessary to adapt to the changing geographical diversification of the institution.

Job Satisfaction

Effective management of human resources is also needed to satisfy the pursuits of individuals in the organization. The bank can contribute to the attainment of employees' personal satisfaction through job enrichment programs and training. On a more basic level, compensation for excellence in work performance is necessary to maintain motivation. Wages, base salaries, and performance bonus compensation should be sufficient to attract and retain quality personnel. Furthermore, compensation structures should be flexible enough to recognize different levels of merit due to outstanding work, as well as the acquisition of new skills. Also, the fringe benefits program, including medical insurance and pension plans, should reflect differences among individuals. In summary, appropriate nonmonetary and monetary compensation for employees is consistent with maximizing job performance.

EXTERNAL PERFORMANCE

External performance is reflected in the ability of the bank to cope successfully with customers, competitors, regulators, and the public.

Market Share

Market share is the proportion of assets, deposits, loans, and total financial services held by a bank in its business region relative to other banks. Failure to meet market demands normally will result in a decline in market share.

Earnings

Market share can affect the earnings of the bank. For example, given that the bank's rate of return on assets did not change, if its asset size declined then earnings per share would decline (because the number of shares does not change while the total earnings of the bank are falling in line with the erosion of the asset base). Conversely, growing too fast can lower equity returns, because assets are expanding but profitability may not be. For example, if the bank's assets grew by 20 percent but the net income after taxes decreased by 10 percent (because higher deposit rates had to be offered to the public to attract sufficient funds to finance the relatively rapid rate of asset expansion), the earnings per share of the bank would decline. Furthermore, growth may not only affect profitability but it may change the perceived riskiness of the bank by the financial market (perhaps because of increased credit risk), which would also result in a loss of share value. Thus, growth for the sake of growth alone is not a suitable goal. Bank managers should set market share goals that are consistent with the internal performance of the bank.

Technology

By implementing new technologies, banks communicate to their customers that they are up to date and progressive. Hence, technology is a marketing tool that can attract customers. Another reason to offer the latest technology to the public is to improve the competitiveness of the bank. Technology enables the bank to reach out to customers beyond traditional market boundaries. It also serves to enhance the convenience of using the bank's financial services; that is, an implicit service return is paid to customers, which increases the attractiveness of the bank. The best examples of this type of technology are credit cards, debit cards, automated teller machines (ATMs), telephone bill-paying services, point-of-sale (POS) payment services, and Internet-based payments and funds management services. Interestingly, the increasing usage of smart phones is changing the financial landscape in the sense that they represent electronic branches to deliver financial services to customers. In response, banks are downsizing brick-and-mortar branches and altering their financial services to fit into this emerging technological change. See Chapter 17, "Electronic Banking" for further discussion of electronic funds transfer services.

Regulatory Compliance

Another dimension of external performance is regulatory compliance. All banks must conform to the laws and regulations of the relevant federal and state authorities. Failure to comply will prompt some form of supervisory action. Such action could take the form of a simple letter explaining a problem with compliance that can be easily rectified by the bank, or it could take the form of a full-blown audit of the bank in an attempt to determine the extent of a major problem. Requests for a plan of action by the bank to overcome the problem(s) could be made and then monitored over time to assess the progress of the bank. Sanctions on bank activities could be imposed by regulators to control risk taking and preserve safety and soundness. Of course, as regulatory risk increases, the costs of compliance increase for the bank. Due to regulation, banks generally must seek to maximize profits subject to the constraint of meeting regulatory requirements (such as capital rules, information disclosure requirements, etc.). If regulation is binding, the unregulated profit level of the bank will be greater than the regulated profit level. Thus, regulation imposes a cost on the banking industry.

Public Confidence

Public confidence relates to the market's ***perception*** of a bank's safety and soundness. No matter how well capitalized a bank is, a loss of public confidence can cause a run on deposits and subsequent closure by regulatory authorities. A case in point is the failure of Hartford Federal, a thrift institution in Hartford, Connecticut, in the 1980s. By coincidence, news that regulatory authorities had placed Hartford

Federal on its watch list appeared in the local paper on the same day that the movie *The Night the Money Stopped* aired on a national TV network. The timing of these two events touched off a run that lasted for a week and ended in the closure and sale of the thrift by regulators. More dramatically, during the 2008-2009 economic and financial crisis (later dubbed the *Great Recession*), subprime residential mortgage market problems spread to global financial markets via exposure to different mortgage-backed bonds sold to investors around the world. Panic ensued that triggered runs on major financial institutions and almost caused a total collapse of the world financial system. Government and regulatory agency intervention eventually worked to help stabilize institutions and markets and begin the long process of recovery. Clearly, public confidence is essential to well-functioning banking and financial systems.

PRESENTATION OF BANK FINANCIAL STATEMENTS

Financial data on commercial banks are presented in two basic documents: the **Report of Condition** (i.e., ***the balance sheet***) and the **Report of Income** (i.e., ***the income statement***).[2]

The Balance Sheet

Table 3-1 (next page) presents a hypothetical balance sheet for State Bank as of December 31, 2016, and December 31, 2015. A bank's balance sheet presents the institution's financial condition at a single point in time. Balance sheets are prepared on a particular date—usually the last day of a month, year, or quarter. Because balance sheets capture a condition at one point in time, it is useful to compare data for several accounting periods. In this way trends in the bank's financial condition over time can be assessed.

Assets: Cash assets include vault cash, deposits at the Federal Reserve (primarily to meet legal reserve requirements), deposits at other banks (for clearing purposes and also to compensate the other banks for providing currency and coin services), and cash items in the process of collection. All of these four categories of assets have one common feature—namely, they earn no interest. As such, bank management should attempt to minimize its investment in these assets.

Interest-bearing bank balances, such as short-term certificates of deposit at other banks and federal funds sold are highly liquid, earning assets. They are generally used as part of the bank's liquidity management program. Most small banks such as State Bank have more federal funds sold than federal funds purchased, indicating relatively high liquidity.

The next major category of bank assets is investment securities. Since banks are generally prohibited from owning equity securities (except in their securities affiliates), the securities that appear on bank balance sheets are almost entirely debt. Regulations force banks to be lenders rather than investors. These investment securities consist of U.S. Treasury securities and U.S. government agencies' obligations (a major portion of which is generally pledged against government deposits); securities issued by states and political subdivisions (i.e., municipalities) in the United States; and all other securities, principally investment-grade corporate bonds. In addition, banks have become major buyers of mortgage-backed securities, most of which are backed by a U.S. government agency. For State Bank, these would be included in Table 3-1 as a part of the U.S. Treasury and agency securities category.

Loans, the least liquid of banking assets and the major source of risk, are the largest asset category for most banking institutions as well as the primary source of bank earnings. Lease-financing arrangements substitute for loans in this section of the balance sheet. Loans and leases are classified into the following categories:

- Loans secured by real estate
- Commercial and industrial loans, including loans to depository institutions
- Loans to individuals for household, family, and other personal expenditures
- Loans to finance agricultural production
- All other loans and lease-financing receivables

Table 3-1: BALANCE SHEET FOR STATE BANK ($ THOUSANDS)

Assets	**Dec. 31, 2016**		**Dec. 31, 2015**	
Cash assets		$ 9,039		$ 10,522
Securities				
Interest bearing bank balances	$0		$1,000	
Federal funds sold	10,500		1,500	
U.S. Treasury and agency securities	54,082		34,219	
Municipal securities	32,789		34,616	
All other securities	0		0	
Total securities		**$97,371**		**$81,857**
Loans and leases				
Real estate loans	$50,393		$38,975	
Commercial loans	9,615		11,381	
Individual loans	8,824		10,640	
Agricultural loans	20,680		19,654	
Other loans and leases	3,684		4,025	
Gross loans and leases	$93,196		$84,675	
Less: Unearned income reserves	(89)		(282)	
Reserve for loan and lease losses	(3,006)		(2,536)	
Net loans and leases		90,101		81,857
Premises, fixed assets, and capitalized leases		2,229		2,398
Other real estate		2,282		3,012
Other assets		4,951		4,014
Total assets		$205,973		$183,767
Liabilities & Capital				
Deposits				
Demand deposits	$23,063		$ 22,528	
All NOW accounts	6,021		5,322	
MMDA accounts	41,402		49,797	
Other savings deposits	3,097		2,992	
Time deposits<$100M	31,707		28,954	
Time deposits>$100M	83,009		57,665	
Total deposits		**$188,299**		**$167,258**
Nondeposit funds				
Fed funds purchased	$0		0	
Other borrowings	0		0	
Bankers' acceptance and other liabilities	3,546		3,101	
Total nondeposit funds		3,546		3,101
Total liabilities		$191,845		$170,359
Subordinated notes and debentures		0		0
All common and preferred equity		14,128		13,408
Total liabilities and capital		$205,973		$183,767

From gross loans and leases, two deductions are made—unearned income and the reserve for loan and lease losses—to arrive at net loans and leases. Unearned income represents the amount of income that has been deducted from a loan (for example, in the case of a discounted note) but has not yet been recognized as income on the income statement because it is distributed over the life of the note.

The amount in the reserve account reflects an estimate by bank management of probable ***charge-offs*** for uncollectible loans and leases on the balance sheet date. Although regulatory authorities are involved in the estimation process, bank management ultimately determines the final valuation of the reserve account. Actual losses are deducted from the reserve account, and recoveries are added back to reserves. The adequacy of the valuation reserve is an important element in the analysis of a bank's risk.

Premises, fixed assets, and capitalized leases represent an important though relatively small portion of assets. Most capitalized leases for banks involve sale-and-leaseback arrangements in which the bank "sells" property and leases it back from the buyer. Terms are structured to allow the bank to maintain control over the property, and these arrangements are made primarily to generate cash. Capitalized leases are recorded under assets rather than under leases, as if the bank still owns the property.

"Other real estate" is any other real estate owned by the bank and usually represents property that has been obtained through collateral foreclosures on problem loans.

The final asset category is all other assets. This includes intangible assets—assets without physical substance—such as goodwill recognized in business combinations.

Liabilities: Bank liabilities consist primarily of the various types of deposit accounts that the institution uses to fund its lending and investing activities.

Depository accounts vary in terms of interest payments, maturity, check-writing privileges, and insurability. Demand deposits are transaction accounts that are payable to the depositor on demand and pay no interest. NOW accounts represent the total of all transaction accounts, less demand deposits. They are accounts that pay interest and permit check-writing but do not include money market deposit accounts. Money market deposit accounts (MMDAs) are savings accounts on which the bank pays market interest, and check writing is limited to a certain number of checks per month. The other savings deposits category comprises all savings deposits other than money market deposit accounts and includes regular passbook accounts with no set maturity and overdraft protection plan accounts. Time deposits under $100,000 are total time deposits (deposits with a fixed maturity) in amounts of less than $100,000. Time deposits over $100,000 are large certificates of deposit (CDs), many of which are negotiable in a well-established secondary market.

Capital: Subordinated notes and debentures are actually liabilities but are shown in the capital section because this type of debt has the characteristics of capital in terms of maturity and permanence and can be counted as capital in meeting certain regulatory requirements.

"All common and preferred equity" capital is the par value of all common and preferred stock outstanding, surplus or additional paid-in capital (the amount by which the original sale of the stock exceeded par value), undivided profits or retained earnings (all of the institution's earnings since its inception less any dividends paid), and capital reserves (a cushion used to absorb unexpected losses on loans and securities).

The Income Statement

The income statement, which shows all major categories of revenue and expenditures, the net profit or loss for the period, and the amount of cash dividends declared, measures a firm's financial performance over a period of time, such as a year, quarter, or month. The income statement and the balance sheet are integrally related and both should be evaluated when assessing bank performance. Table 3-2 presents the income statement format.

Table 3-2: INCOME STATEMENT FOR STATE BANK ($ THOUSANDS)

Revenues and Expenses	Dec. 31, 2016		Dec. 31, 2015	
Interest and fees on loans and leases		$ 8,931		$ 9,192
Income from lease financing	$0		$0	
Fully taxable	8,880		9,142	
Tax exempt	51		50	
Estimated tax benefit	38		21	
Total income on loans and leases		$8,969		$9,213
Investment interest income				
U.S. Treasury and agency securities income	3,735		3,571	
Municipal securities (tax exempt) income	3,097		3,025	
Estimated tax benefit	1,882		2,103	
Other securities income	13		0	
Total investment interest income		8,727		8,699
Interest on federal funds sold		192		194
Interest due from banks		27		5
Total interest income		**$17,915**		**$18,001**
Interest expense				
Interest on CDs over $100,000	3,248		2,924	
Interest on other deposits	6,757		7,167	
Interest on federal funds purchased and repos	16		59	
Interest on borrowed money	0		50	
Interest on mortgages and leases	0		0	
Interest on subordinated notes and debentures	0		0	
Total interest expense		**10,021**		**$ 10,200**
Net interest income		**$ 7,894**		**$7,801**
Noninterest income		571		577
Adjusted operating income		$8,465		$8,378
Overhead expense		3,624		3,876
Provision for loan and lease losses		1,294		3,208
Pretax operating income		$3,547		$1,294
Securities gains (losses)		1,240		3,331
Pretax net operating income		**$4,787**		**$4,625**
Applicable income tax		2,267		2,133
Net operating income		**$2,520**		**$2,492**
Net extraordinary items		0		0
Net income		**$ 2,520**		**$ 2,492**

Interest Income: Loans are the largest asset category for most bank balance sheets, and interest and fees on loans are the primary sources of bank income. This category of revenue, which includes all year-to-date interest and fees on loans, is presented first on the income statement. Income from lease financing is year-to-date income derived from lease financing receivables.

The analyst must realize that income reported on loans and leases is accrued, meaning that it is recognized over the appropriate time period of the loan rather than when cash is actually received. A bank can recognize this income for at least 90 days before the loan goes on ***nonaccrual*** status.

The income reported is divided into fully taxable and tax-exempt portions. The tax-exempt amount includes year-to-date income on loan obligations of state and political subdivisions, and tax-exempt income from direct lease financing. The fully taxable amount is total interest and fees on loans and income from lease-financing receivables less tax-exempt income. The estimated tax benefit results from having tax-exempt loan and lease-financing income from municipal loans and leases. It is estimated and added to income in order to improve the comparability of interest income among different banks over several time periods.

Investment income typically provides the next largest category of income for banking institutions. U.S. Treasury and agency securities income includes interest on U.S. Treasury securities, other U.S. government agencies, and corporate obligations. Interest on municipal securities is interest on securities issued by state and political subdivisions in the United States. Like loans to municipalities, there is a tax benefit resulting from such investments, shown as estimated tax benefit.

"Other securities income" includes income on federal funds sold and securities purchased under agreements to resell, interest on balances due from banks, and income on assets held in trading accounts (excluding gains, losses, commissions, and fees).

Interest expense is the largest expense for most banks. Interest expense is allocated into six categories: (1) interest paid on time deposits of $100,000 or more; (2) interest on other deposits; (3) interest expense on federal funds purchased and securities sold under agreements to repurchase; (4) interest on note balances issued to the U.S. Treasury and on other borrowed money; (5) interest on mortgage debt and capital leases on bank premises, fixed assets, and other real estate owned; and (6) interest on subordinated notes and debentures.

Net interest income on a tax-equivalent basis is total interest income less total interest expense. The relationship between net interest income—the amount by which interest received exceeds interest paid—and total assets is an important analytical tool in assessing a bank's ability to generate profits through the management of interest- earning assets and interest-bearing liabilities.

Noninterest Income: Noninterest income includes all other sources of income: from fiduciary activities, service charges on deposits, gains or losses and commissions and fees on assets held in trading accounts, foreign-exchange trading gains or losses, loan and security guarantees, derivative securities services, and other off-balance sheet activities. These categories of income have increased in relative importance for many banks as a result of deregulation's impact on the permissible financial services.

Other Expense: Three other types of expenses are deducted from adjusted operating income to arrive at pretax operating income. Overhead expense includes salaries and employee benefits, expenses of premises and fixed assets (net of rental income), and other noninterest operating expenses. The provision for loan and lease losses is the year-to-date amount allocated to loan and lease loss reserves (on the balance sheet). Remember that unexpected losses are charged against the balance sheet reserves account.

Gains or losses on the sale, exchange, redemption, or retirement of securities other than those held in trading accounts are netted against pretax operating income to determine pretax operating income on a tax-equivalent basis. Security gains and losses can be an important element in measuring bank performance. The analyst should be aware that a bank can influence operating profit for a period through these securities transactions.

Income Tax Expense: Income tax includes the total estimated federal, state, local, and foreign (if applicable) income taxes on operating income (including securities gains and losses).

Net Income: Income taxes are deducted from pretax operating income to arrive at net operating income. If there are any extraordinary items, defined as transactions that are both unusual in nature and not expected to recur, these are deducted or added, net of taxes, to determine net income.

The preceding discussion has provided a line-by-line description of each account contained in a bank's balance sheet and income statement. It is essential to begin an evaluation of bank financial statements with a basic understanding of the information that is presented in the statements. But what do all of the numbers and accounts mean? How can we use the information contained in a financial statement to assess a bank's historical, present, and future performance? We turn next to these issues.

IMPORTANT TERMS IN UNDERSTANDING BANK FINANCIAL STATEMENTS

Earning assets: Loans, investment securities, and short-term investments that generate interest and yield related fee income.

Federal funds sold/purchased: Excess balances of depository institutions, which are loaned to each other, generally on an overnight basis.

Interest-bearing liabilities: Deposits and borrowed funds on which interest is paid.

Interest rate spread: The difference between the average rate earned on earning assets on a taxable equivalent basis and the average rate paid for interest-bearing liabilities.

Interest-sensitive assets/liabilities: Earning assets and interest-bearing liabilities that can be repriced or will mature within specific time periods.

Interest sensitivity gap: A measure of the exposure of a bank to changes in market rates of interest, its vulnerability to such changes, and the associated effect on net interest income.

Liquidity: The ability of an entity to meet its cash flow requirements. For a bank it is measured by the ability to convert assets into cash quickly with minimal exposure to interest rate risk, by the size and stability of the core funding base, and by additional borrowing capacity within the money markets.

Net charge-offs: The amount of loans written off as uncollectible less recoveries of loans previously written off.

Net interest margin: Net taxable equivalent interest income divided by average interest-earning assets. It is a measure of how effectively a corporation utilizes its earning assets in relation to the interest cost of funding.

Noninterest income: Fee income from on-balance sheet and off-balance sheet activities, where the latter include loan and security guarantees and derivative securities services.

Nonperforming assets: Loans on which interest income is not being accrued, restructured loans on which interest rates or terms of repayment have been materially revised, and real properties acquired through foreclosure.

IMPORTANT TERMS IN UNDERSTANDING BANK FINANCIAL STATEMENTS (continued)

Provision for loan losses: The period charges against earnings required to maintain the allowance for loan losses at a level considered by management to be adequate to absorb estimated losses inherent in the loan portfolio.

Reserve for loan losses: A valuation allowance offset against total loans, which represents the amount considered by management to be adequate to absorb unexpected losses inherent in the loan portfolio.

Return on average assets: A measure that indicates how effectively an entity uses its total resources. It is calculated by dividing annual net income by average assets.

Return on equity: A measure of how productively an entity's equity has been employed. It is calculated by dividing annual net income by total equity.

Taxable equivalent income: Income that has been adjusted by increasing tax exempt income to a level that is comparable to taxable income before taxes are applied.

ANALYZING BANK PERFORMANCE AND FINANCIAL RATIOS

Financial ratios are constructed by forming ratios of accounting data contained in the bank's Reports of Income (i.e., profit and loss) and Condition (i.e., balance sheet). A wide variety of financial ratios can be calculated to assess different characteristics of financial performance. To evaluate a particular financial ratio for a bank, comparisons with peer group banks are often used. Also, it is beneficial to track the ratio over time relative to other banks. Even without comparison with other banks, ratio trends over time may provide valuable information about the bank's performance. A potential shortfall of financial ratio analysis is that other factors are held constant. To overcome this problem, various financial ratios should be calculated that provide a broader understanding of the bank's financial condition. Most of the remainder of this chapter discusses key ratios commonly used by bank analysts to evaluate different dimensions of financial performance, including profitability, capitalization, asset quality, operating efficiency, liquidity, and interest sensitivity.[3]

PROFIT RATIOS

ROE

The ***rate of return on equity (ROE)*** is a good starting point in the analysis of a bank's financial condition for the following reasons:

- If the ROE is relatively low compared with other banks, it will tend to decrease the bank's access to new capital that may be necessary to expand and maintain a competitive position in the market.
- A low ROE may limit a bank's growth because regulations require that assets be (at a maximum) a certain number of times equity capital.
- ROE can be broken down into component parts that help to identify trends in the bank's performance.

Because the ultimate objective of bank management should be to maximize shareholder wealth, this ratio is particularly important.

Defining equity capital as the sum of common and preferred stock, paid-in surplus (above the book value at the time of issuance), undivided profits (or retained earnings), and reserves for future contingencies, the ROE for State Bank using the data in Tables 3-1 and 3-2 is calculated as follows (numbers are in thousands of dollars):

Rate of return on equity (%) = Net income/Total equity capital × 100 (3.1)

Example:

State Bank (Year 2016)	17.8% = \$2,520/\$14,128 × 100
Peer Group	12.4%

The return on equity for State Bank in 2016 was 17.8 percent, considerably higher than the peer ratio of 12.4 percent. If the analyst was interested in exploring the trend of earnings, the ROE for State Bank (and its peer group) could be calculated for earlier years.

ROA

The ***rate of return on assets (ROA)*** measures the ability of management to utilize the real and financial resources of the bank to generate returns. ROA is commonly used to evaluate bank management. For State Bank, ROA can be calculated as follows:

Rate of return on assets (%) = Net income/Total assets × 100 (3.2)

Example:

State Bank (Year 2016)	1.22% = \$2,520/\$205,973 × 100
Peer Group	0.84%

Since the average bank in the State Bank peer group had an ROA of 0.84%, it is obvious that the profitability of State Bank was above average. Again, trends in profitability as measured by the ROA could be calculated.

Unraveling Profit Ratios

In the preceding ratio analyses we found that State Bank had a relatively high ROA compared with its peer group, and also that its ROE was relatively high. The relationship between the ROE and ROA can be expressed as follows:

ROE = ROA × Equity multiplier (3.3)

$$\frac{\text{Net income}}{\text{Total equity}} = \frac{\text{Net income}}{\text{Total assets}} \times \frac{\text{Net assets}}{\text{Total equity}}$$

This formula shows the return on equity ratio as the product of ROA and a ratio indicating the extent to which the bank is using financial leverage, known as the ***equity (or leverage) multiplier***. In the present example the ROE of State Bank can be broken down as follows (where some degree of rounding error is allowed):

Example:

State Bank (Year 2016) $2,520/$205,973 × 100 × $205,973/$14,128

17.8% = 1.22% × 14.6

Peer Group 12.4% = 0.84% × 14.6

State Bank has a higher ROE than its peer group because it earns more on its assets. Its use of financial leverage (as measured by the equity or leverage multiplier) is virtually identical to that of its peer group.

Another useful formula for unraveling profits is as follows:

ROE = Profit margin × Asset utilization × Equity multiplier (3.4)

$$\frac{\text{Net income}}{\text{Total equity}} = \frac{\text{Net income}}{\text{Operating revenue}} \times \frac{\text{Operating revenue}}{\text{Total assets}} \times \frac{\text{Total assets}}{\text{Total equity}}$$

where operating revenue is the sum of total interest income and noninterest income. Notice that this formula breaks down ROA into the product of ***profit margin*** and ***asset utilization***. The profit margin ratio provides information about the ability of management to control expenses, including taxes, given a particular level of operating income. The asset utilization ratio represents the ability of management to employ assets effectively to generate revenues. Together, these two ratios enable the bank analyst to gain insight into the derivation of ROA.

For State Bank, equation (3.4) can be used as follows:

Example:

State Bank (Year 2016) $2,520/($17,915 + $571) × ($17,915 + $571)/$205,973 × $205,973/$14,128

17.8% = 1.36 × 0.90 × 14.6

Peer Group 12.4% = 0.84 × 1.00 × 14.8

State Bank generated a higher ROE than its peer group primarily because of a higher profit margin. Indeed, its asset utilization is lower than the peer group.

Other Profit Measures

A number of other profit measures are commonly used in banking, which provide further insight into a bank's financial performance.

One of these is the ***net interest margin (NIM),*** which is defined as follows:

$$\text{Net interest margin(\%)} = \frac{\text{Total interest income - Total interest expense}}{\text{Average earning assets}} \text{x100} \quad (3.5)$$

where total interest income is on a pretax basis. It should be noted that in the case where municipal bond interest income is not taxable, this interest income must be "grossed up" by dividing by 1 minus the marginal tax rate of the bank to convert it to a pretax-equivalent amount. For example, tax-equivalent yield $(\text{TEY}) = i/(1-t)$ so that a bank with a four percent return on municipal securities and a 34 percent tax rate would report a TEY of 6.06 percent [4/(l – 0.34)]. In the case of State Bank, the net interest margin is as follows:

Example:
State Bank (Year 2016) 4.21% = ($17,915 – $10,021)/$187,472
Peer Group 3.90%

Because interest income and expenses make up the lion's share of total operating income and expenses, respectively, NIM is well worth calculating.

RISK RATIOS

Capitalization

As shown in equation (3.3), *capitalization* directly influences the rate of return on equity. The leverage ratio can affect the growth rate of the bank also. For example, if the policy of the bank was to keep the equity multiplier equal to 10, then each dollar of retained earnings could be used to support $10 of assets, because $9 could be borrowed by the bank to maintain the same equity multiplier. It should be obvious that a high equity multiplier can increase both ROE and the growth rate of the bank as long as ROA is positive.

On the downside, if ROA were negative, ROEs would be magnified in a negative direction. Also, in the preceding example, bank asset size would need to decline tenfold for every dollar lost to keep the equity multiplier constant. In the extreme, if losses exceeded bank capital, the bank would be insolvent and subject to closure by the chartering agency. As discussed earlier, State Bank has an equity capitalization ratio that is very similar to that of its peers.

Asset Quality

Asset quality can be assessed only indirectly using financial ratios. On-site inspection of the bank's outstanding individual loans is certainly the best way to evaluate asset quality.[4] In the absence of this opportunity, some financial ratios can provide at least a historical account of the creditworthiness of a particular bank's loan portfolio.

Provision for Loan Losses: Each bank provides an estimate of future loan losses as an expense on its income statement. This expense may be related to the volume of loans as:

$$\text{Provision for loan loss ratio(\%)} = \frac{\text{Provision for loan losses}}{\text{Total loans and leases}} \text{x100} \qquad (3.6)$$

For State Bank the provision for loan loss ratio is as follows:
Example:
State Bank (Year 2016) 1.38% = $1,294/$93,196
Peer Group 1.18%

This ratio suggests that State Bank has provided more for losses on loans than similar banks.

Loan Ratio: The loan ratio indicates the extent to which assets are devoted to loans as opposed to other assets, including cash, securities, and plant and equipment. The ratio and results for State Bank are as follows:

$$\text{Loan ratio}(\%) = \frac{\text{Net loans}}{\text{Total assets}} \text{x}100 \quad (3.7)$$

Example:
State Bank (Year 2016) 43.74% = $90,101/$205,973
Peer Group 48.70%

These data suggest that the higher provision for loan losses at State Bank compared to its peer group took place despite its relatively lower exposure to loan (or credit) risk.

Additional information on the credit quality of State Bank may be obtained from the footnote to its financial statements. Two measures are particularly important: the amount of charge-offs and the amount of nonperforming assets. ***Charge-offs*** represent the last step in the deterioration of a loan. Once management believes that the loan is uncollectible it is "charged off" the books of the bank and therefore no longer appears as an asset. The charge-off usually reduces the reserve for loan losses and often triggers an increase in the provision for loan losses if the reserve is made inadequate by the charge-offs. The relationship between charge-offs, provision for loan losses, and the reserve for loan losses can be explained as follows (see also Chapter 12). Suppose that a bank has $5 million in the reserve for loan loss account on its balance sheet and that management has determined that the minimum adequate reserve is $4.8 million. Now assume that $500,000 of loans are uncollectible and bank management charges these loans off. This reduces the reserve for loan loss account to $4.5 million. To replenish the reserve, management would then increase the accrued expense item, provision for loan losses, by $300,000. The reserve would also be increased by recoveries of previous loan charge -offs. Algebraically, we have:

$$\text{Reserve for loan losses} = \text{Reserve for loan losses} - \text{Gross charge-offs} + \text{Provision for loan losses} + \text{Recoveries}$$

where

Net charge-offs = Gross charge-offs - Recoveries.

In contrast to charge-offs, which are a lagging indicator of credit quality, ***nonperforming assets*** are a leading indicator. Nonperforming assets equal the sum of nonaccrual loans (those loans whose revenue stream is so uncertain that the bank does not recognize income until cash is received), restructured loans (for example, loans whose interest rate has been lowered or the maturity increased because of problems with the borrower), and other real estate owned (e.g., foreclosed real estate).

Operating Efficiency

A key management area that many studies have found to be the primary factor distinguishing high- and low-profit banks is operating efficiency. ***Operating efficiency*** deals with the production of outputs, such as deposit and loan accounts and securities services, at a minimum cost per dollar (or account).

A number of ratios can be calculated to provide information on cost control by simply dividing various expense accounts by total operating expenses for different expense categories.

Wages and salaries (and related benefits) are normally the largest noninterest expense item. The occupancy expense ratio indicates the level of fixed expenses that the bank is carrying. Relatively high fixed expenses are not always an indicator of poor expense control. In the 1960s and 1970s, for example, banks operated branch offices in part as a means of providing greater convenience to customers (assuming state laws permitted branching). Because Regulation Q prevented banks from paying market rates of interest on deposit accounts at times, branch offices represented an added (implicit) service return to customers. However, the phase-out of Regulation Q in the 1980s caused many banks to trim their branch office facilities to reduce expenses (as interest expenses began to rise dramatically). New electronic technology is also causing many banks to reshuffle the structure of their expenses. More funds are being allocated to ATMs, smart phone innovation, and other automated means of delivering banking services, causing wage expenses to fall (as capital is substituted for labor) along with on-premise occupancy expenses for buildings and furniture.

Liquidity

Liquidity can be defined as the extent to which the bank has funds available to meet cash demands for loans and deposit withdrawals (see Chapter 11 for detailed discussion). Banks require different amounts of liquidity depending on their growth rate and variability in lending and deposit activities.

One problem in measuring liquidity is that liability management has partially replaced asset management at many banks as the way to fund liquidity needs. That is, banks have decreased the quantity of liquid assets they hold for the purpose of meeting loan demands and deposit withdrawals (i.e., asset management) and increased their usage of deposit and nondeposit sources of funds paying market rates of interest (i.e., liability management). These trends have tended to affect banks in the following ways:

- Gross rates of return on assets have increased because longer-term assets normally have higher rates of return than short-term assets (due to upward-sloping yield curves).
- U.S. Treasury security holdings have declined.
- Credit risk has increased in many banks as liquid assets have been replaced by loans.

The shift away from money market assets and toward more lending was motivated in large part by the rising costs of funds in the latter 1970s and early 1980s as Regulation Q ceilings on deposits were phased out and competition for deposit funds intensified. These asset and liability changes have dramatically altered the management of bank liquidity.

Even though liability management has become more prevalent as an approach to meeting liquidity needs, it is still meaningful to calculate financial ratios that focus on the asset liquidity of the bank. If a bank suffered financial distress for any reason, it is likely that other banks and the market in general would reduce their lending to the institution. In this situation the bank would need to rely on its asset liquidity to a greater extent. Thus, asset liquidity is a reserve that the bank can draw on in the event its access to purchased funds is reduced. Another reason for banks to hold liquid assets is to fund loans when interest rates are relatively high. Assuming loan demand is strong, short-term assets bearing little price risk may be a less expensive source of funds than relatively high interest rate deposits. In essence, liquid assets are an alternative source of funds that at times may be cheaper than using liability management methods to raise funds.

Two commonly used measures of liquidity are the ***temporary investments ratio*** and the ***volatile liability dependency ratio***. Temporary investments are a bank's most liquid assets. The higher the ratio of temporary investments to total assets the greater the bank's liquidity. Temporary investments include federal funds sold, trading account assets, investment securities with maturities of one year or less, and cash due from banks. Volatile liabilities are brokered deposits, large (or jumbo) CDs, deposits in foreign offices, federal funds purchased, and other borrowings. Brokered deposits are a particularly important part of volatile liabilities because banks that are experiencing liquidity problems often resort to brokered deposits as their last source of funds.

The volatile liability dependency ratio is somewhat complicated but extremely useful in measuring liquidity. The ratio is calculated as volatile liabilities less temporary investments divided by net loans and leases plus long-term securities. It considers the degree to which the riskiest assets are being funded by unstable or "hot" money funds that can disappear from the bank overnight. The volatile liability dependence ratio varies inversely with liquidity.

These ratios may be calculated as follows:

$$\text{Temporary investments ratio} = \frac{\text{Federal funds sold} + \text{Investment securities with maturities of} \leq \text{one year} + \text{Due from banks}}{\text{Total assets}} \quad (3.8)$$

For State Bank, federal funds sold are \$10,500, and due from banks funds are \$9,039. Since the maturities of investments are not shown in Table 3-1, that information must be obtained from supporting financial statements. In this case, they are \$11,871, so that temporary investments are \$31,410. Hence the temporary investments ratio is:

Example:

State Bank (Year 2016)	15.25% = \$31,410/\$205,973 × 100
Peer Group	43.50%

The ratio for State Bank and its peer group indicate that State Bank has much less funds invested in highly liquid assets (relative to its volatile liabilities) than does the peer group. This may suggest a significant liquidity problem for State Bank. Such a problem is also implied by the volatile liability dependency ratio.

The *volatile liability dependency ratio* is computed as follows:

$$\text{Volatile liability dependency} = \frac{\text{Total volatile liabilities - Temporary investments}}{\text{Net loans and leases \& long-term leases}} \text{x100} \qquad (3.9)$$

Example:
State Bank (Year 2016) 36.31% = ($83,009 – $31,410)/$142,101 × 100
Peer Group –5.41%

State Bank funds a great portion of its nonliquid assets with volatile liabilities. By contrast, peer group banks have a negative ratio indicating that they have large temporary assets relative to volatile liabilities.

Other Financial Ratios

Many more financial ratios than those discussed previously are conceivable. The analyst can construct other financial ratios if it is believed that they will help to reveal the strengths and weaknesses of the bank under study. For example, two areas that might be useful to explore are the ability of the bank to minimize taxes and the interest sensitivity of its mix of sources and uses of funds.

Taxes: The tax exposure of the bank can be assessed by using the following ratio:

$$\text{Tax rate(\%)} = \frac{\text{Total taxes paid}}{\text{Net income before taxes}} \text{x100} \qquad (3.10)$$

where total taxes paid includes the tax consequences of security gains and losses. The tax rate for State Bank is calculated as follows:

Example:
State Bank (Year 2016) 47.4% = $2,267/$4,787 × 100
Peer Group 49.3 %

In general, the marginal tax rate (i.e., the tax rate applicable to the last dollar of income earned) for most banks is the maximum statutory rate.

One way that banks traditionally lowered their tax burden was to purchase municipal bonds, which in the past offered interest payments that were exempt from federal income tax. Under the Tax Reform Act of 1986, this tax reduction technique was substantially lessened because interest expenses incurred on deposits subsequently invested in tax-exempt obligations can no longer be deducted from income for tax purposes. An exception to this law is the purchase of tax-exempt securities (excluding private activity bonds, such as industrial development bonds) issued by municipalities offering $10 million or less of government obligations.

Another means of lowering taxes in the past was to deduct larger provisions for loan losses from income than anticipated charge-offs would suggest. According to 1986 tax law, however, deductions are allowed only as loans are actually charged off.

Interest Sensitivity: Interest sensitivity is the responsiveness of liability costs and asset returns to changes in interest rates. The difference between the quantities of interest-sensitive assets and liabilities is known as the dollar gap ratio. To compare the interest sensitivity of different banks, the following dollar gap ratio can be calculated:

$$\text{Dollar gap ratio (\%)} = \frac{\text{Interest rate–sensitive assets} - \text{Interest rate–sensitive liabilities}}{\text{Total assets}} \times 100 \quad (3.11)$$

where rate-sensitive is defined as short-term assets and liabilities with maturities of less than one year (or that reprice in less than one year). To obtain a more complete picture of interest sensitivity, the analyst will calculate gap ratios for assets and liabilities of different maturity ranges (e.g., 0–90 days, 90–120 days, and 120 days–1 year). By structuring assets and liabilities in terms of maturity ranges, or "buckets," the analyst can determine the extent to which a change in interest rates would affect bank profitability. If interest rates increased (decreased) in the future, positive gap ratios would cause the bank's profitability to increase (decrease). The opposite effects would correspond to negative gap ratios. Chapter 5 discusses interest rate sensitivity and gap management in more detail.

Although the income statement and balance sheet do not provide sufficient information to make such calculations, in the case of State Bank the gap ratio is as follows:

Example:

State Bank (Year 2016)	–18.25%
Peer Group	–6.00%

The large negative gap ratio for State Bank relative to its peer group suggests that its profitability will be affected much more than its peers by a change in interest rates within the next year. If interest rates increase (decrease) in the near future, State Bank's profitability will decrease (increase) dramatically because of the negative gap ratio. It is true that some amount of interest sensitivity may be desirable to take advantage of anticipated movements in interest rates, but excessive sensitivity, as in the present instance, may well be considered "betting the bank" and, therefore, is not prudent management.

Application of Financial Ratios to Evaluating the Performance of Wells Fargo

An overview of the financial performance of Wells Fargo, one of the largest commercial banks in the United States, is provided in Table 3-3. As shown there, Wells Fargo is compared to a peer group comprised of over 60 other banks at year-end 2014 and 2015. With over $1.5 trillion in bank assets in 2015, Wells Fargo outperformed its peers in terms of profitability. The return on assets (ROA) was 1.37 percent (0.98 percent for peers) in 2014 compared to 1.32 percent (1.00 percent for peers) in 2015. However, notice that the net interest margin of Wells Fargo was less than its peers in these years. It is likely that the bank earned relatively high noninterest revenues (e.g., fees, derivatives trading, and off-balance sheet activities) that boosted its return on assets but were not counted in the net interest margin.

In terms of asset quality, Wells Fargo tended to have higher net losses (as a percentage of total loans and leases)—for example, in 2015 this ratio was 0.29 percent versus 0.13 percent for its peers. Additionally, the ratio of provision for loan and lease losses to total assets in 2015 was 0.14 compared to 0.12 for its peers.

Turning to other indicators of financial performance, the bank had a higher liquidity as indicated by a net loans and leases to total assets ratio of about 55 percent versus about 67 percent for peers in 2015. Tier 1 equity capital to total assets (or capital ratio) was 8.01 percent compared to 9.78 percent for peers in 2015 but well above regulatory requirements.

The growth rates for assets, equity capital and reserves, and loans and leases show that the bank was growing more slowly than its peers on average. The main reason for this difference in growth rates is likely related to its large size and higher loan losses in recent years compared to its peers. Slow U.S. economic growth has no doubt contributed to its slower growth compared to smaller peers also. On the whole, Wells Fargo has recovered from the 2008-2009 financial crisis and is poised to expand as the economy rebounds in the years ahead.

Table 3-3: SELECTED FINANCIAL INFORMATION FOR WELLS FARGO AND A PEER GROUP

	December 31, 2015			December 31, 2014		
Percent of Average Assets:	**Bank**	**Peer**	**%Rank**	**Bank**	**Peer**	**%Rank**
Interest Income (TE)	2.92	3.44	20	3.03	3.52	23
- Interest Expense	0.14	0.29	20	0.16	0.3	24
Net Interest Income (TE)	2.78	3.12	26	2.87	3.19	29
+ Noninterest Income	1.74	1.02	84	1.86	1.01	87
- Noninterest Expense	2.44	2.55	44	2.62	2.65	46
- Provision: Loan & Lease Losses	0.14	0.12	59	0.05	0.11	33
Pretax Operating Income (TE)	1.94	1.48	84	2.05	1.46	87
+ Realized Gains/Losses Sec	0.05	0.01	88	0.03	0.01	85
Pretax Net Operating Income (TE)	1.99	1.49	85	2.09	1.47	88
Net Operating Income	1.33	1	83	1.38	0.98	88
Net Income (ROA)	1.32	1	83	1.37	0.98	87
Margin Analysis:						
Avg Earning Assets to Avg Assets	93.38	92.81	58	92.91	92.37	57
Avg Int-Bearing Funds to Avg Assets	83.11	77.84	72	83.04	77.35	71
Int Income to Avg Earn Assets	3.12	3.71	19	3.26	3.83	20
Int Expense to Avg Earn Assets	0.15	0.31	20	0.17	0.33	23
Net Int Inc to Avg Earn Assets (NIM)	2.97	3.37	26	3.09	3.47	28
Loan & Lease Analysis:						
Net Loss to Average Total LN&LS	0.29	0.13	84	0.29	0.18	75
LN&LS Allowance to Total LN&LS	1.16	1.09	59	1.3	1.21	61
Total LN&LS-90+ Days Past Due	1.91	0.14	97	2.53	0.2	97
Liquidity						
Net Non Core Fund Dep New $250M	9.49	13.95	35	7.66	12.87	33
Net Loans & Leases to Assets	54.55	66.74	17	53.82	65.02	21
Capitalization						
Tier One Leverage Capital	8.01	9.78	10	8.06	9.83	13
Growth Rates						
Total Assets	5.08	10.86	34	11.59	11.72	64
Tier One Capital	5.85	11.31	31	8.9	11.51	56
Net Loans & Leases	6.49	13.48	27	6.26	15.41	32
Average Total Assets	1,567,613,250			1,431,489,250		
Total Equity Capital	150,513,000			144,984,000		

MANAGERIAL ISSUES

OVERALL BANK PERFORMANCE MEASURES

There are so many financial ratios that can be computed for a bank that it can be difficult to summarize all of this information. Over the years, computer-based methods have been increasingly applied to this multivariate problem. These multivariate techniques use numerous financial ratios and aggregate them into a single score that represents overall bank performance. For example, bank regulators use these techniques as ***early warning systems (EWSs)*** of bank risk. Let's see how to put together a relatively simple EWS model.

Assume that we have decided to measure bank performance using three financial ratios: the return on assets (denoted X1), total loans/loan charge-offs (denoted X2), and equity capital/total assets (denoted X3). We inverted the asset quality ratio with loan charge-offs so that, as the ratio increases, the bank is considered lower risk. The higher the profit and capitalization ratios, the lower the bank risk also. Two groups of banks with assets between $500 million and $1 billion are constructed: (1) banks that had equity capital/total assets below five percent in 2016, and (2) banks that had equity capital/total assets above five percent in 2016. Suppose that 30 banks are in group 1 and that 2,000 nonfailed banks are group 2. Banks in group 1 are considered to be "capital inadequate" and those in group 2 are "capital adequate." Our goal is to build an EWS model that can predict one year ahead of time if a bank's capital will fall below five percent such that it will be capital inadequate. Such banks are more risky than capital adequate banks, because as their equity capital decreases, the chance that the bank might fail increases. When the bank's equity capital ratio goes below zero, it is technically bankrupt.

We need to construct a database containing our three financial ratios X1, X2, and X3 for our two groups of banks in the year before 2016. So, we compute these three ratios for each bank in 2015. This is the initial data that we will use to build our EWS model.

The first step is to take our initial data and run it using computer software for a multivariate regression model. This software is fairly common—for example, Microsoft Excel can be used. The regression model has the following form:

$$0,1 = a + b1X1 + b2X2 + b3X3$$

where X = independent variables (or our three ratios computed in 2015), b = the regression coefficients for the independent variables, and the dependent variable is either 0 (for capital-inadequate banks in 2016) or 1 (for capital-adequate banks in 2016). Notice that the higher our composite score, the higher the overall performance of the bank. In fact, the composite score is the probability that the bank will have adequate capital. If the score is one, there is a 100 percent chance of having adequate capital. At the other extreme, a score of zero means that the bank has a 0 percent chance of adequate capital. At this stage of the analyses, the score is assigned to be 0 or 1 depending on if the bank is in group 1 or group 2 in 2016. The computer-based regression analyses will tell us whether the coefficients b1, b2, and b3 are significant in terms of discriminating between capital inadequate, or group 1, and capital adequate banks, or group (2). Let's assume that b1, b2, and b3 are all important in this regard. We have completed the model-building step in developing an EWS.

In the next step we need to test our EWS model. To do this we construct another database that is similar to the model-building database, except that we collect 2016 data (instead of 2015 data before). Now we take this data and run it through our model. Assume that b1 = 2, b2 = 1, and b2 = 3. Let's take any bank and multiply its X values by these coefficients. So, if we have a bank with X1 = 0.01, X2 = 0.25, and X3 = 0.06, then its score = 2(0.01) + 1(0.04) + 3(0.06) = 0.20 + 0.40 + 0.18 = 0.78. We can infer that there is a 78 percent chance that this bank will have adequate capital. The 2016 data for each bank is run through the model in a similar way. After all the banks' scores have been computed, we can check to see which banks in 2017 actually did have an equity capital/total assets ratio below five percent and which banks did not. Comparing our scores to the actual capital levels of banks allows us to determine if our EWS model is working in the sense of accurately predicting capital adequacy one year ahead of time. If we rank all banks by their EWS scores (computed with 2016 data), the banks at the bottom near 0 should tend to be the capital inadequate banks (in 2017). Assuming that this is so, we have finished our test phase in developing an EWS. We can apply this model to banks to predict banks' overall performance. We can also use this score to make historical comparisons of banks over the past few years.

Our simple EWS model is only one example of a computer-based approach to assessing overall bank performance. Models can be developed to predict which banks might fail or which banks are most likely to have low profit performance. Bank regulators are known to use EWS models in their supervisory function of overseeing the safety and soundness of the banking industry. Bank analysts can use these models for purposes of making investment decisions. Lastly, bankers can apply EWS models to evaluating themselves relative to their competition.

Internal Performance Evaluation Based on Economic Profit

Expansion of product lines subsequent to the passage of the 1999 Financial Services Modernization Act created new challenges for evaluating bank performance. Confronted with a growing number of financial services, bank managers became concerned about the profitability of different products. One motivation for this is to simply understand the profitability of each financial service. Services that are not profitable need to be either dropped or modified so that they do generate profits. A second motivation is management compensation. Which managers have done the best job and deserve larger increases in their salary, wages, or bonuses? It is important that compensation be tied to management performance. In this section we overview two methods used by banks to evaluate themselves on an internal basis: risk-adjusted return on capital and economic value added. Both of these methods focus attention on economic profit that increases stock prices, as opposed to accounting profits.

Risk-Adjusted Return on Capital (RAROC)

In the 1990s Banker's Trust popularized a method of evaluating loans known as ***RAROC*** that has been expanded to include other areas of internal performance, including product lines and customers. Applied to pricing loans, RAROC allocates equity capital depending on risk of loss, calculates a required rate of return on equity, and then uses this information in pricing loans to make sure that they are profitable to the bank. Assume the following information:

Cost of funds	5.00%
Provision for loan losses	1.00
Direct expense	0.50
Indirect expense	0.25
Overhead	0.25
Total charges before capital charge	7.00%
Capital charge*	2.29
Total required loan rate	9.29%

* The capital charge is determined by multiplying the equity capital allocated to the loan times the opportunity cost of equity and then converting to a pre-tax level. Assume that the allocated equity to loan ratio is 10 percent and the opportunity cost of equity is 16 percent, such that the after-tax capital charge is 1.6 percent. If the tax rate for the bank is 0.3, the pre-tax capital charge is 1.6/(1.0 – 0.3), or 2.29.

In the example above, if the loan rate is 9.29 percent, the bank will earn the target return on equity of 16 percent. Of course, if the bank can price the loan at a rate higher than 9.29 percent, it will earn profit over the target level of equity returns. In this case an economic profit is earned in that the value of equity is increased. Notice that economic profit is different from accounting profit. Loans with a rate of return of eight percent likely would provide a positive return on assets, but equity returns would decline, as equity investors are disappointed by earnings rates below their expectations.

A critical step in applying RAROC is determining the capital assigned to the loan. In the example we assumed that 10 percent equity would be needed to support the loan. One way to arrive at this figure is to use regulatory capital rules for the equity assignment (see Chapter 12 for details). However, capital regulations are only a minimum level, and it is plausible that the bank's risk preferences require more equity be assigned to high-risk loans. In this regard, capital-at-risk (CAR) can be assigned to business units based on either their actual utilized capital or the allocated capital limit or capacity provided by top management (using past performance and expected earnings data). Utilized CAR is a good approach in situations in smaller business units to avoid penalizing them for not using excess capital beyond their control. Allocated capital is more appropriate for larger business units in that it enables some flexibility by managers to expand operations to the point that all capital is profitably invested.

RAROC can be extended to product lines that divide the bank into business units. For example, a large bank will typically have consumer banking, wholesale banking, and securities components. These business areas have different risk exposures that imply varying capital allocations. Also, operating costs can differ across product lines. It should be obvious that business units will tend to have different required rates of return in order to reach equity return targets and generate economic profits. These rates of return are minimum rates that managers need to incorporate in their pricing decisions and risk assessments. Today, many banks employ RAROC to measure managerial performance and tie compensation to earned rates of return relative to benchmark required rates of return.[5] Hence, managers cannot simply earn accounting profits or expand market share at the expense of shareholder earnings. In this way differences between managers' versus owners' goals are mitigated to some degree. One potential drawback of applying RAROC to product lines is that it may not be possible to separate the economic costs and revenues of the different products. The production of outputs may share inputs, such as land, labor, and capital investments, which makes it impossible to individually analyze the product lines. Under these circumstances, either some assumptions on how to allocate costs and revenues must be made or the analyses must be performed on the bundle of jointly produced products.

Economic Value Added (EVA)

A performance metric that is similar in spirit to RAROC is economic value added **(EVA)** [6]. EVA can be defined as follows:

$$\text{EVA} = \text{Adjusted earnings} - \text{Opportunity cost of capital} \tag{3.12}$$

where adjusted earnings is net income after taxes, and the opportunity cost of capital equals the cost of equity times equity capital. The consulting firm Stern, Stewart & Co. developed EVA, but other consulting firms have produced similar performance measures, including Holt Value Associates' cash flow rate of return on investment (CFROI), Boston Consulting Group's total business return (TBR), and LEK/Alear Consulting Group's shareholder value added (SVA).

Managers can apply EVA to loans, projects, product lines, and so on in order to evaluate whether the investment will be justifiable in terms of rewarding shareholders. In this context new investments should undertaken until the marginal contribution of the last investment is zero (i.e., EVA = 0). Contrary to an accounting analysis framework, in which only the investments with the highest ROEs are accepted, EVA accepts all investments that contribute to shareholder wealth.

On a practical level, managers using EVA face tradeoffs in attempting to increase the EVA for investments under their control. A higher EVA can be achieved by boosting adjusted earnings (via lowering costs, increasing sales, etc.), lowering the cost of equity, or by lowering the equity allocated to the investment. However, if earnings are increased by increasing sales, this increased production capacity will imply greater equity investment. Assuming the marginal cost of equity capital remains constant (which may not be true), EVA will increase only if the higher adjusted earnings more than offsets the greater opportunity cost of capital. By focusing attention on the tradeoffs involved in the components of EVA, managers presumably will make decisions more consistent with creating economic value, as opposed to maximizing profits or market share. Like RAROC, EVA is beneficial in assessing managerial performance and developing incentive compensation schemes compatible with shareholder wealth goals (e.g., reducing agency costs). Also like RAROC, EVA presents some difficult challenges in allocation costs, revenues, and equity when applied to lines of business, divisions, products, etc. that are not separate of one another due to joint production of multiple products with shared inputs.

Notice the difference between RAROC and EVA: The former compares business unit profit with the unit's capital-at-risk whereas the latter compares business unit profit with the cost of capital. Critics of RAROC argue that it will reject profitable business opportunities when RAROC exceeds the cost of capital, which will decrease shareholder wealth. However, if the cost of capital is greater than RAROC, then use of EVA would reject profitable opportunities that would improve current performance. One way to resolve this dilemma is to recognize that the cost of capital is a longer-term concept than RAROC. Thus, short-term opportunities can be accepted with RAROC even though their rate of return is below the long-run cost of capital (and therefore would be rejected by EVA). And, investment opportunities must earn returns than exceed the cost of capital in the long run as suggested by EVA.

In sum, RAROC, EVA, and other performance measures based on economic profit help to align the actions of managers with shareholder interests. Normally, they lead to better risk management, efficient control of resources, and informed judgment on the acceptability of investments by the bank. However, they do have weaknesses, especially with respect to their application to jointly produced products in banking. In the years ahead these methods no doubt will be further refined to address these weaknesses. At present most large and regional banks internally employ one or more of these performance evaluation methods.

SUMMARY

The evaluation of bank performance is a complex process involving interactions between the environment, internal operations, and external activities. The ultimate objective of management is to maximize the value of the bank's equity shares by attaining the optimal mix of returns and risks. In this respect bank management needs to develop a comprehensive plan in order to identify objectives, goals, budgets, and strategies that will be consistent with the maximization of share values. Planning should encompass both internal and external performance dimensions. The primary method of evaluating internal performance is by analyzing accounting statements. Financial ratios of accounting items permit an historical sketch of bank returns and risks. External performance is best measured by evaluating the bank's market share, regulatory compliance, and public confidence. Because of increasing innovation and regulatory oversight in the financial services industry, internal and external competitiveness is becoming much more important than in the past.

KEY TERMS AND CONCEPTS

asset utilization
charge-offs
dollar gap ratio
early warning systems
earning assets
equity multiplier
EVA
federal funds sold/purchased
interest-bearing liabilities
interest rate spread
interest-sensitive assets/liabilities
interest sensitivity gap
liquidity
net charge-offs
net interest margin
noninterest income
nonperforming assets
operating efficiency
profit margin
provision for loan losses
RAROC
report of condition
report of income
reserve for loan losses
return on assets (ROA)
return on equity (ROE)
taxable equivalent income
temporary investments ratio
volatile liability dependency

QUESTIONS

3.1 Discuss the difference between bank goals and bank objectives in the planning process. What is the ultimate objective of the bank?

3.2 Why is conserving costs by keeping employee salaries, wages, and benefits down not necessarily a good idea?

3.3 Define bank growth. Why might super growth be a problem for a bank?

3.4 Give at least three reasons for staying up to date with bank technology.

3.5 Why do you think banks are sensitive about news reports concerning them in the financial press?

3.6 ROE and ROA are two key measures of bank profitability. Discuss the importance of these ratios to (a) insured depositors, (b) bank shareholders, and (c) bank management.

3.7 If a bank has a relatively low ROA but a relatively high ROE, what factor would explain this difference? Show an equation to demonstrate your answer.

3.8 In calculating the net interest margin, why does municipal bond interest earnings have to be grossed up?

3.9 If federal regulators require that bank capital be increased to at least 10 percent of total assets, how would bank growth be affected?

3.10 Do loan losses reduce bank profit?

3.11 Bank A operates with an equity to assets ratio of 10 percent and has a return on assets ratio of one percent. What is its return on equity? What would its ROE be if it were allowed to operate with a two percent equity to assets ratio? What does this suggest about the effects of financial leverage?

3.12 Give three explanations for a bank having a lower ratio of interest expenses to total assets than its peers.

3.13 How did the Tax Reform Act of 1986 affect interest deductions on deposits?

3.14 If the dollar gap ratio is negative and interest rates are expected to rise in the near future, what will happen to bank profitability, provided that all else remains the same?

3.15 Why have billion-dollar banks been less affected by deposit rate deregulations than smaller, retail banks?

3.16 What are the principal types of bank risk? Give at least one ratio for each type of risk.

3.17 What is RAROC? EVA? What are their strengths and weaknesses?

3.18 Go to the FDIC Institution Directory at www.fdic.gov/bank and click Bank Data and Statistics. There you can *search* for a specific commercial bank in your town or city. Give an overview of the financial performance of the bank in the past year.

3.19 Go to www.eva.com and click About EVA. Why is EVA important for a bank to know? Can a bank that makes an accounting profit have a negative EVA? Explain.

3.20 Look up the website for a money center bank in the United States. Give an overview of its financial performance based on accounting data over the past three years.

PROBLEMS

3.1 (a) Exhibits 3-1 and 3-2 provide year-end Reports of Condition and Income for Z-Bank in 20XX-1 and 20XX. Exhibit 3-3 shows a list of financial ratios for Z-bank's peer group. Calculate these financial ratios for Z-bank. Round your answers to the hundredths place. For the dollar gap ratio assume that all securities, one-half of loans and lease-financing receivables, and all deposits have maturities less than one year, and exclude cash and due from the calculation of this ratio.

Exhibit 3-1: Report of Condition: Z-Bank

	YEAR-END (IN MILLIONS)	
Report of Condition Items	**20XX-1**	**20XX**
Cash and due from depository institutions	$200	$205
U.S. Treasury securities	50	40
Obligations of other U.S. governmental agencies	20	17
Obligations of state and political subdivisions	70	68
All other securities	20	18
Federal funds sold and securities purchased	35	30
Total cash and securities	$395	$378
Loans	700	600
Lease financing receivables	10	10
Banks premises, furniture, and fixtures	15	16
All other assets	70	65
Total assets	$1,190	$1,069
Demand deposits	267	138
Time and savings deposits	350	250
Deposits in foreign offices	100	100
Deposits of U.S. government	2	2
Deposits of state and political government	50	45
All other deposits	100	170
Total deposits	$869	$705
Federal funds purchased and securities sold	140	180
Interest-bearing demand notes and other borrowings	30	40
Mortgage indebtedness	5	5
All other liabilities	70	65
Total liabilities	$ 1,114	$995
Capital		
Subordinated notes and debentures	5	5
Preferred stock—par value	1	1
Common stock—par value	40	40
Surplus	10	10
Undivided profits and capital reserves	20	18
Total liabilities and capital	$1,190	$1,069

Exhibit 3-2: Report of Income: Z-Bank

	YEAR-END (IN MILLIONS)	
Report of Condition Items	**20XX-1**	**20XX**
Interest and fees on loans	$120	$100
Interest on balances with depository institutions	15	13
Income on federal funds sold and securities purchased	5	4
Interest on U.S. Treasury and other agencies' securities	7	7
Interests on obligations of state and political subdivisions	5	5
Interests on other securities	1	1
Income from direct lease financing	2	2
Income from fiduciary activities	1	1
Service charges on deposit accounts	3	2
Other service charges	6	5
Other operating income	4	3
Total operating income	**$169**	**$143**
Operating expenses		
Salaries and employee benefits	20	18
Interest on CDs of $100,000 or more	15	13
Interest on deposits in foreign offices	35	37
Interest on other deposits	8	14
Interest on federal funds purchased and securities sold	18	23
Interest on demand notes and other borrowings	3	3
Interest on subordinated notes and debentures	1	1
Occupancy, furniture, and fixed expenses	6	6
Provision for possible loan losses	4	4
Other operating expenses	10	10
Total operating expenses	**$120**	**$129**
Income before taxes and securities transactions	49	14
Less: Applicable income taxes	23	7
Income before securities gains or losses	$23	$7
Securities gains (losses), net of taxes	(1)	(1)
Net income	**$22**	**$6**
Cash dividends	12	6
Undivided profits	10	0
Recoveries credited to provision for possible loan losses	1	1
Losses charged to provision for possible loan losses	−3	−7

3.1 (b) Discuss the profitability of Z-Bank by comparing its performance in 20XX-1 and 20XX and by comparing it to its peer group in these years. Break down ROE in your analysis of profitability and discuss the influence of components of roe on Z-Bank's profitability.

3.1 (c) Discuss Z-Bank's risk ratios over time and relative to its peer group. What are Z-Bank's strengths and weaknesses?

3.1 (d) If interest rates rise in the future, what implication is there to Z-Bank's profitability?

Exhibit 3-3: Financial Ratios for Z-Bank's Peer Group

Financial Ratios	20XX-1	20XX
Profit Ratios		
Return on equity (ROE)	20.00%	18.00%
Return on assets (ROA)	1.00%	0.90%
Profit margin	7.00%	6.50%
Net operating margin	2.40%	2.30%
Net interest margin	5.20%	5.00%
Asset utilization		
Risk Ratios		
Capital		
Equity multiplier	16.00	15.50
Asset quality		
Loss rate	0.35%	0.45%
Loan ratio	55.00%	53.00%
Operating efficiency (% of total assets)		
Interest expense	6.50%	6.55%
Wages and salaries	1.72%	1.74%
Occupancy	0.48%	0.49%
PLL	0.30%	0.32%
Other expenses	0.85%	0.85%
Liquidity		
Cash ratio	17.00%	17.00%
Cash and securities ratio	36.00%	37.00%
Other financial ratios		
Tax rate	50.00%	50.00%
Dollar gap ratio	–15.00%-	–10.00%

3.2 NB bank earns one percent on its assets and has a 20 percent tax rate. It earns eight percent on loans, and six percent on investments. It pays four percent on time deposits, and three percent on Federal Funds purchased. Demand deposits pay no interest. Construct an income statement for NB bank (assume a 20 percent tax rate). With this information construct as many ratios of bank performance as you can with the data available.

Balance Sheet for NB

Assets		Liabilities	
Cash and due from banks	$20	Demand deposits	$40
Investments	200	Time deposits	150
Federal funds sold	0	Federal funds purchased	120
Loans	120	Equity	50
Premises	20		$360
	$360		

3.3 Using the information given below, calculate the ROA for each of the banks.

	ROE	Total Equity Capital	Total Assets
Videlia National & Trust	8.16%	$ 14.8 million	$260.5 million
York Savings and Trust	16.24%	11.7 million	$135.4 million
New York State	2.06%	63 million	$972.6 million

3.4 Capital State Bank reports total interest revenue of $86.42 million, total interest expense of $58.62 million, provision for loan losses of $3.6 million, total noninterest revenue of $15.61 million, total noninterest expense of $28.60 million, and an income tax rate of 30 percent. Total assets are $842.16 million. What is Capital's net interest income? What is its net interest margin? Return on assets? Asset utilization? Profit margin?

3.5 Given the following information on Big State Bank, and on its peer group, evaluate the strengths and weaknesses of the bank. What additional information would you want in order to conduct a more in-depth analysis?

	Big State	Peer Group
	For the Year Ended	
	12/31/XX	12/31/XX
Profitability		
Return on assets	0.01%	0.75%
Return on equity	0.24%	14.63%
Earning assets/total assets	89.03%	92.34%
Noninterest expenses/average assets	1.90%	1.72%
Yield on Interest-Earning Assets		
Loans receivable	0.60%	9.63%
Mortgage-backed securities	5.67%	5.82%
U.S. government and other	3.71%	4.98%
Other	3.94%	3.54%
Total	7.28%	8.27%
Yield on Interest-Bearing Liabilities		
Deposits	3.99%	3.44%
Other borrowings	5.11%	4.23%
Total	4.54%	3.86%
Gross Interest Spread	2.74%	4.21%
Interest income/total average assets	6.44%	7.64%
Interest expense/total average liabilities & equity	4.23%	3.66%
Net Interest Spread	2.21%	3.98%
Capital Position		
Equity capital/total assets	4.63%	6.82%

3.6 Given the following information for First National Bank's Reserve For Loan Loss position, answer these questions:
(a) What is the amount of net change-offs in each year?
(b) What trend is evident in the bank's actual loan loss experience? What information is useful in making this assessment?
(c) What trend is evident in the bank's anticipated loan losses?

	20XX	20XX-1
Balance at beginning of period	$1,222	1,206
– Loan charge-offs	61	46
+ Less loan recoveries	32	10
+ Provision for loan losses	40	52
= Balance at end of period	$1,233	$1,222

ENDNOTES

1. The National Information Center (NIC), www.ffiec.gov/nic, provides comprehensive information on banks and other institutions for which the Federal Reserve has a supervisory, regulatory, or research interest. The NIC includes the organizational structure of financial institutions and financial information for some of those institutions. Historical information is available on the structure of all the institutions. Financial information is available for selected time periods.
2. Searching by institution name and FDIC ID number, you can get financial statements of any FDIC-insured bank at the FDIC Institution Directory, www.fdic.gov/bank. The site also has historical information on the banking industry, research and analysis of banking trends across the nation, and more.
3. The Uniform Bank Performance Report (UBPR), available at www.ffiec.gov/UBPR.htm, is an analytical tool created for bank supervisory, examination, and management purposes. In a concise format, it shows the impact of management decisions and economic conditions on a bank's performance and balance-sheet composition. The performance and composition data contained in the report can be used as an aid in evaluating the adequacy of earnings, liquidity, capital, asset and liability management, and growth management. Bankers and examiners alike can use this report to further their understanding of a bank's financial condition.
4. Most on-site inspection information is not publicly disclosed by regulatory supervisors. However, you can review a bank's Community Reinvestment Act (CRA) rating and performance evaluations in meeting the credit needs of communities in which they operate, as well as approved strategic plans, at the Federal Reserve Board's Community Reinvestment Act page, http://www.federalreserve.gov/communitydev/cra_about.htm.
5. For discussion on how to build a best practice RAROC model in banking, see the following excellent article: Robert Durante, Yan An, and Robert Mark, "Designing and Validating Your RAROC Framework," *The RMA Journal*, December 2012-January 2013, pp. 21-28. The Risk Management Association (RMA) is a leader in bank management training programs in the United States.
6. Economic Value Added (EVA) is a registered trademark of financial consultants Stern Value Management. The firm's website, www.eva.com, includes client testimonials and other examples of applying the EVA methodology.

PART 2

Asset Liability Management

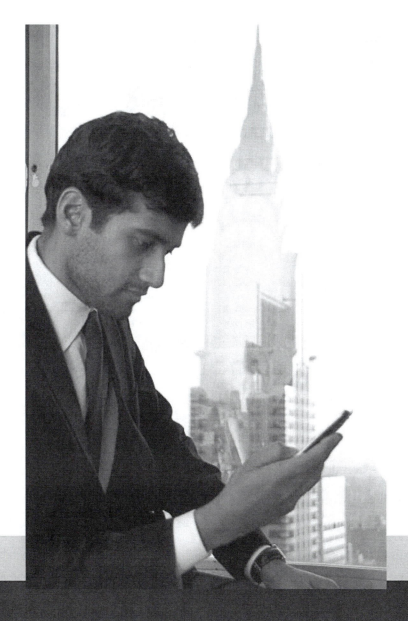

Chapter 4

Bank Valuation

After reading this chapter, you will be able to:

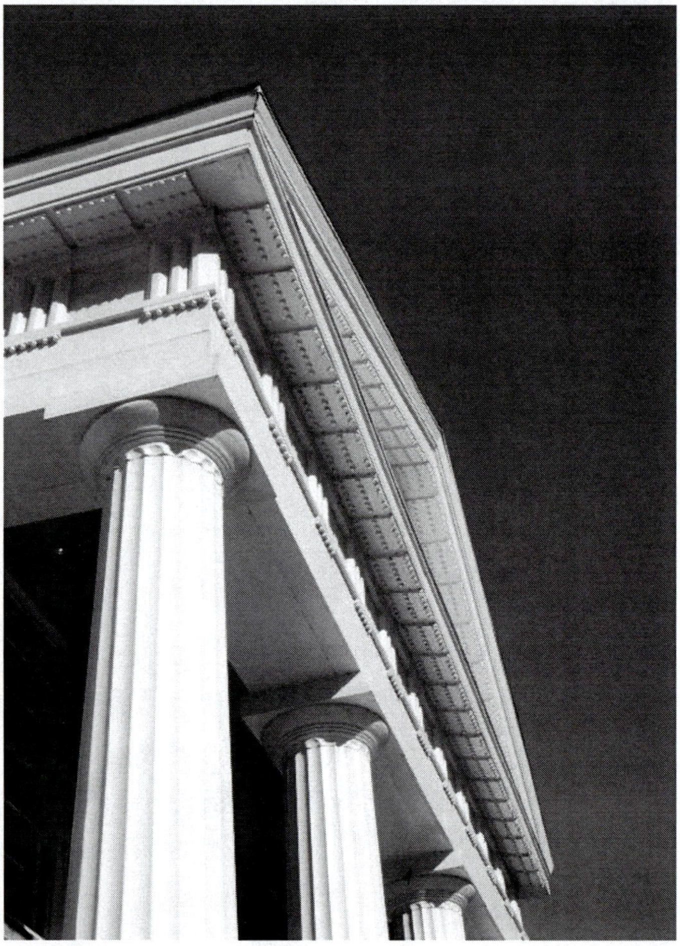

- Define the valuation process for bank stock
- Describe how changes in the amounts and riskiness of cash flows affect the value of a bank
- Discuss the determinants of bank prices in mergers
- Compare the market reaction of bank stocks of bidders and targets in bank mergers
- Identify the factors that define investment value

The management of a commercial bank attempts to balance risk and profitability in making its lending, investing, and funds-raising decisions. For example, issues concerning the pricing of deposits or loans and decisions about buying and selling securities should be thought of within a risk and return framework. Yet just what should be the goal of these decisions?

Under most situations, the goal of bank management should be to maximize the value of the owners' equity. For a publicly traded bank, this involves making decisions that will increase the market value of the stock of the bank. Hence, opportunities that increase the profitability of the bank more than sufficiently to offset the risk exposure and thereby increase the price of the stock should be pursued. In contrast, opportunities that do not increase the profitability of the bank sufficiently to offset the increased risk, and thereby lead to a reduction in share price, should be rejected. For example, a high-risk loan could increase the profitability of the bank, but it could increase its risk even more and therefore should be rejected.

The general rule of pursuing opportunities that increase the value of the stock must be tempered somewhat when discussing a bank whose stock is not publicly traded (and the stock of most banks is not publicly traded). For these banks, since there is no public market price, management must rely more on the income statement and balance sheet implications of various decisions. Moreover, for these closely held banks -- many of which are owned by only a few individuals with a substantial fraction of their wealth committed to the bank -- dividend income and tax considerations are often very important, and may lead to decisions that are different from those taken to maximize share value.

This chapter considers the determinants of the value of shareholder equity for a commercial bank and the strategies that management can follow in attempting to achieve its goals. It begins with a general discussion of the determinants of value. It then analyzes the specific determinants of bank shareholder value. It also considers the implications for shareholder value of the recent wave of mergers and acquisitions that has taken place in the banking industry over the past decade, including megadeals that are causing the formation of financial service giants.

DETERMINING THE EQUITY VALUATION OF A COMMERCIAL BANK

Bank management should make investment, lending, deposit gathering, and other financial management decisions that will result in an increase in the stock price. The focus of these decisions is on the investor in the stock. Given this focus, the immediate question is: How does that investor obtain returns from his or her investment in the stock? To understand this, we need to focus on the ***rate of return*** concept where

$$\text{Rate of return} = \frac{D_t + (P_t - P_{t-1})}{P_{t-1}} \qquad 4.1$$

The rate of return that the investor obtains from holding a share of stock for a year or some other period is composed of two parts: (1) the ***dividend return*** (Dt) and (2) the ***capital gain*** in the value of the stock (Pt – Pt–1). For example, if the price of the stock at Pt–1 was 50, the price at Pt equals 55, and the dividend payment was $1.00 per share, then the rate of return to each shareholder for the year is:

$$\text{Rate of return} = \frac{1.00 + (55 - 50)}{50} = \frac{6}{50} = 12\% \qquad (4.2)$$

Table 4-1 provides the stock rates of return (sometimes called total rates of return or market rates of return) for some of the largest U.S. banking organizations during the period July, 2014 to December, 2014. The returns are divided into that portion due to price change and that part due to dividend return. Large returns for the bank stocks in Table 4-1 reflected price appreciation. ***Dividend yields*** averaged less than two percent in this six-month period, or four percent per year. This pattern is typical -- that is, price changes dominate dividend yields in determining market rates of return. Since these price changes reflect reappraisals of earnings potential and risk for banks, it is the market reacting to an announcement by the bank and by others that fundamentally determines the return.

Table 4-1: RATE OF RETURN FOR SELECTED COMMERCIAL BANKS: JULY 2014-DECEMBER 2014

	Price Change				
	Citicorp	**Bank of America**	**JP Morgan Chase**	**Wells Fargo**	**Capital One**
Jul-14	3.84%	-0.78%	0.09%	-3.16%	-3.70%
Aug-14	5.60	5.51	3.10	1.06	3.17
Sep-14	0.33	5.97	1.33	0.85	-0.54
Oct-14	3.30	0.65	0.40	2.35	1.42
Nov-14	0.82	-0.70	-0.53	2.62	0.53
Dec-14	0.26	4.99	4.02	0.62	-0.78
	Dividend Return				
	Citicorp	**Bank of America**	**JP Morgan Chase**	**Wells Fargo**	**Capital One**
Jul-14	0.02%	0%	0.69%	0%	0%
Aug-14	0	0	0	0.69	0.38
Sep-14	0	0.31	0	0	0
Oct-14	0.02	0	0.66	0	0
Nov-14	0	0	0	0.66	0.36
Dec-14	0	0.29	0	0	0
	Total Return				
	Citicorp	**Bank of America**	**JP Morgan Chase**	**Wells Fargo**	**Capital One**
Jul-14	3.86%	-0.78%	0.78%	-3.16%	-3.70%
Aug-14	5.60	5.51	3.09	1.75	3.55
Sep-14	0.33	6.28	1.33	0.84	-0.54
Oct-14	3.32	0.65	1.06	2.35	1.4
Nov-14	0.82	-0.70	-0.53	3.28	0.88
Dec-14	0.26	5.28	4.02	0.62	-0.78

Source: Center for Research in Security Prices, University of Chicago

In the Great Recession of 2008 to 2009, bank stocks experienced volatile price changes. The severe economic recession at that time contributed to loan and securities losses, and historically low interest rates drove profit margins down for most banks. Citicorp's stock dropped precipitously from almost $50 per share in 2006 to less than $1 dollar per share in early 2009, becoming a penny stock for a brief period of time! By year-end 2014, it recovered into the $50 range. Here we see that economic conditions have a major impact on the earnings and riskiness of bank stocks and, therefore, their valuation.

From equation (4.1), it is obvious that returns to investors are determined by dividend payments and price appreciation. But management can control only dividend payments directly (and dividend policies represent an important dimension of management policies). Management's influences on price changes are, at best, quite indirect. But what determines the stock price (and the change in the stock price) of a bank?

Although many variables enter into the determination of value, three in particular are relevant:

1. The amount of cash flow
2. The timing of cash flow
3. The riskiness of cash flow.

The value of a share of stock is determined fundamentally by the cash benefits (dividends) the buyer expects to receive from the asset. In terms of the present value concept, the value of an asset is the present value of all of its expected cash flows discounted at the appropriate discount rate that reflects the risk of those cash flows. This approach may be expressed algebraically as follows:

$$V_0 = \frac{CF_1}{(1+r)^1} + \frac{CF_2}{(1+r)^2} + \frac{CF_3}{(1+r)^3} + \ldots + \frac{CF_n}{(1+r)^n} \qquad 4.3$$

where Vo is the present value (or price) of the asset at time zero, *CF* is the expected cash flow that accrues to the owner of the asset during the owner's holding period, r is the required rate of return or discount rate, and n is the amount of time the asset is held or is expected to be held. In this valuation model, the appropriate required rate of return is a controversial subject in finance. One possibility is to use the Capital Asset Pricing Model (CAPM), or other asset pricing model. Perhaps the most common method of estimating r is to use observed rates of return for similarly-sized commercial banks as a benchmark and then adjust this rate for specific risk factors associated with the individual bank. Of course, using different realistic values for expected cash flows and discount rates can generate a relevant range of estimated stock values.

In this approach three factors will cause an increase in the value of the asset:

1. An increase in the amount of cash flow (i.e., dividends) to be received from the asset

2. Earlier receipt of the expected cash flow
3. A decrease in the required rate of return.

Conversely, three factors will cause a decrease in the value of the asset:

1. A decrease in the amount of cash flow to be received from the asset
2. Later receipt of the expected cash flow
3. An increase in the required rate of return.

MANAGERIAL ISSUES

HOW BANK MANAGERS CAN CREATE VALUE

In the United States many of the most profitable and highest valued banks are midsize regional banks with from $500 million to $10 billion in total assets. These banks strive to create value for their shareholders by maximizing profits per unit risk from everyday operations. Based on interviews with chief executive officers and comments by industry experts, some of the ways in which bank management can boost earnings and add value to share prices are as follows:

- Minimize operating costs by keeping a careful eye on the ratio of operating expenses to operating income, an often-cited industry measure of how well a bank is managing its costs
- Avoid high concentrations of past-due loans, non-accrual loans, and foreclosed real estate.
- Use branching systems to attract core deposits and sell profitable retail products, such as credit cards, small business loans, and trust services
- Evaluate performance for individual units within a bank branch or office to better understand the profitability of each unit, especially core recurring earnings
- Control the credit quality of the loan portfolio
- Control the market valuation implications of securities investments on accounting statements
- Maintain adequate capital to satisfy regulatory requirements and enable selected acquisitions and de novo (or new) entry to take advantage of profitable market opportunities
- Achieve an excellent reputation with regulatory agencies
- Employ an aggressive sales strategy by encouraging employees to reach out to customers and their needs
- Provide employee training on a regular basis to keep up with recent changes in products and services
- Avoid excessive growth that can unduly stretch management resources and increase bank risk
- Understand that your most valuable asset is quality management

These lessons from past experiences of bank managers are not only important to regional banks but may well be valuable to larger institutions also. The ongoing merger and acquisition wave has been driven primarily by large institutions, whose managements have been occupied with the process of restructuring. Eventually, after the consolidation process slows down, managers of large banks will need to create value from their newly-acquired asset bases.

An example of the determinants of value can assist in an understanding this concept. Assume that the cash benefits from holding an asset for five years are $20 per year. Further assume that the holder expects to be able to sell the asset for $100 at the end of the fifth year, and that the required rate of return is 12 percent. Then the value of the asset is:

$$V_0 = \frac{\$20}{(1.12)^1} + \frac{\$20}{(1.12)^2} + \frac{\$20}{(1.12)^3} + \frac{\$20}{(1.12)^4} + \frac{\$20}{(1.12)^5} + \frac{\$100}{(1.12)^5} = \$128.70 \quad (4.4)$$

What then produces changes in value? First, value obviously changes with changes in investor expectations of dividends. Any event such as a large and unexpected increase in earnings clearly changes expectations of cash dividends. Since cash dividends ultimately are paid out of the earnings created by lending, investing, and deposit gathering, any information that causes investors to change their expectations of future earnings will change the market price of a stock.

As an illustration, suppose that a bank has a sharp reduction in its provision for loan losses due to a strengthening in its local economy, and suppose further that the bank expects the provision for loan losses to continue to be well under prior expectations. This reduction in current and future provision for loan losses will lead to an increase in current reported earnings and in the market's expectation of future earnings (and dividends). Given the announcement of the change in provision for loan losses, we would expect that the market price of the stock would rise. In terms of equation (4.1), Pt would go up because it would capture the effects of higher expected future dividends. As a result, the return to the investor in the stock would rise.

The growth rate of earnings can be incorporated into the valuation formula. Modifying equation (4.3) by assuming that the number of periods n is infinite (i.e., in practical terms stocks do not have a maturity date) and that earnings grow at a constant rate over time, the well-known **Gordon growth model** defines stock value as follows:

$$V_0 = \frac{Div_0}{(r-g)} \quad (4.5)$$

where r is the nominal discount rate, and g is the nominal growth rate of earnings. The nominal discount rate or market capitalization rate equals the current dividend yield (or dividends per share divided by the market price of equity) plus the growth rate of dividends. Here we assume that the bank does not pay out all of its dividends to the shareholders; instead, the bank retains some earnings for reinvestment in capital assets that will generate increased earnings. For example, if a bank retained 40 percent of its earnings (i.e., the payout ratio or dividends per share divided by earnings per share equals 60 percent) and had a 12.5 percent return on equity (i.e., the ratio of earnings to book value of equity), its earnings growth rate would be 10 percent (i.e., 0.40 × 0.125 = 0.05). If the current annual dividend is \$5, and the discount rate is 10 percent, the value of the stock would be Vo = \$5/(0.10 – 0.05) = \$100. Notice that the discount rate equals the sum of the current dividend yield (or \$5/ \$100 = 0.05) plus the growth rate of dividends (or 0.05). It is clear that, as the growth rate of dividends increases, bank value increases also. In this respect, it is important to note that banks normally pay substantial dividends compared to nonfinancial firms. For example, many high tech firms do not pay any dividends and instead reinvest all earnings. For these firms equation (4.5) could not be applied to stock valuation. Banks differ from most nonfinancial firms in terms of higher dividend payouts from profits to their shareholders.

One major reason for dividends to grow over time is inflation. However, since inflation is also embedded in discount and growth rates, its effects should cancel out in equation (4.5). In this regard, Modigliani and Cohn have argued that investors mistakenly undervalue stocks in inflationary times by incorrectly discounting real cash flows in the numerator at nominal discount rates in the denominator. Normally, firms are slow to adjust dividend payments to changes in earnings, including those changes associated with inflation. On the other hand, investors quickly adjust discount rates for expected future inflation. According to Modigliani and Cohn, the difference in the timing of these adjustments to inflation on dividends and discount rates in equation (4.5) causes stocks to be undervalued during times of high inflation.[1] They point out that when inflation is low, these valuation problems are no longer present and, therefore, the real value of stocks is revealed.

After the financial crisis of 2008 and 2009, the Federal Reserve lowered interest rates to near zero levels in an effort to stimulate the economy and prevent deflation that would decrease the values of real estate, stocks, bonds, and the like. Quantitative easing (QE) was implemented by the Fed to buy long-term bonds, raise their prices, and thereby lower long-term interest rates. Inflation was relatively low at below two percent per year from 2009 to 2015. With little or no inflation, bank valuation has been simplified to focusing on earnings and their growth

In the banking industry another major trend affecting bank stock prices is the consolidation movement to be discussed shortly. Banks are expanding across product lines and geographic boundaries, increasing their size, broadening their scope of financial services, forming alliances with nonfinancial firms, developing new electronic payments systems, and upgrading employee expertise. These changes are affecting earnings growth rates and risk profiles, which affects all of the variables in equation (4.5). Today, valuation is a challenging and high-stakes issue in the consolidation wave of bank mergers and acquisitions.

USING THE PRICE-EARNING RATIO

Another approach to understanding the price of a stock and the determinants of changes in that price is in terms of its price-earnings multiple or ratio. The price-earnings ratio is calculated by dividing the current market price by earnings per share:

$$\text{Price-earnings ratio} = \frac{\text{Price per share}}{\text{Earning per share}} \tag{4.6}$$

For example, a bank with a market price per share of $45 and earnings per share of $3 has a price-earnings ratio of 15 times.

The price-earnings (P/E) ratio summarizes the outlook for the future of the bank—the amount of its earnings and dividends, the timing of earnings and dividends, and the risk of those earnings and dividends. A bank that is expected to show rapid growth in earnings will have a higher price-earnings ratio than one with little expected earnings growth. Similarly, a bank in which earnings are highly variable and unpredictable will tend to have a lower price-earnings ratio. Hence, even if two banks have the same current earnings, their market prices can be sharply different. Firms with low P/E ratios are often referred to as **value stocks**, whereas those with high P/E ratios are known as **growth stocks**. Many analyses also compute price/book equity value, price/assets, and price/deposits ratios to compare banks' valuations.

Table 4-2 shows the price-earnings ratios over the period 2008 to 2014 for the same group of banks shown in Table 4-1. These years were marked by major economic events. In 2008 and 2009, banks were struggling with securities and loan losses that caused negative earnings, which explains negative price-earnings ratios around that time. In 2011 most banks were on the road to recovery with positive ratios. Notice that Bank of America had relatively high price-earnings ratios in 2012 and 2014, but these ratios were due more to low earnings than high stock prices in those years. Perhaps the most important uncertainties facing banks in recent years has been the slow pace of economic growth, unemployment overhang from the Great Recession, a slowing global economy, near zero government interest rates, increased regulatory pressures under the 2010 Dodd-Frank Wall Street Reform and Consumer Protection Act, and market volatility related to oil price instability. These external factors slowed bank profits and the merger and acquisition (M&A) wave that was prospering prior to 2008. However, improving economic conditions in 2015 led to higher bank profits and a resumption of M&As among small and regional banks. How do M&As affect bank share values? We turn next to the empirical evidence in search of answers to this question.

Table 4-2: PRICE-EARNINGS RATIOS FOR SELECTED COMMERCIAL BANKS

	Citigroup	Bank of America	JPMorgan Chase	Wells Fargo	Capital One
2008	-1.19	26.07	22.55	42.11	-151.86
2009	-4.14	-51.93	18.34	15.42	51.81
2010	13.36	-36.05	10.62	14.02	7.08
2011	7.25	5.56	7.38	9.77	6.22
2012	16.21	46.44	8.28	10.17	9.40
2013	11.98	17.30	13.34	11.67	11.12
2014	24.6	49.69	11.83	13.37	10.88

Source: http://marketcapitalizations.com/historical-data/pe-ratio-sp-100-companies/

BANK MERGER AND ACQUISITION PRICING

Information from prices set in bank mergers and acquisitions (M&As) provides important insights into the determinants of value at commercial banks and the factors that management should focus on in attempting to increase the value of a bank. Such information is especially relevant for small, closely held banks in which no public market exists for the bank. This comparable transaction method of stock valuation is common is M&As in which the stock is privately held and does not publicly trade. Of course, publicly traded stock is valued continuously in the stock market on a day-to-day basis.

In forthcoming discussion it is important to recognize the difference between a bank ***merger*** and an ***acquisition***. In the former case the target bank is absorbed into the bidding or buying bank. As such, the target loses its bank charter, does not need a chief executive officer and board of directors anymore, and is converted to a branch office of the buying bank. By contrast, in a bank acquisition the target bank retains its bank charter, CEO, and board of directors. It becomes an affiliate member of the bank holding company (BHC) to which the buying bank belongs. Clearly, mergers are a much more drastic form of reorganization than acquisitions, especially in terms of their impact on management.

Changing bank regulations are the driving force behind much of the M&A activity. In the United States, prior to the 1994 Riegle-Neal Interstate Banking and Branching Efficiency Act's deregulation of interstate banking barriers to expansion, BHC acquisitions were more common than mergers. However, after implementation of this legislation, mergers involving conversion to a branch office became the dominant form of reorganization. Clearly, mergers were favored as a means to expansion because they are much less expensive than BHC acquisitions. Subsequently, the 1999 Financial Services Modernization Act triggered a new round of mergers and acquisitions between banks, insurance companies, and securities firms. These conglomerate financial mergers transformed the financial services landscape. In Europe the Second Banking Directive was passed in 1993 and allows nontraditional mergers between different kinds of financial services firms. And in Japan the government in the 1990s mandated the formation of seven financial holding companies in the country that wouldl offer a full menu of different financial services. These global trends in M&As are creating so-called megabanks with global market power.

One of the most comprehensive studies of the determinants of value (measured as the ratio of the market price to the book value of the target bank) was done by the Federal Reserve Board.[2] Research on the determinants of the ***price-book ratio*** in bank acquisitions revealed that three variables were consistently related to bank merger premiums: the growth of the assets of the target firm, the growth of its market, and the target's capital-to-assets ratio. The first two are, to a considerable extent, outside the control of the bank. However, the impact of the capital-assets ratio is under management control.

Another study by academic researchers studied the price-book value ratio for smaller banks involved in both mergers and acquisitions.[3] The banks are first broken down by size (less than or more than $100 million in total assets) and then by high price (price-book ratio greater than 2.0) and low price (price-book ratio less than 1.30). Examination of the financial ratios indicated some important differences between the high-premium banks and the low-premium banks. Net income (as a fraction of total assets) was substantially higher for the high-premium small banks than for the low-premium small banks (0.91 percent versus 0.34 percent). Not surprisingly, highly profitable small banks were able to command higher merger premiums. The high-premium banks also had a larger fraction of their assets financed with non-interest-bearing demand deposits and also experienced sharply lower loan losses. With regard to market conditions, the high-premium small banks were located in markets experiencing greater population growth.

Other research on the determinants of the price-book ratio in bank mergers examined prices paid in 264 bank mergers.[4] It was found that the more profitable the target bank (measured by the return on equity) the higher the merger premium, and that the premium is negatively related to the ratio of U.S. Treasury investments to total assets, the ratio of loans to total assets, and the ratio of the loan loss allowance plus equity (i.e., primary capital) to total assets.

Price-book ratios in bank mergers and acquisitions have varied widely (for example, in a range of 1.0 to more than 3.0) in the 1990s and 2000s. While book values of equity do not change much over time due to regulatory constraints on the maintenance of adequate bank capital, the market values of bank stocks can vary considerably over time. In this regard, the price-book ratio is the conventional way to express the sales price of targets in the banking industry. Higher ratios imply a better price for target shareholders, and vice versa for lower ratios. Higher ratios also imply that management must earn rates of return per unit of risk that exceed historical levels in future years. In the early 1990s the average price-book ratio offered in deals was around 1.5, but this ratio rose to over 2.0 in the late 1990s and early 2000s as M&A activity accelerated at that time. Were the prices paid in too high? In hindsight it would appear to be the case, as the Great Recession of 2008 and 2009 dashed hopes of growth and profits from those deals. In the post-crisis years, the emphasis has shifted from finding target banks with strong financial condition to identifying weak banks that can be bought at relatively low price/book ratios.

BANK EARNINGS AND STOCK PRICES: WHICH EARNINGS MATTER ?

Although bank managers obviously should manage the asset portfolio in order to achieve those earnings that will lead to the highest share price, a question arises as to which measure of earnings is most important. Given the argument that the price of a bank's stock is a function of its earnings and some earnings multiplier (e.g., the price-earnings ratio), it is possible (perhaps likely) that the market may place a different earnings multiple on different sources of earnings. For example, earnings are composed of earnings before securities gains and losses (often referred to as operating earnings) as opposed to securities gains and losses realized when securities are sold.

Earnings before securities gains and losses stem from the fundamental deposit-taking and lending activities of the bank. Changes in these earnings vary with changes in the levels of interest rates in deposit and loan markets, but under traditional historical cost accounting, operating earnings do not change with changes in the market value of assets or liabilities. In particular, earnings before securities gains and losses do not contain any explicit revaluations of the loan portfolio or securities to reflect unrealized gains and losses. In contrast to earnings before securities gains and losses, securities gains and losses consist of changes in the market value of investment securities since their purchase date, and only those gains and losses that are realized. This income is likely to be more transitory and volatile than other components of income.

Given the difference in volatility and permanence between earnings before securities gains and losses on the one hand, and securities gains and losses on the other, we might expect that the market would capitalize the operating earnings at a higher multiple than the securities gains on income. But does it?

Evidence on this issue suggests that this is so.[5] Research relating the market value of bank equity to the composition of earnings -- operating earnings or securities gains and losses -- has found that the market value of bank stock is positively related to operating earnings. Hence, management attempts to structure the bank's portfolio in order to increase operating earnings should result in an increase in the market price of the stock. However, the market value of the bank's stock is negatively related to earnings from securities gains and losses.

The negative relationship between market value and earnings from securities gains and losses is particularly interesting. This suggests that the market interprets the realization of securities gains and losses as an attempt by the bank to manage earnings by means of window dressing that smooths earnings. Thus, management may attempt to take securities gains when operating earnings fall. However, this attempt to "fool the market" apparently does not work. Hence, in the case of earnings smoothing, it is possible that the market will view realized securities gains as bad news rather than good news.

DEREGULATION AND THE VALUE OF BANK STOCKS

The dramatic changes that have taken place in the economic, financial, and regulatory environment within which banks operate have raised questions about the determinants of bank stock prices. Specifically, what factors are important in affecting the price-earnings ratio of bank stocks, and how have those factors changed with deregulation? For example, interest rate deregulation in the 1980s affected large banks' price-earnings ratios.[6] Before interest rate deregulation, the growth rate of deposits, growth rate of earnings, and ratio of capital to assets were positively associated with the price-earnings ratio. The volume of transitory earnings (such as through securities gains and losses) was negatively related to the price-earnings ratio. After interest rate deregulation, the relative influence of these variables changed. In particular, the dividend payout ratio became more significant, while the past earnings growth remained highly important. In contrast, the past five years of deposit growth became less important while the capital/asset ratio became unimportant. Perhaps the most important finding is the decreased emphasis on growth in recent years as a factor that influences bank price-earnings ratios.

Geographic deregulation under the Riegle-Neal Act of 1994 permitted interstate branching in almost all states. Research has shown that, while bank values significantly increased during this legislation's passage, within-state M&As subsequently experienced fewer financial gains than M&As involving expansion across state lines.[7] Apparently, by diversifying across different state economies, banks achieved lower operating risk. This diversification is a benefit to not only bank shareholders but society in terms of greater bank safety and soundness.

More recently, deregulation in the United States and Europe has allowed financial conglomerates comprised of banks, securities firms, and insurance companies. Research has found that European mergers between banks and insurance companies tend to increase the total stock values of these two merging types of financial service firms.[8] However, mergers between banks and securities firms did not increase their stock values. Additionally, domestic mergers between financial service firms tend to increase stock values, but not mergers between financial service firms in different European countries. These results suggest that financial firm diversification across geographic borders and across products is not always beneficial. It is possible that cross-border merger deals face political, cultural, and other barriers that lessen their potential gains to shareholders. Additionally, combinations of banks and insurance companies, which are known as ***bancassurance***, appear to be a successful model for financial conglomerates that is more common in Europe than in the United States.

The Financial Modernization Act (also known as the Gramm-Leach-Bliley Act) in 1999 allowed U.S. commercial banks to form financial holding companies that combine banks with insurance companies and securities firms. One U.S. study examined the shareholder returns of bidders in mergers and acquisitions between banks and insurance companies.[9] Both U.S. and non-U.S. bidders and targets were included in separate analyses of bank bids for insurance companies and insurance company bids for banks. On average, bidders experienced higher share prices. Unlike the European evidence discussed above, shareholders had larger wealth gains when bidders and targets were in different countries. Hence, it is possible for geographic diversification across national borders to be beneficial. Another finding was that the risk profile of acquiring firms was unchanged by the reorganization. This evidence suggests that bancassurance deals are principally driven by increasing operating cash flows rather than risk reduction.

MANAGERIAL ISSUES

SMALL BANK VALUATION

Most banks are small in size and do not trade their stock in public markets. How can these bank stocks be valued? Of course, a starting point is the book value of equity of the bank. In this case the price-book ratio is the primary focus of valuation. This logical procedure is a good reason for the emphasis on this ratio in bank valuation analyses, as opposed to the price-earnings ratio.

Is the market price of equity greater or less than the book value of equity? One possible approach is to use the dividend model in equation (4.5), or Vo = Divo/(r – g), where r is now the dividend yield defined as dividends divided by the book value of equity (instead of the market price of equity) and g is the growth of dividends in recent years. This value will be biased to some extent due to the error in measuring the discount rate r. Nonetheless, this approach offers a value based on readily available accounting data.

As discussed earlier in this chapter, an alternative way to approximate the market value of small bank stocks is to observe their merger and acquisition prices under the ***comparable transaction method***. Small banks of similar size, asset and liability profiles, and local market conditions can be expected to have similar stock values. Due to the large numbers of M&As involving small banks, there is rich data that increases the chances of finding comparable banks.

Another valuation approach is to examine new issues of bank shares by existing or de novo (newly chartered) small banks. De novo banks are especially likely to publicize their stock price in an effort to attract investors. Information on de novo banks can be obtained from federal and state bank regulatory agencies.

Finally, it is possible that some shareholders of a small bank could be approached to assess the potential value of common shares. In this regard, a problem is that different shareholders of the bank may well have different prices at which they would be willing to sell their stock holdings. In this case no single price for the stock could be established.

So what is the value of a small bank's stock? Perhaps the most reasonable answer to this question is that a relevant range of values can be determined based on the above valuation approaches.

EVIDENCE FROM MARKET RESPONSES TO BANK M&A ANNOUNCEMENTS

Insight into the factors that affect the valuation of commercial banks can also be obtained from examining the equity market response to the announcement of a merger or acquisition among commercial banks. A number of studies have focused on the stock market response for the buyer (the bidder) and the seller (the target) banks in M&As. Generally, the studies measure the market reaction by examining a short-term period (usually a few days) around the merger announcement and calculating a measure of the difference between the actual stock price movement on those days and the movement that would have been expected given the movements in the general level of stock prices. This difference between actual and expected returns is commonly referred to as an abnormal return.

Results in one study are representative of others and provide insights useful to bank M&As.[10] Based on samples of target banks and bidder banks involved in M&As, targets tended to do extremely well in M&As. The price of a target bank's shares increased, on average, by about 11.5 percent during the week of the merger announcement (11.5 percent more than would be expected given movements in the stock market during that week). Moreover, the positive stock market response was greater for those transactions in which payment is made in cash, with the stock price increase being 5.76 percent higher for cash than for stock or other securities during the announcement week. And, the target bank's share price appreciates more the larger the assets of the bidding bank.

How do the buyers fare in these mergers? Not very well it would seem. The price of the bidding bank stock decreased, on average, during the week of the M&A announcement, falling generally between one percent and two percent (after adjusting for general market movements). Moreover, the market reaction was more negative when the bidding bank paid for the transaction with stock and when the bidder bank and the target bank were more similar in size.

The findings of a negative market reaction for the stock of the bidding bank raises some important questions concerning the motivation for the management of these banks. Why do banks buy other banks if it causes their stock price to fall? Such behavior is apparently contrary to the stated goal of management to maximize shareholder value. It is, however, consistent with a number of other hypotheses regarding the motivation of management. It may be, for example, that managers are interested in maximizing their own welfare. Thus, if they expand through M&As or through other strategies, they will be able to increase their salaries and fringe benefits associated with their position. Of course, this wealth transfer represents an ***agency cost*** from the standpoint of shareholders, who would bear losses to the extent that management increased their salaries and perquisites (including pensions, office expenditures, vacations, bonuses, etc.). Another explanation is provided by Roll's well known ***hubris hypothesis.***[11] According to this hypothesis, bidders invariably pay too much for targets because they have excessive arrogance about their ability to produce profits from the merged organization. This leads them to believe that their valuation of the target is correct, even though their bid overvalues the target, often by a substantial amount.

Another motive for M&As is ***synergy***, or mutual benefits wherein the combined organization exceeds the sum of its parts, which suggests that both target and acquirer experience gains. Gains could be possible immediately via cost reductions due to cutting duplicate computer, office, employee, and other expenses. Or, gains could be achieved in the long run via cost efficiency and greater management expertise. At first glance this motivation would appear to conflict with the fact that buyers do not gain from mergers. Interestingly, after taking into account losses to buyers due to agency costs and hubris, one study found evidence in favor of synergy.[12]

What do these results imply for bank managers interested in maximizing the value of shareholders' equity? First, it is obviously better to be a seller, not a buyer. Sellers reap substantial gains in the value of their stock, gains that might be difficult or impossible to obtain through operations. Second, sell to a bank that is substantially larger. Third, seek to minimize agency and hubris problems and maximize synergies in M&A deals. Beyond these factors, arrange a cash transaction unless tax factors make that impossible.[13]

What are the lessons for those thinking of making an acquisition? Perhaps "don't do it" is too strong an answer to that question. But clearly the results discussed here should give pause to any bank thinking about embarking on an aggressive M&A strategy. At the least, management should clearly understand the motivation for the structural reorganization. Is it the right motivation? Is it designed to benefit shareholders? Also, management should view with some degree of skepticism any arguments that rest on being able to operate the target bank more effectively than its existing management. Driving forces behind bank M&As nowadays are footprint expansion, market share expansion, product and service enhancement, human capital synergies (such as management talent in the area of enterprise risk management), economies of scale, and management succession.

LONG-TERM EFFECTS OF BANK MERGERS

One possible explanation for the large number of bank M&As that is consistent with the assumption that managers are attempting to increase shareholder value focuses on the longer-term effects of these decisions. Under this view, it may indeed be the case that the announcement of a merger or acquisition does not increase (and may decrease) the bidder's stock price on the announcement date, but the longer-run improved performance of the combined entity more than offsets the temporary decline in stock price. Although only limited evidence exists that relates to this possibility, two studies support the long-term benefits of bank mergers.

Some studies have investigated the post-performance of bank buyers in M&A deals. One study sampled both large interstate acquisitions and large intrastate acquisitions.[14] The analysis focused on the following indicators of bank performance: profitability, capital adequacy, credit quality, efficiency, liquidity, growth, and interest rate risk. Evidence pointed to superior cash flow performance for banks involved in acquisitions, due to their improved ability to attract loans and deposits, increases in employee productivity, and greater asset growth. This higher long-run cash flow resulting from the merger is consistent with a long-run increase in stock price.

Another study of Italian banks found that in acquisitions both return on assets and return on equity increased about 21 percent and 13 percent, respectively, over the long run for the combined bank buyer and target.[15] One factor explaining this increased profitability was lower loan losses in the long run. These results are consistent with the notion that bank mergers and acquisitions have long-run benefits that are not measured by short-run price movements around the announcement date of M&A deals.

STRATEGIES FOR INCREASING STOCK PRICE: BANK MEGAMERGER WAVE

Prior to the mid-1990s, M&As among large banks and other financial service firms (particularly insurance companies and securities firms) were relatively rare. As already mentioned, the main reason for the sudden increase in large M&As that are creating so-called ***megabanks*** is the deregulation of geographic and asset restrictions. Also, the Great Recession caused a number of large home mortgage and securities firms to fail, and they were absorbed into big banks that became even larger in size. In 1985 the top ten banks had an average asset size of about $100 billion; by comparison, a similar list in 2015 would average over $500 billion. The following table gives a sample of multi-billion dollar M&A deals in the banking industry during the Great Recession. These mega deals will have lasting effects on the financial services industry in the years to come.

Date Announced	Target	Acquirer (Buyer)	Type of Target	Value of Deal
April 1, 2008	Bear Stearns, New York City	JPMorgan Chase, New York City	Investment bank	$2,200,000,000
July 1, 2008	Countrywide Financial, Calabasas, California	Bank of America, Charlotte, North Carolina	Mortgage lender	$4,000,000,000
September 14, 2008	Merrill Lynch, New York City	Bank of America, Charlotte, North Carolina	Investment bank	$44,000,000,000
September 17, 2008	Lehman Brothers, New York City	Barclays, London, England	Investment bank	$1,300,000,000
September 26, 2008	Washington Mutual, Seattle, Washington	JPMorgan Chase, New York City	Savings and loan association	$1,900,000,000
October 3, 2008	Wachovia, Charlotte, North Carolina	Wells Fargo, San Francisco, California	Retail and investment banking	$15,000,000,000
October 24, 2008	National City Bank, Cleveland, Ohio	PNC Financial Services, Pittsburgh, Pennsylvania	Bank	$5,580,000,000
October 24, 2008	Commerce Bancorp, Cherry Hill, New Jersey	Toronto-Dominion Bank, Toronto, Canada	Bank	$8,500,000,000

Source: Wikipedia. https://en.wikipedia.org/wiki/List_of_banks_acquired_or_bankrupted_during_the_Great_Recession

While the formation of megabanks no doubt have agency, hubris, and synergy motivations, as discussed above, they could also be driven by diversification and ***market power*** in the case of very large banks. Diversification across products and services as well as geographic areas can reduce operating risk. Also, market power may be needed to maintain a competitive position in national and international banking.

Market evidence is mixed on whether in-market M&As provide improvements in performance compared to cross-market M&As.[16] In this regard, in-market M&As (as measured by the extent of office overlap in shared markets) are more likely to be driven by synergies and market power, whereas cross-market M&As are motivated diversification and growth goals. In general, however, long-run negative stock returns in bank megamergers[17] raise questions about the sudden increase in such activity. It is possible that various benefits from economies of scale and scope do not tell the whole story. For example, some observers contend that: (1) CEOs of larger and more diverse organizations increase their reputation and possibly financial salaries, and (2) when the competitive environment is highly uncertain, it may be advantageous for banks to expand size and scope to reduce their risk.[18] These explanations are useful because they have some degree of support in nonfinancial M&As.[19]

Another implication of megabanks is their potential impact on borrowers. One study found that, for a large sample of more than 3,000 U.S. commercial loan borrowers, average stock prices of borrowers declined in response to a megamerger involving their lending bank.[20] This and other evidence suggests that increased market power among large banks harmed borrowers. Certainly regulatory policy needs to re-evaluate the potential implications of big bank mergers to competitive pricing of financial services.

Megadeals in banking are not confined to the United States. A growing number of large European banks and nonbank financial institutions have been involved in megadeals. For example, during market turmoil in 2007 and 2008, the following multi-billion dollar deals occurred: ABN AMRO in the Netherlands was acquired by Royal Bank of Scotland, Fortis, and Grupo Santander; Alliance and Leicester in the United Kingdom was acquired by Grupo Santander in Spain; both Derbyshire Building Society and Cheshire Building Society were acquired by Nationwide Building Society in the United Kingdom; and HBOS was acquired by Lloyds Bank in the United Kingdom. A number of large, failed financial institutions were bought by the government in some European countries also.

In Japan the 1990s consolidation of 21 large banks and many insurance and brokerage firms into only seven financial-holding companies has resulted in a number of large banks. For example, the Industrial Bank of Japan, Dai-ichi Kangyo Bank, and Fuji Bank merger in 1999 created one of the largest banks in the world, Mizuho, with over $1 trillion in assets. Large, diversified, global entities such as Mizuho raise new challenges in valuation.

Some experts believe that some financial institutions have become so large as to be too big to fail (TBTF). If the failure of a large institution resulted in severe damage to the economy, it would be necessary for government to intervene to preserve economic stability as well as the safety and soundness of the financial system. TBTFs are dangerous to the extent that they might take excessive risks in view of government guarantees to cover losses—in essence, a TBTF bank is "bulletproof." This so-called ***moral hazard problem*** is increasingly a dilemma that governments around the world will need to address as M&A activity among large institutions continues in the years ahead.

Under the FDIC Improvement Act of 1991, a large failing institution would not be rescued (or deemed TBTF) unless the Treasury Department, in agreement with the president, FDIC, and the Federal Reserve Board, believes that the failure would cause systemic risk via damage to the economy. However, in 1998 the failure of Long-Term Capital Management, a hedge fund involved in securities activities, was prevented by the Federal Reserve, which coordinated a bailout by that firm's creditors. It was argued that the collapse of the firm would potentially disrupt capital markets and cause other securities firms and banks to fail in a spillover effect. Thus, TBTF applies not only to banks but to financial services firms in general.

The Financial Services Modernization Act of 1999 charges the Federal Reserve and the U.S. Treasury to recommend ways to implement market discipline to help mitigate the moral hazard problem. One popular proposal is to require large institutions and their parent companies to issue subordinated debt. These debt issues would not carry any government guarantees in the event of failure. As such, the financial market would discipline risky institutions by pricing their debt issues lower than other financial service firms and by not purchasing their debt securities. This market discipline signal could be used by regulators to implement timely measures aimed at curbing excessive risk taking and averting a financial collapse of a major, global financial institution.

More recently, the Dodd-Frank Act of 2010 established the ***Financial Stability Oversight Council (FSOC)*** to evaluate "systemically important" bank and non-bank financial firms with more than $50 billion in assets. Also, under Basel III Accord capital requirements (see Chapter 12), banks deemed as systemically important are subject to higher capital requirements. Higher capital requirements for big banks helps to align societal needs for safety and soundness and bank shareholders' motivation to control risk and reduce the probability of bank failure. In the event of failure, the Dodd-Frank Act designates the FDIC to take the bank into receivership, which would likely lead to restructuring and merger with healthy banks that are well capitalized. While better risk measurement is certainly useful, market discipline exerted by "at risk" claimants such as shareholders and subordinated debtholders would help to reign in excessive risk-taking. Without at-risk claimants, the task of controlling bank risk would fall entirely to bank regulators.

SUMMARY

To achieve its goal of maximizing the value of the owner's investment, management must be able to identify those factors that produce increases in stock prices and those that produce decreases. For publicly traded banks, the equity market produces a rapid evaluation of the importance of different events that affect the bank. However, most banks are not publicly traded. For those banks, management must rely more heavily on the accounting statements to provide insights into bank valuation.

Returns to shareholders include cash dividends and changes in the market price of their investments in the form of capital gains. For most banks, the total return (the sum of cash dividends plus capital gains) is dominated by stock price changes. These stock price changes reflect changes in the amount of anticipated cash flow to be received from the stock, changes in the expected timing of the cash flow, and changes in the riskiness of the cash flow. An increase in stock price results from increases in the amount of the cash flow (i.e., dividends) to be received from the asset, earlier receipt of the cash flow, and a decrease in the riskiness of the cash flow. It is also important to consider the effects of growth in earnings and inflation on stock values. Further insight into the valuation process for bank equity can be obtained from the price-earnings ratio – the ratio of the price per share to the earnings per share. Banks with higher expected growth in cash flow or lower risk should sell at higher price-earnings ratios.

Managers can gain a deeper understanding of the bank valuation process by examining the determinants of merger and acquisition (M&A) prices in the ongoing consolidation movement. Evidence from studies of bank M&As suggests a systematic relationship between bank financial ratios such as equity to assets and net income to assets and bank valuation. Other studies suggest that targets of M&As obtain virtually all the benefits from the merger while the buyer's stock price either stays unchanged or goes down. A variety of motivations for the consolidation movement may affect bank valuation, including agency, hubris, synergy, diversification, and market power.

KEY TERMS

acquisition
agency cost
bancassurance
bidder
capital gain
comparable transaction method
dividend yield/return
Financial Stability Oversight Council (FSOC)
Gordon growth model
growth stock
hubris hypothesis
market power
megabanks
merger
moral hazard problem
price-book ratio
price-earnings multiple or ratio
rate of return
synergy
target
value stock

QUESTIONS

4.1 What is meant by the term "rate of return"? How is it calculated? Why is it important to bank management?

4.2 What is the price-earnings ratio? What information does it provide to management?

4.3 What information is provided from studies of bank merger and acquisitions prices about the determinants of bank stock prices? What appear to be the major determinants of the price-book ratio in bank mergers and acquisitions?

4.4 Are all earnings of equal importance in determining bank stock prices? Why would operating earnings and earnings from security gains and losses differ in their effects on bank stock prices?

4.5 Are the determinants of bank stock prices different since deregulation? If so, in what ways?

4.6 If two banks today announced their agreement to merge, what would you expect to happen to the prices of the buyer's and the seller's stock? Why? What does the evidence of existing studies suggest about the motivation of management?

4.7 What are the motivations for bank mergers and acquisitions? Discuss how these motivations may affect bank value.

4.8 Discuss equation (4.5) as a formula in bank stock valuation. Why is this model fairly reasonable for banks, as opposed to nonfinancial firms? Make up a hypothetical example, plug in the numbers, and show your calculations.

4.9 Go to your favorite internet browser and search for a recent megamerger in banking. Discuss details of the merger using links to related news articles. What were the motives for the merger?

4.10 Go to the FDIC's Bank Data & Statistics Web page at www.fdic.gov/bank/statistical/index.html and use the "Institution Directory" link to look up one of the bank holding companies in your state. What kinds of details about the bank holding company you selected can you collect from this site? You might also try an individual bank rather than a bank holding company if you encounter problems in your search efforts.

PROBLEMS

4.1 Capital National Bank's stock paid a cash dividend of $2.42 per share last year. During the year, the stock price changed from $52 per share at the start of the year to $62 per share at the end of the year. What was its rate of return?

4.2 Pick any five publicly traded banks. Using the Wall Street Journal or the Internet (e.g., Yahoo Finance), record their annual dividends, their prices one year ago, and their most recent prices. Then compute the rate of return for each bank. Finally, compute the fraction of the rate of return for each bank that reflects cash dividends paid. Do they differ significantly? If so, why?

4.3 Pick any five publicly traded electric utility stocks. Compute their rates of return as in problem 4.3. Compare the percent of the rate of return accounted for by cash dividends for these electric utilities with that of the banks from problem 4.3. Do they differ? If so, why?

4.4 The anticipated cash flow per share of stock for Capital National Bank is as follows:

Year 1 = $10

Year 2 = $12

Year 3 = $14

Year 4 = $15

In addition, it is expected that the stock will be sold at the end of Year 4 at $80 per share. Assuming a required rate of return of eight percent, what should be the value of the stock?

4.5 In Problem 4.4, how will the value of the stock change if the required rate of return increases to 10 percent? Decreases to six percent? What might cause the required rate of return to increase or decrease?

4.6 Assume that the current dividend for a bank is $10, its nominal growth rate of earnings is five percent per year, and the nominal discount rate is 15 percent, what is the value of the bank's stock? How should changes in inflation affect this valuation? Based on this formula, how can bank management increase value?

4.7 For the five publicly traded banks you selected in Problem 4.2, calculate their price-earnings ratios. Do they differ? If so, why? How do they compare with the five electric utility companies you selected in Problem 4.3?

CASE: First National Bank of Smithville

Donna Evan is the president of a community bank. In recent weeks the president of another local bank, First National Bank of Smithville, contacted her to propose an acquisition or merger. Ms. Evan's main task at this point is to determine a fair market price for the common stock shares of this bank. Financial statements for First National shown had been faxed to her today. These included the annual report, the most recent quarterly report, and highlights of the bank operations (Exhibits 4-1 through 4-5). She noted that the bank had total assets of $106.6 million at the end of the most recent year and $107.9 million at the most recent quarter. This slow (but steady) growth had typified the bank in recent years. The bank was profitable ($625,477) in the most recent year, although its return on assets of 0.57 percent was significantly below those of its peer group. With 200,000 shares outstanding, the profits to the bank last year equaled $3.12 per share, while book value was $52.64 per share. The relatively low profitability of the bank at a time during which other banks were earning substantial profits was something of a puzzle, although Donna noted that the bank had a very small fraction (24.2 percent) of its assets in loans.

She thus pondered the issue of an offer price and wondered what other information she would need before setting that price.

EXHIBIT 4-1 STATEMENT OF FINANCIAL CONDITION DECEMBER 31, 20XX

Assets		Liabilities and Capital Liabilities	
Cash on hand and due from banks	$ 6,351,751	Deposits	$ 95,635,593
Securities of U.S. government	54,398,942	Cash dividends payable	100,000
Securities of state and political subdivisions	985,567	Other liabilities	384,275
Other investments	11,988,593	Total liabilities	$ 96,119,868
Federal funds sold	7,225,000	Capital	
Commercial loans	19,551,862		
Installment loans	2,144,346	Capital stock	$ 1,000,000
Overdrafts	3,849	Capital surplus	1,100,000
Banking house, net	2,795,873	Undivided profits	8,429,272
Furniture and fixtures, net	59,224	Total capital	$ 10,529,272
		Total liabilities and capital	$106,649,140
Total assets	$106,649,140		

CASE: First National Bank of Smithville (continued)

EXHIBIT 4-2 STATEMENT OF INCOME, YEAR ENDED DECEMBER 31, 20XX

Interest income	
Interest and discounts on loans	$1,998,945
Interest on security investments	3,764,708
Interest on other investments	168,682
Total interest income	$5,932,335
Interest expense	
Interest on deposits	$3,000,828
Net interest income	$2,931,507
Provision for loan losses	460,000
Net interest income after provision for loan losses and bond revaluation	$2,471,507
Other income	
Other income	$1,411,993
Other expenses	
Salaries and wages	$1,033,059
Contribution to profit-sharing trust	25,000
Other operating expenses	$1,955,506
Total other expenses	$3,013,565
Income before income taxes	$ 869,935
Federal income taxes	244,458
Net income	$ 625,477

EXHIBIT 4-3 STATEMENT OF CHANGES IN CAPITAL, YEAR ENDED DECEMBER 31, 20XX

Balance—Beginning of Year	$ 9,704,103
Prior period accrual adjustment	(53,808)
Changes in reserve for mutual fund valuation	225,441
Net income	625,477
Deferred tax adjustment	38,059
Cash dividends paid	(100,100)
Balance—End of Year	$10,529,272

EXHIBIT 4-4 HIGHLIGHTS 20XX

Net profit	$ 625,477
Net earnings per share	$ 3.12
Book value per share	$ 52.64
Total resources	$106,649,140
Total deposits	$ 95,635,592
Total capital and reserves	$ 10,529,272
Number of stockholders	45
Number of employees and officers	49
Number of deposit accounts	9,232

ENDNOTES

1. Franco Modigliani and Richard A. Cohn, "Inflation, Rational Valuation and the Market," *Financial Analysts Journal* 35 (1979), pp. 24–44.

2. Stephen Rhoades, "Determinants of Premiums Paid in Bank Acquisitions," *Atlantic Economic Journal* (March 1987), pp. 20–30.

3. Donald Fraser and James Kolari, "Determinants of Small Bank Acquisition Premiums," Federal Reserve Bank of Chicago, Conference on Bank Structure and Competition (1987), pp. 397–398.

4. Randolph Beatty, Anthony Santomero, and Michael Smirlock, *Bank Merger Premiums: Analysis and Evidence,* Salomon Brothers Center for the Study of Financial Institutions . Monograph Series in Finance and Economics, Monograph 1987-3, (1987).

5. Mary Barth, William Beaver, and Mark Wolfson, "Components of Earnings and the Structure of Bank Share Prices," *Financial Analysts Journal* 46, 1990, pp. J3–J8.

6. John Visser and H.K. Wu, "The Effects of Deregulation on Bank Stock Price Earnings Ratios," *Financial Analysts Journal* 45 (1989), pp. 62–67.

7. See Joseph P. Hughes, William Lang, Loretta J. Mester, and Choon-Geol Moon, "The Dollars and Sense of Bank Consolidation," *Journal of Banking and Finance* 23, 1999, pp. 291–324; and Yaron Brook, Robert Hendershott, and Darrell Lee, "The Gains from Takeover Deregulation: Evidence from the End of Interstate Banking Restrictions,: Journal of Finance 53 (1998), pp. 2185–2204.

8. Alberto Cybo-Ottone and Maurizio Murgia, "Mergers and Shareholder Wealth in European Banking," *Journal of Banking and Finance* 24 (2000), pp. 831–859.

9. L. Paige Fields, Donald R. Fraser, and James W. Kolari, "Is Bancassurance a Viable Model for Financial Firms?, *The Journal of Risk and Insurance* 4 (2007), pp. 777–794.

10. G. Hawawini and I. Swary, *Mergers and Acquisitions in the U.S. Banking Industry: Evidence from the Capital Markets* (Amsterdam: North Holland, 1990).

11. Richard Roll, "The Hubris Hypothesis of Corporate Takeovers," *Journal of Business* 59 (1986), pp. 197–216.

12. Hao Zhang, "US Evidence on Bank Takeover Motives: A Note," *Journal of Business Finance and Accounting* 25 (1998), pp. 1025–1032.

13. For an excellent summaries of bank mergers and performance articles, see Stephen A. Rhoades, "A Summary of Merger Performance Studies in Banking: 1980–93 and an Assessment of the 'Operating Performance' and Event Study Methodologies," Staff Study 169, Board of Governors of the Federal Reserve System (1994); and Ingo Walter, *Mergers and Acquisitions in Banking and Finance: What Works, What Fails, and Why?*, New York: Oxford University Press (2004).

14. Marcia Millon Cornett and Hassan Tehranian, "Changes in Corporate Performance Associated with Bank Acquisitions," *Journal of Financial Economics* 21 (1993), pp. 210–234.

15. Dario Focarelli, Fabio Panetta, and Carmelo Salleo, "Why Do Banks Merge?" *Journal of Money, Credit, and Banking* 34 (2002), pp. 1047–1066.

16. See Thomas F. Siems, "Bank Mergers and Shareholder Wealth: Evidence from 1995's Megamerger Deals," *Financial Industry Studies*, Federal Reserve Bank of Dallas, (1996), pp. 1–9; Yener Altunbas and David Marques, "Mergers and acquisitions and bank performance in Europe: The Role of Strategic Similarities," *Journal of Economics and Business* 60 (2008), pp. 204–222; and Andreas Behr and Frank Heid, "The Success of Bank Mergers Revisited: An Assessment Based on a Matching Strategy," *Journal of Empirical Finance* 18 (2011), pp. 117–135.

17. Atreya Dey, "The Long-Run Performance of Mega Mergers," Working paper, Haverford College (2015). It is worthwhile to note that banks may well learn from previous mergers by themselves and others and thereby improve post-merger performance. See Gayle DeLong and Robert DeYoung, "Learning by Observing: Information Spillovers in the Execution and Valuation of Commercial Bank M&As," *Journal of Finance* 62 (2007), pp. 181–216.

18. Todd T. Milbourn, Arnoud W. A. Boot, and Anjan V. Thakor, "Megamergers and Expanded Scope: Theories of Bank Size and Activity Diversity," *Journal of Banking and Finance* 23 (1999), pp. 195–214.

19. For an excellent overview of the bank M&A literature, see Allen N. Berger, Rebecca S. Demsetz, and Phillip E. Strahan, "The Consolidation of the Financial Services Industry: Causes, Consequences, and Implications for the Future," *Journal of Banking and Finance* 23 (1999), pp.135–194.

20. See Donald R. Fraser and James W. Kolari, "Market Power, Bank Megamergers, and the Welfare of Bank Borrowers," *Journal of Financial Research* 34 (2011), pp. 641–658; Henri Fraisse, Johan Hombert, and Mathias Le, "The Competitive Effects of a Bank Megamerger on Access to Credit," Working paper, HEC Paris (2015); and Hans Degryse, Nancy Masschelein, and Janet Mitchell, "Staying, Dropping, or Switching: The Impacts of Bank Mergers on Small Firms," Review of Financial Studies 24 (2011), pp. 1102–1140.

Chapter 5

An Overview of Asset/Liability Management (ALM)

After reading this chapter, you will be able to:

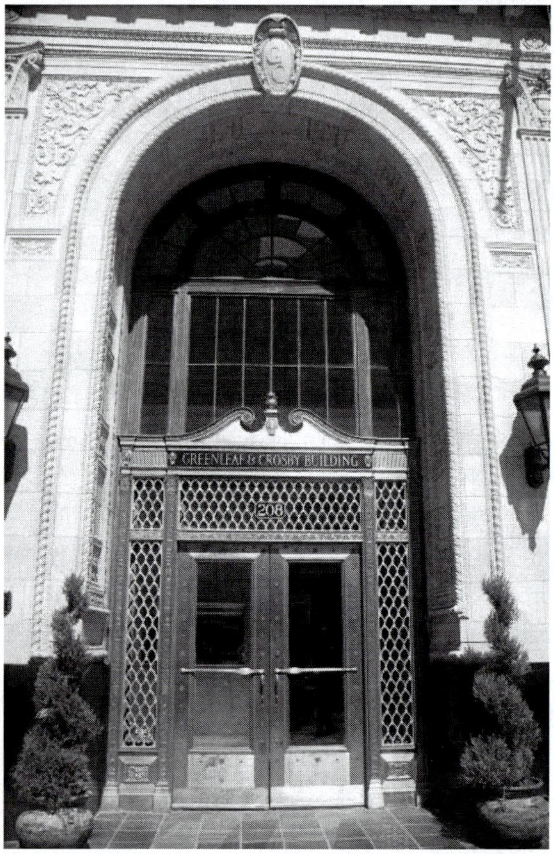

- Describe the nature of asset/liability management
- Discuss alternative approaches to asset/liability management
- Analyze the interest sensitivity position of a commercial bank using gap analysis
- Compare dollar gap management with duration gap management
- Identify the major problems in implementing dollar gap and duration gap strategies.

Jim Fox's first assignment at West American Bank (a $3 billion regional commercial bank) was as assistant to the asset/liability manager. In this capacity Jim was responsible for calculating the interest rate risk position of the bank. On his second day on the job, Jim's boss presented him with the following policy statement that had recently been adopted by the Board of Directors Asset/Liability Management Committee.

The Board Asset/Liability Management Committee directs management to achieve an interest rate risk position that is within the following guidelines:

Change in Interest Rate	Change in Net Interest Income	Change in Market Value of Equity
+300	−80%	−40%
+200	−65	−15
+100	−40	−5
Flat	0	0
−100	−40	−5
−200	−65	−15
−300	−80	−40

The policy itself was relatively clear: if interest rates increased by 200 basis points, the bank should have its portfolio structured so that net interest income did not fall by more than 65 percent and the net worth (the market value of assets less the market value of liabilities) did not decline by more than 15 percent. Similar interpretations could be placed on other movements in interest rates. The problem facing Jim Fox was how to determine whether the interest rate risk position of the bank was within these guidelines. He needed to learn a good deal about dollar gap, duration gap, and simulations that test the sensitivity of income to changes in the composition of the balance sheet when interest rates change.

ASSET/LIABILITY MANAGEMENT

Bankers make decisions every day about buying and selling securities, about whether to make particular loans, and about how to fund their investment and lending activities. These decisions are based, in part, on (1) their outlook for interest rates -- the direction of change in interest rates in the future. Two other factors that they must take into account include (2) the composition of their assets and liabilities, and (3) the degree of risk that they are willing to take. Collectively, these decisions affect the bank's net interest income and balance sheet values. The process of making such decisions about the composition of assets and liabilities and the risk assessment is known as ***asset/liability management (ALM).*** The decisions are usually made by the asset/liability management committee (ALCO) that is responsible for the overall financial direction of the bank. The ALCO's goal is to manage the sources and uses of funds on the balance sheet and off-balance sheet activities with respect to interest rate risk and liquidity. ALM is generally viewed as short run in nature, focusing on the day-to-day and week-to-week balance sheet management necessary to achieve near-term financial goals. The traditional purpose of ALM has been to control the size of the bank's net interest income. This goal is associated with dollar gap. ALM also considers the affects of the changes on the value of balance sheet items. This goal is associated with duration gap. Both the dollar gap and the duration gap will be explained shortly.

ALM can be illustrated with the aid of the following simplified balance sheet. Suppose that a bank has total assets consisting of $100 million in five-year fixed-rate loans at eight percent, and $90 million in liabilities consisting of 30-day time deposits at four percent.

Assets (in millions)	Liabilities (in millions)
$100, 5-year fixed-rate loans @ 8%	$90, 30-day deposits @ 4%
	Equity $10
Total $100	Total $100

The *net interest income (NII)* of $4.4 million is the difference between the interest earned on the assets ($8 million) and the cost of the liabilities ($3.6 million). The *net interest margin (NIM)* is net interest income divided by the earning assets, or 4.4 percent.

$$\text{Net interest income (NII)} = \text{Interest income} - \text{Interest expense} \qquad (5.1)$$
$$= \$8 - 3.6 = \$4.4$$

$$\text{Net interest margin (NIM)} = \text{NII/Earning assets} \qquad (5.2)$$
$$= \$8 - \$3.6/\$100 = \$4.4/100 = 4.4\%$$

The NIM for all FDIC-insured commercial banks in 2015 was about 3.0 percent, down from a high of 3.8 percent in 2010.[1]

If market rates of interest increase, the cost of the short-term borrowing will increase, but the interest earned from the longer-term fixed-rate loans will remain unchanged. Assume that the level of market interest rates increase 200 basis point from four percent to six percent. When the 30-day deposits mature, the interest expense on the new deposits increases from $3.6 million to $5.4 million. However, interest income is not affected because all of the loans are at long-term fixed rates. In this case, the net interest income falls to $2.6 million ($8 million – $5.4 million = $2.6 million), and the NIM decreases to 2.6 percent.

If the bank had made the loans at a variable (floating) rate, the net interest margin would have increased to 4.6 percent because of the higher interest income ($10 million).

$$\text{NIM} = (\$10 - \$5.4)/\$100 = \$4.6/\$100 = 4.6\%$$

Banks make loans with many different maturities and interest rates, and on the other side of the balance sheet they raise funds with different maturities and interest rates. Therefore, the NII depends on (1) the interest rates earned on assets and paid for funds, (2) the dollar amount of the various earning assets and liabilities, and (3) the earnings mix of those funds (rate × dollar amount). Other things equal, an increase in the interest rates earned on assets will increase the NII, whereas an increase in the interest rate paid on funding sources will reduce NII. Other things equal, an increase in the dollar amount of funds raised and invested (e.g., by increasing the size of the bank) will increase NII. Also, other things equal, shifting the earnings mix toward more higher-yielding assets or less costly sources of funds will increase NII. Other things are seldom constant, however. Hence, changes in NII usually reflect changes in each of these three factors. These are some of the decisions that an ALCO must consider.

AN HISTORICAL PERSPECTIVE

Coordinated asset/liability management is a relatively recent phenomenon. From the end of World War II until the early 1960s, most commercial banks obtained their funds from relatively stable (and interest-free) demand deposits and from small time deposits. Interest rate ceilings on deposits (Federal Reserve Regulation Q) limited the extent to which banks could compete for funds by paying higher interest rates. Opening more branches (where permissible by law) in order to attract funds through greater customer convenience or committing more funds to the advertising budget were among the few ways to attract more funds. As a result, most sources of funds were ***core deposits*** (not sensitive to interest rates), which increased with the growth of the national and local economy. Moreover, the volatility of interest rates was quite small. In this environment, bank funds management concentrated on the control of assets. Bank financial management principally was *asset management*. Liability management as it is known today did not exist.

During the 1960s, the demand for bank loans accelerated with the expansion in the economy. The growth in loan demands taxed the ability of commercial banks to fund the loans from existing deposit sources. As a result, banks sought to expand faster than their core deposit growth would allow by acquiring (buying at higher cost) additional funds. As they did this, liability management was created. With liability management, commercial banks bought funds from the financial markets whenever necessary -- either to meet loan demand, to purchase securities, or to replace reductions in other sources of their funds. The acquisition of funds at the lowest possible cost (i.e., the management of liabilities) then became an active part of bank financial management.

During the 1970s, Regulation Q limited the ability of banks to attract funds at market rates of interest. Since deposit rate ceilings limited banks to offering noncompetitive interest rates for many of their deposits, liability management concentrated on nondeposit sources that were not subject to Regulation Q. The purchase of funds in the interbank or federal funds market represents perhaps the most widely used source of funds for liability management. Many large banks used the Eurodollar market (the market for dollars deposited at banks outside the United States) extensively for funds. In addition, during periods when market rates of interest were below Regulation Q ceilings (or when the regulations lifted those ceilings), banks were able to rely upon deposit sources in their liability management.

Liability management fundamentally changed the way banks managed their funds. With liability management, banks had two sources of funds -- core deposits and purchased funds -- with quite different characteristics. For core deposits, the amount of funds is relatively insensitive to changes in interest rate levels; that is, the demand for core deposits by bank customers is relatively interest-inelastic. From the perspective of bank management, core deposits offer the advantages of stability and low cost. The amount of core deposits does not change greatly with relatively large variations in interest rate levels. However, core deposits have the disadvantage of not being overly responsive to management needs for expansion. If the bank experiences a sizable increase in loan demand, it cannot expect to fund the loan growth with core deposits.

For purchased funds, however, the bank can obtain all the funds that it wants (within some reasonable limit) if it is willing to pay the market-determined price. Unlike core deposits, where prices are determined at the local level, interest rates on purchased funds are set in the national money market, and prospective depositors can check certificates of deposit (CD) rates on the Internet. The bank is a price taker in the money market where they can buy funds, whereas it is a price setter in the core deposit market.

Banks that are members of the ***Federal Home Loan Bank*** system can borrow funds (advances) from regional FHLBanks, by using real estate loans as collateral. The maturity of the advances can range from one day to five years or more. The Federal Home Loan Bank system is a government-sponsored enterprise (GSE) whose primary function is to enhance the availability of residential mortgage credit by making low-cost funds available to member institutions. Banks can become member institutions by buying stock in one of the twelve regional Federal Home Loan Banks.

The money market gives the bank flexibility in the amount of funds it is able to raise. However, purchased funds in the money market have two significant risks that the core deposit market does not have. First, the interest rate may be highly volatile. Second, purchased money may be unavailable for banks perceived to be in financial difficulty. This availability risk is particularly significant for banks that finance a large share of their assets with purchased money, such as large banks. Any perception that the quality of the bank is poor may eliminate this source. Then the bank would shift, perhaps overnight, from a position in which it could raise almost unlimited funds at the going market interest rate to that in which it could raise no funds. Given that most purchased money sources of funds are short-term, often overnight, the change in funds availability can quickly cause a crisis as uninsured depositors try to withdraw their funds because of loss of confidence in the bank. Such large-scale withdrawals of deposits, called bank runs or just runs, are an extreme situation that may cause the bank to either fail or suffer liquidity problems.

During the financial crisis of 2008 and 2009, many large U.S. banks experienced difficulties purchasing funds in the money market that constrained their liquidity and even triggered some bank failures. Government intervention by the Federal Reserve and U.S. Department of the Treasury was needed to support large banks, prevent widespread bank runs, and boost bank liquidity. This intervention was an important lesson of the Great Depression from 1929 to 1935. At that time thousands of banks closed their doors due to being unable to meet deposit withdrawals by their customers. Many of these failed banks were actually solvent, profitable enterprises but fell victim to public panic that caused mass bank runs. In view of these historical events, many banks have moved away from exclusive reliance on liability management. Today, management of bank portfolios involves managing both assets and liabilities.

ALTERNATIVES IN MANAGING INTEREST RATE RISK

BALANCE SHEET ADJUSTMENTS

In managing the interest rate risk of a bank's portfolio, management may follow two different approaches (or some combination of the two): on-balance sheet adjustment and off-balance sheet adjustment. On-balance sheet adjustment involves changing the portfolio of assets and liabilities in order to change the manner in which the profitability of the bank or dollar amount of its assets and liabilities changes as interest rates change. For example, management may adjust the maturity, repricing, and payment schedules of its assets and liabilities. Suppose that a small bank or thrift has a substantial amount of long-term fixed-rate mortgages funded by short -term CDs. If interest rates rise, the cost of funds will increase but the earnings on the asset will not, thereby reducing the net interest margin. One approach to dealing with this problem is to shift to adjustable-rate mortgages on the asset side of the balance sheet or to longer-term CDs on the liability side of the balance sheet. Both of these portfolio management decisions represent on-balance sheet portfolio adjustments.

In addition, a bank could securitize some of its assets and sell them to other investors. As noted in previous chapters, securitization is the packaging and selling of otherwise unmarketable loans, such as home mortgage loans. Alternatively, the bank could buy tranches (parts) of securitized loans or participations (parts) of large loans to adjust its loan portfolio.

OFF-BALANCE SHEET ADJUSTMENTS

A bank can change its interest rate risk position without changing the portfolio of assets and liabilities by using off-balance sheet derivatives, such as interest rate swaps and futures. An ***interest rate swap contract*** is an agreement in which a bank and another party (referred to as a counterparty) trade payment streams but not principal amounts. For example, a bank with a long-term fixed-rate mortgage portfolio could agree to receive a floating-rate payment stream and to pay the counterparty an equivalent fixed-rate payment stream. Such a transaction would reduce the interest rate risk from holding this fixed-rate mortgage because rising rates would produce a higher payment to the bank from the swap.

As an alternative, the bank could engage in a futures transaction. An interest rate ***futures contract*** is an agreement between two parties to exchange a commodity for a fixed price at a specified time in the future. Various financial instruments, such as Treasury bonds and Eurodollars, are packaged as interest rate commodities and are actively traded. The holder of the contract earns a gain or incurs a loss based on movements in the price of the contract after purchase. For example, if interest rates fall subsequent to the purchase of a Treasury bond contract, the price of the contract will rise (because bond prices and interest rates move inversely), and, conversely, if interest rates rise the price of the contract will fall. Since the concern of the bank with a long-term fixed-rate mortgage portfolio is that it will be harmed by rising interest rates, it could sell a Treasury bond contract (i.e., take a short position). If interest rates did rise, its profit from the sale of the bond futures contract would offset some or all of the loss on its holdings of fixed-rate mortgages. The use of off-balance sheet adjustment is covered in more detail in Chapter 6.

MEASURING INTEREST RATE SENSITIVITY AND THE DOLLAR GAP

Three techniques of dealing with interest rate risk are examined in this chapter: dollar gap, duration gap, and simulation. The dollar gap is the oldest technique, and the easiest to understand. It also provides a foundation for understanding the other two techniques.

The most commonly used measure of the interest sensitivity position of a financial institution is ***gap analysis***. Under this approach, all assets and liabilities are classified into groups -- interest-rate sensitive or non-interest-rate sensitive -- according to whether their interest return (in the case of assets) or interest cost (in the case of liabilities) varies with the general level of interest rates. Thus, the focus of gap analysis is on net interest income.

Gap analysis classifies assets or liabilities according to their interest sensitivity. Interest-sensitive assets are those that reprice within some defined period (e.g., 0–30 days, 31–60 days, 61–90 days, and so on). Similarly, interest-rate-sensitive liabilities are those that reprice in the same defined periods.

The key to understanding rate sensitivity is that it is determined by how often assets or liabilities are repriced, rather than their maturity. Of course assets and liabilities that have short-term maturities (e.g., 0–30 days, 31–60 days, 61–90 days) are more rate sensitive than those with longer maturities. However, assets and liabilities with longer-term maturities but with variable rates of interest, which are repriced when changes in the general level of interest rates occur (such as a floating-rate, five-year CD), also are interest-rate sensitive. Therefore, rate sensitivity depends on the frequency of repricing.

CLASSIFICATION OF ASSETS AND LIABILITIES

Table 5-1 illustrates the classification of the assets and liabilities of a financial institution according to their interest rate sensitivity. Those assets and liabilities whose interest return or costs vary with interest rate changes over some given time horizon are referred to as ***rate-sensitive assets (RSAs)*** or ***rate-sensitive liabilities (RSLs)***. Those assets and liabilities whose interest return or cost do not vary with interest rate movements over the same time horizon are referred to as ***non-rate sensitive (NRS)***. In other words, assets and liabilities that reprice within the time horizon are rate sensitive.

Table 5-1: CLASSIFICATION OF ASSETS AND LIABILITIES BY INTEREST RATE SENSITIVITY

ASSETS			LIABILITIES AND EQUITY		
Vault cash	NRS	$20	Demand deposits	NRS	$5
Short-term securities	RSA	15	NOW accounts	NRS	5
Long-term securities	NRS	30	Money market deposits	RSL	20
Variable-rate loans	RSA	40	Short-term savings	RSL	40
Short-term loans	RSA	20	Long-term savings	NRS	60
Long-term loans	NRS	60	Federal funds borrowing	RSL	55
Other assets	NRS	10	Equity	NRS	10
		$195			$195

NRs = Non-rate-sensitive asset or liability
RSA = Rate-sensitive asset
RSL= Rate-sensitive liability

Note that the selection of the time period over which to measure the interest sensitivity of the asset or liability is crucial. An asset or liability that is rate sensitive in one time period (e.g., 90 days) may not be rate sensitive in a shorter time period (e.g., 30 days). The time periods are sometimes referred to as ***maturity buckets*** or planning horizons. Over a sufficiently long time period virtually all assets and liabilities are interest-rate sensitive. As the time period is shortened, however, the ratio of rate-sensitive to non-rate-sensitive assets and liabilities falls. At some sufficiently short time period (one day, for example), virtually all assets and liabilities are non-interest-rate sensitive. The industry does not establish standard time periods. Each bank decides on those time periods that match its needs.

In the classification of assets and liabilities used in Table 5-1, short-term securities and short-term deposits are those with a maturity of one year or less. Under this criterion, interest-rate-sensitive assets are all those assets with a maturity of one year or less (short-term securities and short-term loans) and variable-rate loans (assuming that the rates on those loans adjust with interest rate changes within a year). All other assets are non-interest-rate sensitive, including vault cash, long-term securities, long-term loans, and other assets. Interest-rate-sensitive assets in Table 5-1 are $75, and non-interest-rate-sensitive assets total $120. Thus, less than half of the earning assets are rate sensitive.

The total effect of any change in the general level of interest rates on the net interest income of a financial institution depends on the effects on both interest revenue and interest expense. The effect on interest expense depends, in turn, on the interest sensitivity of liabilities. In the example given in Table 5-1, interest-rate-sensitive liabilities are short-term savings deposits, money market deposits (whose interest rates are generally adjusted each week), and federal funds borrowings (whose rates change daily with the federal funds rate). Non-interest-rate-sensitive liabilities are demand deposits (whose interest rate is fixed at zero by federal law), NOW accounts (Negotiable Order of Withdrawal -- checking accounts that pay a positive interest rate but whose interest rate changes infrequently), and long-term savings, such as three- or four-year CDs. Interest-rate-sensitive liabilities total \$115, whereas non-interest-rate-sensitive liabilities are \$70.

DEFINITION OF DOLLAR GAP

The total effect of interest rate changes on profitability can be summarized by its ***dollar gap.*** The dollar gap (also referred to as the funding gap or the maturity gap) is the difference between the dollar amount of interest-rate-sensitive assets (RSA) and the dollar amount of interest-rate-sensitive liabilities (RSL).

$$\text{Gap}(\$) = \text{RSA}(\$) - \text{RSL}(\$) \tag{5.3}$$

Comparison of the interest sensitivity position of different financial institutions using the gap is not meaningful because of differences in the sizes of the institutions. Such a comparison requires some type of "common size" calculations.

$$\text{Relative gap ratio} = \frac{\text{Gap\$}}{\text{Total assets}} \tag{5.4}$$

$$\text{Interest-sensitivity ratio} = \frac{\text{RSA\$}}{\text{RSL\$}} \tag{5.5}$$

The ***relative gap ratio*** expresses the dollar amount of the gap (dollar RSAs – dollar RSLs) as a percentage of total assets. The interest-sensitivity ratio expresses the dollar amount of RSAs as a fraction of the dollar amount of RSLs.

ASSET AND LIABILITY SENSITIVITY

A financial institution at a given time may be asset or liability sensitive. If the financial institution were asset sensitive (for example, it had \$100 million in rate-sensitive assets and \$50 million in rate-sensitive liabilities), it would have a positive gap, a positive relative gap ratio, and interest-sensitivity ratio greater than 1. Conversely, an institution that was liability sensitive (for example, it had \$50 million in rate-sensitive assets and \$100 million in rate-sensitive liabilities) would have a negative gap, a negative relative gap ratio, and an interest-sensitivity ratio less than 1.

Financial institutions that are asset sensitive (they have a positive gap, positive relative gap, or interest-sensitivity ratio greater than 1) will experience an increase in their net interest income when interest rates increase and a decrease in their net interest income when interest rates fall. In contrast, financial institutions that are liability sensitive (they have a negative gap, negative relative gap, or interest-sensitivity ratio less than 1) will experience a decrease in their net interest income when interest rates increase and an increase in their net interest income when interest rates fall. As previously noted, the bank shown in Table 5-1 has rate-sensitive assets of \$75 and rate-sensitive liabilities of \$115. Therefore, its dollar gap is a negative \$40. The negative gap means that the bankers believe that interest rates are going to decline, and they hope to benefit from the lower cost of funds.

$$\text{Gap\$} = \text{RSA(\$)} - \text{RSL(\$)}$$
$$-\$40 = \$75 - \$115$$

The relative gap is

$$\text{Relative gap} = \text{Gap\$/Total assets}$$
$$-0.21 = -\$40/\$195$$

The interest-sensitivity ratio is

$$\text{Interest-sensitivity ratio} = \text{RSA\$/RSL\$}$$
$$0.65 = \$75/\$115$$

GAP, INTEREST RATES, AND PROFITABILITY

The effects of changing interest rates on net income for banks with different gap positions are illustrated in equation (5.6):

$$(\Delta \text{NII}) = \text{RSA\$}(\Delta i) - \text{RSL\$}(\Delta i) = \text{Gap\$}(\Delta i) \tag{5.6}$$

where (ΔNII) is the expected change in the dollar amount of net interest income, and (Δi) is the expected change in interest rates in percentage points.

An example may help to illustrate the effects of changing interest rates on the net interest income of a financial institution. Suppose a financial institution has RSAs of \$55 million and RSLs of \$35 million, and thus has a gap of \$20 million. If interest rates were to rise from eight percent to 10 percent, the net interest income of the institution would rise by \$0.4 million.

$$\text{Gap\$}(\Delta i) = \$20 \text{ million } (0.02) = \$400{,}000 \text{ expected change in NII}$$

Of course, the effect of this interest rate change on net interest margin (which is net interest income divided by earning assets) depends on the previous level of net interest income as well as the size of earning assets of the financial institution. Conversely, if RSAs of the institution were \$35 million and RSLs were \$55 million, the institution would have a negative gap and would be liability sensitive. An increase of two percentage points in interest rates would, in this situation, lower net interest income by \$0.4 million.

The effects of changing interest rates on net interest income is summarized in Table 5-2. For commercial banks with a positive gap, net interest income will rise or fall as interest rates rise or fall. For banks with a negative gap, net interest income will rise or fall inversely with interest rate changes; that is, net interest income will increase with falling interest rates and fall with rising interest rates. In contrast, banks with a zero gap should experience no change in their net interest income because of changing interest rates.[2]

Table 5-2: GAP, INTEREST RATE CHANGES, AND NET INTEREST INCOME

Gap		Change in Interest Rates	Change in Net Interest Income (NII)
Positive	RSA > RSL	Increase	Increase
Positive	RSA > RSL	Decrease	Decrease
Negative	RSA < RSL	Increase	Decrease
Negative	RSA < RSL	Decrease	Increase
Zero	RSA = RSL	Increase	No change
Zero	RSA = RSL	Decrease	No change

INCREMENTAL AND CUMULATIVE GAPS

The gap between interest-rate-sensitive assets and interest-rate-sensitive liabilities can be measured either incrementally or in cumulative terms. The incremental gap measures the difference between rate-sensitive assets and rate-sensitive liabilities over increments of the planning horizon. The ***cumulative gap*** measures the difference between rate-sensitive assets and liabilities over a more extended period. The cumulative gap is the sum of the incremental gaps. Of course, if there is only one planning horizon, the incremental gap and the cumulative gap are the same.

Table 5-3 illustrates the calculation of incremental and cumulative gaps, with a one-year planning horizon broken down into four increments: 0–30 days, 31–90 days, 91–180 days, and 181–365 days. Note that over the entire 365-day period, the institution has a gap of zero, but over a shorter period the institution is not balanced. It has a positive gap for the first gap period (0–30 days) and a positive gap also for the second gap period (31–90 days), but it has negative gaps for the last two gap periods.

Table 5-3: INCREMENTAL AND CUMULATIVE GAPS (in millions)

Days	Assets Maturing or Repriced Within	Liabilities Maturing or Repriced Within	Incremental Gap	Cumulative Gap
0-30	$50	$30	+ $20	+ $20
31–90	25	20	+$5	+$25
91–180	0	20	- $20	+$5
181–365	0	5	- $5	$0
	$75	$75		

GAP ANALYSIS: AN EXAMPLE

Table 5-4 provides a comprehensive dollar gap for City Bank, a community bank with total assets of slightly more than $300 million. In this gap analysis, the interest sensitivity of the bank is divided into five increments or "maturity buckets": daily floating rate, 1–30 days, 31–60 days, 61–90 days, 181–360 days, and 360-plus days. Each asset and liability of the bank is then allocated to one (or more) time horizons. For example, federal funds sold reprice every day. Hence, the $34,800,000 that the bank had outstanding as federal funds sold shows up in the daily floating rate column. Similarly, the $200,000 that the bank had as federal funds purchased shows up in the same column (as a liability). For many asset and liability items, however, the amount of the outstanding balance is distributed among several time horizons. For example, fixed-rate commercial loans are distributed as follows (based on their maturity and repricing characteristics): $1,109,000 in the 1–30 day time horizon, $469,000 in the 31–60 day column, $549,000 in the 61–90 day time horizon, $1,766,000 in the 91–180 day time horizon, $1,954,000 in the 181–360 day time horizon, and $2,202,000 in the 360-plus daytime horizon. Similarly, on the liability side of the balance sheet, CDs of under $100,000 are distributed as follows (based on their maturity): $6,495,000 in the 1–30 day position, $6,741,000 in the 31–60 day time horizon, $5,164,000 in the 61–90 day time horizon, $17,161,000 in the 91–180 day time horizon, and $13,347,000 in the 181–360 day time horizon.

It is important to note the following in understanding the construction of this gap matrix. First, since each asset and liability item must be allocated entirely among the incremental gap positions, reading across each row must produce a sum in each asset or liability category that is the same as the amount shown in the balance sheet. For that reason, the final column in Table 5-4 on the right side of the gap matrix equals the total balance shown on the left side of the matrix.

Second, and more important in understanding the construction of a gap matrix, a considerable amount of judgment is required in the allocation of many balance sheet items among the different maturity positions. This is especially the case for the liability side of the balance sheet. For example, City Bank has chosen to allocate all $21,375,000 of the money market deposit accounts (MMDA) to the 1–30 day time horizon. These are accounts whose interest rates change at the discretion of management, though management responds to changes in open market interest rate in the decisions (made each week) concerning rate adjustments on these deposits. In fact, despite some small changes in market interest rates, management had not changed the rates offered on MMDAs in the three months preceding the date of this gap matrix. Demand deposits also present a difficult problem for the asset/liability analyst. Since these accounts pay no interest, they are by definition not interest sensitive. Hence City Bank has allocated the $48,095,000 in Demand Deposits IPC (Individuals, Partnerships, and Corporations) and the $12,136,000 in Demand Deposits Public Funds (mostly local government) to the 360-plus day time horizon. Yet rising rates will cause customers to shift into interest-bearing accounts such as MMDAs, which will affect the bank's interest expense.

Table 5-4: GAP ANALYSIS FOR CITY BANK, March 31, 20xx

	Total Balance	Daily Floating Volume	1–30 Day Position Volume	31–60 Day Position Volume	61–90 Day Position Volume	91–180 Day Position Volume	181–360 Day Position Volume	360+ Day Position Volume	Total Volume
Assets									
Variable rate comm loans	—	—	8,778	—	—	—	—	—	8,778
Fixed rate comm loans	8,049	—	1,109	469	549	1,766	1,954	2,202	8,049
Variable rate real estate loans	12,890	—	12,890	—	—	—	—	—	12,890
Fixed rate real estate loans	66,949	—	949	1,420	558	8,879	17,578	37,565	66,949
Installment loans	10,618	—	641	523	503	1,389	2,096	5,466	10,618
Student loans	8,934	—	3,311	3,145	2,478	—	—	—	8,934
Credit card loans	1,203	—	—	—	—	—	—	1,203	1,203
Nonaccrual loans	471	—	—	—	—	—	—	471	471
Overdrafts	883	—	—	—	—	—	—	883	883
Loan loss reserve	8,599	—	—	—	—	—	—	8,599	8,599
FNMA/FHLMC ARMs	7,592	—	113	3,808	1,717	1,954	—	—	7,592
Agency issue CMOs/REMICs	64,752	—	1,324	1,289	1,188	8,208	21,771	30,972	64,752
Other U.S. government agency—fixed	8,709	—	1,001	—	—	—	—	2,717	8,709
Other U.S. government agency—variable	5,257	—	1,759	1,756	1,742	—	—	—	5,257
GNMA ARMs	4,840	—	38	38	38	4,726	—	—	4,840
State and political subdivision	60	—	—	—	—	—	5	55	60
Private issue CMOs/REMICs	27,282	—	2,819	1,779	1,304	8,732	4,931	7,717	27,282
Other debt securities	16,414	—	2,375	—	200	4,753	2,375	6,711	16,414
Other marketable securities	8,080	—	673	673	673	2,019	4,038	4	8,080
Investment CDs	291	—	—	—	—	291	—	—	291
Federal funds sold	34,800	34,800	—	—	—	—	—	—	34,800
Cash and due from banks	24,774	—	—	—	—	—	—	24,774	24,774
Fixed assets	6,398	—	—	—	—	—	—	6,398	6,398
Other real estate	4,284	—	—	—	—	—	—	4,284	4,284
Other assets	3,738	—	—	—	—	—	—	3,738	3,738
Total assets	327,547	34,800	37,780	19,891	10,950	42,717	54,748	126,661	327,547

(Continues)

	Total Balance	Daily Floating Volume	1–30 Day Position Volume	31–60 Day Position Volume	61–90 Day Position Volume	91–180 Day Position Volume	181–360 Day Position Volume	360+ Day Position Volume	Total Volume
Liabilities									
Demand deposits IPC	48,095	—	—	—	—	—	—	48,095	48,095
Demand deposits public Fn	12,136	—	—	—	—	—	—	12,136	12,136
NOW	52,482	—	—	—	—	—	—	52,482	52,482
Money market	21,375	—	21,375	—	—	—	—	—	21,375
Super money market	43,197	—	43,197	—	—	—	—	—	43,197
Regular savings	19,268	—	—	—	—	—	—	19,268	19,268
Variable rate IRAs	5,400	—	5,400	—	—	—	—	—	5,400
Fixed rate IRAs	6,411	—	709	909	420	697	1,846	1,830	6,411
CDs < 100M	55,679	—	6,495	6,471	5,164	17,161	13,347	6,771	55,679
CDs > 100M	27,652	—	2,136	1,460	1,512	18,458	2,960	1,126	27,652
Federal funds purchased	200	200	—	—	—	—	—	—	200
Accrued interest payable	781	—	—	—	—	—	—	781	781
Miscellaneous liabilities	1,739	—	—	—	—	—	—	1,739	1,739
Capital stock	2,800	—	—	—	—	—	—	2,800	2,800
Certified surplus	10,200	—	—	—	—	—	—	10,200	10,200
Undivided profits	19,324	—	—	—	—	—	—	19,324	19,324
Current net earnings	808	—	—	—	—	—	—	808	808
Total liabilities	327,547	200	79,312	9,110	7,096	36,316	18,153	177,360	327,547
Gap	—	34,600	–41,532	10,781	3,854	6,401	36,595	–50,699	
Cumulative gap	—	34,600	–6,932	3,849	7,703	14,104	50,699	0	
RSA/RSL	—	174.00%	0.48	2.18	1.54	1.18	3.02	0.71	
Cumulative RSA/RSL	—	174.00%	0.91	1.04	1.08	1.11	1.34	1.00	
Gap/total assets	—	0.11	–0.13	0.03	0.01	0.02	0.11	–0.15	
Cumulative gap/total assets	—	0.11	–0.02	0.01	0.02	0.04	0.15	0.00	

The gap position for City Bank is given at the bottom of Table 5-4. Calculations are made of the gap for each time period, and the cumulative gap. Also, each of the gap measurements is expressed as a fraction of total assets. For example, City Bank's gap for the daily floating rate period is +$34,600,000, reflecting its large amount of federal funds sold. It is thus highly asset sensitive for the one-day period, and its earnings will be significantly affected by changes in the federal funds rate. However, its gap over the 2–30 day period is a negative $41,532,000, producing a cumulative gap of a negative $6,930,000 for the first two periods. The gap then turns positive for each of the remaining periods until the last days when, by definition, the cumulative gap must be zero over the entire gap period.

MANAGING INTEREST RATE RISK WITH DOLLAR GAPS

The principal purpose of asset/liability management traditionally has been to control the size of the net interest income. This control can be achieved through defensive or aggressive asset/liability management. The goal of defensive ***asset/liability management*** is to insulate the net interest income from changes in interest rates; that is, to prevent interest rate changes from decreasing or increasing the net interest income. In contrast, aggressive asset/liability management focuses on increasing the net interest income through altering the portfolio of the institution. The success of aggressive asset/liability management depends on the ability to forecast future interest rate changes. For example, a strategy that anticipates rising interest rates and that restructures the portfolio to benefit from the anticipated rate increase would fail if interest rates remained unchanged or declined. In contrast, defensive asset/liability management does not require the ability to forecast future interest rate levels. The focus of the defensive strategy is to insulate the portfolio from interest rate changes, whether the direction of the interest rate movement is upward or downward, predictable or unpredictable.

No one has perfect foresight with respect to interest rates. However, high-risk strategies combined with imperfect forecasts of interest rate movements can result in disaster. An historical example is the case of First Pennsylvania Corporation. Management of the bank violated one of the basic rules of asset/liability management: Although taking some risk is an acceptable management practice, never bet the bank on any interest rate forecasts. Failure to follow this simple principle produced massive losses for the bank, the threat of failure, and ultimately a rescue by the Federal Deposit Insurance Corporation. Existing management was dismissed, and for a considerable period of time the bank was in effect managed by the FDIC.

In the mid and late 1970s, First Pennsylvania began to increase markedly its securities portfolio, especially its long-term holdings. Securities as a fraction of total assets ranged from 12 percent in 1972 to 28 percent in 1978. Financially, this expansion in longer-term securities with longer-term sources of funds would not have produced any interest rate risk problem. However, the build-up in long-term securities was financed primarily with short-term purchased funds. Federal funds purchased (as a percentage of total assets) increased from eight percent in 1972 to 26 percent in 1978. The bank thus had a large negative gap; it was liability sensitive.

If interest rates had stayed unchanged, First Pennsylvania would have done reasonably well with its strategy of borrowing short and lending long. If interest rates had fallen, First Pennsylvania would have made large profits. Unfortunately, interest rates rose substantially in the late 1970s. Interest rates on three-month Treasury bills soared from about five percent in 1977 to over 10 percent in 1979, and over 14 percent in 1981. The combination of soaring rates and the negative gap virtually destroyed the bank. Profits turned into losses, and the bank experienced a liquidity crisis because it was unable to roll over its short-term purchased funds. The problem was further intensified by large loan losses that made large depositors and other creditors unwilling to put funds in the bank. The financial crisis at First Pennsylvania was stemmed only by an FDIC rescue effort in April 1980 that included a $500 million assistance program from the FDIC and a group of private banks.

HOW MUCH INTEREST RATE RISK IS ACCEPTABLE?

One of the most difficult decisions that bank managers face is determining the appropriate degree of interest rate risk to assume. At one extreme, referred to as defensive interest rate risk management, the bank would attempt to structure its assets and liabilities in order to eliminate interest rate risk. The other extreme would bet the bank on expectations of interest rate changes (i.e., an aggressive strategy, in fact, an extremely aggressive strategy). Few banks follow either extreme, with most banks taking some but very limited interest rate risk. In making decisions about the appropriate amount of interest rate risk, bank management should consider the following.

The profitability of a bank that does not take some interest rate risk might be inadequate. If the bank matches the interest sensitivity of its assets with the interest sensitivity of its liabilities, the spread between the cost of its funds and the amounts that can be earned by investing the funds may be inadequate. Large banks in particular may be unable to earn an adequate return in the highly competitive loan markets in which they operate unless they accept both credit and interest rate risk.

A policy of eliminating all interest rate risk on the balance sheet may be incompatible with the desires of the bank's loan customers. Suppose that loan customers want fixed-rate loans at a time when the bank wants to increase the amount of interest-sensitive assets on its books, or customers want long-term deposits at a time when the bank wants to issue short-term deposits. The bank could ignore the desires of its customers, but if it did so, it would face the substantial risk that they would take their entire banking relationship elsewhere. Within reasonable limits, the bank must accommodate the desires of its customers. Adjustments to the interest sensitivity of its portfolio must then be made elsewhere.

The expertise and risk preference of management are also significant. Managing the assets and liabilities of a bank to achieve a desired risk position often requires extensive knowledge of sophisticated financial market instruments such as futures, options, and swaps. It also requires a management that is comfortable with accepting interest rate risk. Many bankers feel less comfortable in assessing and managing interest rate risk than in dealing with credit risk.

AGGRESSIVE MANAGEMENT

The management of a bank may choose to focus on the dollar gap (also called *maturity* or *funding gap*) in controlling the interest rate risk of its portfolio. With an aggressive interest rate risk management program, such a strategy would involve two steps. First, the direction of future interest rates must be predicted. Second, adjustments must be made in the interest sensitivity of the assets and liabilities in order to take advantage of the projected interest rate changes. The prediction of rising interest rates generally results in shifting the portfolio to a positive gap position.[3]

Rising Interest Rates

If interest rates were expected to increase, a financial institution with a positive gap (i.e., more rate-sensitive assets) would increase interest return more than the liabilities would increase their cost.

A financial institution that expected interest rates to increase but was not in a positive gap position would need to make adjustments in its portfolio. It might, for example, shorten the maturity of its assets by selling long-term securities and using the funds to purchase short-term securities. It could also make more variable-rate loans. Either of these actions would increase the amount of rate-sensitive assets and would thereby allow the higher level of interest rates to be reflected in higher interest income. Another strategy that could be used either as a substitute for the asset portfolio shift or as a complement to it would be to lengthen the maturity of the liabilities of the financial institution. This could be done, for example, by selling longer-term CDs and using the funds to replace federal funds borrowings. With such a strategy, the impact of rising interest rates on the cost of funds of the institution would be reduced, thereby contributing to an increase in the net interest income and net interest margin.

Falling Interest Rates

Expectation of falling interest rates would produce just the opposite adjustment in the portfolio under an aggressive portfolio management strategy. Management would want to shift to a negative gap position to benefit from the falling rates. The maturity of fixed-rate assets should be lengthened, its dollar amount increased, and the amount of variable-rate assets reduced. Finally, the gap position could be shifted to a negative one by shortening the maturity of liabilities by, for example, replacing CDs with federal funds borrowings.

DEFENSIVE MANAGEMENT

The appropriate gap management under a defensive policy is quite different. As discussed earlier, in contrast to an aggressive policy strategy that seeks to profit from anticipated interest rate movements, a defensive strategy attempts to prevent interest rate movements from reducing the profitability of the financial institution. *An aggressive strategy thus seeks to raise the level of net interest income, whereas a defensive strategy attempts to reduce the volatility of net interest income.*

A defensive strategy attempts to keep the dollar amount of rate-sensitive assets in balance with the amount of rate-sensitive liabilities over a given period, so the dollar gap will be near zero. If successful, increases in interest rates will produce equal increases in interest revenue and interest expense, with the result that net interest income and net interest margin will not change. Similarly, falling interest rates will reduce interest revenue and interest expense by the same amount and leave net interest income and the net margin unchanged if the amounts of rate-sensitive assets and liabilities are balanced.

A defensive strategy is not necessarily a passive one. Many adjustments in the asset and liability portfolio under a defensive strategy are often necessary in order to maintain a zero gap position. For example, suppose that a variable-rate loan was paid off unexpectedly. If the gap was zero prior to the loan payoff, it would be negative afterward. To restore a zero gap, the asset/liability manager would have to add to short-term securities or loans or increase the amount of variable-rate loans. Similarly, assume that there was a large and unexpected inflow of funds into short-term CDs, thereby shifting the portfolio from a zero gap to a negative gap. Again the asset/liability manager would have to make portfolio adjustments even under a defensive strategy.

THREE PROBLEMS WITH DOLLAR GAP MANAGEMENT

Time Horizon

Although widely used in practice, dollar gap management has a number of important deficiencies that have caused its modification and, in some cases, abandonment. The first problem concerns the selection of a time horizon. As discussed earlier, separation of the assets and liabilities of a financial institution into rate-sensitive and non-rate-sensitive ones requires the establishment of a time or planning horizon. Although necessary, the selection of a time horizon causes problems because it ignores the time at which the interest rate-sensitive assets and liabilities reprice within the time period, implicitly assuming that all rate-sensitive assets and liabilities reprice on the same day. As an example of the problems caused by such an implicit assumption, suppose that a financial institution had a zero gap (rate-sensitive assets = rate-sensitive liabilities), that the maturity of the rate-sensitive assets was one day, that the maturity of the rate-sensitive liabilities was 30 days, and that the planning horizon was 30 days. Given these assumptions, interest rate changes clearly would affect the net interest income of the financial institution even though the institution had a zero gap. Increases in interest rates would lead to an immediate repricing of the assets upward, whereas the liabilities would reprice upward only after 30 days. Conversely, decreases in interest rates would be reflected in an immediate decrease on earnings on the assets but would produce a decrease in the cost of funds only with a lag.

One solution to this problem is to divide the portfolio of assets and liabilities into separate subcategories, referred to as maturity buckets, and to manage each maturity bucket separately. With the maturity bucket approach, gap analysis becomes the analysis of multiple gaps. Balance sheet items are grouped into a number of maturity buckets and the gap is computed for each one of these buckets. For example, the gap might be computed for one month, one to three months, three to nine months, and so on. The gap for each maturity bucket is referred to as an incremental gap, and the incremental gaps sum to the total gap. The maturity bucket approach would not fully solve the problem, however, unless the time horizon were shortened to a one-day period. Further, expansion of the number of maturity buckets itself causes problems, because it becomes very difficult to determine the overall interest-sensitivity position of the institution.

Correlation with the Market

A second problem with traditional gap analysis is the implicit assumption that the correlation coefficient between the movement in general market interest rates and in the interest revenue and cost for the portfolio of the financial institution is one; that is, when interest rates in the market rise (or fall) by 10 percent, the interest revenue on rate-sensitive assets and the interest cost for rate-sensitive liabilities will rise (fall) by precisely 10 percent. The estimated change in net interest income from the calculations will occur only if this assumption implicit in the calculation is correct. Yet there are reasons to believe that the assumption is not correct. For example, many variable-rate assets are not truly variable – that is, they do not adjust quickly and fully to changes in market interest rates. Residential real estate loans provide an excellent example of the limitations that often exist in variable-rate loans. Variable-rate loans usually adjust their interest rates only over an extended period, sometimes two or three years after the adjustment in market interest rates, and usually have a limit or ceiling on how far upward they can adjust regardless of the changes in market interest rates. Similar constraints exist for a variety of other types of loans. As a result, it would be unusual for the interest returns on rate-sensitive assets to change at the same time by exactly the amount of the change in the general level of market interest rates.

One method of dealing with the problem of imperfect correlation of interest rates is the use of the *standardized gap*. This measure of the gap adjusts for the different interest rate volatilities of various asset and liability items. It uses historical relationships between market interest rates and the interest rates of the bank's asset and liability items in order to alter the maturity and therefore interest sensitivity of the portfolio items. For example, a variable-rate asset whose interest rate has been shown to be rather insensitive to market interest rate movements might be considered as a fixed-rate asset for purposes of short-run gap analysis.

The benefits of the standardized gap approach can be illustrated by looking at Figure 5-1. The rate-sensitivity gap shown in that figure is −30 percent (interest-sensitive assets are 20 percent of total assets, whereas interest-sensitive liabilities are 50 percent of total liabilities). If it is assumed that rate-sensitive assets are $200 and rate-sensitive liabilities are $500, then the dollar gap is –$300. This may be referred to as the "naive" gap, because it ignores the correlation between the interest rate changes of the individual assets and of the market. But if the interest-rate-sensitive liabilities are 90-day CDs and the interest-rate-sensitive assets are 30-day commercial paper, they may, and probably will, respond differently to market rate movements. For example, if the CD rate is 105 percent as volatile as the 90-day T-bill, whereas the 30-day commercial paper rate is 30 percent as volatile, then the standardized gap is –$460. This is computed as follows: The standardized volatility of the 90-day CDs is 1.05 × 500 = 525, and the standardized volatility of the commercial paper is 0.30 × 200 = 60. Comparing the standardized assets with the standardized liabilities produces a standardized gap of –$460. As a result, the potential interest rate risk for this bank is considerably greater than would be indicated by the naive gap. An increase in interest rates would produce a much larger fall in net interest margin than the naive gap would indicate.

FIGURE 5-1 RATE-SENSITIVITY GAP

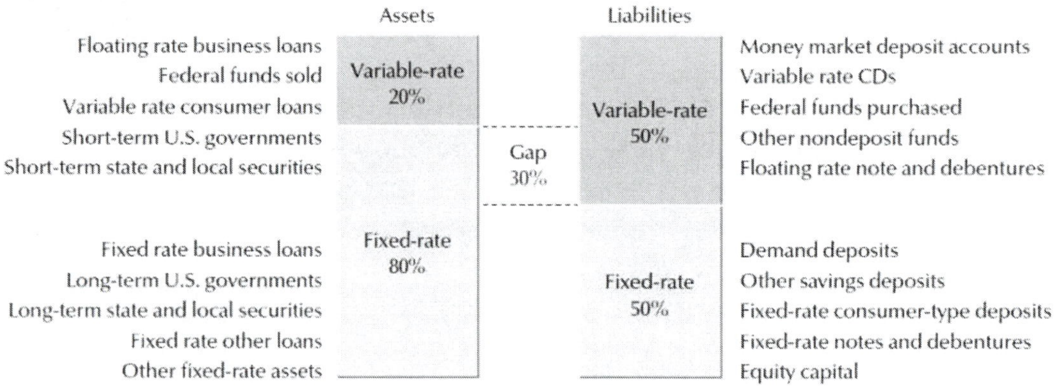

Source: Elijah Brewer, "Bank Gap Management and the Use of Financial Futures," Federal Reserve Bank of Chicago, *Economic Perspectives* (March/April 1985), p. 16.

Focus on Net Interest Income

The final and perhaps the most significant problem with the use of traditional gap analysis is its focus on net interest income rather than shareholder wealth. The asset/liability managers of a financial institution may adjust the portfolio of the institution so that net interest income increases with changes in interest rates, but the value of shareholder wealth may decrease. Aggressive asset/liability management based on predictions of interest rate movements increases the risk of loss. Even if asset/liability management does not "bet the bank" through taking extremely high gap positions (negative or positive) and allows the gap to exceed some desired amount, the attempt to restructure the portfolio still will add some degree of risk to the earnings flow of the financial institution. If successful, aggressive gap management may increase the level of net interest income, but it is also likely to add to the volatility of that income. As a result, aggressive gap management may lessen the value of the institution because of its focus on the wrong goal.

It is possible to take an aggressive position on the balance sheet through positioning of assets and liabilities and yet minimize interest rate risk by using derivatives (such as futures, options, and swaps) to guard against interest rates moving in the wrong direction. However, such techniques have costs and are similar to the costs involved in taking out hazard insurance. Chapter 6 provides insights into these techniques.

Even defensive gap management may produce a decline in shareholder wealth. The main reason would be the possibility that the institution has a zero gap and therefore thought that it was protected from interest rate changes. But, because of the less-than-perfect correlation between asset earnings, liability costs, and general market interest rate movements, it actually was at risk in its net interest income. A more complex but equally valid problem would arise if the dollar amount of rate-sensitive assets equaled the amount of rate-sensitive liabilities, and the amount of non-rate-sensitive assets equaled the amount of non-rate-sensitive liabilities. In that case, even if the interest earnings and costs moved precisely with market interest rate movements, the market value of the institution could drop with rising rates because, despite a constant net interest income, the market value of the assets could fall more than the market value of the liabilities. The market value of the assets would fall more than the market value of the liabilities if the duration of assets exceeded the duration of liabilities. Since ultimately the market value of the equity is equal to the market value of assets less the market value of liabilities, such a policy would lessen the value of the organization to its shareholders.

One final note is important in our discussion of gap analysis. As the use of financial derivatives (such as interest rate swaps, futures, options, floors and caps), and simulation models becomes more widespread, the value of dollar gap report will diminish. More will be said about these other technologies shortly.

DURATION GAP ANALYSIS

The deficiencies of traditional gap analysis, especially the focus on accounting income rather than on equity, have encouraged a search for alternative approaches to measuring and managing the interest rate exposure of a financial institution. One such approach is duration gap analysis. As explained in Managerial Issues: Duration, *duration* is defined as the weighted average *time* (measured in years) to receive all cash flows from a financial instrument. The ***duration gap*** is the difference between the durations of a bank's assets and liabilities.[4] It is a measure of interest rate sensitivity that helps to explain how changes in interest rates affect the market value of a bank's assets and liabilities, and, in turn, its net worth. The net worth is the difference between assets and liabilities (equation 5.7). It follows that changes in the market value of assets and liabilities will change the value of the net worth (equation 5.8). By using duration, we can calculate the theoretical effects of interest rate changes on net worth.

$$NW = A - L \tag{5.7}$$

$$\Delta NW = \Delta A - \Delta L \tag{5.8}$$

where

NW = Net worth

A = Assets

L = Liabilities

Δ = Change in value

A word of caution is in order. The concept of net worth, or value of the equity, as used in the context of duration analysis is not the same as the market value of the firm's outstanding stock. Stock market prices reflect the present value of expected cash flows in the form of dividends. In contrast, duration net worth or duration equity value is the theoretical value of the bank's equity taking into account the market value of its assets and liabilities. Stated otherwise, stock prices reflect future cash flows rather than the market values of balance sheet assets and liabilities.

The actual value of a bank's liabilities cannot be less than the amount owed to its creditors. By way of illustration, suppose that you have a fixed-rate five-year deposit of $1,000 in a bank. Further suppose that interest rates increase from five percent to six percent. Duration theory tells us that the market value of the deposit should decline to, say, $950. While that may be true in theory, the bank's obligation to you is still $1,000. Thus, while the value of marketable liabilities (such as some notes and debentures) may decline when interest rates increase, the value of transaction accounts and other liabilities is insensitive to such changes. For simplicity in the remaining discussion of duration, we will assume that the value of bank liabilities is interest-rate sensitive.

Despite the difference between the theoretical and legal value of some bank liabilities, the duration gap concept provides a valuable guide to bank managers and regulators. The theoretical value of a firm's net worth is one indicator of its solvency. If interest rates increase, and the market value of a bank's assets decline sufficiently, some creditors and regulators may consider it insolvent.

MEASUREMENT OF THE DURATION GAP

The interest-sensitivity position of a financial institution with duration gap analysis may be illustrated with the information in Table 5-5. The financial institution whose balance sheet is shown there has three assets: cash, business loans with a 2.5-year maturity (amortized monthly), and mortgage loans with a 30-year maturity (amortized monthly). On the liability side of the balance sheet, the institution has CDs with two different maturities as well as equity capital. It is assumed that the CDs pay interest only once, at maturity. The interest rate on the loans is assumed to be 13 percent, on deposits 11 percent, and the cash assets are assumed to earn no interest.

The duration of each of the assets and liabilities is also given in Table 5-5. Cash has a zero duration. The durations of both the business loans and the mortgage loans are shorter than their maturities. Except for zero-coupon securities where only a single payment occurs, duration is always less than maturity. The durations of the CDs are the same as their maturities, because they are single-payment liabilities.

Table 5-5: BALANCE SHEET DURATION

Assets	$	Duration (years)	Liabilities	$	Duration (years)
Cash	100	0.00	CD, 1 year	600	1.0
Business loans	400	1.25	CD, 5 year	300	5.0
			Total Liabilities	$900	2.33
Mortgage loans	500	7.00	Equity	100	
	$1,000	4.00		$1,000	

INTEREST RATES, THE DURATION GAP, AND THE VALUE OF EQUITY

Given the preceding information, the duration of the asset portfolio (the weighted duration of the individual assets) is 4.0 years and the duration of the deposits (the weighted duration of the individual types of deposits) is 2.33 years. How will the value of the assets and deposits and theoretical value of the net worth change as interest rates change?

The effect of changing interest rates on the net worth is related to the size of the duration gap, where the duration gap is measured as follows:

$$DGAP = Da - WDL \qquad (5.9)$$

where

DGAP = Duration gap
Da = Average duration of assets
DL = Average duration of liabilities
W = Ratio of total liabilities to total assets

In the example given in Table 5-5, if interest rates were to increase, the value of the net worth would decline. Conversely, if interest rates were to decline, the value of the net worth would increase. For rising interest rates, the value of the assets would drop more than the value of liabilities, and thus the value of the net worth would drop. For falling interest rates, the value of the assets would rise more than the value of the liabilities and the value of the net worth would increase.

The change in the net worth can be determined by measuring the size of the duration gap and by specifying the amount of the change in interest rates. In the preceding example, the duration gap may be determined as follows:

$$DGAP = 4.0 - (.9)(2.33) \tag{5.10}$$
$$= 4.00 - 2.10 = 1.90 \text{ years}$$

Equation (5.11a) gives an approximation for the expected change in the market value of the equity relative to total assets (TA) for a given change in interest rates:

$$\frac{\Delta \text{ Net Worth}}{TA} \cong -DGAP\frac{\Delta i}{1+i} \tag{5.11a}$$

For the dollar amount of the change in net worth, the equation can be rewritten as:

$$\$\,\Delta\text{Net Worth} \cong -DGAP\frac{\Delta i}{1+i}\times TA \tag{5.11b}$$

Suppose that current interest rates are 11 percent and are expected to increase by 100 basis points (1 percentage point), and that the duration gap is as given in equation (5.11a). Then the percentage change in the net worth will be:

$$\%\,\Delta\text{ Net Worth} \cong (-1.90)\left(\frac{1}{1.11}\right) \cong -1.7\%$$

From equation (5.11b), we can determine the dollar amount of the change in equity by multiplying the percentage in net worth by total assets (TA):

$$\$\Delta\text{Net Worth} \cong (-1.90)\left(\frac{1}{1.11}\right)\times TA \cong -1.7\%\times\$1000 = -\$17$$

DEFENSIVE AND AGGRESSIVE DURATION GAP MANAGEMENT

If the duration gap is positive (that is, the duration of assets exceeds the duration of liabilities), then increases in interest rates will reduce the value of net worth, and decreases in interest rates will increase the value of the net worth. Conversely, if the duration gap is negative, with the duration of assets less than the duration of liabilities, rising interest rates will increase the value of the net worth, whereas falling interest rates will lead to a reduction in it. If the institution is immunized from changes in interest rates through a zero duration gap, changes in the values of assets will be exactly offset by changes in the value of liabilities. These relationships are summarized in Table 5-6.

Table 5-6: DURATION GAP, INTEREST RATES, AND CHANGES IN NET WORTH

Duration Gap	Change in Interest Rates	Change in Net Worth
Positive	Increase	Decrease
Positive	Decrease	Increase
Negative	Increase	Increase
Negative	Decrease	Decrease
Zero	Increase	No change
Zero	Decrease	No change

MANAGERIAL ISSUES

MACAULEY DURATION

Duration is a widely accepted measure of a financial instrument's interest rate sensitivity. In its most basic form, *Macaulay duration,* it is a measure of the effective maturity of an instrument. Specifically, duration is the weighted average maturity of an instrument's cash flows, where the present values of the cash flows serve as the weights. The Macaulay duration of an instrument can be calculated by first multiplying the time until the receipt of each cash flow by the ratio of the present value of that cash flow to the instrument's total present value. The sum of these weighted time periods is the Macaulay duration of the instrument. Mathematically,

$$\text{Macaulay duration} = \sum_{t=1}^{n} \frac{PV(CF_t)}{TPV} \times t$$

where

- t = the number of periods remaining until the receipt of cash flow CF_t
- CF_t = the cash flow received in period t
- PV = the present value function $1/(1 + R)^t$, where R is the per-period internal rate of return of the instrument
- TPV= the total present value of all future cash flows (including accrued interest)
- n = the number of periods remaining until maturity.

Because a zero coupon instrument has only one cash flow, its Macaulay duration is equation to its maturity. In contrast, instruments with periodic cash flows, such as coupon bonds and amortizing mortgages, have durations smaller than their maturity.

Duration is measured in units of time, typically years. Relative to the more traditional measure of term to maturity, duration represents a significantly more sophisticated measure of the effective life of a financial instrument. Moreover, when modified to reflect an instrument's discrete compounding of interest, duration measures the instrument's price volatility relative to changes in market yields. Modified duration is calculated as follows:

$$\text{Modified duration} = \frac{\text{Macaulay duration}}{1 + R/c}$$

where R is the per-period internal rate of return of the instrument, and c is the number of times per period that interest is compounded (for example, 2 for a semiannual coupon bond when R is an annual rate).

Modified duration is the price elasticity of an instrument with respect to changes in rates. It represents the percentage change in the present value of a financial instrument for a given percentage point change in market yields; this relationship is defined as follows:

$$\begin{matrix}\text{Percentage} \\ \text{change} \\ \text{in price}\end{matrix} = -\begin{matrix}\text{Modified} \\ \text{duration}\end{matrix} \times \frac{\begin{matrix}\text{Basis point} \\ \text{change in yield}\end{matrix}}{100}$$

For example, with a modified duration of 10, a bond changes 10 percent in price for every 100 basis point change in the market yield of that bond.

In the preceding equation, the inverse relationship between the price of a bond and its market yield is established by the minus sign preceding the term for modified duration. Modified duration acts as a multiplier in translating the effect of changing interest rates on the present value of an instrument: The larger the duration, the greater the effect for a given change in interest rates; and for a given duration, large changes in market rates lead to large percentage changes in price. Therefore, to the extent that the riskiness of an instrument is equated with its price sensitivity, *modified duration acts as a measure of interest rate risk.*

Modified duration provides a standard measure of price sensitivity for different types of instruments. The standardization allows the duration of a portfolio to be calculated as the weighted average of the durations of its individual components. Because a financial institution can be thought of as a portfolio of assets and liabilities, the duration of an institution's net worth is simply a weighted average of the durations of assets and liabilities. Therefore, by weighting assets, liabilities, and off-balance sheet positions by their estimated durations, a single measure of interest rate risk exposure can be derived.

Modified duration is a powerful concept for measuring interest rate risk, but it does have several limitations. The most noteworthy is that the accuracy of duration depends on the assumption of small, instantaneous, parallel shifts in the yield curve. Errors in its use as a measure of interest rate risk increase as actual changes in market yields diverge from these assumptions.

Source: J. Houpt and J. Embersit, "A Method For Evaluating Interest Rate Risk in U. S. Commercial Banks," *Federal Reserve Bulletin* (August 1991), p. 637.

An aggressive interest rate risk management strategy would alter the duration gap in anticipation of changes in interest rates. For example, if interest rates were expected to increase, management would want to shift from a positive to a negative gap position. It could do this by reducing the duration of assets or increasing the duration of liabilities, or both. The expectation of falling interest rates would, of course, produce the opposite type of portfolio management adjustments. Note that the portfolio strategy in response to the expectation of higher interest rates for both duration and dollar gap are similar --more short-term assets and more long-term liabilities. However, such a strategy would produce a positive dollar gap, where the gap is measured as the difference between the dollar amount of interest-sensitive assets and liabilities, and a negative duration gap, where the gap is measured as the difference in the number of years of the duration of assets and liabilities.

Defensive interest rate risk management within this context would seek to keep the duration of assets equal to the duration of liabilities, thereby maintaining a duration gap of zero. As portfolio adjustment occurred at the financial institution because of changes in the demand for loans or in the quantity of CDs, the interest rate risk manager would make adjustments in the duration of assets and liabilities in order to keep the duration gap at or near zero.

PROBLEMS WITH DURATION GAP MANAGEMENT

Although duration gap measurement provides insights that are useful to asset/liability managers, it also has a number of problems. For example, the ***immunization*** or isolation of the market value of equity to interest rate changes will be effective only if interest rates for all maturity securities shift up or down by exactly the same amount (i.e., only if the yield curve moves upward or downward by a constant percentage amount). In fact, yield curves seldom move in this way. In periods of rising interest rates, short-term rates usually move up more than long-term rates; likewise, in periods of falling interest rates short-term interest rates usually fall more than long-term rates. In addition, the earlier discussion of the price changes that occur in the value of a financial asset due to interest rate changes was only an approximation. The relationship between interest rate changes and bond price changes is, in reality, not linear, so that the calculation discussed earlier provides only an approximation of the true relationship for small changes in interest rates. The extent to which bond prices change asymmetrically relative to yield changes is called convexity.[5] Negative yield changes have a greater impact on bond prices than positive yield changes. If the asset and liability have considerably different durations, comparing the effects of interest rate changes on their values may be unwarranted.

Finally, asset/liability managers must deal with the problem of ***duration drift.*** Assume, for example, that a financial institution finances a long-term (seven-year duration) portfolio with a mixture of five- and ten-year duration deposits. After three years the duration of the assets has declined very little, but the duration of the deposits has declined substantially. After four years the duration mismatch is even larger. This happens because maturities were not matched initially even though durations were. This raises the issue of how often you should rebalance the portfolio (annually, quarterly, monthly, etc.) Such rebalancing is costly and would not be undertaken unless there are clearly defined benefits.

SIMULATION AND ASSET/LIABILITY MANAGEMENT

The availability of simulation techniques not only has substantially reduced the mechanical burdens involved in asset/liability management, but also has broadened the scope of possible management techniques. In particular, ***simulated asset/liability management models*** make it possible to evaluate various balance sheet strategies under differing assumptions. Most simulation models require assumptions about the expected changes and levels of interest rates and the shape of the yield curve, pricing strategies for assets and liabilities, and the growth, dollar amounts, and mix of assets and liabilities. Alternative assumptions allow for the creations of various "what if" projections. These projections can include current and expected dollar gaps, duration gaps, balance sheet and income statements, various performance measures (such as net interest margin and return on equity), and complete balance sheet and income statement data.

Many larger banks depend primarily on simulations, and they set limits for their interest rate exposure, and then test those limits. For example, a bank may limit its interest rate exposure to a five percent change in net interest income. Given this limit, it models the balance sheet that will constrain it to that limit when interest rates change by, say, 200 basis points.

In addition, simulation can be used for ***stress testing*** that reveals the effects on income and capital of larger changes in interest rates. Stress testing can be thought of as testing the implications of a worst-case scenario.

Simulation models allow bank management to determine the risk/return trade-offs for different balance sheet strategies. Because of their flexibility in testing different scenarios, they are a superior tool for asset/liability management. They can combine the best features of dollar gap analysis, duration analysis, and other inputs that management wants to consider. Although simulations are used primarily at large banks, their use will spread as the cost of such models declines.

CORRELATIONS AMONG BANK RISKS

The focus of asset/liability management is on interest rate risk. As discussed in Chapter 1, however, bank management is concerned with managing the entire risk profile of the institution, including interest rate risk, credit risk, and other dimensions of risk. If those risks were unrelated (that is, uncorrelated), then management could concentrate on one type of risk, making appropriate decisions, and ignoring the effects of those decisions on the other types of risk. However, there do appear to be considerable interrelationships between the different types of risk, with a particularly significant connection between interest rate and credit risk, especially if commercial banks use their loan portfolio as the principal vehicle to adjust their interest rate risk exposure.

CREDIT RISK

A simple example may best illustrate the relationship between interest rate risk and credit risk. Suppose, for example, that asset/liability management strategy concludes that the bank should increase its emphasis on variable-rate loans. Suppose also that interest rates increase dramatically after a large number of these loans have been made. Rising interest rates lead to higher payments for borrowers, especially if the loans are long-term, such as home mortgages and some automobile loans. The heavier cash outflows burden might reasonably be expected to produce a greater number of defaults in the bank's loan portfolio. A similar situation would result if asset/liability strategy increased the emphasis on fixed-rate loans and interest rates fell dramatically. Unless borrowers were able to refinance these loans at acceptable costs, the incidence of defaults would be likely to increase substantially. And even if refinancing were easy enough to reduce the default rate, the bank would still find its asset/liability management strategy thwarted because assets that were considered fixed rate would in fact be rate sensitive.

LIQUIDITY

Interest rate risk management focuses on the effects of alternative portfolio strategies on the net interest margin (or some other goal) of the bank. Interest rate risk and liquidity risk are different, although closely related, types of risk. Liquidity management focuses on the effects of alternative portfolio strategies on the bank's ability to meet its cash obligation to depositors and borrowers. The two are in fact inextricably intertwined. A few examples may assist in understanding the relationship.

Suppose the bank management decides to pursue a liability-sensitive position; that is, to have more interest-sensitive liabilities than assets. This interest rate management strategy necessarily reduces the liquidity position of the bank. More liabilities are coming due in a shorter period, which creates potential funds strains, and fewer short-term highly liquid assets are available to meet those funding needs. Under most circumstances, this mismatch would not be a problem. However, if there is concern about the bank's ability to meet its obligations, a severe funding problem could exist as the liabilities matured.

As another example, suppose that bank management structured its balance sheet in order to achieve a positive duration gap -- the duration of assets exceeds the duration of liabilities. In that case, the ability to realize liquidity from the assets of the bank is reduced. Long-duration assets will decline more than short-duration assets if interest rates increase. In that case, the sale of assets to raise funds, although still possible, will cause severe losses -- losses that management probably would seek to avoid.

The coordination of interest rate risk and liquidity management is complex, but it is obvious also that they are too interrelated to be managed independently.

SUMMARY

Asset/liability management refers to short-run balance sheet management designed to achieve near-term financial goals. The focus of asset/liability management in connection with the dollar gap is on net interest income, defined as the difference between total interest income and total dollar interest expense. Expressed in relative terms, the focus is on net interest margin, where net interest income is divided by earning assets. Active and aggressive asset/liability management is a relatively recent phenomenon and reflects the increase in volatility of interest rates, the elimination of interest rate ceilings on deposits, and the growth of purchased money (as opposed to "core" deposits.)

Net interest income is affected by the interest rates earned on assets and paid on liabilities, by the dollar amount of assets and liabilities, and by the earnings mix of assets and liabilities. Changes in net interest income (and margin) from one period to the next may be partitioned into those caused by interest rate changes, those caused by changes in the amount of funds, and those caused by changes in the mix of assets and liabilities. Asset/liabilities management generally focuses on the effects of interest rate changes on net interest income.

The most commonly used measure of a bank's interest sensitivity position is its dollar gap, defined as the difference between the dollar amount of interest-sensitive assets and interest-sensitive liabilities. Interest-sensitive assets and liabilities are those whose interest earnings or costs change with the general movement of interest rates within some planning horizon. The focus of this analysis is on the profitability and costs of assets and liabilities rather than on the value of those assets and liabilities. If a bank has more interest-sensitive assets than liabilities, it is said to be asset sensitive and will usually experience an increase in net interest income as interest rates rise (and a decrease in net interest income as interest rates fall). If a bank has more interest-sensitive liabilities than interest-sensitive assets, it is said to be liability sensitive, and will usually experience a decline in net interest income when interest rates increase (and an increase in net interest income when interest rates fall). The gap may be calculated for a variety of time periods and subperiods, resulting in both incremental and cumulative gap.

Bank management may adopt a defensive or an aggressive strategy in managing interest rate risk. With a defensive strategy, the goal is to insulate the net interest margin (or some other measure of bank performance) from fluctuations in interest rates; whereas with an aggressive strategy the goal is to increase the size of the net interest margin (or some other measure of bank performance) by predicting interest rate changes and restructuring the portfolio to benefit from such changes.

If the focus of interest rate risk management were on net interest margin, a defensive strategy would seek to balance the amount of interest-rate-sensitive assets and interest-rate-sensitive liabilities. Properly done, interest revenues and interest expenses would rise and fall together with changing interest rates, so that net interest margin would remain unchanged under this dollar gap strategy. With an aggressive dollar gap program, management would establish a positive gap (rate-sensitive assets greater than rate-sensitive liabilities) when interest rates were expected to rise and a negative gap when interest rates were expected to fall. If the interest rate forecast was correct, the bank would benefit through a higher net interest margin. Of course, if the interest rate forecast was incorrect, the net interest margin would be reduced.

Although widely used, the dollar gap approach has a number of limitations, including the difficulty in selecting a single, appropriate time horizon; the implicit assumption that interest revenue and costs on rate-sensitive assets and liabilities are perfectly correlated with general interest rate movements; and the myopic focus on net interest margin rather than the goal of maximizing shareholder wealth. Such a limited focus may produce portfolio strategies that increase profitability but at the cost of reducing the market value of the equity.

The deficiencies of traditional dollar gap analysis have given rise to an alternative approach that focuses on the market value of the assets, liabilities, and equity of the bank. This is the case with duration gap analysis. The duration of assets is compared with the duration of liabilities. A defensive duration gap management would balance the duration of assets and liabilities, so that the net worth (although not necessarily the profitability of the bank) would not be affected by interest rate changes. With an aggressive strategy, management would establish a negative duration (duration of assets shorter than the duration of liabilities) if interest rates were expected to increase and a positive duration if interest rates were expected to fall.

Both dollar gap and duration gap management have one important similarity that causes problems for asset/liability managers: The adjustments that are required to achieve the appropriate dollar gap or duration gap involve changes in the balance sheet of the bank. Such on-balance sheet adjustments are often difficult or impossible to achieve. For example, appropriate asset/liability management policy may involve concentrating on floating-rate loans in the expectation of rising interest rates. Yet the bank's customers may not want floating-rate loans, especially if they share the view that interest rates will rise. Similarly, assume that asset/liability management strategy calls for the sale of five-year CDs in anticipation of rising interest rates. It may be that there simply is no market for CDs that long (customers may not be willing to commit funds to CDs for longer than three years).

Banks are increasingly using simulation models that allow them to examine alternative interest rate scenarios, and to stress-test their portfolios.

An increasing number of banks, especially larger banks, are dealing with interest rate risk by making their adjustments off-balance sheet through futures, options, and swaps. At the extreme, a bank may let its customers entirely drive its balance sheet --for example, if customers want fixed-rate loans, they get fixed-rate loans; if they want floating-rate loans, they get floating-rate loans. This policy will almost invariably lead to excessive interest rate risk in the balance sheet. But this risk can be offset by taking an appropriate position off-balance sheet through derivatives such as futures, options, and swaps so that the total risk position of the institution (on-balance sheet plus off-balance sheet) is appropriate. The use of these off-balance sheet, derivative financial instruments is the topic of the next chapter.

KEY TERMS AND CONCEPTS

Aggressive/defensive asset liability management
Asset/liability management (ALM)
Core deposits
Cumulative gap
Dollar gap
Duration drift
Duration gap
Federal Home Loan Bank
Gap analysis
Immunization
Interest rate futures contract
Interest rate swap contract
Maturity buckets
Nonrate-sensitive asset/liabilities
Rate-sensitive asset/liabilities
Relative gap ratio
Simulated asset liability models
Stress testing

QUESTIONS

5.1 What is asset/liability management?

5.2 What is the difference between defensive and aggressive asset/liability management?

5.3 Why is it advantageous for banks to accept some amount of interest rate risk? How much interest rate risk should a bank take?

5.4 What kind of aggressive gap management would be appropriate if interest rates are expected to fall?

5.5 Briefly explain the influence of rate, dollar amount, and mix on net interest income.

5.6 Distinguish between the incremental gap and the cumulative gap. Why is this distinction important?

5.7 How would an increase (decrease) in interest rates affect a bank with a positive dollar gap? Negative dollar gap?

5.8 If a bank has a positive duration gap and interest rates rise, what will happen to bank equity? Explain your answer.

5.9 What is immunization in the context of bank gap management?

5.10 What assumptions are made using duration gap analysis?

5.11 How should a bank change its dollar gap as the yield curve changes?

5.12 What is simulated asset/liability management? What benefit is it to a bank?

5.13 How is interest rate risk linked to liquidity risk? Give an example.

5.14 Explain your position on the following statement: Precise identification of the repricing characteristics of each of the assets and liabilities of a bank is possible.

5.15 The ALM committee of your bank is concerned about the recent trends in the secondary market for CDs. Using monthly, weekly, and daily data from the Federal Reserve Statistical Release H.15, Selected Interest Rates (available at www.federalreserve.gov/releases), explain what has been happening to interest rates.

PROBLEMS

5.1 Given the following information:

Assets	$	Rate	Liabilities & Equity	$	Rate
Rate-sensitive	$3,000	10.0%	Rate-sensitive	$2,000	8.0%
Non-rate-sensitive	1,500	9.0	Non-rate-sensitive	2,000	7.0
Nonearning	500		Equity	1,000	
	$5,000			$5,000	

(a) Calculate the expected net interest income at current interest rates, assuming no change in the composition of the portfolio. What is the net interest margin?

(b) Assuming that all interest rates rise by one percent, calculate the new expected net interest income and net interest margin.

5.2 Given the following information:

ABC National Bank (in Millions)

Assets			Liabilities and Equity		
Rate-sensitive	$200	(12%)	Rate-sensitive	$300	(6%)
Non-rate-sensitive	400	(11%)	Non-rate-sensitive	300	(5%)
Nonearning	100		Equity	100	
Total Assets	$700		Total Liabilities and Equity	$700	

(a) What is the gap? Net interest income? Net interest margin? How much will net interest income change if interest rates fall by 200 basis points?

(b) What changes in portfolio composition would you recommend to management if you expected interest rates to increase. Be specific.

5.3 The ALCO has obtained the following information on the interest rate sensitivity of your bank:

		Amount	Rate
90 day	Interest-rate-sensitive assets	$80,000	8.0%
90 day	Interest-rate-sensitive liabilities	$120,000	6.0%

The consensus of forecasting is for interest rates to increase by 50 basis points during the ninety days. But a significant minority of forecasters expects rates to fall by 50 basis points.

(a) How could the bank eliminate its interest rate risk?

(b) What could happen to net interest income if the minority forecast turned out to be the correct one?

5.4 A bank recently purchased at par a $1 million issue of U.S. Treasury bonds. The bond has a duration of three years and pays six percent annual interest. How much would the bond's price change if interest rates fell from six percent to five percent? If interest rates rose from six percent to seven percent? What would your answers be if the duration of the bond was six years?

5.5 Calculate the duration gap of the following bank.

Assets	Amount	%	Duration (Years)	Liabs and Equity	Amount	%	Duration (Years)
Cash	$1000			Deposits	$3,000	4.0	0.5
U.S. gov't secs	2000	4.0	5.0	CDs	9,000	6.0	4.0
Loans	10,000	8.0	4.0	Equity	1,000		
	$13,000				$13,000		

Calculate the percentage and dollar change in the value of equity if all interest rates increase by 200 basis points. How could the bank protect itself from this anticipated interest rate change?

5.6 Assume that the ABC National Bank has the following structure of assets and liabilities:

Assets		Liabilities	
Floating-rate business loans	$250	Variable-rate liabilities (floating-rate CD and money market deposit accounts)	
Federal funds sold	50	Market deposit accounts	$200
Fixed-rate loans and investments	700	Federal funds purchased	200
		Fixed-rate liabilities	500
		Equity	100
Total assets	$1,000	Total liabilities and equity	$1,000

(a) What is the dollar or maturity gap of the bank?

(b) Assuming that floating-rate business loans are 20 percent as volatile as treasury bills, that federal funds are 200 percent as volatile as treasury bills, and that variable-rate liabilities other than federal funds purchased are 10 percent as volatile as treasury bills, what is the standardized gap?

(c) Does the standardized gap suggest a different conclusion about interest rate risk?

5.7 If a bank has a duration gap of 4.0 years, and interest rates increase from six percent to eight percent, what is the change in the dollar value of equity (assume that assets are $1 billion)?

5-8 As a management trainee assigned to the bank's asset/liability management committee, you have been asked to calculate the duration of each of the following loans:

(a) $20,000 principal, $4,500 payments per year for five years

(b) $20,000 principal, $4,200 payments per year for five years

Assume that the bank's current required return on these types of loans is eight percent.

5.9 The balance sheet of Capital Bank appears as follows:

Assets		Liabilities and Maturities	
Short-term securities and adjustable-rate loans Duration: 6 months	$220	Short-term and floating-rate funds Duration: 6 months	$560
Fixed-rate loans Duration: 8 years	700	Fixed-rate funds Duration: 30 months	270
Nonearning Assets	80	Equity	170
Total assets	$1,000	Total liabilities and net worth	$1000

(a) Calculate the duration of this balance sheet.

(b) Assuming that the required rate of return is eight percent, what would be the effect on the bank's net worth if interest rates increased by one percent?

(c) Suppose that the expected change in net worth is unacceptable to management. What could management do to reduce this change?

5.10 Consider the following bank balance sheet:

Assets		**Liabilities**	
3-year Treasury bond	$275	1-year CD	$155
10-year municipal bond	185	5-year note	$180

Assume that the three-year Treasury bond yields six percent, the ten-year municipal bond yields four percent, the one-year CD pays 4.5 percent, and the five-year note pays six percent. Assume that all instruments have annual coupon payments.

(a) What is the weighted average maturity of the assets? Liabilities?

(b) Assuming a one-year time horizon, what is the dollar gap?

(c) What is the interest rate risk exposure of the bank?

(d) Calculate the value of all four securities on the bank's balance sheet if interest rates increase by two percent. What is the effect on the value of the equity of the bank?

5.11 A bank issues a $1 million one-year note paying six percent annually in order to make a $1 million corporate loan paying eight percent annually.

(a) What is the dollar gap (assume a one-year time horizon)? What is the interest rate risk exposure of the bank?

(b) Immediately after the transaction, interest rates increase by two percent. What is the effect on the asset and liability cash flows? On net interest income?

(c) What does your answer to (b) imply about your answer to (a)?

ENDNOTES

1. *FDIC Quarterly: Quarterly Banking Profile*, FDIC.

2. Which way are interest rates going? Each Federal Reserve Bank gathers anecdotal information on current economic conditions in its district through reports from bank and branch directors and interviews with key business contacts, economists, market experts, and other sources. The Beige Book summarizes this information. See http://www.federalreserve.gov/monetarypolicy/beigebook/

3. See www.stls.frb.org/publications/index.html#data for trends in interest rates. Links to many sources of data and information on banking, finance, and economics are available also.

4. For further details about duration and its applications, see Gerald O. Bierwag, *Duration Analysis: Managing Interest Rate Risk* (Cambridge, MA: Ballinger, 1987).

5. For a concise discussion of duration, immunization, and convexity, see William F. Sharpe, Gordon J. Alexander, and Jeffry V. Bailey, *Investments*, 6th ed. (Upper Saddle River, N.J.: Prentice Hall, 1999), Chapter 16.

Chapter 6

Techniques of Asset/Liability Management: Futures, Options, and Swaps

After reading this chapter, you will be able to:

- Describe the nature of interest rate futures, options, and swaps
- Discuss the ways in which a bank can use interest rate futures, options, and swaps as a means to hedge against interest rate risk
- Compare the advantages and disadvantages of interest rate futures, options, and swaps in managing interest rate risk

This chapter concentrates on three techniques used by banks (and other financial institutions) to manage interest rate risk: futures, options, and swaps. Although recent in development and application, they have enjoyed explosive growth and have become relatively common risk management tools. Frequently used in defensive asset/liability management, these techniques can also be used in a more aggressive mode. The chapter discusses each technique separately and then compares and evaluates them as alternative devices for managing interest rate risk.

Banks can deal with interest rate risk either by reducing that risk through dollar and duration gap management of the balance sheet, as discussed in Chapter 5, or by transferring risk to another party. Buying insurance is one device used by individuals, nonfinancial businesses, and banks for transferring risk. Another more commonly used method of transferring risk in interest rate risk management is the use of derivative securities. These securities derive their characteristics from previously existing securities. This chapter focuses on three types of derivatives -- futures, options, and swaps -- and how they can be used to hedge (that is, transfer) interest rate risk and other risks.

FINANCIAL FUTURES

USING FINANCIAL FUTURES MARKETS TO MANAGE INTEREST RATE RISK

The adjustments to a bank's portfolio that were discussed in the previous chapter -- changing the dollar gap and/or the duration gap -- involve alterations in the current cash (i.e., spot) market positions in the portfolio of assets and liabilities.

Equivalent adjustments in the interest sensitivity position of the bank can be achieved through transactions in the futures markets. These transactions, in effect, create new or synthetic assets and liabilities with interest sensitivity positions different from those that are currently held in the portfolio.

NATURE OF FUTURES CONTRACTS

A ***futures contract*** is a standardized agreement to buy or sell a specified quantity of a financial instrument on a specified future date at a set price. The buyer of a futures contract agrees to take delivery at a future date of the specified quantity of the financial instrument at today's determined price, whereas the seller agrees to make delivery of that quantity of the financial instrument on the future date at today's established price. The buyer is said to have established a ***long position*** in the futures market and will benefit if the price of the contract rises. The seller is said to have established a ***short position*** in the futures market and will benefit if the price of the contract falls. The futures market transaction may be contrasted with a cash or spot market transaction. In the futures markets, pricing and delivery occur at different times -- pricing occurs today, and delivery (if it takes place) occurs at some point in the future. In the cash or spot market, pricing and delivery occur at the same time.

Futures contracts are traded in a number of organized exchanges, with most U.S. activity occurring in Chicago (i.e., CME Group and Chicago Board Options Exchange, or CBOE) in addition to New York. Growing markets in Europe (such as Eurex, a German-Swiss electronic exchange, and the London International Financial Futures and Options Exchange, or LIFFE, which is now part of Intercontinental Exchange group that also owns NYSE Euronext) have also become significant.[1] Trading involves a large number of different types of short- and long-term financing instruments, including Treasury bills, notes, and bonds; municipal bonds (munis); Eurodollar time deposits; 30-day federal funds; and one-month LIBOR contracts (or London Interbank Offered Rate, a lending rate between banks). In each case, the contract traded specifies the precise nature of the financial instrument to be delivered at the maturity of the contract. For example, the Treasury bill futures contract traded on the CME is for a $1 million par value of U.S. Treasury bills with 90 days to maturity.

Although futures contracts differ somewhat by type of financial instrument traded and also by exchange, all futures contracts have the following characteristics in common. First, the contracts are for a specified, standardized amount of a financial instrument, with other identical features, such as the date of delivery. Because the contracts are identical, they are easily traded among market participants at low transaction costs.

Second, the ***exchange clearinghouse*** is a counterpart to each contract. Once a futures contract is traded the exchange clearinghouse steps in. The buyer and seller never need to have any relationship with each other. Rather, their relationship is with the exchange clearinghouse. By this device, the risk of default on the contract is minimized. Third, the contracts can be bought and sold with only a small commitment of funds relative to the market value of the contract itself. This commitment of funds is known as the ***margin***. The margin is actually a performance bond that guarantees the buyer and seller of the contract will fulfill their commitments. The fact that the margin is a small fraction of the contract value creates great "leverage," thereby magnifying the potential gain or loss from a futures market transaction. An *initial margin* must be posted to enter into a contract, and a *maintenance margin* is needed as a minimum balance in the margin account. If losses on a contract cause a customer's balance to fall below the maintenance margin, a *margin call* is made by the exchange on the customer to pay funds to replenish the margin account.

Fourth, futures contracts are ***marked-to-market*** each day; that is, market participants must recognize any gains or losses on their outstanding futures positions at the end of each day. Gains are added to the margin balance of traders each day and losses are subtracted from the margin balance each day. If the margin balance falls below the exchange-mandated minimum, the trader will be required to add funds to the margin account.

EXAMPLE OF A FUTURES TRANSACTION

Table 6-1 (next page) provides an example of a simple futures market transaction. It assumes that the trader buys, on October 2, 2015, one December 2015 Treasury bill futures contract at a price of $94.83, or discount yield of 5.17 (100 – 94.83). The trader is now obligated to take delivery of (buy) a $1 million (face value)

13-week bill on the maturity date of the contract in December. On the date of the transaction (October 2, 2015), the buyer pays a commission and deposits the necessary margin. The buyer will gain if the price of the contract rises (i.e., interest rates fall) but will lose if the price of the contract falls (i.e., interest rates rise).

What would happen if the discount rate on Treasury bills rises two basis points immediately after the purchase of the futures contract? Because each basis point is equivalent to $25 on the value of the contract, the buyer loses $50 on the investment. With the practice of marking each contract to market daily, the buyer's margin account value will be reduced by $50 at the end of the day (and the seller's margin account value will increase by $50). Marking to market will occur as long as the buyer holds the contract or until final maturity of the contract, whichever comes first.

Table 6-1: EXAMPLE OF A TREASURY BILL FUTURES TRANSACTION

Suppose that on October 2, 2015, a trader buys one December 2015 Treasury bill futures contract at the opening price of $94.83. Once the transaction is complete the trader is contractually obligated to buy a $1 million (face value) 13-week Treasury bill yielding 100 – 94.83 = 5.17% on a discount basis on the contract delivery date in late December 2010. At the time of the initial transaction, however, the trader pays only a commission and deposits the required margin with a broker.

Effects of Price Changes

Suppose that the final index prices fell two basis points during that day's trading session, meaning that the discount rate on bills for future delivery rose after the contract was purchased. Since each one basis point change in the T-bill index is worth $25 dollars, the trader would lose $50 if he or she were to sell the contract at the closing price.

The practice of marking futures contracts to market at the end of each trading session means that the trader is forced to realize this loss even though the bill is not sold; thus, $50 is subtracted from the margin account. That money is then transferred to a seller's margin account.

Final Settlement

The contract is marked to market one last time at the close of the last day of trading. The final settlement or purchase price implied by the IMM index value is determined as follows:

First calculate the total discount from the face value, $1 million, of the bill using the formula

$$\text{Discount} = \text{Days to maturity} \times \frac{[(100 - \text{Index}) \times 0.01] \times \$1{,}000{,}000}{360}$$

where [(100 – Index) × 0.01] is the future discount yield expressed as a fraction. Second, calculate the purchase price by subtracting the total discount from the face value of the deliverable bill. Note that this is essentially the same procedure used to calculate the purchase price of a bill from the quoted discount yield in the spot market rate.

Suppose that the futures price is $94.81. Then the settlement price for the first delivery day is

$$\frac{\$986{,}880.83 = \$1{,}000{,}000 - 91 \times 0.0519 \times \$1{,}000{,}000}{360}$$

This calculation assumes that the deliverable bill will have exactly 91 days to maturity, which will always be the case on the first contract delivery day except in special cases when a bill would otherwise mature on a national holiday.

Because buying a futures contract during the last trading session is essentially equivalent to buying a Treasury bill in the spot market, futures prices tend to converge to the spot market price of the deliverable security on the final day of trading in a futures contract. Thus, the final futures discount yield should differ little, if at all, from the spot market discount yield at the end of the final trading day.

The settlement price at maturity can be determined by the formula given in Figure 6-1. If the final index price is \$94.81, then the settlement price is \$986,880.83 per \$1 million contracts. In most cases, however, contracts are closed prior to the delivery date (that is, the buyer would offset the long position by selling the identical contract), with the result that no delivery actually occurs. In fact, delivery of the underlying financial instrument seldom occurs in most futures market transactions. [2]

TECHNIQUES IN USING FINANCIAL FUTURES

Although futures might be used both to speculate on future interest rate movements and to hedge against interest rate risk, regulatory policies limit bank use of the futures market to a hedging role. A few examples can help in understanding the ways in which banks can use the futures markets.

USING INTEREST RATE FUTURES TO HEDGE A DOLLAR GAP POSITION

A long, or buy, hedge can be used to protect the bank against falling interest rates. As an example, suppose that the bank has a positive dollar gap -- that is, it has more interest-sensitive assets than liabilities. If interest rates increased, the bank would benefit through higher net interest margins. If interest rates fell, however, the bank's net interest margin would deteriorate. In short, the bank is exposed to interest rate risk. The bank could reduce this interest rate risk by transactions in the spot or cash market such as reducing the interest sensitivity of assets. As an alternative, the bank could engage in a ***long hedge*** by purchasing one or more T-bill contracts for future delivery. In that case, if interest rates fell, the reduction in the net interest margin would be offset by the gain on the long hedge in the futures market. Of course, if interest rates increased, the gain in the net interest margin would be offset by the loss on the futures transaction.

A bank can also adjust its interest sensitivity position through the sale of futures contracts (a ***short hedge***). A short hedge can be used to reduce the interest rate risk associated with a negative dollar gap. If interest rates increased, the unhedged bank would suffer a reduction in its net interest margins. With a short hedge position, however, the bank would experience a gain from the futures hedge that would offset the reduction in the net interest margin. Of course, if interest rates fell, the increased net interest margin would be offset by the loss on the futures contracts.

The number of contracts to be bought (long hedge) to hedge an asset-sensitive position or sold (short hedge) to hedge a liability-sensitive position can be calculated using equation (6.1):

$$\text{Number of contracts} = \left[\frac{V}{F} x \frac{M_C}{M_F}\right] b \tag{6.1}$$

where V is the value of the cash flow to be hedged, F is the face value of the futures contract, MC is the maturity of the anticipated cash asset, MF is the maturity of the futures contract, and b is the ratio of variability of the cash market to the variability of the futures market.

Suppose that a bank wishes to use T-bill futures to hedge a $48 million positive dollar gap over the next six months. The number of futures contracts to be purchased would be (assuming a correlation coefficient of 1):

Number of contracts = (48/1 × 6 months/3 months) (1) = 96 contracts

Balance Sheet Hedging Example

To illustrate the use of financial futures in hedging the dollar gap, we next consider the problem of a bank with a negative dollar gap facing an expected increase in interest rates in the near future. Assume that bank has assets comprised of only one-year loans earning 10 percent and liabilities comprised of only 90-day CDs paying six percent. If interest rates do not change, the following cash inflows and outflows during the next year would occur:

Day	0	90	180	270	360
Loans:					
Inflows	$909.09				
Outflows					$1,000.00
CDs:					
Inflow	$909.09	$922.43	$935.98	$949.71	
Outflows		$922.43	$935.98	$949.71	$ 963.65
Net cash flows	0	0	0	0	$ 36.35

Notice that for loans $1,000/(1.10) = $909.09. Also notice that CDs are rolled over every 90 days at the constant interest rate of six percent [e.g., $909.09 (1.06)0.25, where 0.25 = 90 days/360 days]. Of course, the negative dollar gap of the bank exposes it to the risk that interest rates will rise and CDs will have to be rolled over at higher rates. As a hedge against this possibility, the bank may sell 90-day financial futures with a par of $1,000. To simplify matters, we will assume that only one T-bill futures contract is needed. In this situation the following entries on its balance sheet would occur over time.

Day	0	90	180	270	360
T-bill futures (sold)					
Receipts		$985.54	$985.54	$985.54	
T-bill (spot market purchase)					
Payments		$985.54	$985.54	$985.54	
Net cash flows		0	0	0	

It is assumed here that the T-bills pay six percent and interest rates will not change (i.e., $\$1,000/(1.06)^{0.25} = \$985.54$).

If interest rates increase by two percent in the next year (after the initial issue of CDs), the bank's net cash flows will be affected as follows:

Day	0	90	180	270	360
Loans:					
Inflows					$1,000.00
Outflows	$909.09				
CDs:					
Inflow	$909.09	$922.43	$940.35	$958.62	
Outflows		$922.43	$940.35	$958.62	$ 977.24
Net cash flows	0	0	0	0	$ 22.76

Thus, the net cash flows would decline by \$13.59. In terms of present value, this loss equals \$13.59/1.10 = \$12.35.

We next show the effect of this interest rate increase on net cash flows from the short T-bill futures position:

Day	0	90	180	270	360
T-bill futures (sold)					
Receipts		$985.54	$985.54	$985.54	
T-bill (spot market purchase)					
Payments		$980.94	$980.94	$980.94	
Net cash flows		$ 4.60	$ 4.60	$ 4.60	

The total gain in net cash flows is \$13.80. In present value terms, this equals $4.60/(1.10)^{.25} + 4.60/(1.10)^{.50} + 4.60/(1.10)^{.75} = \$13.16$. Thus, the gain on T-bill futures exceeds the loss on spot bank loans and CDs. As a check on your understanding, work the case problem entitled "Hedging the Balance Sheet" at the end of the chapter.

USING INTEREST RATE FUTURES TO HEDGE A DURATION GAP

Interest rate futures can also be used to hedge a mismatch in the duration of a bank's assets and liabilities. For example, suppose that the bank has a negative duration gap (the duration of assets is less than the duration of liabilities). In that case, the bank could extend the duration of its assets or reduce the duration of its liabilities, thereby reducing the duration gap. As an alternative, it could establish a long position in the financial futures market. Similarly, if the bank had a positive duration gap, it could either reduce the duration of assets, increase the duration of liabilities, or execute a short or sell position in financial futures.

Suppose the bank's portfolio appears as in Table 6-1 (next page). It is assumed that the assets are single-payment loans repayable in 90, 180, 270, and 366 days and are rolled over for 360, 270, 180, and 90 days, respectively. The loan portfolio is financed with a 90-day CD at 10 percent, providing the bank, initially, with a two-percentage-point spread (the loans carry an interest rate of 12 percent).

The present value of the loan portfolio (the total value of the loans portfolio) is \$3,221.50 [$= \$500/(1.12)^{.25} + \$600/(1.12)^{.50} + \$1{,}000/(1.12)^{.75} + \$1{,}400/(1.12)$]. To finance the loan portfolio, the bank borrows \$3,221.50 in 90-day CDs at 10 percent. This is the present value of the amount that the bank will owe in 90 days: $\$3{,}299.18 = 3{,}221.50\,(1.10)^{.25}$.

TABLE 6-1 INTEREST-SENSITIVE ASSETS AND LIABILITIES

Days	Assets	Liabilities
90	$ 500	$3,299.18
180	600	
270	1,000	
360	1,400	

Source: Elijah Brewer, "Bank Gap Management and the Use of Financial Futures," Federal Reserve Bank of Chicago, *Economic Perspectives* (March/April 1985), p. 19.

The bank bears considerable interest rate risk in this example. The duration of its assets is considerably longer than the duration of its liabilities. The duration of the loan portfolio is 0.73 years, whereas the duration of the liabilities is 0.25 years. The bank has a positive duration gap. An increase in interest rates will reduce the value of the equity of the bank. To manage this risk the bank can reduce or eliminate its positive duration gap by implementing a short hedge. Financial futures should be sold until the duration of the assets falls to 0.25, at which point the bank is perfectly hedged.

The duration of a portfolio containing both cash or spot market assets and futures contracts can be calculated with equation (6.2):

$$D_p = D_{rsa} + \frac{N_f FP}{V_{rsa}} \quad 6.2$$

where D_p = duration of the entire portfolio, D_{rsa} = duration of the rate-sensitive assets, D_f = duration of the deliverable securities involved in the hypothetical futures contract from the delivery date, N_f = number of futures contracts, FP = future price, and V_{rsa} = market value of the rate-sensitive assets.

The goal is to reduce the duration of the assets to 0.25 years. With this goal in mind, the bank should sell 64 T-bill futures contracts, assuming that T-bills are yielding 12 percent (such that their price is $\$100/(1.12)^{.25}$). In that case, the number of T-bill futures contracts to be sold is calculated as:

$$0.25 = 0.73 + .25\frac{N_f \$97.21}{\$3,221.50} \quad 6.3$$

$$N_f = -64$$

STEPS INVOLVED IN HEDGING

Seven steps are involved in hedging the interest-sensitivity position of a bank with respect to its dollar gap or duration gap. In summary, these seven steps are:

1. Determine the total interest rate risk either on or off the balance sheet.
2. Select a futures contract. The futures contract selected should be the one most highly correlated with the cash market instrument being hedged. Normally, this would be the same instrument. If the cash market instrument does not have a futures market equivalent, then the bank executes a cross hedge (a hedge using a futures contract in an asset with the highest correlation with the spot market asset).
3. Determine the number of contracts needed. This step takes into account the less-than-perfect correlation that might exist between the cash market instrument and the futures market instrument.
4. Determine the maturity of the hedge.
5. Place the hedge.
6. Monitor the hedge.
7. Lift the hedge.

PERFECT AND IMPERFECT FUTURES SHORT HEDGES

Although it normally does not take place, the following example shows a "perfect hedge" with financial futures contracts (assuming margin and brokerage costs are not considered). In this example the securities firm has agreed in June to purchase long-term municipal bonds (munis) at a fixed yield in October issued by a local city. The securities firm plans to immediately sell these securities into the financial marketplace. If interest rates rise between the commitment and sale dates, the firm will incur a loss of principal value on the munis. The derivatives strategy is to use a short hedge to offset this potential loss and enable a profitable sale of munis bonds in October. Of course, if interest rates fall, the firm forgoes the gain in munis' principal value because the futures position would have an offsetting loss. The fact that the firm's profits are not influenced by changes in interest rates is indicative of a true hedge.

Month	Cash Market	Futures Market
June	Securities firm makes a commitment to purchase \$1 million of munis bonds yielding 8.59% (based on current munis' cash price at $98^{28}/32$) for \$988,750.	Sells 10 December munis bond index futures at $96^{8}/32$ for \$962,500.
October	Securities firm purchases and then sells \$1 million of munis bonds to investors at a price of $95^{20}/32$ for \$956,250.	Buys 10 December munis bond index futures at 93, or \$930,000, to yield 8.95%.
	Loss: (\$32,500)	Gain: \$32,500

Now consider an imperfect short futures hedge for a securities dealer. The dealer holds long cash positions in a bond trading account. The maintenance of these bonds implies that a rise in interest rates will reduce their price. Suppose that the dealer owns corporate bonds purchased on October 4 and then sells an equal amount of Treasury bond futures contracts maturing in March of the following year. The following results of the short hedge are obtained:

Date	Cash Market	Futures Market
October/Year X	Purchase $5 million corporate bonds maturing August 2005, 8% coupon at $87^{10}/_{32}$:	Sell $5 million T-bonds futures contracts at $86^{21}/_{32}$:
	Principal = $4,365,625	Contract value = $4,332,813
March/Year X + 1 futures	Sell $5 million corporate bonds at 79:	Buy $5 million T-bond at $79^{21}/_{32}$:
	Principal = $3,950,000	Contract value = $3,951,563
	Loss: ($415,625)	Gain: $381,250

Here we see that the dealer suffered a loss of $34,375 even with the short hedge, but this loss is much less than the loss of $415,625 that would have been incurred if no hedge had been employed.

Futures contracts are based on the price of a Treasury security. Alternatively, Eurodollar futures contracts are based on LIBOR (London Interbank Offered Rate), which is a commercial lending rate between two banks. Eurodollar futures can be used to hedge short-term interest rates. For example, if a bank held a portfolio of variable rate loans and wanted to hedge a decline in interest rates that would lower its revenues, it could sell short Eurodollar futures contracts. Under this scenario, losses in the cash loan position would be offset by gains in the short futures position. This hedge is likely to be imperfect due to changes in the loan portfolio over time. However, the number of futures contracts can be adjusted as needed to maintain a viable hedge against falling interest rate revenues on loans.

COMPLICATIONS IN USING FINANCIAL FUTURES

Although financial futures are designed to allow banks to reduce interest rate risk, a number of complications must be considered:

- The bank must use the futures markets within the limits prescribed by accounting and regulatory guidelines. These guidelines generally limit a bank's financial futures activities to those transactions that relate to a bank's business needs and the bank's capacity to meet its obligations.

- For ***macro hedges***, in which the bank is hedging the entire portfolio, the bank cannot, under current guidelines, defer gains and losses from marking the futures contract to market daily. As a result, earnings are likely to be less stable in the short term with the practice of macro hedging. However, if the hedge is a ***micro hedge,*** whereby the hedge is linked directly to a specific asset, then gains and losses can be deferred until the maturity of the contract. Hence, accounting policies favor micro hedges even though a macro hedge is generally more appropriate for portfolio management. See Chapter 7 Investments Management for recent accounting standards applied to securities (including derivatives) activities. In general, derivatives held for trading purposes must be reported at their average fair value or current-value balance in the accounting period, in addition to their net gains and losses.

• The bank faces a number of risks in implementing a hedging strategy using financial futures. Perhaps the most important is ***basis risk***. Basis refers to the difference between the cash and futures price of the financial instrument that is used for the hedge. It is the fact that the cash and futures prices move together that provides an opportunity for risk reduction through hedging. Yet the cash and futures prices are not perfectly correlated. As a result, when the basis changes, as it usually does during the period of the hedge, the ability to reduce interest rate risk is compromised. Interest rate risk may be eliminated only if basis does not change, and basis usually does change over the life of the hedge because the cash and futures prices are not perfectly correlated.

• Bank management also must recognize that the existing gap position of the bank may change due to deposit inflows or loan repayments over which the bank has little control. Consequently, a hedge that was appropriate for the portfolio at the time the hedge was created may be inappropriate as the period of the hedge unfolds.

• Futures hedging inherently creates liquidity risk for the bank. The possibility of margin calls requires that the bank maintain money market securities in reserve to cover potential losses to the marked-to-market accounting. Excess margin balances can be transferred to a money market reserve for this purpose. However, daily losses in futures positions will cause temporary liquidity demands on the bank.

USING FUTURES CONTRACTS TO MANAGE CURRENCY RISK

Currency risk arises any time that payments on financial instruments, goods, and services are denominated in foreign currency. For example, assume that you have sold some goods to a European buyer and will be paid 1 million euros in 90 days. The euro/dollar exchange rate is 1.00 at the present time (i.e., 1.00 euros = $1), such that your payment translates to $1 million. However, it is likely that this exchange rate will change over the next 90 days. If the euro falls in value to an exchange rate of 0.80 (0.80 euros = $1), you will be paid only $800,000, which entails a loss of $200,000. To hedge this currency risk, you can sell a euro futures contract. As the euro falls in value relative to the dollar, you would earn a gain on the euro futures position to offset the loss on the cash payment position. Of course, if the euro rose in value over the next 90 days, the gain on the cash payment would be offset by the loss on the futures contract.

USING FUTURES CONTRACTS TO MANAGE STOCK MARKET RISK

Stock market risk can also be hedged using futures contracts. The Standard &

Poor's (S&P) 500 index is traded in futures markets. It allows an investor holding a diversified portfolio of stocks to hedge a decline in stock prices by selling short this index. If an investor has earned a profit in the stock market and wants to lock these gains in, S&P 500 index futures can be employed to do so. Futures on NASDAQ stock indexes are also available for hedging stock price declines.

USING FORWARD CONTRACTS INSTEAD OF FUTURES CONTRACTS

Forward contracts differ from futures contracts in the following ways: forward contracts are less standardized, are traded over the counter (OTC) between large dealer banks (rather than on an organized exchange), and are not marked-to-market daily. Unlike futures contracts, a forward contract is an agreement between two investors, known as counterparties. These contracts are offered in a wider variety of financial instruments and currencies. For example, a corporate bond hedged using Treasury bond futures has considerable basis risk. A better hedge with lower basis risk would be a forward contract on a corporate bond with a similar rating and maturity. Since forward contracts are not marked-to-market, there is no liquidity risk (risk of a margin call) on a daily basis as in the case of futures contracts. However, they are more difficult to close out early due to the need to negotiate with the original counterparty. Most transactions on forward contracts are completed on the expiration date. Also, credit risk is higher, as failure of the counterparty to perform their side of the agreement is not guaranteed by an exchange (and instead requires legal action). Over the past 20 years, the OTC forward market has grown rapidly and now rivals the financial futures market in terms of outstanding volume. Foreign currency and interest rate contracts are the most popular forward agreements.

An option-dated forward contract is a foreign exchange agreement that can be executed within 30 days of the expiration date. This allows flexibility to sell or buy currencies at prices set now for a future transaction within the next month. If you wanted to buy dollars for upcoming payments for goods and services, you can lock in the cost of these dollars in terms of another currency (such as Japanese yen, British pounds sterling, or European euros). Then as you need to take delivery of dollars to make payments, you can exercise option-dated forward contracts.

OPTIONS

CHARACTERISTICS OF OPTIONS

A ***call option*** gives the buyer the right (but not the obligation) to buy an underlying instrument (such as a T-bill futures contract) at a specified price (called the exercise or strike price) and obligates the seller to sell the underlying instrument at the same price. For this right the buyer pays a fee to the seller determined by supply and demand conditions in the options market, which is referred to as a ***call premium***.

A ***put option*** gives the buyer the right (although not the obligation) to sell a specified underlying security at the price stipulated in the contract and obligates the seller to buy the underlying security. As with calls, the premium is determined by the interplay of supply and demand in the options market. Like futures markets, options contracts are standardized contracts that trade on organized exchanges. Fulfillment of the contract is guaranteed by the market clearing corporation. Unlike futures contracts, however, buyers are not required to put forward a margin (because their loss is limited to the premium paid for the option). Due their uncertain potential for losses, sellers of put and call options must maintain margin positions.

Call and put options on Treasury bill and Eurodollar futures are traded on the International Monetary Market (IMM), a division of the Chicago Mercantile Exchange (CME), the largest futures exchange in the U.S. When the contract is exercised, the buyer agrees to take delivery of a T-bill or Eurodollar contract at some future date and the seller agrees to make delivery on a contract. The buyer has a long futures position, whereas the seller has a short futures position. Contract specifications for options in the IMM are given in Table 6-2. It should be noted that interest rate (or bond) options increased in volume in the late 1970s due to interest rate volatility at that time.

TABLE 6-2 CONTRACT SPECIFICATIONS FOR OPTIONS ON IMM MONEY MARKET FUTURES

Options on Treasury Bill Futures

IMM Treasury bill futures options were first listed for trading in April 1986. The underlying instrument for these options is the IMM three-month Treasury bill futures contract. Expiration dates for traded contracts fall approximately three to four weeks before the underlying futures contract matures. IMM futures options can be exercised anytime up to the expiration date.*

Strike Price Intervals

Strike price intervals are 25 basis points for IMM index prices above 91.00 and 50 basis points for index prices below 91.00. Strike prices are typically quoted in terms of basis points. Thus, the strike prices for traded Treasury bill futures options can be 90.50 or 92.25, but not 90.25 or 92.10.

Price Quotation

Premium quotations for Treasury bill futures options are based on the IMM index price of the underlying futures contract. As with the underlying futures contract, the minimum price fluctuation is one basis point, and each basis point is worth $25. Thus, a quote of 0.35 represents an options premium of $875 (35 basis points x $25). The minimum price fluctuation for put and call premiums is one basis point, with no upper limit on daily price fluctuations.

Options on Eurodollar Futures

IMM options on Eurodollar futures began trading in March 1985. Eurodollar options expire at the end of the last day of trading in the underlying Eurodollar futures contract. Because the Eurodollar futures contract is cash settled, the final settlement for Eurodollar options follows the cash settlement procedure adopted for Eurodollar futures. To illustrate, suppose the strike price for a bought Eurodollar futures call option is 91.00 and the final settlement price for Eurodollar futures is 91.50. Exercising the call option at expiration gives the holder the right, in principle, to place $1,000 in a three-month Eurodollar deposit paying an add-on rate of 9 percent. But because the contract is settled in cash, the holder receives $1,250 (50 basis points x $25) in lieu of the right place to place the Eurodollar deposit paying 9 percent.

Strike Price Intervals

Strike price intervals for Eurodollar futures options are the same as Treasury bill strike price intervals.

Price Quotation

Premium quotations for Eurodollar options are based on the IMM index price of the underlying Eurodollar futures contract. As with the underlying futures contract, the minimum price fluctuation is one basis point, and each basis is worth $25.

*The precise rule used to determine IMM Treasury bill futures options expiration dates is as follows. The expiration date is the business day nearest the underlying futures contract month that satisfies the following two conditions: First, the expiration date must fall on the last business day of the week. Second, the last day of trading must precede the first day of the futures contract month by at least six business days.

Options on individual common stocks have been traded on an over-the-counter basis in the United States since the late 1800s. In 1973 the Chicago Board Options Exchange (CBOE) began trading stock options. Their success increased the volume trading in many options contracts to exceed that in the underlying stock itself. Stock index options have become increasingly popular since stock market downturns such as the October 19, 1987, crash and the collapse of the 1990s stock market bubble. These options provide ways to hedge stock portfolios of institutional investors, especially when the market is turbulent. Index contracts based on the S&P 500, Nasdaq 100, Russell 2000, Value Line, Wilshire, NYSE, and more are available. To reduce hedging costs, institutions will often use a *zero-cost collar*. In this strategy a portfolio manager will sell call options on an index and use the proceeds to purchase put options. This combination of options protects the stock portfolio from downside risk but puts a cap on upside market gains if stock prices rise. Such a collar can help protect previous gains that an institution had earned.

Options are available on currencies also. In 1973 world currency markets moved from a gold pegging system to floating currency values. What this meant is that the dollar, yen, pound, and other currencies began to fluctuate in value freely according to supply and demand pressures. The resultant volatility in currency values motivated over-the-counter options contracts on currencies and later trading on exchanges such as the Philadelphia Options Exchange and others. Suppose that you were to receive future payments in euros and so wanted to protect (insure) against a decline in the value of the euro in the near future. The major difference between selling a forward contract and buying a put option contract on euros (for example) is that the latter has a maximum loss equal to the put premium. If the euro rises in value, losses on the forward contract would cancel the gain on the cash position in euro payments. However, by buying a put option, cash position gains would be realized that exceeded the put premium paid to purchase this option. Hence, options on currencies offer insurance against cash position losses but do not totally eliminate cash position gains.

American options can be exercised at any time up to the expiration date. Of course, this means that options with a longer time to maturity, other things being equal, are more valuable and their premium is higher. By contrast, *European options* cannot be executed prior to the expiration date and so their values are unaffected by maturity for the most part. The value of an option is also related to the volatility of the underlying asset price. More price volatility means that the probability of price exceeding or falling below a strike price is increased. And, you could readily infer that, as the asset price gets closer to the strike price, option value increases. For those interested in a detailed explanation of how these variables affect option value, search on the internet using the keywords Black-Scholes option pricing mode.

PAYOFFS FOR OPTIONS CONTRACTS

Figure 6-2 (next page) provides a comparison of payoff possibilities for futures versus options contracts. Figure 6-2 (a) shows the payoff for unhedged long and short futures positions. The horizontal axis measures the market price of the underlying asset (F), and the vertical axis measures any profits or losses due to changes in its market price. Because the buyer of a futures contract gains or loses one dollar for each dollar the contract rises or falls, the 45-degree line passing through F_0 in Figure 6-2(a) provides a representation of the payoff. The payoff from an unhedged short futures position is, of course, the opposite of an unhedged long position.

FIGURE 6-2 OPTIONS PAYOFFS

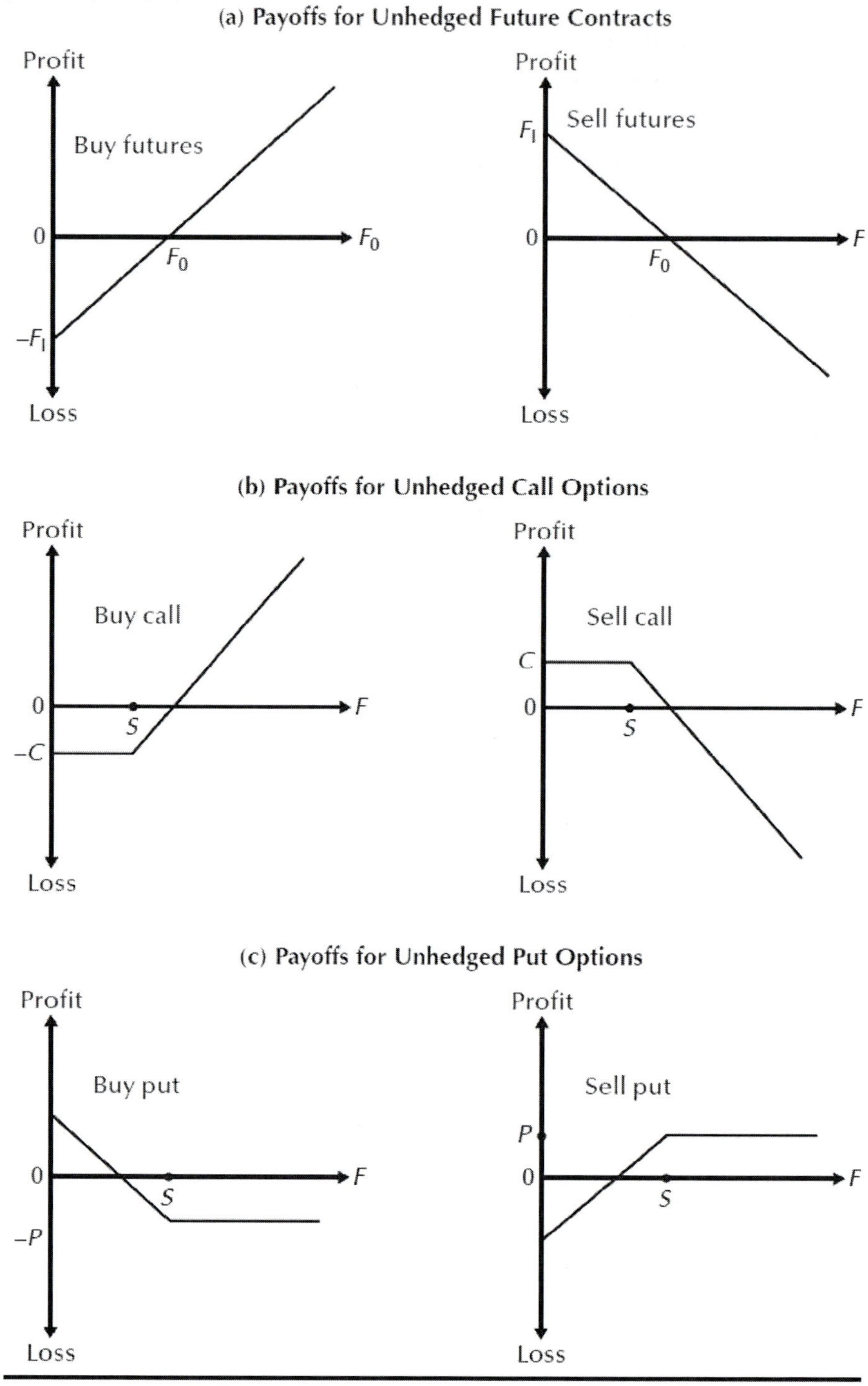

Figure 6-2(b) shows the payoff for an unhedged call option bought and held until expiration. The buyer pays the amount of the call premium (C), which is the maximum that can be lost. As the market value of the underlying asset (F) rises above its strike price (S), the value of the option increases. At a future market price above F_0, the option buyer earns a profit -- that is, call option profit = F – S – C. Notice that this option gain to the buyer is an option loss to the seller. Consequently, sellers must maintain a margin account to cover potential losses on options contracts.

Payoffs for put options are shown in Figure 6-2(c). The buyer of a put option pays a premium (P) and receives the right to sell the underlying asset (at strike price S). As the market price (F) of the underlying asset drops, the premium is recouped and at some (lower) price the buyer of the put has a gain -- that is, put option profit = S – F – P. The logic is comparable although reversed for the seller of a put.

HEDGING THE DOLLAR GAP WITH OPTION AND FUTURES OPTION CONTRACTS

Bank management can use options contracts to hedge interest rate risk. For example, suppose that the bank measured its interest-rate-sensitive assets and liabilities and found that it had a negative dollar gap. Without hedging, the bank would experience a declining net interest income if interest rates were to increase. In that case, the interest rate risk could be reduced by buying an interest rate put option. If interest rates did increase, the prices of underlying bonds would fall. Through buying the put, the bank would earn a profit on the put option and could use it to reduce or eliminate the net interest income loss from the negative dollar gap. If (instead) interest rates decrease, the bank would not exercise its put option, such that it would benefit from an increasing net interest income (minus the put premium).

Conversely, a bank with a positive dollar gap could buy call options in order to hedge its interest rate risk. If interest rates fall, the bank would lose on its cash or spot market portfolio, but the gain from its options position would partially or completely offset that loss. If interest rates rise, the gain in net interest income would only be partially offset by the option cost (premium).

Another hedging strategy is to use an option on a futures contract, or futures ***option contract***. A bank that has a negative dollar gap and is concerned about rising interest rates could buy a put option in T-bill futures contracts. If interest rates increase and T-bill prices fall, the gain in the futures position could be exercised. Of course, the T-bill futures contract would not be exercised if interest rates decrease and T-bill prices rise. Alternatively, a positive dollar gap for a bank concerned about falling interest rates could be hedged by buying a call option in T-bill futures contracts. As rates fall, the call option would earn profits to offset declining net interest income. If rates rise, the call option would not be exercised.

MICRO AND MACRO HEDGES

The preceding discussion focused on a *macro hedge*, where management attempts to hedge an entire portfolio of assets and liabilities. What if management simply wanted to prevent the value of its bond portfolio from falling below $500 million? If the current value of the portfolio was $550 million, it could buy a put option that would earn profits when bond values fell far enough for its portfolio to drop below $500 million.

The bank may also wish, however, to hedge specific portions of the portfolio using a *micro hedge*. For example, suppose that the bank has funded a loan that reprices every six months with Eurodollar CDs that reprice every three months. In that case, the bank could lose considerably if interest rates increase. To protect itself from such a risk, the bank could sell call options on Eurodollar futures. If interest rates increase, the gain from the call options (i.e., the call premium) would offset the loss on the funding of the loan.

CAPS AND FLOORS USING INTEREST RATE OPTIONS

Caps and ***floors*** are versions of interest rate options that are widely used to transfer interest rate risk. An interest rate cap is a contract that reduces the exposure of a floating rate borrower (or a liability-sensitive bank) to increases in interest rates. It essentially involves buying interest rate call options in which the writer guarantees the buyer (the bank) that the writer will pay the buyer any additional interest cost that results from rising interest rates. That is, if interest rates rise, the call option will make profits for the buyer to offset rising costs of debt as interest rates increase. In contrast, an interest rate floor is a contract that limits the exposure of the buyer to downward movements in interest rates. An interest rate floor involves buying interest rate put options in which the writer guarantees the buyer (the bank) that the writer will pay to the bank an amount that increases as the level of interest rates falls. It should be remembered that the strike price of debt instruments varies inversely with the level of interest rates, as their prices and interest rates move opposite to one another. Thus, a call option on a Treasury bill rate is equivalently a put option on its price. Here we use interest rates to discuss the option characteristics of caps and floors (i.e., the X-axis in Figures 6-2b and 6-2c is in terms of interest rates, not prices). In Chapter 14's Off-Balance Sheet Activities, we discuss caps and floors in terms of options on prices of debt securities.

A few examples may provide insight into the use of caps and floors for bank asset/liability management. Suppose that a bank has a portfolio of fixed rate assets that are financed with variable-rate (or very short-term) sources of funds (i.e., positive dollar gap). Suppose that this liability-sensitive bank has a $10 million negative dollar gap. It might choose to purchase an interest rate call option as a cap with a strike price of 8.0 percent and principal value of $10 million. The cap could be purchased with varying maturities, perhaps ranging from three months to five years. The writer of the cap could be an investment bank, a large commercial bank, or another party.

Comparisons are made between market interest rates and the strike price -- often using a Treasury bill or London Interbank Offered Rate (LIBOR) reference rate -- at regular intervals (six months is common) referred to as the *determination date*. If the market yield has risen above the strike price, the cap holder is entitled to receive the difference between the current market interest rate and the strike price multiplied by the principal value of the contract. For example, assuming that on the determination date the relevant market rate for the contract is nine percent, the writer of the call would be obligated to pay $50,000 to the bank:

$$(9\% - 8\%)(\$10,000,000)(0.5) = \$50,000$$

This payment could be used to offset the increased net interest cost produced by the liability-sensitive position of the bank's balance sheet. Of course, if rates do not increase, the bank does not collect on its insurance policy (i.e., the cap) but also does not lose from a liability-sensitive balance sheet.

Suppose on the other hand that the bank is asset sensitive because it has short-term assets financed with longer-term liabilities (i.e., a negative dollar gap). In this case, the bank will benefit if rates rise but will be harmed if rates fall. The bank might then purchase an interest rate put option as a floor with a $10 million principal, a strike price of seven percent, and a six-month determination date. If the interest rate on the appropriate market instrument (say, the three-month Treasury bill) was six percent as of the determination date, the bank would be entitled to receive $50,000 from the writer of the contract:

$$(\$10,000,000)(1\%)(0.50) = \$50,000$$

This payment could then be used to offset the reduced profitability associated with an asset-sensitive position in a falling rate environment. Of course, if rates stay the same, this insurance policy expires without producing any benefit (but the bank has not experienced any loss due to being asset sensitive).

INTEREST RATE SWAPS

One of the most recent techniques devised to manage interest rate risk (and also for other purposes) is the interest rate swap. First developed in Europe in 1981, swaps have dramatically expanded in volume since then, and now total more than $120 trillion in notional value around the world. In an ***interest rate swap***, two firms that want to change their interest rate exposure in different directions get together (usually with the help of some financial intermediary) and exchange or swap their obligations to pay or receive interest (just the interest payment obligations are swapped, not the principal).

Table 6-3 (next page) provides detailed information on the relative size of swaps compared with other derivatives contracts held by U.S. commercial banks from 2003 to 2015. Panel A of Table 6-3 shows that swaps experienced tremendous growth compared with futures and forwards, options, and credit derivatives over this period. Indeed, swap activity almost tripled from about $44 trillion in 2003 to almost $118 trillion in 2015. In Panel B of Table 6-3 we see that interest rate derivatives grew from about $62 trillion in 2003 to about $154 trillion in 2015, which clearly dominates other types of derivatives, including foreign exchange, equities, commodities and credit derivatives. Interestingly, four large U.S. banks hold about 90 percent of all derivatives held in the banking industry, namely JP Morgan Chase Bank, Bank of America, Citibank, and Goldman Sachs. Thus, derivatives activities among U.S. commercial banks tend to be concentrated in the largest institutions.

TABLE 6-3 DERIVATIVES HELD BY U.S. COMMERCIAL BANKS

A. Year-Ends 1991-2002 and Three Quarters of 2003 ($ billions)

	91Q4 $	92Q4 $	93Q4 $	94Q4 $	95Q4 $	96Q4 $	97Q4 $	98Q4 $	99Q4 $	00Q4 $	01Q4 $	02Q4 $	03Q1 $	03Q2 $	03Q3 $
Interest rate	3,837	4,872	7,210	9,926	11,095	13,427	17,085	24,785	27,772	32,938	38,305	48,347	53,447	56,932	58,275
Foreign exchange	3,394	3,789	4,484	5,605	5,387	6,241	7,430	7,386	5,915	6,099	5,736	6,076	6,243	7,092	6,911
Other derivatives	109	102	179	243	378	367	494	684	843	1,080	950	1,016	1,023	1,012	1,059
Credit derivatives							55	144	287	426	395	635	710	802	869
Total	7,340	8,763	11,873	15,774	16,861	20,035	25,064	32,999	34,817	40,543	45,386	56,074	61,423	65,838	67,113

Note: Interest rate swaps, currency (foreign exchange) swaps, and other derivatives are in notional terms and include both OTC- and exchange-traded contracts.

B. Concentration of Derivatives Contracts in Seven Banks in Third Quarter of 2003 ($ billions)

	Top 7 Banks $	Total Derivatives %	Rest 565 Banks $	Total Derivatives %	All 572 Banks $	Total Derivatives %
Futures and forwards	10,049	15.0	810	1.2	10,859	16.2
Swaps	40,069	59.7	1,137	1.7	41,205	61.4
Options	13,300	19.8	880	1.3	14,180	21.1
Credit derivatives	842	1.3	27	0.0	869	1.3
Total	64,260	95.7	2,853	4.3	67,113	100.0

Note: Futures and forward contracts, swaps, options, and other derivatives are in notional terms and include both OTC- and exchange-traded contracts.

Source: OCC Bank Derivatives Report, Office of the Comptroller of the Currency, Washington, D.C. (2003).

Assume that one firm has long-term fixed assets financed with short-term variable-rate liabilities. Further assume that another firm has short-term variable-rate assets financed with long-term fixed-rate liabilities. Both firms are exposed to interest rate risk but their exposure is quite different. If interest rates fall, the first firm gains whereas the second firm loses. Of course, if interest rates increase, the first firm loses and the second firm gains.

For firms having this type of interest rate exposure (e.g., a bank and a savings and loan), the swap of interest payments allows each firm to benefit. The first firm substitutes fixed-rate liabilities for its floating-rate liabilities and thereby reduces its interest rate risk. The second firm substitutes variable-rate liabilities for fixed-rate liabilities and also reduces its interest rate risk.

Figure 6-3 provides an illustration of a swap transaction for a liability-sensitive institution. The liability-sensitive institution has fixed-rate assets (bonds) financed by floating-interest-rate notes. It arranges a swap with a counterparty in which it pays fixed rate and receives floating rate (fixed-rate cash payments are shown as straight lines, whereas floating-rate cash payments are shown as wavy lines). The bottom portion of the illustration shows the net result of the swap, which is that the swap receipt of floating-rate cash payments goes to lower the payment on the floating-rate liabilities on the balance sheet, and the firm is left with the fixed-rate earnings on the bonds financed with fixed-rate payments on the swap.

FIGURE 6-3 USING AN INTEREST RATE SWAP TO HEDGE A LIABILITY-SENSITIVE POSITION

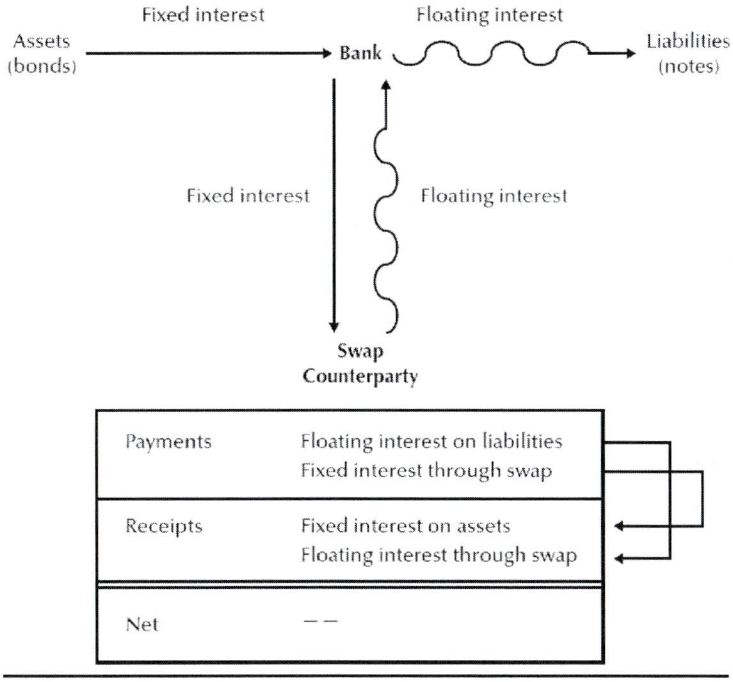

Figure 6-4 (next page) shows a similar example, except that the institution is a bank that has floating-rate assets and fixed-rate liabilities. This institution arranges a swap in which it pays floating rate and receives fixed rate. The net result of the

swap is that the fixed receipts from the swap counterparty are used to pay the fixed payments on the on-balance-sheet liabilities, so that the floating-interest-rate earnings are matched with the floating-interest-rate swap payments.

FIGURE 6-4 USING AN INTEREST RATE SWAP TO HEDGE AN ASSET-SENSITIVE POSITION

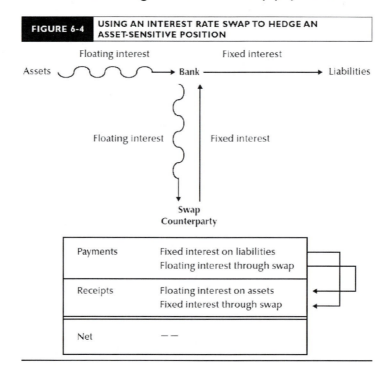

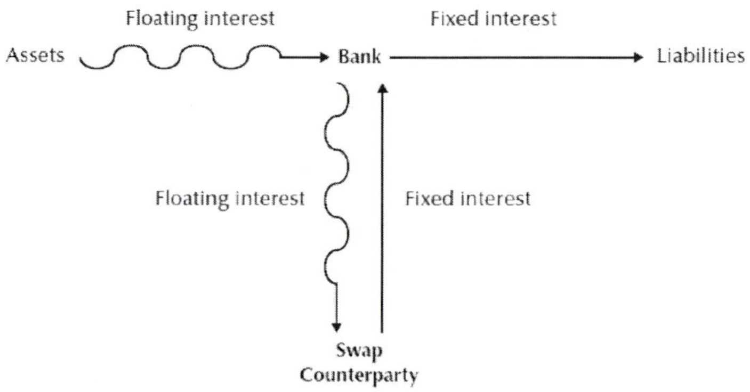

Payments	Fixed interest on liabilities Floating interest through swap
Receipts	Floating interest on assets Fixed interest through swap
Net	— —

Figure 6-5 (next page) provides more detailed information on the mechanics of a swap. It deals with a swap between a thrift institution with a large portfolio of fixed-rate mortgages and a bank with a portfolio consisting primarily of variable-rate loans tied to the LIBOR. On May 10, 200X, the thrift and the bank arrange, through a large investment bank, a swap transaction for $100 million at seven percent. The thrift agrees to pay the bank a fixed rate of 11 percent per year, payable semiannually. This covers the 11 percent rate the bank is committed to pay on a seven-year bond. The thrift also pays the two-percentage-point spread incurred by the bank at the time it issued the bond. In return, the bank agrees to make floating-rate payments to the thrift at 35 basis points below LIBOR. The investment bank earned a fee of $500,000 for bringing the thrift and the bank together.

The swap of the interest payment obligations reduces interest rate risk for both the bank and the thrift. Although interest rate risk is reduced, it is not eliminated. The floating-rate payment that the thrift received is linked to LIBOR, whereas its cost of borrowing is tied more closely to the Treasury bill rate.

A further evolution of the swap concept is embodied in the so-called ***swaption***. A swaption is an option on a swap. In a swaption the buyer has the right (but not the obligation) to enter into an interest rate swap at terms specified in the contract. As with any option, the buyer pays a premium to the seller of the option.

With a payer swaption, the buyer has the option to enter into an interest rate swap in which the buyer pays fixed rates and receives floating rates. (The writer or seller of the option obviously agrees to enter into a swap in which it receives fixed

FIGURE 6-5 HOW A SWAP WORKS

The following example is based on an actual transaction arranged by an investment bank between a large thrift institution and a large international bank.

"Thrift" has a large portfolio of fixed-rate mortgages. "Bank" has most of its dollar-denominated assets yielding a floating rate return based on LIBOR (the London Interbank Offered Rate).

On May 10, 200X, the "Intermediary," a large investment bank, arranged a $100 million, seven-year interest rate swap between Thrift and Bank. In the swap, Thrift agreed to pay Bank a fixed rate of 11 percent per year on $100 million, every six months. This payment covered exactly the interest Bank had to pay on a $100 million bond it issued in the Eurodollar market. Thrift also agreed to pay Bank the 2 percent underwriting spread that Bank itself paid to issue this bond. In exchange, Bank agreed to make floating-rate payments to Thrift at 35 basis points (0.35 percent) below LIBOR. Intermediary received a broker's fee of $500,000.

Twice a year, Intermediary (for a fee) calculates Bank's floating rate payment by taking the average level of LIBOR for that month (Col. 2), deducting 35 basis points, dividing by 2 (because it is for *half* a year), and multiplying by $100 million (Col. 3). If this amount is larger than Thrift's fixed rate payment (Col. 4), Bank pays Thrift the difference (Col. 5). Otherwise, Thrift pays Bank the difference (Col. 6).

The swap allows both Bank and Thrift to reduce their exposure to interest rate risk. Bank can now match its floating rate assets priced off LIBOR with an interest payment based on LIBOR, while the fixed rate interest payments on its bond issues are covered by Thrift. At the same time, Thrift can hedge part of its mortgage portfolio, from which it receives fixed interest earnings, with the fixed rate payment it makes to Bank. However, the floating rate payment that Thrift receives is linked to LIBOR while its cost of borrowing is more closely linked to the T-bill rate. Because LIBOR and the T-bill rate do not always move in tandem, Thrift is still exposed to fluctuations in the relation between LIBOR and the T-bill.

The most common type of swap is the one described here: a dollar fixed rate loan swapped for a dollar floating rate loan, otherwise called the "plain vanilla" swap. However, several variations on this basic swap have emerged in the market. One such variation is a floating-to-floating swap where parties agree to swap floating rates based on different indices. For example, a bank with assets tied to the prime rate and liabilities based on LIBOR may want to swap the interest payments on its liabilities with payments on a prime-tied, floating rate loan. Another type of arrangement involves currency swaps such as a swap of a sterling floating rate loan for a dollar fixed rate loan. For firms whose assets are denominated in a different currency than are its liabilities, this type of swap may be more appropriate. Finally, rather than exchanging interest payments on liabilities, swaps can also be used to exchange yields on *assets* of different maturities or currencies.

The interest rate swap market has proven to be flexible in adjusting its product to new customer needs. This innovativeness all but guarantees that swaps will remain a permanent feature of international capital markets.

Source: Adapted from Jan Loeys, "Interest Rate Swaps, A New Tool for Managing Risk," Federal Reserve Bank of Philadelphia (May/June 1985), p. 20.

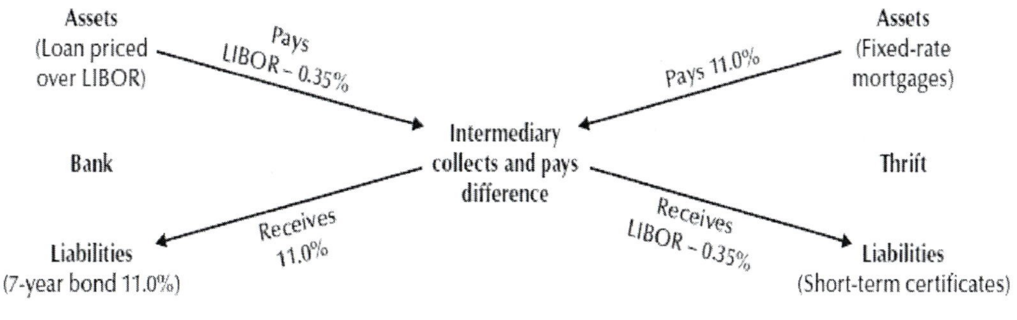

Date	LIBOR	Floating Rate Payment 1/2 (LIBOR—0.35%)	Fixed Rate Payment 1/2 (11%)	Net Payment from Bank to Thrift	Net Payment from Thrift to Bank
May 1999	8.98%	—	—	—	—
Nov 1999	8.43	$4,040,000	$5,500,000	0	$1,460,000
May 2000	11.54	5,595,000	5,500,000	$95,000	0
Nov 2000	9.92	4,785,000	5,500,000	0	715,000
May 2001	8.44	4,045,000	5,500,000	0	1,455,000

rates and pays floating rates.) Buyers are interested in protecting against rising rates (e.g., business firms borrowing funds in the market). In contrast, with a receiver option, the buyer has the right (but not obligation) to enter into an interest rate swap in which the buyer pays floating rates and receives fixed rates (and the seller receives fixed rates and pays floating rates). This swaption protects the buyer against falling rates (e.g., a bank holding a portfolio with fixed-rate loans).

INTEREST RATE SWAPS, THE QUALITY SPREAD, AND THE COST OF FUNDS

The principal purpose of an interest rate swap is to reduce the degree of interest rate risk by more closely synchronizing the interest sensitivity of cash inflows and outflows. However, under certain conditions, the interest rate swap may also result in a reduction in the cost of funds for each of the two parties to the swap. As an example, consider the following:

	High-Quality Bank	Low-Quality Bank	Quality Spread
Floating rate debt	LIBOR + 1.0%	LIBOR + 2.5%	1.5%
Fixed rate debt	8.0%	11.0%	3.0%

High-Quality Bank is assumed to be able to borrow at LIBOR + 1.0% in the short-term, floating-rate debt market or at eight percent in the long-term, fixed-rate debt market. Low-Quality Bank is assumed to be able to borrow on the short-term, floating-rate market at LIBOR + 2.5% or at 10 percent in the long-term, fixed-rate debt market. Notice that while high-quality banks can borrow cheaper in both markets, it has a relative or comparative advantage in the long-term market, as shown by the ***quality spread differentials***. High-quality banks can borrow in the fixed rate market at 300 basis points (three percent) less than low-quality banks but at only 150 basis points (1.5 percent) in the short-term market. But how can an interest rate swap both reduce their interest rate risk and lower their costs of funds?

Suppose that Low-Quality Bank has a negative gap and High-Quality Bank has a positive gap. Both can reduce their interest rate risk if Low-Quality Bank pays fixed rates to High-Quality Bank and if High-Quality Bank pays floating rates to Low-Quality Bank. Further, assume that High-Quality Bank pays LIBOR + 1.0% to Low-Quality Bank and, in return, receives a nine percent fixed rate from Low-Quality bank.

What is the cost of funds for both banks after the swap?

Cost of funds for Low-Quality Bank	=	Borrow floating in Market	−	Receive LIBOR + 1% from High-Quality Bank	+	Pay 9% fixed to High-Quality Bank
	=	LIBOR + 2.5%	−	(LIBOR + 1%)	+	9%
	=	10.5%				

With the swap, Low-Quality Bank has matched its interest rate risk (it now has more fixed rate liabilities) and has lowered its cost of those fixed rate liabilities (10.5 percent with the swap as compared with 11.0 percent without the swap). But High-Quality Bank has also benefited. Its cost of funds is

$$\begin{aligned}\text{Cost of funds for High-Quality Bank} &= \text{Borrow fixed in Market} - \text{Received fixed from Low-Quality Bank} + \text{Pay LIBOR + 1\% to Low-Quality Bank}\\ &= 8\% - 9\% + (\text{LIBOR} + 1\%)\\ &= \text{LIBOR}\end{aligned}$$

High-Quality Bank has obtained the floating rate debt that it wanted in order to positive gap and has lowered its cost for this floating rate debt by one percent with the swap (as compared with LIBOR + 1% without the swap).

Notice that the gain to the two parties in the swap of 1.5 percent (0.5 percent for Low-Quality Bank and 1.0 percent for High-Quality Bank) exactly equals the difference in the quality spreads of the two parties in the floating and fixed rate market of 1.5 percent (3.0 percent – 1.5 percent). It is this difference in relative access to the two markets that creates the opportunity to lower the cost of money for both parties. If the quality spreads had been the same, then both parties could use the swap to reduce interest rate risk but both could not reduce their costs of funds.

SWAPS AND FUTURES

Interest rate swaps provide an alternative to futures (and options) as a device banks can use to manage interest rate risk. Swaps have both advantages and disadvantages when compared with futures. The principal advantages of swaps over futures are twofold. First, swaps can be customized to meet the exact needs of the bank. Because interest rate swaps are negotiated contracts, the terms of maturity and other dimensions of the swap can be tailored to the needs of the bank. Second, the swap can be established for a long-term arrangement—most swaps have maturities of three to ten years. In contrast financial futures are standardized contracts that have a limited number of specified delivery dates and deliverable types of financial instruments. Most important, futures contracts generally are available only for delivery dates at three-month intervals that extend only up to 2.5 years in the future, making hedging interest rate risk with futures contracts impossible over a long-term period.

Swaps do offer some disadvantages, however, relative to futures. Most of these disadvantages stem from the customized nature of the swap contracts. The lack of standardization of swaps increases the search cost of finding counterparts to the swap. Also, it is more costly to close out a swap contract prior to maturity than a futures contract. Equally significant, the bank that enters into a swap agreement faces the possibility that the counterparts may default. Although the bank has no principal at risk, it does have credit risk in the interest payment obligation.

As the swap market has evolved, the importance of these disadvantages has been diminished by the intervention of intermediaries into the market. These intermediaries (generally investment or commercial banks) have been willing (for a fee) to guarantee the payment of interest on a swap contract. Also, to reduce the problems associated with the customized nature of the swap contract, these intermediaries have started to standardize the contract terms, such as the type of floating-rate interest, the repricing dates, and collateral requirements. Secondary markets for swaps have also developed, thereby increasing the liquidity of the swap contracts.

Finally, under the Dodd-Frank Act of 2010, due to increased regulation, many swaps now trade in organized exchanges, as opposed to over-the-counter (OTC). The box below gives a discussion of credit default swap (CDS) contracts that became popular prior to the 2008-2009 financial crisis as a means of insuring against potential default losses on mortgage-related bonds. Unfortunately, they contributed to the collapse of the mortgage market in the crisis. Today, CDSs are widely used to hedge credit risk on bonds but are increasingly traded through organized exchanges to mitigate counterparty risk.

MANAGERIAL ISSUES

CREDIT DEFAULT SWAP (CDS) CONTRACTS

A credit default swap (CDS) provides the buyer with credit risk insurance on a debt instrument (the reference entity or obligor). The buyer pays insurance premiums on a regular basis to the seller in exchange for this credit insurance. If the debt instrument falls into default, the seller pays its par value to the seller. Typical CDS contracts have maturities of one to 10 years and are issued in $10 to $20 million denominations. Debt instruments can be specific loans or bonds.

As credit derivatives, CDS contracts involve two counterparties – the seller takes the risk that payouts on defaulted bonds will exceed the premiums received from buyers, and the buyer bears the risk that the seller will fail and then be unable to honor its insurance obligation to the buyer. The most common usage of CDSs is to hedge risky debt instruments held by the buyer. However, there is a speculative market for CDSs in which buyers do not hold the underlying debt instrument. In the past CDSs were primarily traded in the over-the-counter (OTC) market and have been plagued by transparency problems related to the riskiness of underlying debt instruments.

In the 2008-2009 financial crisis, global insurance and financial company American International Group (AIG) had sold CDS contracts on over $500 billion in debt instruments. Losses on these contracts exceeded $11 billion in 2007 and increased in 2008 due to collateral calls of $8 billion by buyer counterparties due to AIG's downgrading by all three credit agencies. Other losses were incurred on mortgage-related assets purchased with funds raised by making loans on insurance subsidiary assets. Together, CDS and mortgage securities losses reached approximately $50 billion, enough to bring the $1 trillion in assets giant near the brink of collapse. AIG was bailed out by Federal Reserve and Treasury using injections of liquidity and capital to prevent its failure. Under the Dodd-Frank Act of 2010, CDS contracts are increasingly being traded through organized exchanges that guarantee performance, rather than depending entirely on the seller to make payouts to buyers on defaulted bonds.

SUMMARY

Innovations in financial markets have created new instruments that banks can use in managing their interest rate risk. Three in particular have great importance to bank management—futures, options, and swaps. Each allows bank management to alter interest rate exposure, and each has certain advantages and disadvantages when compared with the other. Taken together, however, they give bank managers enormously improved flexibility in managing interest rate risk.

A bank can hedge its interest rate risk in the futures market by taking a position that is the opposite of its existing portfolio position. If, for example, the bank was asset sensitive, it could take a long position in the futures market to hedge risk. If interest rates were to fall, it would suffer a loss with its existing portfolio (because it was asset sensitive) but would incur a gain in its futures position. Conversely, a liability-sensitive bank could protect itself against interest rate movements by establishing a short position in the futures market. Futures market positions could also be used to hedge positive or negative duration gaps. An alternative way of managing interest rate risk is to buy or sell an option on a futures contract. A call option gives the buyer the right (but not the obligation) to buy an underlying instrument (such as a T-bill futures contract) at a specified price (called the exercise or strike price) and the seller the obligation to sell the underlying instrument at the same price. A put option gives the buyer the right (but not the obligation) to sell a specified underlying security at the price stipulated in the contract and the seller the obligation to buy the underlying security. Options on futures would be used similarly to the futures themselves in order to hedge interest rate exposure, although options have the advantage of smaller initial outlay in order to accomplish the interest rate risk management.

The third technique for managing interest rate risk without actually altering the existing portfolio is the swap. With a swap, the bank swaps its obligation to pay interest (but not principal) to another party. The bank agrees to pay the interest of the other party (e.g., fixed-rate interest), whereas the counterparts agree to pay the bank's interest. Whether asset sensitive or liability sensitive, then, the bank is able through the swap to reduce its exposure to interest rate fluctuation.

KEY TERMS AND CONCEPTS

Basis risk
Call option
Call premium
Cap
Derivative securities
Exchange clearinghouse
Floor
Forward contract
Futures contract
Futures option contract
Interest rate swap
Long position
Long/short hedge
Margin
Marked-to-market
Micro/macro hedge
Put option
Quality spread
Short hedge
Short position
Swaption

QUESTIONS

6.1 What are financial futures contracts? What similarities exist among all futures contracts?

6.2 What is meant by a short position in financial futures? A long position? How is each affected by changes in interest rates?

6.3 Why can buyers and sellers of futures contracts ignore possible default by the other party?

6.4 What does marked to market mean?

6.5 Distinguish between a micro hedge and a macro hedge. Are there any inherent conflicts in using both simultaneously in managing interest rate risk?

6.6 How would a bank use interest rate futures to hedge a positive dollar gap? A negative dollar gap?

6.7 How would a bank use interest rate futures to hedge a positive duration gap? A negative duration gap?

6.8 What complications exist in using financial futures to hedge a bank portfolio?

6.9 What is an options contract? Compare and contrast an options contract with a futures contract.

6.10 Compare and contrast the characteristics of and use of put and call options contracts.

6.11 Explain how (a) options contracts and (b) options on futures contracts can be used to hedge interest rate risk.

6.12 What is an interest rate swap? How can it be used to hedge interest rate risk?

6.13 Compare a swap with a swaption.

6.14 Compare the pros and cons of futures, futures options, and swaps as devices to hedge interest rate risk.

6.15 What is an interest rate cap? How is it used? Compare it with a floor.

6.16 Your bank is liability sensitive. To protect itself against rising interest rates, management purchased ten caps from a large investment banking firm. Each contract had a notional value of $1 million, a strike price (based on three-month Treasury bill rates) of 7 percent (rate was currently six percent), and a one-year maturity. Over the next year interest rates in Treasury bills fell, reaching three percent at the end of the year, the cap expired without benefit, and the bank lost the full premium of $46,000. Did management err in its decision to purchase the cap?

6.17 Go to Harvard's Baker Library at www.library.hbs.edu and enter the key words "hedge funds" in the box at the top of the web page. Find material on hedge funds and write a one-page summary report.

6.18 Use a web browser to search on "OCC's Quarterly Report on Bank Trading and Derivatives Activities" and open the most recently published document. What did you find interesting in the report?

6.19 Use a web browser to search on "CBOT and CME Group" and open their homepage. Next, open "View All Products" on their website. Select an interest rate swap product and print out the information provided.

PROBLEMS

6.1 Suppose that an investor holds a $1 million 91-day T-bill futures contract. It is marked to market on the close of the last day of trading at $95. What is the settlement price?

6.2 Assume that on April 1 your bank plans to issue a three-month Eurodollar CD in July. On April 1, the bank could issue a three-month Eurodollar CD for 7.02 percent. The corresponding rate for the six -month Eurodollar contract (due in September) was 7.58 percent.

(a) What position should the bank take in the Eurodollar market?

(b) Suppose that the bank took a position in Eurodollar futures on April 1, and that it closes out its position in July when the futures rate is 7.82 percent. In that situation, has the bank achieved its objective with the hedge?

6.3 Suppose that your bank has a commitment to make a fixed-rate loan in three months at the existing interest rate. To hedge against the prospect of rising interest rates, the bank takes a position in the futures options market. What position should it take? The relevant information is as follows:

T-bill futures prices = $89

Put option = $90

Premium = $2,500

What will be the net gain to the bank if T-bill futures prices fall to $85? If they increase to $93?

6.4 A bank has a spot market asset duration of 1.0 and a liability side duration of 0.50. It seeks to reduce the duration of the asset side to 0.25 using a short T-bill futures hedging strategy. The present value of cash flows on assets is $4,000. If the selling price of the futures contracts is $98, how many T-bill futures contracts are needed to achieve a duration equal to 0.50 for the portfolio containing both spot market assets and futures contracts.

6.5 Corporation XYZ obtains a ceiling agreement from a bank for a five-year loan of $20 million at a rate of seven percent (tied to LIBOR). An upfront fee of two percent is paid by XYZ for the guarantee that rates will not exceed 10 percent.

(a) If LIBOR goes to 12 percent, calculate the quarterly compensation the bank must pay XYZ.

(b) What kind of option is this for the bank? For XYZ? When is the option "in-the-money" in the sense of making a profit?

6.6 Given a forward rate agreement (FRA) on bonds purchased by a bank at 90 for delivery in three months:

(a) If the price of the bonds is 100 on the delivery date, what is the profit (loss) of the bank?

(b) What type of option is analogous to this example?

6.7 Bank A and Bank B have the following opportunities for borrowing in the short-term (floating rate) and long-term (fixed rate) markets.

	Bank A	Bank B
Floating rate	T-bill + 1.0%	T-bill + 2.0%
Fixed rate	8%	10.5%

Bank A has a positive gap and Bank B has a negative gap. Show that both banks can benefit from a swap in the sense of lowering their interest rate risk. Can they also lower their cost of funds?

6.8 State Bank purchased a $10 million floor from a large investment banking firm. The floor has a four percent strike price (based on the three-month Treasury bill) and a three-month determination date. Assuming that the three-month Treasury bill rate is 2.5 percent at the determination date, what is the payment under the contract? Does the bank receive or make payments? Assuming that the bank paid $50,000 for the contract, has the bank gained from the transaction?

6.9Consider a fixed-for-floating LIBOR swap with a notional principal of $200 million and a fixed rate of seven percent. Suppose that the swap cash flows are determined at six-month intervals (t = 0, 1, 2, 3, etc.). Suppose that LIBOR turns out to be

t	LIBOR
0	4.25
1	5.25
2	6.75
3	7.25
4	8.00
5	9.00
6	10.00

What would be the net payments for the counterparties on each of the settlement days?

6.10 Assume the date is August 7, 200X, and you have the following information: (1) the September 13 -week T-bill futures discount is 10.49 percent (which matures on December 20), and (2) the spot quote on September 20 for 13-week T-bills maturing December 20 is 10.39 percent.

(a) Assuming a long position in the futures market, what is the purchase price of the T-bill futures contract? (Note: There are 43 days from August 7 to September 20, and 9.91 percent is the applicable 13-week T-bill rate in this period.)

(b) Assuming a long position in the spot market, what is the purchase price of the T-bills using the spot quote?

(c) What would happen if the futures and spot prices of T-bills differed by an amount larger than the transactions costs of buying and selling them?

ENDNOTES

1. Sydney Futures Exchange (SFE) is the largest open-entry futures exchange in the Asia-Pacific region. Its website, www.sfe.com.au, contains information on futures and their benefits, including an introduction to futures contracts and futures FAQs. 2.
2. Professor Campbell R. Harvey at Duke University has set up a guide to futures and options prices at www.duke.edu/~charvey/options/index1.htm. Case-by-case examples of various derivatives used in the capital markets are provided.

CASE: Hedging the Balance Sheet

Janet Chilton and George Stephens had joined World Trust Corporation (WTC) a few years ago as trainers in the derivatives products group. Part of their responsibilities was to explain to potential clients how their derivatives services could help management with their risk exposures. A small depository institution, First Savings Association, had recently contacted World Trust about hedging its net worth against a possible increase in interest rates. The financial press was regularly speculating that the Federal Reserve would continue raising interest rates to hold down incipient inflation in the economy. During its latest Board of Directors meeting, First Savings decided that the probability of a significant increase in interest rates was sufficient to warrant the implementation of a derivatives hedging strategy. However, the board wanted the selected dealer to clearly present its hedging plan at its next meeting the following month. A number of the board members expressed concern due to past news stories of major blunders by derivatives dealers in properly managing client risk.

Janet and George collected the latest reports on the maturities of assets and liabilities held by First Savings. After checking the data, they agreed that First Savings did indeed face interest rate risk due to a positive maturity gap, that is, the maturity of assets exceeded the maturity of liabilities on average. They decided to set up a simple example of this type of mismatch and present it to the Board of First Savings.

Assume the institution made a one-year loan at 10 percent with receipts of $1,000 (i.e., its present value is $909.09). This loan is funded with 90-day CDs paying eight percent. Put together a schedule of receipts and payments for the loan and CDs in each quarter for the upcoming year.

Assume further that the date is September 15 and that you sell 13-week T-bill futures in December, March, and June as a hedge on the CDs. Calculate the price of the T-bill futures contract using a 10 percent discount rate. Assuming further that interest rates do not change, show the results of First Savings purchasing T-bills in the spot market and selling T-bills in the futures market on the delivery date.

We are now ready to demonstrate the effects of an interest rate increase of two percent on the receipts and payments associated with the balance sheet and the futures hedge strategy. Assume that interest rates increase after the first 90-day is sold at eight percent, such that all subsequent CDs must pay the higher interest rate of 10 percent. Assume also that First Savings has already sold T-bill futures for the upcoming year prior to the interest rate increase and therefore has locked in its sales price.

As a member of the staff at World Trust, you have been asked by Janet and George to show how the net receipts on the balance sheet and futures hedge are affected. In anticipation of their upcoming meeting with the board of First Savings, they also want you to write up some short answers to the following questions for distribution to the members of the board.

- What is the present value of the net receipts if interest rates rise two percent?
- How does this change in net receipts compare with the result assuming no change in interest rates
- If interest rates declined rather than increased, what would be the effect on the balance sheet and futures hedge results?
- How might the bank use an option on a futures contract to achieve the same result?
- What are the advantages of using the option on a futures contract over a futures contract alone? What is the disadvantage of the options approach compared with using only a futures contract?
- Finally, should World Trust seek to pair a hedge contract to each individual asset or liability on the balance sheet of First Savings, or should it seek to look at the "big picture" and hedge the overall risk of the balance sheet?

PART 3

Investment, Lending and Liquidity Management

Chapter 7

Investment Management

After reading this chapter, you will be able to:

- Overview the development of investment policies and goals
- Define investment securities that banks purchase
- Describe the different institutional goals that the securities portfolio can be employed to meet
- Discuss unique aspects of managing a securities portfolio in a banking institution, especially regulatory restrictions and tax treatment of securities
- Compare the types of risk that are involved in securities investments
- Identify investment strategies used by banks to achieve bank goals

The second largest asset item on a bank's balance sheet is security investments. As a general rule, investment securities are purchased to produce income in the form of interest paid and capital gains, but liquidity is another role that these securities can fulfill. During recessionary periods when demand for commercial credit is relatively low, investment securities are a good alternative source of income. As economic recovery proceeds and loan demand increases, maturing investment securities can be rolled into loans, or shorter-term securities can be sold to fund higher-earning loan and investment security opportunities. To some extent, therefore, investment securities provide an additional reserve of funds over and above secondary reserves to meet the liquidity need of banks.

Investment securities also play other roles in bank management. For example, they can be pledged as collateral on public deposits of federal, state, and local governments, borrowing from Federal Reserve banks, and securities sold under agreement to repurchase. Some municipal securities can be used to reduce income taxes. Moreover, investment securities can be purchased to increase the diversification of the bank's total asset portfolio or to take advantage of interest rate movements that would yield capital gains, both of which are portfolio adjustments that attempt to maximize return per unit risk. More recently, banks have been using securities to adjust their interest rate risk and to help meet risk-based capital standards. In this chapter we overview investment policies and goals, types of investment securities, methods of evaluating investment risk, and investment strategies. As we will see, securities investments play an important role in bank risk management and profitability.

DEVELOPING INVESTMENT POLICIES AND GOALS

Bank ***investment policy*** should be formally established so that managers can make decisions that are consistent with the overall goals of the organization. In general, investment policy seeks to maximize the return per unit risk on the investment portfolio of securities, although regulatory requirements, lending needs, tax laws, liquidity sources, and other factors can limit return/risk performance. Bank policy should have sufficient flexibility to enable it to shift investment goals in response to changes in financial and economic conditions and competition from rival institutions. For example, a bank must decide how to divide assets between liquidity and securities investment. Higher asset liquidity reduces the risk of missing profitable lending opportunities because of a shortfall of available funds; however, higher returns on longer-term investment opportunities are normally sacrificed. Liability management tends to decrease the emphasis on asset liquidity (as discussed in the previous chapter), which implies that investment securities are more likely to constitute a significant part of the asset base of today's banks. Furthermore, volatile bond and stock markets in the 2008 and 2009 financial crisis serve as potent reminders that the potential risks and returns on investment securities can be substantial. In this context investment policies are essential to successfully managing the inherent risks and potential returns in a securities portfolio.

The investment policy should be written out as a guide to managers in allocating responsibilities, setting investment goals, directing permissible securities purchases, and evaluating portfolio performance. In this respect, securities should be classified according to their credit risk. In 2013 the Office of the Comptroller of the Currency, Federal Reserve, and Federal Deposit Insurance Corporation agreed on guidelines for appraising the credit risk of securities held by banks. Securities are generally classified into two categories:

- Investment grade debt securities – the issuer of the securities has adequate capacity to meet the financial commitments for the life of the asset. Default risk is low in terms of full and timely payment of interest and principal.
- Sub-investment grade debt securities – securities that do not meet the investment grade standard. These securities are distinctly or predominantly speculative and considered substandard.

In some cases a security could be designated as doubtful, which indicates that the security has experienced significant credit deterioration and decline in fair value accompanied by uncertainty about the extent of impairment. Further information is needed to classify the security. Banks need to continually assess the credit risk of securities, especially in the context of potential adverse economic conditions. Some securities may have to downgraded to Doubtful or Substandard due to weakening credit conditions in an economic downturn. Among these securities, assets classified as "loss" are considered uncollectible and should be written off (although there could be some salvage value in the future). Conversely, as credit conditions improve a security may warrant an upgrade to "pass."

Banks with asset sizes greater than $500 million need to devote greater effort toward developing investment policies and goals than do smaller institutions. Larger banks typically manage trading accounts that conduct a variety of securities services, including diversification, liquidity, expert advice to clients, government securities management, trading desk activities, and speculation in price movements. Many times smaller banks follow the investment recommendations of larger "correspondent" banks. Smaller banks also subscribe to a variety of other investment services that correspondent banks offer (such as safekeeping of financial instruments, trading services, and computer portfolio analyses).

Some examples of different investment goals are

- Income
- Capital gains
- Interest rate risk control
- Liquidity
- Credit risk
- Diversification
- Pledging requirements

Income can be achieved by purchasing bonds with high coupon rates or when loan demand is weak and securities represent an alternative source of revenues. If forgoing current income for future income is desired, capital gains are an appropriate investment goal. Deeply discounted bonds have relatively low coupon rates and emphasize capital gains. Moreover, interest rate conditions can affect these two earnings goals. For example, if interest rate levels are declining, income will also decline, but this loss of earnings on securities can be more than offset by purchasing long-term securities that will increase in price (yielding a capital gain) as interest rates fall.

Interest rate risk control is another factor for management to consider. Loans cannot easily be sold in many cases, which decreases management's ability to adjust dollar and duration gaps, as discussed in Chapter 5.[1] By contrast, securities can be sold at management's discretion, so that if management expected interest rates to change in the near future, it could buy and sell securities with various maturities to diminish interest rate risk effects on the bank.

As an example, in low interest rate periods, depositors will be hesitant to purchase long-term CDs, and borrowers will prefer longer-term loans than usual to take advantage of the low interest rates. This difference in deposit and loan demands would tend to cause the average maturities of deposits to be less than the average maturity of loans. An increase in interest rates would squeeze profit margins, as deposit accounts would be rolled over more rapidly than loan accounts -- in effect, interest costs rise more rapidly than earnings on assets over time. Also, an increase in interest rates would diminish the value of bank equity due to the greater price risk of assets compared with liabilities. (For an illustration of these concepts, see *A Simple Example of Interest Rate Risk and Securities Management* on the next page.) To offset these potentially harmful interest rate risk effects, the maturity of the investment securities portfolio could be shortened to lower the average maturity of assets comprised of loans and securities. An excellent choice to accomplish this defensive strategy is adjustable-rate agency securities.

While longer-term securities are less liquid than shorter-term securities, they can offer some degree of liquidity in the sense that management can sell them to take profits and meet cash needs. Because balance sheets reflect book values (or purchase prices) of securities, banks at times "cherry pick," or sell securities with large gains. This practice became controversial over time. The Securities and Exchange Commission (SEC) argued that by using historical book values, rather than market values, bank financial condition is distorted. Cherry picking left securities selling below book value on the balance sheet and therefore overstated their value, further implying that the level of bank capital was lower than reflected by its book value. Others defended book value accounting by pointing out that fair value accounting treatment of securities would give investors and depositors a false impression of bank risks. The greater balance sheet volatility associated with market value accounting could hamper bank lending, especially during times of market volatility. For example, during the 2008 and 2009 financial crisis a number of large

MANAGEMENT OF RISK

A SIMPLE EXAMPLE OF INTEREST RATE RISK AND SECURITIES MANAGEMENT

Assume that a bank funds \$100 of two-year securities with \$100 of one-year deposits. To simplify matters, also assume that both securities and deposits are discount instruments that pay par at maturity so that there are no interest payments during the year. The securities earn a yield of 10 percent, and the deposits cost 8 percent. The income and expenses for the bank for the bank over these two years is as follows:

	Year 1	Year 2
Income	\$0	\$121 (= \$100 × 1.10 × 1.10)
Expense	–8	–108
Profit	–\$8	\$ 13

Discounting all cash at 8 percent, which is the cost of funds, we get $\$13/(1.08)^2 - \$8/(1.08) = \$3.74$, such that the net present value of the investment portfolio is positive.

Suppose that interest rates rise to 10 percent for deposits in the second year. Given that the securities purchased and deposits acquired in the first year have their interest rates locked in at the rates that prevailed at the beginning of the first period, the income and expenses for the bank would now be

	Year 1	Year 2
Income	\$0	\$121 (= \$100 × 1.10 × 1.10)
Expense	–8	–110 (= 100 × 1.10)
Profit	–\$8	\$ 11

Discounting all cash at 8 percent in the first period and 10 percent in the second period, we get $\$11/(1.10)^2 - \$8/(1.08) = \$1.68$. Notice that the net present value of the investment portfolio has declined by over 50 percent from \$3.74 before the rise in interest rates. This drop in profitability was due to the decrease in profits in Year 2 from \$13 to \$11 (before discounting to present values).

We can also calculate the effect of the increase in interest rates on the equity value of the bank in Year 2. For this purpose we make use of equation (10.2) covered later in this chapter. That equation shows how the concept of duration can be employed to estimate changes in asset values in response to interest rate changes (see also Chapter 5). In the above example securities have a duration equal to 2, while deposits have a duration equal to 1. Substituting this information into equation (10.2), the change in the value of securities is $-(2)\$100(0.02/1.10) = -\$3.64$, while for deposits the change is $-(1)\$100(0.02/1.08) = -\$1.85$. So, the net change in equity must be –\$1.79 in Year 2.

The bank could have avoided the negative profit and equity capital implications of the increase in interest rates with an accurate interest rate forecast in Year 1 of the 2 percent increase in Year 2. In this event some of its securities could have been sold and the resultant funds used to purchase shorter-term securities with less price risk. Rearranging the maturity structure of deposits or loans is also possible but is more difficult from the standpoint that, while bank pricing of deposits and loans with different maturities can influence their maturities, depositor and borrower preferences for different maturity ranges comes into play. With securities investments, interest rate risk can be adjusted without taking into account deposit and loan demands.

banks with sizeable investments in mortgage-related securities suffered large losses that impacted their net income and asset values (as well as capital on the other side of the balance sheet).

In the 1990s the Financial Accounting Standards Board (FASB) approved ***market value accounting*** rules that require banks to classify securities for valuation purposes on their accounting statements. These rules have evolved over time. After the financial crisis, FASB established three classes of securities: (1) assets held to maturity, (2) trading securities, and (3) assets available for sale. Most bonds are held to maturity and therefore are carried on the books at historical cost. However, traded assets are marked to market on a quarterly basis. If a bond's value falls from \$1,000 to \$900, a \$100 decrease in assets on the left side of the balance sheet will occur as well as a \$100 pretax loss on the income statement. Normally, observable market prices are used to determine traded securities valuation, but at times other market information could be utilized to value these securities (e.g., market prices are not available or the market is illiquid). In this regard, during the financial crisis, regulators temporarily relaxed strict fair value accounting rules to take into consideration the market turmoil at that time. The last classification of securities – assets available for sale – must be marked to market value each quarter but does not affect the bank's regulatory capital. Note that derivatives must always be reported at fair market value but loans are typically reported at book value. Also, liabilities can be marked to market (e.g., a bank with $100 million debt outstanding can mark its value down to $90 million to increase its earnings and capital by $10 million).

One problem for investment managers under market value accounting is that many times securities are held for trading or available for sale to meet liquidity demands, rather than to maximize yields or to trade at a profit. For many small banks this problem is particularly troublesome. To minimize the effect of market value accounting, shorter-term securities should be held for trading or sale and longer-term securities can be held for maturity. In this way liquidity needs are met without exposing the investment portfolio to considerable interest rate risk.

In the context of investment goals, bank management needs to consider the risk preferences of shareholders. Risk by itself is not undesirable; instead, it is risk in excess of some level appropriate for the shareholders that is unsatisfactory. Thus, bank management must understand shareholder risk preferences in order to establish investment goals.

Securities held to meet *pledging requirements* mentioned earlier should be selected with other goals in mind to avoid conflicts among investment goals. For example, if U.S. government deposits must be collateralized with Treasury securities, or state government deposits require pledged municipal securities, bank management should purchase instruments with income and capital gains earnings that coincide with goals in these particular areas. Other liabilities, such as repurchase agreements (RPs) and discount window borrowings, must also be collateralized with qualifying assets.

Development of an investment policy that maximizes returns per unit risk involves defining the various goals discussed above. Even though policies generally are oriented toward a long-run perspective, the investment policy should incorporate some degree of management flexibility to accommodate changing market conditions. If tax laws or regulatory standards change to more favorably treat a particular type of security (e.g., new risk-based capital standards have zero capital requirements on some types of securities and higher capital requirements on other securities), management should take such changes into account in their investment decisions. Because internal and external conditions change over time for banks, management must periodically review and update investment goals.

TYPES OF INVESTMENT SECURITIES

Investment securities can be arbitrarily defined as those securities with maturities exceeding one year. Two categories of securities dominate over 90 percent of bank investment portfolios -- U.S. government and agency securities, and obligations of state and political subdivisions, or municipal securities. Other bonds and equity securities are heavily restricted by regulations; for example, high-quality corporate bonds are allowed but are subject to restrictions, and common stock investment is allowed in subsidiaries of banks or bank holding companies that are legally separate entities under the Financial Services Modernization Act of 1999.

U.S. GOVERNMENT AND AGENCY SECURITIES

U.S. Treasury Securities

Most ***treasury notes*** and bonds purchased by banks have maturities ranging from one to five years. Unlike Treasury bills, which are sold at a discount and pay no coupon interest, Treasury notes and bonds are coupon-bearing instruments, consistent with their income function.[2] Because the market for Treasuries in the one-to-five-year range is relatively deep and broad, these securities provide an extra measure of bank liquidity. Additionally, these securities serve to secure both deposits of public money (e.g., tax and loan accounts of the U.S. Treasury) and loans from Federal Reserve banks, and they are widely accepted for use in repurchase agreements.

Agency Securities

Many federal agencies issue securities that are not direct obligations of the U.S. Treasury but nonetheless are federally sponsored or guaranteed. Some examples of federal agencies are the Government National Mortgage Association (GNMA or Ginnie Mae), Federal Home Loan Mortgage Corporation (FHLMC or Freddie Mac), Federal Housing Administration (FHA), Veterans Administration (VA), Farm Credit Administration (FCA), Federal Land Banks (FLB), and Small Business Administration (SBA). Ginnie Maes, for instance, represent a claim against interest earnings on a pool of FHA and VA mortgages issued by private mortgage institutions. The principal and interest on these so-called "pass through" bonds are guaranteed by the full faith and credit of the U.S. government. Similarly, securities issued by the Federal National Mortgage Association (FNMA or Fannie Mae) and the Mortgage Guarantee Insurance Corporation (MGIC or Maggie Mae) and other agencies represent claims on mortgage pools; however, because FNMA is a federally sponsored agency and MGIC is a private mortgage bank, FNMA securities have lower interest rates than do MGIC securities. There is also a modest risk distinction between federally guaranteed issues (e.g., GNMAs) and federally sponsored issues (FNMAs and FHLMCs).

Other mortgage-backed securities (MBSs) (otherwise known as *agency securities*) include participation certificates (PCs), guaranteed mortgage certificates (GMCs), and collateralized mortgage obligation (CMOs). PCs are ownership claims on conventional mortgages held by Freddie Mac with monthly payments of interest and principal. GMCs are also claims on a pool of mortgages held by Freddie Mac, but the interest payments are made semi-annually like a corporate bond and principal is paid once a year. CMOs are an important innovation that repackages the cash flows from both pooled mortgages and MBSs (with standardized terms of payment and maturity) into different payment combinations -- for example, interest only (IO), principal only (PO), and mixed payment streams -- and different maturity ranges. In so doing CMOs are designed to appeal to diverse investor demands.

All mortgage-derivative securities are exposed to ***prepayment risk***. For example, when interest rates decline, refinancings of mortgages by homeowners to take advantage of the lower interest payments can cause prepayments of outstanding mortgages.[3] While homeowners clearly benefit from refinancing at lower interest rates, MBS investors now must reinvest at lower interest rates as MBSs effectively mature. In turn, as interest rates fall to low levels, the prices of MBSs can decline due to negative investor reaction to prepayment risk. This price behavior is known as "reverse convexity"[4] (i.e., prices decline as interest rates decline, the opposite of the normal experience in which prices rise in response to falling interest rates). Interestingly, one advantage of CMOs is that investors can select bonds with varying levels of prepayment risk, for shorter-term bonds have lower risk than longer-term bonds in this respect.

In recent years banks have held about $3 trillion in securities, of which about $2.2 trillion is comprised of Treasury and agency securities. Of the latter, about $1.5 trillion is mortgage-backed securities (MBSs). The major reason for this emphasis on MBSs is that these agencies earn a slightly better yield than Treasuries without sacrificing much liquidity, as secondary markets for agencies have become well developed over the last 20 years. For comparison purposes, banks held about $8.5 trillion in loans and leases to their customers. Hence, investments represent about 20 percent of bank assets.

MUNICIPAL BONDS

Municipal bonds are issued by state and local governments to finance various public works, such as roads, bridges, schools, fire departments, parks, and so on. They normally offer higher yields than do the U.S. government and agency securities because they are exposed to default risk. General obligation municipal bonds (GOs) are backed by the "full faith and credit" of the taxing governmental unit. Revenue bonds are somewhat riskier than GOs because they are backed by the earning power of a public project, such as a toll road. In the event of default, bondholders would likely suffer large losses, because the physical assets are not marketable, especially if construction is not completed. The supply of revenue bonds has risen over time because of the desire by communities to borrow funds and thereby avoid further taxation of local residents.

Taxes

Historically, due to the exposure of banks to federal (and state) income taxes, the primary advantage of "munis" compared with other securities was their exemption from federal income taxes (as well as from state income taxes if issued by a governmental unit within the state). In this case, a muni yielding seven percent before taxes may well have had an after-tax yield exceeding that of a comparable-risk corporate bond yielding 10 percent before taxes. To see how the interest tax exemption on munis affects the income statement, assuming only federal income taxes, consider the following short-form income statement for a bank (on the next page):

Notice that net operating income (NOI) is just offset by municipal interest earnings such that the bank does not have any taxable income. If NOI were less than municipal interest earned, the bank would obtain no benefits from the tax exemp-

	In Thousands
Total interest on securities	$1,000
Municipal bond interest	600
Other interest on securities	400
Total interest on loans	2,000
Total operating income	$3,000
Total interest expenses	(2,100)
Total noninterest expenses	(300)
Total operating expenses	$(2,400)
Net operating income (NOI)	600
Less municipal bond interest	(600)
Taxable income	$0
Less taxes	(0)
Net income after taxes	$0

tion on munis.[5]

This type of situation occurred for many U.S. banks in the past, because profit margins narrowed due to deregulation, regional economic doldrums, and farming sector problems.

However, under the Tax Reform Act of 1986 (TRA86), the attractiveness of munis as investments for banks was substantially reduced. Generally, banks no longer can deduct interest expenses on borrowed funds used to purchase tax-exempt securities.[6] The loss of this deduction offsets the tax exemption on munis interest earnings for the most part. In the example above, if interest paid on funds acquired to purchase munis was $400, interest expenses would be reduced to $1,700 from $2,100, and taxable income would rise to $400 from $0. An important exception is that banks are permitted to deduct 80 percent of the interest paid to acquire funds to purchase munis issued by local governments with no more than $10 million of new issues in any one year (so-called "bank qualified" munis[7]).

To compare the yields on munis with yields on taxable bonds, the following tax equivalent yield for munis with comparable risk and maturity can be applied:

$$YTM_m/(1 - T) = (1.0 \times \text{Average cost of funds} \times T)/(1 - T) = YTM_{TE} \qquad (7.1)$$

where YTMm = the yield-to-maturity on the munis bond, T = the tax rate of the bank, the average cost of funds is calculated based on IRS rules, and YTMTE = the tax equivalent yield-to-maturity on munis. The factor of 1.0 in the numerator of the second term indicates that 100 percent of interest is nondeductible under TRA86 rules. For qualified munis bonds this factor would be 0.20. To demonstrate the use of this formula, assume YTMm = 8 percent, tax rate = 34 percent, average cost of funds = 7 percent, and 100 percent of interest is nondeductible. The tax equivalent munis yield is:

$$[0.08/(1 - 0.34)] = [(1.0 \times 0.07 \times 0.34)/(1 - 0.34)] = .0852$$

or 8.52 percent. As a check, if we consider (for example) a $1 million corporate bond, the after-tax earnings would be the same as the munis bond:

	Taxable Bond	Munis Bond	
Interest	$85,200	$80,000	
Less taxes	(29,000)	0	
Nondeductible interest	0	(23,800)	(= 1,000,000 × 0.07 × 0.34)
After-tax earnings	$56,200	$56,200	

Another relevant tax item under TRA86 is that banks pay the higher of (1) regular income tax or (2) alternative minimum tax at a 20 percent tax rate. Today, the maximum corporate tax rate is 35 percent. The alternative minimum tax prevents banks from paying no taxes, as in the example above. If the alternative minimum tax method is used, one-half of munis' interest will be exposed to taxes (i.e., a 10 percent tax rate on munis interest). Clearly, the net effect of these changes in tax laws is a reduction in the attractiveness of munis for commercial banks.

Additionally, risk-based capital rules (see Chapter 12) have altered banks' interest in GO versus revenue bonds. New rules phased in during 2014 and 2015 require a 20 percent risk weight in computing risk-based capital requirements for GOs compared with a 50 percent risk weight for revenue bonds. For every dollar of investment, this implies that two-and-a-half times more capital is needed for revenue bonds than for GOs. Clearly, bank investment in revenue bonds is disadvantaged by capital rules, while investment in GO bonds is advantaged.

Of course, at least from a tax management perspective, bank management should not hold municipal securities beyond the point where their after-tax yield to the bank (after taking into account lost interest deductions) is less than the after-tax corporate bond yield of comparable risk. However, even if munis' yields exceed corporate yields, for various reasons, such as liquidity needs and capital regulations, management may opt to invest in corporate securities. Also, it is possible that taxes can be reduced by other means than municipal securities, such as utilizing leasing, making loans subject to foreign tax credits, timing loan and security losses, and accelerating depreciation.

CORPORATE BONDS

A corporate bond is a long-term debt security issued by a private corporation. Because the historical failure rate of corporations far exceeds the default rate by state and local governments on their debt obligations, it is necessary to evaluate carefully the default risk of this type of bond. Bond ratings and financial analysis of firms' accounting statements are two approaches to evaluating this risk (to be discussed shortly).

RECENT PORTFOLIO COMPOSITION

Table 7-1 shows the composition of the securities portfolio of all insured U.S. commercial banks during the five-year period 2010-2014. The mix of total securities was dominated by U.S. Treasury and government agency securities, which normally accounted for 10 percent to 17 percent of total assets during this period. State and local government (or municipal) securities accounted for only about one percent to two percent of total assets. In this regard, investment in municipal securities has gradually diminished from a level of about six percent since 1986, when the Tax Reform Act was signed, as discussed earlier. All other securities, which are corporate bonds and private mortgage-backed securities for the most part, were five percent to eight percent of total assets, with an upward trend in the 1995–2002 period. Over this period of time, there was a shift toward increased purchases of U.S. government agencies comprised of MBSs and CMOs. Notice that securities investments declined from 24 percent of total assets in 1994 to 19 percent in 2001 but thereafter increased somewhat to about 21 percent in 2002. The decrease in securities holdings in the late 1990s was due to strong loan demand. The subsequent increase in securities investments in 2002 was no doubt related to falling loan demand during the economic recession.

Of total securities held, about 25 percent had maturities of less than one year and, therefore, were purchased primarily for liquidity purposes. The majority of securities, about 75 percent, had maturities exceeding one year and might be considered the investment portfolio. Of these securities, about one-half had maturities in the range of one to five years, and one-half had maturities exceeding five years. Thus, most investment securities will mature at different times within one business cycle. This provides banks with some degree of flexibility in their allocation of funds throughout the business cycle.

Table 7-1 (next page) shows that banks increased their securities investments from a book value of $2.4 trillion in 2010 to $2.94 trillion in 2014. Market values of these investments were close to their book values due to very low and stable interest rates. During this period, U.S. Treasury holdings more than doubled from $157 billion to $391 billion, and municipal securities (i.e., states and political subdivisions) increased markedly from $206 billion to $303 billion. Holdings of agencies' securities grew by about $240 billion due to increasing normalization of the housing market after the 2008 to 2009 financial collapse. And, holdings of corporate bonds remained little changed due to the slow economic recovery and related demand for corporate credit at that time.

EVALUATING INVESTMENT RISK

The investment risk involved in purchasing securities can be evaluated either on an individual security basis or in the context of the total asset portfolio of the bank. Thus, both security-specific and portfolio considerations should be taken into account to understand the risk of investment securities. Finally, an important consideration is potential inflation effects on investment values.

SECURITY-SPECIFIC RISK

Default Risk

Default risk is the probability that promised payment of interest and principal

Table 7-1: COMPOSITION OF SECURITIES PORTFOLIO FOR ALL U.S. COMMERCIAL BANKS: 2010-2014 (dollar amounts in thousands)

	Obligations of			Other Obligations			
Year	U.S. Treasury	U.S. Agencies and Corporations	States and Political Subdivisions	Corporate Bonds and Other Securities	Equity Securities	Total Investment Securities (Book Value)	Market Value
2014	390,676,649	1,545,226,644	302,627,369	688,009,443	10,608,258	2,937,148,363	2,944,605,529
2013	187,971,043	1,493,700,622	279,832,367	750,898,563	10,901,746	2,723,304,341	2,716,816,675
2012	200,214,744	1,527,252,852	249,975,567	760,402,956	13,604,171	2,751,450,299	2,757,487,231
2011	157,302,131	1,432,506,290	206,379,832	733,949,769	12,857,598	2,542,995,622	2,546,058,440
2010	185,959,060	1,303,039,289	171,218,604	679,198,817	14,925,527	2,354,341,297	2,356,907,712

Source: Federal Deposit Insurance Corporation, https://www5.fdic.gov/hsob/HSOBRpt.asp.

will not be made on time. In general, municipal and corporate bonds (and some agency bonds) have greater credit risk than do federal government securities. Standard & Poor's and Moody's both provide credit risk ratings that indicate the long-run probability of timely payment of promised interest and principal. ***Investment grade bonds*** are assigned letter ratings by Moody's/S&P's as follows:

Aaa/AAA	Highest-grade bonds that have almost no probability of default
Aa/AA	High-grade bonds having slightly lower credit quality than triple-A bonds
A/A	Upper-medium-grade bonds that are partially exposed to possible adverse economic conditions
Baa/BBB	Medium-grade bonds that are borderline between definitely sound and subject to speculative elements, depending on economic conditions

Junk bonds are rated as follows:

Ba/BB	Lower-medium-grade bonds that bear significant default risk should difficult economic conditions prevail
B/B, Caa/CCC, Ca/CC, C/C	Speculative investment of varying degree that have questionable credit quality
DDD, DD, D	Bonds in default, differing only in terms of their probable salvage value

Except in rare instances (e.g., a bond may have been downgraded subsequent to its purchase), banks restrict themselves to investment-grade securities, which fall within the "prudent person" rule of law.

Bond ratings provide general guidelines for gauging default risk. However, what if a bank is attempting to decide between three different firms' bonds that all have the same bond rating? In this situation financial analysis can be helpful. Typically, a wide variety of financial ratios are calculated from the firms' accounting statements. Ratios should be calculated over time to gain insight into trends. Also, ratios need to be compared with industry averages or peer group averages. Industry averages are reported by a number of sources, including the Risk Management Association, Dun & Bradstreet, the Federal Trade Commission, and trade associations. Alternatively, a peer group of firms that are close competitors of the firm can be sampled by the analyst.

Table 7-2 gives an example of financial ratios for three hypothetical firms that we will assume have the same bond rating. Firm B has the highest rate of return on assets (net profits/total assets), Firm C has the highest rate of return on equity (net profits/net worth), and Firm A is in the middle of this peer group. Firm C has the highest current ratio (current assets/total liabilities) but its quick or acid test ratio ([current assets – inventory]/current liabilities) is not the highest. Higher activity ratios reflect stronger short-term solvency, as more liquid assets are available to cover short-term creditor claims. Since inventory commonly is not as liquid as other current assets, and losses can occur on inventory if liquidated, the quick ratio is a stronger (acid) test of liquidity than the current ratio. The data in Table 7-2 show that Firm C is more highly levered (indebted) than Firms A and B. This difference explains the high rate of return on net worth for Firm C (i.e., lower net worth in the denominator of this ratio). Finally, Firm C has a moderate level of inventory turnover (sales/inventory) but has low total assets turnover (sales/total assets). The latter low figure suggests that it does not produce as much in sales per dollar of assets as the other firms. Thus, assuming equal bond yields, Firm C should be dropped from consideration due to higher financial risk associated with relatively higher leverage and lower ability to generate sales to pay debt charges. Comparing Firms A and B, Firm B has lower leverage, stronger activity, more liquidity, and higher profitability than A. Firm B is favored over Firm A for these reasons.

Table 7-2: EXAMPLE OF FINANCIAL RATIO ANALYSIS

Financial Ratios	Firm A	Firm B	Firm C
Profitability			
Net profits/net sales	0.04	0.05	0.03
Net profits/net worth	0.15	0.12	0.18
Net profits/total assets	0.06	0.07	0.06
Liquidity			
Current assets/current liabilities	2.00	2.30	2.40
(Current assets – inventory)/current liabilities	1.30	1.40	1.30
Leverage			
Total debt/total assets	0.40	0.35	0.50
Gross income/interest charges	4.00	4.20	3.00
Activity			
Sales/inventory	10.00	8.50	9.00
Sales/total assets	1.50	2.00	1.40

Note: All ratios are calculated using book values as reported on accounting statements.

Our purpose here is to simply introduce some basic concepts within the context of investment decisions. In general, a complete financial ratio analysis involves analyses of trends over time, a broader set of financial ratios and other financial information, and industry or peer group comparisons. If the bank is planning to purchase large quantities of bonds issued by an individual entity where default risk is a relevant concern, an in-house analysis by bank investment managers would be warranted.

Bondholder Losses in Default

Readers should recognize that both bond ratings and financial analyses capture default risk as reflected in the probability of default and expected losses in default. Potential losses to bondholders arise from two sources: (1) priority of claims and (2) bankruptcy costs. In bankruptcy court proceedings, bondholders receive the prorated cash flows of the firm, depending on their order of claim. It is important to note that nonsubordinated bonds have more senior claims than subordinated bonds. The amount paid out to bondholders depends largely on various bankruptcy costs, such as the administrative costs of legal, accounting, and other court procedures. Another bankruptcy cost relates to the value of the firm's assets. If the court sells off portions of the firm, merges it out with a solvent firm, or liquidates all of its assets, bondholders receive returns based on the proceeds of any such "distressed" sale. If a firm's assets are easily transferred to other firms and are valued highly due to market demand (e.g., commercial airplanes), then bondholders will have lower default losses. While bond ratings give some estimate of expected losses in default based on historical evidence, it is prudent for bank management to assess potential default losses before making bond investments. Thus, although Firm C was dropped from consideration in the financial analysis above, this decision may well be reversed by relatively higher expected values of assets than Firms A and B in the event of default. Unfortunately, there is no agency or firm that supplies publicly available information on distressed sale values of assets held by firms. This information could be either purchased from consultants or researched by investors by studying recent (or historical) liquidation results of comparable firms with similar assets.

Bond Prices and Default Risk

Bond prices are inversely related to credit risk, which means that lower-quality bonds have higher yields on average than do higher-quality bonds. This difference in yields between low- and high-quality bonds (or ***yield spread***) tends to vary with economic conditions. During recessionary periods, when default is perceived to be most likely to occur, yield spreads are greater than they are during economic expansions. For bank management, this cyclical behavior of yield spreads implies that lower-quality bonds offer relatively favorable yields per unit of risk during recessionary periods (when loan demand is depressed and the bank has greater excess cash to invest). While interest rates normally increase after a recession and this would depress bond prices, bonds purchased during an economic downturn could be timed to mature at different points in the future in order to both avoid capital losses and provide added liquidity throughout the expansionary phase of the business cycle.

Price Risk

Price risk refers to the inverse relationship between changes in the level of interest rates and the price of securities. This relationship is particularly relevant to bank managers of investment securities, because securities purchased when there is slack loan demand and interest rates are relatively low may need to be sold later at a capital loss (to meet loan demand) in a higher interest rate environment. In light of this potential pitfall, securities should be timed to mature during anticipated future business-cycle periods of increased loan demand. Bonds maturing beyond five years normally fall outside of this range and so are not generally emphasized in the investment portfolio. Moreover, because the yield curve tends to be upward-sloping and flattens out after about five years, there is typically little income incentive to purchase securities beyond the five-year range.

When interest rates are relatively high and the expansionary phase of the business cycle is peaking, purchasing securities with terms longer than five years may well be justified. At such times loan demand is beginning to fall as business firms decide that interest rates are so high that borrowing would not be profitable (i.e., the net present value of projects declines as interest rates rise and expectations for future business revenues fall). The next-best income-producing alternative is to purchase long-term securities. Earning high yields for an extended period of time is clearly one benefit of purchasing such securities, because interest rates will probably decline during a downturn in business activity. Another (and perhaps more important) benefit is that if these long-term securities are later sold to meet load demand (for example), a capital gain could be realized, because interest rates will likely be lower than they were when the securities were originally purchased. The longer the term-to -maturity of the securities that are sold, the larger this capital gain would be. Thus, longer-term securities can be purchased as an aggressive approach toward price risk. Such an approach is not without its potential pitfalls, for there are uncertainties in forecasting both expected future interest rates and business cycle movements. Bank management needs to weigh the expected returns against the expected risks in order to evaluate price risk properly in this situation.

To evaluate the amount of price risk on a bond, it is necessary to consider not only the expected change in interest rates but also the duration of the bond. As previously discussed in Chapter 5, duration is a measure of bond maturity that considers the timing of cash flows. Relevant to the current discussion, duration is a proxy for price risk. The following formula shows how duration links interest rate changes to bond price changes:

$$\Delta P = -D \times B \times \Delta i/(1 + i) \qquad (7.2)$$

where ΔP is the change in the price of the bond, D equals the duration (in years),[9] B is the original price of the bond, and Δ is the change in interest rates from some original level i. To demonstrate, if a bond currently selling for \$1,000 has a duration of five years and interest rates are expected to increase from five percent to seven percent in the coming year, the bond's price will decline by approximately $95 (i.e., –5 × $1,000 × 0.02/1.05). Because high-coupon bonds have shorter durations than do low-coupon bonds of the same yield and term-to-maturity, high-coupon bonds have relatively less price risk. For example, consider two five-year bonds with equal yield to maturity and risk. One bond is a zero-coupon bond and the other a high-coupon bond. The "zero" would have a duration equal to its maturity, or five years, whereas the high-coupon bond, say, has a duration of three years. If interest rates increase by two percent, this change is multiplied by five for the zero-coupon versus three for the high-coupon bond in calculating their respective price declines. Clearly, duration is a valuable price risk measure that management can use to gauge their exposure to potential future changes in interest rates.

Duration analysis can be used to "immunize" the investment portfolio from the opposing forces of price risk and reinvestment risk. If interest rates increase, prices of securities decline but periodic coupon returns on bonds can be reinvested at higher rates of return. Conversely, if interest rates decrease, prices of securities rise but earnings on bonds must be reinvested at lower rates of return. Assuming coupon-bearing securities on average are sold at about their duration date, these opposing risks will approximately offset one another. The net result is that the promised yield-to-maturity is earned on a security. Alternatively, if the holding period for a bond is other than the duration date, it is unlikely that the promised yield will be realized. For example, suppose a manager purchases a five-year bond with a promised yield-to-maturity equal to 10 percent and plans to hold the bond to its maturity date. In the calculation of the promised yield, it is assumed that all coupons earned over time on the bond are reinvested at the promised yield of 10 percent. However, it is almost impossible that interest rates will not change over time; thus, it is obvious that holding a bond to maturity will likely not result in a realized yield of 10 percent. In order to more accurately estimate ahead of time the actual yield to be earned on securities, duration must be set equal to the holding period. In this way the bank can immunize itself from price and reinvestment risks and thereby increase control over the returns per unit risk on securities.

Even if a bank uses duration to immunize securities' risks, market value accounting for securities held for sale requires that duration analysis be employed to evaluate the expected future prices of securities in the investment portfolio in response to potential changes in interest rates. Of course, a key ingredient to such an analysis is the estimation of expected future changes in interest rates. In this regard, market analysts examine the ***yield curve***. Figure 7-1 (next page) shows the yield curve for U.S. Treasury securities as of November 7, 2014. Normally, the yield curve has an upward slope, with longer-term securities offering higher yields than shorter-term securities.

Figure 7-2 (next page) shows how the yield curve typically changes its level and shape over the business cycle. In a recession, interest rate levels are low due to the weak demand for funds by business firms, and the shape is steeply upward sloping than at other times. During a business expansion, the level of the yield curve will rise in response to increased demand for funds by business firms and will gradually

FIGURE 7-1 **YIELDS ON U.S. TREASURY SECURITIES**

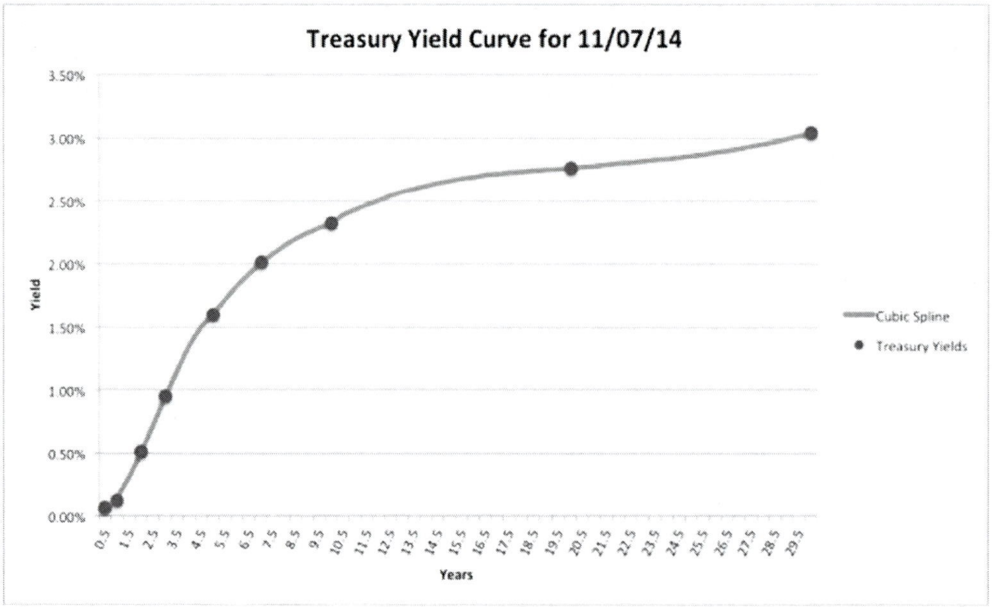

flatten in shape but remain generally upward sloping. Finally, at the end of an economic expansion, the yield curve will be at its highest level and take on a variety of shapes. Figure 7-2 shows an inverted shape at this point, but humped shapes and a flat shape are possible also. At some point high interest rates will precipitate a business slowdown, and the yield curve can collapse in a matter of months. The StockCharts.com website (http://stockcharts.com/freecharts/yieldcurve.php) has an animated yield curve feature that allows you to see how the yield curve has been moving over time over the last few years.

FIGURE 7-2 **THE YIELD CURVE AND THE BUSINESS CYCLE**

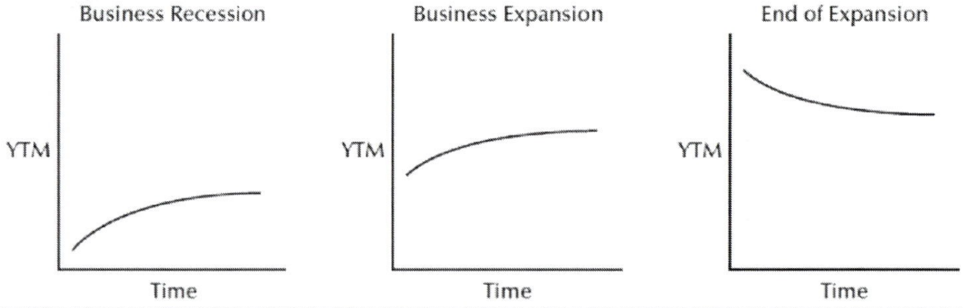

Many observers have attempted to explain the shape and dynamics of the yield curve throughout the business cycle. Four theories have gained favor over the years: the expectations theory, the liquidity premium theory, the market segmentation theory, and the preferred-habitat theory.

According to the expectations theory of the yield curve, investors earn the same rate of return regardless of their holding period. This means that an investor would earn the same amount by either purchasing a two-year bond and holding it for two years or purchasing a one-year bond now and another one-year bond next year. Formally stated, the following geometric average relationship is hypothesized to hold between long- and short-term interest rates over time:

$$(1 + {}_0R_2)^2 = (1 + {}_0R_1)(1 + {}_1r_2) \tag{7.3}$$

where ${}_0R_2$ is the two-year (spot) rate at the present time, ${}_0R_1$ is the one-year (spot) rate at the present time, and ${}_1r_2$ is the one-year future implicit rate that will exist one year from now. In effect, the future implicit rate is a forecasted rate of interest. The future implicit rate is not known with certainty at time 0 (now) but it nonetheless is reflected in the two-year spot rate of interest. To demonstrate, assume that ${}_0R_2$ = 10 percent and ${}_0R_1$ = 9 percent. Given this information, the rate ${}_1r_2$ can be calculated to be 11 percent; that is, ${}_1r_2 = (1 + 0.10)^2/(1 + 0.09) - 1 = 0.11$. Thus, one-year interest rates are expected to increase by about two percent within the next year. Naturally, market expectations are not always correct and this forecasted interest rate may well be in error. But we would anticipate that the forecasts of future implicit rates would be too high 50 percent of the time and too low 50 percent of the time. On average, it should not matter what the holding period of the investor is.[10]

Based on the expectations theory, interest rate forecasts in any period and for any maturity range of bonds can be estimated. To forecast the two-year bond rate two years from now, or ${}_2r_4$, four-year and two-year spot rates could be gathered and used as follows:

$$(1 + {}_0R_4)^4 = (1 + {}_0R_2)^2\,(1 + {}_2r_4)^2$$

To forecast the one-year bond rate three years from now, or ${}_3r_4$, four-year and three-year spot rates could be used:

$$(1 + {}_0R_4)^4 = (1 + {}_0R_3)^3\,(1 + {}_3r_4)$$

Equations of this form can be readily developed to derive other interest rate forecasts.

Empirical evidence has repeatedly shown that future implicit rates in equation (7.3) provide upwardly biased estimates of actual future rates of interest. For this reason it is advisable to adjust the interest rate forecast based on the expectations theory for other possible influences on yields over time. One factor is the liquidity preference of lenders in the financial market. Risk-averse lenders prefer to lend funds for short periods of time, unless a premium is paid for foregoing greater liquidity and lending funds for longer periods. This added return, or premium, is known as a ***liquidity premium***.[11]

Many analysts believe that liquidity premiums cause expectations theory forecasts to be biased upward; that is, the actual yield curve is a summation of the expectation yield curve plus liquidity premiums. For example, in our previous example, ${}_0R_2$ = expected yield on two-year bonds + liquidity premium. If the liquidity premium were 0.5 percent, the expected two-year rate would equal 9.5 percent (i.e., 10 = 9.5 + 0.5). Substituting this adjusted long-term rate into equation (7.3), the new forecast for the one-year rate next year is 10 percent, which means interest rates can be expected to increase by only one percent, rather than two percent before accounting for the potential liquidity premium.

Another factor that could affect yields over time is the relative supplies and demands for short- and long-term financial instruments by various market participants, especially government and institutional investors. It is generally acknowledged that there are ***segmented markets*** in the financial system because there are different participants and needs in the money and capital markets. Commercial banks, the Federal Reserve, and corporations requiring inventory and other working capital are the key participants in the money market, whereas life insurance companies, pension funds, and corporations demanding capital funds for investment projects dominate the long-term bond market. This segmentation occurs due to the desire by firms to maintain maturity structures of assets and liabilities that are matched for the most part. Generally speaking, short-term interest rates tend to be more volatile than long-term rates. Consequently, short-term variations in supply and demand factors will have the greatest influence on the shape of the yield curve and, therefore, on forecasts of expected future interest rates. Adjusting for liquidity preferences, for example, we earlier estimated one-year interest rates to increase by about one percent next year. This short-term forecast could be adjusted further for anticipated changes in Federal Reserve monetary policy, corporate working capital needs, and commercial bank effects on the supply and demand for money.

Finally, the ***preferred-habitat*** theory takes into account all three of these yield curve factors. It hypothesizes that investors will switch from their normal maturity preference (or habitat) to a different maturity range of securities if yield differentials are sufficiently high to compensate for the potential price risks associated with mismatched asset and liability maturities. As such, interest rate forecasts would be based on market expectations, liquidity preferences, and market segmentation. Forecasts of potential future changes in interest rates enable investment managers to evaluate the influence of these changes on security prices. These estimates can be valuable in making purchase and sale decisions, particularly if the bank is seeking aggressively to manage the investment portfolio throughout the business cycle.

Table 7-3 (next page) shows an example of how price risk can affect the investment portfolio at two points in time. Assume that all securities are held for sale, such that market value accounting is a key concern of bank management. Further assume that at time 0 information contained in the yield curve forecasts a one percent in interest rates. Given that this forecast is accurate, notice that at time 1 (i.e., one quarter later) the market values of securities declined, with larger declines associated with longer-term securities. Since these securities are marked-to-market, losses must be subtracted from retained earnings to obtain the net addition (loss) to equity on the balance sheet. It is possible that the securities losses could diminish equi-

TABLE 7-3	EXAMPLE OF PRICE RISK IN A SECURITIES PORTFOLIO ($ MILLIONS)

Quarter 1 Values:

Quarters to	One-Year U.S. Bonds		Five-Year U.S. Bonds		State and Munis Bonds	
Maturity	Par Value	Market Value	Par Value	Market Value	Par Value	Market Value
2	5.000	5.000	15.000	15.000	10.000	10.000
3	5.000	5.015	15.000	15.050		
4	10.000	10.061	15.000	15.089	5.000	5.011
8					27.000	27.085
12			15.000	15.412	1.250	1.197

Quarter 2 Values (after a 1% increase in the level of interest rates):

Quarters to	One-Year U.S. Bonds		Five-Year U.S. Bonds		State and Munis Bonds	
Maturity	Par Value	Market Value	Par Value	Market Value	Par Value	Market Value
1	5.000	5.000	15.000	14.945	10.000	9.978
2	5.000	4.997	15.000	15.001		
3	10.000	9.993	15.000	14.985	5.000	4.979
7					27.000	26.635
11			15.000	14.929	1.250	1.160

ty capital sufficiently to fall below regulatory standards. In this event the bank would be under regulatory and market pressure to maintain adequate capital. A common solution to this problem is to purchase a short (or sell) position in financial futures contracts. As interest rates rise, the futures contracts can be sold at higher prices than their original purchase prices, with resultant gains on sale. Thus, the gains on shorting futures offset losses on long (buy) cash positions in securities held on the balance sheet (see examples in Chapter 6).

Duration analysis and interest rate cycles can be useful in estimating the ***value-at-risk (VAR)***. VAR considers the maximum amount that could be lost in investment activities in a specified period of time. More specifically, given a certain probability and holding period, VAR measures the maximum amount by which the investment portfolio will decline in value. Based on the historical movements in interest rate series over time, a distribution of interest rate changes over a chosen holding period can be constructed. Assuming the distribution is normal, the probability of any particular change in interest rates can be selected. For example, based on an historical distribution of interest rate changes, suppose that the probability of a 50 basis point increase in interest rates in a ten-day period is five percent. Using this interest rate increase in equation (7.2), in combination with the average duration of securities held for sale, an estimate of the maximum loss in market value of these securities that will occur in one-out-of-20 ten-day holding periods can be calculated. If the average duration is three years, the securities are worth $1 billion at the present time, and interest rates are currently at six percent, this data would yield a VAR of $15.6 million (= −3 × $1 billion × 0.0050/1.06).

Obviously, there is considerable flexibility in the application of VAR to measuring price risk in the investment portfolio. The selection of probabilities and holding periods is ad hoc and subject to manager judgment. Volatility can change over time and cause the historical analyses to be invalid. If interest rate forecasts suggest an increasing trend in market volatility, VAR estimates could be adjusted to reflect these changing conditions. Of course, banks can buy and sell futures contracts to either offset long cash positions or change their duration and thereby alter their VAR. Due to the dynamic nature of VAR estimates, it is now routine for banks to simulate the performance of their securities portfolios under alternative conditions. Assumptions are changed and input parameters in calculating VAR are altered to reflect the latest market conditions and hedging strategies. These stress tests consider normal and worst-case scenarios in order to give management a complete picture of securities portfolio risks. Despite the inherent subjectivity of VAR due to uncertainty in financial markets, it is a popular tool in investment practice that is commonly applied to estimating maximum potential losses on securities.

Marketability Risk

Not all bonds can be sold quickly without loss of principal. If the bank has to sell investment securities to meet liquidity demands, it will likely sell U.S. government securities before municipal and corporate bonds because the secondary market for the former securities is deeper and broader than for the latter bonds. Viewed from another perspective, to guard against ***marketability risk***, investment managers should evaluate the likelihood of liquidity demands exceeding secondary (or liquid) reserves and then purchase investment securities to take into account this potential added liquidity.

For both municipal and corporate bonds the volume of outstanding securities by a particular borrower can significantly affect marketability. Small issue size reduces marketability simply due to the fact that the issue is unknown to most investors. By purchasing widely traded bond issues, bank management can reduce marketability risk.

Call Risk

Municipal and corporate bonds issued when interest rates are at relatively high levels commonly have a call provision in their indenture agreements. The call provision gives the borrowing firm or institution the right to redeem the bond prior to maturity. The bond is callable only if the call deferment period has expired and the current price of the bond has risen to at least the call price, which exceeds the original price of the bond. As interest rates decline over time, the bond's price rises and eventually "strikes" the call price. If the call deferment period has lapsed, the bond can be redeemed. The bank's ***call risk*** in this situation is the reinvestment of the par value in bonds bearing lower interest yields. As compensation for this reinvestment risk, the indenture agreement will state call premiums (i.e., an added "sweetener" paid to the bondholder) payable on various dates in the future. When bonds are called early, the call premium is higher, which offsets in part or whole the call risk.

When banks attempt to purchase bonds during high interest rates periods and later plan to sell them for sizable capital gains as rates fall, call risk is especially worth evaluating. Because callable bonds have an additional element of uncertainty, they tend to offer higher yields than other bonds.

PORTFOLIO RISK

According to portfolio theory, the riskiness of any security should not be evaluated in isolation but in the broader context of all assets held by an investor. In this way the effect of a security on the risk per unit of return of the bank's total portfolio of assets can be considered. It is possible for a securities portfolio to decrease the portfolio risk of the bank's assets, especially if the returns on securities over time are not perfectly correlated (or synchronized) with the returns on loans over time. As a descriptive example, if loan rates of return are falling due to declining interest rates, but rates of return on securities are rising due to increasing capital gains, the overall pattern of earnings of the bank are smoother over time and therefore less risky due to securities holdings than if all bank assets were loans. This type of risk reduction is known as a diversification effect. Notice that diversification is a more complicated concept than merely purchasing a bundle of different assets. It also is necessary that the returns of the assets follow different patterns over time (i.e., less than perfect positive correlation) to obtain diversification benefits.

Few banks make a conscious effort to set up a securities portfolio to decrease the total risk of bank assets due to greater emphases on credit risk, interest rate risk, and liquidity risk objectives. However, most banks consciously purchase securities to help protect themselves from a potential economic downturn that could increase loan losses. In this circumstance securities offset to some extent falling earnings in the loan portfolio. This income stream smoothing is an important benefit of diversification in bank asset portfolios. Appendix A gives a more detailed treatment of modern portfolio theory, including an example of its application to bank management.

INFLATION RISK

Another potential risk in purchasing securities, which is not security-specific, is inflation. Here the investor is concerned that the general price level will increase more than expected in the future. Unanticipated increases in inflation lower the purchasing power of earnings on securities. An unexpected surge in inflation can cause interest rates on bonds to suddenly increase with potentially large price declines. In this case securities held for sale would suffer losses that could diminish bank liquidity and lower trading profits. Such losses would increase as the average maturity of the investment portfolio increases. For these reasons banks should be cautious about long-term investments subject to substantial price risk in periods of inflation uncertainty.

In the period from the 1960s to the early 1980s, periodic bouts with inflation motivated investment managers to shorten security maturities and seek securities with sufficiently high yields to offset inflation risk. However, since the 1990s, the U.S. and other industrialized countries have experienced historically low levels of inflation. As nominal interest rates declined due to lower inflation rates, long-term securities experienced strong capital gains. In recent years the Federal Reserve and other central banks around the world have kept short-term interest rates near zero to help stimulate credit demand and boost economic growth. Quantitative easing (QE) has been implemented also by buying longer-term bonds to lower long-term interest rates and thereby decrease the cost of long-term borrowing for business and households.

INVESTMENT STRATEGIES

Investment strategies should be guided by the principle that income be maximized within the constraints of regulations, taxes, liquidity needs, correspondent banking relationships, management expertise, and various types of investment risk. Management can choose between passive investment strategies that do not require active management and aggressive investment strategies that are designed to take advantage of prevailing or expected market conditions.

PASSIVE INVESTMENT STRATEGIES

Two passive strategies used in managing the investment portfolio are the spaced-maturity, or ladder, approach and the split-maturity, or barbell, approach. Smaller banks commonly use these methods because they are simple to implement and thus conserve management resources. Also, the investment goals of many small banks are often of secondary importance because the majority of their excess funds is transferred upstream to larger correspondent banks in return for competitive money market rates of interest in addition to financial services, such as wire transfers, foreign exchange, and the like.

Spaced-Maturity Approach

Otherwise known as the *ladder approach*, the spaced-maturity investment strategy involves spreading available investment funds equally across a specified number of periods within the bank's investment horizon. For example, if the bank had an investment portfolio of $10 million, and its investment horizon was five years, then it would purchase $2 million of one-year securities, $2 million of two-year securities, and so on until the $10 million was evenly distributed over the five-year planning period.

This strategy is simple not only to set up but also to maintain, as principal redeemed on one-year securities coming due would be rolled over into five-year securities to keep an evenly spaced maturity of securities over five years. Other advantages of this approach are that trading activity (and, therefore, transactions costs) is minimized, and that an average rate of return is earned because investment securities are spread out evenly at different points in time on the yield curve. The major drawbacks of this approach are that the bank is passive with respect to interest rate conditions, and that liquidity is sacrificed to some extent should loan demands exceed short-term investment securities.

Split-Maturity Approach

Another relatively conservative strategy is to purchase larger proportions of short- and long-term securities and smaller proportions of intermediate-term securities. This so-called *barbell approach* offers a balance of higher income on the long-term securities (assuming the yield curve is upward-sloping) and good liquidity through substantial purchases of short-term securities. One way to maintain the barbell strategy is to reinvest matured short-term securities in the longest-maturity, short-term securities, and sell shortest-maturity, long-term securities and reinvest in the longest-maturity, long-term securities. The periodic sales of securities result in modest capital gains or losses depending on changes in the level or shape of the yield curve. Of course, there is a trade-off here between transactions costs versus both liquidity and income benefits from using the barbell strategy relative to the spaced-maturity strategy. Variations on the barbell strategy include holding more short-term securities, which is known as a *front-end loaded approach*, and holding more long-term securities, or a *back-end loaded approach*. These strategies may be implemented by the bank to stress either liquidity or income, respectively, in the investment strategy.

AGGRESSIVE INVESTMENT STRATEGIES

Larger banks with sizable investment portfolios and more volatile loan demands than smaller banks typically engage in one or more aggressive investment strategies intended to maximize their investment income. Because these strategies require a certain level of management expertise and trading activity, management must weigh the added costs against the potential benefits when selecting an appropriate strategy. In general, aggressive strategies can be classified into two groups: yield-curve strategies and bond-swapping strategies.

Yield-Curve Strategies

"Playing the yield curve" is a widely used phrase that means the bank is attempting to take advantage of expected future changes in interest rates by coordinating investment activities with the shape and level of the yield curve. When the yield curve is at a relatively low level and is steeply upward-sloping, short-term securities are usually purchased. As interest rates rise in the months (or years) ahead, the securities are repeatedly rolled over into higher earning securities. At the same time, they provide added liquidity should investment securities be needed to meet loan demands. When the yield curve is flatter in shape and at a relatively high level, the bank would switch to longer-term securities. This strategy provides higher yields to maximize interest income. Liquidity is not as relevant at this point in the business cycle because it is expected that loan demand will decline due to the high interest rates. As interest rates in future periods decline, capital gains are earned on these long-term securities because of favorable price risk. When interest rates have fallen substantially, long-term securities are sold and the principal and capital gains are rolled over into short-term securities.

This *switching strategy* in playing the yield curve is not without its potential problems, however. Market timing is pivotal to success. For example, if interest rates continued to rise after the maturity of investment securities is lengthened (in anticipation of a decline in rate levels), the bank would be forced to meet liquidity needs either by purchasing funds at increasingly higher costs or selling the long-term securities at a capital loss (plus transactions costs). Such a mistake could have a significant impact on the bank's profitability. Thus, it is recommended that some amount of short-term securities not be rolled over into longer-term securities to maintain an element of liquidity in the investment portfolio.

Another approach to playing the yield curve is known as *riding the yield curve.* For this strategy to work, (1) the yield curve must be upward-sloping and (2) the level of interest rates must not be expected to move upward as much as indicated by the shape of the yield curve in the near future. According to this strategy, the investment manager would purchase securities with a longer maturity than the investment horizon of the bank. With an upward-sloping yield curve, as time passes and the term-to-maturity of the securities declines, their yields fall in line with the upward shape of the yield curve. The increasing prices of the securities yield a capital gain when they are sold at the end of the investment horizon.

To estimate the holding period yield of riding the yield curve, the following formula can be used:

$$Y_h = Y_o + T_r(Y_o + Y_m)/\ T_h \tag{7.4}$$

where Y_h = the holding period yield, Y_o = the original yield on the security purchased, Y_m = the security's market yield at the end of the holding period when it is sold, T_r = the remaining maturity of the security when sold, and T_h = the holding period (or investment horizon) equal to the lapsed time between the purchase and sale of the security. As an example, suppose that Y_o = .10, T_r = 1 year, T_h = 1 year, and Y_m = .09. The holding period yield obtained from riding the yield curve is then

$$0.10 + 1\,(0.10 - 0.09)/1 = 0.11$$

or 11 percent, which exceeds the original yield by one percent. As long as the yield on the security declines from its original yield on the purchase date such that Y_m is less than Y_o, the second term on the right-hand side of equation (7.4) gives an estimate of the approximate capital gain earned by riding the yield curve. On the other hand, if interest rates increased in line with the expectations theory of the yield curve, then Y_m is greater than Y_o and Y_h is less than Y_o, or a capital loss would cause the holding period yield to fall short of the original yield.

Obviously, playing the yield curve by using a switching strategy or by riding the yield curve requires considerable market forecasting expertise. According to expectations theory, the expected return is identical across all maturities for any holding period. Thus, playing the yield curve involves forecasting changes in interest rates that are not expected by the market as a whole. In this regard, although "outguessing" the market is surely possible, such an aggressive strategy may well be imprudent on a large scale. For this reason playing the yield curve is a strategy that should not be overemphasized in investment management and should be coupled with one or more other investment strategies.

Bond-Swapping Strategies

Exchanging one bond for another for return and risk reasons is known as a bond swap. A swap might be undertaken in anticipation of future changes in interest rates or simply because the swap would clearly be a superior choice. For example, management may perform a tax swap if the corporate bond yield is higher than the pretax equivalent municipal bond yields currently held by the bank. If the municipal bond is sold at a capital loss, tax savings equal to the bank's marginal tax rate multiplied by the capital loss are realized. Alternatively, if the bank's marginal tax rate declined from some reason (e.g., a decline in earnings or change in applicable tax laws), the bank might choose to swap municipal bonds for corporate bonds. Opposite reasoning would apply to swapping corporate for municipal bonds.

A *substitution*, or *price, swap* entails selling securities comparable to the ones being purchased because the latter have a lower price. In an efficient market, where securities' prices reflect all publicly available information, it is not common to find imbalances of this sort, but it is possible to find mispriced securities at times (i.e., a temporary market disequilibrium).[12]

Trading banks that have day-to-day market operations in various securities are most likely to execute substitution swaps. A trading account must be maintained for regulatory purposes, and the resultant trading profits (and losses) must be reported as a separate account in the bank's operating earnings. It should be mentioned that other portfolio profits (and losses) and associated taxes on securities are reported after net operating earnings are adjusted for federal income taxes.

A *yield-pickup*, or *coupon, swap* involves the exchange of a low-coupon bond for a high-coupon bond, or vice versa. The trade-off between coupon earnings and capital gains in such a swap could be influenced either by interest rate risk (duration) differences or tax differences.

A *spread*, or *quality, swap* implies the exchange of two bonds with unequal risk. For regulatory capital or risk management reasons a bank could sell higher-risk securities and replace them with lower-risk securities. Or, in an effort to boost earnings, a bank could sell off lower-risk securities and replace them with higher-risk securities.

Finally, a *portfolio shift* (bond swap) strategy entails selling securities with low yields and replacing them with higher-yielding instruments. If a bank purchased securities during a period of low interest rates, as interest rates gradually rise over time, the cost of funds at the bank would increase until there was a negative spread between security yields and average interest costs. In this case the bank might opt to sell the old securities, take the capital loss due to increased interest rate levels, deduct the loss from taxes, and purchase new higher-yielding securities with the sale proceeds plus tax savings. As an example, suppose that the bank purchased at par value $1 million of five-year Treasury bonds with an annual coupon rate of six percent. Also, initially average deposit costs are three percent but rising interest rates push up this cost to five percent two years after the bonds are purchased. Assume that allocable operating expenses equal 1.5 percent. Under these circumstances, the following cash flows are available to the bank:

	Year 1	Year 2	Year 3	Year 4	Year 5
Interest income	$60,000	$60,000	$60,000	$60,000	$60,000
Average deposit expense	(30,000)	(30,000)	(50,000)	(50,000)	(50,000)
Allocable operating expense	(15,000)	(15,000)	(15,000)	(15,000)	(15,000)
Net profit on bonds	$15,000	$15,000	$(5,000)	$(5,000)	$(5,000)

It is clear that after Year 3 the bond is an unprofitable investment that cumulates larger losses over time. Now consider the possibility of selling the bond at the beginning of Year 3. The two percent increase in interest rates would decrease the value of the Treasury bond to say $950,000. Given that the bank's marginal tax rate equals 30 percent, the tax savings earned by the bank on the capital loss would be: $50,000 (1 – 0.30) = $35,000. Thus, the bank could invest $950,000 + $35,000 = $985,000 in three-year Treasury bonds selling at par value and offering a eight percent coupon yield. The cash flows with this portfolio shift are as follows:

	Year 1	Year 2	Year 3	Year 4	Year 5
Interest income	$60,000	$60,000	$78,800	$78,800	$78,800
Average deposit expense	(30,000)	(30,000)	(50,000)	(50,000)	(50,000)
Allocable operating expense	(15,000)	(15,000)	(15,000)	(15,000)	(15,000)
Net profit on bonds	$15,000	$15,000	$13,800	$13,800	$13,800

The new higher coupon earning Treasury bonds purchased at the beginning of Year 3 generate a net profit stream that is $1,200 less than the initial years of the five-year investment horizon but boost net profits from $5,000 losses to $13,800 gains in the later years.[13] Hence, changes in interest rate levels can force banks to undertake portfolio shifts to protect profit margins.

SUMMARY

Investment securities provide an alternative source of income for commercial banks, especially when loan demand is relatively low during slowdowns in economic activity. Bank policy should aim to maximize the return on the securities portfolio per unit of risk within regulatory and market constraints. In this regard, bank management needs to consider the tax implications of municipal securities, default risk and call risk of municipal and corporate bond securities, interest rate risk of longer-term securities, and marketability of securities. The effects of investment policy on the risk and return of the bank's total assets should also be evaluated in a portfolio context, where diversification benefits can be gained by purchasing securities with return patterns that are not perfectly positively correlated with the return patterns of other bank assets.

Once bank policy is established, an investment strategy needs to be chosen. Passive strategies, such as the spaced-maturity, or ladder, approach and the split-maturity, or barbell, approach do not require much expertise, conserve management resources, and are inexpensive to implement.

Aggressive strategies, such as playing the yield curve and bond swapping, require more management expertise, involve more trading activity, and are riskier in nature than passive strategies but offer higher earnings potential.

KEY TERMS AND CONCEPTS

Agency securities
Aggressive investment strategies
Call risk
Corporate bond
Expectations theory
Inflation risk
Investment grade bonds
Investment policy
Junk bonds
Liquidity premium
Market value accounting
Marketability risk
Municipal bonds
Passive investment strategies
Portfolio risk
Preferred habitat
Prepayment risk
Price risk
Segmented markets
Treasury bonds
Treasury notes
Value-at-risk (VAR)
Yield curve
Yield spread

QUESTIONS

7.1 Why are Treasury bills not considered to be investment securities?
7.2 Why might agency securities be preferred to Treasury notes and bonds?
7.3 How do municipal bonds reduce taxes for a bank?
7.4 What do bond ratings indicate? How do bond yields vary with these ratings?
7.5 Why is investment policy affected by the interest rate cycle?
7.6 Why do most investment securities have maturities in the range of one-to-five years?
7.7 Why do banks generally avoid junk bonds?
7.8 Discuss two components of bond risk premiums.
7.9 Define price risk. How can a bank take advantage of price risk in a relatively high interest rate period?
7.10 Why might forecasts of future interest rates using the expectations theory of the yield curve be wrong? How would you adjust for other interest rate influences?
7.11 Why do bonds issued in relatively low interest rate periods have low call risk?
7.12 Why is call risk an important factor for an investment manager purchasing bonds in a relatively high interest rate period?
7.13 How does diversification affect portfolio return? How does it affect portfolio risk?
7.14 Show a graph of two assets that offer no diversification benefit. Also draw graphs illustrating both partial and complete diversification of risk.
7.15 What is the key to diversification?
7.16 Why might the split-maturity approach to investment management be preferred to the spaced-maturity approach?
7.17 What does "playing the yield curve" mean? How is it different from "riding the yield curve?"
7.18 Briefly discuss four kinds of bonds swaps.
7.19 Explore two of the following popular websites. Write a summary of the information located there.

- E-Trade, www.etrade.com—Online services by online brokers are provided.
- Hollywood Stock Exchange, www.hsx.com—A stock-trading game can be found here.
- The Motley Fool, www.fool.com – One of the original stock-trading communities, this site contains message boards, tips, and investing philosophy.
- Bankrate.com, http://calculators.bankrate.com – Calculators for solving typical financial problems can be accessed.
- Big Charts, http://bigcharts.marketwatch.com/ – Stock trends, technical analysis, charts and graphs, and more can be viewed.
- Morningstar, www.morningstar.com – One-stop shopping for mutual funds with ratings, top holdings, returns, and more is available.

7.20 Go to the Securities and Exchange Commission website at www.sec.gov. Look under "Latest News" and write an abstract on its content.

7.21 Go to the BAI website at www.bai.org. Search for "investments." Select an article and write an abstract on its content.
7.22 Go to the International Finance and Commodities Institute (IFCI) website at risk.ifci.ch and find "Case Studies." Select one of the case studies and write a two-page paper summarizing the material there.

PROBLEMS

7.1 (a) Given a five-year municipal bond yielding 10 percent, a comparable five-year corporate bond yielding 15 percent, and a federal income tax rate of 34 percent facing the bank, which bond should be preferred by the bank?
(b) Given the following income statement information, calculate the bank's net income after taxes. Assume a tax rate of 34 percent on income. What if $400 of interest tax deductions are lost due to the municipal bond purchases?

	(In Thousands)
Total interest on securities	$2,000
Municipal bond interest	500
Other securities' interest	1,500
Total interest on loans	4,000
Total operating income	$6,000
Total interest expense	(4,100)
Total noninterest expense	(900)
Total operating expense	($5,000)

7.2 A munis bond selling at par has a yield-to-maturity equal to 10 percent. A bank investment manager wishes to calculate its tax equivalent yield. Assume that it is a qualified bond, the bank's tax rate is 34 percent, and the average cost of funds for the bank is eight percent. If the bond was not qualified, what would be the answer?
7.3 Refer to the Appendix to work this problem. Given the following information about security j in states of nature i:

State of Nature	P_i = Probability	R_{ji}
1	.10	.08
2	.25	.10
3	.30	.12
4	.25	.14
5	.10	.16

(a) Calculate the mean and variance of security j's rate of return.
(b) Given further the rate of return on the bank's portfolio of assets is as follows:

State of Nature	P_i	R_{pi}
1	.10	.16
2	.25	.14
3	.30	.12
4	.25	.10
5	.10	.08

Find the mean and variance of the rates of return on the bank's portfolio of assets.
(c) If the bank invests in security j such that 10 percent of its funds are allocated to security j and 90 percent of its funds are allocated to its previous portfolio of assets, what will be the mean and variance of rates of return for the bank?
7.4 You are given the responsibility to conduct a financial analysis of three firms issuing bonds that your bank is evaluating. All three firms are regional manufacturing firms in the same industry. Your bank's loan officer has requested that you evaluate their potential default risk. After collecting ac-

counting statements from last year, you construct the following table of financial ratios for the three firms:

	Firm X	Firm Y	Firm Z
Profitability			
Net profits/net sales	0.08	0.05	0.06
Net profits/net worth	0.20	0.24	0.13
Net profits/total assets	0.10	0.06	0.08
Liquidity			
Current assets/current liabilities	2.50	2.00	2.60
(Current assets-inventory)/current liabilities	1.50	1.20	1.50
Leverage			
Total debt/total assets	0.50	0.75	0.40
Gross income/interest charges	3.80	2.50	5.00
Activity			
Sales/inventory	8.00	10.00	9.00
Sales/total assets	2.00	1.80	2.20

CASE: The Case of the Missing Gap

Jack Brothers had recently taken over the management of the securities portfolio at Community Bank & Trust, a $100 million asset-size bank in a suburb of a large U.S. city. Previously, Jack worked in the loan portfolio of a bank in another state. He had gained favorable recommendations from his prior employers in large part due to his innovative work in securitizing loans, a growing area of management in the banking industry involving the issuance of mortgage-backed securities on home loans. A meeting with CEO George Willis the day before had raised some unsettling evidence concerning the gap management of the bank. The accounting department reported that, while the dollar gap of the bank over the past year was zero, with equal dollar holdings of interest rate sensitivity of assets and liabilities, the bank had lost $500,000 in interest income over the last year as interest rates had rapidly fallen 300 basis points. Mr. Willis asked Jack to identify the "missing gap" problem that appears to exist and make recommendations in the securities portfolio that would help solve the problem. He wanted a fast turnaround on these questions, with a preliminary report due tomorrow afternoon. He also made clear that, according to investment policy, securities portfolio management was a means to effective and efficient asset/liability management. The recommendations made by Jack to Mr. Willis would be forwarded to the Asset/Liability Management Committee in order to coordinate activities in the bank.

Jack reviewed asset/liability materials that evening in his study at home and decided to go forward with a standardized gap analysis (see Chapter 5). The short period of time allowed for the preliminary report required that only a general analysis of the problem be attempted at this stage.
In the morning he visited the accounting department staff, who helped him obtain some rough historical figures from the past year on the interest rate sensitivity of broad asset and liability accounts in response to a change of 100 basis points in the prime rate of interest.
It occurred to Jack that the rapid decline in interest rates this past year may imply that interest rates will increase in the future. Consequently, he also checked the financial newspaper in the morning and found that the two-year Treasury bond rate was 5.0 percent and the one-year Treasury rate was 4.0 percent. He estimated that approximately a 50 basis point liquidity premium likely exists in the two-year bond rate to compensate investors for the added price risk of these bonds relative to the one-year bonds.

Based on standardized gap analysis, why did the 300 basis point drop in interest rates so adversely affect the bank's net interest earnings in the past year? How could securities management have reduced or eliminated the recent loss of $500,000? What is the interest rate forecast using expectations and liquidity premium theories of the yield curve? What are the implications of anticipated future interest rate movements for net interest earnings, the bank's gap position, and securities management in the near future?

EXHIBIT 7-1: SUMMARY OF INTEREST RATE SENSITIVITY: COMMUNITY BANK & TRUST

Accounts	Change per 100 Basis Point Change in the Prime Rate	Dollar Holdings
Liabilities		
Retail deposits	25 basis points	$40,000,000
Wholesale deposits	100 basis points	30,000,000
Nondeposit funds	100 basis points	23,000,000
Assets		
T-bills (< 1 year)	91 basis points	$10,000,000
Govt. (1 year)	77 basis points	10,000,000
Govt. (5 year)	20 basis points	10,000,000
Munis (1 year)	60 basis points	3,000,000
Munis (5 year)	20 basis points	2,000,000
Loans	80 basis points	70,000,000

Note: While interest rates on five-year government and munis securities are fixed, a portion of the portfolio either matures or is sold during the year, most of which is normally replaced by rolling over the funds in investments of the same type. Also, while most loans have variable rates, some portion of fixed rate loans mature and are replaced each year with new fixed rate loans.

Appendix 7A: Modern Portfolio Theory and Bank Securities Management

Markowitz's (1959) now famous work on individual investment choice under uncertainty established modern portfolio theory as a foundation of financial market investment behavior. Markowitz believed that investors not only evaluate the expected rates of return on investment but their risks as well. In the forthcoming discussion, we assume for simplicity that the bank holds two general classes of assets—securities and loans—and desires to examine the effect of the securities portfolio j on the total risk of the bank's assets after taking account the loan portfolio k. Note that the same portfolio concepts apply to individual securities and loans.

Measuring Expected Rates of Return

To estimate expected rates of return, the following equation can be used:

$$E(R_j) = \sum_{i=1}^{n} P_i R_{ji} \qquad (7A.1)$$

where P_i = the probability that a particular (random) state of nature i will occur (with a total of n states of nature considered), R_{ji} = the rate of return on the security portfolio in the *i*th state of the nature, and $E(R_j)$ = the expected rate of return on the securities portfolio. By "state of nature," we refer to a possible future business environment from among all possible scenarios that may exist. A rough approach is simply specifying pessimistic, average, and optimistic business scenarios. Table 7A-1 provides an example of this calculation using hypothetical data.

Table 7A-1 HYPOTHETICAL CALCULATION OF THE EXPECTED RATE OF RETURN

State of Nature	P_i = Probability	R_{ji}	P_iR_{ji}	$R_{ji} - E(R_j)$	$[R_{ji} - E(R_j)]^2$	$P_i[R_{ji} - E(R_j)]^2$
1	.10	.05	.005	−.02	.0004	.00004
2	.20	.06	.012	−.01	.0001	.00001
3	.40	.07	.028	.00	.0000	.00000
4	.20	.08	.016	.01	.0001	.00001
5	.10	.09	.009	.02	.0004	.00004
	1.00	$E(R_j)$	= .070			$\sigma^2(R_j)$ = .00010
						$\sigma(R_j)$ = .010

Measuring Variability

The total risk of an investment is directly linked to the variability of its rates of return over time. To measure the risk of the securities portfolio, the variability of the rate of return in different states of nature can be proxied by their standard deviation, or σ. The standard deviation is calculated by taking the square root of the variance of returns, or $\sigma^2(R_j)$, where

$$\sigma^2(R_j) = \sum_{i=1}^{n} P_i[R_{ji} - E(R_j)]^2 \tag{7A.2}$$

and

$$\sigma(R_j) = \sigma^2(R_j)^{1/2} \tag{7A.3}$$

Based on these equations, Table 7A-1 shows that the standard deviation of rates of return is 1.0 percent.

Assuming that rates of return are normally distributed, $E(R_j)$ and $\sigma(R_j)$ can be used to understand the risk and return characteristics of the securities portfolio. Figure 7A-2 graphically depicts the probability of rates of return on the vertical axis and rates of return themselves on the horizontal axis. Notice that 65 percent (95 percent) of the normal distribution falls within one (two) standard deviations of the mean, or $E(R_j)$. Given $E(R_j) = 7$ percent and $\sigma(R_j) = 1.0$ percent, we can infer that 65 percent of the security portfolio's rate of return will fall within the range of 6.0 percent to 8.0 percent and 95 percent of the time it will be from 5.0 percent to 9.0 percent.

Portfolio Effects

With these risk and return concepts in hand, consider the effect of the securities portfolio on the expected return and risk of all bank assets including the loan portfolio. We define the expected return and standard deviation of the bank's portfolio of loans as $E(R_k)$ and $\sigma(R_k)$. The bank's expected rate of return and variance of rates of return *after* purchasing securities can be calculated as follows:

$$E(R_{bank}) = aE(R_j) + (1 - a)E(R_k) \tag{7A.4}$$

where a = the proportion of funds invested in the securities portfolio with expected rate of return $E(R_j)$, and $(1 - a)$ = the proportion of funds invested in the loan portfolio with expected rate of return $E(R_k)$, and

$$\sigma^2(R_{bank}) = a^2\sigma^2(R_j) + (1 - a)^2\sigma^2(R_k) + 2a(1 - a)\,\text{Cov}(R_j, R_k) \tag{7A.5}$$

where $\text{Cov}(R_j, R_k)$ = the covariance of the rates of return of securities portfolio j and loan portfolio k, or

$$\text{Cov}(R_j, R_k) = \sum_{i=1}^{n} P_i[R_{ji} - E(R_j)][R_{ki} - E(R_k)] \tag{7A.6}$$

Table 7A-2 shows an example of how the securities portfolio might affect the expected rate of return and risk of bank assets as a whole. The loan portfolio is calculated to have $E(R_k) = 6$ percent and $\sigma(R_k) = 2.2$ percent. If the securities portfolio is considered in combination with the loan portfolio, then $E(R_{bank}) = 6.1$ percent and $\sigma(R_{bank}) = 1.9$ percent.

Figure 7A-1 NORMAL DISTRIBUTION OF HYPOTHETICAL INVESTMENT OPPORTUNITIES

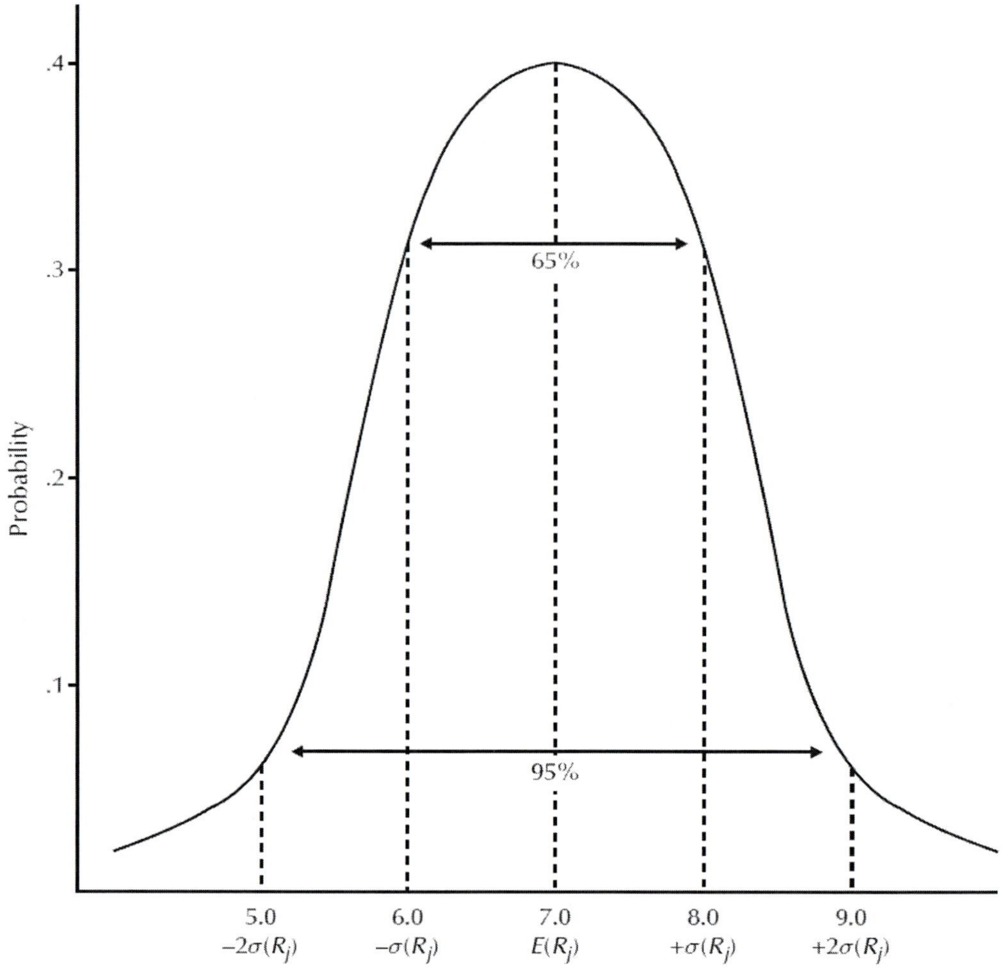

Thus, the securities portfolio would not only increase the bank's total expected rate of return above that earned by the loan portfolio, it would also reduce the bank's risk by decreasing the standard deviation of rates of return below that of the loan portfolio.

Notice that bank risk declines both because the standard deviation of the securities portfolio was less than the loan portfolio's standard deviation and because the covariance term was negative. Hence, we can infer that the effect of the securities portfolio on the risk of the bank's portfolio of assets is not a simple weighted average of the loan portfolio and securities portfolio risks (where weights are the proportional investment), instead, an adjustment must be made for the relationship of the securities portfolio's pattern of rates of return to the loan portfolio's rates of return in different states of nature (i.e., the covariance term affects the bank's total risk).

To elaborate on covariance adjustment, we can redefine the last term in the variance formula shown in equation 7A-5 as

$$2a(1-a)\text{Cov}(R_j,R_k) = 2a(1-a)\,\rho_{jk}\sigma(R_j)\sigma(R_k) \quad (7A.7)$$

where ρ_{jk} = the correlation of the securities portfolio with the loan portfolio. If $\rho_{jk} = 1$, we say that the two patterns of rates of return are perfectly positively correlated. If $\rho < 1$, the variance measure of risk is reduced, with maximum variance reduction occurring at $\rho = -1$, which is perfectly negative correlation. The reduction of variance caused by less than perfect positive correlation is technically known as *diversification*.

Table 7A-2 HYPOTHETICAL EXAMPLE OF SECURITIES PORTFOLIO EFFECTS ON THE RISK AND RETURN OF TOTAL BANK ASSETS INCLUDING LOANS

State of Nature	P_i = Probability	a = 10% R_{ji}	(1 − a) = 90% R_{ki}	$P_i[R_{ki} - E(R_k)]^2$	(1) $R_{ji} - E(R_j)$	(2) $R_{ki} - E(R_k)$	(3) (1)×(2)	P_i ×(3)
1	.10	.05	.10	.00016	−.02	.04	−.008	−.00008
2	.20	.06	.08	.00008	−.01	.02	−.0002	−.00004
3	.40	.07	.06	—	—	—	—	—
4	.20	.08	.04	.00008	.01	−.02	−.0002	−.00004
5	.10	.09	.02	.00016	−.02	−.04	−.0008	−.00008
		$E = (R_j) = .07$	$E(R_k) = .06$	$\sigma^2(R_k) = .00048$				$\text{Cov}(R_j,R_k) = -.00024$
				$\sigma(R_k) = .022$				

$$E(R_{bank}) = aE(R_j) + (1 - a)(E(R_k)$$
$$= (.10)(.07) + (.90)(.06)$$
$$= .061$$
$$\sigma^2(R_{bank}) = a^2\sigma^2(R_j) + (1 - a)^2\sigma^2(R_k) + 2a(1 - a)\text{Cov}(R_j, R_k)$$
$$= (.10)^2(.00012) + (.90)^2(.00048) + 2(.10)(.90)(-.00024)$$
$$= .0003468$$
$$\sigma(R_{bank}) = .019$$

Figure (7A.2) graphically depicts three different correlation possibilities and their effects on risk. The rates of return patterns for two assets (or portfolios) of equal value considered separately in different states of nature are shown by thin lines, and their combination is shown by the bold line. The variability, or risk, of each rate of return pattern can be visually compared by observing the amount of its movement up and down over different states of nature. Panel A in Figure (7A.2) shows that combining perfectly positively correlated assets does not reduce risk. At the other extreme, panel B shows the total elimination of risk by combining perfectly negatively correlated assets. In the real world, correlations between financial assets are normally positive but not perfectly so. Panel C shows that risk is reduced by combining assets with less than perfect positive correlation; that is, the combined pattern is flatter in shape than either asset alone.

While we have discussed the diversification effects of the securities portfolio on the bank as a whole, investment managers could also consider the effect of individual securities on the bank. Because most bank assets are debt instruments, and these assets' yields tend to follow interest rate changes, the correlations among bank assets' rates of return are usually highly positive. Evidence reported by the Federal Reserve, for example, has indicated that securitization of home loans by commercial banks and other financial institutions has caused mortgage rates to follow U.S. Treasury security rates more closely. A partial offset to this trend is that differences in maturity cause prices (and therefore yields) of bank assets to be less than perfectly positively correlated as interest rate levels change over time. Because investment securities are longer-term than most other bank assets, they tend to have a significant diversification effect on the bank's portfolio. Also, many loans—for example, consumer and commercial loans—likely have different rate of return patterns than Treasury and agency securities that dominate the investment portfolio.

Figure 7A-2 CORRELATION OF ASSETS' RATES OF RETURN AND RISK REDUCTION

A. Perfect positive correlation: $\rho_{12} = 1$

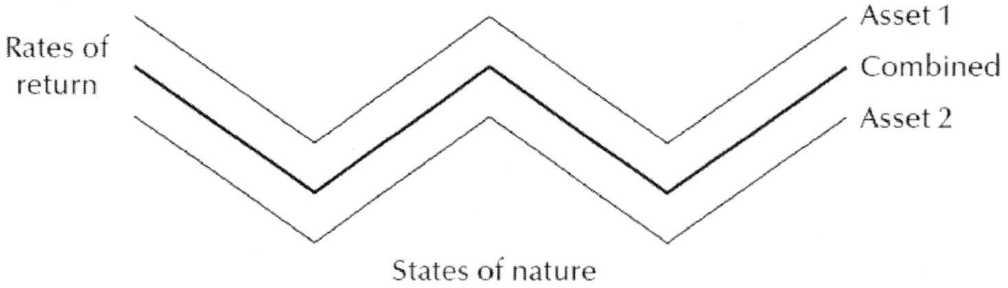

B. Perfect negative correlation: $\rho_{12} = -1$

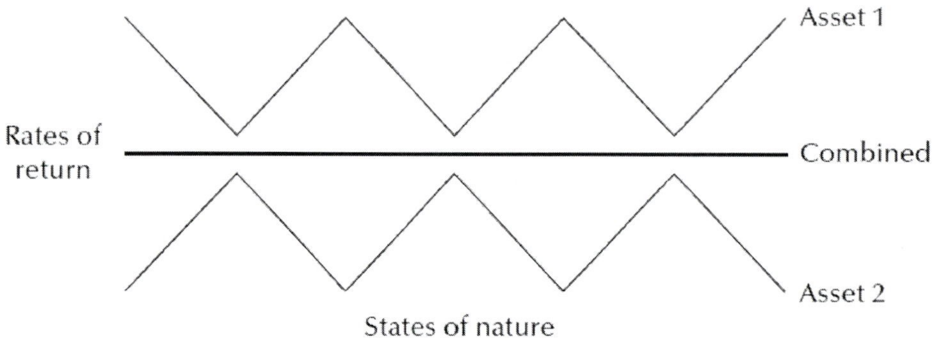

C. Positive but not perfect correlation: $0 < \rho_{12} < 1$

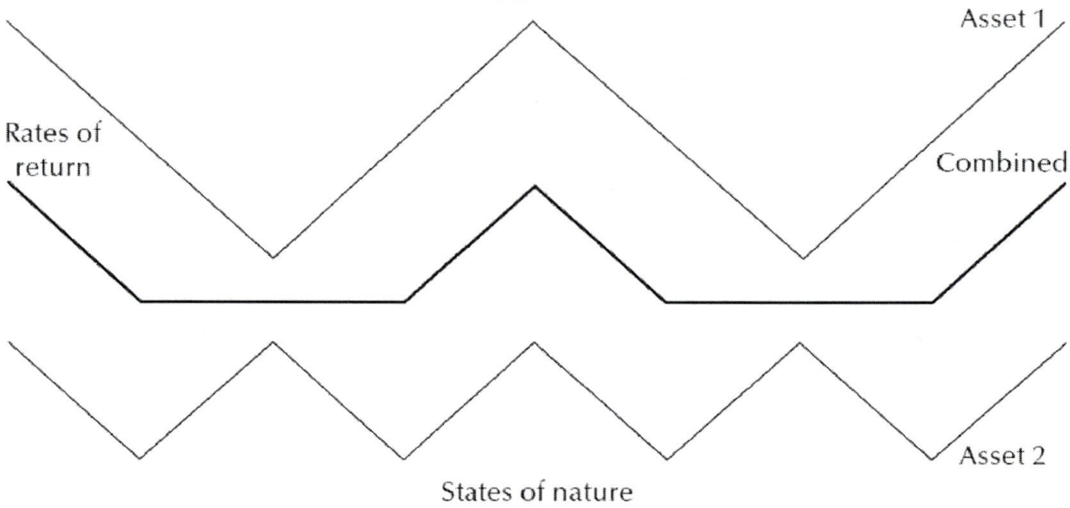

ENDNOTES

[1] The growing securitization of loans is changing their flexibility of maturity composition and risk-taking. Credit card and automobile loans are commonly securitized today, and small business loans have become another growing area of securitization.

[2] Discount money market instruments, such as Treasury bills, commercial paper, repurchase agreements, and bankers acceptances, have a peculiar convention of using discount basis yields, otherwise simply referred to as the *discount rate* (DR):

$$DR = [(\text{Par Value} - \text{Discounted Sale Price})/\text{Par Value}](360/n),$$

where *n* is the days to maturity. For a $1 million, 90-day T-bill selling at 98.5 (or $985,000), we have

$$DR = [(100 - 98.5)/100](360/90) = 0.06, \text{ or } 6\%.$$

This yield is lower than normal due to using 100 in the denominator of the rate of return calculation in brackets, as well as due to using 360 days instead of 365 days. To instead obtain a coupon equivalent rate (CER), the following formula is used:

$$CER = [\text{Par Value} - \text{Discounted Sale Price})/\text{Discounted Sale Price}](365/90)$$

$$CER = [100 - 98.5)/98.5](365/90) = 0.062 \text{ or } 6.2\%$$

An effective annual rate (EAR) can be estimated by assuming that the security will be rolled over at the same CER, or 6.2 percent, each quarter during the year:

$$EAR = \{1 + [0.062/(365/90)]\}^{365/90} - 1 = 0.063, \text{ or } 6.3\%$$

[3] Prepayment of home loans can occur for other reasons also, such as moving to a new home due to family, economic, and other conditions.

[4] Convexity measures the second derivative of prices with respect to interest rates, or $d^2P/di^2(1/P)$, while duration represents the first derivative, or dP/di. Since convexity is the nonlinear slope of the price curve (where price is the y-axis and interest rates are the x-axis), reverse convexity simply means that the slope of the price curve is positive rather than negative. See footnote 9 later in this chapter for the formula for duration. For further discussion of convexity and its relationship to duration, see G. O. Bierwag, George G. Kaufman, and Cynthia M. Latta, "Duration Models: A Taxonomy," *Journal of Portfolio Management* 14 (Fall 1988), pp. 50–55.

[5] As another example, suppose that a bank issues $10 million in CDs. The CDs require no reserves, so the full amount can be invested. The cost of CD money is 5.4 percent and the marginal tax rate of the bank is 35 percent. At the moment taxable security interest rates are equal to nine percent, while tax-exempt rates are equal to seven percent, such that the latter are more attractive than taxable securities. We can now calculate the dollar amount of taxable and tax-exempt securities to purchase as

$$[(0.09 \times \text{Taxable}) + (0.07 \times \text{Tax-exempt})] - \$540{,}000 - (0.07 \times \text{Tax-exempt}) = 0$$

where the term in brackets is the total interest income, $540,000 is total interest expense, and the last term in parentheses subtracts out tax-exempt interest income to get zero taxable income. This equation simplifies to

$$(0.09 \times \text{Taxable}) = 0$$

such that $6 million is the quantity of taxable securities to purchase, which implies that $4 million of tax-exempt securities should be purchased. If the bank purchases more than this amount of tax-exempt securities, it will not benefit from further tax exemptions. By contrast, at $4 million of tax-exempt securities it will maximize the value of the interest tax exemption.

[6] Also, not all munis are exempt from taxes under TRA86 (e.g., securities classified as private activity bonds, which are used by communities to support private companies, are taxable).

[7] To be classified as "bank qualified," the bonds must also be used to finance essential government services, such as schools, water and sewer utilities, highways, and so forth. Since most munis are issued for these purposes, small muni issues normally are bank qualified.

[8] This formula assumes that the bonds are sold at par and held to maturity. In this case all income is earned in the form of interest payments with no capital gains.

[9] More specifically, D = [Σ (Coupon payment × t)/(1 + i)^t + (Principal value × m)/(1 + i)^m]/B, where t is the time a coupon payment is paid, m is the maturity date, i is the discount rate, and B is the price of the bond. Notice that time is weighted by the cash flows such that duration is a weighted average of time to maturity. It is obvious that if a bond has no coupon payments, then D = m (i.e., the duration reaches a maximum limit equal to the maturity of the bond). As coupon payments increase, duration decreases in line with greater weighting of earlier time periods. As mentioned in note 6, for a typical bond paying coupons over time and principal value at maturity, taking the partial derivative of bond price with respect to a change in interest rates results in equation (7.2), including the aforementioned formula for duration. Some investors prefer to use a modified duration calculated as MD = D/(1 + i). Now ΔP = −MD × B × Δi, which simplifies the relationship between changes in interest rates and prices. Finally, we should note that duration is a fairly good measure of price risk for small Δi. Due to the nonlinear relationship between interest rates and prices, however, large changes in interest rates (e.g., Δi = 2 percent or more) will cause price changes that are considerably different from equation (7.2) predictions. For further discussion and an example, see James C. Van Horne, *Financial Market Rates and Flows,* 6th ed. (London: Prentice Hall International, 2001).

[10] The geometric average relationship between long- and short-term interest rates shown in equation (7.3) holds because of the arbitrage activities of investors. Arbitrage takes place, for example, if the two-year rate, or $_0R_2$, is greater than 10 percent. Now investors could earn higher returns by purchasing the two-year bond, as opposed to purchasing one-year securities in two consecutive years. Investors would sell one-year bonds and purchase two-year bonds. As this process proceeds, the price of the one-year securities would fall, causing their yield to rise, and the price of the two-year bonds would rise, causing their yield to fall. Eventually, an equilibrium would be reached in which it would no longer be advantageous to purchase two-year bonds. At this point equation (7.3) would hold once again.

[11] For a more complete discussion of liquidity premiums, see J. R. Hicks, *Value and Capital,* 2nd ed. (London: Oxford University Press, 1946).

[12] See Fischer Black, "Bank Funds Management in an Efficient Market," *Journal of Financial Economics,* Vol. 2, 1975, pp. 323–339, for an excellent discussion of the implications of an efficient market to bank management in general.

[13] Losses on bonds held for more than 12 months must be used to first offset long-term capital gains, and losses in excess of long-term capital gains can then be applied to short-term gains. Likewise, losses on bonds held for 12 months or less must first be applied to short-term gains. This distinction can be significant as short-term gains are taxed as ordinary income with rates as high as 35 percent compared with the 15 percent top rate for long-term gains.

Chapter 8

Credit Evaluation Process

After reading this chapter, you will be able to:

- Learn about credit scores.
- Understand the importance of financial analysis.
- Recognize some pitfalls that financial analysts face.
- Differentiate between what happened and why it happened.
- Perform ratio analyses to measure profitability, liquidity, efficiency, and financial leverage.

Alex Morrow, senior loan officer at American Bank, N.A., reviewed a list of large corporations that he is going to visit in order to solicit their business. The bank can offer them loans, cash management services, pension fund management (in the trust department), swaps, derivative products, and other fee-generating activities.

Ajax Manufacturing Corporation is the first firm on his list. As a matter of practice, Alex has the bank's credit department analyze the financial condition of those firms before the visit in order to assess the quality of their management and whether they are likely loan customers. The financial analysis is done in order to avoid soliciting loan business from firms that might not be good customers for the wide variety of financial services offered by his bank. The more Alex knows about the firm he visits, the better chance he has of getting their business.

Banks do not want to make loans to borrowers who cannot repay them. Therefore, prior to making loans, banks evaluate the credit risk of prospective borrowers and their ability to repay loans. Over the years, the process of credit evaluation has changed. The traditional method involves the financial analysis of balance sheets and income statements. However, the use of credit scores and credit ratings for all types of loans (such as commercial, consumer, mortgages) has become increasingly popular. While bank credit departments usually do their own financial analysis, credit scores and ratings are provided by a variety of vendors.

CREDIT SCORING

Credit scoring is the use of statistical, operational research, and data mining models to determine the credit risk of prospective borrowers.[1] The credit score is a number that is calculated by a credit bureau, or another company, such as the Fair, Isaac and Company's FICO score that is used in making credit decisions and for other purposes. According to the FDIC, "Credit scoring models *inform decision making*, providing predictive information on the potential for default or delinquency used in the loan approval process and risk pricing."[2]

The major advantages of using credit scoring models are that they reduce the cost of evaluating credits and increase the speed, consistency, and accuracy of credit decisions.[3] They are widely used in making consumer loans, home mortgage loans, and some commercial loans.

CONSUMER CREDIT AND HOME MORTGAGE LOANS

Credit scores are based on the past financial performance of groups of borrowers who are similar to the one being scored. The three major credit bureaus (Equifax, Experian, and TransUnion) maintain credit reports, credit scores, and other information.[4] They use software provided by the Fair Isaac Corporation (FICO) and they also provide other credit scores. Their information covers individuals and some businesses.

As economic conditions change over time, the credit scoring models also change. To keep up with behavioral trends of consumers and to suit the evolving needs of lenders, the FICO® Score model has been redeveloped over the years by the Fair Isaac Corporation. The result is that there are multiple FICO® Score versions available in addition to the most widely used version, FICO® Score 8.[5]

The models employ variables that are associated with default risk. Past due payments, debt load relative to income, and employment status are examples of factors related to consumer credit and home mortgage loans. However, under the Equal Credit Opportunity Act, items such as race, religion and sex are illegal to use in such models.

In general, a high credit score signals low credit risk. Base FICO scores range from 300-850, and industry-specific FICO scores range from 250-900. The higher the score, the better. The median score is 720.

The score is designed to rank the likelihood that a prospective borrower will default on a loan, fall 90 days past due on at least one loan, or file for bankruptcy within the next two years. The higher the score, the lower the likelihood of default. Scores of 800 or higher have a one percent likelihood of default. Scores of 700 have a five percent chance of default, scores of 680 have a 15 percent chance, and scores of 500 have a 71 percent chance. Scores below 680 are commonly considered *subprime*, which is another way of saying high credit risk.

Each lender has its own cut-off points depending on the risks they are willing to take. Thus, a lender may use a rating system such as:

- FICO scores of 720 and above: Excellent credit
- 680-719: Good credit
- 620-679: Conditional credit
- 585-619: High risk credit
- 584 and below: Very high risk credit

Five of the major factors that FICO considers, and their weights are:[6]

1. Payment history (35 percent). For example, are bills paid on time? Are there missed payments?

2. How much is owed (30 percent). For example, what is the amount owed on all accounts, and on different types of accounts?

3. Length of credit history (15 percent). How long credit accounts have been established.

4. New credit (10 percent). Are you taking on more debt?

5. Credit mix (10 percent). What is the mix of retail credit, installment loans, mortgage, and the like?

Equally important, FICO scores do not consider the following factors:[6]

1. Your race, color, religion, national origin, sex and marital status. U.S. law prohibits credit scoring from considering these facts, as well as any receipt of public assistance, or the exercise of any consumer right under the Consumer Credit Protection Act.

2. Your age. Other types of scores may consider your age, but FICO Scores don't.

3. Your salary, occupation, title, employer, date employed or employment history. Lenders may consider this information, however, as may other types of scores.

4. Where you live.

5. Any interest rate being charged on a particular credit card or other account.

6. Any items reported as child/family support obligations.

7. Certain types of inquiries (requests for your credit report). Your scores do not count "consumer-initiated" inquiries – requests you have made for your credit report, in order to check it. They also do not count "promotional inquiries" – requests made by lenders in order to make you a "pre-approved" credit offer – or "administrative inquiries" – requests made by lenders to review your account with them. Requests that are marked as coming from employers are not counted either.

8. Any information not found in your credit report.

9. Any information that is not proven to be predictive of future credit performance.

10. Whether or not you are participating in a credit counseling of any kind.

RATING BUSINESSES

Some banks and vendors (such as Fair Isaac, Equifax, Experian, TransUnion, and Dun & Bradstreet) have developed different credit scoring models for commercial loans up to $250,000, although many banks only use them for loans up to $100,000. The models include such factors as:

- Number of years in the company has been in business
- Lines of credit applied for and used in the last nine months
- Collections amounts in the last seven years
- Payment history in the last 12 months
- Percentage of available credit used
- Number of late payments
- And other factors

Loans that are considered higher risk are charged higher rates. Banks also use credit rating agencies to evaluate the credit worthiness of their borrowers.

CREDIT RATINGS

Credit rating agencies, such as Standard & Poor's (S&P), Moody's Investor Service, Fitch and Fitch Ratings, and Duff and Phelps provide credit ratings that reflect their opinions about the general creditworthiness of debt and equity issuers in the capital markets. The ratings also take into account the type of security, collateral, and other factors. The ratings indicate the credit agencies' view of the obligors' ability to meet its financial obligations. The ratings for bonds, for example, range from AAA (S&P)/Aaa (Moody's) indicating the highest investment grade and least default risk, to C, the lowest grade and highest default risk. An S&P rating of D means that there is a default on a payment. The ratings have finer gradations, AAA, AA, A, and + and - to show their relative standings.

Investment grade bonds meet the minimum standards as legal investments for trusts and fiduciaries. The ratings of AAA, AA, A, and BBB are considered investment grade. ***Junk bonds*** are those with a BB/Ba rating or lower, and they are speculative in quality. Investors in the riskier bonds or companies require higher rates of return.

Credit rating agencies also provide detailed financial reports. For example, Moody's Financial Metrics™ provides information about selected large non-financial companies.[8] Information includes:

- Adjusted Financial Data and Ratios: Globally comparable financial data and ratios presented "as-reported" by companies and "as-adjusted" by Moody's analysts.
- Powerful Analytics and Reports: Custom querying and reporting tools shed light on key credit issues and help the reader conduct meaningful peer comparisons.
- Scorecards and Models: Analytic models and scorecards provide insight into rating drivers and allow readers to anticipate rating changes and run their own scenarios.

FINANCIAL ANALYSIS

The analysis of financial statements is the traditional way that banks evaluate business loans. Such analysis is done for the following reasons. The first is to determine the *financial condition* and *creditworthiness* of potential and existing customers. Making loans results in credit risk to the bank. ***Credit risk*** means that the customers to whom credit has been extended may default on their payment for the goods and services they received, resulting in a loss to the bank.

The second reason for using financial analysis is to *monitor* the financial behavior of customers after credit has been extended. This is necessary to detect activities that could impair their ability to pay their loans and accounts payable or to honor commitments to buy products that take a long time to produce. For example, retail firms in distress might liquidate inventory at unprofitable prices in order to increase their cash flow in the short run. An increase in sales at unprofitable prices can only result in bankruptcy over time.

DIFFERENT PERSPECTIVES

Financial analysis provides information about the past and most recently reported financial condition of a firm. The information can yield clues about the firm's performance in the future. Because not all analysts have the same objectives in mind, they focus on different aspects of a firm's condition and outlook. For example, bank credit analysts want to know if a firm can repay its loans, and they focus on liquidity and cash flow. Security analysts are interested in earnings growth and profitability, so they focus on earnings and dividends, which affect stock prices. Financial managers are interested in the overall well-being of the firm, so they are concerned with all aspects of financial analysis.

Because of the perspectives of a banker, a security analysts, and a financial manager are different, they can examine the same data and have three different opinions about the condition of a firm. Consider the case of Northern Supply Company, which has been experiencing some difficulties. A bank credit analyst examined Northern's quarterly financial statement, and then reported to her supervisor that Northern may not have sufficient earnings six months later to repay its loan. A security analyst examined the same quarterly report and recommended to the stock brokerage firm's customers that they continue to hold the stock (not buy or sell it) because the work stoppages that have been depressing earnings will be ending soon. The financial manager is optimistic about the future because Northern is planning to sell some outlets to another firm. The sale will provide sufficient funds to repay the loan and eliminate its less profitable operations. Therefore, Northern's dependence on borrowed funds will be reduced and its profitability increased. This example illustrates that the interpretation of information depends on what the observer is looking for and on the amount of private information to which they have access. Private information or ***asymmetric information*** is information used by one party that is not available to others. The financial manager had private information that was not available to the bank credit analysts or to the stock analyst. In this example, Northern would have been better off sharing that information with the credit and stock analysts. If those analysts had known that the outlets were going to be sold, their reports would have been more favorable.

QUALITY OF THE DATA

Fiscal year-end data are better quality data than interim reports. Year-end data should be used for making decisions, whereas interim reports can be used for monitoring the financial condition of a firm. The reason for this is that interim reports do not reflect year-end adjustments that may substantially alter a firm's financial condition. Unexpected write-offs are one example of a year-end adjustment

The quality and reliability of financial statements also differs among a compilation, a review, and an audit. A ***compilation*** is defined by the American Institute of Certified Accountants (AICPA) "as presenting, in the form of financial statements, information that is the representation of management without undertaking to express assurance on the statements."[9] Compilations may or may not have disclosures, and may or may not have been compiled by qualified persons.

A ***review*** is defined as "performing inquiry and analytical procedures that provide the accountant with a reasonable basis for expressing limited assurance that there are no material modifications that should be made to the statements in order for them to be in conformity with generally accepted accounting principles, or, if applicable, with another comprehensive basis of accounting." [10] The review provides "limited assurance" with respect to meeting accounting standards.

An *audit* "is the process by which a competent, independent person accumulates and evaluates evidence about quantifiable information related to a specific economic entity for the purpose of determining and reporting on the degree of correspondence between quantifiable information and established criteria." [11] The audited statement assures the reader that the financial statements followed generally accepted accounting principles (GAAP) instead of following cleverly rigged accounting practices (CRAP). It is the most reliable accounting data for recording the economic events that occurred during that accounting period. In other words, if a person is given a choice, the person should analyze audited financial statements in preference to reviews or compilations.

Carefully read the independent auditor's report for qualifications. A *qualification* is a statement in the report that comments on limitations to the audit examination or doubts concerning a reported item.

Finally, there are differences in the quality of auditors. Some firms have a better reputation than others. The auditor's reputation must be considered when evaluating their reports and the statements they audited. The following is an example of an auditor's opinion:

"We have audited the accompanying consolidated balance sheet of XYZ Company and its subsidiaries for the years December 31, 2015, and December 31, 2014, and the related consolidated statements of operations, shareholder's equity, and cash flows for each of the three years in the period ended December 31, 2015. These consolidated statements are the responsibility of company's management. Our responsibility is to express an opinion on these financial statements based on our audits.

We conducted our audits in accordance with generally accepted auditing standards. Those standards require that we plan and perform the audit to obtain reasonable assurance about whether the consolidated statements are free of material misstatement. An audit includes examining, on a test basis, evidence supporting the amounts and disclosures in the consolidated financial statements. An audit also includes assessing the accounting principles used and the significant estimates made by management, as well as evaluating the overall consolidated financial statement presentation. We believe that our audits provide a reasonable basis for our opinion.

In our opinion, the consolidated financial statements referred to above present fairly, in all material aspects, the consolidated financial position of XYZ Company and its subsidiaries as of December 31, 2015, and December 31, 2014, in conformity with generally accepted accounting principles."

EFFECTS OF INFLATION

Inflation can distort some data and it may contribute to misinterpretation of information. For example, the annual report of Northern Supply boasted that sales revenues increased 10 percent in each of the last four years. Management considered 10 percent good until it was pointed out that inflation had increased 12 percent per year. When sales were deflated (divided by the inflation index), sales growth was negative. In ***constant dollars*** (inflation adjusted) sales had declined from $100 million in year 1 to $88 million in year 4.

Year	1	2	3	4
Sales ($ millions)	$100	$110	$121	$123
Inflation index	1.00	1.12	1.25	1.40
Adjusted sales (Sales/inflation index)	$100	$ 98	$ 97	$ 88

During this same period, the number of sales outlets increased from 10 to 13. The annual report stated that the increased number of outlets was a positive sign of growth. However, had management divided the number of sales outlets by adjusted sales each year, they would have seen that in constant dollars sales declined from $10.0 million to $6.8 million per outlet.

COMPARISONS ARE RELATIVE

Suppose that you read that the score of a football game was 32 for your team. The problem is that your team's 32 points could be a winning or losing score, depending on what the other team did. Thus, scores are relative. Similarly, analysis of data, such as the growth of sales or profitability, cannot be examined in isolation. The data must be judged relative to (1) historical trends and (2) other firms that are peers.

Historical Trends

Analysis of historical data is important. While data for one or two years may be an aberration, data for five years or longer provide a good basis for trend analysis. Substantial deviations from a trend may be considered red flags. Red flags are simply warning signs that something is happening that warrants further investigation. The deviation from the trend may be good or bad.

The red flag tells you what happened -- the figures deviated from a trend, or there was a large change in some important figure such as total assets. The important issue is why the deviation occurred. The key to meaningful financial analysis is explaining both what and why changes that deserve your attention occurred.

Comparisons with Other Firms and Life Cycle Considerations

Financial data should be compared to firms of similar size, in the same industry, and located in the same geographic region. By way of illustration, it does not make sense to compare a small start-up firm to an industry average that consists of well-established, large, mature firms. The two should have substantially different financial profiles. Along this line, the life cycle of a firm should be kept in mind when analyzing financial data. It is common practice to use industry average to make financial comparisons. However, firms that are just beginning to grow are not going to have the same financial characteristics as mature firms. For example, mature firms are expected to pay cash dividends, but start-up firms are not in a financial position to do so. Similarly, the growth rate of revenues is generally lower for mature firms than for start-ups. Without understanding the life-cycle concept, one could misinterpret the data to mean that the new firm is performing poorly in comparison to the industry average; whereas in reality, it may be doing very well, given its stage of development.

Average Data

Comparing data for a firm to an "average" for other firms can be misleading too. Average is a measure of central tendency. There are different types of averages: arithmetic mean, median, mode, and geometric. By definition, half of the firms are more profitable than the median average return, and the other half are below it. The real issue is not whether a firm is above or below the average of comparable firms, but how much the firm deviates from the average. A small deviation is no cause for concern. A large deviation is a red flag -- something that warrants further investigation.

LIFO/FIFO

Differences in accounting practices between firms may distort comparisons. For example, some firms use the *LIFO* (last in, first out) method of inventory valuation, and others use *FIFO* (first in, first out). During periods of inflation, FIFO can result in the overstatement of profits and, thus, in the overstatement of profitability. Even during periods of price stability, the two methods yield substantially different profits. By way of illustration, suppose that a firm purchases 10 items of inventory at $5 each and then 10 more items at $8 each. For simplicity, we assume that the firm has no other inventory. If the firm uses the FIFO method, items are sold in the order in which they were purchased. If 15 items are sold, 10 items will be assigned a cost of $5 each, and 5 items will be assigned a cost of $8 each. The total cost of the goods sold is $90. Because inventory purchases total $130, and the cost of goods sold is $90, the remaining inventory is valued at $40. Let's say the 15 items sold were priced at $12 each, giving a gross sales figure of $180. With the cost of goods sold at $90, the profit is $90.

If, instead, the firm uses LIFO, the results are quite different. With LIFO the cost of the last items purchased is assigned first. Profit under the LIFO method is $75. Similarly, different methods of depreciating fixed assets can affect profitability and financial ratios (Table 8-1 on next page).

RATIO ANALYSIS

To illustrate the process of financial analysis, we will refer to the financial statements for Ajax Manufacturing Corporation. Ajax Manufacturing Corporation designs and produces parts used in household appliances and industrial equipment. Ajax's true identity has been disguised to eliminate any prior knowledge that readers might have concerning the company or its operations.

Many banks use Annual Statement Studies™,[12] financial analysis software and spreadsheets to perform ratio analysis and make comparisons to industry data. Com-

Table 8-1: Comparison of LIFO Versus FIFO Inventory Methods

	FIFO	LIFO
First inventory purchase (10 items at $5 each)	$ 50	$ 50
Second inventory purchase (10 items at $8 each)	80	80
Total inventory purchases	$130	$130
Cost of goods sold (15 items)		
10 at $5 = $50 10 at $8 = $80	$ 50	$ 80
5 at $8 = $40 5 at $5 = $25	40	25
Total cost of goods sold	$ 90	$105
Inventory balance at end of period		
Beginning inventory (assumed)	$ 0	$ 0
Total inventory purchases	130	130
Less total cost of goods sold	(90)	(105)
Value of ending inventory	$ 40	$ 25
Profit		
Gross sales (15 items at $12 each)	$180	$180
Less total cost of goods sold	(90)	(105)
Gross profit	$ 90	$ 75

puterized systems are useful because they reduce the amount of time required to compute financial ratios and measures. Nevertheless, this chapter explains how to do it manually in order to give the reader "hands-on" experience.

Our analysis will be from the point of view of a loan officer who wants to evaluate the overall condition of Ajax, to assess its strengths and weaknesses, before he visits the firm to offer them his bank's services.

BALANCE SHEET

The ***balance sheet*** shown in Table 8-2 (next page) represents a statement of financial condition on one particular date. It is analogous to a snapshot of Ajax's financial condition on one day, December 31. ***Assets*** represent resources that the company owns or controls. Assets include financial assets (cash, investments, receivables and the like), real assets (property, plant, and equipment), and some firms have intangible assets (patents, trademarks, etc.). Assets that are expected to be converted into cash within one year, or an operating cycle, are called current assets. An operating cycle refers to the time when inventory is purchased until cash is collected when the goods are sold.

Ajax had total assets of $818,219,575 at the end of 2015, compared to $794,521,255 at the end of the previous year. The increase in assets indicates that Ajax is growing in size. But bigger may not be better. More analysis is required.

Liabilities represent what the company owes to others. It is the amount that various creditors have invested in the business. Liabilities due to be paid within one year, or within an operating cycle, are called *current liabilities*. The remainder of the

Table 8-2: Consolidated Balance Sheets for Ajax Manufacturing Corporation and Subsidiaries (Years Ended December 31, 2015, 2014)

	2015	2014
Assets		
Current assets		
Cash	$ 3,344,075	$ 1,487,676
Temporary investments	10,073,726	11,734,261
Trade accounts receivable, less allowances	137,299,371	135,065,650
Inventories	162,086,784	173,168,270
Prepaid expenses and other current assets	7,896,024	7,269,878
Future income tax benefits	6,406,485	5,725,166
Total current assets	327,106,465	334,450,901
Other assets	35,976,963	36,815,088
Property, plant, and equipment		
Land	2,593,311	3,223,368
Buildings	173,661,175	151,716,975
Machinery and equipment	546,629,604	504,747,066
Construction in progress	46,727,823	32,118,483
Less allowances for depreciation and amortization	(314,475,766)	(268,550,626)
Net property, plant, and equipment	455,136,147	423,255,266
Total assets	$ 818,219,575	$ 794,521,255
Liabilities and Stockholders' Equity		
Current liabilities		
Notes payable	$ 7,167,285	$ 6,684,796
Accounts payable and accrued expense		
Trade accounts	23,896,090	38,826,568
Employee compensation	14,355,414	10,523,668
Other	4,456,928	4,921,527
Total accounts payable	42,708,432	54,271,763
Federal and state income taxes	10,709,170	11,528,267
Current maturities of long-term debt and capital lease obligations	11,129,575	12,283,430
Total current liabilities	71,714,462	84,768,256
Long-term debt and capital lease obligations (less current maturities and unamortized debt discount)	180,338,551	191,257,695
Deferred Liabilities		
Federal and state income taxes	$ 48,656,564	$ 49,727,625
Accrued pension and other	9,424,669	6,815,997
Total deferred liabilities	58,081,233	56,543,622
Redeemable Cumulative Preferred Stock		
Par value $0.01 per share; authorized 10,000,000 shares; issued and outstanding 558,443 shares in 2006 and 559,943 shares in 2005	5,584,430	5,599,430
Stockholders' Equity		
Common Stock, par value $0.01 per share; shares outstanding: 40,889,909 in 2006; 40,919,638 in 2005	414,200	414,200
Paid-in capital	47,383,897	48,494,262
Retained earnings	465,552,899	422,221,703
Treasury Stock	(13,601,818)	(15,811,931)
Currency translation adjustment	2,751,721	1,034,018
Total stockholders' equity	502,500,899	456,352,252
Total liabilities and stockholders' equity	$ 818,219,575	$ 794,521,255

liabilities includes long-term debts and leases and deferred liabilities. *Deferred taxes*, for example, represent amounts that may be owed in taxes due to timing differences in income earned but not yet recognized for tax purposes.

Not all liabilities are shown on the balance sheet. For example, post-retirement benefits are described in the notes at the end of the financial statements. Financial Accounting Standards Board Statement No. 106 requires employers that provide certain post-retirement benefits to recognize those costs and to report them. Other firms may have commitments, contingent liabilities, or be engaged in hedging (buying and selling futures contracts), all of which are described in the notes. The point is that you must read all of the notes!

Stockholders' equity represents the owners' investment in the business. It is a claim against assets. *It is not funds that the stockholders can withdraw from the firm.* For Ajax, stockholders' equity includes the value of the stock purchased by the stockholders, earnings that have been retained, stock that has been repurchased by the company *(treasury stock)*, and an accounting adjustment representing changes in the value of foreign currencies in connection with their foreign operations.

By definition, total assets must equal total liabilities plus stockholders' equity.

INCOME STATEMENT

The ***income statement*** represents a firm's revenues and expenses during an accounting period such as a year or a quarter. The statement is reported on an accrual basis rather than a cash basis. An ***accrual basis*** means that revenues are recognized in the accounting period when they are earned, regardless of when the cash is received. Similarly, expenses are recognized in the accounting period when they are incurred, regardless of when the cash is paid. This explains why there were deferred taxes on the balance sheet. A ***cash basis*** means that revenues and expenses are recognized when they are received or paid.

Table 8-3 (next page) reveals that Ajax's net sales increased during the three-year period shown. The major categories of expenses include cost of goods sold; selling, general, and administrative expenses; interest expense; and taxes. When the expenses were deducted from the revenues, net income declined. This suggests that Ajax is doing some things that appear to be beneficial to stockholders, such as increasing sales. However, Ajax has problems too, as evidenced by the decline in income. We will use data from these and other tables to analyze Ajax and try to find the cause of its problems. Selected industry data will be used for comparisons. Only two consecutive years of balance sheet data are presented here for ease of exposition. However, the use of longer periods, such as five years, is recommended for trend analysis.

AVERAGE VERSUS YEAR-END DATA

There are two ways to calculate ratios using data from both the balance sheet and income statement. Because the balance sheet represents one day

Table 8-3: Consolidated Statements of Income for Ajax Manufacturing Corporation and Subsidiaries (Years Ended December 31, 2015, 2014, 2013)

	2015	2014	2013
Net sales	$804,584,939	$713,812,344	$687,954,312
Cost of goods sold	553,159,643	461,280,501	457,874,872
	251,425,296	252,531,843	230,079,440
Selling, general, and administrative expenses	142,773,638	126,269,548	109,724,386
	108,651,658	126,262,295	120,355,054
Other deductions (income)			
Interest expense incurred	18,096,696	18,884,674	15,643,287
Other-net	(310,980)	(2,294,670)	1,983,444
	17,785,716	16,590,004	17,626,731
Income before income taxes	90,865,942	109,672,291	102,728,323
Federal and state income taxes			
Currently payable	35,779,380	38,897,000	32,314,689
Deferred	(1,752,380)	2,828,000	5,678,891
	34,027,000	41,725,000	37,993,580
Net income	56,838,942	67,947,291	64,734,743
Preferred stock dividends	559,568	568,943	571,943
Net income applicable to common shareholders	$ 56,279,374	$ 67,378,348	$ 64,162,800
Net income per common and common equivalent shares	$ 1.38	$ 1.65	$ 1.57
Dividends per share	$ 0.32	$ 0.32	$ 0.28

(December 31), and the income statement may represent one year (365 days), the first method uses the same time period when computing ratios that involve both statements. This is accomplished by averaging data from two balance sheets so that the data cover the same period as the income statement. For example:

Assets at Year End December 31 (From Table 8-2)	
2015	$818,219,575
2014	794,521,255
Total	$1,612,740,830
Average	$806,370,415

This amount represents the average assets of the firm during the course of one year. This figure can be used when comparing, say, net income to average total assets:

$$\frac{\text{Net Income 2015}}{\text{Average total assets}} = \frac{\$56,838,942}{\$806,370,415} = 0.0705 \text{ or } 7.11\%$$

The second method uses year-end balance sheet data instead of average balance sheet data. Computing the same ratio for 2015 using year-end data yields a different result:

$$\frac{\text{Net Income 2015}}{\text{Year-end assets 2015}} = \frac{\$56{,}838{,}942}{\$818{,}219{,}575} = 0.0695 \text{ or } 6.95\%$$

The first method is more accurate because the average balance sheet data and the income statement cover the same time period. One drawback of this method is that it requires the use of two years of balance sheet data to calculate one average balance sheet figure. Because many publicly held companies provide only two years of balance sheet data in their annual and quarterly reports, it makes comparisons difficult. Therefore, some credit analysts use year-end data because (1) they can calculate the ratio for two years and (2) it's easier to calculate. Both methods provide similar insights into the financial condition of a firm as long as they are used consistently. Only two years of balance sheet data are shown in the examples given here. Therefore, we will use year-end balance sheet data for the computations.

PROFITABILITY RATIOS

Profitability is the ultimate test of the effectiveness of management. Profitability can be measured in terms of returns on assets, net assets, equity, and sales. All of the measures presented here indicate that Ajax's profitability declined.

Return on Assets

The ***return on assets*** (ROA) is the most comprehensive measure of profitability, measuring the productivity for shareholders, bondholders, and other creditors. ROA is calculated by dividing net income (NI) by total assets. Recall that we are going to use year-end balance sheet figures in our computations. The ratios reveal that overall profitability declined and was less than the industry average. The industry average is based on the results of three similar firms.

ROA = NI/total assets (8.1)

$$\frac{\text{Net income 2015}}{\text{Year-end assets 2015}} = \frac{\$56{,}838{,}942}{\$818{,}219{,}575} = 0.0695 \text{ or } 6.95\%$$

$$\frac{\text{Net income 2014}}{\text{Year-end assets 2014}} = \frac{\$67{,}947{,}291}{\$794{,}521{,}255} = 8.55\%$$

Industry average = 7.83%

Return on Equity

The ***return on equity*** (ROE) measures the rate of return on the stockholders' investment in the corporation, which includes their paid-in capital as well as retained earnings. ROE is calculated by dividing net income by total stockholders' equity.

If a firm has large amounts of preferred stock outstanding, a similar ratio can be computed by dividing income available to common stockholders by common equity. Notice that Ajax has redeemable cumulative preferred stock outstanding (see the balance sheet of Table 8-2). The preferred stock is redeemable at the stockholder's option, and all of the dividends due to the preferred stockholders must be paid to them before any dividends can be paid on common stock. Technically, preferred stockholders are owners of the corporation. However, they have limited voting rights and they receive fixed cash payments (dividends), similar to the fixed interest payments on debt. Thus, this hybrid preferred stock has some features of both debt and equity investments. Therefore, it is listed in the liability section of the balance sheet, and it is not considered part of stockholders' equity.

ROE = NI/Common stockholders' equity (8.2)

ROE 2015 = $\frac{\$56,838,942}{\$502,500,899}$ = 11.31%

ROE 2014 = $\frac{\$67,947,291}{\$456,352,252}$ = 14.89%

Industry average = 12.54%

Let's examine the ROE and ROA in further detail. The ROE is equal to the ROA times LR, which is a leverage ratio. The LR is one indicator of financial leverage. It indicates the dollar amount of assets that are financed by each dollar of equity:

ROE = ROA X LR (8-3)

NI/E = NI/A A/E

where

NI = net income

E = stockholders' equity

A = total assets

LR = leverage ratio (A/E)

Using 2015 data for Ajax companies, we see that the leverage ratio is 1.63. In other words, every dollar of equity finances $1.63 dollars in assets. The remainder of the assets are financed by debt (including current liabilities). The relationship between debt and equity is called financial leverage. More will be said about financial leverage shortly.

ROE = ROA X LR

NI/E = NI/A X A/E

11.31% = 6.95% X 1.63 times

Suppose that the leverage ratio was 1.00, which means that every dollar of equity finances only $1 dollar in assets. If net income remains the same, ROE will decline to 6.95 percent. This means that ROE is a function of both financial leverage and net income. Observe that ROA is not affected directly by financial leverage. Both measures are affected indirectly because interest expense affects NI.

ROE = ROA X LR

6.95% = 6.95% X 1.00 times

Net Profit Margin

As previously mentioned, profitability can be measured in terms of returns on assets, net assets, equity, and sales. The ***net profit margin*** on sales, computed by dividing net income by net sales, is the percent of profit earned for each dollar of sales. Both the numerator and the denominator in this ratio come from the income statement. The sharp decline in the profit margins is a red flag telling us that further analysis of the income statement is required. We do this analysis when we examine common size financial statements.

$$\text{Net profit margin} = \frac{\text{Net income}}{\text{Net sales}} \quad (8\text{-}4)$$

$$\frac{\text{Net income 2015}}{\text{Net sales 2015}} = \frac{\$56,838,942}{\$804,584,939} = 7.06\%$$

$$\frac{\text{Net income 2014}}{\text{Net sales 2014}} = \frac{\$67,947,291}{\$713,812,344} = 9.52\%$$

Industry average = 9.48

Earnings per Share

Earnings per share (EPS) is the statistic that is often quoted when profitability is discussed. The reason for its popularity is that it is relatively easy to understand and easy to relate to stock prices. Earnings per share is derived by dividing income available for common stock by the number of shares outstanding. The EPS can be reported as "basic EPS" and "diluted EPS." Basic EPS represents the income from continuing operations and net income. Diluted EPS takes into account the effect of conversion of convertible securities, warrants, and stock options.

Because the number of shares outstanding can change from year to year, a firm with no change in income could have higher EPS if the number of shares declined. Many firms buy their own stock for Treasury stock, employee stock option plans (ESOP), and for other purposes. One effect of such purchases is to increase EPS.

If a firm has an extraordinary charge to earnings, such as a one-time adjustment for a change in accounting methods, earnings before and after the charge should be examined to gain a better understanding of the trend.

Net income available for common stockholders is net income less preferred stock dividend payments. Some companies have sinking fund payments that must be deducted too. Sinking fund payments are periodic payments made to retire debts.

The number of shares outstanding for Ajax is listed in the Stockholders' Equity portion of the balance sheet (Table 8-2). The data reveal that the EPS has $1.38 in 2015 compared to $1.65 in the previous year.

$$\text{Earnings per share} = \frac{\text{Net income available for common stock}}{\text{Number of shares outstanding}} \quad (8.5)$$

$$2015 \quad = \frac{\$56,279,374}{40,889,909} = \$1.38 \text{ per share}$$

$$2014 \quad = \frac{\$67,378,348}{40,919,638} = \$1.65 \text{ per share}$$

Dividend Payout Ratio

Earnings might be retained by the firm to help finance growth, or they might be paid out to the shareholders in the form of cash dividends. The extent to which earnings are paid to common stockholders in the form of cash dividends is called the ***dividend payout ratio***. Strictly speaking it is not a measure of profitability, but it does relate to the distribution of profits. The payout ratio is computed by dividing cash dividends per share on common stock by earnings per share. The cash dividends per common shares are listed in Table 8-3.[13] Ajax paid a cash dividend of $0.32 cents per share in both years. Because the dividend remained unchanged and earnings per share declined in 2015, the payout ratio increased from 19 percent to 23 percent, slightly above the industry average.

The average payout ratio for this industry is far below the national average for all corporations. The ratio of dividends to profits after taxes for all corporations was 50.65% in 2015.[14] Ajax's relatively low payout ratio indicates that management believes that it has growth opportunities that they want to fund, in part, with retained earnings. Equally important, it suggests that this industry is still in the expansion stage of the life cycle, while the national average may be dominated by mature firms.

$$\text{Payout ratio} = \frac{\text{Cash dividends per share}}{\text{Earnings per share}} \quad (8.6)$$

$$2015 \quad = \frac{\$0.32}{\$1.38} = 23\%$$

$$2014 \quad = \frac{\$0.32}{\$1.65} = 19\%$$

Industry average = 20%

As noted at the beginning of this section, all of the measures indicate that Ajax's profitability declined. That is what happened. Now we will try to determine why it happened.

LIQUIDITY RATIOS AND MEASURES

A company must survive the short run in order to prosper in the long run. If a firm does not have sufficient liquidity, it may not survive the short run, which is why liquidity measures are so important. The following measures of liquidity assess the ability of a firm to meet its short-run, or current obligations -- those that are due within one year.

Net Working Capital

As a general rule, companies use current assets to pay their current liabilities. For example, cash is used to pay accounts payable. The arithmetic difference between current assets and current liabilities is called *net working capital* (NWC), and it represents a cushion for creditors' short-term loans. In other words, creditors view more working capital as being better than less. However, too much working capital may be a detriment to the company, because it may indicate that funds are not being used effectively. Holding excess nonearning assets, such as cash and accounts receivable, can hold down profits. Cash, for example, might be better employed in inventory or fixed assets. An examination of Ajax's balance sheet (Table 7A-3) reveals that net working capital increased from about $250 million in 2014 to $255 million in 2015:

Net working capital = Current assets - Current liabilities

$$\text{NWC 2015} = \$327{,}106{,}465 - \$71{,}714{,}462 = \$255{,}392{,}003 \quad (8.7)$$

$$\text{NWC 2014} = \$334{,}450{,}901 - \$84{,}768{,}256 = \$249{,}682{,}645$$

Current Ratio

The ***current ratio*** is a broad measure of liquidity derived by dividing current assets by current liabilities. It is considered a broad measure because it includes all current assets and all current liabilities. The current ratio for Ajax increased sharply in 2015 and was well above the industry average. This is a red flag that requires further analysis. The high current ratio suggests that Ajax may be too liquid.

$$\text{Current ratio} = \frac{\text{Current assets}}{\text{Current liabilities}} \quad (8.8)$$

$$\text{Current ratio 2015} = \frac{\$327{,}106{,}465}{\$71{,}714{,}462} = 4.56 \text{ times}$$

$$\text{Current ratio 2014} = \frac{\$334{,}450{,}901}{\$84{,}768{,}256} = 3.95 \text{ times}$$

$$\text{Industry average} = 2.97 \text{ times}$$

Acid Test Ratio

The ***acid test ratio*** is a narrow measure of liquidity derived by dividing cash, marketable securities, and accounts receivable by current liabilities. It is considered narrow because it excludes the least liquid current assets -- inventory, prepaid expenses, and future tax benefits -- from the numerator of the equation. The acid test ratio for Ajax increased in 2015, which may account for the high current ratio and lower profits.

Notice that Ajax's acid test ratio is high when compared to the industry average. Sometimes a high acid test ratio is due to conservative financial policies. Alternatively, the firm may be building its cash and investments in anticipation of capital expenditures or an acquisition. Finally, the firm may not be collecting its receivables. Further analysis is required to determine which explanation is correct.

$$\text{Acid test ratio} = \frac{\text{Cash + Securities + Accounts receivable}}{\text{Current liabilities}} \quad (8.9)$$

$$\text{Acid test 2015} = \frac{\$150,717,172}{\$71,714,462} = 2.10 \text{ times}$$

$$\text{Acid test 2014} = \frac{\$148,287,587}{\$84,768,256} = 1.75 \text{ times}$$

Industry average = 1.48 times

Average Collection Period

The ***average collection period*** indicates the average number of days that a firm waits before receiving cash from sales made on credit. All of Ajax's sales are made on credit, so it is important for the firm to minimize the collection period in order to be paid as soon as possible.

Two steps are required to calculate the average collection period. Step 1 involves determining the dollar amount of credit sales per day. We do this by dividing net sales (Table 8-3) by 360 days. The use of 360 days to represent a financial year was developed in an era before hand-held calculators and computers, but is still widely used by analysts. Either 360 or 365 days can be used as long as one is used consistently. Step 2 is to divide accounts receivable by credit sales per day. The data revealed that the average collection period declined from 68 to 61 days, indicating that Ajax is doing a better job of collecting its funds. Therefore, the high level of the acid test ratio noted earlier is either a result of conservative management policies or Ajax is increasing liquid assets for future expansion.

$$\text{Credit sales per day} = \frac{\text{Net sales}}{\text{360 days}} \quad (8\text{-}10a)$$

$$\text{Credit sales per day 2015} = \frac{\$804,584,939}{\text{360 days}} = \$2,234,958$$

$$\text{Average collection period} = \frac{\text{Accounts receivable}}{\text{Credit sales/day}} \quad (8\text{-}10b)$$

$$\text{Average collection period 2015} = \frac{\$137,299,371}{\$2,234,958} = 61.42 \text{ days}$$

$$\text{Credit sales per day 2014} = \frac{\$713,812,344}{\text{360 days}} = \$1,982,812$$

$$\text{Average collection period} = \frac{\$135,065,650}{\$1,982,812} = 68.11 \text{ days}$$

Industry average = 63 days

Average Payment Period

The ***average payment period*** is one indicator of how a firm is managing its current liabilities. This ratio is computed using two steps. Step 1 determines the dollar amount of credit purchases per day. Credit purchases amount to 80 percent of the cost of goods sold for Ajax. Step 2 divides accounts payable by the credit purchases per day. There was a sharp decline in the dollar amount of accounts payable and in the average payment period. It is currently far below the industry average. We don't have the information here to explain the sharp reduction in time. Nevertheless, we can guess that if they had sufficient liquidity, the reduction in the payment period may be to allow Ajax to take advantage of trade discounts for early payment of bills.

$$\text{Average payment period} = \frac{\text{Accounts payable}}{\text{Credit purchases/day}} \tag{8.11}$$

$$\text{2015 credit purchases/day} = \frac{0.80(\$553{,}159{,}643)}{360 \text{ days}} = \$1{,}229{,}244$$

$$\text{2015 average payment period} = \frac{\$23{,}896{,}090}{\$1{,}229{,}244} = 19 \text{ days}$$

$$\text{2014 credit purchases/day} = \frac{0.80(\$461{,}280{,}501)}{360 \text{ days}} = \$1{,}025{,}068$$

$$\text{2014 average payment period} = \frac{\$38{,}826{,}568}{\$1{,}025{,}068} = 38 \text{ days}$$

$$\text{Industry average} = 35 \text{ days}$$

MEASURING EFFICIENCY

Efficiency indicators measure how effectively certain assets and liabilities are being used in the production of goods and services. The average collection period can be thought of as both a measure of liquidity and efficiency.

Inventory Turnover Ratio

The objective in managing inventories is to hold the minimum amount necessary in order to serve customers' needs and make sales. The ***inventory turnover ratio*** is calculated by dividing the cost of goods sold by inventory.

As a general rule the higher the turnover, the faster the company can realize profits. Inventory turnover ratios vary widely from industry to industry. One would expect a daily newspaper to have a very high inventory turnover ratio (about 365 times per year), because few people want to buy last month's newspaper. In contrast, the inventory turnover ratio for a jewelry store may be relatively low, perhaps once or twice per year.

$$\text{Inventory turnover ratio} = \frac{\text{Cost of goods sold}}{\text{Inventory}} \tag{8.12}$$

$$\text{Inventory turnover 2015} = \frac{\$553{,}159{,}643}{\$162{,}086{,}784} = 3.41 \text{ times}$$

$$\text{Inventory turnover 2014} = \frac{\$461{,}280{,}501}{\$173{,}168{,}270} = 2.66 \text{ times}$$

Industry average = 3.00 times

Age of Inventory

Another way to examine inventories is to determine the average number of days that the inventory remains on hand. This is accomplished by dividing 360 days by the inventory turnover ratio. The age of the inventory declined in 2015, reflecting the higher inventory turnover ratio and more efficient use of inventories.

$$\text{Age of inventory} = \frac{360 \text{ days}}{\text{Inventory turnover ratio}} \quad (8.13)$$

Age of inventory 2015	= 360/3.41	= 106 days
Age of inventory 2014	= 360/2.66	= 135 days
Industry average		= 120 days

Asset Turnover Ratio

The ***asset turnover ratio*** is a broad measure of efficiency because it encompasses all assets. It is computed by dividing net sales by total assets. The ratios indicate that Ajax is using its assets more efficiently. This is consistent with the improvements noted in the management of accounts receivable and inventory.

$$\text{Asset turnover} = \frac{\text{Net sales}}{\text{Total assets}} \quad (8.14)$$

$$\text{Asset turnover 2015} = \frac{\$804,584,939}{\$818,219,147} = 98.33\%$$

$$\text{Asset turnover 2014} = \frac{\$713,812,344}{\$794,521,255} = 89.84\%$$

Industry average = 93.15%

FINANCIAL LEVERAGE

Financial leverage refers to the relationship between borrowed funds, such as loans and bonds, and common stockholders' equity. Some analysts consider preferred stock to be in the same category as debt because of the obligation to pay preferred dividends. We will follow that practice because the balance sheet for Ajax (Table 8-2) does not include the preferred stock in stockholders' equity.

Companies with a high proportion of borrowed funds are said to be highly leveraged. Financial leverage increases the volatility of earnings per share and the risk of bankruptcy. Several measures of financial leverage are described here.

Debt Ratio

The ***debt ratio*** indicates the proportion of a firm's total assets that is financed with borrowed funds. It is calculated by dividing total liabilities by total assets. The easy way to compute total liabilities is to subtract common stockholders' equity from total assets. Recall that we are not considering the preferred stock as equity.

The data reveal that the debt ratio declined in 2015. An examination of the balance sheet reveals both an increase in equity and a decrease in liabilities. The principal changes in liabilities were lower accounts payable and long-term debts.

Debt ratio	= Total liabilities / Total assets		(8-15)
Debt ratio 2015	= \$315,718,676 / \$818,219,576	= 38.59%	
Debt ratio 2014	= \$338,169.003 / \$794,521,255	= 42.56%	
Industry average		= 40.18%	

Long-Term Debt as a Percent of Total Capital

Total capital includes long-term debt and equity. In 2015, for example, total capital for Ajax was:

Long-term debt	\$180,338,551
Preferred stock	5,584,430
Stockholders' Equity	502,500,899
Total capital	\$688,423,880

Long-term debt as a percent of total capital = Long-term debt / Total capital (8-16)

Long-term debt/capital 2015	= \$180,338,551 / \$688,423,880	= 26.19%
Long-term debt/capital 2014	= \$191,257,695 / \$652,939,377	= 29.29%
Industry average		= 32.13%

Ajax reduced its long-term debt and is currently below the industry average.

Times Interest Earned

By reducing the amount of debt outstanding, Ajax was better able to cover (i.e., pay) its outstanding debts, thereby reducing its financial risk. Debt coverage is measured by ***times interest earned***, which is computed by dividing earnings before interest and taxes (EBIT) by interest expense. In 2015, EBIT was:

Income Before Income Taxes	\$90,865,942
Interest Expense	18,096,696
EBIT	\$108,962,638

The decline in the coverage ratio in 2015 reflects the lower EBIT. Nevertheless, the firm still has ample coverage and is above the industry average by a substantial margin.

Times interest earned	= EBIT / Interest expense		(8-17)
Times interest earned 2015	= \$108,962,638 / \$18,096,696	= 6.02 times	

Times interest earned 2014 $= \frac{\$128{,}556{,}965}{\$18{,}884{,}674} = 6.81$ times

Industry average $= 5.38$ times

REVIEW OF FINANCIAL INDICATORS

Table 8-4 provides a review of the financial indicators as well as the results for Ajax Manufacturing Corporation. The financial indicators reveal that Ajax's profitability declined. The liquidity measures indicate that Ajax is very liquid, but their high degree of liquidity did not account for the decline in profitability. The efficiency measures show that Ajax has become more efficient in the most recent period. Finally, the firm has reduced its financial leverage. The reason for the decline in profitability will be revealed shortly.

TABLE 8-4 REVIEW OF FINANCIAL INDICATORS

ROA = NI/total assets

$$\frac{\text{Net income 2006}}{\text{Year-end assets 2006}} = \frac{\$56{,}838{,}942}{\$818{,}219{,}575} = 0.0695 \text{ or } 6.95\%$$

$$\frac{\text{Net income 2015}}{\text{Year-end assets 2015}} \quad \frac{\$67{,}947{,}291}{\$794{,}521{,}255} = 8.55\%$$

$$\frac{\text{Net income 2014}}{\text{Year-end assets 2014}} \quad 7.83\%$$

(8.1)

ROE = NI/Common stockholders' equity

$$\text{ROE 2006} = \frac{\$56{,}838{,}942}{\$502{,}500{,}899} = 11.31\%$$

$$\text{ROE 2015} \quad \frac{\$67{,}947{,}291}{\$456{,}352{,}252} = 14.89\%$$

Indu ROE 2014 | 2.54%

(8.2)

ROE = ROA × LR

NI/E = NI/A × A/E

11.31% = 6.95% × 1.63 times (for 2006)

6.95% X 1.63 (for 2015)

(8.3)

$$\text{Net profit margin} = \frac{\text{Net income}}{\text{Net sales}}$$

$$\frac{\text{Net income 2006}}{} = \frac{\$56{,}838{,}942}{\$804{,}584{,}939} = 7.06\%$$

$$\frac{\text{Net income 2015}}{\text{Net sales 2015}} \quad \frac{\$67{,}947{,}291}{713{,}812{,}344} = 9.52\%$$

$$\frac{\text{Net income 2014}}{\text{Net sales 2014}} \quad .48\%$$

(8.4)

$$\text{Earnings per share} = \frac{\text{Net income available for common stock}}{\text{Number of shares outstanding}}$$

$$\text{Earning per share 2015} \quad \frac{\$56{,}279{,}374}{40{,}889{,}909} = \$1.38 \text{ per share}$$

$$\text{Earning per share 2014} \quad \frac{\$67{,}378{,}348}{40{,}919{,}638} = \$1.65 \text{ per share}$$

(8.5)

$$\text{Payout ratio} = \frac{\text{Cash dividends per share}}{\text{Earnings per share}}$$

$$\text{Payout ratio 2015} \quad \frac{\$0.32}{\$1.38} = 23\%$$

$$\text{Payout ratio 2014} \quad \frac{\$0.32}{\$1.65} = 19\%$$

Industry average = 20%

(8.6)

Net working capital = Current assets − Current liabilities

NWC 2006 = \$327,106,465 − \$71,714,462 = \$255,392,003

NWC 2015 = \$334,450,901 − \$84,768,256 = \$249,682,645

(8.7)

NWC 2014

$$\text{Current ratio} = \frac{\text{Current assets}}{\text{Current liabilities}}$$

$$\text{Current ratio 2006} = \frac{\$327{,}106{,}465}{\$71{,}714{,}462} = 4.56 \text{ times}$$

$$\text{Current Ratio 2015} = \frac{\$334{,}450{,}901}{\$84{,}768{,}256} = 3.95 \text{ times}$$

Current Ratio 2014 = 2.97 times

(8.8)

$$\text{Acid test ratio} = \frac{\text{Cash + Securities + Accounts receivable}}{\text{Current liabilities}}$$

$$\text{Acid test 2006} = \frac{\$150{,}717{,}172}{\$71{,}714{,}462} = 2.10 \text{ times}$$

Acid test 2015

$$\text{Acid test 2005} = \frac{\$148{,}287{,}587}{\$84{,}768{,}256} = 1.75 \text{ times}$$

Asset test 2014

Industry average = 1.48 times

(8.9)

$$\text{Credit sales per day} = \frac{\text{Net sales}}{\text{360 days}}$$

$$\text{Credit sales per day 2006} = \frac{\$804{,}584{,}939}{\text{360 days}} = \$2{,}234{,}958$$

Current sales per day 2015

(8.10a)

$$\text{Average collection period} = \frac{\text{Accounts receivable}}{\text{Credit sales/day}}$$

$$\text{Average collection period 2015} = \frac{\$137{,}299{,}371}{\$2{,}234{,}958} = 61.43 \text{ days}$$

$$\text{Credit sales per day 2014} = \frac{\$713{,}812{,}344}{\text{360 days}} = \$1{,}982{,}812$$

$$\text{Average collection period} = \frac{\$135{,}065{,}650}{\$1{,}982{,}812} = 68 \text{ days}$$

Industry average = 63 days

(8.10b)

(Continues)

TABLE 8-4 REVIEW OF FINANCIAL INDICATORS *(CONTINUED)*

$$\text{Average payment period} = \frac{\text{Accounts payable}}{\text{Credit purchases/day}}$$

$$\text{Current purchases/day 2015} = \frac{0.80(\$553{,}159{,}643)}{360 \text{ days}} = \$1{,}229{,}244$$

$$\text{Average payment period 2015} = \frac{\$23{,}896{,}090}{\$1{,}229{,}244} = 19 \text{ days}$$

$$\text{Current purchases/day 2014} = \frac{0.80(\$461{,}280{,}501)}{360 \text{ days}} = \$1{,}025{,}068$$

$$\text{Average payment period 2014} = \frac{\$38{,}826{,}568}{\$1{,}025{,}068} = 38 \text{ days}$$

Industry average = 35 days (8.11)

$$\text{Inventory turnover ratio} = \frac{\text{Cost of goods sold}}{\text{Inventory}}$$

$$\text{Inventory turnover 2015} = \frac{\$553{,}159{,}643}{\$162{,}086{,}784} = 3.41 \text{ times}$$

$$\text{Inventory turnover 2014} = \frac{\$461{,}280{,}501}{\$173{,}168{,}270} = 2.66 \text{ times}$$

Industry average = 3.00 times (8.12)

$$\text{Age of inventory} = \frac{360 \text{ days}}{\text{Inventory turnover ratio}}$$

$$\text{Age of inventory 2015} = \frac{360}{3.41} = 106 \text{ days}$$

$$\text{Age of inventory 2014} = \frac{360}{2.66} = 135 \text{ days}$$

Industry average = 120 days (8.13)

$$\text{Asset turnover} = \frac{\text{Net sales}}{\text{Total assets}}$$

$$\text{Asset turnover 2015} = \frac{\$804{,}584{,}939}{\$818{,}219{,}575} = 98.33\%$$

$$\text{Asset turnover 2014} = \frac{\$713{,}812{,}344}{\$794{,}521{,}255} = 89.84\%$$

Industry average = 93.15% (8.14)

$$\text{Debt ratio} = \frac{\text{Total liabilities}}{\text{Total assets}}$$

$$\text{Debt ratio 2015} = \frac{\$315{,}718{,}676}{\$818{,}219{,}575} = 38.59\%$$

$$\text{Debt ratio 2014} = \frac{\$338{,}169{,}003}{\$794{,}521{,}255} = 42.56\%$$

Industry average = 40.18% (8.15)

$$\text{Long-term debt as percent of total capital} = \frac{\text{Long-term debt}}{\text{Total capital}}$$

$$\text{Long-term debt/capital 2015} = \frac{\$180{,}338{,}551}{\$688{,}423{,}880} = 26.20\%$$

$$\text{Long-term debt/capital 2014} = \frac{\$191{,}257{,}695}{\$652{,}939{,}377} = 29.29\%$$

Industry average = 32.13% (8.16)

$$\text{Times interest earned} = \frac{\text{EBIT}}{\text{Interest expense}}$$

$$\text{Times interest earned 2015} = \frac{\$108{,}962{,}638}{\$18{,}096{,}696} = 6.02 \text{ times}$$

$$\text{Times interest earned 2014} = \frac{\$128{,}556{,}965}{\$18{,}884{,}674} = 6.81 \text{ times}$$

Industry average = 5.38 times (8.17)

COMMON-SIZE STATEMENT ANALYSIS

BALANCE SHEET

Common-size financial statements present each item listed on the balance sheet as a percent of total assets, and each item listed on the income statement as a percent of net sales. This format facilitates comparisons of financial statements because the data are expressed as percentages instead of dollar amounts. Consider Ajax's balance sheet (refer back to Table 8-2). Total current assets for Ajax decreased from $334.4 million in 2014 to $327.1 million in the following year, while total assets increased from $794.5 million to $818.2 million. Although it is difficult to comprehend the significance of these changes, it is easy to understand that total current assets declined from 43 percent of total assets to 39.9 percent. Similarly, common-size statements are useful in comparing financial statements of different companies, and for comparing financial data from large and small companies because all of the data are expressed as percentages of total assets or sales.

Table 8-5 (next page) is the common-size balance sheet for Ajax Manufacturing. The common-size balance sheet and income statement for Ajax are based on the balance sheet and income statements presented in Tables 8-2 and 8-3. As previously noted, total current assets declined in both absolute and relative terms. Keeping in mind that we know that sales increased during the period under review, the reduction in current assets is consistent with the improvement in the average collection period of accounts receivable and the higher inventory turnover that we observed. In other words, Ajax is using these assets more efficiently. Also note that Ajax increased its investments in property, plant, and equipment.

On the other side of the balance sheet, there was a substantial decline in both total current liabilities and long-term debt, whereas total equity increased. This is consistent with the downward trend in the debt ratio that we observed. We did not find any surprises examining the common-size balance sheet.

TABLE 8-5 COMMON-SIZE CONSOLIDATED BALANCE SHEETS FOR AJAX MANUFACTURING CORPORATION AND SUBSIDIARIES (YEARS ENDED DECEMBER 31, 2015, 2014)

	2015	2014
Assets		
Current assets		
Cash	0.41%	0.19%
Temporary investments	1.23	1.48
Trade accounts receivable, less allowances	16.78	17.00
Inventories	19.81	21.80
Prepaid expenses and other current assets	0.97	0.93
Future income tax benefits	0.78	0.72
Total current assets	39.98	43.35
Other assets	4.39	4.63
Property, plant and equipment		
Land	0.32	0.41
Buildings	21.22	19.11
Machinery and equipment	66.81	63.53
Construction in progress	5.71	4.04
	94.06	87.07
Less allowances for depreciation and amortization	(38.43)	(33.80)
Net	55.63	53.27
Total assets	100.00%	100.00%
Liabilities and stockholders' equity		
Current liabilities		
Notes payable	0.88%	0.84%
Accounts payable and accrued expenses:		
Trade accounts	2.92	4.89
Employee compensation	1.75	1.33
Other	0.55	0.62
	5.22	6.81
Federal and state income taxes	1.31	1.45
Current maturities of long-term debt and capital lease obligations	1.36	1.55
Total current liabilities	8.77	10.67
Long-term debt and capital lease obligations (less current maturities and unamortized debt discount)	22.04	24.07
Deferred Liabilities		
Federal and state income taxes	5.95	6.26
Accrued pension and other	1.15	0.86
	7.10	7.12
Redeemable cumulative preferred stock		
Par value $.01 per share, authorized 10,000,000 shares, issued and outstanding 558,443 shares in 2006 and 559,943 shares in 2005	0.68	0.71
Stockholders' equity		
Common stock, par value $.01 per share, shares outstanding: 40,889,909 in 2006; 40,919,638 in 2005	0.05	0.05
Paid-in capital	5.79	6.10
Retained earnings	56.90	53.14
Treasury stock	(1.66)	(1.99)
Currency translation adjustment	0.34	0.13
	61.41	57.44
Total liabilities and equity	**100.00%**	**100.00%**

Note: Figures may not add to totals due to rounding.

INCOME STATEMENT

Table 8-6 is the common-size income statement. It shows that the net profit margin [Eq. (8-4), net income expressed as a percent of net sales], declined from 9.5 percent in 2014 to 7.1 percent in 2015. We examined this ratio previously, but we were not able to determine the reason for its decline. Now, by using the common-size income statement, we can delve into the problem further. A careful examination of Table 8-6 reveals that the reason for Ajax's poor performance is the increase in the cost of goods sold. The cost of goods sold is the total cost of the finished goods inventory in a period (annual in our example). The cost of goods sold is the cost of goods available for sale less cost of finished goods in inventory. In manufacturing accounting, the cost of goods sold includes direct materials and work-in-process. Work-in-process includes labor and manufacturing expenses. Some manufacturing concerns have high levels of fixed operating and financial costs, or high operating and financial leverage. Fixed costs are those that are incurred regardless of the level of short-term production. Over the long term, such costs may change if, for example, new plant and equipment are acquired.

The cost of goods sold increased from 64.6 percent of net sales in 2014 to 68.7 percent in 2015. The reason for the higher cost was explained in footnotes and in management's discussion and analysis of their financial condition that were attached to the financial statements, but were not presented here. The higher cost of goods sold was due to a reduced production schedule. In the first half of 2015, unit sales had increased, but prices had declined, and Ajax had excess inventory. By the second half of the year, the imbalance was corrected and improved sales resulted in the higher inventory mentioned previously.

Net sales less cost of goods sold is the gross margin, which is the profit before all of the other expenses are considered. The other expenses listed in the table did not change appreciably.

TABLE 8-6 COMMON-SIZE CONSOLIDATED STATEMENTS OF INCOME FOR AJAX MANUFACTURING CORPORATION AND SUBSIDIARIES (YEARS ENDED DECEMBER 31, 2015, 2014, 2013)

	2015	2014	2013
Net sales	100.0%	100.0%	100.0%
Cost of goods sold	68.7	64.6	66.5
Gross margin	31.3	35.4	33.5
Selling, general and administrative expenses	17.7	17.7	15.9
Other deductions (income)			
Interest expense incurred	2.2	2.6	2.2
Other-net	0.0	(0.3)	0.3
	2.2	2.3	2.5
Income before income taxes	11.3	15.4	14.9
Federal and state income taxes			
Currently payable	4.4	5.4	4.6
Deferred	(0.2)	0.4	0.9
	4.2	5.8	5.5
Net income	7.1	9.5	9.4

Note: Figures may not add to totals due to rounding.

Let's review the process of financial analysis. We began by examining the raw data listed in Ajax's balance sheet and income statement. The raw data revealed that Ajax was growing, but its net income had declined. The ratio analysis showed that Ajax was operating more efficiently and that it had reduced its financial leverage. However, it was not until we examined the common-size income statement that we discovered that the increased cost of goods sold was one of the principal factors that contributed to the lower earnings. That is why computing common-size statements was essential in this case.

SUMMARY

Banks analyze credit risk before and after making loans. They do it before making loans to determine if prospective borrowers can repay the loans. They also monitor the borrowers throughout the life of the loan.

Credit scoring is growing in importance in evaluating and monitoring loans. The FICO score is widely used in making consumer and home mortgage loans loans. Scores above 680 are considered good, and those below 620 are considered subprime. Credit scoring models are also used for small and large business C&I loans. Likewise, credit ratings (such as Moody's) are used to measure the quality of debt and equity securities as well as firms.

Traditional financial analysis refers to using various financial ratios and indicators to evaluate the financial condition of firms. In this chapter, we examined seventeen financial indicators (see Table 8-4), as well as common size financial statements. The data for firms should be compared with peers, and examined over time. Life cycle considerations also should be taken into account when evaluating the data.

KEY TERMS AND CONCEPTS

Acid test ratio
Accrual basis
Asset turnover ratio
Assets
Asymmetric information
Audit (financial statements)
Average collection period
Average payment period
Balance sheet
Cash basis
Common-size financial statements
Compilation (financial statements)
Constant dollars
CreditGrades™
Credit ratings
Credit risk
Credit scoring
Current ratio
Debt ratio
Dividend payout ratio
Earnings per share (EPS)
Equifax Risk Rating™
FICO score
FIFO (inventory)
Financial leverage
Income statement
Inventory turnover ratio
Investment grade bonds
Junk bonds
Liabilities
LIFO (inventory)
Moody's KMV
Net profit margin
Qualification (financial statements)
Return on assets (ROA)
Return on equity (ROE)
Review (financial statements)
Stockholders' equity
Subprime
Times interest earned

QUESTIONS

8.1 Why do banks use credit scoring models?

8.2 What does a FICO score of 650 mean?

8.3. Explain the meaning of the Standard & Poor's BBB and BB credit ratings.

8.4 Which financial ratio is the most important?

8.5 There is a saying that in order to survive in the long-run, you have to survive in the short-run.

What ratios can be used to determine if a firm can meet its current financial obligations?

8.6 What ratio provides the best measure of liquidity?

8.7 The inventory turnover ratio measures how many times an inventory is sold each year. What would be the expected turnover ratios for TIME magazine and for a high-priced jewelry store?

8.8 When comparing a firm's ratios to an industry, is it bad to be below average?

8.9 Is it possible to make a meaningful comparison of the financial statements of Ford and a small company?

8.10 Why is a high degree of financial leverage considered risky?

8.11 Why are high degrees of financial leverage more acceptable in some industries than in others?

8.12 What does an increase in the average collection period suggest?

8.13 What does an increase in the average payment period suggest?

PROBLEMS

Chipco is a manufacturer of specialized computer chips. In 2015, Chipco sales slumped as a result of a recession. The expectations are for an economic recovery. Using all of the financial indicators listed in Table 8-4, evaluate the financial condition of Chipco, whose balance sheet and income statements are shown in Table 8-7 and 8-8.

TABLE 8-7 CHIPCO'S CONSOLIDATED BALANCE SHEETS--DECEMBER 31, 2015 and 2014

	2015	2014
Assets		
Current assets:		
Cash and cash equivalents	$ 211,706	$ 321,106
Short-term investments	1,340,324	1,227,896
Accounts receivable, net of allowance for doubtful accounts of $1,302 ($803 in 2005)	81,447	89,836
Inventories:		
Raw materials	2,997	6,990
Work-in-process	22,941	14,090
Finished goods	3,004	4,512
Total inventories	28,942	25,592
Deferred tax asset	43,754	43,482
Prepaid expenses arid other current assets	21,408	19,936
Total current assets	1,727,581	1,727,848
Property, plant and equipment, at cost:		
Land, buildings and improvements	140,468	136,978
Manufacturing and test equipment	326,388	316,501
Office furniture and equipment	3,384	3,343
	470,240	456,822
Accumulated depreciation and amortization	(209,388)	(167,596)
Net property, plant and equipment	260,852	289,226
Total assets	$ 1,988,433	$ 2,017,074
Liabilities and stockholders' equity		
Current liabilities:		
Accounts payable	$ 5,098	$ 10,615
Accrued payroll and related benefits	36,517	65,930
Deferred income on shipments to distributors	46,168	44,481
Income taxes payable	63,354	51,335
Other accrued liabilities	17,860	29,863
Total current liabilities	168,997	202,224
Deferred tax liabilities	37,982	32,893
Stockholders' equity:		
Common stock, $0.001 par value, 2,000,000 shares authorized; 316,150 shares issued and outstanding at Dec. 31, 2006; 318,908 shares at Dec. 31 2005	316	319
Additional paid-in capital	672,600	607,883
Retained earnings	1,108,538	1,173,755
Total stockholders' equity	1,781,454	1,781,957
Total liabilities and stockholders' equity	$ 1,988,433	$ 2,017,074

TABLE 8-8 CHIPCO'S CONSOLIDATED STATEMENTS OF INCOME -- YEARS ENDED -DECEMBER 31, 2015, 2014 and 2013

	2015	2014	2013
Net sales	$512,282	$972,625	$705,917
Cost of sales	144,719	231,122	178,949
Gross profit	367,563	741,503	526,968
Expenses:			
Research and development	79,839	102,487	78,299
Selling, general and administrative	62,625	92,731	74,273
	142,464	195,218	152,572
Operating income	225,099	546,285	374,396
Interest income	53,251	64,366	42,858
Income before income taxes	278,350	610,651	417,254
Provision for income taxes	80,721	183,195	129,348
Net income	$197,629	$427,456	$287,906
Earnings per share:			
Basic	$ 0.63	$ 1.34	$ 0.93
Diluted	$ 0.60	$ 1.29	$ 0.88
Weighted average shares outstanding:			
Basic	317,215	316,924	310,953
Diluted	328,538	332,527	328,002
Cash dividends per share	$ 0.17	$ 0.13	$ 0.09

ENDNOTES

1. For detailed explanations of credit scoring, see Elizabeth Mays, *Credit Scoring for Risk Managers: The Handbook for Lenders*, Mason, OH, Thomson-South-Western, 2004.
2. FDIC Supervisory Insights, Model Governance, Robert L. Burns, 12/5/2015, https://www.fdic.gov/regulations/examinations/supervisory/insights/siwin05/article01_model_governance.html
3. Alan Greenspan, Chairman, Federal Reserve Board, Remarks before the American Bankers Association, Phoenix AZ (via satellite), October 7, 2002.
4. The three major credit bureaus are Equifax - www.equifax.com/OfficialSite , Experian - www.experian.com, and TransUnion-www.transunion.com/CreditBureau
5. FICO® Score versions, http://www.myfico.com/CreditEducation/FICO-Score-Versions.aspx
6. For additional information, see www.myfico.com, and " What's in my FICO Scores," www.myfico.com/crediteducation/WhatsInYourScore.aspx
7. "What's not in my FICO Scores," myFICO, http://www.myfico.com/CreditEducation/WhatsNotInYourScore.aspx
8. Moody's Investor Service, Moody's Financial Metrics™ http://www.moodysanalytics.com/~/media/Brochures/Credit-Research-Risk-Measurement/Credit-Research/Corporate-Finance-Data-Analytics/Moodys-Financial-Metrics-Brochure.pdf
9. Alvin A. Arens and James K. Loebbecks, *Auditing: An Integrated Approach*, 5th ed., Englewood Cliffs, N.J.: Prentice Hall, 1991. For additional information, see "Compilation Reports on Financial Statements Included in Certain Prescribed Forms", AR §300.03, ©2015, AICPA, http://www.aicpa.org/Research/Standards/CompilationReview/DownloadableDocuments/AR-00300.pdf
10. *Ibid.*
11. *Ibid.*
12. The Risk Management Association (RMA; www.rmahq.org) publishes Annual Statement Studies™ that provide financial data for industry comparisons. RMA also publishes industry default probabilities based on their data and Moody's RiskCalc™.
13. If "per share" data are not available, then divide cash dividends by net income available for common stockholders.
14. *Economic Indicators*, July, 2015, U. S. Government Printing Office, Corporate Profits. Data are for the Quarter, 2015.

Chapter 9

COMMERCIAL AND INDUSTRIAL LENDING

After reading this chapter, you will be able to:

- Explain the role of asymmetric information in lending.
- Understand how competition affects lending.
- Evaluate the lending process.
- Describe the various types of loans.
- Understand loan pricing.

This is the first of two chapters about lending and managing loan portfolios. This chapter deals primarily with ***commercial and industrial loans (C&I loans)*** and the process of lending. C&I loans are those made to businesses to finance their day-to-day activities (such as inventories and receivables), longer-term needs (such as plant and equipment), and for other business purposes. The next chapter deals with real estate and consumer loans.

THE ROLE OF ASYMMETRIC INFORMATION IN LENDING

Three theoretical concepts are examined in this section concerning the relationships between banks and the customers who borrow from them. These concepts underlie much of the material that is presented in this chapter and the next one.

ASYMMETRIC INFORMATION AND ADVERSE SELECTION

Before banks make loans, they must evaluate imperfect information about prospective borrowers to determine if they are creditworthy. Information is difficult and costly to obtain. Information about large firms that are publicly traded, such as Microsoft, is easier to obtain than information about small, privately held firms. The information that prospective borrowers provide to the banks might be sufficient to make a credit decision. However, it is usually incomplete in the sense that borrowers know more about the risk of their proposed investment projects than they reveal to the bank. We are using the term "investment project," but the concept applies to the use of any funds borrowed from the bank including consumer loans. The inequality of information between the bank and the borrower is called asymmetric information. Simply stated, ***asymmetric information*** means that the borrowers have more information about themselves than is available to the bank.

Because of asymmetric information, banks tend to charge an interest rate that reflects the average rate of risk of all borrowers. The average interest rate is too high for borrowers with low-risk investment projects, and too low for borrowers with high-risk investment projects.

Adverse Selection

Adverse selection means that high-risk borrowers try to obtain loans from banks because they are willing to pay the average rate of interest, which is less than those borrowers would have to pay if their true condition were known to the bank. It also follows that low-risk creditworthy borrowers might be able to borrower directly from the money and capital markets at lower rates than those offered by banks. Market rates of interest confirm this. In April, 2016, the prime rate was 3.5 percent. The rate is the base rate on corporate loans made by banks. However, the rate on Aaa (top quality) corporate bonds was 3.62 percent, and the rate on 30-day commercial paper (short-term paper issued by major corporations) was 0.45 percent.[1] The banks tend to attract the higher-risk borrowers that do not have direct access to the money and capital markets. Note that adverse selection occurs before the loan is made.

Moral Hazard

The asymmetric information also gives rise to a moral hazard problem after the loan is made. ***Moral hazard*** is the risk that the borrower, who now has the loan, might use the funds to engage in higher-risk activities in expectation of earning higher returns. The higher-risk activities increase the probability of default on the loan. The moral hazard problem is most likely to occur when the lender is unable to monitor the borrower's activities.

THE COMPETITIVE ENVIRONMENT

THE BUSINESS OF LENDING

Lending money can be profitable, but it is risky. The profits come from collecting the interest income and fees earned on the loans. To the extent possible, banks and other lenders try to charge high-risk borrowers higher interest rates than low-risk borrowers. Therefore lenders have an incentive to take greater risks in expectation of earning higher returns. The major risk they face is credit risk.

Credit risk is "the risk of repayment, i.e., the possibility that an obligor will fail to perform as agreed," and adversely affect earnings and capital.[2] Credit risk applies to loans, derivatives, foreign exchange transactions, the investment portfolio, and other financial activities. With respect to loans, it is the risk that borrowers may default on their loans, causing losses to the lender.

Banks do not intentionally make bad loans. They do, however, make loans that can go bad over time. For example, two years after granting a loan, a severe recession could adversely affect a borrower's ability to repay the loan, and the borrower defaults. The fact that economic conditions changed for the borrower helps to explain why banks must monitor their loans.

The decision to default on a loan belongs to the borrower. In theory, borrowers have a "put option" to put the loan back to the lender when it is to their advantage to do so. This usually occurs when borrowers are unable to make the required loan payments or meet other terms of the loan agreement. If a large number of borrowers exercise their put options to default, and the losses are sufficiently large, the lender may fail. Fearing losses and failure, lenders try to control their credit risk.

INCREASING COMPETITION

Economic theory tells us that the expectation of high returns attracts competition, and the loan business is no exception. In the past, banks dominated commercial and consumer lending. It was thought that banks were special because they had particular expertise in making, monitoring, and collecting loans. However, banks did not have a sustainable competitive advantage, and today they are facing increasing competition from nonblank financial firms such as General Electric Capital Corporation, Ford Motor Credit Company, Commercial Credit Company, Merrill Lynch, and credit unions. In addition, there are online services that make loans, market loans, and provide other financial services. Bankrate, Lendingtree, LendingClub, LoanDepot and On Deck Capital are examples of online firms that provide such services.

Trade credit is another major source of competition. Trade credit is credit granted by a selling business concern to finance another firm's purchase of the sellers' goods. For example, General Motors may extend credit to its automobile dealers to buy their cars. Trade credit is the largest single source of short-term business credit in the United States.[3] Trade credit can be more expensive than most bank loans. For example, suppose that the terms are 2/10/net 30. This means that there is a two percent discount if the bill is paid in 10 days, or the full amount is due in 30 days. If the buyer does not pay the bill in 10 days, the cost of financing is two percent for the 20 additional days is 36% (365 days/20 = 18.25 x 2% = 36.5%). Most buyers take advantage of the discount.

Some specialized financial institutions have developed that deal with particular markets. For example, venture capital firms played an important role in the development of high technology companies in the Silicon Valley of California. Specialized lenders have developed to deal with "subprime" (high credit risk) consumer lending, and "monoline" (one line of business) banks have developed expertise in credit card lending.

The growth of nonbank lenders has resulted in highly competitive terms of lending on loans and the standards used to make those loans. Stated otherwise, some lenders who are trying to maximize revenue, or market share, may not give credit risk the weight it deserves in their lending decisions. Nevertheless, there is some differential in pricing risk. The average interest rate on all C&I loans at all commercial banks in August, 2015, when interest rates were at very low levels, was 2.22 percent. The daily rate was 1.05 percent and 3.13 percent for loans of more than 365 days. The lowest-risk loans of more than 365 days was 3.13 percent and 4.45 percent for the highest-risk ones.[4] No data were available for nonbank lenders.

Competition also affects the "non-price" terms of loans, such as the degree of restrictions in loan covenants, and the releasing of guarantees to make it easier to obtain loans. Loan covenants are conditions in the loan contract that the borrower must meet. For example, the borrower must provide audited financial statements annually.

Both nonbank and bank lenders have shifted their portfolios to longer-term higher- yielding and higher-risk loans in recent years. During the 1988-2015 period, C&I loans for all U.S. banks declined from 19.5 percent to 16.8 percent of assets, while real estate loans increased from 20.9 percent to 33.1 percent.[5]

Consider the market for home equity loans (second mortgages). Because of competition, many banks have raised their *loan-to-price ratios* on home equity loans, and they may be as high as 100 percent. The loan-to-price ratio reflects the amount of equity that a borrower must invest in a loan. An 80 percent ratio means that the borrower must invest 20 percent of his/her own money in the home. A 100 percent ratio means that the borrower has nothing invested. The implication of this is that banks are operating in a higher-risk environment to meet competition from finance companies that make home equity loans for 125 percent or more of the value of the homes.[6]

CHANGES IN TECHNOLOGY

Recent developments in financial technology are changing the way that banks and other lenders operate their lending activities. These developments are the securitization of loans, credit scoring, and banking online. Other changes in technology, such as the use of credit derivatives to manage portfolio risks are emerging, but their use is not widespread.

Securitization

Securitization is the packaging and selling of otherwise unmarketable loans to other financial institutions and investors. For example, residential mortgage loans are packaged in large volumes and sold as mortgage pools, some of which are guaranteed by government agencies. Other securitized loans include automobile loans, credit card loans, and small business loans. The small business loans may be guaranteed by the Small Business Administration. Alternatively, the issuer may "overcollateralize" the loans – putting up more collateral loans than is required – to enhance the package.

The growth of securitization means that loans that were formerly funded in local markets are now being funded in global capital markets. Removing geographic financial constraints for borrowers and lenders allows demand for such loans and the supply of funds to grow and provides increasing liquidity for the secondary loan market. It also provides lenders and investors who buy those loans a means of diversifying their portfolios.

Prior to the development of securitization, the loan market tended to clear more on quantity (the dollar amount of the loan) than on price. With the development of the secondary market, securitized loans are behaving more like bonds, where the quantity is set by the issuer and the price by the market.

Unbundling of Loans

The growth of securitization has contributed to the "unbundling of loans." Traditionally, banks made and held loans in their portfolios. Today, the lending process can be divided into the following activities:

1. Originating loans
2. Packaging loans for sale to others
3. Servicing loan portfolios, and
4. Investing in loan-backed credit instruments.

A bank, or some other organization, can do any one or all of these activities. Accordingly, one firm might originate the loans, another package them for resale, and so on.

Credit Scoring

Credit scoring is the use of statistical models to determine the likelihood that a prospective borrower will default on a loan. As noted in Chapter 8, credit scoring models are widely used to evaluate business, real estate and consumer loans. In the case of small business loans, for example, the models might be based on data from credit applications, personal financial statements, business financial statements, and business and credit bureau reports. The base FICO scores range from 300-850, and industry-specific FICO scores range from 250-900. A higher sore is better.[7] The cutoff scores (e.g., a FICO score of 680) used by lenders depend on the degree of risk they are willing to take. Therefore different lenders use different scores, and they have "override" policies. A customer who receives a low score might still receive a loan if the lender decides to "override" the model because of other considerations.

The advantages of credit scoring models are the reduced time and lower cost of processing loans. Another advantage is that the same measures are applied to all customers, thereby demonstrating a consistent credit policy.

Some lenders "pre-approve" loans and solicit large numbers of customers. Typically, this approach is used in connection with unsecured loans (not backed by collateral). Lenders making such loans can diversify their loan portfolio risk by making a large number of relatively small loans spread over large geographical areas.

Online Banking and Financial Services

All large banks and many smaller banks have their own web pages. The banks are encouraging their customers to take advantage of online services, such as paying bills. The increased use of such information technology can broaden the customer base, provide new services, and reduce the operating costs. However, the internet knows no geographic bounds, and banks and nonbanking financial firms vie for customers wherever they are located. More will be said about banking and financial services online in Chapter 17.

THE BOARD OF DIRECTORS WRITTEN LOAN POLICY

THE ROLE OF DIRECTORS

A bank's board of directors has the ultimate responsibility for all of the loans made by that bank. Because the board delegates the task of making loans to others, it must have a written loan policy that establishes the guidelines and principles for the bank's credit risk strategies and policies. The credit risk strategy must recognize the goals of credit quality, earnings, and growth – that is the risk/reward tradeoff.

Loan policies vary widely from bank to bank. The loan policies for a small bank that lends primarily to local consumers are going to differ from the policies of a large bank that specializes in lending to business concerns. In either case, a policy would state that the bank is in the business of making sound and profitable loans. Therefore, the loan policy must make it clear that an important part of the lending process is that all loans should have a repayment plan at the time the loan is made.

Other parts of the loan policy deal with:

- Loan authority - Who has the authority to make loans. The lending limits relative to capital, deposits, or assets. The loan approval process.
- Loan portfolio - The types of loans the bank wants to make, such as consumer loans, loans to start up businesses, loans to large businesses, farm loans, international loans, and so on. The policy should also put limits on the concentration of particular types of loans.
- Geographic limits of the bank's trade area where it might grant loans. The overwhelming majority (97 percent) of small- and medium-sized businesses use financial institutions within 30 miles of their principal office.
- Policies for determining interest rates, fees, and contractual terms of the loans.
- Limits and guidelines for off-balance sheet exposures from loan commitments, letters of credit, securitized loans, and derivative products (swaps, options, futures, etc.).
- A loan review process to evaluate lending procedures and the quality of the loan portfolio.

Although this listing is incomplete, it is sufficient to give you an overview of some of the key topics that are covered in a loan policy. The policy also may specify the types of loans that the board considers undesirable. For example, the bank should not make loans to persons whose integrity or honesty is questionable. It should not make loans to a business where the loan cannot be repaid within a reasonable period except by liquidation of the business. And finally, it should not make loans secured by stock in a closed corporation where there is no market for that stock.

REDUCING CREDIT RISK

Banks use a wide variety of techniques to reduce their credit risk. The following eight techniques are listed below in alphabetical order.

1. *Avoid* making high-risk loans. For example, a small bank located in Cincinnati, Ohio should reject a loan proposal to buy deep sea fishing boats in New England. While this might be a good loan for a bank in New England that is familiar with that industry, it would be a high-risk loan for a midwest bank that has no expertise in lending on deep sea fishing boats.
2. *Collateral* reduces the risk to the lender, and the threat of loss of the collateral provides an incentive for the borrower to repay their loans. Collateral is considered a secondary source of repayment in the event of loan default.
3. *Diversify* the loan portfolio. Diversification means making loans to a variety of borrowers whose cash flows are not perfectly positively correlated, and avoiding undue concentration to a borrower, or in a particular type of loans whose returns are related. In other words, small loans made to a large number of borrowers in a wide variety of industries is less risky than a few large loans made to a small number of borrowers in the same industry.

4. *Documentation* refers to all of the documents needed to legally enforce a loan contract and to protect a bank's interest. Documents typically include promissory notes, guarantees, financial statements, UCC (Uniform Commercial Code) filings for collateral, notes about meetings with the customers, and so on. An unsigned promissory note is not enforceable. Moreover, failure to renew a UCC filing on collateral can turn a secured loan into an unsecured loan. The successful collection of loans may depend on documentation.

5. *Guarantees* do not eliminate default risk or the riskiness of a loan portfolio. In fact, they may contribute to increased risk as banks substitute financial guarantees for high credit standards or higher rates charged on risky loans. Nevertheless, federal government loan guarantees pay important roles in agriculture, commerce, and housing. The Small Business Administration (SBA), for example, assists small businesses by guaranteeing all or parts of qualifying loans made by banks and other lenders. Government-guaranteed loans are one way that the government channels benefits to targeted sectors in the economy. Direct loans are another method. A Federal Reserve Bank of Richmond study revealed that guaranteed loans do not make the economy more efficient because the government does not have better information or a technical advantage over private lenders.[10]

Private guarantees (those not backed by government) are also widely used by borrowers. A parent company guaranteeing the loan of a subsidiary is one example.

6. *Limit* the amount of credit extended to any single borrower, or groups of borrowers with related cash flow patterns in order to avoid undue loan concentration. For example, banks that are members of the Federal Reserve System are limited in the amount of their capital that they can lend to a single borrower. The maximum amount is 15 percent of the total capital in the case of a loan that is not fully secured, and an additional 10 percent for loans that are secured by readily marketable collateral.[11] However, loans secured by bills of lading or warehouse receipts covering readily marketable staples have higher loan limits.[12]

7. *Monitor* the behavior of the borrower after the loan is made to ensure compliance with the loan agreement. Recall that the decision to default on a loan is a put option held by the borrower. Some borrowers have a moral hazard problem and take excessive risks. Other borrowers may be adversely affected by external factors such as oil price shocks, recessions, floods, droughts, and so on. Therefore, the monitoring should take into account those external factors that might impede the borrower's ability to repay the loan.

As shown on the next page, the outside monitor may know that the borrower has used the loan funds to buy assets, such as inventory or equipment. However, the monitor may not be able to verify the value of those assets.[13] The difference between what the monitor knows and what they can verify contributes to the agency problems between the lender and borrower. Agency problems as used here refers to the ability of the lender (the principal) to influence the behavior of the borrower (the agent).

Outside Monitor

	What they "know"	Is it "verifiable?"
1	What is there	Yes
2	The value of what is there	No

8. *Transfer* risk to other parties by selling securitized loans and loan participations, and by hedging with interest rate and credit derivatives. For example, a bank may use a credit default swap to transfer the risk of loans defaulting to a counterparty such as an insurance company or pension fund. The credit event that triggers the default swap may be a bankruptcy, insolvency, or receivership. The payment that is contingent on that event may be defined in terms of the price of a reference obligation, such as a bond. One of the advantages of using credit derivatives is that they reduce a bank's credit exposure without removing the assets from the balance sheet. Also, the sale of a large loan may affect the bank's relationship with its customer. The size of credit default swaps ranges from a few million dollars to billions of dollars.

SEVEN WAYS TO MAKE LOANS

The seven ways that banks make loans are presented in alphabetical order.

BANKS SOLICIT LOANS

Banks actively solicit loans in person, by mail, and on the internet, offering loans and other services provided by their respective banks. These sales efforts are typical of banks seeking new customers, and those trying to cross-sell their services. For example, a branch manager or loan officer might explain to a prospective borrower how the bank's cash management services, including lock boxes and cash concentration accounts, can improve the firm's cash flow. Lock boxes are mail boxes where retail customers send their payments for goods and services purchased. The lock boxes are serviced by the bank, and funds can be concentrated and forwarded to the firm's treasury for investment.

BUYING LOANS

Banks buy parts of loans, called *participations*, from other banks. The acquiring banks have pro rata shares of the credit risk. Participations by three or more unaffiliated banks in loans or formal loan commitments in excess of $20 million are called *shared national credits*.[15] Suppose that a large bank is making a $100 million loan to an airline, but the originating bank does not want to keep such a large loan in its loan portfolio. It may sell parts (participations) of that loan to other banks. The sale of participations "down stream" to smaller banks allows smaller banks to participate in loans that they could not originate. In addition, it is one way for a bank with slack demand for loans to increase its loan portfolio. It also allows all of the banks involved to diversify their loan portfolios. Participations can originate from small banks too. Suppose that a small bank wants to make a loan that exceeds its lending limits. It can make the loan and sell participations "up stream" to larger banks. Banks also buy and sell securitized loans.

COMMITMENTS

About 84 percent of all commercial and industrial loans are made under loan commitments.[16] A ***loan commitment*** is an agreement between a bank and a firm to lend funds under terms that are agreed upon in writing. Loan commitments specify the amount of the commitment fee and the amount of funds to be borrowed, but the cost of borrowing depends on the prevailing rates at the time the loan is made. The pricing on the loan is usually specified when the commitment is made. For example, the bank may charge the *prime rate* (the base rate on commercial and industrial plus one or two percentage points when the funds are borrowed. The prime rate was 3.25 percent in November, 2015.[17] The prime rate plus one percentage point was 4.25 percent. To put that interest rate in perspective, the interest rate on a 30-year home mortgage loan was 3.98 percent. This means that banks considered the best C&I to have greater credit risk than 30-year mortgage loans. However, it is interesting to note that most of the bank failures during the financial crises in the 1980s were due to interest rate risks associated with mortgage lending, not from credit risk on C&I loans.

Firms pay a commitment fee to banks for the call option of borrowing at some future date. Commitment fees range from 0.25 percent to 0.50 percent per annum of the total amount to be borrowed. Commitment fees contribute to bank's income and they do not require immediate funding. For example, assume a 45 day commitment for $5 million, and the commitment fee is 0.50 percent per annum computed on a 360 day basis. The bank earns $3,125.00 without investing any assets, but it does have a contingent claim.

Commitment x 0.50%

$5,000,000 x 0.005 = $25,000

Daily fee = total fee/360

$25,000/360 = $69.444

Fee for 45 days = daily fee x 45 days

$69.444 x 45 = $3125.00

Banks may compute the fee on a 365 day basis. Using 365 days, the daily fee is $68.493 and the bank earns $3,082.19. The bank is better off using 360 days.

CUSTOMERS REQUEST LOANS

A customer asks for a commercial loan. Unfortunately, many potential borrowers are denied loans or do not get what they need because they do not know what information the bank needs in order to grant a loan request. Some borrowers, for example, do not know what type of loan (line of credit, term loan) will meet their financial needs, or what type of collateral (accounts receivable, order bill of lading, second mortgage) is suitable for their loans. Good loan officers work with prospective borrowers, who do not know the procedures, by explaining to them what information they must provide to the bank.

LOAN BROKERS

Loan brokers sell loans to banks and other lenders. Loan brokers are individuals or firms who act as agents or brokers between the borrower and the lender. For example, a loan broker may contract with a real estate developer to find financing for a particular project. The broker will seek out lenders and arrange for the loan. Once the loan is made and the fees are paid, the broker is out of the picture.

OVERDRAFTS

An ***overdraft*** occurs when a customer writes a check on uncollected funds, or when there are insufficient funds in the account to cover the withdrawal. If a bank pays on a check written against insufficient balances, it is extending an unsecured loan.

Some overdrafts are written with prior permission of the bank, but most are not. In the latter case, the overdraft represents a loan that the bank may not want to make. The borrower did not ask the bank for the funds in advance.

Overdrafts can be for less than one day (***daylight overdraft***) when a check is written or funds transferred out by wire in the morning and the deposit to cover that check or wire transfer is not made until that afternoon. Suppose that a firm located in New York City deposits a check drawn on a bank located in El Paso, Texas. It will take about two days for the check to be collected by the New York bank from the bank in Texas. Although the New York firm's balance has increased, it cannot use those funds to write checks without the bank's permission. Many banks analyze their customers' "out of town" checks and permit them to write checks only on their average collected balances. Under the Competitive Banking Equality Act of 1987, no more than one business day may intervene between the deposit of a local check and the availability for withdrawal of those funds, and four business days for nonlocal checks.

REFINANCING

Borrowers refinance loans. Suppose that interest rates on loans have declined from 10 percent to 6 percent, and that borrowers with high fixed rate loans want to take advantage of the lower rates. They can make a new loan at the lower rate and pay off the high rate loan. The refinancing is at the borrower's option, and only occurs when it is to their advantage.

COLLECTING LOANS

Making loans is the easy part of the lending process. Collecting the loans the hard part. There are *two primary sources of repayment* that lenders consider when they make loans. The primary sources of repayment are from the borrowers 1) cash flow (such as earnings), and 2) the sale of the assets being finance (such as inventory). Collateral serves as a *secondary source of repayment.*

In the event that neither the primary nor the secondary sources of loan repayment satisfy the debt, the bank will have to take appropriate action to protect its interests. If the loan is guaranteed (such as a guarantee from the Small Business Administration) the bank will turn to the guarantor for repayment. Alternatively, the bank may force the borrower into bankruptcy. This is the least effective method of repayment.

PRINCIPAL LENDING ACTIVITIES

The principal lending activities include loans and leases. The types of loans presented here are lines of credit, revolving loans, term loans and bridge loans. Banks make other types of loans that are not described here. Each type of loan has its own purpose. The concept of "different types of loans for different purposes" is illustrated in Figure 9-1. As shown in the figure, the total assets of a firm can be divided into two categories, permanent assets and temporary assets. Permanent assets include plant and equipment as well as that portion of working capital (cash, accounts receivable, and inventory) that will be sustained over time. Temporary assets include that portion of working capital that fluctuates with periodic changes in sales and revenues. For example, the inventory of The Toy Store is expected to increase before Christmas. When the toys are sold, the inventory will be reduced but the accounts receivable will increase. As the receivables are collected and the cash is used to repay debts or acquire new long-term assets, working capital will be reduced.

FIGURE 9-1 THE FINANCING MIX

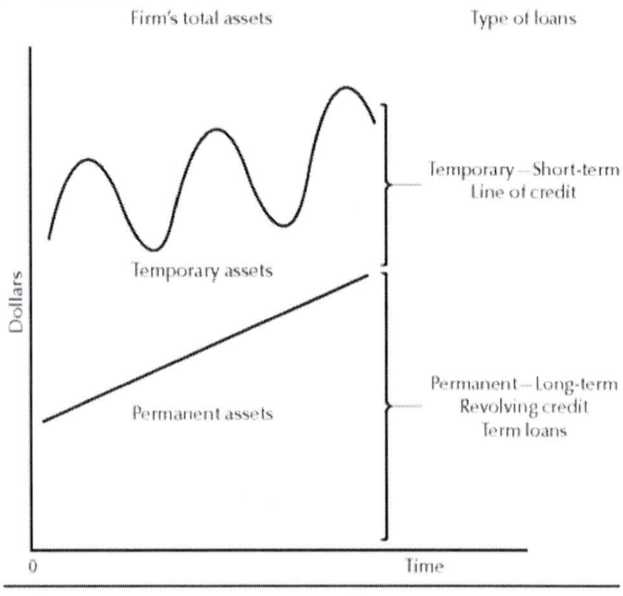

The figure also shows that temporary assets should be financed with temporary loans and permanent assets with permanent loans. Stated otherwise, a safe lending strategy is to match the maturity of the asset being financed with the maturity of funds used to finance it. For example, it makes sense to finance The Toy Store's seasonal inventory loan for up to one year, although one would expect it to be repaid in a less time. It does not make sense to provide funds for five years to finance an inventory of toys for one Christmas season. Sometimes this kind of a mismatch occurs when funds are lent to finance both temporary and permanent assets in one loan rather than being treated as separate loans.

Next, we examine specific types of loans and ***credit facilities*** (agreements which may or may not result in loans).

LINE OF CREDIT

A ***line of credit*** is an agreement between a customer and the bank, that the bank will entertain requests from that customer for a loan up to a predetermined amount. The line of credit is established when the bank gives a letter to the customer stating the dollar amount of the line, the time it is in effect (i.e. 1 year), and other conditions or provisions such as the relationship the customer must maintain with the bank and the customer's financial condition. If the borrower does not meet all of the terms and conditions of the letter, the bank is not obligated to make the loan or continue the line of credit.

The line of credit is the maximum amount that can be borrowed under the terms of the loan. The loans are made for periods of one year or less; and they should be used to finance seasonal increases in inventory and accounts receivable. When the inventory is sold, receivables are collected, and the funds are used to reduce the loan. The loans are usually payable on demand by the bank, or within 90 days.

Business credit and debit cards are another form of a line of credit. However, the credit is provided by a *credit card company* (such as Amex, Chase, Capital One, and others) rather than a *commercial bank*. Both large and small business concerns use business credit cards, but the terms of each vary. In the case of small business credit cards for unincorporated businesses, the bank may require personal guarantees based on the credit worthiness of the borrower.

REVOLVING LOAN

Revolving loans are similar to a line of credit because they too are used to finance borrowers' temporary and seasonal working capital needs. One difference between a revolving loan and line of credit is that the bank is obligated to make the loans up to the maximum amount of the loan, if the borrower is in compliance with the terms of the agreement. Revolving loans commonly specify the minimum amount of the increments that may be borrowed. For example, the loan could be for $30,000 increments up to a maximum limit of $3 million.

Another difference is that revolving loans usually have a maturity of two years or more, while lines of credit are usually for shorter periods.

TERM LOAN

A *term loan* is usually a single loan for a stated period of time, or a series of loans on specified dates. They are used for a specific purpose, such as acquiring machinery, renovating a building, refinancing debt, and so forth. They should not be used to finance day-to-day operations.

Term loans may have an original maturity of five years or more. From the lender's point of view, the maturity of the loan should not exceed the economic life of the asset being financed if that asset is being used as collateral for the loan. Equally important, the value of the asset being financed always should exceed the amount of the loan. The difference between the value of asset and the amount being financed is the borrower's equity. The borrower's equity represents the borrower's investment in the asset being financed. It also provides the bank with a "cushion" in the event of default. The borrower will lose his or her funds before the bank experiences a loss. Borrowers not wanting to lose their equity investment have an incentive to operate their business so that the loan will be repaid.

Term loans can be repaid on an amortized basis or at one time. Recall that the planned repayment of loans should come from the borrower's operating revenues, or from the sale of assets. These concepts are illustrated in the top panel of Figure 9-2. The point of these concepts is to help protect the bank's security interest in the loan.

The lower panel illustrates improper lending procedures -- a loan that exceeds the value of the asset that it is financing. In addition, the maturity of the loan exceeds the life of the asset. If the borrower defaults when the value of the equipment is less than the amount of the loan, the bank will incur a substantial loss.

FIGURE 9-2 TERM LOANS FOR MACHINERY

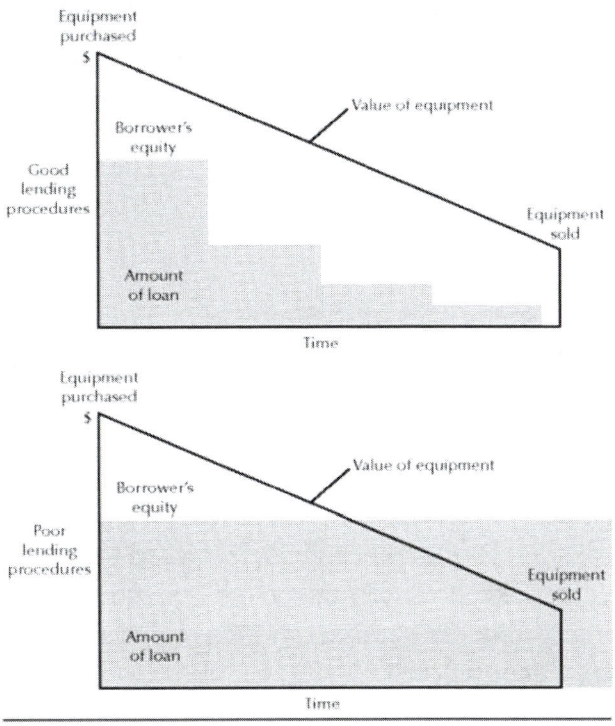

BRIDGE LOAN

Bridge loans "bridge a gap" in a borrower's financing until some specific event occurs. For example, a firm wants to acquire a new warehouse facility, but needs funds to finance the transaction until the old warehouse can be sold. Thus, a bridge loan is short-term financing that is made in anticipation of receiving longer-term financing on which an agreement has been reached.

Similarly, a firm needs working capital now; and next week it is going to issue commercial paper to provide those funds. A bank can provide temporary financing. In this case the bank loan is being used as a short-term substitute for other debt financing by the firm.

ASSET-BASED LENDING

Asset-based lending is a form of commercial lending where the assets of a company are used to secure the company's obligation to the lender. Most asset-based lenders are finance companies, although some banks do asset-based lending too. In the broadest sense, all secured loans could be classified as asset-based lending. Asset-based loans have as their collateral base accounts receivable, inventory, machinery and equipment and real estate, single or packaged in various combinations (that is, receivables and inventory, receivables and machinery, and so forth).
The major distinctions between asset-based loans and other secured loans is that much greater weight is given to the market value of the collateral in asset-based lending than in regular C&I loans. In addition, asset-based lenders place greater emphasis on monitoring than do bank lenders. Moreover, if the borrower defaults, the asset-based lenders are more willing to liquidate the borrower's collateral than is the case for regular C&I loans.

Asset-based loans require a higher level of monitoring than do other "secured" commercial loans. The degree of monitoring to ensure the existence, value, and integrity of the collateral further differentiates asset-based loans from other secured commercial loans. The combination of a higher level of monitoring and a greater willingness to liquidate in the event of default may help explain why asset-based lenders tend to have higher spreads and fees and lower write-offs than other secured lenders.

LEVERAGED LENDING

The Office of the Comptroller of the Currency (OCC) "broadly considers a leveraged loan to be a transaction where the borrower's post-financing leverage, when measured by debt-to-assets, debt-to-equity, cash flow-to-total debt, or other such standards unique to particular industries, significantly exceeds industry norms for leverage."...[18] "Leveraged lending is a type of corporate finance used for mergers and acquisitions, business recapitalization and refinancing, equity buyouts, and business or product line build-outs and expansions. It is used to increase shareholder returns and to monetize perceived "enterprise value" or other intangibles. In this type of transaction, debt is commonly used as an alternative to equity when financing business expansions and acquisitions."[19]

LEASING

Leases are used to finance tangible assets such as cars, airplanes and ships. A lease is contract that enables a user, the lessee, to secure the use of a tangible asset over a specified period of time by making payments to the owner, the lessor. The contract also specifies the details of the payments, the disposition of income tax benefits, provisions for maintenance, renewal options, and other clauses that permit the contract to qualify as a true lease under the Internal Revenue Code. We will consider two types of leases, operating leases and financial leases.

Operating leases are short-term leases used to finance equipment such as computers, where the term of the lease is a fraction of the economic life of the asset. The asset is not fully amortized over the term of a lease. Operating leases may be canceled.

Financial leases are used in connection with financing long - term assets and have a term that is equal to the economic life of the asset. For example, a communications satellite might be leased for 12 years. Such leases are usually not canceled.

COLLATERAL

Sound banking practices require that certain types of loans be backed by collateral. Collateral refers to an asset pledged against the performance of an obligation. If a borrower defaults on a loan, the bank takes the collateral and sells it. Therefore, it is frequently referred to as a *secondary source of repayment*.

Collateral reduces the bank's risk when it makes a loan. However, collateral does not reduce the risk of the loan per se. The risk of the loan is determined by the borrowers' ability to repay it and other factors.

While collateral reduces the bank's risk, it increases the costs of lending and monitoring. The higher costs are due to the need for documentation and the costs of monitoring the collateral. In an effort to cut costs, some banks are not requiring collateral on lines of credit issued to small businesses. However, without collateral some borrowers could not obtain loans.

Collateral benefits both borrowers and lenders in certain type of loans. In other types of loans collateral is not used. For example, a large creditworthy corporation borrowed $20 million for one day until it sold its own commercial paper. The minimal risk and the large volume of paperwork to obtain liens against specific assets mitigated the need for collateral in this case.

CHARACTERISTICS OF GOOD COLLATERAL

Almost anything that is lawful can be used as collateral, but some things are better than others. The five factors listed below determine the suitability of items for use as collateral.

Durability

This refers to the ability of the assets to withstand wear, or to its useful life. Durable goods make better collateral than nondurables. Stated otherwise, crushed rocks make better collateral than fresh flowers.

Identification

Certain types of assets that are readily identifiable because they have definite characteristics or serial numbers that cannot be removed make good collateral. Two examples are 1) a large office building and 2) an automobile that can be identified by make, model and serial number.

Marketability

In order for collateral to be of value to the bank, the collateral must be marketable. That is, you must be able to sell it. Specialized equipment that has limited use is not as marketable as trucks that have multiple uses.

Stability of value

Bankers prefer collateral whose market values are not likely to decline dramatically during the period of the loan. Common stocks, for example, are not as desirable as real estate for collateral because the stock prices are more variable than real estate prices.

Standardization

Certain types of grains have been graded by the U.S. Department of Agriculture. For example, soybeans are graded as No. 1 yellow, No. 2 yellow, or No. 3. yellow. These grades indicate the quality of the beans. Likewise, other types of commodities and merchandise have been graded to facilitate their use in trade and as collateral. The standardization leaves no ambiguity between the borrower and the lender as to nature of the asset is that is being used as collateral.

TYPES OF COLLATERAL

The most common types of collateral that are used in commercial lending are examined here.

Accounts Receivable

There are three ways that accounts receivable can be used as collateral. They are pledging, factoring, and Bankers' Acceptances.

Pledging: A borrower can pledge accounts receivable with his or her bank. In this case the borrower retains ownership of the receivables; and there is usually no notification made to the buyer of the goods for which the receivables have been pledged.

The percentage of face value of the accounts receivable that the banker is willing to advance depends on the size, number, and quality of the receivables. Most bankers prefer to advance funds from receivables from a few well established firms with good credit ratings.

Factoring: Factoring is the sale of accounts receivable to a factor that is usually a bank or finance company. When the receivables are sold, the buyer of the goods is usually notified to make payments to the factor. Like pledging, factors prefer receivables from well established firms. One important difference between the two methods is that factors usually buy receivables on a nonrecourse basis. Nonrecourse means that it cannot be returned to the firm that is selling the receivables. Thus, the factor accepts the credit risks for the receivables that they purchase. To reduce their risk, the factor may only advance 80 or 90 percent of the face value, the remainder being held in reserve until the receivables are collected or until some predetermined date. In addition, the factor charges a commission that ranges from one to three percent of the total face value, and monthly interest charges on the advances. For example, suppose that Southern Mill Outlet wants to factor $100,000 in receivables. The factor holds a reserve of 10 percent (advances 90 percent), charges a three percent commission, and a two percent monthly interest charge. The Southern Mill Outlet receives $85,260 and the factor earns $4,740 plus what they can earn on investing the reserve.

Face value of the accounts receivable	$100,000
Reserve held by factor (10%)	10,000
Commission (3%)	- 3,000
Funds that may be advanced	$87,000
Less monthly interest charge (2%)	- 1,740
Funds available to Southern Mill Outlet	$85,260

Bankers' Acceptance: A Bankers' Acceptance usually arises from foreign trade. Suppose that an American exporter sells computer parts to a French concern. The French importer agrees to pay for the parts 30 days after they have been delivered. The means of payment is a time draft, which is similar to a predated check. The American manufacturer can send the time draft, which from exporter's point of view is the same as an account receivable, to the French importer's bank and have it accepted. This means that the French bank becomes responsible for the payment of the draft, and will collect the funds from the importer when the draft becomes due. In other words, the French bank is guaranteeing payments of the French importer's obligation. The accepted draft is called a Bankers' Acceptance. It is a negotiable instrument that can be traded in the securities markets. The American manufacturer can sell the Bankers' Acceptance at a discount (i.e., below face value) to compensate investors who bought it and cannot collect the full value until it matures.

Inventory

Inventory is widely used as collateral against commercial loans. The inventory might consist of raw materials or finished goods, such as automobiles. Other types of inventory might include natural resources, livestock and crops, and so on.

Marketable Securities

Marketable securities including, corporate stocks and bonds, Certificates of Deposit, U.S. Treasury securities, and others, can be used as collateral for business loans. The amount of credit extended on such securities varies widely. One problem with securities as collateral is that the market value of publicly held stocks and bonds can vary widely from day to day. The value of publicly traded securities is readily available in the press. In contrast, the market value of privately held companies may not be determinable without going to considerable expense.

Real Property and Equipment

Real property refers to real estate that includes houses, office building, shopping centers, factories, and so on. Such property is widely used as collateral. In addition, equipment of various sorts might be used. Equipment includes trucks, fork lifts, drill presses, robotics, and other items. Appraisals by qualified real estate appraisers and equipment appraisers are essential before the loan is made.

Guarantees

Bankers can improve their security by having a third party guarantee the payments. The third party may be an individual, insurance company, or U. S. government agency such as the Small Business Administration. For example, a parent company may guarantee a loan made by a subsidiary. Without the guarantee, the loan would not have been made. With the exception of the government agencies, the quality of a guarantee depends on the financial strength of the guarantor.

In summary, many banks require collateral or a guarantee when they make business loans. Small businesses frequently use the personal assets of the principals as collateral. Personal assets include real estate, cars, the surrender value of life insurance policies, or anything else of value.

THE LENDING PROCESS

The process of lending begins before a loan is made. The Board of Directors establishes a loan policy, and considers the risk reduction techniques previously described. The process ends when the loan is repaid or when it is determined to be uncollectible. At that point, if it no longer has value, it is removed as an asset from the bank's balance sheet. Even then, the bank still may be able to collect some of the proceeds. Both the lender and the borrower perform certain tasks over the term of the lending process.

EVALUATING A LOAN REQUEST

A key part of the lending process involves the Six Cs of credit. Banks that use credit scoring models incorporate data from credit reporting agencies and other sources that cover some of the Six Cs. While the use of credit scoring models is growing in importance, many loans must be evaluated using the traditional methods described below.

1. Character (personal characteristics of the borrower, honesty, and attitudes about willingness and commitment to pay debts).
2. Capacity (the borrower's success in running a business – cash flows).
3. Capital (the financial condition of the borrower – net worth).
4. Collateral (pledged assets).
5. Conditions (economic conditions).
6. Compliance (compliance with laws and regulations).

Character

Banks must know their customer before they make loans, and character is the place to start. Character refers to a combination of qualities that distinguishes one person or a group from another. To some extent, the words character and reputation overlap in meaning. We use the term character here to refer to a borrower's honesty, responsibility, integrity, and consistency on which we can determine their willingness to repay loans. Evidence of character traits can be found in reports from credit bureaus and credit reporting agencies such as D&B.[20]

Capacity

This refers to success of the borrower's business as reflected in its financial condition and ability to meet financial obligations via cash flow and earnings. Banks generally require prospective borrowers to submit their financial statements and/or federal and state income tax statements in order to determine their credit worthiness. Chapter 8 provided a detailed description of credit scoring and financial analysis.

Capital

Capital represents the amount of equity capital that a firm has which can be liquidated for payment if all other means of collection of the debt fail. Equity capital is equal to total assets less total liabilities. However, there can be a substantial difference between the *book value* and the *market value* of assets and liabilities. For example, land purchased 20 years ago can be carried on the books at its historical cost. However, the market value of the land could be substantially higher or lower than the book value.

Collateral

Collateral refers to assets that are pledged for security in a credit transaction. The fact that borrowers may lose their collateral if they default on their loans serves as an incentive for them to perform in accordance with the loan contract.

Conditions

Conditions refers to external factors that are beyond the control of a firm, but that may affect their ability to repay debts. Excess capacity in commercial real estate is one example. If there is excess capacity in that market, the lender should take it into account before granting a loan to add to the capacity. It is changes in conditions, such as recessions, interest rate shocks, and asset price deflation, that adversely affect borrowers and contributes to their defaulting on loans.

Compliance

While the previous "Cs" concerned the borrower, compliance applies to the lender. Compliance with court decisions, laws, and regulations is an increasingly important part of the lending process. Banks must comply with the Community Reinvestment Act (CRA), the Environmental Superfund Act, the USA Patriot Act, and dozens of other laws to operate in accordance with the law and bank regulations, and to avoid lender liability. ***Lender liability*** means that the lender might be sued by borrowers or others for losses and damages. For example, in the case of *U.S. v. Maryland Bank and Trust Company*, the Environmental Protection Agency (EPA) sued the bank for reimbursement of cleanup costs of a hazardous waste dump after the bank foreclosed on the property. However, in *U.S. v. Fleet Factors*, the Eleventh Circuit

Court of Appeals ruled that a secured lender can be liable under federal environmental laws, even absent foreclosure, if the lender participates in management to a degree that it influences the firm's treatment of hazardous waste.

STRUCTURING COMMERCIAL LOAN AGREEMENTS

When a bank decides to grant a loan, all of the terms of the loan are put into a contract called a *loan agreement*. The contract is structured to control the borrower to the extent necessary to assure timely repayment of the loan. All commercial loans have the following six elements:

1. The type of credit facility (e.g., term loan) and amount to be borrowed.
2. The term of the loan (e.g., 2 years).
3. The method and timing of repayment (e.g., the loan is to be repaid monthly from the sale of inventory)
4. Interest rates and fees to be paid by the borrower to the banker. The interest rates can be fixed rate, or floating rate, based on the prime rate, or the London interbank offered rate (LIBOR), etc.
5. Collateral if required.
6. Covenants – promises by the borrower to take or not to take certain actions during the term of the loan. For example, the borrower will provide the bank with quarterly financial statements. The borrower will not incur additional long-term debt without the bank's prior permission.

PRICING COMMERCIAL LOANS

One key element in the process of commercial lending is loan pricing -- determining what interest rate to charge the borrower and how to calculate that rate. The interest rate can be determined by using a ***loan pricing model***. The purpose of loan pricing models is to determine the minimum price that a bank should charge on a commercial loan. Before we examine loan pricing, let's consider the effective yield.

How to Calculate Effective Yield

There is a difference between the *nominal interest rate* -- the interest rate that is stated in the loan agreement -- and the *effective yield*, which takes the payment accrual basis and the payment frequency into account. The method for calculating effective yields is explained after some terms have been defined.

The *payment accrual basis* refers to the number of days used in the interest rate calculation. One part of the calculation involves the number of days in a year. Interest can be calculated on the basis of a 365-day year or a 360-day year. To illustrate the difference, consider a $1 million loan at a 10 percent nominal rate of interest. The daily interest payment (interest income to the bank and interest expense to the borrower) of the loan is determined by multiplying the amount of the loan by the nominal interest rate and then dividing by the appropriate number of days (365 or 360), and multiplying that figure by the amount of the loan. Accordingly, the cost of a $1 million loan at 10 percent interest is $273.97 on a 365-day basis and $277.78 on a 360-day basis. These calculations will be presented again.

Another part of the calculation involves the number of days that the loan is outstanding. One can use the actual number of days the loan is outstanding, or one can use a 30-day month base.

The final variable is the frequency of interest payments. Typically, term loans are structured with monthly, quarterly, or annual payments. Because of the time value of money (money is worth more today than if the same amount is received in the future), frequent payments are favored by bankers but harder to sell to borrowers. The effect of payment frequency on interest earned and yields will be explained shortly.

To illustrate the effective yield, let's consider a 345-day term loan beginning on January 1 and ending on December 11. The principal amount is $1 million and the interest rate is 10 percent. The calculations for a 360-day year and 30-day month are as follows:

1.	$1,000,000	Principal amount
2.	× 0.10	Annual interest rate
3.	$100,000	Annual interest amount
4.	360	Divide by number of days in year (360 or 365)
5.	$277.78	Daily interest payment
6.	× (30 days × 11 months + 11 days)	Times 11 months of 30 days plus 11 days (341 days) or the actual number of days
7.	$94,722.22	Total interest paid

$$\text{Effective yield} = \frac{\text{Total interest paid}}{\text{Principal amount}} \times \frac{365}{\text{Term of loan in days}} \qquad (9.1)$$

$$= \frac{\$94{,}722.22}{\$1{,}000{,}000.00} \times \frac{365}{345} = 10.02\%$$

The same process (with the appropriate number of days in lines 4 and 6) can be used to calculate the effective yields for 360-day years with actual number of days and 365-day year with actual number of days. The effective yields for the three methods are as follows:

Effective Yield

360-day year/30-day month	10.02%
360-day year/actual number of days	10.14%
365-day year/actual number of days	10.00%

Effect of Payment Frequency on Interest Earned and Yields

The frequency of loan payments has a major impact on interest earned and the yield received on loans. Suppose that a bank is considering making a one-year, $100,000 loan at 12 percent interest. The $100,000 loan will be repaid at the end of the year. The bank earns $12,000.00 if interest is paid annually, and $12,747.46 if it is paid daily. The bank earns more when interest is collected frequently.

Payment Periods	Interest earned on $100,000 loan	Yield
Continuous	$12,748.28	12.748%
Daily	$12,747.46	12.747%
Monthly	$12,682.50	12.683%
Quarterly	$12,550.88	12.551%
Annually	$12,000.00	12.000%

The amount that the bank receives at the end of the period can be determined by the equation for the future value of $1:

$$FV_n = PV_o(1 + i/m)^{nm} \tag{9.2}$$

where

FV_n = future value at end of n periods

PV_o = present value ($100,000 in this example)

i = interest rate

n = number of periods

m = number of interyear periods (days, months, quarters).

Thus, the amount earned if interest is collected monthly is:

$$FV_{12} = \$100{,}000(1 + 0.12/12)^{1X12}$$
$$= \$112{,}682.50$$

Interest earned is the difference between FV_{12} and PV_O, which is:

$$\$112{,}682.50 - \$100{,}000 = \$12{,}682.50$$

It follows that the annual yield is [21]

$$FV_n = PV_O(1 + 0.12/12)^{nX12}$$
$$= 12.683\%$$

Many loans are amortized, which means that the principal is reduced with periodic payments. Methods for computing the annual interest rates (APR) on such loans are explained in connection with consumer loans in Chapter 10.

Loan Pricing

When profit margins on commercial loans are razor thin, precise estimates of cost are necessary to price the loans correctly. Overpricing of loans results in some borrowers going elsewhere to obtain loans. Underpricing of loans results in banks earning less than they should for a given level of risk. Consistent underpricing could adversely affect both the profits and the value of banks making that error.

Many banks price commercial loans by using an index rate (i.e., prime rate) plus a markup of one or more percentage points. Other banks use the cost of borrowed funds (i.e., 90-day CD rate) plus a markup. The advantage of using markups above prime of the cost of CDs is that they are simple and easy to understand. Markups are supposed to compensate the bank for the risk it takes in making a loan, as well as providing a return on its investment. The disadvantage of using markups is that they may not properly account for risk, the cost of funds, and operating expenses. The result may be that some loans are mispriced. The alternative is to use loan pricing models that properly account for risk, costs, and returns.

Return on Net Funds Employed

There are many types of loan pricing models. The one presented here is to illustrate some of the factors going into loan pricing. This loan pricing model establishes the required rate of return that the bank wants to earn on the loan, and then it must determine the net income that the loan must generate to provide that return. If the loan cannot generate sufficient net income to earn the required rate of return, the bank should consider rejecting it. We will examine each of the components of the model below, and then solve for loan income.

$$\text{Marginal cost of funds} + \text{Profit goal} = (\text{Loan income} - \text{Loan expense})/\text{Net bank funds employed} \quad (9.3)$$

Required Rate of Return

In this model, the required rate of return is equal to the marginal cost of funds plus a profit goal. The marginal cost of capital (funds) is the rate of return required by debt and equity investors on newly issued funds they provide to the bank.[22] That rate may differ from the rate of return required by the bank's management. We make the simplifying assumption that the marginal cost of capital is the weighted average cost of capital (WACC).[23] In this example, we further assume that WACC is six percent. A detailed explanation of how to calculate WACC for a bank appears in appendix 7B at the end of this chapter.

$$k_w = k_d(1 - T)L + k_e(1 - L) \quad (9.4)$$

where

k_w = weighted average cost of capital of new funds

k_d = cost of interest-bearing liabilities

k_e = cost of equity

T = corporate tax rate

L = ratio of liabilities to assets.

Profit Goal

While the cost of capital takes into account the average risk of the bank, the profit goal must consider the specific risk of each loan. The percentages we discuss here reflect the profit goal and are added to the WACC. The size of the markup is directly related to the risk of the loan under consideration. High-risk loans require larger markups than low-risk loans. The criteria for classifying the riskiness of the loan may include the strength of the financial statement, relative position the firm holds in the industry, collateral, and other factors. When all of these factors are considered, the firms might be classified as having, say, very low, low, average, or high risk.

Liquidity, measured in terms of years, must be considered when evaluating the profit goal. Short-term loans are more liquid than long-term loans.

The combination of risk and liquidity can be used to determine a profit goal. For example, the profit goal shown here for a very low risk loan made for one year or less is 1.0 percent. If the loan had a maturity of three to five years, a 1.2 percent return would be required. The profit goal increases with the risk and the maturity of the loan. The determination of the profit goals based on risk and liquidity are based on management's judgment. Thus, they will vary from bank to bank.

	Profit Goal for Term of Loans:	
Class of Risk	Under 1 year	3-5 years
Very Low	1.0	1.2
Low	1.5	1.8
Average	2.0	2.4
High	2.6	3.1

Loan Expense

Loan expense includes all direct and indirect costs associated with making, servicing, and collecting the loan. However, it does not include the bank's cost of funds. Making effective cost estimates to be used in the model is difficult to do. To illustrate the difficulty, suppose that a loan officer spent 35 hours of working time trying to attract a new loan customer. Let's consider only the officer's time, which is worth $100 per hour. The cost is $3,500. If the customer borrows $10,000 for 90 days, the equation suggests that the bank would have to charge more than $3,500 (35 percent) to cover that cost along. Obviously, the bank would not attempt to charge that amount. Nevertheless, someone has to pay for the loan officer's time. This is done by using cost accounting data and trying to make reasonable estimates about the cost of making, servicing, and collecting loans.

Net Bank Funds Employed

The net bank funds employed is the average amount of the loan over its life, less funds provided by the borrower, net of Federal Reserve System reserve requirements. Borrowers provide funds in the form of compensating balances or other balances held at the bank. The bank cannot use the entire amount on deposit because it is required by the Federal Reserve System to maintain a specified amount of reserves against those balances.

To illustrate the use of Eq. (9.4), let's make the following assumptions:

1. Marginal cost of funds is 6%.
2. Profit goal is 2%.
3. Loan expense is $2,000.
4. Net bank funds employed is $100,000.

Given these assumptions, we use Eq. (9.4) to solve for loan income, which comes out to $10,000.

(6% + 2%) = (Loan income - $2,000)/$100,000

Loan income = $10,000

The $10,000 is the amount of income this loan must generate in order for the bank to earn its required rate of return. This figure understates the correct amount because it does not take the time value of money into account. Nevertheless, it is a good "ballpark" estimate of the income that is needed.

This loan pricing model is best suited for banks that have effective cost accounting data and that can estimate the order data that are required. If this model is used to price variable rate loans, the rate of return to the bank will change whenever the loan rate changes. This problem is resolved in the next model.

Relationship Pricing

The loan pricing model that was examined did not take into account other business relationships that the borrower may have with the bank. For example, the borrower might be using cash management services, have a pension fund managed by the bank, and use the other bank facilities. Each of these activities generates positive income. When, and under what circumstances, should a borrower's relationships be considered?

To answer that question, we must think about making a loan as a new investment opportunity. All of the relevant cash flows must be evaluated. If the loan is the only business that the borrower has with the bank, then only the cash flows associated with the loan are relevant. However, if the loan is one of many services provided by the bank, then all of the cash flows associated with that borrower's relationship with the bank must be evaluated. The projected cash flow from each service, including the loan, should be adjusted to take risks into account. In *relationship pricing*, the rate charged on a loan may differ from the rate indicated by the loan pricing model presented previously.

Minimum Spread

Some banks price loans by determining the minimum spread they will accept between their lending rate and their costs plus a profit margin. For example, assume that a bank's costs are 12 percent and the profit margin is two percent. If the bank wants to encourage lending, it will accept a smaller profit margin and charge borrowers 13 percent. If the bank wants to retard lending, it will increase the spread and charge borrowers 15 percent. Encouraging and discouraging lending is a common practice and reflects banks' changing financial needs. The banks know that many large commercial loans are repriced every day or every 30, 60, or 90 days. Large borrowers regularly shop for the lowest rates. A bank that increases its lending rate in one period to discourage a borrower may decide to make the loan the next time it is repriced. Loans to corporations waiting to sell commercial paper are an example of loans that are repriced frequently.

Average Cost Versus Marginal Cost

The costs used in this model include the cost of funds and operating costs. Here too there are problems determining the relevant costs. Since operating costs have been discussed previously, let's focus on the cost of funds. Should the bank use the average cost of funds or the marginal cost of funds? In the explanation of the cost of capital, the marginal and average costs were the same. But that is not always the case. To illustrate this problem, suppose that a firm wants to borrow $1 million for 90 days. The bank's lending rate is the cost of funds plus one percentage point per annum. The hypothetical bank raised $0.5 million by selling a 90-day CD at 12 percent. In addition, the bank has $0.5 million in other interest-rate sensitive liabilities that cost eight percent. For simplicity, we ignore equity. The average cost of borrowed funds, which is determined by dividing total interest cost by total funds employed, is 10.0 percent. The marginal cost of funds, or the 90-day CD rate, is 12 percent.

Should the bank use the average cost of funds or the marginal cost of funds to price the loan? When market rates of interest are rising, the bank is better off using the marginal cost of funds because it is higher than the average cost of funds. However, when market rates of interest are falling, it is better off using the average cost of funds, which is higher than the marginal cost.

Another consideration is how the loan is funded. If the $1 million, 90-day loan was *match funded* by selling a $1 million 90-day CD, the CD rate could be used to represent the borrowed funds. Although not mentioned previously, the bank would have to raise more than $1 million in order to cover reserve requirements. Suppose that reserve requirements are five percent. The bank would have to raise $1,052,632 ($1,000,000/0.95 = $1,052,632) in order to lend $1 million.

If the bank views all of its deposits as a "pool" of funds used to finance loans, the answer is still the marginal rate. In theory, the marginal loan (the next loan to be made) should be charged the marginal cost of funds including the cost of equity.

All of the examples used here suggest that in order to make a profit, a bank's lending rate should be greater than its cost of funds, including equity.

Performance Pricing

The price of a loan reflects the riskiness of the borrower. When the borrower's riskiness changes, the price of the loan should be changed accordingly. One way to do this is with performance pricing, which allows banks and borrowers to change the price of a loan without renegotiating it. The price can be tied to specific financial ratios, the amount of the loan outstanding, the borrower's debt ratings, or other criteria that are mutually agreeable.

MONITORING AND LOAN REVIEW

After the loan has been granted, the bank must monitor the loan to determine if the borrower is complying with the terms of the loan agreement. Part of the monitoring process is a loan review. This is an internal audit system for the lending functions of the bank. Loan reviews help to identify potential problems with particular loans and weaknesses in loan procedures. In addition, they are used to help quantify the risk in the loan portfolio.

PAYOFFS OR LOSSES?

One of four things can happen to an outstanding loan: 1) it can be repaid on schedule; 2) it can be renewed or extended; 3) the bank can sell the loan to another investor; and 4) the loan can go into default and the bank may sustain losses. Items 1-3 are desirable outcomes. Item 4 is the worst case scenario for the bank.

SUMMARY

Banks make most of their money by lending, and lending accounts for most of their risk – credit risk. Recall from Chapter 1 that credit risk is the primary cause of bank failure. Simply stated, credit risk is the risk to earnings and capital that an obligor will fail to meet the terms of a contract with the bank. Asymmetric information and adverse selection play an important role in credit risk. Asymmetric information refers to the fact that borrowers know more about their business prospects than banks, and the banks tend to attract the higher-risk borrowers. This, coupled with increased competition for lending from nonbank lenders, has resulted in banks shifting their portfolios to higher -risk loans in hopes of increasing their profitability. Changes in technology, such as securitization and credit scoring, also have affected the ways loans are made and serviced.

The process of lending begins with the Board of Director's written loan policy that sets out the guidelines within which the bank must operate. Given those limits, which will vary from bank to bank, various techniques for reducing credit risk (avoiding high risk loans, diversification, etc.) were presented. Against this background, the ways (soliciting loans, buying loans, commitments, etc.) that banks make C&I loans was explained. A loan should be made with the expectation that it will be repaid from earnings or the sale of assets. Collateral is a secondary source of repayment.

Banks make different types of C&I loans for different purposes. Lines of credit, for example, are used to finance temporary or seasonal working capital needs; term loans are used to finance the acquisition of real assets and for other purposes. The use of collateral is a common practice in C&I lending. Collateral reduces the risk to a bank and serves as an incentive to the borrower to repay the loan. Almost anything that is legal can be used as collateral. However, the most common forms of collateral include accounts receivable, inventory, equipment, and real estate.

Before loans are granted, the lender must evaluate the creditworthiness of the prospective borrower. The borrower's character, financial condition, and ability to repay the loan from future income or the sale of assets are of primary importance. (A detailed description of financial analysis appears in Chapter 8.) The bank must also comply with numerous federal regulations before and after credit is extended. In addition, the bank must price the loan so that it is fair to the customer and profitable for the bank. Different pricing models result in different interest earnings. Once all of this is done, the loan agreement is developed that provides details about how the funds will be used, how they will be repaid, and other terms. After the loan is granted, the bank must monitor the loan to assure repayment. The best outcome is that the loan is repaid in full. The worst outcome is that it is charged off as a loss.

KEY TERMS AND CONCEPTS

Adverse selection
Asset-based lending
Asymmetric information
Bankers Acceptance
Bridge loan
Board of Directors written loan policy
Business credit and debit cards
Charged-off (loan)
Collateral
Commercial and Industrial Loan (C&I)
Credit default swap
Credit facility
Credit risk
Credit scoring
Daylight overdraft
Factoring
Leasing
Lender liability
Leveraged Lending
Line of credit
Loan broker
Loan commitment
Loan pricing model
Loan-to-price ratio
Moral hazard
Overdraft
Pledging
Prime rate
Revolving loan
Shared national credit
Term loan
Trade credit
USA Patriot Act

QUESTIONS

9.1 How can banks reduce their credit risk?

9.2 Explain the concepts of asymmetric risk and adverse selection in connection with commercial lending.

9.3 What is credit scoring and how is it used in commercial lending?

9.4 Explain the difference between a line of credit and a revolving loan.

9.5 What type of loan should be used to finance:

a. seasonal inventory needs?
b. construction of a warehouse?
c. refinancing debt?
d. acquiring equipment?

9.6 What are the sources of repayment of term loans repaid?

9.7 How does asset-based lending differ from other types of lending?

9.8 Explain the role of "documentation" in the lending process.

9.9 Does the payment of a commitment fee and a loan commitment guarantee that a bank will make funds available to a borrower?

9-10 List the five characteristics of good collateral.

9-11 What do trust receipts and floating liens have in common?

9-12 True or false. Explain your position: The quality of a loan guarantee depends on the quality of the guarantor.

9-13 How does "pledging" accounts receivable differ from "factoring?"

9-14 What is the role of the Board of Directors in the lending process? Why is a written loan policy important?

9-15 How does the effective yield differ from the nominal interest rate on a loan?

9-16 Why do many loan pricing models ignore the cost of equity?

9-17 Many banks use "relationship pricing." What does that mean? What is the implication for loan pricing.

9.18 Under what circumstances is a loan charged off, and what does that mean? What is the effect on earnings?

9.19 Carla Fernandez owns a fleet of taxi cabs. The cabs are leased to taxi drivers for periods of one year or longer. The cabs are used for about two years before they are sold. She asked her attorney for advice on borrowing money from a bank to acquire more cabs. He recommended a line of credit so that she could borrow the funds when she needed them. He further suggested that the lease agreements could be used as collateral for the loans. If you were a bank loan officer, what would you tell Carla about her attorney's suggestion?

9.20 The Board of Directors of Commonwealth Bank's key performance objectives include: 1) Achieving a secure and sustainable return on shareholder investment. 2) Achieving a profit performance which compares well in our industry. At the same time, we manage our business with prudence to avoid levels of risk that could threaten our profitability. Are these performance objectives consistent? Explain your answer.

9.21 Suppose that you served on a large bank's management committee. One issue facing the committee today is how to fund a $15 million three-year loan, and whether the interest rate charged on the loan should be floating or fixed. The loan request has been approved, but the details of the credit facility have not yet been worked out. Given the current economic and financial outlook, what is your recommendation?

9.22 According to the Survey of Term of Lending (Federal Reserve statistical release E.2, which can be found on the web at http://www.federalreserve.gov/releases/, what is the average size and maturity for all C&I loans? What percentage of the C&I loans are secured by collateral? What is the most common base pricing rate?

PROBLEMS

9.1 Alpine Cotton Mill wants to factor $312,500 in accounts receivable. The Northern Bank is willing to factor 80 percent of that amount. Northern charges a three percent commission, requires eight percent of the factored amount to be held in reserve, and charges 18 percent per annum on the amount advanced. Northern can invest its funds at a seven percent per annum return. How much will Northern earn during the first month of factoring?

9.2 Newton Mfg. is shopping for a loan commitment for $10 million for 60 days. Bank A is willing to make the commitment for 3.33 percent on a 360 day year basis. Bank B is offering the same rate but uses a 365 day year. Which one should Newton take, and how much will be saved?

9-3 A $500,000 loan is made for 90 days at eight percent per annum. Compute the effective yield using a) 360-day year/30 day months, and b) 365-day year/actual number of days.

9-4 Using the net bank funds employed pricing model, determine how much loan income the following loan must generate to produce the required returns. Marginal cost of funds is 12 percent, profit goal is three percent, loan expense is $5000, and the amount of the loan is $220,000.

9-5 Compute the annual interest earned on a $350,000 loan, at 10 percent interest compounded monthly, quarterly, and annually.

9-6 Compute the weighted average cost of capital for a bank using the following information:

Equity = 8%, Tax rate = 25%, Cost of debt 8%, Cost of equity = 12%.

9-7 A five percent (5%) commitment fee on a $1 million loan for 6 months (180 days) is equal to?

CASE: MADISON NATIONAL BANK[24]

Asset-Liability Management and Loan Pricing

Judy Langer, Vice-President of Funds management for Madison National Bank, was reviewing Madison's loan position during a coffee break at the Asset-Liability Management Committee (ALCO) meeting. The ALCO decides the composition of earning assets, which include loans, time deposits at other banks, Federal Funds sold, and security investments. The committee also decides the different funding options of the liability side of the balance sheet. Examples are the amount of C.D.s versus transaction accounts. Members of the committee include the vice-presidents of funds, bonds, and securities (which include all non-bond security investments) management as well as commercial lending. The chairman of the committee is the executive vice-president of investments and financial planning.

Madison has a reputation for having conservative lending policies. Madison's loan position, established by the board of directors, is governed by two lending policy guidelines, First, total loans cannot exceed 100 percent of core deposits, which are defined as demand, savings, and time deposits as well as certificates of deposit less than $100,000. Second, earning assets cannot exceed 140 percent of core deposits. (See Table 9-1).

ALCO Meeting

Sam Rogers, chairman of the committee, started the meeting by discussing their current posture with respect to transaction- based loans. He informed the members that several large companies are in the market for these transactions-based loans, which are to be repriced. They want quotes from Madison as well as other banks. Sam then asked for comments and opinions on what Madison's position should be regarding these opportunities.

Mike Clayman, vice-president of commercial lending, started the discussion by raising the issue of strong commercial loan demand. Mike stated that in the past year the demand for loans has been increasing. In addition, it is expected to remain strong in the months ahead due to the continued economic expansion in such areas as housing construction as well as commercial and industrial modernization of plant and equipment. Judy Langer wanted more information about both points and wrote herself a note on the pad in front of her.

Willie Morgan, vice-president of securities management, then pointed out that these loan requests are for transactions-based loans. Transactions-based loans are short-term loans to large corporate borrowers for the purpose of meeting inventory and other operational needs. The typical size of such loans is about $10 million.

He also stated that these corporations are very interest-rate sensitive; that is, they will shop around for the lowest loan prices and borrow from banks offering the best terms. He stressed the fact that losing such a loan is not disastrous because the corporations will come back to shop for prices again when their loans are repriced.

Denise Wright, vice-president of bonds management, asked about the bank's current pricing policy. Judy Langer told her that the borrower selected the maturity of the loan. Three maturity options currently available at Madison are 30, 90, and 180 days. In addition, the borrower selects the pricing base to be used in pricing the loan. Again, there are usually four choices: the "all-in" C.D. rate, the Fed funds rate, the prime rate, and the London Interbank Offering Rate (LIBOR). However, LIBOR was not considered in this case. The "all-in" C.D. rate is the market rate plus the cost of deposit insurance and the reserve requirement on C.D.s. The insurance fee and reserve requirement adds about eight basis points to the market rate of C.D.s. Finally, the maturity of the pricing option is matched with the maturity of the loan. Thus, a 30-day loan is priced off of a 30-day C.D., for example.

Judy also reviewed the spread set for each pricing option. The spread when using the prime rate, which is more stable than other pricing options, averages around 100 basis points. When the bank wants the loan, the spread is lowered five to 10 basis points. On the other hand, when the bank does not want the loan, the spread is increased.

The C.D. and Fed fund rates, being more volatile than the prime rate, usually have a premium of five to 10 basis points, respectively. For example, if the spread is set off of Prime of 10 percent, the "all-in" CD rate of 8.5 percent, and Fed funds rate of 8.0 percent with a 100-basis point spread to start with, the following loan prices would be derived: The prime would not have any additions other than the 100 basis point spread, making its related price 11.0 percent. The "all-in" CD rate would have the 100 basis points and five additional basis points added due to the volatility of such rates; this would give a price of 9.55 percent. The Fed funds rate would have the 100 basis points and 10 additional points added giving a price of 9.10 percent.

Available Options

After hearing the information presented at the meeting, Sam Rogers stated that the committee must decide what to do about the demand for transactions-based loans. He went on to present the following options.

A. Run off the loan - By pricing the loan above competitive rates, Madison can avoid absorbing a large volume of transactions-based accounts as the potential borrower will go elsewhere for available funds. Plus, funds would become available for possible higher-yielding lending opportunities of longer maturity. Experience indicates that an increase in spread of 8-10 basis points above the market rate will remove Madison from consideration by the borrowers.

B. Accept the loan using purchased funds - This method, which has been used in the past, generally involves purchasing funds and setting the desired spread off of the average monthly rate. For December, the Fed funds rate ranged between 8.83 percent and 7.95 percent for an average monthly rate of 8.38 percent. (See Table 9-2 below).

C. Accept the loan and sell participations - This arrangement allows Madison to make these loans and share the principle funding responsibility (and interest income generated) with other interested banks that buy parts of the loan. This may be done either upstream (sharing with larger banks) or downstream (through a network of smaller correspondent banks). Additionally, Madison could sell off a portion of their current loan portfolio already on the books to other banks through a participating agreement. This would free a portion of current funds tied up in transactions-based lending for alternative uses.

D. Liquidate Securities - This would allow Madison to exchange assets by selling securities and making loans from the funds generated by the sale.

Sam Rogers instructed the committee to take a short recess and think about the alternatives discussed for handling transactions-based loans. Judy Langer contemplated these options relative to Madison's current loan position and tried to decide what to do.

TABLE 9-2 PRICING OPTIONS FOR TRANSACTION-BASED LOANS*

			Certificates of Deposit		
	Prime	Fed Funds	1-mo.	3-mo.	6-mo.
September	12.97	11.30	11.20	11.29	11.47
October	12.58	9.99	10.18	10.38	10.63
November	11.77	9.43	9.09	9.18	9.39
December	11.06	8.38	8.47	8.60	8.85
January	10.60	8.35	8.05	8.14	8.45
February	10.50	8.45	8.15	8.23	8.49

*Predicted monthly averages.

TABLE 9-1 **BALANCE SHEET (IN MILLIONS)**

($ Millions)	2015	2014
Assets		
Cash and due from banks	$ 820,268	$ 676,448
Earning assets		
Time deposits in other banks	0	398,000
Federal funds sold and securities purchased under agreement to resell	418,550	16,900
Trading account securities	19,606	15,292
Investment securities	1,211,300	1,330,017
State and local government securities	352,462	452,689
Loans	5,419,424	4,187,428
Less: allowance for loan losses	(73,488)	(56,478)
Unearned income	(152,622)	(153,258)
Net loans	5,193,314	3,979,692
Total earning assets	7,195,232	6,192,590
Premises and equipment, net	170,060	155,628
Customer's acceptance liability	126,694	23,232
Accrued interest receivable and other assets	251,504	255,262
Total assets	$8,563,758	$7,273,160
Liabilities and shareholders' equity		
Deposits and interest-bearing liabilities		
Deposits:		
Noninterest-bearing transaction	$1,698,846	$1,846,068
Interest-bearing transaction	1,173,072	977,844
Savings	465,610	494,398
Time	1,431,344	1,107,208
Certificates of deposits less than $100,000	715,670	553,600
Certificates of deposits of $100,000 or more	952,610	643,856
Total deposits	6,437,152	3,622,974
Federal funds purchased and securities sold under agreement to repurchase	866,808	799,224
Commercial paper	32,530	36,990
Other interest-bearing liabilities	457,124	162,600
Total deposits and interest-bearing liabilities	7,793,614	6,621,788
Acceptances outstanding	126,662	23,158
Accrued expenses and other liabilities	121,676	115,004
Total liabilities	$8,041,952	$6,759,950
Shareholders' equity:		
Preferred stock	$ 0	$ 800,000
Common stock	22,782	22,612
Capital surplus	274,710	271,200
Retained earnings	270,196	224,038
	567,688	525,850
Less cost of common stock in treasury	45,882	12,640
Total shareholders' equity	521,806	513,210
Total liabilities and equities	$8,563,758	$7,273,160

Note: Figures may not add to totals due to rounding.

ENDNOTES

1. Interest rate data are from the Federal Reserve Bank of St. Louis, *USFinancialData*. For the latest data, see http://www.stlouisfed.org.

2. Loan Portfolio Management: Comptroller's Handbook, Washington, D.C., Office of the Comptroller of the Currency, April 1998, 4.

3. Mitchell Berlin, "Trade Credit: Why do Production firms Act as Financial Intermediaries?" *Business Review*, Federal Reserve Bank of Philadelphia, Third Quarter, 2003, 21-28.

4. Board of Governors of the Federal Reserve System, "E2 Survey of Terms of Business Lending" August 3-7, 2015

5. Board of Governors of the Federal Reserve System, H.8 Release, Assets and Liabilities of Commercial Banks in the United States –November 13, 2015. Page 2. Gup found that real estate loans were more commonly associated with bank failures than any other category of loan (Benton E. Gup, *Bank Failures in the Major Trading Countries of the World: Causes and Remedies,* Westport, CT: Quorum Books, 1998, Chapter 4). Also see Benton E. Gup, *International Banking Crises: Large-Scale Failures, Massive Government Interventions,* Westport, CT. Quorum Books, 1999, Chapter, 2.

6. Google "mortgage lenders." Mortgage lenders may show what percentage of value they are willing to lend and other terms of lending.

7. See http://www.fairisaac.com. for information about their credit scoring models.

8. For details, see "Principals of the Management of Credit Risk," Basel Committee on Banking Supervision, Bank for International Settlement, September 2000, www.bis.org. http://www.bis.org/publ/bcbs75.htm

9. Comments by Joseph E. Stiglitz, Bank Lending to Small Business, Washington, DC, Office of the Comptroller of the Currency, November 15, 1994, 9.

10. Li, W., "Government Loan, Guarantee, and Grant Programs: An Evaluation," Federal Reserve Bank of Richmond, *Economic Quarterly*, Fall 1998, 25-51.

11. The limits apply to a bank's total unimpaired capital and surplus, which equals their Tier 1 and Tier 2 capital. For additional details, see 12 USC 84.

12. 12 CFR 32.3 - Lending limits. https://www.law.cornell.edu/cfr/text/12/32.3

13. Stewart C. Myers, "Outside Equity Financing," National Bureau of Economic Research, NBER Working Paper 6561, May 1998.

14. For a discussion of credit derivatives, see: Moser, J.T., "Credit Derivatives: Just-in-time Provisioning for Loan Losses," Federal Reserve Bank of Chicago, *Economic Perspectives*, Fourth Quarter 1998, 2 -11; Jose A. Lopez, "Financial Instruments for Mitigating Credit Risk," *FRBSF Economic Letter*, Federal Reserve Bank of San Francisco, November 23, 2001.

15. The Shared National Credit Program was established in 1977 by the Board of Governors of the Federal Reserve System, the Federal Deposit Insurance Corporation, and the Office of the Comptroller of the Currency to provide an efficient and consistent review and classification of any large syndicated loan. Today, the program covers any loan or loan commitment of at least $20 million that is shared by three or more supervised institutions.

16. Board of Governors of the Federal Reserve System, "Survey of Terms of Business Lending – E.2", August 3-7, 2015.

17. *The Wall Street Journal* section on "Consumer Rates and Returns to Investor," gives the current prime rate, and other market rates of interest. Data are for November 23, 2015.

18. Office of the Comptroller of the Currency, Leveraged Lending, Comptroller's Handbook, Assets,

February 2008, p. 3.

19. Ibid. p. 1

20. For information about D&B, see: http://www.dnb.com/us/

21. The continuous yield is determined by calculating ein = (2.718)0.12x1 = 12.7483%, where e = Euler's constant, and ein is the limit of (1 + i/m)nm.

22. Risk-based capital weights are not considered here because commercial loans have a 100 percent risk weighting.

23. If the increased equity results in the bank being perceived by investors as being less risky, the cost of borrowing may be reduced, which may lower the WACC.

24. The original field based research for this case was conducted by graduate students taking Dr. Gup's banking classes.

25. If the increased equity results in the bank being perceived by investors as being less risky, the cost of borrowing may be reduced, which may lower the WACC.

26. The cost of equity may be computed by using the CAPM, the dividend valuation model, or by using a bond yield plus a risk premium. Although questions have been raised about the validity of the CAPM, as well as questions about the other methods, the CAPM is still widely used.

27. The expected return on the market may be estimated by several methods. For simplicity, we used 7.5 percent. From 1926-2000, the arithmetic mean return on common stocks was 7.5 percent on large company stocks according to Roger G. Ibbotson and Rex A Sinquefield, *Stocks, Bonds, Bills and Inflation: 2000 Yearbook* Chicago: Ibbotson Associates, 2001.

APPENDIX A: THE COST OF CAPITAL

This appendix explains how to calculate the weighted average cost of capital for banks. We make the simplifying assumptions that total liabilities are interest-rate sensitive and that interest expense divided by total liabilities represents the marginal cost of borrowed funds. Considering liabilities to be interest-rate sensitive means that they are repriced when market rates of interest change. In this example, the marginal cost of capital is the weighted average cost of capital (WACC).

25

$$k_w = k_d(1 - T)L + k_e(1 - L) \quad (9A.1)$$

where

k_w = weighted average cost of capital of new funds
k_d = cost of interest-bearing liabilities
T = corporate tax rate
L = ratio of liabilities to assets
k_e = cost of equity

Equation (9A.1) reveals that the cost of capital for all new funds raised is equal to the proportionate after-tax cost of liabilities, plus the proportionate cost of equity. The WACC is expressed as a percentage.

The cost of equity may be computed by the *capital asset pricing model* (CAPM).[21] The CAPM asserts that the cost of equity capital is equal to the risk-free rate of interest plus beta times a market premium. The risk-free rate of interest refers to the rate paid on default-free Treasury securities. Beta is a measure of systematic risk—risk that is common to all stocks. 26

The market premium is the difference between the expected return on the stock market and the risk-free rate of interest. The CAPM may be expressed as:

$$k_e = rf + b(k_m - rf) \quad (9A.2)$$

where

rf = the risk-free rate of interest on Treasury bills
b = stock market beta of a stock
k_m = expected return on the stock market

To illustrate the use of these equations, we will compute the cost of capital of Major Bank, a large money center bank. Using the following data, Major Bank's cost of equity capital is estimated to be 11.45 percent:

rf = risk-free rate on Treasury bills = 0.0412
b = beta = 1.2
k_m = expected return on the market[22] = 0.075
k_d = interest expense/total liabilities = 0.0858
T = tax rate = 0.40
L = ratio of liabilities to assets = 0.955

$$\begin{aligned} k_e &= rf + b\,(k_m - rf) \\ &= 0.0412 + 1.2\,(0.075 - 0.0412) \quad 27 \\ &= 8.18\%. \end{aligned}$$

Using the 8.18 percent cost of equity, the WACC for Major Bank is 5.29 percent:

$$\begin{aligned} k_w &= k_d(1 - T)L + k_e(1 - L) \\ &= (0.0515 \times 0.955) + (0.0818 \times 0.045) \\ &= 5.29\% \end{aligned}$$

Although the cost of equity is relatively high (8.18 percent), it only accounts for a small portion (4.5 percent) of the total capital structure. Therefore, the proportionate cost of equity (0.8818 × 0.045 = 0.0037) in the WACC is relatively small, but nevertheless important.

Chapter 10

Real Estate and Consumer Lending

After reading this chapter, you will be able to:

- Explain the characteristics of residential mortgage loans
- Understand alternative mortgage instruments
- Understand how commercial real estate loans differ from residential loans
- Explain the various types of consumer loans
- Understand how finance charges on consumer loans are computed
- Explain the major federal laws governing real estate and consumer credit.

Times have changed. In the past, people who wanted to obtain mortgage loans or personal loans had to go to the bank and ask for them. Today, they can do it from the comfort of their homes by using the internet, or they can do it from anywhere using their cell phones. Technology is changing the ways that home buyers and consumers borrow money, and technology also affects the ways that lenders are making real estate and consumer loans. Electronic banking is examined in Chapter 17. In this chapter, we examine the real estate and consumer lending from the lender's point of view.

THE EFFECTS OF THE RECESSION – 2007-2009[1]

The recession that ran from December, 2007 to June, 2009 definitely earned the title the Great Recession. Real GDP fell four percent, employment fell six percent, and the unemployment rate crossed the 10 percent mark for only the second time in postwar U.S. history. Housing was at the epicenter of the crisis. Home prices fell 25 percent, the first time since the Great Depression of the 1930s that home prices decreased nationally. Residential investment cratered and skilled workers exited the construction industry, many permanently. Over 2.7 million households lost their homes to foreclosure or a foreclosure alternative such as a short sale. As a result, the homeownership rate plummeted and stands today no higher than it did in the first quarter of 1967.

These statistics illustrate the impact of the recession on the U.S. as a whole. However the recession affected each state differently. Some states suffered disproportionately while others avoided the worst of the downturn.

Many of these differences in impact can be traced to differences in the state economies. For example, Michigan had the bad luck to depend heavily on the automotive industry, a sector that collapsed at the start of the recession... In contrast, states in the oil patch – Texas, Oklahoma, Arkansas, Louisiana – suffered less than average."

REAL ESTATE LENDING

Banks need to "know your customers" (KYC) in making any kind of a loan in order to assure that a loan can be repaid. However, with real estate loans, they also need to know their customer's property. Under the Environmental Superfund Act of 1980, and the amendments in 1986, banks can be held responsible for cleaning up environmental damage done by their borrowers. Potentially hazardous materials include chemicals, gasoline, and asbestos. Asbestos was widely used in older buildings for insulation. In the case of U.S. v. Maryland Bank Trust Co., for example, the Environmental Protection Agency (EPA) sued the bank for reimbursement of cleanup costs of a hazardous waste dump after the bank had foreclosed on the property. The bank had held the property for four years, and the court held that the bank should pay for the cleanup cost. However, foreclosures were not a necessary condition in U.S. v. Fleet Factors Corporation. The Eleventh Circuit Court of Appeals held that a secured lender can be liable under federal environmental laws, even absent foreclosures, if the lender participates in the financial management of the borrower's facility to a degree indicating a capacity to influence the corporation's treatment of hazardous waste.

MORTGAGE DEBT OUTSTANDING

The term mortgage is used in connection with real estate lending. In general terms, a mortgage is a written conveyance of title to real property. It provides the lender with a security interest in the property, if the mortgage is properly recorded in the county courthouse. It also provides that the property being used as collateral for the loan will be sold if the debt is not repaid as agreed. The proceeds from the sale of the property are used to reimburse the lender. As shown in Table 10-1, mortgage debt for residences of one to four members accounts for 73 percent of the total mortgage debt outstanding. Nonfarm, nonresidential mortgage debt, which we will call commercial mortgage loans, are the second largest category of mortgage loans, accounting for about 18 percent of the total mortgage debt outstanding. Multifamily residences and farm mortgages account for the remainder.

Table 10-1: MORTGAGE DEBT OUTSTANDING BY TYPE OF PROPERTY 2015, 2nd Quarter ($ millions)

1-4 family residences	9,901,059
Multifamily residences	1,041,887
Nonfarm, nonresidential (commercial)	2,437,884
Farm	204,107
Total	13,584,937

Source: *Federal Reserve Bulletin*, September, 2015, Mortgage Debt Outstanding

Mortgage loans are originated by commercial banks and other financial institutions. *Conventional mortgage* loans are those that are not insured or guaranteed by the government [i.e., Federal Housing Administration (FHA), Department of Veterans Affairs (VA), or Department of Agriculture]. They are usually for less than $417,000, may require lower down payments, and do not meet certain other requirements that allow them to be sold.[2] Mortgage loans that are insured by the FHA or guaranteed by VA are called *government backed or insured mortgages*. However, some conventional mortgages are insured against default by private mortgage insurance companies.

The originating institutions might hold the mortgages in their loan portfolios or sell them in the secondary market. The *secondary mortgage market*, in which securities representing pools of mortgage loans are purchased and sold, increases the liquidity of residential mortgages and lessens the cyclical disruptions in the housing market. The pools of mortgage loans are referred to as *asset-backed securities*.

The process of transforming individual loans into marketable asset-backed securities is called *securitization*. The process involves the issuance of securities that represent claims against a pool of assets (i.e., mortgages, car loans, credit card receivables, and small business loans) that are held in trust. The originator of a loan sells the assets to a trust. It must be a *true sale*, which means that the assets cannot be returned to the originator's balance sheet. The trustee then issues securities through an investment banker (underwriter) to investors. Some banks act as packagers of asset-based loans, and they take on the risk of an underwriter. Some act as originators, packagers, and they service (collect loan payments, deal with delinquencies, etc.) the loans too. As the principal and interest payments are made on the loans, they are paid out to investors by the trustee or *servicer* who retains a small transaction fee. In most cases, the cash flows to investors are guaranteed *(credit enhanced)* by bank guarantees (standby letters of credit), by government agency guarantees (i.e., Government National Mortgage Association), or by having more loans than is necessary to secure the value of the pools (***overcollateralize***). Credit rating agencies, such as Standard and Poor's, assign ratings to asset-backed securities just as they do for stocks and bonds. The quality of the credit enhancement is an important part of the rating. The credit enhancements, credit ratings, and the reputations of the investment banker or packager help to standardize the quality of asset-backed loans.

One benefit of the secondary mortgage market is that it permits lenders to increase the liquidity of their mortgage portfolios. Stated otherwise, they can package otherwise unmarketable individual mortgage loans and sell them to investors. Another benefit is that the secondary market has attracted investors from outside the traditional mortgage investment community who want to buy mortgage- backed securities. Thus, the secondary mortgage market has increased the breadth, depth, and liquidity of the capital market that is available for mortgage financing.

The three major participants in the secondary market are:

1) Depository institutions (banks, savings and loan associations, and nondeposit trust departments).

2) The Federal National Mortgage Corporation (Fannie Mae), the Federal Home Loan Mortgage Association (Freddie Mac), and the Farmers Home Administration. These three organizations were created by Congress, and they developed a secondary mortgage market. They issue mortgage pools or trusts of one-to-four family, multifamily real estate, and certain other properties. Congress also created the Government National Mortgage Association, but it is a very small factor in the secondary mortgage market. Some private organizations also operate in the secondary mortgage market.

3) Mortgage pools and trusts hold 20 percent the total mortgage debt outstanding.

The ***Federal Home Loan Banks*** also play an important role in providing liquidity to the mortgage market. At the end of 2014, 4,739 commercial banks, 4,878 credit unions, 1,299 thrifts, 882 insurance companies, and other financial organizations joined the Federal Home Loan Bank System, and they are eligible to borrow funds from the FHLBanks for residential real estate lending.[3] The FHLBanks also hold mortgage-backed securities.

Table 10-2: MORTGAGE DEBT OUTSTANDING BY TYPE OF HOLDER 2015, 2nd Quarter ($ millions)

Depository Institutions	$4,248,235	31%
Life insurance companies	399,260	3
Federal and related agencies	5,004,130	37
Mortgage pools and trusts	2,764,124	20
Individuals and others	1,169,188	9
Total	$13,584,937	100%

Source: *Federal Reserve Bulletin*, September, 2015, Mortgage Debt Outstanding

"Industry concentration is declining. In 2009, the peak year for concentration, the top five mortgage originators accounted for 62 percent of all mortgage loans. In 2014, the top five firms accounted for only 34 percent of the market."[4] Part of this is due to the declining role of commercial banks in mortgage lending and increasing role of nondeposit independent mortgage companies.

CHARACTERISTICS OF MORTGAGE LOANS

In October 2015, the average purchase price of an existing single family home in the United States was $263,700.[5] However, home prices ranged from a low of $204,100 in the midwest to a high of $357,300 in the western part of the country.

The geographic locations make a big difference in housing prices and mortgage lending. For example, Fannie Mae, Freddie Mac, and the Federal Housing Finance Agency (FHFA) set the maximum amount for loans that they will buy from lenders. The loan limits for jumbo loans ranged from $417,000 to $625,500 in high-cost areas of the U.S. (such as San Jose, CA, San Francisco, New York) and Puerto Rico, and higher still in Alaska, Hawaii, Guam, and U.S. Virgin Islands. [6]

Mortgages that exceed those limits are call "jumbo loans." A *Wall Street Journal* article reported that "You can't find anything decent in San Francisco or under a million bucks. With 20% down, you're at $800,000. That is not even close to the confirming limit."[7]

The Census Bureau reported that in 2014, the average size of new houses being built was 2,690 square feet, compared to1,660 square feet in 1973.[8] During that same period, the average number of people per household declined from 3.01 to 2.54, and the average living space per person living in the house has almost doubled.

No matter where the borrower lives, the Consumer Financial Protection Bureau (CFPB) requires mortgage lenders to evaluate a borrower's ability to repay the loans in order to have a "Qualified Mortgage," or "QM." A borrower for a QM must have a total monthly debt-to-income ratio including mortgage payments of 43 percent or less. In addition, QMs cannot have certain harmful features:

. Interest only loans (paying only the interest without paying the principal). . Negative amortization (allowing the principal to increase over time).

. Balloon payments (larger than usual payments at the end of the loan – but which are allowed under certain conditions for small lenders).

.Loan terms longer than 30 years.

. No excess upfront points or fees.

. Certain legal protections for lenders.

Assume that the average purchase price of a new home is $300,000, and the average amount lent is $220,000. The difference between those two amounts, $80,000, represents the *down payment*, or borrower's equity. Equity is the difference between the market value of the property and the borrower's mortgage debt. From the lender's perspective, the percentage loaned to the borrowers, or the loan-to-price ratio, was 73.3 percent. Bank regulators have established loan-to-price (value) limits for different categories of loans.

According to "Interagency Guidelines for Real Estate Lending," high loan-to-value (HLTV) one- to four-family residential property loans include (1) a loan for raw land zoned for one- to four-family residential use with an loan-to-value (LTV) ratio greater than 65 percent; (2) a residential land development loan or improved lot loan with an LTV ratio greater than 75 percent; (3) a residential construction loan with an LTV ratio greater than 85 percent; (4) a loan on nonowner-occupied one- to four-family residential property with an LTV ratio greater than 85 percent; and (5) a permanent mortgage or home equity loan on an owner-occupied residential property with an LTV ratio equal to or exceeding 90 percent without mortgage insurance, readily marketable collateral, or other acceptable collateral."[9] Table 10-3 (next page) shows the FDIC's supervisory loan-to-value limits.[10]

In option pricing theory, bank loans are considered compound options containing the rights to prepay (call options) and to default (put options) on each of the scheduled payment dates.[11] When the put options are in the money (the value of the asset is less than the loan amount), borrowers have an incentive to exercise their put options and default on the loans. The lower the loan-to-price ratio (i.e., the higher the borrower's equity), the less likely it is that borrowers will default.

When market rates of interest rates decline below the interest rate on the loan, borrowers with fixed interest rate loans can exercise their call options and prepay the loans. That is, they refinance their loans at lower rates.

Table 10-3: SUPERVISORY LOAN-TO-VALUE LIMITS [a]

Institutions should establish their own internal loan-to-value limits for real estate loans. These internal limits should not exceed the following supervisory limits:

Loan category	Loan-to-value limit (percent)
Raw land	65
Land development	75
Construction:	
Commercial, multifamily,[b] and other nonresidential	80
1- to 4-family residential	85
Improved property	85
Owner-occupied 1- to 4-family and home equity[c]	–

[a] Appendix A to Part 365 of FDIC Rules and Regulations, http://www.fdic.gov/regulations/laws/rules/2000-8700.html#2000appendixatopart365

[b] Multifamily construction includes condominiums and cooperatives.

[c] A loan-to-value limit has not been established for permanent mortgage or home equity loans on owner-occupied 1- to 4-family residential property. However, for any such loan with a loan-to-value ratio that equals or exceeds 90 percent at origination, an institution should require appropriate credit enhancement in the form of either mortgage insurance or readily marketable collateral.

THE REAL ESTATE PORTFOLIO

Banks make an investment decision as to the percentage of their loan portfolio that they want to invest in various types of real estate loans. The decision takes into account risks and returns of the various types of real estate loans they make (residential and commercial). The risks include defaults, declining real estate values, prepayments, and lack of liquidity. Bankers also must decide what proportions of their loans should be made at fixed rates, or at adjustable rates. These decisions reflect the characteristics of the lender, the market, and the borrowers. Lenders mitigate some of these risks by raising their credit standards and excluding less creditworthy borrowers, by requiring borrowers to make larger down payments (lower loan-to-price ratios), by selling real estate loans in the secondary market, and by changing origination fees to influence borrowers' behavior. The returns banks receive on real estate lending come from interest earned on the loans, fees for transaction, settlement and closing costs, and fees for servicing loans that are sold. In addition, *points* -- fees paid to the lender -- are often linked to the interest rate. One point equals one percent of the loan. Finally, some lenders require *private mortgage insurance (PMI)* when the down payment is less than 20 percent. The PMI protects the lender in the event of default.

Collateral

Residential real estate is good collateral because it is durable, easy to identify, and most structures cannot be moved elsewhere. Despite these fine qualities, the value of real estate can go up or down. During periods of inflation, residential real estate in many parts of the country appreciates in value, thereby enhancing its value as collateral. During deflation and recessions, however, the value of residential real estate in some areas declines. As shown in Table 10-4, when real estate values declined during the financial crisis in 2008, net charge-offs in banks with mortgage concentrations where relatively high compared to banks in 2015 when the economy was strong.

Table 10-4: PERCENT OF NET CHARGE--OFFS FOR All FDIC INSURED INSTITUTIONS WITH MORTGAGE CONCENTRATIONS

	Banks Second Qtr. 2008	Banks Second Qtr. 2015
Net charge-offs to loans and leases	1.85%	0.13%

Source: *FDIC Quarterly Banking Profile*, Second Quarter 2008, Table III-A., FDIC Quarterly Banking Profile, Second Quarter, 2015, Table III-A.

The fact that real estate has a fixed geographic location is both good and bad. It is good in the sense that the collateral cannot be removed. It is bad in the sense that its value is affected by adjacent property. If a toxic waste dump site were to locate in what was previously a golf course, the value of the adjacent residential property would decline.

Finally, real estate is illiquid. That is, it is difficult to sell on short notice at its fair market value. These comments on residential real estate also apply to commercial real estate.

RESIDENTIAL MORTGAGE LOANS

Residential mortgage loans differ from other types of loans in several respects. First, the loans are for relatively large dollar amounts. As previously noted, the average purchase price of an existing single family home in the United States was $263,700 in October, 2015. Second, the loans tend to be long-term, with original maturities as long as thirty years. Third, the loans are usually secured by the real estate as collateral. However, real estate is illiquid, and its price can vary widely.

The two basic types of 1-4 family residential mortgage loans are ***fixed- rate mortgages*** and ***adjustable rate mortgages (ARMs).*** The interest rate charged on fixed rate mortgages does not change over the life of the loan. In contrast, ARMs permit lenders to vary the interest rate charged on the mortgage loan when market rates of interest change. The basic idea behind ARMs is to help mortgage lenders keep the returns on their assets (mortgage loans) higher than the costs of their funds. However, it is the borrowers who decide what type of mortgage loans they want, and that choice is influenced by the level of interest rates. When interest rates are high, borrowers prefer ARMs that will provide lower rates when interest rates decline. Alternatively, they can refinance their fixed rate mortgages, but that costs more to do.

When interest rates are low, borrowers want to lock in the low rates and prefer fixed-rate loans. Lenders, on the other hand, prefer ARMs so that they can benefit when interest rates increase. The lenders can hold the mortgage loans, or sell them to investors who are willing to hold them.

Fixed-Rate Mortgages

Fixed-rate, fully amortized, level payment mortgages are the predominant form of financing residential mortgage loans. *Fixed-rate, fully amortized, level payment mortgage* means that the interest rate does not change and the debt is gradually extinguished through equal periodic payments on the principal balance. In other words, the borrower pays the same dollar amount each month until the mortgage loan is paid off. *Partially amortized, fixed-rate mortgages* also are used for financing home loans. In this case, only a portion of the debt is extinguished by level periodic payments over a relatively short period, say five years, and the unamortized amount is paid in one large lump sum payment -- *a balloon payment*. Alternatively, the loan can be refinanced when it matures.

Monthly Mortgage Payments

The dollar amount of monthly payments depends on the size of the loan, the interest rate, and the maturity. Table 10-5 shows the monthly mortgage payments for a $1,000 mortgage loan with selected annual interest rates and maturities. A close examination of the body of the table reveals two important facts. First, the dollar amount of the monthly mortgage payment increases as the interest rate increases. For example, the monthly mortgage payment for a loan with 10 years to maturity ranges from $11.10 when the interest rate is six percent to $16.76 when the interest rate is 16 percent. Second, the dollar amount of the monthly mortgage payment declines as the maturity of the loan is extended. When the interest rate is six percent, the monthly mortgage payment declines from $11.10 when the maturity is 10 years maturity to $6.00 when the maturity is 30 years.

Table 10-5: MONTHLY PAYMENTS FOR A $1,000 MORTGAGE LOAN

Annual Interest	Years to Maturity				
	10 years	**15 years**	**20 years**	**25 years**	**30 years**
6%	$11.10	$8.44	$7.16	$6.44	$6.00
8	12.13	9.56	8.36	7.72	7.34
10	13.22	10.75	9.65	9.09	8.78
12	14.35	12.00	11.01	10.53	10.29
14	15.35	13.32	12.44	12.04	11.85
16	16.76	14.69	13.92	13.59	13.45

The monthly mortgage payments shown in Table 10-5 can be determined by using equation 10 -1 to solve for the present value of an annuity. By way of illustration, we will compute the monthly mortgage payment for a $1,000 mortgage loan at six percent interest for 10 years.[12] Because we are solving for a monthly payment, the number of payments over the 10 years is 120 (10 years x 12 months per year). Moreover, only one-twelfth of the six percent annual interest rate (0.06/12 = 0.005) is charged each month. The present value of the annuity is the $1,000 mortgage loan in this example. The monthly payment is $11.10.

$$\text{PV of annuity} = PMT\ \frac{1-(1+i)^{-n}}{i} \qquad (10\text{-}1)$$

$$\$1{,}000 = PMT\ \frac{1-(1+0.005)^{120}}{0.005}$$

$$PMT = \$11.10$$

where:

PV = Present value of the annuity.
PMT = Payment per period
i = *Interest rate per period*
n = Number of periods

Maturity

Don't be fooled by low monthly payments. For a given interest rate and maturity, the *total* cost of the loan is higher with longer maturities (smaller monthly payments) than shorter maturities (higher monthly payments). The total cost is determined by multiplying the mortgage payment per $1,000 of loan for each interest rate by the dollar amount of the loan (in thousands) and the number of months. By way of illustration, consider a $100,000 mortgage loan at 12 percent with a maturity of 10 years. The monthly payment is $1,435 ($14.35 x 100 = $1,435) and the total cost over the life of the loan is $172,200 ($1,435 x 120 months = $172,000). If the maturity were 25 years, the monthly payment would be reduced to $1,053, but the total cost would be $315,900, which is $143,900 more than the cost of the shorter-term loan.

Principal and Interest

Let's examine the monthly mortgage payment in greater detail and consider the amount that is allocated to principal and to interest. Table 10-6 shows the breakdown between principal and interest for the first year's payments of a $100,000 loan at 12 percent for 25 years. The striking feature of this table is the disproportionate amount of the monthly payment that is applied to interest payments. Total mortgage payments amounted to $12,636 ($1,053 x 12 = $12,636) during the first twelve months of the loan. Of that amount, $11,361.52 was applied to interest and only $1,274.48 was used to reduce the principal amount of the loan.

The implication of the data presented in Table 10-6 (next page) is that lenders earn most of their interest income during the early years of a mortgage loan. Therefore, all other things being equal, a high turnover of the mortgage loans contributes more interest income to earnings than having mortgage loans remain in their portfolio until they mature.

Table 10-6: MORTGAGE AMORTIZATION $100,000 @ 12% for 25 years, Months 1-12, MONTHLY PAYMENT= $1,053.00

Month	Principal	Interest	Balance
1	$53.00	$1,000.00	$99,000.00
2	63.00	990.00	98,010.00
3	72.90	980.10	97,029.90
4	82.70	970.30	96,059.60
5	92.40	960.60	95,099.00
6	102.01	950.99	94,148.00
7	111.52	941.48	93,206.53
8	120.93	932.07	92,274.46
9	130.26	922.74	91,351.72
10	139.48	913.52	90,438.20
11	148.62	904.38	89,533.82
12	157.66	895.34	88,638.48
Totals	$1,274.48	$11,361.52	

Adjustable Rate Mortgages

An ***adjustable rate mortgage (ARM)*** is one in which the interest rate changes over the life of the loan. The change can result in changes in monthly payments, the term of the loan, or the principal amount.

Index

The idea behind ARMs is to permit lenders to maintain a positive spread between the returns on their mortgage loans (assets) and their cost of borrowed funds (liabilities) when benchmark interest rates change. This is accomplished by linking the mortgage rate to a standard benchmark rate, such as the rate on one-year Constant Maturity Treasury yield or the Federal Reserve's District Cost of Funds.

When an index changes, the lender can 1) make periodic changes in the borrower's monthly payments, 2) keep the monthly payment the same and change the principal amount of the loan, 3) change the maturity of the loan, or 4) any combination of the above. Some mortgage loans have fixed rates for three, five, seven, or 10 years, but might adjust one time, or annually, after that.

The best adjustment, from the lender's point of view, depends on whether interest rates are expected to rise or fall over the life of the mortgage. If they are expected to rise, increased monthly payments will increase the lender's cash flow. If they are expected to fall, the second option listed above will permit the lender to more or less maintain its spread between earning assets and costs of funds. The *adjustment period* may be monthly, annually, or any other time period, and changes are made according to the terms of the contract.

Caps

ARMs have ***caps*** that limit how much the interest rate or monthly payments can change annually or over the term of the loan. For example, the interest rate may change no more than two percentage points annually, nor more than six percentage points over the life of the loan. Alternatively, a $50 payment cap means that the monthly payment cannot increase more than $50 per year.

Margin

Margin is the number of percentage points that the lender adds to the index rate to determine the rate charged on the ARM each adjustment period. The equation for the ARM rate that is charged is:

$$\text{ARM interest rate} = \text{index rate} + \text{margin} \qquad (10\text{-}2)$$

Suppose the index rate is 6 percent and the margin is two percent. The interest rate that will be charged on the ARM is eight percent (6% + 2% = 8%). The margin usually remains constant over the life of the loan. However, the size of the margin can vary from lender to lender.

Rates

Lenders may offer prospective home buyers a lower interest rate or lower payments for the first year of the mortgage loan to induce the buyer to use an ARM. After the discount period, the ARM rate will be adjusted to reflect the current index rate. The lower rate is commonly called a *teaser rate*, because lenders expect it to increase in future years.

Even without teaser rates, the initial interest rates charged on ARMs are lower than the rates charged on fixed rate mortgages. The extent to which they are lower depends on the maturity of the loans, and varies widely, but differences of 100 or more basis points are not uncommon. For example, in November, 2015 the average 5/1-year ARM available in the U.S. was 3.01 percent, while the average 15-year fixed rate mortgage was 3.18 percent and the 30-year rate was 5.46 percent.[13] The 5/1 ARM means that the interest rate is fixed for five years, and then adjusted on an annual bases thereafter. The interest rate for a 30-year fixed rate mortgage is 3.95 percent. A *jumbo mortgage* is one that is larger than the limits set by Fannie Mae and Freddie Mac. In 2016, that amount was $417,500 in the 48 states and $625,500 in Alaska and Hawaii. The amount is adjusted annually.

Shifting the Risk

Lenders shift some of their interest rate risk of holding mortgage loans from themselves to borrowers by using ARMs. However, the lenders may trade reduced interest rate risk for increased default risk and lower income. First, ARMs are riskier than fixed-rate mortgages because they generate less interest income during periods of declining interest. Second, ARMs have higher delinquency and default risk than fixed-rate mortgages. One reason for this may be that loan-to-value ratios are higher for ARMs than for fixed rate mortgages. Another may be that ARMs are used more frequently by younger, first-time buyers. The delinquency rates reported here occurred during a period of falling interest rates. The delinquency rates could get worse if interest rates increase because the borrower's ability to repay the loan might be diminished. This is so because the borrower's disposable income may not increase sufficiently to cover the higher interest payments. These risks are reflected in the relatively narrow spread between the effective rates charged on fixed-rate mortgages and ARMs that was mentioned above.

Lenders can reduce their risk by requiring the borrowers to have *private mortgage insurance* on their loans. Private mortgage insurance is usually required when the down payment, or borrower's equity, is less than 20 percent. Private mortgage insurance companies consider ARMs riskier than their fixed- rate counterparts, and the insurance premiums on ARMs are higher than those on fixed-rate mortgages.

ADDITIONAL TERMS

Assumable Mortgage

Some mortgage loans such as Veterans Administration (VA) backed home loans are assumable, which means that they can be passed on to a new owner if the property is sold. Most mortgage loans are not assumable.

Buydown

A high mortgage interest rate is offset by paying points at the time of closing.

Due-on Sale Clause

Some mortgage loans contain a *due-on-sale clause*, which means that the mortgage loan is not transferable to the new buyer, and the balance of the loan must be paid to the lender when the house is sold. The clause is exercised at the option of the lender. Other loans, however, are assumable, which means that the mortgage loan can be transferred to the buyer, if the buyer meets the lender's credit requirements and pays a fee for the assumption.

Late Charges

Borrowers are required to make their monthly payments by a certain date or pay a late charge. Late charges cover the costs of handling delinquent accounts and add to the lender's fee income.

Mortgage Insurance

Private mortgage insurance for conventional mortgage loans is required by some lenders to reduce the default risk by insuring against loss on a specified percentage of the loan, usually the top 20 to 25 percent.

Points

In addition to paying interest on the borrowed funds, lenders charge both fixed rate and adjustable rate mortgage borrowers additional fees or points, to increase their income, and to cover the costs of originating and closing mortgage loans. A **point** is one percent of the principal amount of a mortgage loan, and points are prepaid interest. One point on a $100,000 mortgage is $1,000. The points usually are paid by the borrower at the time of the closing. They may be deducted from the face amount of the loan or paid as a cash cost. If they are deducted from the face amount of the loan, a one-point closing cost on an $100,000 mortgage loan would result in a disbursement to the borrower of $99,000. Points are charged on government-backed (FHA, VA, FmHA) mortgages when the market rate of interest on conventional mortgage loans exceeds the rate permitted on such mortgages. The points make up the difference in rates between the two types of mortgages.

Points increase the *effective interest rate* of a mortgage loan. The effective interest rate is contract interest rate plus points and other costs amortized over the payback period of the loan. As a rule of thumb, each point (1 percent of the loan amount) increases the interest charge by one-eighth (1/8 or 0.125) of one percent. The 1/8 factor corresponds to a payback period (number of years until the loan is paid off) of about 15 years. For example, suppose that the contract interest rate on a mortgage loan is 13 percent and four points are charged at the closing. The effective interest rate for a 15 year payback is 13.5 percent (13% + 0.125 x 0.04 = 0.135). If the loan is repaid before or after 15 years, the rule of thumb does not apply.

Settlement Charges

Settlement is the formal process by which ownership of real property, evidenced by the title, is transferred from the seller to the buyer. The settlement process for most residential mortgage loans is governed by the ***Real Estate Settlement Procedures Act (RESPA)***. Part of the settlement costs may include fees that enhance the lender's income. Examples of such fees are:

. Loan discounts or points.

. Loan origination fees, which cover the lender's administrative costs.

. Lender's inspection fees to inspect the property.

. Assumption processing fees, which may be charged when the buyer takes on the prior loan from the seller.

. Escrow, funds held to ensure future payment of real estate taxes and insurance. No interest is paid on the funds.

. Settlement or Closing fee, a fee paid to the settlement agent.

. Title search and guarantee.

. Survey of the property.

These settlement fees and others not mentioned here may amount to three percent, or more, of the total amount borrowed.

ALTERNATIVE MORTGAGE INSTRUMENTS

Alternative mortgage instruments is a generic term that cover a smorgasbord of mortgage instruments where the terms of the contract can change or where they differ from the traditional mortgage loan. Listed below are the principal types of alternative mortgage instruments.[14]

Balloon Mortgage

Balloon mortgage loans are relatively short-term loans, such as five years. At the end of that period, the entire amount of the loan comes due and a new loan is negotiated. The initial payments are usually based on a 20- to 30-year amortization. This is similar to the *Canadian rollover mortgage or renegotiable mortgage*, where the maturity is fixed, but the interest payments are renegotiated every three to five years.

Graduated Payment Mortgage

Because of the high cost of housing, many young buyers cannot afford large monthly mortgage payments. GPMs address this problem by making a fixed-rate loan where monthly payments are low at first and then rise over a period of years.

Because the monthly payments on GPMs are so low in the early years, there is *negative amortization* -- the monthly payments are insufficient to pay the interest on the loan. The unpaid interest accrues, and borrowers pay interest on the interest. If the borrowers decide to sell their residence in the early years and it did not appreciate in value, the principal balance on the loan would increase due to negative amortization. In other words, the borrowers would owe more than they originally borrowed on the house, and the sale of the mortgaged property might not provide sufficient funds to pay off the loan.

Growing Equity Mortgage

GEMs are 15-year fully amortized home mortgage loans that provide for successively higher debt service payments over the life of the loan. They are made at a fixed rate and the initial payments are calculated on a 30-year schedule. However, they are paid off more rapidly because there is an annual increase in the monthly payments, all of which goes to reduce the principal balance of the loan. In addition, the interest rate is made below the prevailing rate for 30-year loans. Borrowers who can afford the increased payments can save thousands of dollars in interest payments over the term of the loan.

Interest-Only Mortgages

The interest-only mortgage lets the borrower pay only the interest portion of the loan for some predetermined period, and then the loan payments are adjusted to fully amortize over the remaining life of the loan. For example, a 30-year mortgage loan may be interest only for the first 10 years and then the loan payments are changed to amortize the loan over the remaining 20 years. One of the major advantages from the borrower's point of view is that monthly payments during the interest-only period are lower than they would be for a fully amortized mortgage. On the other side of the coin, the borrower may have little or no equity stake in the real estate.

Shared Appreciation Mortgage

A SAM is a mortgage loan arrangement whereby the borrower agrees to share in the increased value of the property (usually 30 to 50 percent) with the lender in return for a reduction in the fixed-interest rate at the time the loan is made. The increased value of the property is determined at some specified date in the future when the loan can be refinanced or when the property is sold. Sharing a decline in value is not part of the loan agreement.

The Internal Revenue Service considers the bank's portion of the appreciation as contingent or residual interest, which means that it is ordinary income. Thus, the bank has no equity position in the property. Similar arrangements can be applied to other types of mortgage loans, such as large commercial mortgage loans and reverse annuity mortgages. While such arrangements between banks and real estate borrowers are not common, they are used by insurance companies and other long-term lenders making commercial real estate loans.

Reverse Mortgages

The reverse mortgage is designed for senior citizens, 62 and over, who own their houses free and clear and want to increase their incomes by borrowing against the equity in their houses.[15] In this case, the lender pays the property owner a fixed tax-free annuity based on a percentage value of the property. The owner is not required to repay the loan until his or her demise, at which time the loan would be paid from the proceeds of the estate, or until the house is sold. The interest rate on the loan may be adjustable and the loan may have a refinancing option.

Second Mortgage/Home Equity Loan

Many homeowners use a second mortgage when they need funds for business or as a substitute for consumer loans. Other than selling their homes, a home equity loan is the only way homeowners can convert their equity into funds they can spend. As previously noted, equity is the difference between the market value of the property and the mortgage debt, A traditional second mortgage is made in addition to the first mortgage and uses the same property as collateral. Second mortgages usually provide for a fixed dollar amount to be repaid over a specified period of time requiring monthly payment of principal and interest. Second mortgages have a subordinated claim to property in the event of foreclosure.

A *home equity loan* can be a traditional second mortgage, or a revolving line of credit in which case the line of credit has a second mortgage status, but would be the first lien if the borrower has no mortgage debt outstanding when the credit line was established. The line of credit has more a flexible repayment schedule than the traditional second mortgage. Under the home equity line of credit, the borrower with a fixed credit line can write checks up to that amount. In the case of a home equity loan, the loan is a lump sum that is paid off in installments over time. Interest charges on home equity loans may be tax deductible, unlike the interest on consumer loans. Moreover, since home equity loans have the borrower's home as collateral, the interest rate charged on such loans may be less than the interest rate on credit cards. The home equity loan can be for a fixed amount, or it can be line of credit.

TECHNOLOGY

Credit scores have been in use since the 1950s to evaluate automobile and credit card loans, but today they are also widely used to as a credit determinant in real estate lending. The higher the credit score, the lower the interest rate and monthly payment that the borrower will have to pay. On a $200,000 fixed-rate mortgage for 30 years, the monthly cost of a loan at four percent is $954.83, and at five percent it is $1,073.64. Saving one percent point on the interest rate amounts to saving $42,771.60 on the cost of the loan.

Total Cost @ 5% for 30 years	= $386,510.40
Total Cost @ 4% for 30 years	= $343,738.80
Difference	= $42,771.60

The role of technology in mortgage lending is not limited to credit scoring. Automated underwriting technology at the Federal National Mortgage Association (Fannie Mae) has reduced the time it takes to originate a mortgage loan from four weeks to four minutes, and has cut the cost of origination by $800.[17]

There are substantial economies of scale of having large numbers of applications scored in one place. Because this is so, specialized banks -- limited purpose or monoline -- have developed that deal primarily in credit cards, and to a lesser extent in mortgage lending.

COMMERCIAL REAL ESTATE LOANS

Commercial mortgages includes loans for land, construction and real estate development, and loans on commercial properties such as shopping centers, office buildings or warehouses. Commercial real estate loans often are linked to commercial loans. For example, suppose a delivery firm wants to expand and buy new trucks and build a warehouse. The bank would make a term loan to finance the trucks, a construction loan to build the warehouse, and then refinance it with a mortgage loan when it is completed. The mortgage loan on the warehouse cannot be pooled and sold like home mortgage loans. Nevertheless, it is a profitable loan. It is financed on a floating rate basis for seven years, and it is cross collateralized with the trucks.

After land is acquired and financed, *construction loans* call for the bank to make irregular disbursements to the borrower or builder. One method of making the disbursements is based on completion of certain phases of construction. For example, 30 percent may be paid when the foundation is completed, 30 percent when the project is under roof and the plumbing and wiring have been completed, and the remainder when the structure is completed and ready for occupancy. Another method is to pay the builder upon presentment of bills from suppliers and subcontractors as the building progresses. Construction loans have to be flexible to meet the needs of the borrower and the lender.

Construction and development loans are considered "interim" financing. That is, the loans are only in effect during the development and construction phase of the real estate project. When the project is complete, the builder is expected to get "permanent" (i.e., long-term) financing. The permanent financing is usually determined before interim financing is provided.

In the case of home loans, the permanent financing will be provided when the homes are sold and the buyers obtain mortgage loans. In the case of commercial property, long-term financing can be obtained from life insurance companies, Fannie

Mae, Freddie Mac, pension and retirement plans, as well as banks. It is common practice of life insurance companies to share in the equity or profits from large commercial real estate ventures they finance.

During the development and construction phase of development, the land and partially completed structures serve as collateral for the loan. If the developer or builder is unable to complete the project for one reason or another, and defaults on the loan, the lender may take possession of the partially completed structure. Then the lender has to consider finishing the structure or liquidating it. Because there may be considerable risk involved with interim financing, the interest rates charged are relatively high for some borrowers.

Interest rates on construction loans are frequently priced at the prime rate plus one or more percentage points depending on the risk involved. In addition, an origination fee of one to three percent of the amount of the loan might be charged. This fee is charged to cover the cost of the paperwork involved and to increase the effective yield on the loan to the bank.

CONSUMER LENDING

Consumer credit outstanding was $3.5 trillion in September, 2015. Depository institutions (U.S.-chartered commercial banks and the savings institutions) held 41 percent, and the remainder was held by finance companies, credit unions, the federal government (student loans and other loans), pools of securitized loans, and others.[18] ***Consumer credit*** consists of loans to individuals for personal, household, or family consumption. Consumer lending is the heart of retail banking -- banking services provided to individuals and to small business concerns. Services provided to medium- and large-size business concerns and governments is called wholesale banking. Most banks do both retail and *wholesale banking*, although some specialize more than others. Small banks tend to specialize in retail banking because they do not have sufficient assets to do large-scale wholesale lending.

TYPES OF CONSUMER LOANS MADE BY FINANCIAL INSTITUTIONS

Consumer loans differ from commercial and industrial loans and real estate loans (including home equity loans) in several respects. First, except for large motor vehicle loans, automobile and mobile home loans, most consumer loans are for relatively small dollar amounts compared to a home loan. Second, most consumer are not secured by collateral because they are used to buy nondurable goods and services where collateral is not practical. Airline tickets, food, gasoline, and doctor bills are examples of such goods and services. Third, with the same exceptions, many consumer loans are *open-end* (no maturity) lines of credit whereby consumers may increase their loans and pay off the loans over an indefinite period of time. Credit card loans are one example of open-end loans. Loans with definite maturities are called *closed-end loans*. Automobile loans that must be repaid within 48 months are an example of closed-end loans.

Although the major focus of this book is on commercial banks, it should be noted that the Federal government and nonprofit educational institutions make student loans under the Federal Direct Loan Program, the Perkins Loan Program, Federal Family Education Loan Program, and loans purchased under the Ensuring Continued Access to Student Loans Act. In September, 2015, total student loans amounted to $1.303 trillion, which was only slightly less than the $1.383 trillion in consumer credit held by depository institutions.[19]

The greatest risk associated with consumer installment credit is default risk -- the risk that the borrower will not repay the loan. Defaults tend to increase with the size of the loan, with longer-term maturities, and they are inversely related to the value of the collateral relative to the size of the loan. Defaults also tend to increase during recessions when unemployment is high.

Because the market for consumer loans is highly competitive, there is competition on interest rates, amounts lent, fees, and noncredit services provided by issuers of credit issuers. The services offered include liability insurance on automobile rentals, frequent flyer mileage on airlines, travel accident insurance, discounts on long-distance phone calls, extended warranties on items purchased, and other benefits. Some credit cards have a cash back bonus that pays their cardholders a small percentage of the items charged on their credit card. In addition, *affinity card plans* offer bank credit cards to members of a particular organization (such as universities, clubs, and unions). Affinity cards carry the organization's logo, and the organization may benefit financially from the cards being used.

Consumer installment loans can be profitable. One obvious reason is that the rates charged on such loans are relatively high when compared to rates charged on commercial and real estate loans. A credit card loan, for example, may have an interest rate of 15 percent, while the commercial loan may have a 10 percent rate and the real estate loan an eight percent rate. Of course the size, risk, and maturity of each of the loans differs substantially. Another reason for the high profitability is that the much of the processing and monitoring work concerning consumer loans (that is, credit cards) can be automated. The automation provides economies of scale when managing large portfolios of such loans. A large consumer loan portfolio consists of many small loans over a wide geographic area. This allows the lender to diversify its risk of lending. It also means that the few loans that default will not have a major impact on the bank's capital. In contrast, banks that have small loan portfolios of large commercial real estate loans may not have sufficient capital to withstand the failure of a few large commercial real estate loans. As noted earlier in this chapter, failures of real estate loans were one of the primary causes of bank failures in the United States and other major countries.[20] More will be said about income from the credit card business shortly.

Motor Vehicle Loans

Motor vehicle loans include loans for passenger cars, minivans, vans, sport-utility vehicles, and pickup trucks and other light trucks used for personal use. Loans for boats, motorcycles and recreational vehicles (RVs) are not included.

Automobile loans account for 40 percent of the nonrevolving credit that is shown in Table 10-7 . Forty-eight month new car loans issued by commercial banks in 2015 Q2 had an interest rate of 4.31 percent, whereas 24-month personal loans cost 9.69 percent. Thus, the automobile serving as collateral had a beneficial effect on the cost of the personal loan.

The average loan-to-value ratio -- the amount financed for a car loan divided by the current value of the vehicle -- varies among dealers and lenders. It may be as high as 95 percent for new cars and 100 percent for used ones. Although most automobile loans are paid off in installments, some are balloon loans with a repurchase agreement that makes them "look like" a closed-end lease from the customer's point of view. (Closed-end leases will be discussed shortly.) Under a *repurchase agreement*, the bank (or some other third party) will repurchase the automobile at the end of the term of the loan, at the customer's option, for a price that is equal to the balloon obligation. In other words, the bank takes the automobile instead of the final payment. Suppose that the amount borrowed for the loan is $18,000 and the automobile is expected to have a value of $10,000 at the end of the loan period -- which is the same dollar amount as the balloon payment. At the end of the loan period, the customer can:

1) sell or trade in the car and pay off the balance of the loan,

2) keep the car and pay off or refinance the balance,

3) exercise the repurchase agreement instead of paying off the loan.

The repurchase agreement stipulates that the vehicle must be within certain standards for mileage and wear and tear. The mileage limit may be 15,000 miles per year and the buyer is required to provide normal maintenance. The trade-in value of the automobile is usually supported by an insurance policy, thereby reducing the risk to the bank.

The monthly payments on balloon loans are often 300 to 500 basis points higher than the monthly payments on a lease because the lender does not get the tax advantage of the depreciation from the vehicle.

Like mortgage loans, automobile loans can be pooled and sold to investors. Thus, securitization provides lenders with increased liquidity and flexibility in managing their loan portfolios.

Table 10-7: CONSUMER CREDIT OUTSTANDING, SEPTEMBER 2015

Type	Amount ($ billions)	Percentage
Nonrevolving	$2,574.0	74%
Revolving	925.2	26%
Totals	$3,499.2	100%

Source: Federal Reserve statistical release, Consumer Credit, September 2015, G19.

Revolving Consumer Loans

Revolving loans accounted for 26 percent of consumer credit (Table 10-7). *Revolving loans*, or *open-end credit*, are those where the borrower has a line of credit up to a certain amount, and may pay off the loans and credit charges over an indefinite period of time. Revolving loans have no definite maturity. The terms of repayment are flexible and are largely at the discretion of the borrower. Most revolving loans only charge interest on the amount borrowed if the borrower pays less than the full amount of the loan at the end of a grace period of 25-30 days or less. This does not apply to cash advances that can incur finance charges beginning on the transaction date. Bank credit cards, such as VISA and MasterCard, account for most of the revolving loans.

Credit and Debit Cards

A *credit card* is any card, plate, or device that is used from time to time and over and over again to borrow money, or buy goods and services *on credit*.[21] The major credit card businesses are owned by Visa, MasterCard, American Express, and Discover Card.[22] All four credit card companies are publicly traded on the New York Stock Exchange.

A credit card should not be confused with a debit card, or prepayment card. A *debit card* looks like a plastic credit card, and can be used to make purchases, but no credit is extended. The funds are withdrawn or transferred from the cardholder's account to pay for the purchases. Debit and credit cards are the preferred method of payment for in-store sales. More will be said about payments methods in Chapter 17.

In the case of *prepayment (stored-value) cards*, a certain dollar amount is prepaid and deductions are made for each transaction. They are widely used to make telephone calls, and in New York, San Francisco, and Washington in lieu of coins for subway fares. Smart cards, cards containing silicon chips that are capable of storing data and making simple computations, are being used in China, Europe, and the United States.

A study by the Consumer Payments Research Center of the Federal Reserve Bank of Boston found that cash and debit cards accounted for the largest share of consumer payments (31.1 and 26.3 percent, respectively), and the credit card share reached 22.5 percent. Almost half of the consumers had access to mobile payments, and over a third reported using them during the year.[23]

In 2015, the Consumer Payments Research Center reported that:[24]

- Check payments continued to decline while noncheck payments increased.
- Almost half of consumers had access to mobile banking in 2013.
- More than one-third reported that they had used mobile payments in 2013.

Another study that was published by "CreditCards.com" revealed the following:[25]

- Average credit card debt per U.S. adult, excluding zero-balance cards and store cards: $5,232.

- Average debt per credit card that usually carries a balance: $7,494.
- Average debt per credit card that does not usually carry a balance: $1,128.
- Average number of cards held by cardholders - bankcards: 2.24. Average number of cards held by cardholders - store cards: 1.55.
- Average APR charged on credit cards: 12.10 percent as of Q3 2015. Average APR on credit cards that carry a balance: 13.93 percent as of Q3 2015.
- Total U.S. outstanding revolving debt: $925.2 billion as of September, 2015.
- Total U.S. outstanding consumer debt: $3.5 trillion as of September, 2015.
- Charge-off rate on credit card loans from top 100 banks: 2.9 percent as of Q3 2015.

The growth of credit card-related consumer debt is attributable to automation and the fact that credit cards are mass-marketed like a commodity. That is, credit cards are sold as a cluster of services at one price, and there is no personal contact with the issuer. Mass mailings of credit card applications are sent to selected segments of the population based on demographic criteria, such as income and housing. The applications are evaluated by computer programs using credit scoring. Qualified applicants receive cards, and their accounts are monitored by computer programs. The use of automation keeps labor cost at a minimum for the large number of transactions processed. This process allows credit card issuers located in Delaware, North Dakota, or elsewhere to sell their cards anywhere in the United States. Obviously, they must be sold in sufficient quantity to justify the cost of credit card operations.

In addition to the mass marketing of credit cards, individual banks issue them to their customers. There are three types of credit card plans for banks. The first type utilizes a single principal bank to issue the credit card, maintain accounts, bill and collect credit, and assume most of the other functions associated with credit cards.

In the second type, one bank acts as a limited agent for the principal bank. The principal bank issues the card, carries the bulk of the credit, and performs the functions described in the first plan. The functions of the agent bank are to establish merchant accounts and accept merchant sales drafts; it receives a commission on the business it generates without incurring costs of a credit card operation. The limited agent bank may have its own name and logo on the card. Cardholders assume that the card is issued and managed by that bank, which is not the case.

In the third plan, a bank affiliates with one of the major *travel and entertainment card* (T & E) plans such as American Express. A travel and entertainment card is a credit card; but cardholders must pay the amount owed when billed. They do not have the option of making small payments over time. However, American Express also issues the "Optima" card and other credit cards which are credit cards in the true sense of the word.

All bank credit cards have the following common features:

1. The credit card holder has a prearranged line of credit with a bank that is-

sues credit cards. Credit is extended when the credit card holder buys something and signs (or approves) a sales draft at a participating retail outlet. The retail merchant presents the sales draft to its bank for payment in full, less a *merchant discount* that is based on:

a) the retail outlet's volume of credit card trade, or

b) the average size of each credit card sale, or

c) the amount of compensating balances kept at the bank, or

d) some combination of the above factors.

The merchant discounts range from nothing to six percent or more. Some merchants do not accept certain credit cards that have high merchant discounts. Thus, not all credit cards are equal in the eyes of the merchants.

The merchant's bank will get part of the merchant discount for handling the transaction and routing it to the major credit card company (such as VISA) that issued the card. The credit card company determines the amount that the card-issuing bank owes. The card-issuing bank pays the credit card company, and the credit card company pays the merchant bank. Finally, the card-issuing bank presents the sales draft to the credit card holder for payment.

2. Most banks allow the credit card holder to pay for the draft in full within a grace period (say 25 days from the billing date), and not be charged interest on the outstanding balance -- or pay some minimum amount each month on an installment basis. However, some banks have no grace period, and they state in their contracts, "There is no period during which credit extended can be repaid without incurring a finance charge." Banks depend on interest income earned on these credit balances as the major source of income from their credit card operations.

Banks also earn *fee income* from credit cards. For example, a bank may charge an annual fee (say $50) for the privilege of having a credit card. However, for competitive reasons, some banks charge no annual fees.

Fees are also charged for other account activities such as:

- Cash advances, three percent of the cash advance or a minimum of $3 and no maximum amount;
- Late payments, the issuer will add $20 to the purchase balance for each billing period the borrower fails to make the minimum payment due;
- Exceeding the credit line, the issuer will add $20 to the purchase balance for each billing period the balance exceeds the line of credit;
- Returned check fees when payments are not honored, $20.
- Finally, banks earn fees for the sale of products, vacation packages, magazine subscriptions, and insurance in connection with their credit cards.

3. The plastic credit card itself serves special purposes. First, it identifies the customer to the merchant. Some Citibank credit cards have the customer's picture on the card in order to enhance its security.

Chip-bearing credit cards are the latest cybersecurity measure to stop in-store point-of-sale fraud. The chip is a microprocessor that contains information about the credit card holder that makes it more difficult to counterfeit. The cards may also require the user to have a Personal Identification Number (PIN), or a signature.[26] The chip and pin technology, called EMV which stands for Europay, MasterCard and Visa, was created by major U.S. credit card issuers MasterCard, Visa, Discover and American Express to enhance credit card security. Cards containing chips are known as "EMV" cards, as well as "chip-and-signature," "chip-and-pin," or "smart" cards." After an Oct. 1, 2015, the liability for card-present fraud shifted to whichever party was the least EMV-compliant in a fraudulent transaction deadline.[27]

According to the Federal Bureau of Investigation (FBI), "Although EMV cards provide greater security than traditional magnetic strip cards, an EMV chip does not stop lost and stolen cards from being used in stores, or for online or telephone purchases when the chip is not physically provided to the merchant (referred to as a card-not-present transaction). Additionally, the data on the magnetic strip of an EMV card can still be stolen if the merchant has not upgraded to an EMV terminal and it becomes infected with data-capturing malware. Consumers are urged to use the EMV feature of their new card wherever merchants accept it to limit the exposure of their sensitive payment data." [28]

About half of credit card debt outstanding is *convenience* use, in which the cardholder uses the credit card instead of cash or checks and pays the amount owed in full when billed, thereby avoiding interest charges.[29] Therefore, the amount of consumer credit shown in Table 10-7 is overstated.

Mobile Home Loans

Because of their origins as trailers being pulled behind cars, mobile home loans are included in consumer credit. Mobile home loans are direct and indirect loans made to individuals to purchase mobile homes. A mobile (manufactured) home is a moveable dwelling unit, 10 feet or more wide and 35 feet or more in length that can be moved on its own chassis. They are not considered the same as travel trailers, motor homes, or modular housing. In the case of indirect loans, banks may require the dealers from whom they purchased loans to stand behind them in the event of default. This can be accomplished by the dealer keeping a reserve account at the bank until the loan is repaid. Additional protection for the lender can be obtained in the form of insurance. Mobile home loans can be guaranteed by the FHA or VA. Mobile (manufactured) home loans that are backed by FHA/VA qualify as collateral in GNMA mortgage-backed securities. In addition, the Department of Housing and Urban Development (HUD) insures approved lenders against losses on manufactured home loans, lots and parks for manufactured homes, made in accordance with the National Housing Act (Titles, I, II, and Section 207). The loan must be for the purchase of a manufactured home to be used as the principal single-family residence, or for manufactured home lots and parks. The manufactured homes must meet certain design, construction, and performance standards.

MANAGEMENT OF RISK

History of Consumer Credit in the United States

During the eighteenth century and first half of the nineteenth century, the principal non-bank agencies that extended credit were small merchants, physicians, and pawnbrokers. The Industrial Revolution brought about changes in credit demands and institutions. Industrialization made more goods available for consumers and created a class of wage earners, which was bolstered by large-scale immigration into the United States. The credit needs of the industrial wage earners differed from the credit needs of farmers, who generally borrowed on "open-book" accounts (without formal agreements) and paid off their debts with the crops that were sold. In contrast, industrial wage earners received steady incomes and could pay their debts on a regular basis throughout the year. Accordingly, the concept of installment credit evolved, since many workers received low wages and required credit to raise their standard of living above substance levels.

These credit needs were partially satisfied by small-loan companies that concentrated on making personal loans secured by personal property and wage assignments. Those who could not obtain credit from legitimate small-loan companies borrowed from loan sharks, individuals who charged excessive rates of interest -- sometimes in excess of 200 percent -- and sometimes required the borrower's physical well-being as collateral. Today such interest rates are a violation of the federal extortion and credit statutes (Title 18, U.S.C. 891-896).

By the turn of the twentieth century, installment credit and loan sharks were widespread throughout the United States. The first legislation concerning installment credit and the abuses of loan sharks was enacted in Massachusetts in 1911. This law permitted lenders to make loans of up $300 and charge an interest rate of 42 percent per year. Other states enacted similar legislation. A direct result of the effort to curb and regulate loan sharks was the development of consumer finance companies.

After World War I, new types of credit institutions developed. The availability of consumer durables such as automobiles and washing machines expanded the demand for consumer credit. Sales finance companies, which buy consumer installment credit contracts from retail dealers and provide wholesale financing to those dealers, grew from this demand. Commercial banks were the next institution to enter the consumer loan field. The National City Bank of New York opened the first personal loan department in 1928. Revolving retail credit appeared when John Wanamaker, a large Philadelphia department store, introduced it in 1938. The next major innovation was the development of the credit card. In 1951, Franklin National Bank of New York issued the first bank credit card. This plastic money was the forerunner of the credit cards issued by banks, retailers, oil companies, and others.

Noninstallment Loans

Commercial banks also make *noninstallment consumer loans*. These are loans that are scheduled to be repaid in a lump sum. The largest component of the noninstallment loans are single payment loans that are used to finance the purchase of one home while another home is being sold. Loans used for this purpose are called bridge loans. Other noninstallment loans are used to finance investments and for other purposes.

LEASES

Leasing is an alternative method of financing consumer durables such as automobiles, trucks, airplanes, and boats. In the case of cars, low monthly costs and getting a new car every few years are two reasons for their popularity.

Under a lease, the bank owns the automobile and "rents" it to the customer.[30] The lease may be *open-end,* in which case the bank is responsible for selling the automobile at the end of the lease period. If the amount received is less than a previously agreed upon residual value, the customer pays the difference -- a balloon payment. Suppose that an automobile is leased under a three-year open-end lease. The lessor estimates that the car will be worth $15,000 after three years of normal wear. If the auto is returned in a condition that reduces its value to $12,000, the lessee may owe a balloon payment of $3,000. The value can be determined by an independent appraiser, but the lessee must pay the appraisal fee. The balloon payments are usually no more than three times the usual monthly payment. If the monthly payment is $600, the balloon payment would not be more than $1,800, unless there was unusual wear and tear on the auto. If the appraised value is more than the residual value, the customer receives the difference.

Under a *closed-end lease,* the bank assumes the risk of the market value being less than the residual value of the automobile. National banks must have insurance on the residual on closed-end leases. The monthly payments for closed-end leases are higher than those for open-end leases because the bank has a greater risk, but there is no balloon payment. However, since the bank owns the automobile and gets the tax benefit (depreciation), the monthly payments may be less than that of a loan of an equivalent amount to buy the automobile outright.

Under the Consumer Leasing Act of 1976 (and Federal Reserve Regulation M), consumer leases must meet the following criteria:

- A lease of personal (not real) property
- The term of the lease must exceed four months
- It must be made to a natural person (not a corporation)
- The lease must be for personal, family or household purposes. It covers leases for cars, furniture, and appliances, but does not cover daily car rentals or apartment leases.

FINANCE CHARGES

The Truth in Lending Act (Title I of the Consumer Protection Act of 1968), which is implemented Federal Reserve Regulation Z, requires lenders of consumer loans to provide borrowers with written information about finance charges and annual percentage rates (APR), before they sign a loan agreement, so that may compare credit costs. The extent to which consumers use the information to make intelligent decisions is not clear. Few consumers have the time or the knowledge to compare the nuances of the costs of financing. As we will see shortly, costs are not always what they appear to be on the surface.

The finance charge is the total dollar amount paid for the use of credit. It is the difference between the amount repaid and the amount borrowed. The finance charge includes interest, service charges, and other fees that are charged the borrower as a condition of or incident to the extension of credit. For example, a customer borrows $1,000 for one year and pays $80 in interest, a $10 service charge, and a $10 origination fee, The finance charge is $100.

Four methods of assessing finance charges on revolving credits are presented here. As previously mentioned, some methods of computing charges have a higher profit potential for lenders than others. To illustrate the differences in potential profits, or costs to consumer, consider the following transactions.

On June 5, Andrew Earl receives a statement with the total amount due of $100 for the billing period ending May 31. There will be no finance charge if the balance is paid by June 30. On June 1, Andrew made a $100 purchase that will appear on his next monthly statement. On June 15, he made a $20 payment on the loan. The interest rate charged on the unpaid balance is 1.5 percent monthly (18 percent annually).

Adjusted Balance Method

Using this method, the finance charge is applied against the amount that has been billed less any payments made prior to the due date. Purchases are not counted. The amount billed in this example is $100 and the payment was $20, resulting in $80. The finance charge is 1.5 percent times $80, which amounts to $1.20.

Previous Balance Method

According to this method, the finance charge is applied against the original amount billed and no consideration is given to the $20 payment. The finance charge is 1.5 percent times $100, which amounts to $1.50.

Average Daily Balance Method Excluding Current Transactions

According to this method, the finance charge is based on the average daily balance outstanding over the current 30-day period, but does not include current transactions. The average daily balance is $90 ($100 for 15 days and $80 for 15 days), such that the finance charge is $1.35 ($90 x 1.5% = $1.35).

Average Daily Balance Method Including Current Transactions

According to this method, the finance charge is based on the average daily balance outstanding during the current 30-day period, including new purchases made during that time. The average daily balance is $200 for the first 15 days ($100 from April and $100 purchased on June 1) and the $180 for the last 15 days ($200 less $20 = $180), so the average balance for the entire period is $190. The finance charge is 1.5 percent times $190, which amounts to $2.85.

If a borrower skips a payment on a month's purchases, or makes a partial payment, they may lose the "grace period." The grace period is the time in which the bill can be paid in full to avoid interest on the most recent month's charges. The reason is that many card issuers calculate interest on the account's average daily balance retroactive to the first purchase. The average daily balance including the current transactions method illustrates the impact this has on finance charges. Some banks which promote their low interest rates use the most expensive methods of computing their finance charges.

In review, by using different methods for determining the unpaid balance, finance charges on the same transaction based on an 18 percent annual interest rate (1.5 percent monthly) ranged from a low of $1.20 to a high of $2.85! All of these methods for determining unpaid balances are widely used.

Methods	Finance Charge
Adjusted balance	$ 1.20
Previous balance	$ 1.50
Average daily balance excluding current transactions	$ 1.35
Average daily balance including current transactions	$ 2.85

The Truth in Lending Act does not tell creditors how to calculate the finance charges, it only requires that they inform borrowers of the methods that are used and provide them with information about the annual percentage rate.

ANNUAL PERCENTAGE RATE

Single Payment, End of Period

The ***annual percentage rate (APR)*** is the percentage cost of credit on an annual basis. The APR can be used to compare credit costs of loans of various sizes and maturities. The APR is the annualized internal rate of return (IRR) on the loan. Readers who are familiar with financial management will recognize that the IRR is that rate of interest that equates the present value of the periodic payments with the principal amount of the loan.

The APR for a given series of payments can be calculated easily by calculators programmed to calculate the IRR. For textbook exercises, we recommend such calculators. Most banks use computer programs or tables to compute the APR. Finally, the IRR can be determined by using the following equation when the payments are the same in each period:

$$P = \sum_{t=1}^{n} PMT[1/(1+i)^t] \qquad (10\text{-}3)$$

P = original principal amount ($), or the amount received by the borrower in the case of discount loan rate

PMT = periodic payments ($)

i = periodic interest rate (%)

n = number of periodic payments (number)

Other equations (methods) also can be used to calculate APRs.[34] The Federal Reserve allows some flexibility in how to compute APRs. The APRs are considered acceptable as long as they are within one-eighth of one percent of one of the two "actual APRs" computed by the Federal Reserve. The Federal Reserve uses the internal rate of return (actuarial method) and/or the U.S. Rule method (not described here) to compute the "actual APR." The methods give slightly different results.

By way of illustration of the use of the IRR to compute APRs, assume that a customer wants to borrow $1,000 for one year at 10 percent. The bank can offer the customer monthly amortization, an add-on rate, or a discount rate. The APRs for each method are substantially different.

Monthly Amortization

Amortization refers to the gradual repayment of debt over time. In this example, the loan is amortized by 12 monthly payments of $87.92 each. Using equation (10-3), we determine that the IRR/periodic rate is

$$P = \sum_{t=1}^{n} PMT[1/(1 + i)^t]$$

$$\$1{,}000 = \sum_{t=1}^{12} \$87.92\, [1/(1+i)^t]$$

$$i = 0.83407$$

$$APR = 0.83407 \times 12 = 10.01\%$$

Because the periodic rate is monthly, the nominal annual rate is determined by multiplying the periodic rate by 12 to get the percentage. Accordingly, the APR in this example is 10.01 percent (12 x 0.83407 = 10.01%).

Add-on Loan Rate

The term "add-on" means that the finance charge is added on to the amount borrowed. Consider a $1,000 loan for one year at 10 percent add-on interest. For purposes of illustration, the finance charge FC is determined by multiplying the amount borrowed P by the add-on interest rate expressed as a decimal R, times the life of the loan in years T. The FC may include fees and charges not considered in these examples. In this example, one year is used, so T = 1. If the loan had been for 15 months, T would be equal to 1.25; if it were for 18 months, T would be equal to 1.5, and so on.

$$FC = P \times R \times T \tag{10-4}$$

$$= \$1{,}000 \times .10 \times 1$$

$$= \$100$$

The $100 finance charge is added on to the amount borrowed, so that the total amount owed is $1,100. The monthly payments PMT are determined by dividing the total amount owed, which is principal amount plus the finance charge, by the number of payments n.

$$PMT = (P + FC)/n \quad (10\text{-}5)$$
$$= (\$1{,}000 + \$100)/12 = \$91.67$$

Using equation (10-3), the APR is 17.98 percent.

$$P = \sum_{t=1}^{n} PMT[1/(1 + i)^t]$$

$$\$1{,}000 = \sum_{t=1}^{12} \$91.67\,[1/(1+i)^t]$$

$$i = 1.498$$

$$APR = 1.498 \times 12 = 17.98\%$$

Discount Loan Rate

In a discount loan, the creditor deducts the finance charge from the principal amount of the loan and the borrower receives the difference. Consider a $1,000 loan discounted at 10 percent. The creditor deducts the $100 finance charge from the $1,000 principal amount and the borrower receives $900. Nevertheless, the borrower must repay $1,000 in 12 monthly payments of $83.33 ($1,000/12 = $83.33). When calculating the APR on discount loans, P the amount received by the borrower ($900) is set equal to the discounted monthly payments. The APR for the discount loan is 19.90%.

$$P = \sum_{t=1}^{n} PMT[1/(1 + i)^t]$$

$$\$900 = \sum_{t=1}^{12} \$83.33\,[1/(1+i)^t]$$

$$i = 1.6587$$

$$APR = 1.6587 \times 12 = 19.90\%$$

In summary, the APRs are:

Monthly amortization	10.01%
Add-on rate	17.98%
Discount rate	19.90%

From the bank's point of view, the discount method produces the highest returns followed by the add-on method.

As mentioned previously, the APR can be used to compare the cost of credit. The concept of cost of credit is multidimensional, and it includes the amount of the monthly payments, the amount of the down payment, method of payment (i.e., cash, payroll deduction, etc.), and other factors. By way of illustration, consider loans A and B, each for $6,000, and each having an APR of 14 percent. Loan A has a maturity of three years and loan B has a maturity of four years. Because loan B has a longer maturity, the monthly payments are lower than those of loan A. However, the total finance charge and total payments of loan B are higher than those of loan A. Although the finance charges are lower with loan A, consumers who prefer lower monthly payments may choose loan B.

	APR %	Maturity Years	Monthly Payments	Finance Charge	Total Payments
Loan A	14	3	$205.07	$1,382.52	$7,382.52
Loan B	14	4	163.96	$1,870.08	$7,870.08

Real Estate and Consumer Credit Regulation

Federal laws prescribe certain terms and conditions under which lenders can make residential real estate and consumer loans. Highlights of selected laws are presented here. The legislation and regulations impose substantial costs on lenders. They must maintain detailed records of their actions and submit to examinations to determine if they are complying with the legislation and relevant regulations. A recent study revealed that the costs of complying with all bank regulations is about 12-13 percent of banks' noninterest expense.[34]

Community Reinvestment Act (CRA)

The ***Community Reinvestment Act*** is directed at federally regulated lenders that take deposits and extend credit. Such institutions are required to serve the needs and convenience of their respective communities. The intent of the legislation is to facilitate the availability of mortgage loans and other types of loans to all qualified applicants, without regard to their race, nationality, or sex.

Equal Credit Opportunity Act (ECOA) and the Fair Housing Act

The ***Equal Credit Opportunity Act*** (Federal Reserve Regulation B) and ***Fair Housing Act*** collectively prohibit lenders from discriminating against borrowers on the basis of age (provided that the applicant has the capacity to contract), color, family status (having children under age 18), handicap, marital status, national origin, race, receipt of public assistance funds, religion, sex, or the exercise of any right under the Consumer Protection Act.

Fair Credit Billing Act

If a customer believes that there is an error on a bill, he or she must contact the lender, *in writing*, within 60 days after the first bill in which the error appears is sent. A telephone call to the lender does not preserve the customer's rights. The amount in dispute, including finance charges, accrues until the issue is resolved. The lender has 90 days to correct the error or explain why the bill is correct.

Home Mortgage Disclosure Act

The HMDA (Federal Reserve Regulation C), enacted by Congress in 1975 and amendments, were intended to make available to the public information concerning the extent to which financial institutions are serving the housing credit needs of their communities. HMDA data are also used by government officials to assess public sector investments in housing, and to identify possible discriminatory lending patterns.

Real Estate Settlement Procedures Act (RESPA)

Settlement is the process by which the ownership of real estate, which is represented by the title, passes from the seller to the buyer. The intent of RESPA is to provide buyers and sellers with information about the settlement process. RESPA covers most residential real estate loans including lots for houses or mobile homes. When a buyer applies in writing for a loan covered by RESPA, the lender must send the borrower "good faith estimates" of the settlements costs within three business days of the application, and a booklet called *Settlement Costs – a HUD Guide*, describing the settlement and charges. One day before settlement, the borrower has the right to see the completed Uniform Settlement Statement that will be used.

Truth in Lending Act

The purpose of the Truth in Lending Act (Federal Reserve Regulation Z) is for creditors to disclose to individual consumers who are borrowers (not business borrowers) the amount of the finance charge and the annual interest rate (APR) they are paying to facilitate the comparison of finance charges from different sources of credit. In addition, credit card issuers are required to disclose, in written applications or their telephone solicitations, fees, grace period and the method of calculating balances. Finance charges and APR were discussed earlier in this chapter. The law requires that the disclosures be clear and conspicuous, grouped together, and segregated from other contractual matters to make it easier for consumers to understand.

If Credit is Denied

Credit denial must be based on the creditworthiness of the applicant. If credit is denied, the creditor must notify the applicant within 30 days. The notification must be in writing and explain the reasons for the denial, or state that the applicant has the right to ask for an explanation if one is not provided. Frequently, the denial is based on information received from a *credit bureau* -- a firm that provides credit information for a fee to creditors. Credit bureaus obtain their information from creditors, and sometimes errors are made or information is out of date. For example, bankruptcies must be removed from credit histories after 10 years, and suits, judgments, tax liens, and arrest records must be removed after seven years.

Under the *Fair Credit Reporting Act*, applicants who have had credit denied based on information from a credit bureau have the right to examine the credit file and correct errors or mistakes in it. If the request is made within 30 days of the refusal, the credit bureau may not charge a fee for providing the information. The credit bureau is required to remove any errors that the creditor who supplied the information admits are there. If a disagreement still remains, the applicant can include a short statement in the file with their side of the story. However, removal of incorrect information from one credit bureau does not change the files of the other credit bureaus.

Under the *Fair and Accurate Credit Transactions Act of 2003* (the Fact Act), everyone can obtain a free credit report once a year from the three major credit bureaus, Exquifax Inc., Experian, and Transunion. It also provides for another free credit report for victims of identity theft.

Privacy Issues

Banks collect information about their customers from the customers themselves, from third parties such as credit reporting agencies, and from the customer's transactions with the bank and its affiliates.

Under the *USA Patriot Act* (Section 326), financial institutions are required to implement reasonable procedures to verify the identity of their customers, maintain information about that person, and determine if that person is on any list of known or suspected terrorists or terrorist organizations. This is part of an effort to prevent money laundering, terrorist financing, identity theft, and other forms of fraud.

The ***Gramm-Leach-Bliley Act of 1999*** gives consumers of financial institutions the right to "opt out" of sharing some of their personal financial information with unrelated third parties. Examples of personal private information include your Social Security number, assets, income, and your transactions history and account balances.

SUMMARY

Real estate and consumer lending are the heart of retail banking. Mortgage lending for residences of one to four members accounts for about 76 percent of the mortgage debt outstanding and revolving credit accounts for 41 percent of consumer credit. Changes in technology are having a major influence in the conduct of retail banking. The use of credit scoring to make lending decisions and securitization to manage portfolios are changing the way that lenders operate. The economies of scale in both credit scoring and securitization favor both increased concentration (size) of lenders, and increased specialization. In addition, an increasing number of lenders are using the internet to sell their products, thereby expanding the geographic markets in which they operate from local markets to global markets.

This chapter examined some of the details of real estate and consumer lending. One significant difference between commercial and industrial loans that were examined in the previous chapter, and real estate and consumer loans is that the latter are becoming standardized commodity products that can be securitized. Nevertheless, there are still a very large number of real estate and consumer loans that are not securitized and remain on the lender's books.

Finally, retail banking is more heavily regulated than wholesale banking in order to help consumers make informed credit decisions, to protect their financial interests, and to meet social goals mandated in the CRA and other acts.

Key Terms

Alternative mortgage instruments (Balloon mortgage, Home equity loan, etc.)
Adjustable rate mortgage loans (ARMs)
Annual percentage rate (APR)
Asset-backed securities
Caps
Commercial real estate loans
Community Reinvestment Act (CRA)
Consumer credit
Conventional mortgages
Credit cards
Credit enhanced
Debit cards
Down payment
Equal Credit Opportunity Act (ECOA)
Equity
Fair and Accurate Credit Transactions Act (Fact Act)
Fair Credit Reporting Act
Fair Housing Act

Federal Home Loan Banks
Fee income
Finance charges
Fixed rate mortgage loan
Government backed mortgages (insured mortgages)
Gramm-Leach-Bliley Act
Home Mortgage Disclosure Act (HMDA)
Jumbo mortgage
Laws pertaining to real estate and consumer credit
Leases
Margin
Mortgage (Commercial, multi-family, residential)
Nonrevolving consumer loans
Origination of the mortgage
Overcollateralize
Points
Private mortgage insurance
Residential mortgage loans
Real Estate Settlement Procedures Act (RESPA)
Reverse mortgages
Revolving consumer loans
Secondary mortgage market
Securitization
Servicer (of a mortgage loan)
Settlement
True sale
Truth in Lending Act
USA Patriot Act

QUESTIONS

10.1 Is real estate good or bad collateral?

10.2 What are the two basic types of 1-4 family residential mortgage loans. Which is more widely used? Why?

10.3 What is a balloon loan?

10.4 What factors affect monthly payments on a residential mortgage loan? Explain the effect of each factor.

10.5 Why do lenders charge points on mortgage loans?

10.6 Explain the following terms: settlement charges and RESPA; buydown; due-on-sale clause.

10.7 What are the advantages and disadvantages of an ARM from the lender's point of view?

10.8 Briefly distinguish between the following types of loans: graduated payment mortgages, shared appreciation mortgages, reverse annuity mortgages, home equity loan.

10.9 In what respects are the Home Mortgage Disclosure Act and the Community Reinvestment Act similar?

10.10 Describe the secondary mortgage market.

10.11 Explain the meaning of the term "consumer installment credit."

10.12 Distinguish between open- and closed-end consumer loans. Give an example of each

Explain what is meant by nonprice competition in credit cards.

What is the difference between a debt card, a credit card, and prepayment card?

10.15 Distinguish between open- and closed-end leases for automobiles.

10.16 Explain the intent of the Truth in Lending Act.

10.17 What is the difference between a finance charge on a loan and the APR?

10.18 Which method produces the highest APR on a $50,000 loan, an add-on rate or a discount loan rate? Why?

10.19 What method of computing interest charges on credit cards produces the largest finance charges? Explain why.

10.20 What is the purpose of CRA?

10.21 The Truth in Lending Act protects consumers against unauthorized use of their credit cards, if the loss or theft is reported. What happens if the loss or theft is not reported?

PROBLEMS

10.1 Compute the finance charges on the following transaction due at the end of the billing period using: 1) adjusted balance method, 2) previous balance method, 3) average daily balance method excluding current transactions, and 4) average daily balance method including current transactions. On August 31, the amount outstanding from the previous billing period is $500. No interest, which is computed at 18 percent annually, is due if the bill is paid by September 30. On September 15, an additional charge of $500 is made. On September 20, a 100 dollar payment is made.

10.2 Compute the APRs for the following loans (next page). Which yield the highest return on investment to the lender?

	Principal	Maturity	Periodic Payment
1.	$1,000	12 months	$88.85
2.	$5,000	15 months	$360.62
3.	$10,000	18 months	$609.82

10.3 What is the APR on a) 9.33 percent, 18 month, $1,000 add-on loan; b) a 7.95 percent, 15 month, $1,000 add-on loan.

10.4 What is the APR on a) 9.33 percent, 18 month, $1,000 discount loan; b) a 7.95 percent, 15 month, $1,000 discount loan.

10.5 An advertisement for a $25,000 installment loan provided the following information:

Loan amount: $25,000	Loan Payments:
36 months	$825
48 months	$653
60 months	$550
72 months	$483
84 months	$435

a. Compute the APR.
b. What is the total interest payment for each of the maturities?
c. What is the interest cost as a percent of the loan amount for each maturity? Divide the total interest payment by $25,000.
d. Which maturity would you recommend if you were 1) a borrower, and 2) a lender?

CASE: WHAT'S IT GOING TO COST?

Bloch Realty Inc. is headquartered in the city where you are now. It owns and manages commercial real estate properties in the surrounding states. The company specializes in large-size multi-family units. Germaine Bloch, the principal stockholder in Bloch Realty, has decided to expand the scope of the firm's operations and is considering some properties in New York City. Germaine knows that the cost of living in New York City is different from her current location, but she does not know what it's going to cost to live and operate there. She asks you to prepare a brief report comparing some of the costs of living in your city with those in New York City. Give her some comparative data, especially with respect to mortgage rates, credit card rates, and other costs. She suggests the following internet sites that may be helpful in writing your report:

- For information about credit cards, mortgage rates, home equity loans, etc., see the State of New York Banking Department's website, and look at "Consumer Services," www.banking.state.ny.us. Also see the Bank Rate Monitor and CNNfn: http://www.cnnfn.com.
- The U.S. Department of Housing and Urban Development, http://www.hud.gov.
- Mortgage surveys and data from the Federal Home Loan Mortgage Corporation (Freddie Mac) at http://www.freddiemac.com, and the Federal National Mortgage Association (Fannie Mae) at http://www.fanniemae.com.
- Bureau of the Census, for economic surveys and other data, http://www.census.gov

ENDNOTES

1. Freddie Mac, Office of the Chief Economist, "Insight & Outlook," October 26, 2015.
2. Consumer Financial Protection Bureau, Understanding loan options/owning-a-home/loan options/conventional-loans/.
3. FEDERAL HOME LOAN BANKS Combined Financial Report for the Quarterly Period Ended September 30, 2015, Table 41, page 52. http://www.fhlb-of.com/ofweb_userWeb/resources/2015Q3CFR.pdf.
4. Freddie Mac, Office of the Chief Economist, "Insight & Outlook," October 26, 2015.
5. National Association of Realtors, "Sales Price of Existing Single Family Homes," October 2015, preliminary data.

6. "What is a jumbo loan?" Consumer Financial Protection Bureau, 1/22/14. "What is a Qualified Mortgage?" Consumer Financial Protection Bureau, 12/30/13, "Mortgage Rules," Consumer Financial Protection Bureau, Beginning January 2014.
7. Joe Light, "Mortgage Limit to Pinch Home Buyers," The Wall Street Journal, November 27, 2015, A2.
8. Mark J. Perry, "Today's new homes are 1,000 square feet larger than in 1973, and average living space per person had doubled," American Enterprise Institute, June 26, 2015.
9. Office of the Comptroller of the Currency, Comptroller's Handbook, "Residential Real Estate Lending" June 2015, 50.
10. FDIC, Supervisory Insights - From the Examiner's Desk. Examiners Report on Commercial Real Estate Underwriting Practices, Last Updated, 12/14/06. https://www.fdic.gov/regulations/examinations/supervisory/insights/siwin06/examiners_desk.html
11. For additional discussion of this point, see B. W. Ambose and C. A. Capone, Jr., "Cost-Benefit Analysis of Single Family Foreclosure Alternatives," Journal of Real Estate Finance and Economics, 13, November 1996, 105-120.
12. To solve the problem on a financial calculator, such as a Hewlett-Packard 12C, clear the calculator then enter n = 10 years (multiplied by 12 monthly payments, blue key), i = 6 (divided by 12 monthly payments, blue key), PV = $1,000, (also press END button, blue key) and then press PMT. The monthly payment PMT = - $11.10. Each model and brand of calculators has unique features. Your operator's manual should explain how to compute loan payments for amortized loans.
13. Freddie Mac, "Mortgage Rates Survey," 11/25/15, http://www.freddiemac.com/pmms/
14. For additional information, see the New York State Banking Department web site: http://www.banking.state.ny.us/index.htm, and Bankrate: http://www.bankrate.com.
15. For additional information about reverse mortgages, see the website for the National Reverse Mortgage Lenders Association, www.reversemortgage.com.
16.The Federal Reserve System's Mortgage Credit Partnership Credit Scoring Committee collected and published information about credit scoring in real estate. See: "Perspectives on Credit Scoring and Fair Mortgage Lending," Profitwise, Federal Reserve Bank of Chicago, Fall 2000.
17. Johnson, J. A., "Remarks by James A. Johnson, Chairman and Chief Executive Officer, Fannie Mae, before the New York Society of Security Analysts, New York, New York, October 28, 1998.
18. "Consumer Credit," Federal Reserve Statistical Release, G. 19, Consumer Credit Outstanding., September 2015.
19. Ibid.
20. Benton E. Gup, Bank Failures in the Major Trading Countries of the Word: Causes and Remedies. Westport CT., Quorum Books, 1998.
21. Credit cards are defined by Regulation Z, and in 12 CFR 226.2 (a)(15).
22. For information about these cards, see www.visa.com; www.mastercard.us/en-us.html; www.americanexpress.com; and www.discover.com.
23. Scott Schuh and Joanna Stavins, "The Survey of Consumer Payment Choice: Summary Results, No. 15-04, Federal Reserve Bank of Boston, Updated July 27, 2015.
24. Ibid. updated September 2015.
25. CreditCards.Com. http://www.creditcards.com/credit-card-news/credit-card-industry-facts-personal-debt-statistics-1276.php, accessed 12/1/15.
26. Gilliam E. Duvall, "Chip-Bearing Credit Cards Present New Vulnerabilities," SIGNAL, December 1, 2015. http://www.afcea.org/content/?q=Article-chip-bearing-credit-cards-present-new-vulnerabilities
27. Sienna Kossman, "8 FAQs about EMV credit cards," CreditCards.com, updated October 6, 2015, http://www.creditcards.com/credit-card-news/emv-faq-chip-cards-answers-1264.php
28. Federal Bureau of Investigation, Public Service Announcement, "New Microchip-enabled Credit Cards May Still Be Vulnerable to Exploitation By Fraudsters," Alert Number I-100815(REVISED)-PSA, October 13, 2015.
29. U.S. Department of Commerce, Statistical Abstract of the United States 1998, Table 823. The latest data are for 1995.
30. When a customer leases a car, he or she pays a monthly rental use tax. This is in lieu of a sales tax that would be charged if the car were purchased.
31. In the case of automobile leases from banks, the interest cost is referred to as a "money factor," and may be converted to an APR.
32. For detailed information about interest rate calculations, see: David Thorndike, Thorndike Encyclopedia of Banking and Financial Tables, Revised Edition, Boston: Warren, Gorham & Lamont, 1980.
33. An alternative method for computing APR is presented in Chapter 17, Electronic Banking.
34. Gregory Elliehausen, "The Cost of Bank Regulation: A Review of the Evidence," Federal Reserve Bulletin, April 1998, 252-253.

Chapter 11

Liquidity Management

After reading this chapter, you will be able to:

- Define the basic liquidity problem facing banking institutions
- Describe how banks can estimate their liquidity needs
- Discuss the resources available to meet bank liquidity needs
- Compare alternative management approaches to meeting liquidity needs
- Consider the problem of optimal liquidity that trades off the cost of liquidity against the cost of insufficient liquidity
- Understand the regulatory perspective of adequate liquidity

The concept of liquidity is well known in business -- namely, the ability to sell assets on short notice with minimal loss in value. However, bank liquidity management is a much more complex concept than liquidity per se. In general, liquidity management consists of two interrelated parts. First, management must estimate funds needs, which is based on deposit inflows and outflows and varying levels of loan commitments. Deposit flows are affected by movements of interest rates relative to other financial instruments, as well as the competitive rates posted by banks in their respective geographic markets. For example, the period from the last half of the 1990s to 2015 was marked by 50-year lows in interest rates levels. The record low interest rates made it difficult for banks to attract transactions deposits. Also, the economic expansion since the 2008 and 2009 financial crisis put considerable pressure on banks to supply credit. At least for large banks, another credit problem is competition for loans from other financial institutions and even nonfinancial firms. Also, loan commitments, letters of credit, and other off-balance-sheet activities are creating new liquidity demands on large banks. Thus, recent market trends have challenged bankers to accurately estimate liquidity needs.

The second part of liquidity management involves meeting liquidity needs. Two types of liquidity are available to meet potential liquidity requirements—asset management and liability management. ***Asset management*** refers to meeting liquidity needs by using near-cash assets, including net funds sold to other banks and money market securities.[1] Also, asset-backed securities derived from securitizing loans is a growing source of asset liquidity in the banking industry. ***Liability management*** refers to meeting liquidity needs by using outside sources of discretionary funds (such as fed funds, discount window borrowings, repurchase agreements, certificates of deposit, and other borrowings). However, in order to access these sources of liquidity, a bank must maintain sound financial condition. In general, smaller banks tend to emphasize asset management in meeting liquidity needs, in contrast to large banks with an emphasis on liability management.

From a policy standpoint, bank management should develop a liquidity plan or strategy that balances risks and returns. Excessive asset liquidity offers safety but can decrease bank profits. The reason for this is that liquid assets are shorter term and lower risk than other assets, both of which cause their rate of return to be lower than could be earned on investment securities and loans. On the other hand, aggressive liability management can increase bank profits via shifting funds to longer-term and higher-earning assets; however, this strategy can expose the bank to unexpected risks that could trigger sudden withdrawals of interest-sensitive deposit and nondeposit funds. Indeed, during the financial crisis in 2008 and 2009, when many large banks suffered unprecedented losses on mortgage-related investments, a severe liquidity crisis occurred due to problems in nondeposit funding that threatened their solvency. The lesson learned from the crisis is that each bank must determine the appropriate level of asset versus liability management in view of liquidity risk and associated tradeoffs in terms of bank profitability.

Finally, liquidity management is related to prudential regulation of the banking industry. Bank regulators seek to evaluate bank safety and soundness to prevent serious liquidity crises that could lead to unexpected bank failures. In this regard, international liquidity principles have been recommended to help protect the banking system as well as individual banks. Regulatory supervisors work closely with banking institutions to prudently manage liquidity risk.

ESTIMATING LIQUIDITY NEEDS

The first step in any analysis of bank liquidity is the estimation of liquidity needs. These needs primarily arise from deposit withdrawals and loan demands (including off-balance-sheet commitments). To estimate them, the bank must forecast the level of future deposit and loan activity. Although loan growth generally will not exceed deposit growth in a community, differences can arise temporarily, especially in urban areas. Forecasting month-to-month or seasonal liquidity needs is a process based normally on the experience of the bank, with appropriate adjustments for specific future events that would alter typical liquidity needs. A recent trend in liquidity management is the ability to meet cash needs arising from securities activities, which in many cases are off-balance-sheet exposures for hedging or market-making purposes. Admittedly, the complexity of liquidity management involves considerable subjectivity due to uncertainty in forecasting the future. Consequently, it is prudent to adjust the estimated need upward to some extent to avoid a liquidity squeeze in the form of a cash shortage that could result in lost lending opportunities, reduced depositor confidence, or regulatory agency suspicions concerning safety and soundness.

SOURCES AND USES OF FUNDS METHOD

One method of estimating future liquidity needs is to develop a sources and uses of funds statement. To do this, bank management must evaluate potential future changes in its individual asset and liability accounts. For example, the loan portfolio can be divided into its component parts: commercial and industrial loans, residential real estate loans, consumer loans, agricultural loans, and other loans. The demand for funds by businesses and individuals in these different lending areas are estimated from past loan histories and future economic projections. Commercial and industrial loan demand, for instance, would be influenced by the production and growth of the business sector in the past and future. In 2008 and 2009 the rate of growth of business loans dramatically declined due to a sluggish economy; however, by 2011 the economy was on the rebound and business loan growth had increased. Since 2011 the demand for credit has steadily increased to more normal levels, with slow but moderate economic growth, and banks responded by increasing business loans. Although it is not easy to forecast the amount of bank financing needed by business firms, experience and judgment concerning local and regional loan demands, in addition to information on national and international economic trends, are valuable guides to making reasonable estimates of loan demands.

Similarly, deposit levels are influenced by economic and competitive market conditions. As interest rates rise, corporate treasurers move funds out of demand deposits and into interest-bearing assets; therefore, banks will tend to experience increasing competition for deposit funds from nonbank financial service companies such as money market mutual funds. Also, during periods of relatively low interest rates, as experienced over the past 15 years, depositors are motivated to "reach" for higher yields by investing their funds in bonds and stocks, thereby increasing liquidity demands at banks. Other variables may periodically influence deposit levels also, such as changes in monetary policy and international financial markets. If the Federal Reserve moves to decrease the money supply, deposit levels in the banking system as a whole will contract. Also, if U.S. money market securities are viewed in global markets as a safe haven relative to other countries experiencing financial crises (a scenario repeated a number of times in the 1990s and 2000s due to periodic problems in emerging market countries), foreign investors will transfer holdings of dollars into CDs issued by U.S. banks, in addition to other U.S. money market instruments, thereby increasing domestic deposit levels.

As an example, Table 11-1 (next page) gives a hypothetical *sources and uses funds statement* for a bank over a six-month period. The expected increase in total loan demand in the spring and subsequent decline in early summer is a common seasonal trend in agricultural banking. When loan demands increase, deposit balances often decline, as many bank customers obtain both deposit and loan services from the same bank. Notice that *decreases* in loans and *increases* in deposits are sources of funds; conversely, increases in both loans and deposit withdrawals are uses of funds. Subtracting deposit changes from loan changes provides an estimate of liquidity needs.

With regard to sources and uses of funds, it should be recognized that there are discretionary items versus nondiscretionary items, based on the ability of management to control the flow of funds. Obviously, deposit withdrawals are nondiscretionary because the bank cannot control depositors' activities; however, loans (and securities sales and purchases) are discretionary for the most part due to the fact that management can play an active role in their quantity.

To estimate the figures shown in Table11-1, past seasonal trends are reviewed by bank management. Next, these trends are adjusted for cyclical movements in economic and financial conditions. For example, a bank with a large proportion of its assets invested in commercial and industrial loans needs to adjust loan estimates downward if a recession in the business sector is forecasted. Although loan demand will fall and therefore ease liquidity needs, rising unemployment will tend to depress deposit balances, offsetting the decline in loans. A bank with a relatively high proportion of residential real estate loans would be particularly affected by movements in interest rates. As interest rates rise to relatively high levels, loan demand can be expected to fall at some point, as many potential home buyers can no longer qualify to meet the higher interest expenses. As rates fall, demand for home loans increases and is aggravated by homeowners seeking to refinance at lower rates of interest.

TABLE 11-1 ESTIMATING LIQUIDITY NEEDS BASED ON A SOURCES AND USES OF FUNDS STATEMENT

End of Month	Estimated Total Loans	Estimated Total Deposits	Estimated Change: Loans	Estimated Change: Deposits	Estimated Liquidity Need
December	$68,000	$85,000	$ —	$ —	$ —
January	70,000	90,000	2,000	5,000	(3,000)
February	79,000	86,000	9,000	(4,000)	13,000
March	89,000	83,000	10,000	(3,000)	13,000
April	96,000	78,000	7,000	(5,000)	12,000
May	95,000	79,000	(1,000)	1,000	(2,000)
June	88,000	80,000	(7,000)	1,000	(8,000)

Local and regional economic factors must also be evaluated and used to adjust estimated liquidity needs. A dramatic example is the passage of the North American Free Trade Agreement (NAFTA) in the early 1990s and its subsequent impact on U.S. states that border Mexico since that time. Increased traffic and business trade on the border greatly increased infrastructure needs, including roads, bridges, warehouse facilities, and water treatment facilities. Loan demands far surpassed deposit growth which forced many border banks to seek assistance from other banks in the form of loan syndications, fed funds, and correspondent relationships. In some cases bank mergers and acquisitions were motivated by liquidity pressures that only larger organizations could manage. Another example is the Great Recession in 2008-2009 that resulted in cutbacks in jobs across the nation. While national in scope, the economic recession hit some parts of the country harder than others. Faced with regulatory requirements to meet risk-based capital standards (see Chapter 12), banks in some communities were forced to raise their equity and cut back on liabilities, thereby reducing their ability to borrow funds to meet liquidity needs and causing reductions in loans. Thus, local and regional business conditions can have a significant impact on the sources and uses of bank funds and, therefore, bank liquidity.

In 2008, in response to the financial crisis at that time, the international Basle Committee[2] proposed the following Sound Principles for assessing and managing bank liquidity:

- the importance of establishing a liquidity risk tolerance;
- the maintenance of an adequate level of liquidity, including a cushion of liquid assets;
- the necessity of allocating liquidity costs, benefits and risks to all significant business activities;
- the identification and measurement of the full range of liquidity risks, including contingent liquidity risks;
- the design and use of severe stress test scenarios;

- the need for a robust and operational contingency funding plan;
- the management of intraday liquidity risk and collateral; and
- public disclosure in promoting market discipline.

These liquidity principles are most appropriate for medium and large banks, but the same concepts can be applied to smaller banks. Bank supervisors were provided guidance in assessing the adequacy of a bank's liquidity risk management framework as well as liquidity levels. A bank's size, financial services, complexity, and role in the financial system are taken into account in liquidity assessments.

STRUCTURE-OF-DEPOSITS METHOD

Another way to estimate liquidity needs is the ***structure-of-deposits method***. The basic idea of this approach is to list the different types of deposits that the bank is using to acquire funds and then assign a probability of withdrawal to each type of deposit within a specific planning horizon. High risk, or unstable, deposits require substantial liquidity to support them, whereas low risk, or stable, deposits require relatively less liquidity. Core funds represent deposits of loyal, local depositors and tend to be relatively stable. A strong and positive relationship typically exists between the bank and these depositors. Noncore deposits tend to be unstable sources of funds, as these depositors are likely very price sensitive and influenced primarily by the interest rate on their funds. If other competing banks post higher interest rates, these funds can rapidly be withdrawn and thereby cause liquidity demands on the bank.

The major strength of the structure-of-deposits method is that it directs management attention to the probable cause of liquidity pressures—namely, deposit withdrawals. On the other hand, its main weakness is ignoring other liquidity demands stemming from loans. Despite this drawback, as well as the subjectivity of the deposit classification process, the structure-of-deposits method is a useful technique for controlling liquidity risk.

TABLE 11-2 DEPOSIT SOURCES

	Probability of Amount Held (in Millions)	×	Expected Withdrawal in Next Three Months	=	Withdrawals (in Millions)
Short-term (unstable):					
Demand deposits	$ 2		.90		$ 1.8
Other transactions accounts	$10		.60		$ 6.0
Medium-term:					
Small time and savings deposits	$50		.30		$15.0
Long-term (stable):					
Large time deposits	$10		.20		$ 2.0
Expected deposit withdrawals					$24.8

As a simple example, suppose that bank management structured its deposit sources as shown in Table 11-2. Notice that the bank has relatively low amounts of short-term and long-term deposits. The major deposit source is medium-term small time and savings deposits, which are relatively stable components of core deposits. In this case liquidity demands from deposit withdrawals should be fairly modest. Of course, this same structuring method can be applied to nondeposit funds sources also, particularly if these sources are important to the bank. In any application the evaluation of the probability of withdrawal, or volatility, of various sources of funds must be determined on a case-by-case basis. A careful examination of the stability characteristics of each source of funds by management is essential due to the large differences that can exist among banks in this respect.

FUNDING AND MARKET LIQUIDITY NEEDS

Banks with significant investment portfolios are exposed to liquidity needs that arise from trading activities. ***Funding-liquidity risk*** refers to maintaining sufficient cash to meet investment objectives. For example, suppose that a bank has large holdings of securities on its balance sheet and that interest rates are expected to increase in the near future. In this case the price of the securities will fall and the bank will incur a capital loss. To hedge the price risk in this spot position, the bank sells short Treasury bill contracts. If interest rates do later increase as expected, the bank can simultaneously buy T-bills at the now lower price and sell T-bills at the earlier contracted higher price. Netting out the spot and futures positions, the losses in the spot position will be offset by the futures position (see Chapter 6 for numerical examples). However, T-bill futures contracts are marked-to-market daily, which means that gains and losses are reckoned at the end of each day. Losses in the futures position that prompt margin calls must be paid in cash, whereas the profits on the spot position are simply paper gains unless the securities are actually sold. This mismatch in cash outflows versus inflows in these and other securities activities creates a liquidity problem. For large banks the funding-liquidity risk attached to their considerable exposures to securities risks involved in derivatives and foreign-exchange trading operations puts constant pressure on their cash flows. Indeed, the sheer complexity of multifaceted derivatives strategies can make liquidity needs difficult to measure for many large banks. Since such banks are continuously either putting up or unwinding different parts (or legs) of complex securities strategies, they are always exposed to some degree of cash flow imbalance.

Market-liquidity risk is another source of potential cash flow problems for banks with sizeable securities activities. Consider the liquidity effects of a market disruption (such as the October, 1987 stock market crash, 1998 Asian currency crisis, 2000 stock market technology bubble, and 2008-2009 mortgage-related financial crisis). Sudden shifts in supply and demand forces in the financial markets cause bid/ask spreads to widen—that is, the price difference between what buyers and sellers are seeking in the market increases. Given that bid/ask spreads are normally representative of the depth of a market, market participants could have difficulty closing out open positions in derivatives, securities, and so on without sustaining losses. At such times large institutional investors may pull out of the market and further widen bid/ask spreads. Thus, volatile financial markets can cause temporary illiquidity in securities positions held by banks.

ASSET LIQUIDITY

Historically, ***asset liquidity*** was the primary means by which banks met cash demands. Money market instruments, such as Treasury bills and short-term obligations of state and political subdivisions (municipal securities), are "liquid" in the sense that they can be sold readily with minimal loss of capital. Relatively large loan demands and deposit withdrawals were typically met by liquidating the required quantity of these near-money instruments. This approach to liquidity management traditionally fell under the rubric of *asset management*.

Asset management was the dominant method of bank management until the 1960s, when *liability management* became popular as an alternative means of meeting cash needs. Liability management involves the acquisition of external funds from deposit and nondeposit sources as liquidity needs arise. As discussed later in this chapter, liability management substantially altered the role of liquidity management in banking.

ROLE OF ASSET LIQUIDITY

There are two basic roles of asset liquidity management in modern banking. First, liquid assets serve as an alternative source of funds for the bank; the bank can use either assets or liabilities to meet cash needs. Its selection of sources of funds will depend heavily on their relative costs. If it is less costly to sell off some liquid assets than to issue certificates of deposit (CDs), internal liquidity will be favored over external liquidity to acquire funds. Consider a situation in which interest rates are relatively high. Increased loan demand at this time might be better met by selling Treasury bills than by issuing CDs with interest rates at or near the Treasury bill rate. By selling Treasury bills, funds effectively are shifted to higher-earning assets such as commercial loans, which will boost bank profitability.

The second role of asset liquidity management is as a reserve. If the financial market loses confidence in a bank's safety and soundness, it is likely that borrowed sources of funds would become inaccessible. In this case the bank would have to rely upon its liquid assets to maintain business operations. Thus, asset liquidity is a reserve to forestall problems that threaten bank solvency. In keeping with this rationale, regulators impose ***primary reserve*** requirements that apply to cash held in their vaults and on deposit at a Federal Reserve district bank. ***Secondary reserves*** are near-money financial instruments that have no formal regulatory requirements and provide an additional reserve of liquid assets to meet cash needs. While there are no formal liquidity requirements imposed by bank regulators, it is considered in the onsite examination process. Also, professional analysts compare the asset liquidity of banks to their large, uninsured liabilities to see how many times these liabilities are "covered" in the event of a loss of market confidence and rapid funds withdrawals.

Finally, one should note that use of liability management increases the asset size of the bank and so requires appropriate increases in capital reserves to stay within regulatory guidelines. By contrast, liquidating money market assets (with no capital requirements) does not change bank size and, therefore, does not affect bank capital reserves, unless the funds are used for loans or investments that require capital backing.

PRIMARY RESERVES

Most primary reserves are cash assets held to satisfy legal reserve requirements. Banks seek to minimize cash accounts because there is an opportunity cost to holding idle funds. That is, cash[3] does not earn interest. Thus, total cash reserves generally equal legal reserves. As of 2016, banks are not required to carry reserves against the first $15.2 million of net transactions deposits (mostly checking deposits). A three percent reserve is required against transactions accounts from $15.2 million to $110.2 million (known as the low reserve tranche adjustment). And, a 10 percent reserve is required for transactions accounts greater than $110.2 million. To the extent that legal reserves exceed the cash reserves that banks would hold in the absence of these requirements, banks are *taxed* by the government. Taxation is an appropriate interpretation here because the Federal Reserve invests banks' deposits held at its district banks in Treasury securities, and most of the resultant earnings are transferred to the U.S. Treasury to help pay the fiscal budget. This reserve tax has been opposed by bankers. Indeed, an exodus of member banks from the Federal Reserve system occurred in the 1960s and 1970s, as bankers complained of relatively high reserve requirements imposed on member banks compared with nonmember banks. In the 1990s banks' legal reserves declined considerably, due in large part to banks' efforts to avoid noninterest (or idle) funds. In an effort to address this issue, the Financial Services Regulatory Relief Act of 2006 authorized the Federal Reserve Banks to pay interest on balances held by depository institutions at Reserve Banks, subject to regulations of the Board of Governors. The effective date of this authority was October 1, 2008 (as revised by the Emergency Economic Stabilization Act of 2008). The interest rate on required reserves (IORR rate) is determined by the Board but is generally set at the federal funds target rate under monetary policy.

In 1980 the Monetary Control Act was passed as part of the Depository Institutions Deregulation and Monetary Control Act of 1980. This legislation requires all depository institutions to carry legal reserves set by the Federal Reserve under Regulation D. It eliminated any reserve requirement incentive for banks to leave the system, while establishing uniform reserve rules for banks. Moreover, it tightened the linkage between reserves and money supply and thus served to facilitate monetary control (because reserve requirements are a monetary policy tool used by the central bank to achieve its monetary and economic objectives). To further enhance its ability to control the money stock and so rein in inflation, in 1984 the Federal Reserve began using ***contemporaneous reserve requirement accounting methods (CRR)*** on transactions deposits, as opposed to ***lagged reserve requirement accounting (LRR)*** previous to that time. Under CRR rules, the computation and maintenance periods overlap to a great extent, such that from a banking perspective reserve management was a daily activity. Due to difficulties encountered by depository institutions in managing reserves under CRR, in 1998 the Federal Reserve returned to a lagged system of reserve accounting.

Currently, required reserves using LRR under Regulation D are computed on the basis of daily average balances of transactions deposits during a 14-day period ending every second Monday *(the computation period)*. Figure 11-1 gives an example for illustrative purposes. Reserve requirements are computed by applying the ratios shown in Table 11-3 (to be discussed shortly). It should be noted that average daily vault cash held in a subsequent 14-day computation period are counted as reserves, which means they are deducted from the amount required based on transactions accounts to get the required reserve balance. The reserve balance that is required must be maintained with the Federal Reserve during a 14-day period *(the maintenance period)* that begins on the third Thursday following the end of the transactions computation period. Thus, there is a 17-day lag between the end of the transactions computation period and the beginning of the maintenance period. This lagged reserve accounting procedure is advantageous in terms of allowing banks and the Federal Reserve to lower management costs and improve the quality of information on required reserve balances.

FIGURE 11-1 LAGGED RESERVE REQUIREMENT ACCOUNTING

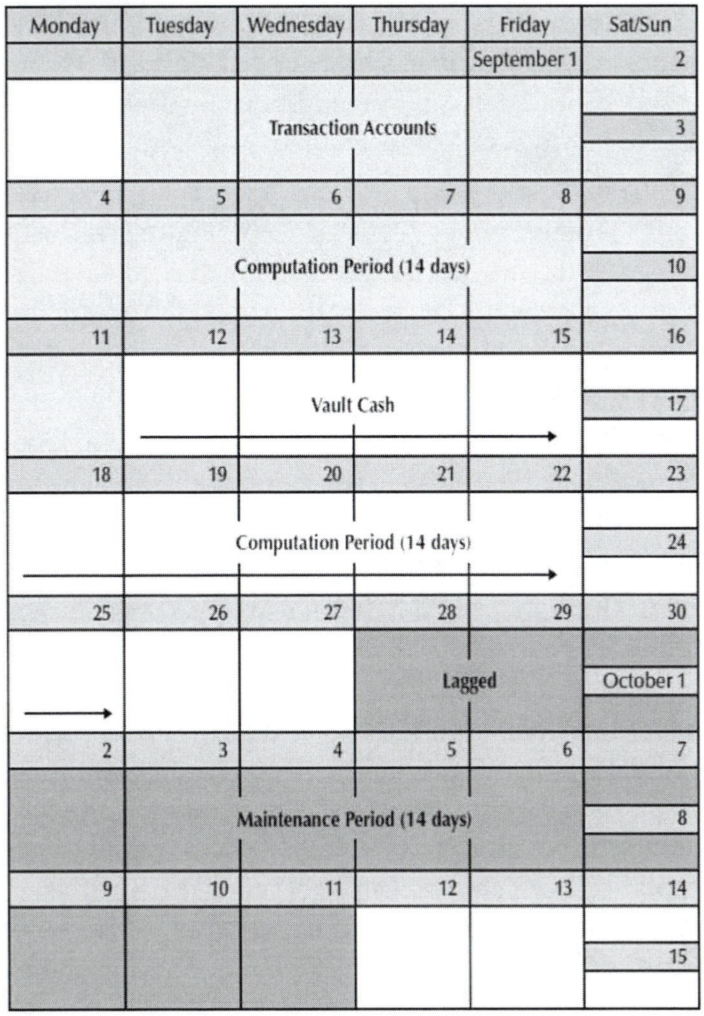

MANAGING THE MONEY POSITION

Managing the money position of a bank relates to minimizing cash holdings. Because legal reserve requirements exceed bank preferences in general, the money position is synonymous with reserve management.[4] Table 11-3 (next page) shows an example of how a bank would calculate its required reserves. The three basic categories of deposits shown in Table 11-3 are defined as follows.

Transactions Accounts

All deposits are included for which the account holder is permitted to make withdrawals by negotiable or transferable instruments, payment orders of withdrawal, and telephone and preauthorized transfers (in excess of three per month) for the purpose of making payments to third persons or others. Examples of ***transactions accounts*** are demand deposits, NOW accounts, and share draft accounts (offered by credit unions).

Nonpersonal Time Deposits

Nonpersonal time deposits are time deposits, including savings deposits, that are not transactions accounts and that in general are not held by an individual. However, certain transferable time deposits held by individuals and other obligations are included. For example, money market deposit accounts (MMDAs) and similar accounts with no more than six preauthorized, automatic, or other transfers per month (of which no more than three can be checks) are included.

Eurocurrency Liabilities

Eurocurrency liabilities represent net borrowings from related foreign offices, gross borrowings from unrelated foreign depository institutions, loans to U.S. residents made by overseas branches of domestic depository institutions, and sales of assets by U.S. depository institutions by their overseas offices. Eurocurrencies (or so -called Eurodollars) are used mainly by large banks as an alternative source of deposit funds.

Total reserves required according to the calculations in Table 11-3 (next page) are $12,850,000. Because the bank has an average daily vault cash balance of $500,000 (which is based on the two-week period ending three days prior to the beginning of the two-week maintenance period under LRR), it needs to hold cash reserves of $12,350,000 at the Federal Reserve Bank to comply with Regulation D.

If a bank has deficient reserves, as in Table 11-3, it must correct this shortfall or face penalties. In the latter case, the Federal Reserve Banks are authorized to assess charges for deficiencies or require additional reserves be maintained in subsequent reserve maintenance periods.

If the bank had a deficiency (or excess) in reserves, the federal funds market is a likely source (use) of funds. Also, the Federal Reserve's ***discount window*** is another source of funds that banks commonly tap for cash needs.[5] Sometimes unexpected payments on loans and deposits will cause cash balances to increase substantially above legal requirements. In this event, the money manager would seek first to evaluate the nature of this increase. If the increase in reserves is strictly temporary, short-term money market instruments (such as Treasury bills, bankers' acceptances, or commercial paper) could be purchased to earn interest on the excess cash. If the increase in cash appears to be more permanent, the money manager would consider longer-term investment opportunities, such as capital market securities (e.g., longer-term government securities, including municipal securities and corporate bonds) and loans. On the other hand, significant drains on cash balances could be met either by selling short-term, liquid securities or by purchasing deposit and nondeposit funds in the market. The deregulation of interest rate ceilings on deposits has made the latter strategy more feasible than it was in the past, because posting relatively competitive deposit rates can rapidly attract funds.

TABLE 11-3 CALCULATING RESERVE REQUIREMENTS FOR COMMERCIAL BANKS

Type of Deposit and Deposit Interval	Average Dollar Amount (In Millions) In Computation Period	Reserve Requirement	Average Dollar Amount (In Millions) In Maintenance Period
Net transactions accounts:			
$0–$15.2 million	$15.2	0%	$0*
$15.2–$110.2 million	$95.0	3%	2.850*
Over $110.2 million	100.0	10%	10.000
Nonpersonal time deposits	150.0	0%	0
Eurocurrency liabilities	40.0	0%	0
Total reserves required			$12.850
Less vault cash			(0.500)
Federal Reserve Bank			$12.350

*The cutoffs for the low reserve tranche adjustment and three percent reserve requirement regularly change as amendments are made by the Board of Governors of the Federal Reserve System. For the latest details on applicable cutoffs, browse on the key words "reserve requirements and Federal Reserve."

Small and large banks generally differ in their approach to managing their money positions. During the beginning of the reserve maintenance period, small banks will tend to run a surplus volume of reserves at the Federal Reserve. After this point, they will sell their excess reserves in the federal funds market. By contrast, large banks tend to experience an increasing shortfall in reserves as the maintenance period proceeds. They become purchasers of fed funds later in the maintenance period, which are supplied primarily by small banks. This general pattern of reserve holdings at large banks does not always occur, however. It may be altered because of anticipated fed funds rates -- for example, if a money manager believed interest rates in the fed funds market were going to rise substantially near the end of the maintenance period (perhaps due to tight money conditions), it would be less costly to purchase fed funds at the beginning of the maintenance period and to sell any surplus at the end of the period or use the discount window later. Alternatively, larger banks may experience relatively volatile reserve levels throughout the maintenance period because of changes in loan demands and deposit activity that occur as the bank reacts aggressively to changing market conditions.

SECONDARY RESERVES

Once future liquidity needs have been estimated, the bank must decide what sources of liquidity will be tapped to cover these needs. If deposits are forecasted to decline in the near future, some amount of cash reserves is likely to become available for use because reserve requirements will decline. Remaining liquidity needs must be covered either with liquid assets or by borrowing funds.

Assuming liquid assets are to be used, banks normally seek to match the maturities of their assets with specific future liquidity needs. This ***money market approach*** enables the bank to avoid transactions costs, as well as price risk, while maximizing interest revenues.

Secondary reserves can also be used to provide collateral for repurchase agreements, discount window borrowings, and public deposits by the government. Pledging requirements in the form of near-cash assets for these purposes must follow regulatory guidelines. Once pledged, these secondary reserves cannot be employed for other liquidity needs. Thus, pledged securities should be netted out to determine unencumbered liquid securities.

Cyclical monetary policies to restrain strong inflationary pressures can cause liquidity pressures that force banks to rely more on their internal liquidity than on their external liquidity. This possibility influences the decision concerning the choice of liquid assets to hold. For example, Treasury bills (and notes and bonds nearing maturity) are most liquid because of an active secondary market with large trading volume. By contrast, commercial paper has a thinner secondary market, such that it may have to be discounted depending on buyer demand. Bankers' acceptances and negotiable certificates of deposit (CDs) have a good secondary market and, thus, fall somewhere between these two extremes. Of course, the bank must trade off liquidity risk against interest earnings in selecting the asset securities it will purchase. Commonly-used money market instruments are as follows:

- ***Treasury bills (T-bills)*** are direct obligations of the U.S. government that have an original maturity of one year or less. T-bills are discount instruments that are sold at a weekly auction. The minimum denomination is $10,000, with larger denominations available in multiples of $5,000 above this minimum. Original maturities of T-bills are three months, six months, and one year.
- ***Federal agency securities*** are issued by various government agencies (e.g., Federal Land Banks, Federal Home Loan Banks, Banks for Cooperatives, Government National Mortgage Association, Federal National Mortgage Association, Federal Home Mortgage Loan Association, and Tennessee Valley Authority). Some agencies are backed directly by the federal government whereas others carry the implicit assumption of government support (such as government-sponsored entity, or GSE, status). Nonetheless, significant price risk is possible as experienced by mortgage-related securities in the 2008-2009 financial crisis. Agency securities are interest-bearing instruments with varying maturities and minimum denominations of $50,000 or more.
- ***Repurchase agreements (RPs or repos)*** are securities purchased (sold) under agreement to resell (repurchase) with a securities dealer. RPs may or may not have a set maturity date, but generally their term does not exceed three months. They have low default risk because T-bills are normally pledged as

collateral. Interest is paid on transactions that involve at least $1 million.

- ***Bankers' acceptances*** are time drafts used in international trade that are "accepted" by a large bank. For example, an importer may obtain a letter of credit from a bank, which is used by the exporter to draw a draft on the bank for payment of goods. Upon accepting the draft, the bank can market it if desired. Maturities normally extend throughout the transit period for shipment of goods (that is, from 30 to 180 days).
- ***Negotiable certificates of deposit (CDs)*** are interest-bearing liabilities of banks and other depository institutions that may be sold to third parties and carry minimum denominations of $100,000. Maturities range from about one to 18 months, and rates may or may not vary with interest rate conditions. Eurodollar CDs are dollar-denominated securities issued by foreign branches of major U.S. banks and foreign-owned banks. Yields on CDs can differ depending on the size and risk of issuing banks and exceed Treasury yields on instruments of equal maturity.
- ***Federal funds (fed funds)*** are immediately available funds that represent interbank loans of cash reserves, either held on deposit at Federal Reserve district banks or elsewhere (including correspondent banks). Government intervention may cause fed fund rates to move sharply in response to monetary policy operations of the Federal Reserve. Fed funds "sold" are liquid assets of the lending institution that appear as fed funds "purchased" on the borrowing institution's liability side of the balance sheet. Fed funds are not considered deposits and, therefore, do not require that reserves be held against them. Most fed funds' transactions are "overnight loans" and expire in a single day. Typically, fed funds flow from small banks (or so-called respondent banks) with excess liquidity to larger banks (or so-called correspondent banks) with liquidity demands.
- ***Commercial paper*** is a short-term, unsecured promissory note issued by major U.S. corporations. Denominations normally are in multiples of $1,000, with a minimum of $25,000. Maturities range from three days to nine months. Commercial paper may or may not be a discount instrument, and rates closely track the prime rate quoted by major U.S. banks. Little or no secondary market exists for this security.

Although timing securities to mature in order to meet liquidity demands is the most common approach to managing asset liquidity, there may be an opportunity to take advantage of yield curve relationships by using an ***aggressive liquidity approach***. For example, if the yield curve were upward-sloping and expected to remain at the same level in the near future, the purchase of longer-term securities would not only offer higher yields than shorter-term securities but also could offer the realization of capital gains if they were sold before maturity to meet liquidity needs. Capital gains are possible because, as time passes and the securities' maturities shorten, their interest rate declines in line with the upward slope of the yield curve. To demonstrate, suppose a bank knows that it will have a cash deficiency in six months.

Further, assume that the yield curve now is upward sloping and is forecast to have approximately the same shape and level in six months. If $500,000 of one-year Treasury securities were purchased now at a price of 92 (or 92 percent of par value), and six-month Treasury securities have a price of 94 due to an upward sloping yield curve, the expected capital gain on the sale of the Treasury securities in six months would be 0.02 × $500,000 = $10,000. These potential earnings gains would have to be weighed against transactions costs and risks associated with this aggressive approach. If the level of the yield curve rose over the next six months, instead of remaining about the same, the sale of the two-year bonds after holding them one year would result in a reduced capital gain and perhaps even a capital loss (however, the capital loss may not completely offset the higher interest earnings on one-year securities compared with six-month securities earned over the next six months).

FIGURE 11-2 **AGGRESSIVE LIQUIDITY MANAGEMENT AND THE YIELD CURVE**

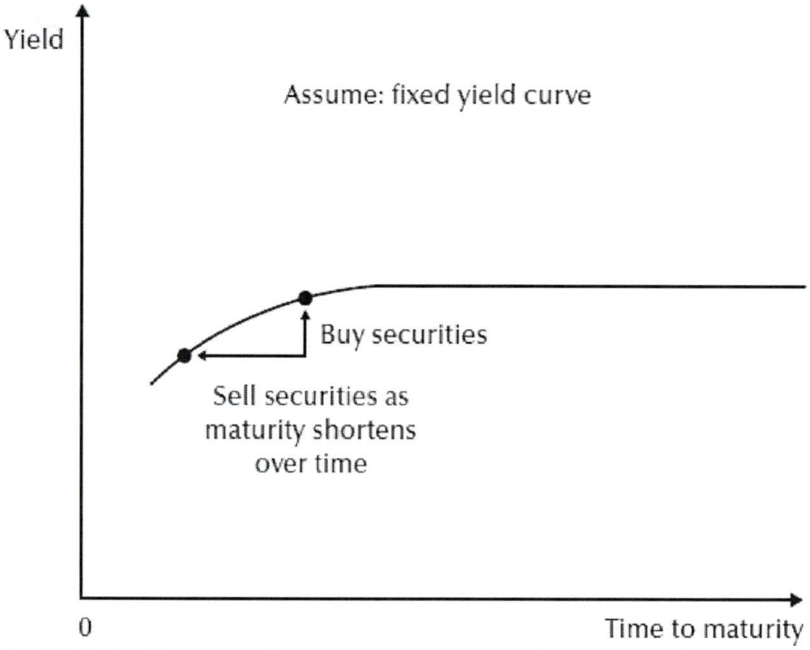

An important liquidity innovation is the securitization of certain types of loans. For example, a bank may sell securities to investors that represent claims on a pool of auto loans. If they are sold without recourse, the bank is not liable to security holders, as in the case of issuing CDs or raising other funds by issuing IOUs. Instead, the security investors obtain a pro rata share of the monthly payments on auto loans, net of a service fee charged by the bank. This type of *asset-backed financing* (via securitization) is most likely to be feasible for loans that can be standardized and do not require the bank to obtain confidential, nonpublic information on borrowers. It is possible that the bank could, in effect, certify the quality of business loans without divulging sensitive information to security investors, but the bank may then expose itself to some degree of liability should investors lose funds due to loan defaults. The securitization of commercial loans is in its initial stage of development, as some banks have begun to package large numbers of small business loans. The main effect on bank liquidity of securitization is the increase in marketability of these loans in the financial marketplace. In effect, asset liquidity is improved with the added benefit that credit risk can be geographically diversified and, therefore, reduced. Whether the reduction in credit risk is passed on to borrowers (in the form of, say, lower auto loan interest rates compared with no securitization of such loans), holders of the securities, or bank shareholders is an issue for further study. It is logical to believe that these different parties in the securitization process will share the risk benefits in some way.

LIABILITY MANAGEMENT

An alternative approach to liquidity management is to purchase the funds necessary to meet loan demands and deposit withdrawals. This approach falls under the heading of liability management, a topic that was covered in the more general context of asset/liability management in Chapter 5. In this section our purpose is to discuss liability management as applied to the more general problem of liquidity management.

There are substantial differences between small and large banks in their use of liabilities to manage liquidity. Large banks that are active in the money market have a natural advantage over smaller banks in terms of their ability to cost-effectively raise funds through federal funds, the discount window, repurchase agreements, negotiable CDs, Eurocurrency deposits, and other types of purchased funds. By contrast, smaller banks often obtain purchased funds in the money market through their larger correspondent banks. Because smaller banks tend to have deposits in excess of loan demands, they will deposit excess funds at correspondents in exchange for money market services. ***Correspondent balances*** thus serve as an additional source of asset liquidity for smaller banks and as an additional source of borrowed liquidity for larger banks.

The primary advantage of liability management is that assets can be shifted from lower-earning money market instruments to higher-earning loans and longer-term securities. Greater asset diversification also may be possible in this instance.

On the downside, there are risks involved in liability management. If interest rates increase suddenly, the cost of funds could rise substantially as purchased funds come due and must be rolled over at higher rates of interest. Thus, *interest rate risk* is increased under liability management of liquidity. If the bank's assets are less sensitive to interest rate changes than its liabilities are, profit margins would suffer and capital may become inadequate. As profit margins decline, the bank could be forced to sell off assets to reduce its need for purchased funds and improve its capital ratios. Capital losses on the sale of assets could further squeeze profit margins, however. Because liquid assets would minimize capital losses, larger banks need to carry some amount of money market instruments to help offset interest rate risk. Furthermore, in the event that the public loses confidence in the bank's safety and soundness, deposit withdrawals may increase temporarily, and liquid assets will help absorb these withdrawals.

At times banks use liability management to aggressively pursue profits on interest rate risk. For example, suppose that the yield curve is upward sloping and stable due to monetary policy. After the 2008-2009 financial crisis, the Federal Reserve followed a monetary policy of keeping interest rates low in an effort to stimulate an economic recovery. Given that short-term interest rates were less than long-term interest rates and both of these rates were not changing, some banks practiced a bond ***carry trade strategy***. This strategy is implemented by borrowing short-term funds (such as fed funds) and invest in longer-term securities (such as one- and two-year Treasury securities). As long as interest rates do not increase, the carry trade can earn a positive yield spread. However, there is interest rate risk, as rising interest rates would collapse the positive yield spread and result in capital losses on the Treasury debt securities. For example, in 1994 Orange Country, California, experienced large losses on its carry trade strategy as interest rates rose at that time.

Liability management also increases the bank's financial risk. As discussed in Chapter 12, *financial risk* is the increase in the variability of earnings per share that is associated with an increase in debt as a proportion of total assets (i.e., financial leverage). Bank managers thus need to consider the risk preferences of shareholders when using liabilities to meet liquidity needs.

Finally, a new risk that is related to liability management is ***capital market risk***. This risk occurs due to low interest levels that motivate investors to transfer deposit funds to the capital market in an attempt to earn higher rates of return. Over the past 20 years, interest rate levels remained relatively low from an historical perspective, causing CD rates to drop below three percent. Banks lost billions of dollars of "hot money" (i.e., sources of funds sensitive to interest rates) to the capital markets due to low interest rates. During such times, banks must find alternatives to retain deposits and, more important, customers. For example, many banks offer customers mutual funds managed by the bank (i.e., proprietary funds) or by nonbanking institutions (i.e., nonproprietary funds). Investment consultants have been retained by banks to assist customers in portfolio decisions concerning deposits, mutual funds, and individual stocks and bonds. The main idea of this relationship banking is to view the customer as a client of the bank and, therefore, encourage future deposits when interest rates move up again.

It should be obvious that one of the greatest difficulties in using liabilities to meet liquidity needs is estimating the availability and cost of external funds. The quantity and cost of deposit and nondeposit funds depends on many factors, including monetary policy actions by the Federal Reserve, economic conditions, and the bank's financial strength. Uncertainties associated with these factors require that banks have more than sufficient access to different kinds of liabilities to make sure that liquidity needs are adequately covered. Chapter 13 provides detailed discussion of different sources of bank funds.

Some new liquidity sources that banks have developed to better meet liquidity needs are collateralized commercial paper programs and medium-term notes. In the former case, the bank sets up a *special purpose corporation* (SPC). Commercial paper is issued by the SPC to raise funds for credit card loans, consumer loans, commercial loans, leases, and other uses. The SPC is not legally linked to the bank or its holding company, but for all practical purposes is another way to practice asset securitization and thereby generate fee income. SPCs essentially are off-balance-sheet entities for accounting purposes and under Regulation D of the Federal Reserve. Investors in commercial paper of SPCs hold claims on the portfolio loans originated by the bank.

Medium-term notes (MTNs) is jargon for debt securities that are continuously offered by a firm (either financial or nonfinancial), as opposed to underwritten debt securities sold within a relatively short time period. MTNs have maturities ranging from nine months to 30 years, can be counted as senior or subordinated debt by bank holding companies, and can be issued by banks themselves as deposits or senior debt. While large banks have been most active in MTNs, they also could be attractive to smaller banks that either want to raise small amounts of funds not sufficient to justify underwriting costs of new debt issues or do not have access to traditional debt markets. Also, MTNs help to avoid price risks in underwriting that could affect the cost of debt to the bank. Best of all, MTNs can be sold in the exact quantities and maturities demanded by investors. These advantages help to explain the growing popularity of MTNs among both financial and nonfinancial firms.

Recognizing the difficulties of liability management for banking organizations, the Federal Home Loan Bank (FHLB) System offers credit services to member[6] depository institutions and insurance companies in an effort to support housing finance and economic development in communities. Due to the decline of thrift institutions in the 1980s, banks now play a more important role in the home loan market than in the past. While most banks have access to fed funds, the Federal Reserve's discount window, and lines of credit from other banks, these sources can be costly at times due to tight money conditions or simply increased demands for cash around days near the end of the reserve maintenance period. As a federal agency, the FHLB prices its credit competitively based on Treasury rates and has a broad range of maturities to fit any liability need. Loans from the FHLB are normally collateralized with a "blanket pledge" of mortgage-related assets, such as residential mortgages and mortgage-backed securities, and deposits held at the FHLB, U.S. Treasury, and other agency obligations.

FUNDS MANAGEMENT OF LIQUIDITY

As suggested by the preceding discussion, management of liquidity is best handled by combining asset liquidity and liability management, or a funds management approach. Funds management involves comparing total liquidity needs with total liquidity sources.

LIQUIDITY RATIOS

From the standpoint of bank analysts, bank liquidity can only be roughly estimated using Call Reports of Condition. Four common ratio measures of bank liquidity are

- Loans/deposits
- Loans/nondeposit liabilities
- Unencumbered liquid assets/nondeposit liabilities
- Near-cash assets/large-denomination liabilities

These ratios must be evaluated together in order to gain insight into a bank's liquidity position. For example, if the loans/deposits ratio is high, we can infer that the bank either has a large loan portfolio or is using large amounts of nondeposit, or purchased, funds to finance assets. If the loans/nondeposit liabilities ratio is also high, it must be that the loan portfolio is large, rather than that the bank is relying heavily on nondeposit funds. To examine liquidity further, the unencumbered (nonpledged) liquid assets/nondeposit liabilities ratio is valuable. If it is relatively high, the bank has considerable secondary reserves; alternatively, a fairly low ratio would imply that the bank had used up a large part of secondary reserves and was borrowing funds to finance loans and investments. The last ratio, or near-cash assets/large-denomination liabilities, was mentioned earlier and is a good measure of the ability of the bank to use liquid assets to cover wholesale funds that are for the most part uninsured. It should be clear that bank liquidity is a multidimensional concept that requires management to consider many factors and their interrelationships.

Another approach to measuring liquidity is to account for changes over time in both liquidity needs and sources. This approach is superior to focusing on one or the other parts of the liquidity problem because it evaluates liquidity relative to bank needs. To do this, the following ratio can be calculated:

$$\frac{\text{Liquid assets and liabilities in period } t}{\text{Estimated liquidity needs in period } t} \qquad (11\text{-}1)$$

Table 11-4 (next page) calculates this ratio for a hypothetical bank using the estimated liquidity needs from Table 11-1 and other information on the bank's liquid assets and estimated access to liability sources of funds. (Detailed information of this kind is probably available only internally to bank management.) Asset liquidity is restricted to unencumbered assets, and liability sources are based on estimates of low-cost external funding sources. Notice that estimated liability sources are assumed to stay the same from month to month. It is possible, however, that changing economic and financial market conditions could affect the ability of the bank to access purchased funds over time. Asset liquidity is under greater management control and can be varied to ensure that adequate total liquidity is available to meet deposit and loan needs. As shown in Table 11-4, the bank has negative liquidity needs (or excess liquidity) in January, May, and June, such that negative liquidity ratios result in these months. In the other months the ratio exceeds one, which indicates that sufficient liquidity was available to meet normal operating needs. If the ratio had been in the range between zero and one, the bank could experience a potential liquidity problem and should begin developing a plan to overcome this shortfall.

TABLE 11-4 EVALUATING BANK LIQUIDITY BY COMPARING NEEDS AND SOURCES OVER TIME

End of Month	(1) Estimated Liquidity Needs*	Asset Liquidity	Estimated Liability Sources	(2) Total Liquidity	(2)/(1) Liquidity Ratio
January	(3,000)	5,000	10,000	15,000	-5.00*
February	13,000	6,000	10,000	16,000	1.23
March	13,000	7,000	10,000	17,000	1.31
April	12,000	7,000	10,000	17,000	1.42
May	(2,000)	4,000	10,000	14,000	-7.00*
June	(13,000)	3,000	10,000	13,000	-1.00*

*A negative liquidity need causes the bank liquidity ratio to be negative, which can be interpreted to mean that the bank has sufficient liquidity.

OPTIMUM BANK LIQUIDITY

A question that bank management must ultimately face is whether the liquidity ratio is optimal. Optimality in this context is a dynamic concept because liquidity conditions in a bank change from day to day and week to week. For this reason bank liquidity must be regularly monitored and adjusted to reflect changing bank financial condition and market demands.

Optimum liquidity is achieved by balancing risks and returns. To be more specific, measures of liquidity need to be high enough to meet even *unexpected* changes in liquidity needs and sources. On the other hand, liquidity should not be too high because there is an opportunity cost in the sense of excessive near-cash assets that could be earning higher rates of return if sold and funds were invested in other assets. Also, liquidity management can conflict with other management goals in areas such as interest sensitivity management, loan management, and portfolio management. As a case in point, excessive use of liability management could force the bank to use relatively high-cost funding if interest rates unexpected surged upward.[7] Thus, the bank must trade off the cost of maintaining excessive liquidity and the cost of insufficient liquidity. As shown in Figure 11-3 (next page) , at some point an optimum liquidity level is reached, at which liquidity costs are minimized.

Because of the reliance on forecasted needs and sources, a reasonable margin for error should be considered. Greater uncertainty tends to increase the potential costs of maintaining liquidity, as well as the potential costs of insufficient liquidity. As such, the optimum quantity of bank liquidity is increased by uncertainty. To evaluate uncertainty and its effects on bank liquidity more formally, a graphical comparison of the probability distributions of both liquidity needs and sources can be constructed as shown in Figure 11-4 (next page). The overlapping area is proportion-

FIGURE 11-3 TRADING OFF THE COST OF MAINTAINING LIQUIDITY AGAINST THE COST OF INSUFFICIENT LIQUIDITY

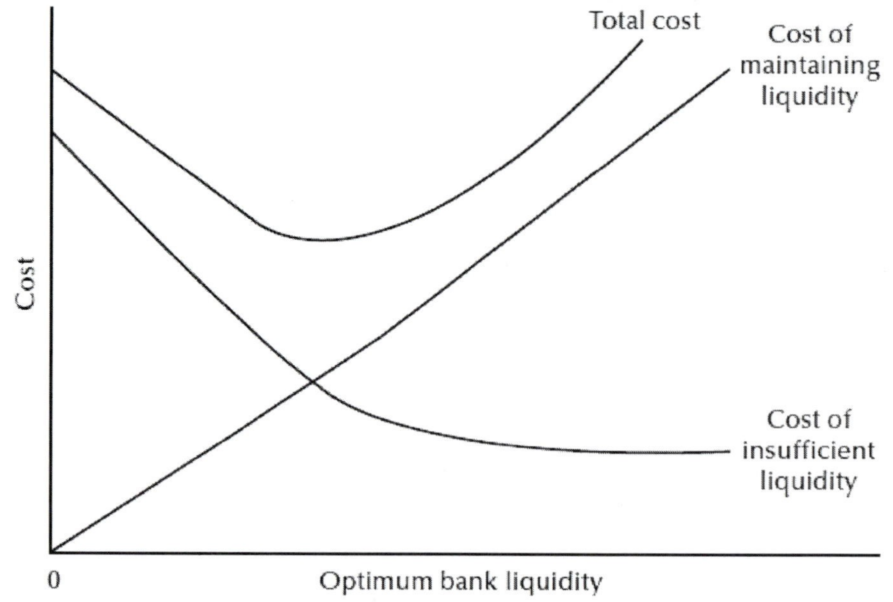

al to the probability that the bank will use up all of its liquidity; that is, liquidity needs could exceed liquidity sources. As the amount of overlap in these two distributions increases, it becomes more likely that the bank will be illiquid at some point during the period of time under consideration.

FIGURE 11-4 GRAPHICAL ANALYSIS OF BANK LIQUIDITY

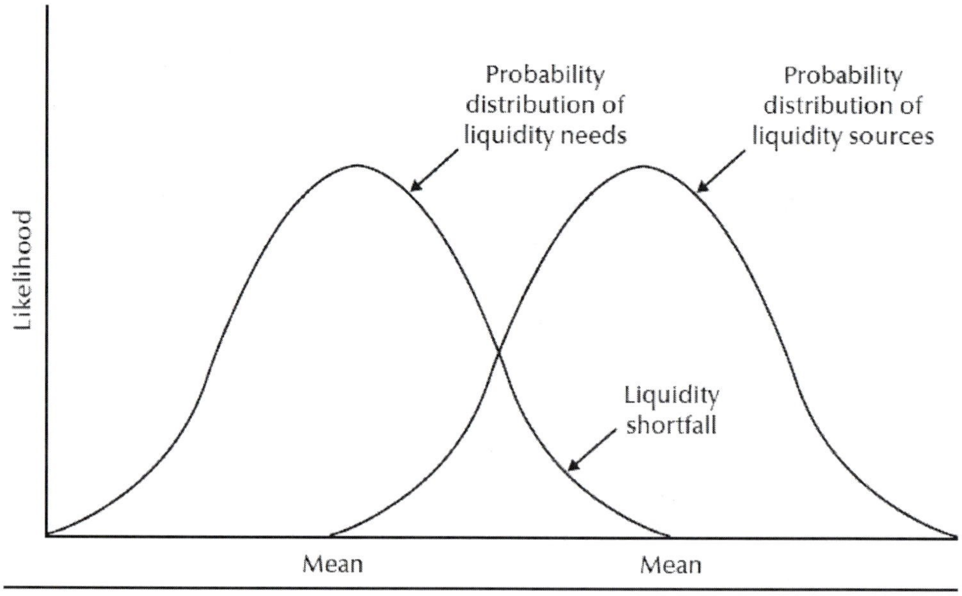

It should be obvious that liquidity management is a complex balancing of risks and returns over time. Banks today differ considerably not only in their liquidity needs and sources but also in the extent to which they use different liquidity management strategies. As banks expand their asset base, changes in liquidity management should be assessed. Also, changes in bank condition could require management to modify its approach to liquidity. Less liquidity is necessary if the bank has large amounts of (unpledged) long-term securities, loan cash flow, and marketable loans. Also, as alluded to earlier, the bank may be using a considerable quantity of large-denomination liabilities, but the risk associated with these funds would depend on their apportionment between core funding and volatile funding.

REGULATORY VIEW OF BANK LIQUIDITY

Regulators are concerned with the adequacy of a bank's liquidity, as opposed to the least-cost liquidity strategy. The Uniform Bank Performance Report (UBPR) published by the Federal Financial Institutions Examination Council gives liquidity analyses of individual banks, as well as different groupings of banks. It provides an important analytical tool used by bank examiners to evaluate a bank's liquidity position. Current liquidity ratios and their trends relative to peer group average ratios are compared to obtain a comprehensive view of bank liquidity. Some of the more common ratios used by examiners include:

- Net non-core funding dependence
- Net loans and leases to deposits
- Net loans and leases to total assets
- Short-term assets to short-term liabilities
- Pledged securities to total securities
- Brokered deposits to deposits, and
- Core deposits to total assets.

Of course, such an evaluation must consider the quality, stability, and unique characteristics of asset and liability accounts before analyzing liquidity ratios. In particular, loans, securities, deposits, and borrowings should be evaluated before using UBPR ratios to draw conclusions concerning the liquidity position. For example, a bank with a relatively risky loan portfolio financed by large CDs could be prone to extreme liquidity risk in the sense that it is "reaching" for interest income on risky loans with "hot" deposits, which are relatively expensive and can disappear overnight. If loan problems arose such that the CDs could not be rolled over, the bank would suffer a severe liquidity crisis. It is therefore important to distinguish between ***operational liquidity*** and ***crisis liquidity*** management. The former term applies to liquidity practice in normal everyday operations, whereas the latter type of liquidity relates to a temporary or enduring problem situation that threatens the bank's solvency. Crisis liquidity can be differentiated further into problems specific to the institution versus systemic problems that affect all institutions. Referring to the preceding example, the bank may be considered operationally liquid but relatively illiquid in a crisis situation.

Almost all banks employ a staff to oversee ***management information systems*** to measure and respond to liquidity needs. Such systems collect information both on and off balance sheet and are especially helpful for institutions with global operations. They also are valuable tools to forecasting operational and crisis liquidity positions under alternative scenarios in a simulation setting. As a further check on liquidity management, banks routinely audit their information systems and their management success in achieving the bank's liquidity goals and policies. And, yet another layer of protection is afforded by ***comprehensive contingency funding plans***. These plans outline courses of action to various liquidity problems and define coincident management responsibilities.

The wide variety of data collected by federal regulators to gauge bank liquidity amply suggests that it is a multidimensional concept. No single index is currently available that captures all of the factors included in an evaluation of liquidity, including the liquidity of assets, stability of liabilities, access to borrowed funds, and liquidity needs. Instead, each bank must be analyzed on an individual basis. In this regard, an extenuating circumstance could be the evaluation of bank liquidity in periods of financial crisis, i.e., crisis liquidity. Due to liquidity problems among especially large banks during the 2008-2009 financial crisis, the Basle Committee is phasing in a new ***Liquidity Coverage Ratio (LCR)*** for large, internationally active banks. Effective January, 2015, large banks must assume a period of economic stress like the recent financial crisis and estimate the following ratio:

$$\text{LCR} = \frac{\text{High-quality liquid assets (HGLA)}}{\text{Total net cash outflows over the next 30 days}} \qquad (11\text{-}2)$$

While somewhat subjective due to hypothetical stress levels, it seeks to ensure that large banks have sufficiently high liquidity to protect the financial system as well as individual banks themselves under difficult conditions. The new liquidity requirement will be gradually phased in over a five-year period ending 2019. Bank supervisors consider both the LCR and earlier Sound Principles established by the Basle Committee to assess bank liquidity. A potential problem with the new LCR for large banks is that increasing cash and near-cash holdings will decrease loanable funds and reduce credit supplies. Despite this drawback, it is believed the new liquidity rules are needed to maintain a safe and sound banking system should future economic and financial shocks occur.

BANK LIQUIDITY: AN EXAMPLE

Southwest National Bank and Rocky Mountain Bank are two medium-sized, regional banks located in a city with a population of approximately five million people. Southwest is oriented primarily to serve large commercial and industrial business firms in the area, while Rocky Mountain has sought to meet the needs of both individuals and businesses, most of which are smaller retail and light manufacturing firms. The two banks are not in direct competition with each other because of emphases on different market niches but do share a common economic base in the same city.

In the last two years the local economy has experienced a sharp downturn due to cutbacks in military spending that have seriously affected some large electronic components firms in the area. The slowdown has caused losses of jobs and outflows of workers, which triggered failures of retail merchants and restaurants and a decline in real estate values due to a rising supply of homes for sale.

These events have affected the financial condition of both Southwest and Rocky Mountain. Table 11-5 shows a number of financial ratios over the last three years for these banks. Both institutions have been under some degree of financial distress, as net income/total asset ratios have markedly slipped and equity capital/total assets ratios have declined also. Southwest appears to have experienced a sharper downturn in profit rates and capital ratios than Rocky Mountain.

TABLE 11-5 FINANCIAL CONDITION OF SOUTHWEST NATIONAL BANK AND ROCKY MOUNTAIN BANK OVER TIME

	Southwest			Rocky Mountain		
Financial Ratios	**2014 (%)**	**2015 (%)**	**2016 (%)**	**2014 (%)**	**2015 (%)**	**2016 (%)**
Net income/total assets	2.1	1.0	0.5	1.2	0.9	0.8
Equity capital/total assets	6.5	6.0	5.5	6.0	5.6	5.5
Business loans/total assets	50.0	52.0	53.0	20.0	22.0	19.0
Home loans/total assets	5.0	5.0	4.0	30.0	28.0	26.0
Consumer loans/total assets	6.0	8.0	9.0	15.0	16.0	18.0
Temporary investments/total assets	20.0	18.0	16.0	15.0	14.0	12.0
Core deposits/total assets	50.0	48.0	45.0	80.0	82.0	83.0
Volatile liabilities/total assets	40.0	42.0	44.0	12.0	11.0	12.0

Comparing their loan portfolios, we see that Southwest has tended to increase business lending, as well as consumer lending, on a percentage of assets basis. These changes could be due to a desire by bank management to increase asset risk and, therefore, loan yields in an effort to make up for declining earnings. Rocky Mountain has maintained its business loan activity, cut back on home loans, and shifted to greater consumer lending. These changes likely had little or no effect on its overall credit risk.

Finally, and most relevant to our discussion, Southwest and Rocky Mountain clearly have different approaches to liquidity management. Southwest has relatively higher temporary investments than Rocky Mountain, but it uses much larger proportions of assets funded by volatile liabilities and much smaller proportions of assets funded by core deposits than Rocky Mountain. These differences are not unexpected, as greater use of volatile liabilities naturally should be backed up with higher secondary reserves. However, notice that Southwest has decreased its temporary investments while increasing volatile liabilities and decreasing core deposits. Rocky Mountain has also drawn down its temporary investments somewhat, but its mix of core deposits and volatile liabilities has stayed about the same over time.

We can infer that Southwest has significantly weakened its liquidity position. It is reasonable to believe that this change was prompted by a shift to higher-risk loans, as funding for these loans was essentially purchased as needed. By contrast, Rocky Mountain has been under earnings and capital pressures but has not compromised its safety and soundness by increasing credit risk or substantially altering its liquidity. Instead, Rocky Mountain is using some of its secondary reserves for meeting liquidity needs otherwise covered by bank earnings. This hypothetical example helps to illustrate that liquidity is a relative concept that varies not only from bank to bank but over time.

SUMMARY

Banks are under constant liquidity pressures. Since no bank can function without adequate liquidity, it is one of the most fundamental aspects of bank management. While adequate liquidity to avoid a crisis is one dimension of the problem, for most ongoing banks it is operational liquidity that is the real challenge. In this respect the central issue that management must evaluate is the risk and return tradeoffs.

Liquidity management involves estimating future expected liquidity needs and then planning to meet those needs by converting assets to cash, acquiring external funds, or both. To estimate liquidity needs the sources and uses approach can be used to evaluate the effects of deposit inflows and outflows and changing loan demands on bank liquidity. The structure-of-deposits method is another way to estimate liquidity needs and focuses on the stability of deposits as a source of funds. Another major bank liquidity consideration is meeting the Federal Reserve's legal reserve requirements under Regulation D. Contemporaneous reserve requirement (CRR) accounting procedures must be used for transactions deposits as specified by the Federal Reserve.

Once liquidity needs are estimated, bank management must plan to meet those needs. Asset liquidity is a traditional approach, whereas liability management is a more modern approach. Asset liquidity refers to holding secondary reserves of money market instruments that can be quickly converted to cash with little or no capital loss. Use of cash and short-term financial instruments to meet liquidity needs does not affect the capital position of the bank, while liability management can affect the bank's capital position, which must be sufficient to satisfy regulatory requirements.
Liability management of liquidity enables the bank to shift funds from lower-earning money market instruments to higher-earning loans and investment securities. It also tends to increase the financial flexibility of the bank in dealing with liquidity needs. If it is cheaper to acquire funds than it is to liquidate assets to finance new loans, the former should naturally be used, barring the influence of other factors in the decision. However, this liquidity approach is not without risks. Debt interest obligations rise as a percentage of total assets, which tends to increase the bank's exposure to interest rate risk, as well as its financial risk because of increased financial leverage.

Optimally, bank managers must weigh the cost of maintaining excessive liquidity against the cost of insufficient liquidity in an attempt to minimize the total costs of liquidity management. By contrast, regulators are more concerned with the adequacy of the bank's liquidity, as measured in the Liquidity Coverage Ratio (LCR) and *Sound Principles* of liquidity risk management employed by supervisors.

KEY TERMS AND CONCEPTS

Aggressive liquidity approach
Asset liquidity
Asset management
Banker's acceptances
Capital market risk
Carry trade strategy
Commercial paper
Comprehensive contingency funding plans
Contemporaneous reserve requirement accounting
Correspondent balances
Crisis liquidity
Discount window
Eurocurrency liabilities
Federal agency securities
Federal funds
Funding-liquidity risk
Funds management
Lagged reserve requirement accounting
Liability management
Liquidity Coverage Ratio (LCR)
Management information systems
Market-liquidity risk
Money market approach
Negotiable certificates of deposit
Nonpersonal time deposits
Operational liquidity
Optimum liquidity
Primary reserves
Repurchase agreements
Secondary reserves
Sources and uses of funds method
Structure-of-deposits method
Transactions accounts
Treasury bills

QUESTIONS

11-1. What is the first step in any bank liquidity analysis? Discuss two methods of accomplishing this first step.

11.2 Why has asset management been less emphasized over the last 30 years?

11.3 When would asset liquidity be preferred to liability management of liquidity?

11-4. Why are legal reserves considered a tax on banks? What did the Federal Reserve to recognize this issues?

11-5. What are collateralized commercial paper programs and medium-term notes? How do they help meet liquidity needs?

11-6. What are lagged reserve requirements? How is vault cash counted in maintaining reserves using LRR?

11-7. How are reserve requirements calculated for MMDAs?

11-8. How do small and large banks differ in the management of their money positions?

11.9 What is the money market approach to liquidity management?

11-10. Discuss the risks and returns associated with using liability management to meet liquidity needs. Why can a carry trade strategy be risky?

11-11. What is funds management? What does it seek to do?

11-12. Discuss optimality in bank liquidity management. How does uncertainty affect optimal bank liquidity?

11-13. How do regulators evaluate bank liquidity? How much liquidity is adequate?

11-14. How does operational liquidity management differ from crisis liquidity management?

11-15. If the ratio of liquid assets and liabilities in period t divided by estimated liquidity needs in period t is between zero and one, might there be a problem with bank liquidity?

11-16. What is the Liquidity Coverage Ratio (LCR) under new regulations adopted by the Basle Committee? How is it related to financial crisis?

11-17. What is funding-liquidity risk and market-liquidity risk? How might banks use management information systems to control these risks?

11-18. Review the Federal Financial Institutions Examination Council's (FFIEC) "UBPR User's Guide" (www.ffiec.gov/UBPR.htm). What is contained in the report? How is it useful to banking institutions?

11-19. Google "FDIC and bank liquidity" and go to the FDIC's website overviewing different aspects of liquidity management. Pick one of the articles there and write a summary of its content.

11-20. Go to the National Information Center (NIC) website at www.ffiec.gov/nic, look up an individual bank, and collect data on its liquidity. Write a short report based on your data.

PROBLEMS

11.1 (a) Given the Sources and Uses of Funds Statement in Exhibit 11-1, calculate the estimated changes in loans and deposits from month to month, as well as the estimated liquidity need.

(b) Given the results of part (a) above, in which months does the bank have excess or deficient liquidity? If there is a deficiency, what sources of liquidity are there to meet the liquidity need? In the month(s) in which there is excess liquidity, what uses of funds are there to avoid holding too much idle cash?

(c) Given the information in Exhibit 11-2, calculate the bank's ratio of estimated liquidity sources to liquidity needs. Is there a possibility that the bank will have a liquidity problem at some time in the coming months?

EXHIBIT 11-1. SOURCES AND USES OF FUNDS STATEMENT

End of Month	Estimated Total Loans	Estimated Total Deposits
June	$180,000	$190,000
July	190,000	180,000
August	210,000	190,000
September	240,000	200,000
October	200,000	210,000
November	180,000	200,000
December	170,000	190,000

EXHIBIT 11-2. ESTIMATED SOURCES OF LIQUIDITY

End of Month	Estimated Asset Liquidity	Estimated Sources of Liabilities
June	$3,000	$ 5,000
July	4,000	10,000
August	4,000	5,000
September	3,000	3,000
October	2,000	5,000
November	3,000	10,000
December	4,000	10,000

11.2 Given the following deposit data, calculate the total reserves required:

	Average Dollar Amount (in millions) in Computation Period
Net transactions accounts	
$0–$15.2 million	$15.2
$15.2-$110.2 million	95.0
Over $110.2 million	30.0
Nonpersonal time deposits	25.0
Eurocurrency liabilities	
All types	2.0

Note: The first $15.2 million of transactions deposits are exempt from reserve requirements.

11.3 You are given the responsibility to review your bank's liquidity position by top management, as reflected by balance sheet and income statement information. To do this your assistant assembled the following financial data per your request:

	Metropolitan Bank			Peer Group of Banks		
Financial Ratios	2014 (%)	2015 (%)	2016 (%)	2014 (%)	2015 (%)	2016 (%)
Net income/total assets	0.8	0.9	1.1	0.8	0.9	0.9
Equity capital/total assets	5.5	5.7	6.0	5.6	5.7	5.9
Business loans/total assets	50	53	56	48	47	48
Home loans/total assets	10	9	8	12	13	13
Consumer loans/total assets	9	8	6	10	9	9
Temporary investments/ total assets	20	18	15	20	21	20
Core deposits/total assets	55	50	45	53	55	54
Volatile liabilities/total assets	35	39	45	37	36	37

CASE: NORTHEAST NATIONAL BANK

The last few years had been quite profitable for Northeast National Bank, despite increasing competition from out-of-state competitors in its home state. Northeast had increased total assets over the last five years from $300 million to $500 million and was starting to enjoy some scale economies from the larger size of operations and recent organizational changes. Ten years ago changes in federal banking laws had opened up interstate branching in the nation. A low-cost opportunity to enter new markets presented itself -- branch offices did not require (1) applying for new bank charters, (2) a CEO or board of directors, and (3) high operating and overhead costs. Instead, branch offices could be operated with a manager and many operations of the branch channeled through the main bank office, including paperwork on mortgage loans, most computerized record keeping, wire transfers of funds, payrolls, etc. The cost savings of branch banking had enabled Northeast to increase its profits despite growing competition and use the retained earnings to expand its reach in the area. At the present time, Northeast had five branch offices located within a 20-mile radius of the main office, with two of these offices located across a nearby state line.

The larger size and different configuration of operations of Northeast had changed its liquidity management. It had become essential that the main office for a branch network work closely with the branch managers on their liquidity needs and sources. Unfortunately, no formal system of control over the liquidity function had formally developed over the last ten years, as most liquidity issues were overcome by strong cash flows from recent cost savings on branch operations.

However, other banks in the state also have been modifying their organizational structure to take advantage of operating cost savings from branching. A competitive trend that has been emerging in the last year is the use of these savings by other banks to lower loan rates and raise deposit rates relative to Treasury rates of interest. Thus, profit margins are beginning to return to previous levels that existed prior to the federal relaxation of branch banking laws.

John Thorpe, vice president of operations for Northeast, arrived at work Monday morning to find a memorandum from CEO George Schindler requesting a strategic report on liquidity management issues that would need more in-depth analyses in the next six months. Mr. Schindler asked that the following questions be discussed in the report:

- How is liquidity defined?
- How is liquidity measured at the branch office level in relation to the bank organization as a

whole?

- How does the branching structure change liquidity risks for the main office?
- How does the branching structure affect the liquidity risks of each individual branch office?
- Does it make sense to evaluate the liquidity of the consolidated branching organization or should liquidity analyses focus on each operating branch as well as the main office?
- How can the bank communicate its liquidity strengths to outside observers who only can obtain data on the consolidated bank organization?

After calling the branch managers, John learned that each branch had a different market niche and normally (but not always) referred larger customer needs for credit and other services to the main office. The main office was located in a large suburb of a major U.S. city. One branch was located near a university and specialized in small, retail deposit accounts for students with few credit services, except for auto loans and some other consumer installment loans. A second branch was located on the main street of a small nearby community and offered small business deposit and loan services for the most part. A third branch was not far from the main office at a convenient customer location that helped support both retail and commercial services for the main office. The fourth branch tended to emphasize auto loans due to its close proximity to a number of automobile dealerships that were concentrated in one part of town. The fifth, and last, branch office was larger than the other branches and offered a full line of financial services, with the exception of wholesale banking services to large corporate clients.

With this information in mind, John Thorpe has asked you, as his assistant, to write a two-page report briefly addressing each of the above questions. He has encouraged you to stick to fundamentals but, at the same time, show some creativity in handling the issue of branch offices.

ENDNOTES

1. Cash and due from banks is not a near-cash asset. Cash and due is comprised of fed reserves, float, and vault cash, all of which are frozen assets and not available for purchasing other assets or decreasing liabilities.

2. The Basle Committee was founded in 1975 and today is comprised of senior representatives of banking supervisory authorities and central banks from Belgium, Canada, France, Germany, Italy, Japan, Luxembourg, the Netherlands, Spain, Sweden, Switzerland, the United Kingdom and the United States. Other countries that participated in the new liquidity principles were: Australia, China, Hong Kong SAR, Singapore and the Committee on Payment and Settlement Systems.

3. Cash assets include vault cash, bank deposits at Federal Reserve banks, bank deposits at other banks, and other available cash (e.g., cash items in the process of collection, in addition to cash and due from banks, which are holdings of other banks' certificates of deposit).

4. For this reason cash reserves are not liquid assets for most banks. However, the money position is still relevant to liquidity management due to its short-term nature and daily adjustment using internal and external liquidity sources.

5. Regulation A restricts banks from using the discount window to "supplement capital," which means that chronic use of the window to meet liquidity needs is not permitted.

6. Lenders eligible for Federal Home Loan Bank membership include savings banks, savings and loan associations, cooperative banks, commercial banks, credit unions, and insurance companies that are active in housing finance. The 11 Federal Home Loan Banks have more than 7,500 member financial institutions.

7. Evaluating the costs of various liabilities sources involves an all-in-cost approach. Deposits have interest payments, FDIC insurance premiums, and operating costs. Commercial paper has interest payments, underwriting fees, and (at times) credit enhancement costs (through standby letters of credit and other guarantees). Likewise, costs of repurchase agreements, bankers' acceptances, fed funds, and other external funding sources need to be fully assessed.

PART 4

CAPITAL, LIABILITIES, AND OFF-BALANCE SHEET MANAGEMENT

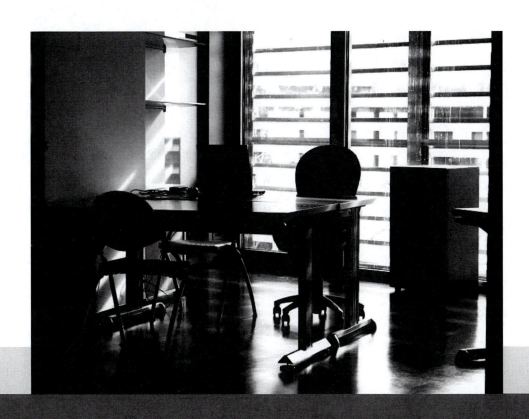

Chapter 12

Capital Management

After reading this chapter, you will be able to:

- Define the components of bank capital, which differs in some respects from nonfinancial firms
- Describe the role of bank capital in the banking industry
- Discuss the capital adequacy of banking institutions from the perspective of both regulators and shareholders.
- Compare the different capital standards utilized by regulators over the years, including those that are applied today
- Identify trends in the capitalization of U.S. commercial banks and their relationship to regulatory standards

Bankers and regulators view bank capital differently. From the banker's perspective, using less capital is a way to magnify (or lever) asset earnings and so earn higher equity rates of return. By contrast, regulators prefer that banks increase their capital to ensure their safety and soundness in the event earnings become negative. Despite these different views, on one point there is total agreement -- namely, capital is a fundamental building block of the banking business that is essential to survival and growth.

This chapter begins by defining bank capital and then discusses its role in managing both bank operations and financial risk. With these basics in hand, we cover the issue of capital adequacy from the alternative viewpoints of bank regulators and bank shareholders. The international risk-based capital requirements applicable to banks today are presented in some detail. Finally, capital trends over time for U.S. commercial banks are presented and discussed.

DEFINITION OF BANK CAPITAL

Like nonfinancial firms, capital in banking includes equity plus long-term debt. Equity is a residual account in the sense that it is the difference between total assets on the left-hand side of the balance sheet and total liabilities on the right-hand side of the balance sheet. Unlike nonfinancial firms, however, ***bank capital*** also includes reserves that are set aside to meet anticipated bank operating losses from loans, leases, and securities. Moreover, bank capital is subject to detailed regulatory requirements that attempt to ensure adequate capital to absorb normal levels of operating losses. In so doing, depositors are protected, as well as the deposit insurer.

EQUITY

Equity is constituted of ***common stock, preferred stock, surplus,*** and ***undivided profits.*** The accounting value of common (and preferred) equity is equal to the number of shares outstanding multiplied by their par value per share. Surplus is the amount of paid-in capital in excess of par value realized by the bank upon the initial sale of stock. Finally, undivided profits equal retained earnings, which are the cumulative net profits of the bank not paid out in the form of dividends to shareholders. The sum of these components is the ***book value of equity.***

An alternative way to measure common stock and preferred stock is in terms of the ***market value of equity.*** Market values reflect not only the past, such as the historical book value of equity, but also the expected future value of the bank. Indeed, stockholders are most concerned about future earnings available to them and the associated risks of those earnings. Thus, it is not surprising that the book value and market value of equity differ from one another.

As an example, suppose that a newly chartered bank sold one million common shares with a par value of $9 per share for $10 per share. During the first three years of business, the bank had undivided profits of $100,000, $110,000, and $120,000, respectively. Equity capital, as indicated in the Report of Condition, would be as follows:

Preferred stock	$ 0
Common stock	9,000,000
Surplus	1,000,000
Undivided profits	330,000
Total equity	$10,330,000

Normally, the market value of equity would exceed the ex post (or historical) book value of equity on the balance sheet, because most banks expect to have positive earnings per unit of risk in the future. Unfortunately, the equity stock of most banks is not traded in the open market, either because they are closely held by a small group of investors or because trading activity is too low to warrant listing on a stock exchange. In this case the historical accounting (or book) value traditionally has served as a benchmark in comparing the equity positions of different banks.

LONG-TERM DEBT

Subordinated notes and ***debentures*** are sources of long-term debt that banks can utilize to raise additional external funds. Because this debt is second in priority to depositor claims in the event of bank failure, it is said to be "subordinated." Banks use far less long-term debt than do nonfinancial firms because most of their debt is in the form of short- and intermediate-term deposit and nondeposit funds, which essentially are money market sources of funds. However, in the 1960s especially large banks began to increase their usage of long-term bank debt. This increase was motivated by a change in regulatory requirements that allowed notes and debentures (with maturities of at least seven years) to be used to meet capital standards for national banks. In the context of regulatory capital, however, it should be noted that the long-term debt only serves to absorb operating losses in the event of failures.

A major advantage of using debt capital (as opposed to equity capital) is that interest payments are tax deductible, whereas equity earnings are fully exposed to federal income taxes. Consequently, debt is a less expensive after-tax source of external capital than equity in general.

For small banks the use of long-term debt is much more costly than it is for large, billion-dollar banks. Fixed transactions costs can raise the marginal cost of small debt issues to an unreasonably high level. Moreover, small issues normally are less liquid than larger issues, causing investors to demand a higher rate of return, which raises the cost of borrowing for small banks. Nonetheless, under regulatory capital standards (to be discussed shortly) banks have incentives to issue long-term debt. By inducing banks to issue long-term debt, regulators intend to increase "market discipline," whereby creditors monitor bank safety and soundness and reflect their views in bond prices. Of course, for small banks, scanty trading activity for bonds would diminish market discipline to some extent.

RESERVES

Banks set aside earnings for loan (and lease) loss reserves. When a loan defaults, the loss does not necessarily reduce current earnings because it can be deducted from the reserve account. To establish reserves to meet anticipated loan losses, banks expense an account known as the ***provision for loan losses (PLL)*** on their income statement. By expensing PLL, banks reduce their tax burden. In the past banks used either the experience method or the percentage method to calculate their PLL. The experience method involves using the average loan losses over the previous six years. The percentage method simply takes 0.6 percent of eligible loans. Since the passage of the Tax Reform Act of 1986, however, banks with more than $500 million in assets can expense only actual losses from pre-tax income. This change prevents banks from overstating loss reserves to reduce their income and, in turn, their taxes.

Another reserve account is the ***reserve for loan losses***. This account is reported on the liability side of the balance sheet and is also known as the allowance for loan losses. The reserve for loan losses is calculated as the cumulative PLL minus net loan charge-offs. Since this reserve is subtracted from total loans to get net loans, it is a contra-asset account. Part of the reserve for loan losses is counted as capital on the right-hand-side of the balance sheet. These ***capital reserves*** are employed by regulators in measures of capital adequacy. Typically, capital reserves are comprised of funds set aside to pay dividends or retire stocks and bonds outstanding, as well as funds held for unexpected losses.

As an example of what happens when banks charge off loans, assume that a bank has a PLL equal to $1 million and the reserve for loan losses is $3 million. Given that the bank charged off $800,000 in loan losses during the year, but recovered $80,000 on previous charge-offs, the reserves for loan losses is calculated as follows:

Reserves for loan losses, beginning of 20XX	$3,000,000
Less: Charge-offs during 20XX	800,000
Plus: Recoveries during 20XX on loans previously charged off	80,000
Plus: Provision for loan losses, 20XX	1,000,000
Reserves for loan losses, end of 20XX	$3,280,000

Because reserves absorb most losses in the banking industry, they are a key component of bank capital. Losses that exceed these reserves would have to absorbed by stockholders' equity.

ROLE OF BANK CAPITAL

Bank capital serves three basic roles. The first, and most obvious, is that it is a source of funds. A new bank requires funds to finance start-up costs of capital investment in land, plant, and equipment. Established banks require capital to finance their growth, as well as to maintain and modernize operations. They normally rely upon internal capital (retained earnings) to a much greater extent than external capital (long-term debt and equity stock). However, external capital is often used to finance major structural changes, such as acquisitions and mergers.

The second function of capital is to serve as a cushion to absorb unexpected operating losses. Relatively high loss rates on loans that surpass the loan loss provisions covering anticipated operating losses are charged against capital. Banks with insufficient capital to absorb losses are declared insolvent by their regulatory agency and are handled by the Federal Deposit Insurance Corporation (to be discussed in greater detail later in this chapter). It should be recognized that long-term debt instruments are a capital source of funds that cannot be used to absorb losses except in a liquidation of a failed institution. Thus, in contrast to reserves and equity sources of capital, long-term debt only weakly satisfies the role of capital as a cushion to absorb losses.

The third, and last, function of bank capital bears on the question of adequate capital. Unlike nonfinancial firms with capital/asset ratios commonly in the 40 percent to 60 percent range, banks generally have less than 10 percent of assets funded by capital. This means that banks "skate on thin ice" such that relatively small (unanticipated) asset losses can significantly affect bank capital and threaten bank solvency. As discussed in the forthcoming section, "adequate capital" to maintain a reasonable margin of safety is a difficult concept in practice. Bank regulators establish minimum requirements to promote safety and soundness in the banking system. They also seek to mitigate the moral hazard problem in deposit insurance by using capital requirements to increase the exposure of bank shareholders to potential losses and so motivate prudent management. Additionally, market confidence is another factor in evaluating adequate capital. If the market perceives a shortage of bank capital, bank stock prices will be adversely affected. Conversely, a record of strong and stable capital over time tends to favorably affect bank stock prices.

DEPOSITORY INSTITUTION FAILURES AND CAPITAL

Waves of depository institution failures occurred throughout U.S. financial history. The Great Depression in the 1920s and 1930s saw about 15,000 banks fail and the remaining 20,000 or so banks severely weakened with relatively low capital levels. Over 4,000 federally insured depository institutions failed from 1980 to 1991 (including commercial banks, thrift institutions, and credit unions). After reckoning the damage, it is believed that taxpayers paid over $200 billion in losses (or about 20 percent of these depository institutions' assets). Also, while most failures in the Great Depression were small institutions, large banks were increasingly at risk. For example, in 1992 the number of failed banks declined to 120 from over 200 in 1989, but their combined total assets exceeded $40 billion. Confirming this trend, in the 2008-2009 financial and economic crisis, now dubbed the *Great Recession,* the largest 15 U.S. banks experienced financial distress that threatened their solvency. A government bailout was implemented to bolster bank capital in these banks and prevent a national financial disaster like the banking collapse in the Great Depression.

Many reasons have been cited for these catastrophic losses, including interest rate management problems, high and volatile interest rates, local and regional economic declines, turmoil in money and capital markets, deregulation that expanded risk-taking opportunities, changes in the market for home loans, bad management, regulatory failures, and illegal or unethical practices. Central to the debate concerning the reasons for these losses at depository institutions is deposit insurance. Deposit insurance at fixed rates or premiums creates incentives for bank managers and shareholders to take excessive risks, as losses are paid by the insuring agency (e.g., the FDIC). This is known as the ***moral hazard problem***. In nonfinancial firms creditors monitor the degree of risk taking by the firm and use this information to constrain borrowing. By contrast, in depository institutions, insured depositors are indifferent to bank risks so that risk must be monitored by regulators. With over 10,000 depository institutions (including banking and thrift institutions) in the United States, the regulatory tasks of measuring risks and undertaking disciplinary actions are formidable. Indeed, this regulatory approach to controlling risk in depository institutions clearly is deficient in view of repeated financial crisis that have shocked the banking system.

For these reasons capital has become a centerpiece of regulatory policy. The basic idea is that shareholders with significant stakes in the institution will act to control risk taking to protect their investment. Thus, capital requirements are being imposed on depository institutions. Greater equity investment in banks tends to discourage risk taking behavior by increasing market discipline. While some institutional losses can be explained by other reasons (such as regulatory forbearance in terms of keeping insolvent institutions with negative net worth open and able to incur further losses), the moral hazard problem can be diminished via equity and debt investment in the banking industry.

CAPITAL ADEQUACY

As mentioned earlier, bank regulators and bank shareholders tend to have differing views about the adequacy of capital. Regulators normally are concerned about the downside risk of banks; that is, they focus on the lower end of the distribution of bank earnings. By contrast, shareholders are more concerned with the central part of the earnings distribution, or the expected return available to them. Both regulators and shareholders also consider the variability of bank earnings, albeit from different perspectives once again. Regulators perceive earnings variability in the context of the likelihood that earnings will fall so much that capital is eliminated and the bank becomes insolvent. Shareholders require higher earnings per share as the bank profitability becomes more variable. Of course, shareholders receive compensation for bank risk, whereas regulators do not.

REGULATORY VIEWPOINT

From the viewpoint of regulators, financial risk increases the probability of bank insolvency. Greater variability of earnings after taxes means that interest and noninterest expenses are more likely to exceed bank earnings and that capital will be required to absorb potential losses. If there is insufficient capital to absorb losses, regulators must close the bank due to ***capital impairment***.

The problem faced by regulators is that, although requiring banks to maintain higher capital tends to lower financial risk, such requirements may inhibit the efficiency and competitiveness of the banking system -- that is, capital requirements that exceed unregulated levels act as a constraint on the lending operations of banks. In this instance, banks may not allocate loanable funds in the most efficient way. The productivity of the economic sector could therefore be lessened by this constraint on the financial system. Regulatory restrictions on bank capital could also hinder their competitiveness relative to other sellers of financial services. For example, relatively high capital requirements tend to constrain the rate at which bank assets can be expanded. Unable to grow as rapidly as other financial service companies, banks would be at a competitive disadvantage. Thus, regulatory policy regarding ***capital adequacy*** must weigh the potential benefits of safety and soundness against the potential costs of efficiency and competitiveness.

CAPITAL STANDARDS

In general, regulators favor added capital as a buffer against insolvency to promote the safety and soundness of the financial system. "Safety and soundness" in this instance implies protecting depositor funds and preventing financial panics through the provision of a stable money supply. Regulators historically have maintained different standards for capital adequacy and have changed those standards many times. For example, because deposit runs were the major threat to bank soundness in the early 1900s, the ***Office of the Comptroller of the Currency (OCC)*** focused on banks' capital-to-deposit ratio to measure capital adequacy, as deposit problems were perceived to be the major cause of failure. During World War II, banks accumulated large proportions of default-free government securities to help finance federal debt, which caused regulators to utilize a capital-to-risk-asset ratio, where the term risk assets was defined as total assets minus cash and government securities. In this case losses on risky assets was perceived to the main reason for bank failure.

Over the last 50 years, a wide variety of methods for assessing capital adequacy have been applied by regulators. In the 1950s for example, the ***Federal Reserve Board (FRB)*** began using the ***Form for Analyzing Bank Capital (FABC)*** to classify assets into six different risk categories. Banks were required to hold a different percentage of capital against each asset category (e.g., 0.4 percent capital against U.S. Treasury bills and 10 percent capital against business loans). Also, smaller banks had higher capital requirements because of the perception that their portfolio diversification was less than larger banks. By contrast, the OCC abandoned the use of strict guidelines in the early 1960s in favor of more subjective evaluations based on many factors, including management quality, asset liquidity, ownership, operating expenses, and deposit composition. Because OCC standards applied to national banks, FRB standards applied to state member banks and banks affiliated with holding companies, and FDIC standards applied to state-chartered banks, the capital adequacy of an individual bank was determined to a certain degree by its particular regulatory agency. Of course, for banks subject to multiple federal regulatory agencies (such as national banks in bank holding companies), compliance with capital requirements could become confusing.

Another problem with capital standards has been their enforceability. In the past, regulators relied primarily upon persuasion to enforce capital standards. Seldom were cease and desist orders employed to obtain compliance, because regulators were not supported by force of law. A steady decline in capital/asset ratios in the banking industry in the 1960s and 1970s made clear that this approach to capital regulation was not working. This problem was solved by the ***International Lending Supervision Act of 1983*** under which regulators were given legal authority to establish minimum capital requirements and enforce them. Normally, the regulator requires violating banks to submit a plan to correct the capital shortfall, which is now enforceable in the courts.

Yet another problem with previous capital standards is the question of fairness. In the past, small banks had more restrictive capital requirements than large banks. Presumably, bank size was directly related to safety and soundness, according to this dichotomy. However, the historical evidence on bank failures in the United States has not proved failure risk to be greater in small banks than in large banks.

UNIFORM CAPITAL REQUIREMENTS

In 1981 federal bank regulators established minimum primary capital-to-asset ratios. ***Primary capital*** was defined as common stock, perpetual preferred stock, capital surplus, undivided profits, capital reserves, and other nondebt instruments. The FRB and OCC adopted a six percent minimum for banks with less than $1 billion in assets and five percent for banks over $1 billion assets. The FDIC applied a five percent minimum ratio to all banks. Multinational banks, which are the 15–20 largest banks in the United States, were evaluated on a case-by-case basis. Under the 1983 International Lending and Supervision Act, however, multinationals were required also to meet the five percent minimum primary capital requirement.

Further improving uniformity, in 1985 the three federal bank regulators settled on a 5.5 percent primary capital ratio for all banks. In this regard, regulators established zones for billion-dollar banks that considered ranges of ratios for primary and ***total capital*** (defined to also include debt instruments), as well as asset quality and other factors that are relevant to capital risk. Finally, if a bank was judged to be undercapitalized, it had to make up the shortfall under the supervision of its regulatory agency. Progress toward compliance with capital standards was monitored over time.

In response to this uniform capital/asset ratio measurement of capital adequacy, undercapitalized larger banks generally raised new capital, reduced their holdings of liquid assets, and increased off-balance-sheet activities (because only booked assets were counted in the calculation of the capital ratio). Some larger institutions, forced to increase capital, also sought to cut operating costs, raise service prices, and make riskier loans. These changes tended to offset the advantage of added capital in many cases and so defeated to some extent the capital adequacy goals of regulators.

BASEL I

In 1987, U.S. federal regulatory agencies, in conjunction with the Bank of England and authorities from ten other leading industrial countries, agreed to release for public comment proposed ***risk-based capital rules.***[1] The major rationale for this proposal was that historical evidence indicated no obvious relationship between bank capital and failure risk. In the Great Depression, for example, capitalization was not linked directly to failures. Not only would the proposed standards be more closely related to failure risks, they would also promote convergence of supervisory policies on the adequacy of capital among countries with major banking centers. This convergence was needed due to the rising competition in international banking. If U.S. regulators raised capital standards for U.S. banks, but other countries did not do so, U.S. banks would be disadvantaged relative to international competitors. In June, 1988 the so-called ***Basel Agreement*** was signed by 12 industrialized nations under the auspices of the Bank for International Settlements (BIS). By year-end 1992 all U.S. banks were required to comply with the new rules.

Credit Risk and Capital Rules

Known as *Basel I* today, the international risk-based capital rules maintained a minimum threshold for all banks, which was consistent with previous uniform standards, and classified assets into *four credit risk categories* with different levels of capital requirements, not unlike the Federal Reserve's previous FABC approach. Additionally, starting January, 1998 an amendment by the Basel Committee was implemented to extend Basel I rules to new market risk capital requirements that focus on securities trading by commercial banks. There are two categories of capital: (1) Tier 1 or "core" capital, and (2) Tier 2 or "supplemental" capital. ***Tier 1 capital*** measures equity holdings and is equal to the sum of tangible equity, including common stock, surplus, retained earnings, and perpetual preferred stock. Unlike primary capital under uniform rules, capital reserves are excluded from equity. Tier 2 capital is comprised of loan loss reserves, subordinated debt, intermediate-term preferred stock, and other items counted previously as primary capital (such as mandatory convertible debt and cumulative perpetual preferred stock with unpaid dividends). Since year-end 1992, the minimum capital levels have been as follows:

Capital	Risk-Adjusted Assets	Total Assets
Tier 1	4%	3%
Tier 1 + Tier 2 (Total Capital)	8%	No requirement

Table 12-1 (next page) gives details of the minimum requirements for Tier 1 and Tier 2 capital.

TABLE 12-1 COMPONENTS AND RULES OF GOVERNMENT QUALIFYING CAPITAL UNDER RISK-BASED CAPITAL RULES

Components	Minimum Requirements
Tier 1 (Core) Capital	Must equal or exceed 4% of risk-weighted assets (RWAs)
Common shareholder's equity and retained earnings	No limit
Qualifying noncumulative perpetual preferred stock and related surplus*	No limit, but regulatory warning against "undue reliance"
Minority interests in equity accounts of consolidated subsidiaries	No limit, but regulatory warning against "undue reliance"
Less:	
Goodwill and some intangible assets†	
Subsidiaries of S&Ls engaged in activities not permitted national banks	
Tier 2 (Supplementary) Capital	Limited to 100% of Tier 1
Allowance for loan and lease losses	Limited to 1.25% of RWAs
Perpetual preferred stock not qualifying for Tier 1 capital	No limit within Tier 2
Hybrid capital instruments and equity-contract notes‡	No limit within Tier 2
Subordinated debt and intermediate- term preferred stock	Limited to 50% of Tier 1
Deductions from Total Capital	
Investments in unconsolidated subsidiaries	
Reciprocal holdings of other depositories' capital securities	
Other activities of S&L's not permitted national banks	
Other deductions required by supervisory agents	
Total Capital	Must equal or exceed 8% of RWAs
= Sum [Tier 1 + Tier 2] – Deductions	

* Bank holding companies can include both cumulative and noncumulative perpetual preferred stock in Tier 1, but the total amount is limited to 25 percent of Tier 1 capital.

† Other intangible assets are those that do not meet a three-part test (see 54 Fed. Reg. 4,168, 4,179, Jan. 27, 1989).

‡ Hybrid capital instruments include instruments that are essentially permanent in nature and that have characteristics of both equity and debt.

Table 12-2 (next page) gives the Basel I weighting scheme for calculating risk-adjusted assets for purposes of credit risk capital requirements. Weights for on-balance-sheet assets increase as credit risk increases:

- Zero default risk items have a zero percent weight
- Mortgaged-backed bonds issued by U.S. government and U.S. government-sponsored agencies and general obligation municipal bonds have a 20 percent weight
- Home loans, revenue bonds, and some other mortgage-backed securities carry a 50 percent weight
- All other assets have a 100 percent weight

To calculate the minimum capital requirements for a bank in dollar terms, the following formula can be used:

$$K = \text{minimum ratio} \times [0.00\,(A_1) + 0.20\,(A_2) + 0.50\,(A_3) + 1.00\,(A_4)] \qquad (12.1)$$

where minimum ratio is the Tier 1 or total capital minimum requirement, and A1..., A4 is the dollar amounts held in four asset categories. The term is brackets is known as ***risk-adjusted assets.***

As an example, assume a bank has the following assets:

Assets	(1) ($ Thousands)	(2) Risk Weight	(1) × (2) Risk-Adjusted Assets
Cash	$ 100	0.00	$ 0
FNMA securities	1,000	0.20	200
General obligation municipal bonds	1,500	0.20	300
Home loans	3,000	0.50	1,500
Commercial loans	5,000	1.00	5,000
	$10,600		$7,000

The minimum capital requirements using the risk-adjusted assets procedure would be:

Tier 1 capital = 0.04 ($7,000) = $280

Total capital = 0.08 ($7,000) = $560

Tier 1 capital would also have to be greater than 3.0 percent of total assets, or $318. In this case the capital required under the risk-adjusted assets procedure of $280 is irrelevant because at least $318 Tier 1 capital is required on total assets. Thus, the risk-adjusted method of calculating primary capital is important only for banks with larger amounts of risky assets. For less risky banks Tier 1 capital ratios are based on the uniform 3.0 percent requirement.

TABLE 12-2 COMPONENTS OF ON-BALANCE-SHEET RISK-WEIGHTED ASSET CATEGORIES

Risk-Weight Category	On-Balance-Sheet Assets
0%	Cash
	Securities backed by the full faith and credit of U.S. and OECD governments and some U.S. government agencies
	Balances due from Federal Reserve banks and central banks in other OECD countries
20%	Cash items in the process of collection
	Mortgage-backed U.S. government or U.S. government-sponsored agency securities
	U.S. and OECD interbank deposits and guaranteed claims
	Assets collateralized by securities backed by the full faith and credit of U.S. and OECD governments
	Assets conditionally guaranteed by U.S. and OECD governments
	Securities issued by and direct claims on U.S. government-sponsored agencies
50%	Loans fully secured by first liens on 1–4 and multifamily properties
	Mortgage-backed securities backed by home mortgage loans with at least 80% loan-to-value ratios
	U.S. state and local government revenue bonds
100%	All other claims on private obligers, including consumer and commercial loans
	Long-term claims on, or guaranteed by, non-OECD banks
	Residential construction loans
	Premises, plant, and equipment; other fixed assets; and other real-estate owned
	Commercial paper and most private-issue debt
	Investments in unconsolidated subsidiaries, joint ventures, or associated companies not deducted from capital
	Mortgage-related securities with residual characteristics
	All other assets, including intangible assets not deducted from capital

Table 12-3 shows the risk-weighting scheme for ***off-balance-sheet activities.*** These items must first be converted to on-balance-sheet "credit equivalent" amounts. The items are assigned to the appropriate on-balance-sheet risk category, and the capital requirements can then be calculated as before. For example, assume that a bank has the following off-balance-sheet items:

Items	(1) Amount ($ thousands)	(2) Conversion Factors	(3) Risk Weight	(1) × (2) × (3) Risk-Adjusted Assets
Performance standby letters of credit	$1,000	0.50	0.20	$ 100
Commercial letters of credit	2,000	0.20	1.00	400
Guaranteed letters of credit	1,500	1.00	1.00	1,500
Total off-balance-sheet items	$4,500			$2,000

Tier 1 capital and total capital requirements under the risk-adjusted assets procedures would now be:

Tier 1 capital = 0.04 ($7,000 + $2,000) = $360

Total capital = 0.08 ($7,000 + $2,000) = $720.

Including off-balance-sheet items, primary capital of $360 exceeds the minimum using total assets of $318. Thus, the risk-adjusted requirement for primary capital is now relevant or binding. It should be mentioned that a more complicated formula is used for interest rate swaps, forward contracts, and options, as well as foreign exchange contracts (see Table 12-3 on the next page).

Market Risk and Capital Rules

As already mentioned, ***market risk capital requirements*** were fully implemented in January, 1998. These rules supplement the credit risk capital requirements by invoking some adjustments to the risk-based capital ratio. Insured state member banks and bank holding companies with significant securities trading activity are exposed to market risk rules; namely, institutions with more that 10 percent of total assets or $1 billion or more in trading account positions. The trading account includes both on- and off-balance-sheet positions in financial instruments, currencies, and commodities held for profitable resale in the event of price and rate changes. These assets are marked-to-market daily and banks must hold on a daily basis a minimum eight percent risk-adjusted capital ratio adjusted for market risk. Two types of market risk adjustments are necessary: (1) ***general market risk*** associated with the financial market as a whole, and (2) ***specific risk*** due to other risk factors (including credit risk of the securities issuer). A "covered position" implies that adequate capital is held to support these two market risks.

The primary adjustment to the risk-adjusted capital ratio due to market risk takes place in the denominator. In the denominator the value of market-risk equivalent assets must be added to an adjusted value of credit-risk-weighted assets (i.e., the previous value of credit-risk-weighted assets less covered positions in the trading

TABLE 12-3 COMPONENTS OF OFF-BALANCE-SHEET RISK-WEIGHTED ASSET CATEGORIES

Conversion Factor	Off-Balance-Sheet Assets
	20% Risk Weight
50%	Performance standby letters of credit conveyed to others
	Participations in commitments with an original maturity exceeding one year conveyed to others
100%	Financial standby letters of credit conveyed to others
	50% Risk Weight
0%	Unused commitments with an original maturity of one year or less
	Other unused commitments if unconditionally cancelable and a separate credit decision is made before each draw
20%	Commercial letters of credit and similar instruments
50%	Performance standby letters of credit less those conveyed to others
	Unused portion of commitments with an original maturity exceeding one year less those conveyed to others
	Revolving underwriting facilities, note issuance facilities, and similar arrangements
100%	Financial guarantee standby letters of credit less those conveyed to others
	Participations in acceptance acquired
	Securities loaned
	Farmer Mac loans (Farm Credit Administration)
	Other off-balance-sheet items
	Sale and repurchase agreements and assets sold with recourse
	Forward agreements and other contingent obligations with a specified draw down
	Subordinated portions of senior/subordinated mortgage-pool securities

Note: The notional value of off-balance-sheet items are converted to on-balance-sheet "credit equivalent" amounts. These "credit equivalent" amounts are then assigned the risk weights that would be applicable to the counterparty or underlying collateral. Interest-rate and exchange-rate contracts are converted to on-balance-sheet credit equivalent amounts by summing the current credit exposure and the potential credit exposure. Current credit exposure is the replacement cost of the contract (in U.S. dollars). The potential credit exposure is an estimate of the potential increase in credit exposure over the remaining life of the contract.

account). Thus, in the previous example, assume that the $1,500 in general obligation (GO) municipal bonds is all in the trading account of the bank. Given the risk-adjusted assets for these securities was $300 (=$1,500 × 0.20), the adjusted value of credit-risk-weighted assets would be $7,000 – $300 = $6,700. The calculation of market-risk equivalent assets is determined by individual banks using their own internal risk model. As discussed in Chapter 7, such a model estimates the daily value-at-risk (VAR) for the trading account assets plus an add-on capital charge for specific risk. VAR is normally calibrated to the ten-day 99th percentile standard. As an example, assume that on a particular day a bank calculates from past records over the last year that there is only a 1 in 100 chance of losing $66.67 in any ten-day period. This VAR is typically multiplied by a scaling factor of 3 (but it can be higher if required by regulators), such that market-risk equivalent assets equals $200 (= $66.67 × 3) on the chosen day in the present case. Under the new rules, banks must use: (1) an average VAR over the last 60 business days times 3, or (2) the previous day's VAR. Because the second criterion is only relevant to periods in which the financial markets are extremely volatile, the first criterion is more commonly employed. Banks must use a minimum of one year in their historical calculations of VAR on any particular day. Assuming that \$200 is the average VAR over the last 60 business days, the new value for risk-adjusted assets in the denominator of the risk-adjusted capital ratio is \$6,900 (= \$6,700 + \$200).

Specific risk can be calculated either using standardized measurement methods or using the bank's individual internal model. Capital charges for specific risk are intended to cover losses not captured by the VAR model estimates. Recall that general market risk captures movements in prices and interest rates; consequently, it does not reflect risk in a trading position involving securities that are illiquid due to infrequent trading. In the context of our previous example, if specific risk was estimated at \$50, the capital charge would be \$200 (= \$50 × 4) and, in turn, the denominator of the risk-adjusted capital ratio would become \$7,100 (= \$6,900 + \$200). We can see that the new market risk capital requirements have increased risk-adjusted assets from \$7,000 for credit risk alone to \$7,100 for credit risk and market risk. If total capital was nine percent of credit-risk-adjusted assets (or \$630), it would decline to about 8.9 percent due to market risk. Most experts believe that total capital ratios have declined 30 to 40 basis points due to market risk.

All banks must implement control procedures in market risk assessments. Each bank must have a risk-control unit that is separate from the business-trading function. The risk-control unit is required to regularly perform backtests to determine the accuracy of the internal VAR model and specific risk estimates. Internal models should be updated at least every three months, and (as mentioned in Chapter 7) stress tests of simulated changes in various risk factors checked against actual trading experience. Backtesting results enable VAR models to evolve over time and provide regulators with important information on changing risk levels in banks' trading accounts. While criticisms about the ad hoc application of scaling factors and potential risks of turning over some degree of regulatory control to banks themselves are certainly warranted, market risk capital requirements represent a major advance in both regulatory oversight and bank risk management.

Potential Weaknesses of Basel I

In general, risk-based capital requirements should tend to decrease risk by forcing equity holders to take a greater stake in banks. However, there were a number of potential weaknesses in Basel I capital requirements. First, related to credit risk, differences in the default probabilities and potential recovery rates in default were generally not addressed. In this regard, because bank loans are not actively traded, VAR methods that are easily applied to traded securities are difficult to implement for loans. Second, another problem is that book values rather than market values were used in the weighting scheme. By favoring (nontrading) securities over loans in the weighting scheme, risk-based capital requirements may curtail bank credit, as banks shift more funds to investments. Third, Basel I rules did not account for other kinds of bank risk, such as operating, liquidity, and legal risks. Of these, operating risk is increasingly being recognized by regulators. Operating risk considers the competitive risks the bank faces in its market, as well as payments and accounting system failures and fraud. Fourth, a lack of portfolio diversification is another consideration that is not explicitly taken into account. Despite these weaknesses, the combination of credit risk and market risk capital requirements was a significant improvement over previous capital rules. The new capital rules (1) were sensitive to some extent to differences in bank risk taking; (2) incorporated off-balance-sheet activities into risk assessments; (3) did not penalize banks for holding low-risk, liquid assets; and (4) increased the consistency of rules applied to large banks around the world.

BASEL II

In view of the aforementioned weaknesses in the Basel I capital requirements, the Basel Committee, comprising central banks and bank supervisors and regulators from the major industrialized countries and meeting at the Bank for International Settlements (BIS) in Basel, Switzerland, issued a proposal to replace the Basel I with a more risk-sensitive framework referred to as Basel II. After numerous revisions to Basel II, the new Accord was implemented in 2007. Basel I and II can be compared as follows:[2]

Basel I

- Focus on a single measure of capital adequacy
- One size fits all
- Broad-brush approach

Basel II

- More emphasis on banks' own internal risk models, supervisory review, and market discipline
- Flexibility, menu of approaches, incentives for better risk management
- More risk sensitivity

Basel II contains three pillars:

I. ***Minimum capital requirements:*** The definition of capital was unchanged and the minimum capital requirement remained eight percent, but risk-adjusted assets were calculated differently. Now credit risk is evaluated more precisely to get the weights for different kinds of loans. Banks had the choice between a standardized approach (similar in most respects to Basel I) versus internal credit risk models of banks (similar to market risk capital requirements). Also, operational risk was now taken into account, including computer failures, poor documentation, fraud, and risks external to the bank.

II. ***Supervisory review process:*** Supervisors evaluate bank measurement techniques with respect to credit and operational risks.

III. ***Market discipline:*** Banks are required to increase their information disclosure, especially on the measurement of credit and operational risks.

As shown in equation (12.2), pillar I retains the current definition of capital and the minimum eight percent requirement in the numerator. In the denominator the measures for credit risk are more complex than Basel I (as mentioned above, market risk was unchanged but operational risk was added).

$$\frac{\text{Total Capital (definition unchanged)}}{\text{Credit risk + Market risk + Operational risk}} \geq 8\% \text{ Minimum capital ratio} \tag{12-2}$$

where

Credit risk can be measured by:

1. Standardized approach -- a modified version of the existing method, based on external credit ratings when available.
2. Advanced internal ratings based (IRB) approach

Market risk can be measured by:

1. Standardized approach
2. Internal models approach

Operational risk can be measured by:

1. Basic indicator approach
2. Standardized approach
3. Internal measurement approach

Under pillar I, smaller banks favored the standardized approach, whereas larger banks typically chose the internal models for evaluating credit and operational risks. Banks selecting the standardized approach are required to obtain external risk assessments by (for example) a rating agency for each borrower. Most firms issuing public debt obtain credit ratings from Moody's and Standard & Poor's. If a borrower has no credit rating, supervisors can assess the risk. Basel I uses a weight of 100 percent on all corporate loans. The new Basel II Accord, using the standardized approach, would provide four credit risk categories with weights of 20 percent, 50 percent, 100 percent, and 150 percent.

If a bank opts for an internal-ratings-based (IRB) approach for measuring credit risk, it can employ the advanced method (i.e., the bank computes the probability of default and the loss given default to assess capital required for each loan). It should be noted that the advanced method applies only to the 10 largest banks and that another 15 to 20 large banks were anticipated to adopt this method also. Internal credit risk models allow for far more diverse risk weights on loans. One way to measure default risk is to observe the default histories of bank loans. Another approach is to track credit ratings over time. Credit ratings or scores for loans generated on a quarterly basis enable banks to track the credit quality of their loan portfolio over time. Internal credit risk models attempt to forecast changes in average rating levels over time. The models seek to link changes in credit ratings with changes in the value of the loan portfolio, which is the key variable from the perspective of bank capital management. The probability that capital will be impaired by any particular decline in credit ratings can then be estimated. Perhaps most important, the bank can take appropriate actions with regard to its allowance for loan loss account to ensure that capital does not become impaired by credit losses. Regulatory capital requirements would use internal credit risk models of banks to establish weights for different levels of credit risk. Also, they could take into account the risk-reducing effects of diversification in the loan portfolio. While model validation is an ongoing problem in measuring default risk, an accumulation of experience for many banks over a number of business cycles should strengthen the reliability of the credit risk estimates. Such backtests can be used to periodically make adjustments to credit risk models and further refine their accuracy.[3]

BASEL III

Basel II was a controversial regulatory reform due to its complexity and the need to coordinate rules across numerous countries. As such, it was expected that the Basel Committee would periodically revise or amend Basel II as needed. Indeed, before Basel II was fully implemented, the 2008-2009 financial crisis made obvious the need to entirely rethink regulation, supervision, and risk management of banks. Building on Basel I, in 2010-2011 the Basel Committee proposed ***Basel III*** to:

- improve the banking sector's ability to absorb shocks from financial and economic stress
- improve risk management and governance
- strengthen banks' transparency and disclosures.

Two levels of reforms were implemented:

- microprudential or bank-level regulation
- macroprudential or system-wide regulation.

These reforms raise capital requirements for derivatives activities, reduce potential banking industry risks from systemically important institutions, and promote a buildup of capital buffers in good times that can be drawn down in periods of stress. The new rules are scheduled to be gradually phased in by March, 2019 among signatory countries.

Table 12-4 (next page) overviews the Basel III capital requirements. The Common Equity Tier 1 (CET1) must be at least 4.5 percent. An Additional Tier 1 (AT1) of 1.5 percent is added to CET1 to get a Tier 1 Capital ratio of at least six percent. The mandated "capital conservation buffer" boosts the CET1 capital ratio to seven percent. And, a "discretionary counter-cyclical buffer" of up to 2.5 percent can be required by regulators during periods of high credit growth. Moreover, Basel III added a non-risk-based ***leverage ratio*** (i.e., Tier 1 capital/total assets) of three percent. The Federal Reserve requires eight Systematically Important Financial Institution (SIFI) banks to maintain a six percent leverage ratio and insured bank holding companies to have a five percent leverage ratio. This ratio seeks to establish contain excessive system-wide leverage.

Table 12-5 shows FDIC guidelines for Prompt Corrective Action related to the new capital rules. Undercapitalized institutions are deemed in violation of capital rules and engaged in unsafe and unsound management practices. Discretionary or mandatory supervisory actions will be initiated in an attempt to resolve the deficiencies.

TABLE 12-4 CALIBRATION OF BASEL III CAPITAL FRAMEWORK (PERCENT)

	Common Equity Tier 1 (CET1)	Tier 1 Capital (CET1 + AT1)	Total Risk-Based Capital
Minimum risk-adjusted assets ratio	4.5	6.0	8.0
Conservation buffer	2.5		
Minimum plus conservation buffer	7.0	8.5	10.5
Counter-cyclical buffer range	0 – 2.5		

Leverage ratio (Tier 1 capital/total assets) = 3

TABLE 12-5 FDIC GUIDELINES FOR PROMPT CORRECTIVE ACTION (PCA)

PCA CATEGORY	Total RBC Ratio	Tier 1 RBC Ratio	CET1 RBC Ratio	Tier 1 Leverage Ratio
Well Capitalized	10%	8%	6.50%	5%
Adequately Capitalized	8%	6%	4.50%	4%
Undercapitalized	<8%	<6%	<4.5%	<4%
Significantly Undercapitalized	<6%	<4%	<3%	<3%
Critically Undercapitalized	Tangible Equity/Total Assets equal to or less than 2%			

Source: *Risk Management Manual of Examination Policies*, FDIC.

The Federal Reserve introduced new liquidity rules also. The ***Liquidity Coverage Ratio*** (LCR) is defined as follows:

$$LCR = \frac{\text{High quality liquid assets}}{\text{Total net liquidity outflows over 30 days}} \geq 100\% \qquad (12\text{-}3)$$

where high quality liquid assets can be quickly liquidated to meet liquidity needs in a short period of time, and the denominator is total expected cash outflows minus total expected cash inflows. Only banks with more than $10 billion in assets are subject to the liquidity rule. Also, new metrics are being developed by the Basel Committee to assist supervisors in identifying and analyzing bank liquidity risk trends at the micro (bank) and macro (systemwide) levels.

Basel capital requirements will continue to evolve in the years ahead. To keep up with the latest developments, visit the webpage for the Basel Committee on Banking Supervision (BCBS) at https://www.bis.org/bcbs/.

FDIC

The ***Federal Deposit Insurance Corporation (FDIC)*** has a vested interest in bank capital adequacy. It insures deposits held by approximately 98 percent of all U.S. commercial banks. Banks are required to pay premiums to insure deposit accounts up to $250,000. Rebates, determined by the FDIC's collections minus disbursements and operating expenses, have been paid to sound institutions at the end of the year.

Created in 1933, the FDIC has two policy objectives. First, deposit insurance is intended to protect depositors of modest means against bank failures. Second, the insurance is supposed to protect communities, states, or the nation from the economic consequences of a breakdown in the payments system. The record shows that since its inception the FDIC has effectively met these objectives, with 100 percent recovery of insured deposits and about 99 percent recovery of total deposits.

When a distressed bank situation arises, the FDIC handles it in one of five ways: (1) depositor payoff, (2) purchase and assumption, (3) provision of financial aid, (4) charter of a Deposit Insurance National Bank (or bridge bank), or (5) reorganization. In a depositor payoff, each insured depositor receives up to $250,000 from the FDIC within one week. Liquidated proceeds from the bank are used for this purpose, and remaining funds are used to pay off other deposit and nondeposit claims, as well as the FDIC itself. It is normally less costly, however, for the FDIC to use the purchase and assumption (P&A) method of disposition. Under this approach, the bank is merged with a healthy bank. The FDIC accepts the lower-cost bid for the bank and pays off part (or all) of the acquiring bank's losses in the merger.

If the closure of a bank would severely disrupt banking services to a community or cause creditors to suffer extraordinary losses, the FDIC can choose among the latter three approaches cited previously. Financial aid can be used temporarily to assist a distressed bank. A ***Deposit Insurance National Bank (DINB***, or so-called bridge bank) can be chartered by the FDIC to take over operations until the bank is either closed or acquired by another bank. Finally, the major creditors can reorganize the bank with or without regulatory intervention. Of the five approaches, liquidations and mergers are the most commonly used.

Deregulation of financial institutions has caused new problems for the FDIC. Now banks can choose among a broader opportunity set of risks and returns in their liability and asset management. Intuitively, it is inappropriate for all banks to pay the same deposit insurance costs, but prior to 1993 premium rates were fixed for all banks. It is believed that some banks took excessive risks in an attempt to exploit the mispricing of deposit insurance by the FDIC -- the moral hazard problem mentioned previously. For these reasons, the FDIC implemented a ***risk-based deposit insurance*** scheme in 1994; the strongest institutions would pay lower insurance premium rates per $100 of domestic deposits than the weakest institutions. Premiums could vary depending on risk measures and supervisory ratings.

Table 12-6 shows the list of risk measures currently used the FDIC for banks, which are different for those banks with less than versus more than $10 billion. Since 2011 the assessment rates in cents per $100 of insured deposits are based on four bank risk categories: (I) 2.5-9, (II) 9-24, (III) 18-33, and (IV) 30-45. Large and highly complex organizations are assessed in the range 2.5 to 45 based on the risk factors shown in Table 12-6. In effect, the variable-rate premiums increase deposit (debt) costs as capital ratios decline and the probability of bank failure increases. This pricing system mimics to some extent the higher interest costs of debt demanded by creditors of nonfinancial firms as risk increases. Of course, deposit premiums reduce earnings available to shareholders. This exerts further control on bank managers, who are accountable to shareholders. On the other hand, some banks may be willing to pay higher insurance premiums if risky investments are well managed and earn relatively high returns.

It may seem that risk-based capital requirements and risk-based deposit insurance are redundant. However, while capital forces shareholders to "co-insure" (with the FDIC) against bank losses, deposit insurance pays for losses beyond the co-insurance level. Naturally, banks with higher co-insurance (equity capital) should pay lower premiums. Therefore, capital adequacy and deposit insurance pricing are interrelated rather than redundant.

SHAREHOLDERS' VIEWPOINT

Shareholders view bank capitalization in a substantially different way than regulators do. Shareholders seek an optimal mix of debt and equity finance to maximize the value of their common stock. Because share values are a function of both expected future cash flows available to equity owners and their associated risks, shareholders focus on the expected value of rates of return on equity and their variability. In this section we review some of the major factors that influence capital structure decisions of bank shareholders.

FINANCIAL RISK AND SHARE VALUATION

Financial risk is associated with borrowing funds to finance assets. As a bank substitutes debt (including both deposit and nondeposit liabilities) for equity, there is less margin for error in lending, liability management, investment, and other bank operations. This financial risk is reflected in the variability of earnings per share (EPS). Table 12-7 gives an example of the effect of financial risk on EPS. It is clear from the results there that greater use of debt, or financial leverage, causes the percentage change, or variability, of EPS to increase. More specifically, the relationship between debt usage and EPS variability can be written simply as:

$$\text{\% change in EPS} = \text{\% change in EBIT} \times (\text{EBIT} - \text{Interest Expenses})/\text{EBIT} \quad (12.4)$$

TABLE 12-6 **FDIC RISK MEASURES TO DETERMINE RISK-BASED PREMIUM RATES ON INSURED DEPOSITS FOR BANKS**

A. Assets Less than $10 Billion
- Tier 1 leverage ratio
- Loans past due 30-89 days / Gross assets
- Nonperforming assets / Gross assets
- Net loan charge-offs / Gross assets
- Net Income before Taxes / Risk-weighted assets
- Rapid asset growth funded by brokered deposits
- Weighted average examination component ratings

Additional adjustments for:
- High reliance on brokered deposits (only applies to higher risk small institutions)
- Reliance on long term unsecured debt

B. Assets Greater than $10 Billion
- Tier 1 Leverage Ratio
- Higher risk assets / Tier 1 capital and reserves
- Level of, and growth in, risk concentrations
- Core earnings / Average assets
- Past due assets / Tier 1 capital and reserves
- Criticized and classified assets / Tier 1 capital and reserves
- Core deposits / Total liabilities
- Highly liquid assets / Potential cash outflows
- Projected loss given default / Domestic deposits
- Weighted average examination component ratings

Additional risk measures for highly complex institutions:
- Largest counterparty exposure / Tier 1 capital and reserves
- Top 20 counterparty exposures / Tier 1 capital and reserves
- Trading revenue volatility / Tier 1 capital
- Market risk capital / Tier 1 capital
- Level 3 trading assets / Tier 1 capital
- Short-term borrowing / Average assets

Additional adjustments for all large banks:
- High reliance on brokered deposits (only applies to higher-risk large institutions)
- Reliance on long-term unsecured debt

Source: Staff paper, "Deposit Insurance Funding: Assuring Confidence," FDIC (November, 2013).

where EBIT equals expected net operating earnings before interest expenses and taxes. In Table 12-7 (next page), for the low-debt scenario, the percentage change in EPS for a 10 percent change in EBIT is 10% × ($10,000)/($10,000 – $7,000) = 10% × 3.33 = 33.33%, which agrees with our findings shown there. (As a check, students should calculate the same result for the high-debt scenario.)

Although shareholders must bear more variation in earnings if they use greater financial leverage, tax deductions on interest payments lower the costs of making loans. For example, suppose debt and equity rates were equal to 10 percent (after adjusting for risk differences) and the bank's marginal tax rate was 40 percent. The after-tax cost of debt to the bank would be only six percent because of the tax deductibility of interest expenses (i.e., 10% × [1 – 0.40]). The relatively lower cost of debt compared with equity on an after-tax basis causes a preference for debt financing by shareholders.

In nonfinancial corporate enterprises, shareholders cannot necessarily increase their wealth by using debt to obtain tax deductions beyond some leverage point. As compensation for the increased probability that the firm will be unable to pay the higher debt load, debt claimants can be expected to raise the required interest rate that the firm must pay. Also, debtors use covenants to place limits on the extent to which corporations can borrow in the future, as well as on the kinds of debt that can be used and other restrictions on business operations. At some level of financial leverage, the tax gains on leverage are offset by higher interest payments and restrictions on debt usage.

TABLE 12-6 FINANCIAL RISK AND VARIABILITY OF EARNINGS PER SHARE (IN THOUSANDS)

	Low Debt			High Debt		
	Bad	**Expected**	**Good**	**Bad**	**Expected**	**Good**
Net earnings before interest and taxes	$9,000	$10,000	$11,000	$9,000	$10,000	$11,00
Interest expenses	(7,000)	(7,000)	(7,000)	(9,000)	(9,000)	(9,000
Net earnings	2,000	3,000	4,000	0	1,000	2,00
Taxes (@34%)	(680)	(1,020)	(1,360)	0	(340)	(680
Earnings after taxes	$1,320	$1,980	$2,640	$ 0	$ 660	$1,32
Common Shares Outstanding = 1 Million						
Earnings per share	$1.32	$1.98	$2.64	$0	$0.66	$1.3
% change in EBIT relative to expected outcome	–10%	0%	+10%	–10%	0%	+10
Percentage change in EPS relative to expected outcome	–33%	0%	+33%	–100%	0%	100

In banking, however, because of deposit insurance, the debt usage of shareholders normally is not limited by debtors, many of whom are bank depositors. Depositors of insured banks generally do not require a higher rate of interest depending on the bank's leverage, nor do they place restrictions on the issuance of new debt. In the absence of these forms of market discipline, regulators must control bank leverage by setting capital standards and imposing compliance costs on banks that violate those standards. Also, as mentioned earlier, risk-based deposit premiums increase debt costs as leverage increases. We can formally state the effects of debt, taxes, and regulation on bank valuation (and therefore shareholder wealth) as follows:

$$V_L = V_U + tD - C, \tag{12.5}$$

where V_L is the value of the levered bank, V_U is the value of the unlevered (no debt) bank, t is the tax rate on bank income, D is the market value of debt (insured deposits), and C is costs imposed by regulators, such as deposit insurance premiums, reporting requirements, and other compliance costs of regulation. To simplify matters, we have assumed all debts (deposits) are insured and, consequently, are riskless. Without any regulatory costs (or C = 0), the maximum value of the bank is obtained by borrowing as much as possible through deposits and reducing equity capital. This result is consistent with the famous Modigliani and Miller (1963) model of corporate valuation; however, Buser, Chen, and Kane (1981) have argued that regulatory costs cause banks to temper their use of deposits to finance assets.[4]

At some point, further use of deposits will impose such high regulatory costs that bank valuation will decline. Under the new risk-based capital rules, exceeding the minimum requirements will cause C to rise substantially, thereby reducing bank (and stock) value. As banks approach the minimum equity capital boundary, management must be increasingly careful not to make decisions that will later decrease equity capital below the regulatory standard. Moreover, deposit insurance premiums are tied to equity capital levels. Thus, C gradually increases as banks approach minimum equity capital levels. The "optimal" use of debt occurs where V_L is maximized. Of course, bank management seeks to use an optimal financing mix of debt and equity to maximize the value of the firm.

As an example, assume the bank has made investments in loans and securities that are expected to earn $1 million per year based on a rate of return of 10 percent. The unlevered value of the firm, or V_U, equals $1 million/0.10 = $10 million. The bank borrows $12 million in insured deposits and has a 30 percent income tax rate, such that tD = 0.30 × $12 million = $3.6 million. Regulatory costs are as follows: (1) deposit insurance premium is $0.10 × ($12 million/$100) = $12,000, (2) management compliance costs (e.g., compliance officer salary, office space, equipment) are $200,000 per year, and reporting requirements (e.g., loan officers must document that loans are consistent with regulatory guidelines) are $300,000 per year. The value of the bank then is

$$V_L = \$10 \text{ million} + \$3.6 \text{ million} - \$12{,}000 - \$200{,}000 - \$300{,}000 = \$13{,}088{,}000$$

Clearly, the tax deductions of deposit interest exceeds regulatory costs, such that the bank would likely benefit from further increasing its use of deposits and decreasing equity capital. Figure 12-1 (next page) summarizes this analysis and shows an optimal debt level corresponding to bank value maximization. The equity position of the bank currently equals $S = V_L - D$ = $13,088,000 – $12 million = $1,088,000, such that the equity/total assets ratio is $1,088,000/$13,088,000 = 0.083, or 8.3 percent. Because this equity ratio well exceeds regulatory minimums of three percent, assuming the bank does not have abnormally high asset-risk levels, increased leverage likely would boost bank (and share) valuation.

CORPORATE CONTROL

It is possible that greater debt usage increases stockholders' ***corporate control*** of management and, therefore, the bank's operations. That is, more concentrated ownership in the hands of fewer shareholders tends to enhance management control. In closely held banks, because the owners are often the executive officers, minimal conflicts of self-interest arise. In banks that are not closely held, however, it is possible that (for example) managers may make decisions to protect and enhance

FIGURE 12-1 **BANK VALUATION WITH INTEREST TAX DEDUCTIONS ON DEBT AS WELL AS REGULATORY COSTS (IN MILLION $)**

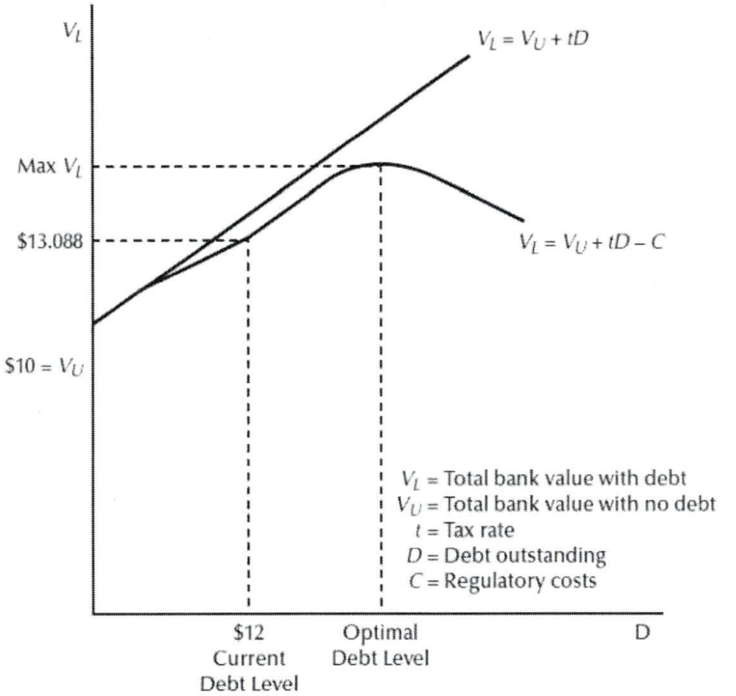

their careers at the expense of shareholders. This potential conflict between principals (shareholders) and agents (managers) is known as an "agency cost" problem.

Although shareholder meetings should normally resolve conflicts of this kind, management might dominate such meetings under some circumstances. For example, if equity ownership is diluted among a large number of owners, individual owners might view themselves as having a negligible effect on the outcome of stockholder meetings. Faced with the costs of collecting information necessary to vote intelligently on issues raised at meetings, many owners may opt out of bank control. This does not necessarily mean that bank managers can act imprudently. Poor performance will tend to stir interest among shareholders concerning management capability. Also, the bank may become a ***hostile takeover*** target—that is, if its shares are undervalued, well-managed banks might seek to purchase a controlling interest in the bank and remove existing management. If shareholders finance bank assets with greater proportionate amounts of debt, individual owners have a greater vested interest in stockholder meetings and, in turn, management control is more easily achieved.[5] Agency costs also can be reduced by linking management compensation to stock prices by offering stock options and bonuses. Finally, shareholders have preemptive rights that enable them to maintain their proportionate ownership share in the event a new issue of stock is made. This right reduces dilution of ownership across many owners and increases the vested interest of existing shareholders. In doing so, the agency cost problem is mitigated to some degree.

MARKET TIMING

Cyclical price movements in the debt and equity markets can affect bank financing decisions. If the level of interest rates is relatively high and debt prices are depressed, it may be cheaper to use equity financing, even accounting for the tax deductibility of interest. Thus, general market conditions may at times favor equity over debt. Alternatively, if inflation is expected to increase in the near future, debt may be preferred over equity because interest payments could be made in "cheaper" dollars (as the nominal value of currency falls over time).

Bank income can also affect debt usage by banks. For example, the marginal tax rate of the bank may be sufficiently low to warrant the use of equity over debt. This might occur because of considerable income earned from municipal bonds not exposed to ordinary income taxes, loan losses, depreciation, and other noncash expenses. Alternatively, marginal tax rates may decline due to low net operating income.

ASSET INVESTMENT CONSIDERATIONS

Bank asset and capitalization decisions are interrelated to some extent. For example, national banks are generally allowed to lend no more than 15 percent of their capital on an unsecured basis to a single borrower. Many states have higher limits for the banks they charter. In 2001 the Comptroller of the Currency implemented a pilot program allowing national banks with the highest supervisory ratings to lend up to the state limit – but no more than 25 percent of capital – to single borrowers for small business loans and for loans secured by a perfected first-lien security interest in 1–4 family real estate in an amount that does not exceed 80 percent of the property's appraised value. Restrictions also exist on the purchase of various securities investments held by the bank (as opposed to a securities subsidiary). Additionally, as asset risk increases, more bank capital is needed to absorb potential losses. As already discussed, risk-based capital rules tie capital closely to the risks of different bank assets and commitments.

DIVIDEND POLICY

Shareholders usually desire the payment of some proportion of bank earnings in the form of cash dividends. This is because they either wish to consume part of their investment income or because they want to diversify their investment holdings. Most owners also want regular and predictable dividend payments. A sudden decrease in dividends would likely raise questions among shareholders concerning the bank's profitability and cause share prices to decline. Thus, bank management should establish and maintain a dividend policy.

In developing a dividend policy, the bank needs to determine its payment strategy. One approach is to use fixed dividend payments. This strategy satisfies shareholder demands for consistent returns, but if earnings decline, this approach may force the bank to raise external debt and equity to finance operations, regardless of their costs. Alternatively, a fixed dividend payout ratio strategy could be implemented, which means that a specific percentage of net income is distributed to owners. This strategy does not constrain the bank's financing choice as much as the fixed dividend strategy; however, it causes dividends to vary with net income over time.

Considerable controversy surrounds the question of why shareholders wish to receive income in the form of dividends instead of capital gains. If shareholders sold shares of stock to consume income or diversify more fully, they could do so when they wished to rather than when the firm distributed dividends. Also, receiving income in capital gains form defers income taxes until such gains are realized, which is a clear advantage relative to receiving periodic dividends. Despite these (and perhaps other) disadvantages of dividends, it is generally true that banks pay out a sizeable proportion of earnings as dividends to shareholders. A long-standing rationale for this is that individuals simply prefer to receive cash returns sooner rather than later because of risk aversion concerning uncertainty in the future. In this way the duration (concerning the timing of cash flows) of the stock is reduced to reflect lower price risk. Alternatively, some individuals may prefer the convenience of regular dividends, which involve no transactions cost. In general, differences in individuals' preferences cause "clienteles" to exist, which firms attempt to attract by setting dividend policy appropriately. A more recent argument is that firms pay dividends as a way to signal shareholders of expected future changes in earnings. Unfortunately, the "optimal" dividend policy in the sense of maximizing share price remains somewhat of a puzzle. Perhaps management's best approach here is historical experience and keeping in touch with the needs of the bank's shareholders.

DEBT CAPACITY

It is generally preferable to avoid using the maximum amount of debt possible in order to preserve some amount of financial flexibility. If a bank borrowed to the limit of capital regulations, for example, it might be unable to take advantage of an unexpected investment opportunity. Some amount of borrowing capacity provides slack that can be used to meet unanticipated liquidity problems. Also, an unexpected loss could push borderline capital below regulatory requirements, thereby provoking added compliance costs. Thus, a reasonable amount of debt capacity is needed as a reserve to help cover potential capital demands.

TRANSACTIONS COSTS

Costs of issuing securities can affect bank financing plans. The acquisition of debt is normally much more costly for nonfinancial corporations than it is for banking institutions. Banks have easier access to credit markets than do nonfinancial firms, mainly because of their intermediary role as depository institutions and their access to insured deposits.

In contrast to most nonfinancial firms, however, all but the largest banks would find the transactions costs of equity issues relatively high. This is because bank issues of equity stock are smaller on average than nonfinancial, corporate issues. Transactions costs, including registration with the Securities and Exchange Commission (SEC), underwriting expenses, legal fees, and other expenses, have a large fixed component that raise the per-share cost of smaller issues. Thus, scale economies in transactions costs make public offerings of equity fairly expensive for most banks. To sidestep the costs of a public offering, banks can use a private stock issue to raise new equity capital. Other reasons for private sale of stock are that the funds can be raised in a relatively short period of time, no SEC registration is required, and underwriter fees can be avoided.

MERGERS AND ACQUISITIONS

External growth through mergers and acquisitions generally requires raising new capital to purchase a controlling equity interest in the target institution(s). The mix of debt and equity used to finance external growth is complicated by the existing capital structures of the bank itself and the target institution(s). The consolidated banking organization must meet regulatory capital requirements, be consistent with the desires of the acquiring (and possibly the target) shareholders, and fulfill other management criteria previously discussed. For example, a common-for-common (stock) exchange in an acquisition would dilute the earnings per share of the buyer (or bidder) if the seller's (target) stock had a relatively high price/earning ratio. If a buyer could use excess debt capacity plus cash to purchase the seller's shares, however, no dilution of earnings per share would occur.

On the other hand, banks anticipating a takeover attempt by another institution may repurchase equity. By repurchasing equity and increasing concentration of ownership, the ability of outsiders to seize voting control through buying publicly available shares (known as takeover) is diminished. However, such a capital strategy could compromise other factors influencing the capital position of the bank, such as excessive financial risk due to higher leverage.

Experts anticipate continued consolidation of the banking industry in the years to come. Merger and acquisition (M&A) activity can be broken down into mega, regional market, and small bank deals. As previously covered in Chapter 4, megamergers involve the world's largest banks. Numerous mergers among large institutions took place in the 2008-2009 financial crisis to rescue especially large home lenders and securities firms from bankruptcy. The top 15 banks substantially increased their size and scope of financial services in response to the crisis. M&As involving purchases of institutions with assets in the $500 million to $5 billion range represent the regional market. At least in the United States, the major buyers have been large national organizations that are taking advantage of interstate banking deregulation, in addition to the fact that internal growth is more expensive under the more restrictive risk-based capital requirements. Finally, many small banks are being purchased by regional banks, who are seeking to strengthen their regional market power. Many small banks have been unable to cope with increasing regulatory costs and seek to exit the industry via M&A. Together, mega, regional, and small bank M&A activity is reshaping the structure of the banking industry.

INTERNAL EXPANSION

The rate at which a bank can internally expand its assets and still maintain its capital ratio is known as the ***internal capital generation rate (ICGR).*** This rate can be calculated as follows:

$$\text{Internal Capital Generation Rate (ICGR)} = \frac{1}{\text{Capital ratio}} \times \frac{\text{Return}}{\text{on assets}} \times \frac{\text{Earnings}}{\text{retention rate}} \quad (12\text{-}6)$$

where the capital ratio is total equity divided by total assets, return on assets is net income after taxes divided by total assets, and the earnings retention ratio is net income available to shareholders minus preferred and common stock dividends divided by net income available to shareholders.

According to the ICGR ratio, decreasing the capital ratio allows a more rapid expansion of bank assets, all else the same.[6] Conversely, higher capital requirements increase the role of internally generated profits, as opposed to externally borrowed funds, in growing the asset base of the bank. It should be recognized that management's approach to financing asset growth is a function not only of the ICGR but regulatory rules concerning capital adequacy, competitive pressures, financial market conditions, and various internal factors (such as shareholder preferences for debt).

As an example of management usage of ICGR, assume that the bank has a total equity/total assets ratio of four percent. If the return on assets ratio is one percent and the retention ratio is 0.50, then ICGR = $(1/0.04) \times 0.01 \times 0.50 = 0.125$, or 12.5 percent. Thus, total assets can be expanded 12.5 percent within the next year with no decrease in the capital ratio. In view of regulatory requirements on bank capital, ICGR is a useful tool for maintaining adequate capital. Also, it highlights the importance of capital in management planning of profit rates, growth rates, and dividend policy.

TRENDS IN BANK CAPITAL

Figure 12-2 (next page) shows trends in the leverage ratio (Tier 1 equity/total assets) for all insured U.S. commercial banks during the period 1984–2015. Average leverage ratios have trended upward for all asset size categories with smaller banks garnering higher leverage ratios than larger banks. Large banks with assets more than $10 billion increased from about four percent in the 1980s to over eight percent in 2015. In general, leverage ratios increase with bank size. Small banks with assets less than $100 million increased from about nine percent in the mid-1980s to about 12 percent by 2015. Also notice the fluctuations in leverage ratios over time. Recessions in the early 1990s and 2008-2009 financial crisis are marked by declining capital ratios, with later recovery as economic conditions improved.

The growing equity base in the industry has enabled banks to increase their assets throughout the 1990s and 2000s. This association highlights the fact that bank asset growth is related to equity capital growth. That is, if a bank sought to increase its size by 10 percent, it would have to raise capital by 10 percent to maintain the same capital ratio. Thus, a bank's ability to increase capital directly affects its ability to expand its asset base.

Lastly, Figure 12-3 illustrates the trends in different capital ratios for banks from 2007 to 2015. All capital ratios increased after the 2008-2009 financial crisis. As of 2015, the total risk-based capital ratio was slightly greater than 14 percent for all insured commercial banks, and the Tier 1 risk-based capital ratio was about 12 percent. The leverage ratio was about nine percent. Strengthening capital ratios in recent years are a direct result of increasing capital standards under the Basel Agreement.

FIGURE 12-2 **TRENDS IN BANK LEVERAGE RATIOS**

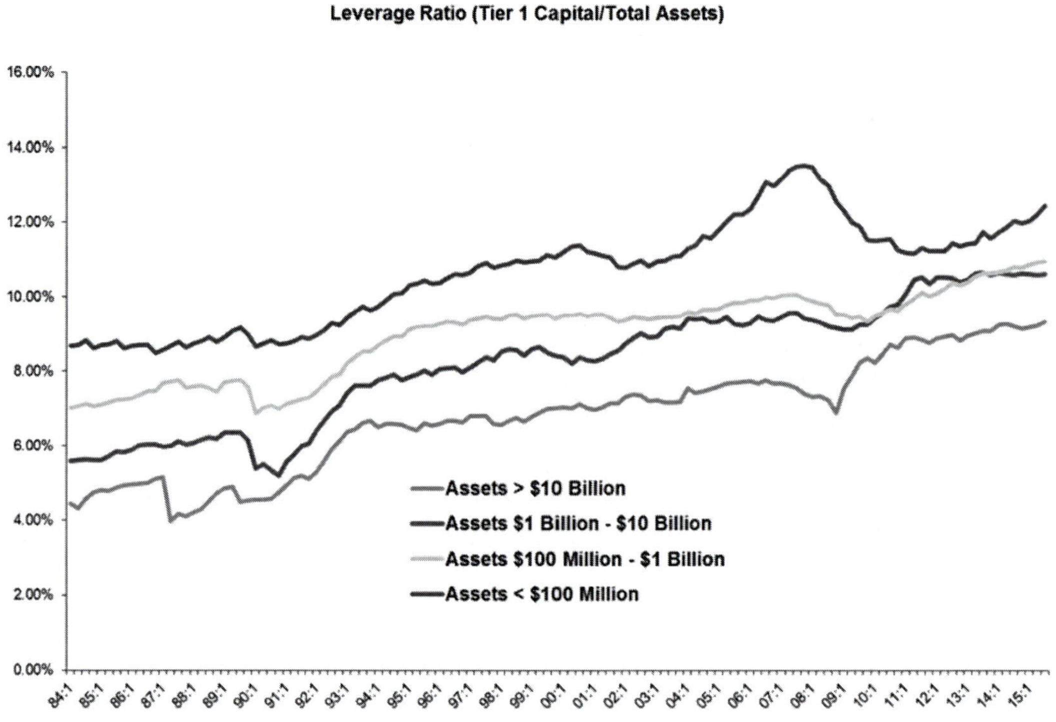

Source: FDIC.

FIGURE 12-3 **TRENDS IN BANK CAPITAL RATIOS**

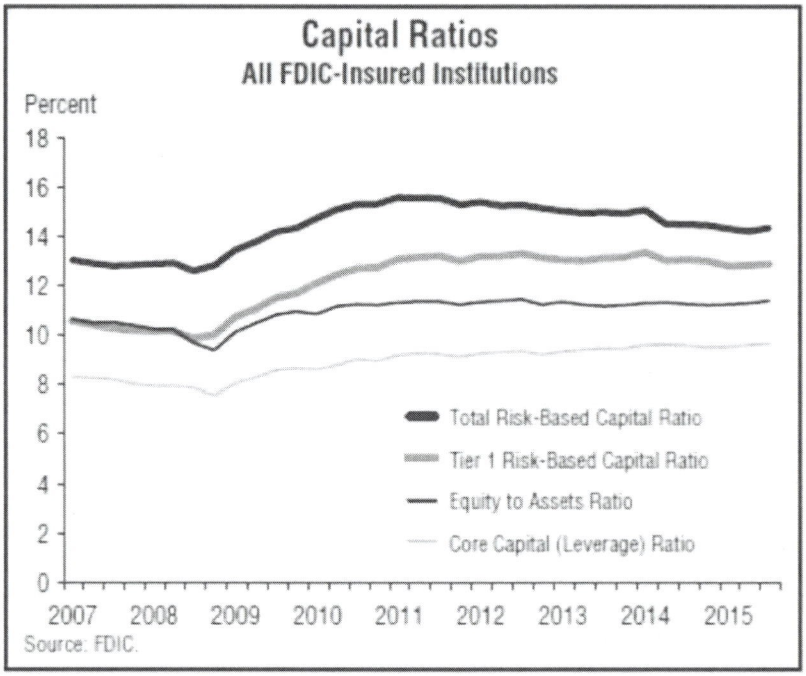

Source: FDIC. FDIC Quarterly, 2015.

SUMMARY

Bank capital management is a controversial subject because regulators and shareholders have differing viewpoints concerning the adequacy of capital. Regulators consider bank capital as a cushion to absorb operating losses. Bank capital for regulatory purposes has two components: Tier 1 capital and Tier 2 capital. New international risk-based capital requirements under the Basel Agreement became effective at year-end 1992 (known as Basel I) and caused U.S. banks to raise equity capital as a percentage of both risk-adjusted assets and total assets. Basel I was amended in 1998 to take into account the market risk of securities, currencies, commodities, and other tradable assets held by banks. Due to deficiencies in Basel I, in 2007 Basel II capital rules were implemented based on three pillars: (1) minimum capital requirements, (2) supervisory process, and (3) market discipline. Among other changes, the new capital rules allowed banks to choose between the standardized approach and internal credit risk model approach. Finally, in response to the 2008-2009 financial crisis, the Basel Committee proposed Basel III, which builds on Basel II by adding further refinements in capital requirements plus new liquidity rules to better protect individual banks and the banking system as a whole from economic and financial shocks.

New risk-based deposit insurance pricing became effective in 1994. Today, the FDIC prices deposit insurance premiums on the basis of risk measures and supervisory ratings. Riskier banks pay higher premiums than safe and sound banks.

Shareholders view capitalization (or the mix of debt and equity funds used to finance bank assets) from the standpoint of maximizing the value of their ownership claims. Although added debt increases the interest burden of the bank and also increases the probability of failure, the tax deductibility of interest expenses lowers the cost of debt financing relative to equity financing. In nonfinancial, corporate enterprises, debtors would require higher interest rates as financial leverage increases or would impose limitations on corporate borrowing; by contrast, banks obtain a large proportion of their funds from federally insured depositors, who are not exposed to default risk and, therefore, do not monitor bank borrowing. As such, capital requirements are the main limitations on borrowing faced by banks. Given the regulatory requirements on capital adequacy and deposit insurance costs, bank shareholders need to consider the following areas in making capital structure decisions: (1) financial risk, (2) ownership control, (3) management control, (4) market timing, (5) asset investment considerations, (6) dividend policy, (7) debt capacity, (8) transaction costs, (9) mergers and acquisitions, and (10) internal expansion.

Trends in bank capital reveal that the U.S. banks bolstered their capital positions by increasing their leverage ratios subsequent to the implementation of the Basel Agreement in 1992. Smaller banks tend to have higher capital ratios than larger banks. And, while economic recessions have reduced bank capital ratios, subsequent economic recoveries have reversed these trends.

KEY TERMS AND CONCEPTS

Bank capital
Basel I
Basel II
Basel III
Basel Agreement
Book value of equity
Capital adequacy
Capital impairment
Capital reserves
Common stock
Corporate control
Credit risk capital requirements
DINB
EPS
FABC
FDIC
Financial leverage
FRB
General market risk
Hostile takeover
Internal capital generation rate
International Lending Supervision Act
Leverage ratio
Liquidity Coverage Ratio (LCR)
Market discipline
Market risk capital requirements
Market value of equity
Minimum capital requirements
Moral hazard problem
OCC
Off-balance-sheet activities
Preferred stock
Primary capital
Provision for loan losses (PLL)
Reserve for loan losses
Risk-adjusted assets
Risk-based capital rules
Risk-based deposit insurance
Specific risk
Subordinated notes and debentures
Supervisory review process
Surplus
Tier 1 capital
Tier 2 capital
Total capital
Undivided profits

QUESTIONS

12.1 What is bank capital? Why is the reserve for loan losses not counted as part of equity capital?

12.2 Is the balance sheet an accurate source of information in calculating bank capital?

12.3 What are the three key functions of bank capital? How do banks differ from nonfinancial firms in terms of capital levels?

12.4 Why are notes and debentures considered bank capital?

12.5 How are notes and debentures related to "market discipline"?

12.6 How much capital is "adequate"?

12.7 Why is measuring adequate capital from a regulatory viewpoint difficult?

12.8 Define Tier 1 and Tier 2 capital under Basel I rules. What are the risk-adjusted capital requirements?

12.9 Explain the problems of using uniform capital requirements.

12.10 Why has there been a switch to risk-based capital requirements?

12.11 What is the credit risk formula for the risk-based capital requirement under Basel I rules? How does market risk affect capital requirements?

12.12 How do Basel II capital rules differ from Basel I rules? What are the three pillars?

12.13 After the 2008-2009 financial crisis, Basel III rules were proposed. How did capital and liquidity requirements change under these new rules?

12.14 What five options does the FDIC have in handling a distressed bank?

12.15 How are variable-rate deposit insurance premiums determined by the FDIC? What is the "moral hazard" problem inherent in deposit insurance?

12.16 What are the advantages of debt finance to bank shareholders?

12.17 What are the disadvantages of debt finance to bank shareholders?

12.18 Why are the capital ratios of small and large banks different? Will this change in the future?

12.19 What is the "agency cost" problem? How can it be reduced?

12.20 Go to the Federal Deposit Insurance Corporation (FDIC) website at www.fdic.gov/bank/historical/bank and look up recent bank failures. Print out the information about one of the banks. Given the alternatives discussed in the text, how did the FDIC handle the failure?

12.22 Visit the website for the Office of the Comptroller of the Currency (OCC) at www.occ.treas.gov. Search on "working papers" in the box at the top of the page. Select one of the research papers in their working paper series and write a one-page abstract of the article.

12.23 The Bank for International Settlements (BIS) routinely updates information on risk-based capital requirements. Go to its website at www.bis.org. Search for Basel III in the box at the top of the page. Print out the latest updates on Basel III rules.

PROBLEMS

12.1 Given the following information, calculate Tier 1 and Tier 2 capital under Basel I rules:

	($ thousands)
Common stock	$ 30,000
Perpetual preferred stock	5,000
Surplus	2,000
Undivided profits	100,000
Capital reserves	1,000
Reserves for loan and lease losses	5,000
Subordinated notes and debentures	2,000

(a) If the bank has total assets (in thousands) of $2,840,000, does it have adequate capital under regulatory standards?
(b) If risk-adjusted assets equal $2,000,000, is capital adequate?
(c) If an analysis of market risk revealed that the bank had a value-at-risk (VAR) of $300,000, and its adjusted value of credit-risk-weighted assets are $1,500,000, is capital still adequate?

12.2 Given the following information, calculate risk-adjusted assets for credit risk purposes under Basel II rules for a small, community bank:

	($ thousands)
Vault cash	$ 50
Cash balances at district Federal Reserve Bank	100
U.S. government securities	250
Mortgage-backed bonds	300
Home loans	200
Corporate bonds	100
Commercial loans	800

12.3 In problem 12.2 assume that the $300 invested in mortgage-backed bonds is in the bank's trading account. If VAR and specific risk for these securities are estimated to be $50 and $25, respectively, what are the bank's (a) market-risk equivalent assets and (b) modified risk-adjusted assets?

12.4 In problem 2.2 assume that Basel III was relevant for community bank. Would the bank pass Common Equity Tier 1 (CET1) and Tier 1 (CET1 + AT1) capital requirements? Consider both minimum risk-adjusted assets ratio and minimum plus conservation buffer capital requirements.

12.5 Suppose Bank One has earnings before interest and taxes (EBIT) equal to $10 million and interest expenses equal to $8 million. There are 1 million shares of common stock outstanding. If EBIT increased by 10 percent, what would be the percentage change in earnings per share (EPS)?

12.6 Calculate the internal capitalization rate using the following information:

Net income	$ 100
Dividends	40
Total equity	800
Total assets	10,200

(a) What does this rate mean to the bank?
(b) If the regulatory standard for capital is three percent, what is the maximum asset growth rate implied for the bank?
(c) How would a higher capital standard affect the bank's asset growth?

CASE: OVERALL ASSESSMENT OF CAPITAL ADEQUACY

In the past, First National Bank (FNB) had maintained its capital ratios according to Basel Agreement standards. However, in recent years the bank's capital ratios decreased to the point where its capital position was marginal or near the borderline.

Jack Mead was a bank examiner reporting to the Federal Reserve district office in the region. He received news yesterday that FNB was coming up for review by his staff next month. In preparation for the upcoming on-site visit, he has gone over a chart of FNB's capital ratios and is concerned about their trends. Peer group banks did not exhibit similar downward trends; indeed, strong economic growth in the region had contributed to strengthening capital ratios at some of FNB's competitors.

He decided to call the CEO to discuss the timing of the review and express some preliminary concerns about FNB's capital adequacy. The CEO's attitude was positive and a copy of management's strategic plan was faxed to Jack to help him better understand the bank's goals, objectives, and business conditions.

Jack brought the plan home with him that evening to begin reviewing the situation. His first reaction to seeing the concise and well-organized five-page strategic plan was one of relief. Effective strategic plans enable management to be proactive rather than reactive in responding to market forces. Such plans are long-term in nature and integrate a variety of management areas, including asset deployment, funding sources, capital formation, management, marketing, operations, and information systems. They serve not only to provide management direction and leadership but to communicate bank goals and objectives throughout the organization.

In the capital section of the plan, Jack noted the following key areas and related discussion:

- ***Growth:*** The bank sought to keep pace with the region's strong economic growth by rapidly expanding the loan portfolio. Many new credit opportunities were opening up due to the bank's ability to offer a wider menu of financial services to its customers under the Financial Services Modernization Act of 1999. There was some evidence that loan concentration had increased, especially with respect to certain local industries that had been particularly successful and, subsequently, had increased their credit lines with the bank. Bank management appeared to have become more risk tolerant in light of the long period of good economic times.

- ***Dividends:*** The bank is owned by a bank holding company and is dedicated to paying substantial dividends to fund the holding company's expansion goals. The bank holding company is attempting to expand beyond its traditional home state into adjacent states.
- ***Access to additional capital:*** Since the bank is relatively small, its access to capital markets is limited. However, this limitation is not considered to be restrictive due to the fact that the bank holding company can be relied upon to assist them with capital funds. The bank indicated that it was sensitive to current shareholders' desire to avoid the diluting effect of new capital. Under Federal Reserve policy, the bank holding company is expected to be a source of strength in terms of liquidity or capital funds for subsidiary banks.
- ***Earnings:*** Net interest margins (NIMs) had been exceptionally high from an historical standpoint. The NIM had been favorably affected by low interest rates and strong loan demand that allowed the bank to widen the spread over interest costs. Nonetheless, NIM and the rate of return on assets (ROA) had fluctuated more than peer group banks over the last five years. The bank had recently adopted securities policies to better hedge the interest rate risk on its balance sheet. Also, in an effort to address ROA volatility, the bank had strengthened its collateral and guarantees to upgrade the credit quality of its loan portfolio. Finally, the bank had increased its allowance for loan and lease losses in the last two years.
- ***Bank stock prices:*** FNB's stock price relative to book value was below its peer group by about 25 percent. Management made clear that it believed the stock was undervalued, as opposed to low-valued due to a lack of investor confidence.
- ***Fixed bank assets:*** The bank had a central location for its main office plus three local branch offices. All facilities were refurbished in recent years by the bank holding company and electronic payments services installed to ensure that the bank could offer a full array of banking, securities, and insurance services.

Given this preliminary information, step into Jack's role and write a report for his staff prior to their visit to the bank. The report should cover each of the above strategic plan areas and provide an evaluation of capital strengths and weaknesses implied by the plan. Most important, it should set the stage for their overall assessment of FNB's capital adequacy.

ENDNOTES

1. The proposal was adopted in 1988 by the Basel Committee on Banking Regulations and Supervisory Practices, which is comprised of representatives of the central banks and supervisory authorities of Belgium, Canada, France, Germany, Italy, Japan, Netherlands, Sweden, Switzerland, United Kingdom, United States, and Luxembourg. The Committee continues to work toward strengthening the capital resources of international banks.

2. See Secretariat of the Basel Committee on Banking Supervision, *"The New Basel Capital Accord: An Explanatory Note,"* Bank for International Settlements, January, 2001.

3. For readers interested in the technical details of credit risk modeling, see Jose A. Lopez and Marc R. Saidenberg, *"Evaluating Credit Risk Models,"* Working Paper, Federal Reserve Bank of San Francisco and Federal Reserve Bank of New York, respectively (April, 1999), and citations to other literature therein. Companies such as KMV (PortfolioManager), McKinsey (CreditPortfolio View), and Credit Suisse (CreditRisk+) have developed approaches to estimate credit losses in a portfolio context. Regulatory agencies, including the Bank for International Settlements (BIS), Board of Governors of the Federal Reserve System, Comptroller of the Currency, Federal Deposit Insurance Corporation, and other national bank regulators, regularly publish papers on bank credit risk modeling.

4. See Franco Modigliani and Merton Miller, "Corporate Income Taxes and the Cost of Capital: A Correction," *American Economic Review,* June, 1963, pp. 433–443, and Stephen A. Buser, Andrew H. Chen, and Edward J. Kane, "Federal Deposit Insurance, Regulatory Policy, and Optimal Capital Structure, *Journal of Finance,* March, 1981, pp. 51–60.

5. For banks using large amounts of nondeposit liabilities, it is possible that the degree of financial leverage employed by shareholders could be limited. Uninsured debtholders seeking to protect their claims from new debtholders' claims as well as from potential bankruptcy costs incurred in failure can be expected to require debt covenants that place an upper bound on bank leverage. To the extent that this occurs, concentration of ownership would tend to be reduced, as well as the associated control of bank management by shareholders.

6. From a regulatory viewpoint, higher capital requirements are favored for this same reason, as rapid rates of growth increase the risk of bank failure according to historical evidence.

Chapter 13

Liabilities Management

After reading this chapter, you will be able to:

- Define the structure of bank liabilities
- Describe the unique characteristics of different types of bank liabilities
- Discuss the pricing decisions facing bank management, including pricing policy and strategy, relationship pricing, promotional pricing, and other related marketing elements
- Compare the trends in sources of bank funds over time in the U.S. banking industry
- Identify the methods of estimating the cost of bank funds, including average costs and marginal costs

Inflationary surges in the 1960s and 1970s, competition in the financial services industry, and deregulation of deposit rates in the 1980s spurred banks to develop many new sources of funds, which have dramatically transformed the liability side of their balance sheets and put pressure on banks' operating costs. The higher interest cost of liabilities significantly affected banks' profitability and interest rate risk exposure. Many banks sought to increase noninterest sources of revenues due to narrowing spreads on interest income and interest expenses. More recently, in the 1990s and 2000s interest rate levels dropped to historic lows that decreased cost pressures on banks. However, the low rates offered on deposit accounts caused outflows of deposit funds, as customers searched for higher yields in the money and capital markets. Interest-sensitive deposit costs and competition from financial markets for sources of funds have increased the challenges for liabilities management in the banking industry. For these reasons it is essential to understand the different types of bank liabilities. In this chapter we begin by summarizing each source of bank funds and their distinguishing features. Next, historical trends of the mix of different liabilities employed by U.S. banks are covered. Finally, various aspects of estimating the costs of bank funds are discussed, including how those costs can affect bank profitability.

STRUCTURE OF BANK LIABILITIES

Demand deposits have historically dominated the liability structure of commercial banks. Savings and time deposits normally played a significant but secondary role in the acquisition of deposit funds, and ***nondeposit funds*** were almost nonexistent. Beginning in the 1960s, however, the liability structure of commercial banking began to change substantially. For example, by the mid-1960s, time and savings deposits surpassed demand deposits as the primary source of bank funds. In the 1970s nondeposit borrowings grew rapidly and emerged as a major new source of funds for larger banking institutions. Additionally, the variety of deposit and nondeposit accounts and securities offered to the public by commercial banks greatly expanded. Deregulation of deposit rates of interest in the 1980s further expanded the variety of deposit accounts offered by banks. Finally, low interest rate levels in the 1990s and 2000s prompted banks to offer deposit customers alternative money market and investment accounts. In this section deposit and nondeposit sources of bank funds are overviewed, as well as the historical developments that shaped the new liability structure of commercial banking. Table 13-1 (next page) gives a summary of the structure of liabilities for U.S. banks of different size.

DEPOSIT SOURCES OF FUNDS

Bank deposits are categorized as either ***core deposits*** or ***purchased deposits***. Core deposits are typically deposits of regular bank customers, including business firms, government units, and households. Purchased deposits are acquired on an impersonal basis from the financial market by offering competitive interest rates. Core deposits provide a stable, long-term source of funds, whereas purchased deposits serve as a liquidity reserve that can be tapped when needed.

TABLE 13-1 **SOURCES OF BANK FUNDS FOR U.S. COMMERCIAL BANKS: SEPTEMBER, 2015 (percent of average total assets)**

		Total Asset Size of Banks		
Liability Item	**All Commercial Banks**	**Less Than $100 Million**	**Assets $100 Million to $1 Billion**	**More Than $1 Billion**
Total liabilities	88.63	87.73	88.89	88.61
Total deposits	75.80	84.33	83.75	75.16
Interest-bearing deposits	55.45	66.25	65.77	54.61
Deposits held in domestic offices	66.69	84.33	83.74	65.31
Federal funds purchased and repurchase agreements	1.83	0.56	1.17	1.89
Trading liabilities	1.74	0	0	1.88
Other borrowed funds	6.28	2.21	3.22	6.53
Subordinated debt	0.62	0.01	0.02	0.67
All other liabilities	2.35	0.61	0.73	2.48
Volatile liabilities	17.61	5.30	6.96	18.48
FHLB advances	2.56	2.06	3.12	2.53

Source:* FDIC, *Statistics on Depository Institutions Report.

Extensive use of purchased deposits can expose a bank to liquidity problems. In contrast to core deposits, a large proportion of purchased deposits may not be insured by the Federal Deposit Insurance Corporation (FDIC), which covers up to $250,000 per deposit account. Also, unlike core deposits that normally provide both *explicit interest earnings* and *implicit service returns* (such as free checking and convenient branch offices), purchased deposits provide only explicit interest earnings. These differences cause purchased deposits to be much more sensitive to changes in both bank risk and interest rates than core deposits are. If the financial market perceives a decline in a bank's safety and soundness, its purchased deposits would have to be rolled over at higher rates and may even cease to be available (as depositors shy away from placing liquid assets in institutions that may become insolvent). Thus, the risks and returns of core deposits and purchased deposits differ considerably from each other.

Deposit accounts can be categorized as follows: demand deposits, ***small time and savings deposits***, and ***large time deposits***. As a consequence of deposit rate deregulation, both small and large time deposits can serve the dual roles of core and purchased deposit sources of funds. Historically, financial crises in the late 1800s, and particularly the Great Depression in the 1930s, motivated Congress to pass the Glass-Steagall Act as part of the 1933 Banking Acts. Under Glass-Steagall, payment of interest on demand deposits was prohibited. It was believed that interest payments caused intense competition between banks that induced them to make riskier loans in an effort to pay the high costs of deposits. The same logic was applied to a 1935 extension of the Glass-Steagall Act that gave the Board of Governors of the Federal Reserve System the power to set deposit rate ceilings ***(Regulation Q)*** affecting all federally insured banks.

Deposit rate ceilings led to a series of "credit crunches" in the 1960s and 1970s. In 1966, for example, market rates rose above deposit rate ceilings. On previous occasions ceiling rates were increased; however, the Fed did not change the ceiling rate this time. Large certificate of deposit (CD) sales dropped considerably, causing bank credit to dry up. Similar episodes of high interest rates in the periods 1969–1970 and 1973–1974 likewise caused credit contractions.

In an attempt to meet credit demands during these periods, banks and other depository institutions began innovating around deposit rate barriers. In 1966, for example, large banks acquired time deposit funds from the Eurodollar market. Subsequent extension of Regulation Q to these deposits led large banks in 1969 to make greater use of nondeposit sources of funds, including nonbank federal funds, repurchase agreements, and commercial paper issued by holding companies.

Banks also began developing new transactions accounts. As the general level of interest rates edged upward in the 1960s and 1970s, they began to offer *payments in kind* and to indirectly pay interest on demand deposit balances. Payments in kind involved nonprice benefits such as free checking and branch facilities offering greater convenience. Indirect payments of interest were offered in the form of gifts for opening new accounts and ***sweep accounts*** for large depositors that automatically transferred checking balances over a certain amount to repurchase agreements, money market funds, and other short-term, interest-bearing assets at the end of each day. Smaller depositors were offered ***automatic transfer service (ATS)*** accounts that allowed them to minimize transactions balances by automatically transferring funds from their interest-bearing savings account to their checking account as overdrafts occurred.

Bank innovation and rising competition for consumer deposits prompted Congress to deregulate applicable deposit rate ceilings. A summary of this deregulation is as follows:

- ***Depository Institutions Deregulation and Monetary Control Act (DIDMCA of 1980)***: Authorized all depository institutions to sell negotiable order of withdrawal (NOW) accounts to individuals and nonprofit organizations in December, 1980 as well as automatic transfer service (ATS) accounts. These interest-bearing demand deposit (or checking) accounts had interest rate ceilings initially imposed on them.

- ***Garn-St. Germain Depository Institutions Act of 1982:*** Authorized all depository institutions to issue money market deposit accounts (MMDAs) in December, 1982 with no interest rate restrictions and limited check-writing privileges.

- ***Depository Institutions Deregulation Committee (DIDC):*** Established by DIDMCA of 1980, the DIDC authorized Super NOW (SNOW) accounts effective January, 1983 that payed market interest rates. Later deregulation of interest rates in 1986 eliminated the distinction between NOWs and SNOWS. Also, these accounts were extended to commercial business depositors in the 1990s.

Checkable Deposits

Checkable deposits, including demand deposits, are transactions balances subject to reserve requirements. They are classified into three categories: (1) consumer deposits, (2) corporate deposits, and (3) government deposits. Consumer deposit accounts may not be interest-bearing but normally are NOW accounts that pay interest based on deposit balances.

The "NOW experience" of banks indicates that interest-bearing transactions accounts are not much more costly than regular checking accounts. The reason for similar costs is that regular checking accounts have relatively higher *implicit*, or noninterest, service costs than NOW accounts, and banks tend to increase service charges on NOW accounts to offset some of the differences in interest costs. From the customer's standpoint, the mix of implicit, or noninterest, and explicit, or interest, pricing offered by banks influences the type of transactions account that is opened. From the perspective of bank management, both operational costs and consumer demands must be evaluated to price transactions accounts correctly.

Until recently, corporate demand deposit balances were prohibited from earning interest. However, under the 2010 Dodd-Frank Act, banks can offer NOW accounts that pay interest on corporate checking accounts effective July 21, 2011. This Act repealed long-standing Regulation Q restrictions imposed by the 1933 Banking Act. Prior to this change, as a way to compensate corporate depositors, banks typically offered sweep accounts that moved excess deposit funds to separate accounts that earned interest. Also, banks would offer earnings credit allowances that would lower bank service fees for various financial services. Nowadays, banks offer some combination of interest, sweeps, and earnings credit allowances on corporate checking accounts. One factor influencing the mix -- interest is taxable but earnings credit allowances are not. All corporate transactions accounts are insured by the FDIC up to $250,000 per depositor.

Small Time and Savings Deposits

Small deposits of less than $100,000 may be acquired through time deposits (otherwise known as ***savings certificates***, or ***retail CDs***) and savings deposits. Small time deposits can be offered with denominations as low as $1,000. These deposits have fixed maturities and yields that approximate those of Treasury securities of equal maturity. A slight premium is normally required by depositors over the Treasury yield, however, because these deposit instruments are nonnegotiable and have early withdrawal penalties attached to them. Small time deposits are normally categorized by maturity as (for example) seven to 31 days, 32 days to one year, and greater than one year.

In the early 1980s high interest rates increased demand for retail CDs. As rates surpassed 10 percent, many individuals began shifting funds from the stock and bond market to these savings accounts. However, this so-called *consumerism movement* was short lived. Low inflation and associated interest rates in the 1990s reversed the flow of funds from retail CDs back into long-term, capital market securities.

Savings deposits are interest-bearing deposits that do not have fixed maturities. Savings deposits can be set up periodically to cover overwithdrawals of transactions accounts (called ATS, or automatic transfer service) or to provide transactions funds by means of limited check-writing privileges. A good example of the latter type of savings account is the ***money market deposit account (MMDA).*** MMDAs have no rate restrictions and allow consumers to make up to six transfers (three by check) per month. Authorized under the Garn-St. Germain Act of 1982, MMDAs were designed to compete with ***money market mutual funds (MMMFs).*** The accounts were highly successful, surpassing the $218 billion held by MMMFs only one year after their introduction in December, 1981. Although their growth has been less spectacular since then, they represent a major source of savings deposits in banking today. An important advantage of MMDAs over MMMFs is that they are FDIC insured up to $250,000 per depositor.

Small banks rely upon retail CDs as a major source of funds. Even though larger banks place less emphasis than small banks on retail CDs, they can be a valuable source of liquidity for larger banks, especially in the event of a liquidity crisis. In such circumstances, uninsured depositors typically withdraw their funds from the bank. On the other hand, insured retail CDs reduce the outflow of funds and so limit the extent of a liquidity crisis.

Due to the unattractiveness of low-interest bearing CDs in recent years, banks have been developing new CD products. One such product is the market-indexed CD. This CD pays returns based on a market index such as the Standard & Poor's 500 or Chicago Board of Exchange Internet index. For example, the CD could offer 80 percent of capital gains and dividends earned on the market index. If the stock market falls in value, depositors receive at a minimum their principal upon maturity. Thus, investors can participate in market upswings (such as the 2010 to 2015 stock market rebound) but be protected from losing their original investment capital. While a major advantage of these CDs is deposit insurance up to $250,000, they are generally longer-term CDs with maturities from three to ten years. As such, only depositors interested in long-run savings would be inclined to purchase these CDs.

Large Time Deposits

Time deposits issued in denominations of $100,000 or more are known as ***negotiable certificates of deposit (NCDs or simply CDs).*** Large, or "jumbo," CDs are marketable securities with maturities ranging from 14 days to 18 months. First issued by First National City Bank of New York (now Citibank) in February, 1961, NCDs were quickly offered by other money center banks and dealers, causing the volume of NCDs to expand rapidly. By 1966 these CDs were second only to Treasury bills among outstanding money market instruments.

Originally, large CDs were issued by New York banks in an attempt to retain corporate demand deposits that paid no interest. Rising short-term interest rates in the post-World War II period motivated corporate treasurers to draw down demand deposits and buy Treasury bills, commercial paper, and repurchase agreements with dealers. To stem this deposit outflow and retain their share of credit flows, large banks designed the CD to appeal to corporate depositors. Initially subject to Regulation Q interest rate ceilings, these caps were removed on large CDs by May,1973.

Later, large CDs became the primary source of funds for liability management. Most CD buyers are still nonfinancial corporations, but other market participants, such as MMMFs, now buy CDs also. Because CDs are commonly issued in denominations exceeding the $250,000 FDIC insurance limit (for example, a round lot in the secondary market is usually $1 million), the default risk of the issuing bank can affect rates of interest on these CDs. Indeed, a tiered CD market has evolved in which money center and large regional banks tend to offer CDs at lower rates than smaller banks.

Eurodollar Deposits

A ***Eurodollar deposit*** is a dollar-denominated deposit in a bank office outside of the United States. Originally dominated by European-based bank offices, the term still applies to out-of-country dollar deposits in general. Eurodollar deposits have grown with international business expansion, as firms maintain dollar deposits in foreign countries.

Large banks normally tap Eurodollar deposits through their foreign branch offices. For example, foreign branches sell Eurodollar CDs, which are dollar-denominated negotiable CDs. These funds are then loaned to domestic offices. Because the secondary market is smaller compared with domestic CDs, and FDIC deposit insurance is unavailable, Eurodollar CDs usually have higher yields than domestic CDs. Eurodollar deposits, like domestic deposits, can be issued in many different maturity ranges and denominations. Fixed-rate and variable-rate deposits are available.

Brokered Deposits

Brokered deposits are small and large time deposits obtained by banks from brokers seeking insured deposit accounts on behalf of their customers. Deposit brokers appeared in the early 1980s when depositors began to face increased risk of loss because of bank failure. An often-cited example of this risk was the failure of Penn Square Bank in July, 1982. For the first time since the Great Depression, federal regulators liquidated a large bank, rather than allowing the bank to be merged into or acquired by a solvent bank with no loss to depositors. Depositors that were not insured (because their balances exceeded the $100,000 FDIC limit at that time) suffered large losses, with only 55 percent of uninsured claims eventually covered.

Because interest rates on large, negotiable CDs in denominations of $100,000 were unregulated, and rates on smaller, retail-level CDs were deregulated for the most part by year-end 1982, brokers entered deposit markets to bring together depositors (sellers) seeking insured accounts with banks and other depository institutions (buyers) demanding lower-cost, insured deposit funds. Electronic funds transfer technology enabled brokers to cost-effectively "split" $1 million (for example) into ten $100,000, fully insured deposit accounts at ten different depository institutions. Alternatively, brokers can offer smaller depositors better yields by pooling their deposits and selling "shares" in "participating" large CDs offering higher yields than smaller CDs.

Federal regulators have opposed the use of brokered deposits. In April, 1982, for example, the FDIC announced that brokers could obtain only $100,000 of deposit insurance per bank, as is the case for any depositor. It was believed that, because insured depositors are less likely to "discipline" bank management by withdrawing their funds or charging higher rates on deposits, bank safety and soundness might be compromised to the extent that banks used nationally brokered deposits to grow excessively or to take excessive loan risks. However, the FDIC's rule on brokered deposits was struck down by a court decision in June, 1984.

The FDIC Improvement Act of 1991 prohibits depository institutions that are not well capitalized from accepting brokered deposits. Adequately capitalized banks can use brokered deposits subject to prior waiver by the FDIC, while well-capitalized banks can freely use these deposits without restriction (see Chapter 12 for definitions of these three capital categories for banks). Bank networks can act to split large deposits into $250,000 increments among participating banks to obtain 100 percent FDIC insurance. In this case, the network bank acts as a deposit broker. Interest rates on brokered deposits must be in line with competitive market rates. These regulatory changes preclude institutions from acquiring deposits (by posting interest rates above those on insured deposits) to cover earnings losses. This type of behavior was repeatedly found in failing saving and loan associations in the 1980s and resulted in large increases in the later costs of closing many of those institutions. Also, banks with low supervisory ratings tended to use more brokered deposits than higher-rated institutions.

IRA and Keogh Plans

IRA and Keogh plans are personal pension plans that individuals can use to defer federal income taxes on contributions and subsequent investment earnings. Keogh plans have been available to self-employed individuals since 1962. They allow up to 25 percent of earned, nonsalaried income, but not more than $47,000 (as of 2007), to be deposited in a tax-deferred account. Individual Retirement Account (IRA) plans were allowed for all individuals under the Economic Recovery Tax Act of 1981. IRAs enable individuals to set aside earnings for retirement up to an allowable maximum of $5,500 per year ($6,500 if age 50 years or older). IRS rules determine how much of these contributions (if any) can be deducted from income to reduce taxes. Both of these personal retirement accounts are subject to a 10 percent tax penalty if withdrawn before age 59½. No penalty is paid under certain circumstances, including withdrawals for emergencies such as disability, medical expenses, or decreased life expectancy and for higher education or first-time home purchase.

IRA products have expanded in recent years with the introduction of the Roth IRA under the Taxpayer Relief Act of 1997. Unlike traditional IRAs, contributions by savers are exposed to income taxes but later investment earnings and distributions are not taxed. Since withdrawals are not reportable income, they do not affect adjusted gross income during retirement or estate taxes paid by beneficiaries such as a surviving spouse or children.

IRAs and Keoghs have become a major source of long-term, stable deposit funds for banking institutions, which serve as account custodians. One problem with these new accounts is the intensity of market competition. IRAs can be offered by banks, savings institutions, brokerage firms, insurance companies, mutual funds, and employers with qualified pension, profit-sharing, or savings plans. To be competitive, banks must offer attractive interest rates and good service, both of which trim profit margins. Even so, these accounts are a source of funds that should not be overlooked.

MANAGERIAL ISSUES

ARE YOUR DEPOSITS INSURED?

The Federal Deposit Insurance Corporation (FDIC) insures deposits of any individual or entity holding an account in a U.S. insured commercial bank or savings association. A variety of deposit accounts are eligible for insurance, including checking accounts, NOWs, savings accounts, certificates of deposit (CDs), money market deposit accounts (MMDAs), and trust accounts. These accounts are insured up to a legal limit of $250,000 and in some cases higher amounts.

Some important insurance rules to keep in mind are:

- Only deposits payable in the United States (not overseas) are covered.
- Mutual funds, securities, and related investment products sold to customers are not covered.
- Official checks (including cashiers' checks, officers' checks, expense checks, loan disbursement checks, interest checks, outstanding drafts, negotiable instruments, and money orders drawn on an institution) as well as certified checks, letters of credit, and travelers' checks are covered.
- Customers can have deposits in different FDIC-insured institutions that are separately covered. However, if the deposits are in various offices of a branch bank, they are added together to determine insurance coverage.
- Insurance coverage extends for six months beyond the date of death of a depositor.
- More than $100,000 of insurance is possible at a single institution due to the fact that each of the following types of accounts can be separately insured: single (or individual) accounts, joint accounts, testamentary accounts, and retirement accounts.
- Single ownership offers $250,000 for the sum of all deposit accounts held by a depositor. As such, a person could not obtain more than $250,000 insurance by opening NOW, MMDA, savings, and other accounts at a single bank.
- Joint accounts owned by two or more individuals are insured up to a limit of $250,000 per person. Thus, if a person held three joint accounts with different persons at the same bank, the sum of their portion of deposits in each account would determine the extent of insurance coverage. If not specified, it is assumed that joint deposits are equally divided among the owners, unless otherwise stated on the deposit records.
- A testamentary account (otherwise known as a tentative or Totten trust account, revocable trust account, or payable-on-death account) is separately insured from single and joint accounts. In this account the grantor or depositor has indicated an intent upon death to transfer ownership of funds to a beneficiary. If there is more than one beneficiary, each beneficiary is eligible for $250,000 of insurance.
- Revocable living trusts, which appoint a trustee to oversee the funds for a beneficiary, are insured as single accounts, unless they are set up as testamentary trusts.
- Irrevocable trust accounts are insured separately from other accounts owned by an individual.
- IRA and Keogh funds are separately insured from nonretirement funds held by a depositor. These retirement accounts are added together for insurance purposes. The new Roth IRA is considered to be an IRA and receives no special treatment. By contrast, the new Education IRA is considered to qualify as an irrevocable trust account and, therefore, is separately insured.

Since there are specific definitions of each type of eligible account, it is wise to check with the insuring institution about the specific FDIC rules for these different types of insured accounts. Also, deposit insurance rules for pension plans, profit-sharing plans, and business accounts should be carefully evaluated. Nondeposit investment products, such as annuities, mutual funds, bonds, stocks, government securities, municipal securities, and U.S. Treasury securities, are not insured. For further information, email the FDIC at Consumer@FDIC.gov, visit the FDIC's website at www.fdic.gov, or call a regional FDIC office.

NONDEPOSIT SOURCES OF FUNDS

Nondeposit funds are money market liabilities that are purchased for relatively short periods of time to adjust liquidity demands. Because they are typically used in liability management, they are often referred to as managed liabilities. The use of these purchased funds came about as a consequence of tight money periods in which deposit rate ceilings caused banks to have difficulty attracting deposit funds. Unlike deposit funds, nondeposit funds typically are exempt from federal reserve requirements, interest rate ceilings, and FDIC insurance assessments.

Federal Funds

In general, *federal funds* are short-term, unsecured transfers of immediately available funds[1] between depository institutions for use in one business day (overnight loans). About 20 percent of federal funds have maturities longer than one day. Banks typically either purchase or sell "fed" funds, depending on their desired reserve position, which is normally based on legal reserve requirements. Because Federal Reserve open market operations directly affect the quantity of bank reserves, fed funds rates are relatively more volatile than other money market rates. Also, in the last few days of the reserve maintenance period, the fed funds rate may jump significantly, if relatively low supplies of excess reserves are in the banking system.

Overnight loans usually are booked by verbal agreements between corresponding officers of depository institutions. Written contracts or brokers, or both, can be employed if the parties are unfamiliar with one another. Overnight loans can be put on a continuing-contract basis in which they are automatically renewed unless otherwise notified. Such contracts are often arranged between large correspondent banks and smaller respondent institutions and tend to lower transactions costs (such as brokers' fees and funds transfer charges).

Repurchase Agreements

Nonbank firms supply funds to banks through *repurchase agreements* (RPs, or repos). An overnight RP can be defined as a secured, one-day loan in which claim to the collateral is transferred. Multiple-day RPs can be arranged for a fixed term ("term RPs") or on a continuing basis. An RP is created by the sale of securities in exchange for immediately available money with the simultaneous promise to buy back the securities on a specific date at a set price within the next year. The repurchase price is typically the initial sale price plus a negotiated rate of interest. U.S. Treasury and federal agency securities are normally used as collateral (which allows depository institutions to avoid reserve requirements), but CDs, mortgage-backed securities, and other securities might be used on occasion. The transaction is known as a *reverse RP (or matched sale-purchase agreement)* from the perspective of the purchaser of the securities (supplier of funds).

Because RP purchasers acquire title to the securities for the term of the agreement, they may use them to create another RP or to meet the delivery of a forward or futures contract, a short sale, or a maturing reverse RP. This flexibility makes the RP a low-risk money market instrument that dealers can use to meet diverse liquidity needs among investors, including business firms, depository institutions, state and local governments, and other financial institutions. RPs usually are available in denominations of at least $1 million in the wholesale market, but smaller denominations under $100,000 can be found in the retail market also. Retail RPs must have maturities of 89 days or less and, like wholesale RPs, are not subject to interest rate ceilings. However, deposits obtained from retail RPs are not federally insured.

RP contract provisions can be altered to fit the needs of the participants. If a corporate treasurer needs funds to make payroll payments on a Friday afternoon, a bank can repurchase securities from the treasurer at a specified time to efficiently make those payments. As another example, *dollar repurchase agreements* (dollar rolls) allow the seller to repurchase securities that are similar to but not identical to the securities originally sold. A further example is the "flex repo," in which a customer can sell back securities to the dealer before the final maturity date.

Discount Window Advances

Banks can borrow funds from the 12 regional Federal Reserve banks by means of a ***discount window advance*** (subject to the provisions of Regulation A). Advances can be used by banks to meet unanticipated reserve deficiencies or to meet more persistent outflows of funds that are transitory in nature (such as an unexpected loss of deposits, surge in credit demands, or natural disaster). Funds cannot be borrowed, however, either to arbitrage profits through acquiring higher-earning financial assets with advances or to supplement bank capital. Also, if alternative sources of funds are readily available, discount window borrowing is discouraged. Discount window borrowings normally are overnight loans that are deposited in the bank's reserve account at its Federal Reserve district bank. Extended credit is possible under exceptional circumstances to assist banks in adjusting to changing market conditions. Advances must be secured by approved collateral, such as U.S. Treasury securities and government agency securities, municipal securities, residential mortgages, short-term commercial notes, and other marketable securities. Also, interest and principal are due at maturity. The interest rate is normally 50 basis points above the Fed's target rate for federal funds.

Prior to the Monetary Control Act of 1980, only Federal Reserve System member banks could use the discount window for reserve management purposes. However, this act enabled all depository institutions with transactions balances or nonpersonal time deposits (except bankers' banks) to access the discount window. One caveat here is that banks with less-than-adequate capital levels or low CAMEL bank ratings (that is, 5 on a 5-point scale) are limited in their use of the discount window. Primary credit is available to financially sound institutions. Secondary credit may be available to other institutions. Seasonal credit is offered to small depository institutions that have intra-year swings in funding needs.

Federal Home Loan Bank Borrowings

The Federal Home Loan Bank (FHLB) in the past provided discount window services for savings and loans, but the Financial Institutions Reform, Recovery, and

Enforcement Act (FIRREA) of 1989 allowed banks access also. FHLB borrowings (known as advances) are less restrictive than the Fed's discount window. Maturity ranges from overnight to 30 years are available at competitive market rates. At times FHLB facility funds may have wholesale market rates below the deposit rates available in competitive local markets. Borrowings are not intended to meet liquidity deficiencies and must be collateralized with bank assets (such as residential mortgage loans and mortgage-backed securities). Also, the composite CAMEL rating of an institution can affect its borrowing authority and collateral requirements. Member institutions can be commercial banks, thrifts, credit unions, and insurance companies.

Banker's Acceptances

A ***banker's acceptance*** is a time draft drawn on a bank by either an exporter or an importer to finance international business transactions. The bank may discount the acceptance in the money market to (in effect) finance the transaction.

An example perhaps best explains how banks use acceptances to acquire loanable funds. A U.S. importer (buyer) might obtain a *letter of credit* in its behalf from its bank. The letter of credit authorizes the foreign exporter (seller) to draw a draft at its foreign bank at a specified time in the future,[2] which then forwards the draft and shipping documents to the U.S. bank issuing the letter of credit (perhaps through its U.S. correspondent bank). If everything is in order, the issuing bank stamps "accepted" on the face of the time draft, and a negotiable instrument known as a banker's acceptance is created. The acceptance can be discounted by the issuing bank for the account of the foreign bank. At this point the acceptance is a financial asset of the bank and a liability of the importer. Normally, however, the issuing bank also sells the acceptance in the secondary market. In this case the acceptance is being used as a source of funds in the sense of recouping funds committed to the foreign bank.

It is noteworthy that all parties concerned benefit from the acceptance transaction. Exporters receive payment for goods at the time of shipment, importers receive credit for the transit period of the goods, foreign banks usually obtain service fees, domestic banks obtain a new source of funds to finance loans (plus service fees), and money market participants have another interest-bearing instrument in which to invest funds temporarily.

The maturities on banker's acceptances range from 30 to 180 days and are timed to coincide with the transit (and disposal) of goods. Market yields are only slightly above those of U.S. Treasury bills, as issuing banks are large institutions with good international reputations. Banks earn not only the discount on the acceptance from corporate borrowers but a fee equal to a minimum of 1.5 percent (i.e., 1/8th of one percent per month), depending on the credit rating of the borrower.

Commercial Paper

Commercial paper is a short-term, unsecured promissory note sold by large companies with strong credit ratings. Banks can use their holding companies to issue commercial paper and acquire loans and investments from them. Bank holding companies (BHCs), therefore, are another channel through which funds can be raised.

Banks have also established independent companies, which are not holding companies, to issue commercial paper and then funnel the proceeds to one or more subsidiary banks by purchasing bank loans and investments.

Commercial paper is sold in $100,000 denominations with maturities normally ranging from 30 to 270 days. They are issued as part of continuous rolling program that can be years in length. There is little or no secondary market for commercial paper; however, some dealers may redeem notes prior to maturity. Most BHCs place new issues directly with institutional investors (i.e., direct paper) as opposed to using a securities dealer to make a public sale (i.e., dealer paper).

Capital Notes and Debentures

Banks can purchase long-term funds by issuing ***capital notes and debentures***, or senior debt capital. During the Great Depression, distressed banks raised much-needed funds by selling these kinds of debt issues. The stigma of this experience prompted the Comptroller of the Currency to discourage national banks from issuing *senior debt securities* until the 1960s. To provide banks more flexibility in managing their capital, the Comptroller ruled in 1962 that these debt securities could be counted as part of (unimpaired) capital in calculating lending limits on unsecured loans to any one borrower. Many banks quickly moved to sell notes and debentures due to this ruling.

Changing definitions of bank capital and associated regulatory requirements have caused banks to increase their usage of notes and debentures. Because capital notes and debentures are uninsured, as discussed in Chapter 12, it is believed that the marketplace prices these issues according to risk and, therefore, provides some amount of "market discipline." Additionally, bank regulators can use bank debt prices as another way to detect possible problem situations.

Capital notes and debentures are subordinated, or second in order of claims, to bank deposits in the event of bank failure. Issues are made in a wide assortment of denominations and maturities in order to tailor them for sale to specific bank customers, including correspondent banks of the issuing bank. Normally, senior debt securities are issued by large banks, because small banks do not have such ready access to the capital markets, and transactions costs are relatively high for smaller issues.

BALANCE SHEET STRUCTURE OF BANK LIABILITIES

Table 13-2 (next page) provides information on the balance sheet composition of bank liabilities from 2010 to 2014 for all insured U.S. commercial banks. A number of trends can be observed in the data reported there. Deposit liabilities increased by about 25 percent over these years. No doubt the declining and volatile stock market in the 2008-2009 financial crisis increased demand for safe and liquid assets among the public. Another explanation for increased deposits is *quantitative easing* (QE) by the Federal Reserve that purchased bonds to help lower longer-term interest rates, prevent potential deflation, and boost the sluggish economy in those years. QE increased the monetary base (or cash in circulation and cash reserves deposited by banks in their accounts at the Fed) as well as deposit base of the banking system, especially core deposits (including transactions, savings, and small time deposits). Sweep accounts became more popular, which move funds from transactions accounts (such as NOW accounts) with reserve requirements to savings accounts with no reserve requirements. In many cases the deposits over a designated level are upstreamed from the bank to the parent bank holding company or another affiliate bank for reinvestment in commercial paper and other money market instruments. As such, these programs offer better average yields to depositors than transactions accounts alone and enable the bank to free up some reserves for investment in loans and other assets. Due to rising deposits, available loanable funds on the credit side of the balance sheet expanded.

Another trend shown in Table 13-2 is decreased use of higher-rate borrowed funds (or managed liabilities), such as large time deposits and other interest-bearing liabilities (such as repurchase agreements, banker's acceptances, and commercial paper). This decline is likely explained by the lower cost of deposit funds for banks. Also, notes and debentures declined. Altogether, total liabilities increased by almost 20 percent from 2010 to 2014, with deposit growth more than offsetting nondeposit declines. It should be noted that bank deposits have been steadily growing at this rate since the early 2000s.

TABLE 13-2 **LIABILITIES OF U.S. COMMERCIAL BANKS: 2010-2014 (thousands of dollars)**

Year	No. Banks	Total Deposits	Borrowed Funds	Subordinated Notes	Other Liabilities	Total Liabilities
2014	5,643	10,953,329,342	1,197,340,488	96,841,822	629,933,204	12,877,444,856
2013	5,877	10,396,437,358	1,110,171,632	99,033,210	549,822,614	12,155,464,814
2012	6,097	10,021,082,372	1,141,537,310	117,532,500	615,417,589	11,895,569,771
2011	6,292	9,263,083,011	1,193,589,016	131,788,580	644,837,842	11,233,298,449
2010	6,531	8,519,600,438	1,448,843,607	144,824,463	593,917,247	10,707,185,755

Source: FDIC.

The liability mix among different sizes of banks varies considerably. Smaller banks ranked below the top 1,000 banks in total asset size hold negligible foreign deposits, whereas the ten largest U.S. banks finance more than 10 percent of their assets with foreign deposits (i.e., a component of other liabilities). The ten largest banks also differ from smaller institutions in holding a higher proportion of notes and debentures than smaller banks. In general, as bank size decreases, greater emphasis is placed on retail deposits and less on nondeposit sources of funds. This changing structure of bank liabilities reflects the wholesale nature of larger banks. An unexpected increase in loan demand at a large bank could not be handled solely by retail CDs. Thus, the greater use of large-denomination CDs, RPs, foreign CDs and the like at larger banks is a natural consequence of their loan operations.

Over the period from the 1980s to 2015, typically five-year CDs have higher interest rates than shorter-term six-month and one-year CDs but at times their rates differ little if at all. Interest rates over time have generally trended downward in large part due to declining inflation rates. More recently, in response to Federal Reserve monetary policy targeting near zero federal funds rates and QE, CD rates declined to historically low levels after 2009. These trends have significantly reduced the interest costs of bank liabilities.

Figure 13-1 shows that ***net interest margins*** have held steady for community banks, but not all commercial banks, from 2007 to 2015. The most likely explanation for this trend is that many community banks were less affected by the mortgage market collapse during the 2008-2009 financial crisis. Larger banks have lower proportions of assets devoted to consumer and small business loans compared to community banks and higher proportions in mortgage-related assets and medium-to-large business loans. Historically, it should be recognized that net interest margins tend to increase as bank size decreases. Larger banks rely more on noninterest sources of revenues (including fees, off-balance sheet assets, and derivatives activities) than smaller banks, whose profits are determined to a greater extent by net interest margins.

FIGURE 13-1 **NET INTEREST MARGINS FOR U.S. COMMERCIAL BANKS: 2007-2015**

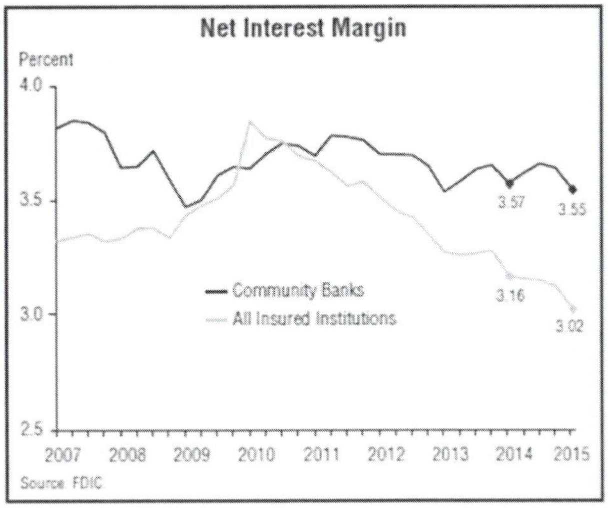

The 2000s ushered in a period of record low interest rates that presented different liability management problems from those arising from by double-digit deposit rates in the 1980s. In the 1980s high deposit rates allowed banks to readily attract funds from the financial marketplace. Brokerage firms often assisted customers in finding the highest yielding bank CDs in the country. The problem was not acquiring deposits but paying their high interest costs and earning a reasonable net interest margin. An opposite problem began to appear in the 2000s. Low deposit rates challenged banks to retain their deposit customers' funds. Due to low rates, banks have sought to expand their relationship with deposit customers by offering more electronic banking services, credit cards with cash back, travel, and other rewards programs, and investment services (such as stocks and bonds through mutual funds and other securities firms). In 1999, the Financial Services Modernization Act improved banks' ability to retain deposit customers. The act allows financial holding companies to offer a full menu of financial services, including investment and insurance services. These changes are expanding the scope of liability management and thereby enabling bankers to create packages of financial services for their customers. Today, many banks seek to cross-sell a variety of securities and insurance services to their deposit customers.

MANAGING BANK LIABILITIES

Deregulation of deposit interest rate ceilings and restrictions on financial services as well as rising competition for deposit funds has resulted in a wide variety of deposit products and associated services. This growing diversity of liability services has caused banks to use product differentiation as a way of distinguishing themselves from competitors. For example, Table 13-3 (next page) compares the pricing strategies of five hypothetical banks in the same city with respect to NOW and MMDA accounts. The total ***pricing strategy*** is a combination of convenience (such as ATMs, or automated teller machines), service charges, minimum balances to avoid service charges or earn interest, electronic funds transfer services (including mobile phones), and other unique characteristics of the particular account. In general, these pricing features are traded off against one another; for instance, banks with low service charges either had higher minimum balances or lower numbers of ATMs. Of course, the pricing strategy of individual banks is also influenced by their desired liability mix. Due to the competition for funds, customers that seek minimum idle cash balances, and disintermediation (or movement of deposit funds by customers to higher-rate money and capital market instruments), bank management must implement a deposit development and retention program. In this section we discuss different aspects of the pricing decision that should be considered in the management of bank liabilities, in addition to the control of costs involved in acquiring funds.

FORMULATING PRICING POLICY

The pricing policy is a written document that contains the pricing details of deposit services. Some key areas to be covered in the bank's pricing policy are:

- Service fees versus minimum balance requirements
- Deposit costs and volumes and their relationship to profits
- Credit availability and compensating balances
- Customer relationship pricing
- Promotional pricing of new products
- Other marketing elements such as product differentiation and technology

Obviously, the pricing process is based on many variables that require experience and judgment to evaluate effectively. We next discuss these aspects of pricing policy in greater detail.

TABLE 13-3 PRICING NEW DEPOSIT ACCOUNTS:A HYPOTHETICAL EXAMPLE

Bank	# of ATMs in City/State	Service Charges NOW	Minimum Balance to Avoid Service Charges NOW	Minimum Balance to Earn Interest MMDA	Additional Restrictions on MMDAs
I	60/300	$3/mo $0.25/ck $0.25/ATM transaction	$1,000	$1,000	No more than six automatic, preauthorized, or ATM withdrawals or transfers per month
II	80/350	$5/mo $0.15/ck $0.10/ATM transaction	$1,000	$2,500	No more than six withdrawals per month
III	30/100	$1.50/mo $0.25/ck $0.20/ATM transaction	$ 500	$2,500	No more than six transfers per month to checking account and ten withdrawals per month
IV	90/300	$7/mo	$1,000	$1,000	$0.50 per transaction over ten per month
V	25/80	$6/mo $0.10/ck	$ 600	$1,000	No checks

DEPOSIT PRICING MATRIX

In banking, both ***explicit and implicit pricing*** of products and services are used. Explicit pricing relates to interest expenses, whereas implicit pricing concerns noninterest expenses, such as free checking and other services, which are payments in kind. Figure 13-2 (next page) shows a pricing matrix that gives some examples of explicit and implicit pricing of bank liabilities and their effects on bank revenues and costs.

Deregulation of deposit accounts has caused banks to move toward greater use of explicit pricing and decreased use of implicit pricing. This shift has been the result of unbundling costs, which means simply using explicit pricing to reflect more closely the true costs of producing specific products and services. Prior to deregulation of deposit interest rates, free checking was normally available as an implicit payment of interest to customers. Free checking was justifiable, because no interest could be earned on transactions balances, and individuals included some amount of savings balances in their transactions accounts for the sake of convenience. Deregulation of deposit rates allowed retail depositors to choose from alternative new accounts, some of which had predominantly checking features (such as demand deposits), savings features (such as MMDA accounts), or a mixture of both (such as NOW accounts). Naturally, banks price each type of deposit account differently to distinguish them from one another. As interest rates change over time, customer preferences for implicit and explicit pricing can shift. For example, when interest rates are at relatively high levels, banks must emphasize explicit pricing over implicit pricing or suffer disintermediation. When interest rates are low (as in the 1990s), customers are less interest sensitive (due to lower opportunity costs) and, therefore, implicit pricing becomes more important (such as offering electronic banking services). In general, banks are continuing to adjust their pricing strategies as they learn more about customer preferences for implicitly and explicitly priced deposit services.

FIGURE 13-2 DEPOSIT PRICING MATRIX

Effect on Bank Cash Flows	Pricing Strategy: Explicit Prices	Pricing Strategy: Implicit Prices
Bank Costs	• Interest payments • Gifts (e.g., appliances) • Compounding interest (e.g., daily)	• Below cost provision of services (e.g., free checking) • Added convenience (e.g., branch offices, ATMs, business hours)
Bank Revenues	• Service charges (e.g., charge per check) • Fees (e.g., overdrafts)	• Minimum balance requirements • Restrictions (e.g., limited check-writing privileges)

THE PRICING COMMITTEE

The pricing committee should be staffed by employees from throughout the bank. Because pricing decisions greatly affect the deposit base, they must be coordinated with other bank activities, including lending, marketing, accounting, data processing, operations, and trust services. Top management should appoint members to the pricing committee and periodically review its performance.

Committee assignments should address the primary objectives of deposit maintenance, market competitiveness, cost minimization, and adequate funding to meet lending goals. Information pertaining to these objectives must be gathered and reviewed periodically. Subsequent changes in pricing existing products need to be monitored for their effects on costs and deposit flows. Also, the committee should play a major role in the development and introduction of new products.

COMPONENTS OF THE PRICING DECISION

The Federal Reserve Bank of New York conducted a series of interviews with senior commercial and savings bankers on the pricing of their institutions' deposits.

Bankers were asked what factors they considered in pricing consumer deposit products. The following key factors were identified:

- Wholesale cost of funds
- Pricing strategy of competitors
- Interest elasticity (or responsiveness) of consumer demand
- Past deposit flows for various kinds of consumer accounts
- Maturity structure of deposits

The ***wholesale cost of funds***, or large CD rates, was viewed by bankers as an alternative cost of money. Adjustments for differences in maturity (such as MMDAs, NOWs, and savings deposits that can be immediately withdrawn and have no fixed maturity), reserve requirements, and servicing were made to estimate retail costs of funds.

Various market factors influenced the pricing decision. The pricing strategy of competitors was monitored regularly, as well as the deposit flows of their own institution regarding various types of accounts. Additionally, the interest elasticity of demand for different deposit accounts was considered to assess the potential influence of price changes on deposit flows.

Bankers also reviewed the maturity structure of their institution's deposits to determine what deposits were maturing and when they would come due. In general, bankers indicated that they did not consider the bank's short-term funding needs in making pricing decisions for consumer deposits. Such liquidity needs were met for the most part by wholesale deposits. This pricing behavior suggests that retail deposits are perceived primarily as core deposits.

Pricing decisions were reviewed on a weekly basis by most of the banks surveyed. Of course, changes in pricing were implemented less frequently. For example, even though large CD rates may have changed, the rate on MMDAs may not have been changed because MMDAs are less interest sensitive than CDs (presumably because MMDAs are shorter-term and tend to be used by customers as temporary accounts to "park" cash until it can be reinvested). Savings accounts were believed to be relatively insensitive to interest rate changes also. Rates on consumer (or retail) CDs, however, were changed more frequently following a change in large CD rates. Generally, among revisions that were made, bankers observed that changes in implicit prices (such as service convenience) were seldom implemented, perhaps only once a year. Thus, most price changes involved explicit interest, service charges, and fees.

PROFITABILITY OF DEPOSIT PRICING

The goal of bank management should be to maximize deposit revenues and minimize deposit costs in an effort to maximize bank profitability. Cost/revenue analysis is one way in which managers can better understand how deposit pricing decisions are affecting bank profitability.

Figure 13-3 (next page) shows how bank costs and revenues change as the deposit base is expanded. The S-shaped cost curve assumes economies of scale as deposits initially are expanded, which gradually reduce costs per unit deposits; however, diseconomies at some deposit level increase costs per unit deposits and cause the cost curve to increase at an increasing rate. Total bank costs equal fixed costs of land, buildings, and equipment, plus variable costs of deposits and other activities. Total bank revenues include deposit revenues, loan and security portfolio revenues, and other revenues. Profit maximization requires the following: (1) minimization of total costs at each output level; (2) maximization of total revenues at each output level; and (3) marginal total costs equal marginal total revenues (i.e., the cost of an additional dollar of deposits equals the revenue it would provide when invested by the bank). The latter marginal cost/revenue condition is represented in Figure 13-3 at the deposit level where the slopes of the total cost and total revenue curves are equal. Upper and lower breakeven points occur where costs and revenues equal one another in absolute (rather than marginal) terms. These points describe the output range within which the bank can profitably operate.

FIGURE 13-3 COST/REVENUE ANALYSIS

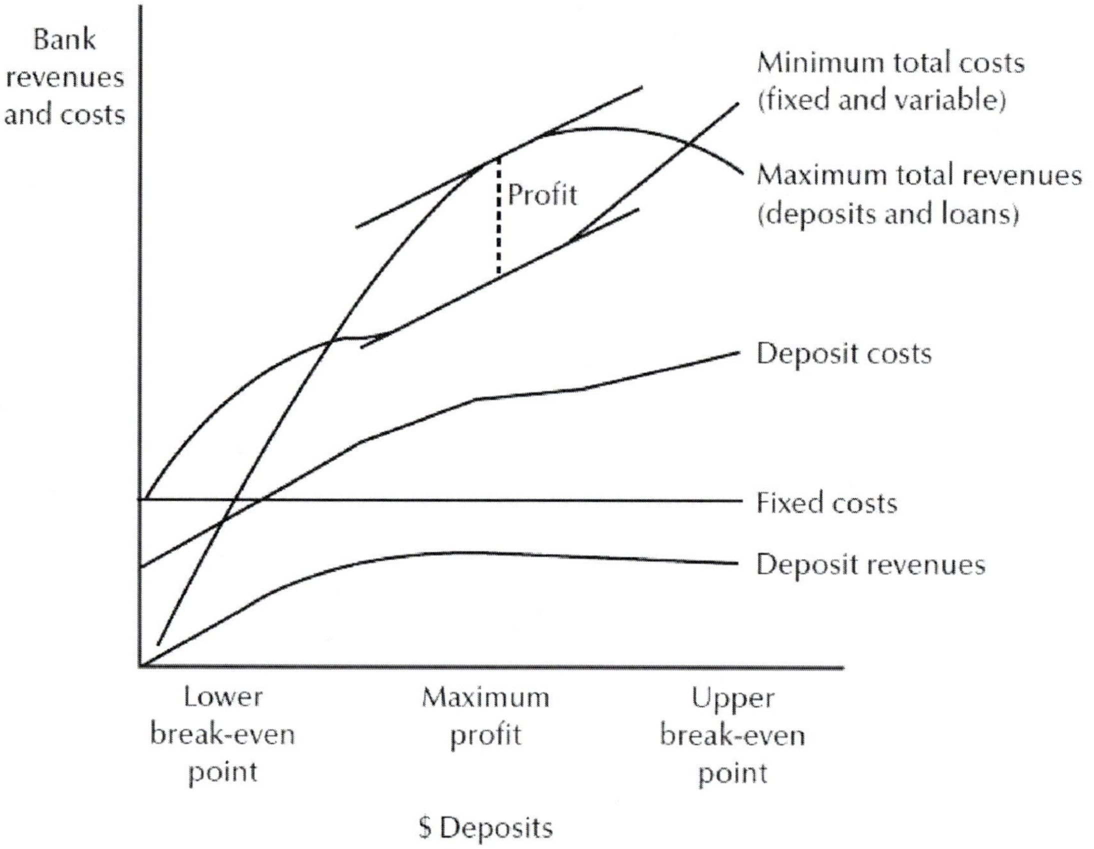

Once an optimal deposit level is estimated, the task of the pricing committee is to minimize net deposit costs for the target deposit base. Some of the ways in which banks reduce deposit costs are (1) truncating checks (i.e., not returning cleared checks to customers); (2) levying stricter penalties for early withdrawal on time deposits; (3) reducing the number of deposit products to avoid spreading resources too thin; (4) using weekly or monthly interest compounding instead of daily compounding; (5) waiting for customers to ask for higher-interest products rather than automatically moving their funds to these products; and (6) offering electronic banking services when possible to reduce operating costs associated with checks and physical bank facilities (such as branch offices). Obviously, these cost-cutting techniques are not always successful because customers might become dissatisfied with the bank's service and withdraw their deposits.

LENDING AND DEPOSIT COSTS

Deposit costs can be affected by bank loan policies. For example, most loans require that compensating (deposit) balances be maintained by the borrower. Such balances are inexpensive to maintain because they usually pay no interest, require no promotional expenditures, and have minimum transactions costs (for example, customer information is already on file). Another advantage of compensating balances is that they are a relatively stable source of deposits that is less likely to be withdrawn than other deposits, thus lowering the cost per unit risk of deposits.

Another way in which loan policy can lower deposit costs is through *tie-in arrangements* between deposit and loan services. Those customers that have deposit accounts could be provided greater access to credit. For instance, many farm operators hold deposit accounts at rural banks not so much to earn interest but to establish a banking relationship that would enable them to obtain loans when needed. Thus, the credit function can be used by banks not only to raise deposit funds (i.e., compensating balances) but to reduce deposit costs.

CUSTOMER RELATIONSHIP PRICING

Relationship banking is an expression that includes the *total* financial needs of the public rather than just specific needs. It also includes fulfilling long-term needs, as opposed to immediate needs, such as cashing a check. This can be done by cross-selling a variety of services that tends to lower user costs and increase convenience compared with selling each service separately. Also, patrons are viewed as clients, as opposed to customers, according to this viewpoint. This pricing strategy greatly increased in importance subsequent to the Financial Services Modernization Act of 1999, which expanded the array of products and services that banking institutions can provide to full-blown securities and insurance activities. Many banks set goals of selling (on average) three to five financial services to each customer. Managers are appropriately rewarded in their compensation for achieving multiple product sales.

PROMOTIONAL PRICING

Promotional pricing is used to introduce new products. In brief, the product is priced below cost to attract market attention. More frequently, promotional pricing is used to support or rejuvenate demand for existing products. Some of the potential reasons for such promotions include increasing or protecting market share, modifying existing products, developing brand recognition or overall bank image, targeting particular market segments of the population in certain geographic areas, and increasing sales to a cost-efficient level at which economies of scale can be obtained.

OTHER MARKETING ELEMENTS RELATED TO PRICING

Product Differentiation

Designing products and services to meet the needs of specific market segments is known as ***product differentiation***. As mentioned earlier, banks typically must price their liabilities in different ways to compete effectively for funds. If banks did not differentiate their products, and instead competed side-by-side for the same customers, many customers might be forced to purchase products that are not priced to fit their needs. For example, a bank could offer a company a business card that offers a rewards program to receive free travel costs for its employees. The card could help simplify the company's accounting processes, slow down accounts payables, and increase employee convenience.

Distribution

Another part of the pricing decision that bank managers should consider is the physical delivery of deposit services to the public. The problem here is one of logistics, namely, how to optimize the time and place preferences of customers, while minimizing bank operating costs net of associated revenues. Banks have two basic distribution channels from which to choose: (1) *retail channels* that distribute services to the general public (such as drive-in teller windows, ATMs, and internet access), and (2) *wholesale channels* that distribute large volume services to corporate enterprises and government units (such as lock boxes, electronic transfers of funds, and oversight of cash management functions).

ESTIMATING THE COST OF BANK FUNDS

Cost Definitions

The acquisition of bank funds entails incurring both financial and operating costs. Financial costs pertain to explicit payments to lenders minus revenues obtained from service charges and fees, whereas operating costs relate to land, labor, and equipment expenditures. When discussing the costs of bank funding, it is also necessary to distinguish between average costs and marginal costs. ***Average costs*** are simply calculated by dividing the total dollar costs of funds by the dollar amount of funds. ***Marginal costs*** are the incremental costs of acquiring an additional dollar of funds. Marginal costs are superior to average costs because they more accurately reflect current costs as opposed to past costs.

WEIGHTED AVERAGE COST OF FUNDS

On an aggregate basis, costs of bank funds are measured in weighted average terms. The *weighted-average cost of funds* can be calculated by summing the average cost of each source of funds times the proportion of total funds raised from each respective source of funds. We can write this average cost of funds as follows:

$$CT = C_1 \frac{F_1}{TF} + C_2 \frac{F_2}{TF} + \ldots + C_n \frac{F_n}{TF} \qquad (13\text{-}1)$$

where CT is the weighted average cost of funds, C_n is the average cost of the *n*th source of funds, F_n is the funds acquired from the *n*th source of funds, and TF is the total funds acquired by the bank. The ratio F_n/TF is the proportion of total funds obtained from a particular source of funds, or the weight used for this source's average cost of funds. Theoretically, the average costs of the individual sources of funds, or C_n, are equal to one another as well as to CT, after adjusting for differences in risk. This must be so because the bank would naturally acquire funds from the cheapest risk-adjusted source until its cost per unit risk rose to the cost per unit risk of other funds' sources.

PURPOSES OF COST ANALYSES

Performance Reports

Table 13-4 (next page) provides example historical cost data for different sources of funds (excluding equity) that could be included in a performance report. Funds available for investment are less than the amount of funds acquired by the amount of reserves required (because of either legal requirements or management preferences). Financial costs equal total interest costs net of service revenues,[3] and operating costs are based on allocated expenses for labor, premises, occupancy expenses, and other operations associated with physically producing accounts. The total cost of funds is divided by funds available for investment to obtain the average cost of each type of fund. Notice that reserve requirements raise the *effective cost of funds,* which is associated with funds usable for investment purposes. The final step is to calculate the weighted average cost of funds by applying equation (13.1). As shown in Table 13-4 this historical cost equaled 7.12 percent.

The information displayed in Table 13-4 can be used by the pricing committee to identify both problems and opportunities. For example, public deposits were costing an average of 10 percent, which exceeds the average cost of any other type of funds, even though the risk associated with these funds is relatively low (because government accounts are a fairly stable source of deposits). Thus, management could work on reducing the cost of public deposits. On the other hand, the average cost of demand deposits was only about one percent, well below the cost of other kinds of funds. Bank management could increase promotional expenses, lower service charges and fees, or increase implicit service returns (by increasing operating expenses) to expand this relatively inexpensive source of funds. This kind of historical overview of costs can help guide bank management in minimizing the costs of funds in the future. In turn, cost minimizing behavior of bank managers causes the marginal costs of all sources of funds to remain about the same, including the cost of equity funds, on a risk-adjusted basis.

To obtain detailed information about a bank's liabilities and their costs, a convenient resource is the Uniform Bank Performance Report, or UBPR (www.ffiec.gov/UBPR.htm). The UBPR was created for bank supervisory, examina-

TABLE 13-4 HISTORICAL COST ANALYSIS (IN THOUSANDS OF DOLLARS)

Sources of Funds*	(1) Funds Acquired	(2) Funds Available for Investment	(3) = (1)/1,000,000 Proportion of Funds Acquired	(4) Financial Cost†	(5) Operating Cost‡	(6) = (4) + (5) Total Cost	(7) = (6)/(2) Average Cost of Funds	(8) = (3) × (7) Weighted Average Cost of Funds
Deposit sources								
Demand deposits	$20,000	$18,000	0.02	$ −10	$200	$ 190	1.06%	0.212%
NOW accounts	8,000	7,200	0.08	480	40	520	7.22	0.578
Passbook savings	5,000	4,500	0.05	350	20	370	8.22	0.411
MMDAs	7,000	7,000	0.07	525	30	555	7.93	0.555
Retail CDs	14,000	14,000	0.14	1,120	20	1,140	8.14	1.140
Large CDs (≥$100,000)	25,000	25,000	0.25	2,125	60	2,185	8.74	2.185
Public deposits	10,000	8,800	0.10	800	80	880	10.00	1.000
Nondeposit sources								
Fed funds and repos	4,000	4,000	0.04	360	30	390	9.75	0.390
Other borrowed money	5,000	5,000	0.05	450	30	380	9.60	0.480
Notes and debentures	2,000	2,000	0.02	140	30	170	8.50	0.170
Total	$100,000	$95,500	1.00	$6,340	$540	$6,880 Cost	Wtd. Avg. = 7.12 percent	

* The following simplified reserve requirements are assumed to apply to various sources of funds: transactions accounts (10%), nonpersonal time deposits (0%), personal time and savings deposits (0%), and nondeposit funds (0%).

† Financial costs equal interest expenses minus revenues from service charges and fees.

‡ Operating costs equal total expenses involved in physically producing accounts.

tion, and management purposes. In a concise format, it shows the impact of management decisions and economic conditions on a bank's performance and balance-sheet composition. The performance and composition data contained in the report can be used as an aid in evaluating the adequacy of earnings, liquidity, capital, asset and liability management, and growth management. Bankers and examiners alike can use this report to further their understanding of a bank's financial condition, and through such understanding, perform their duties more effectively.

The UBPR data is the most widely used source of bank data due to its breakdown of balance sheet and income statement information by individual banks, peer group, states, and the nation. For example, you can enter the name of a bank in your area and obtain detailed UBPR data. In this way you can conduct bank performance analyses of individual banks. A convenient comparison for any individual bank's data is its peer group. Data for peer groups are organized by asset size. For example, Peer Group 1 contains the largest banks in the United States. From the list of banks in Peer Group 1, you can select an individual large bank and then quickly download comparative data to conduct a case study of its financial condition.

MARGINAL COSTS OF FUNDS

The average cost of funds is historical and, therefore, is not useful in making investment decisions in the future. For example, if a bank manager is contemplating making a loan at 10 percent to a potential borrower, the relevant cost of funds for the purpose of evaluating the profitability of the loan is the cost of funds at the time the loan is made. In this sense, the marginal cost of funds can be interpreted as the minimum yield on bank investments in loans and securities that must be earned to avoid a loss in equity share values. This interpretation is based on the notion that funds should continue to be acquired and invested as long as shareholders earn yields in excess of the minimum required rate of return.

Investment Decisions

Care must be taken not to use the marginal cost of any particular source of funds as the cutoff rate in investment decisions. In the case of the pending loan decision mentioned above, it would be a mistake to measure the cost of funds by linking it with (say) six-month CDs issued on the day of the loan. This approach to investment decisions is short run in nature and ignores the long-run implications of intermediating savings flows from different sources to investment in different loans and securities.

Instead, it is the marginal cost of the entire *mix* of funds that must be used as a cutoff criterion in investment decisions. Table 13-5 shows the marginal cost of each type of funding, which is equal to the incremental percentage cost of acquiring an additional dollar of funds from that source. The weighted average of these costs, where the weights are the proportions of each source of funds in the long run, is the marginal cost of funds to be used in bank investment decisions. In Table 13-5 the marginal cost is calculated to be 8.79 percent. In order to be worthwhile to shareholders, an investment would have to yield 8.79 percent or more.

An adjustment to the marginal cost of funds for purposes of investment decisions is needed if there is some proportion of funds that is nonearning, such as excess cash reserves. In this case the effective marginal cost of funds is increased. This adjustment is similar to calculating effective loan rates when there is a stated interest rate but compensating balances are required. In the above example, if five percent of total funds raised are placed in nonearning assets, the effective marginal cost equals 0.0879/(1 – 0.05) = 0.0925, or 9.25 percent. This cost is a more appropriate hurdle rate to use for earning assets that the bank is evaluating.

The greatest difficulty in applying the marginal cost concept to real-world investment decisions is the estimation of individual marginal costs for different sources of funds. The earnings/price ratio for common stock is a good proxy for the after-tax marginal cost of equity funds (see the second footnote in Table 13-5 concerning the distinction between before-tax and after-tax equity costs). Also, the Capital Asset Pricing Model (CAPM) could be used to estimate the cost of equity from market stock price and interest rate information.[4] Unfortunately, most banks do not have actively traded common stock. In this case, some multiple of book value must be used to estimate market value. Neither are liabilities' marginal costs readily calculable in many cases. Although marginal financial costs can be estimated fairly accurately from market and internal information, marginal operating costs of acquiring an additional dollar of deposit funds may be difficult to assess. Experience and judgment are the best resources that can be used to avoid this problem. Thus, even though there are some drawbacks to marginal cost analysis in investment decisions, management expertise normally is sufficient to make appropriate estimates.

FIGURE 13-5 MARGINAL COST ANALYSIS

Source of Funds	Funds Acquired	Proportion of Funds Acquired	Marginal Cost*†	Marginal Weighted Average Cost of Funds
Deposit sources				
Demand deposits	$20,000	0.18	6.50%	1.170%
NOW accounts	8,000	0.07	7.80	0.546
Passbook savings	5,000	0.05	7.90	0.395
MMDAs	7,000	0.06	8.10	0.486
Retail CDs	14,000	0.13	8.30	1.079
(≥$100,000)	25,000	0.23	8.40	1.932
Public deposits	10,000	0.09	8.00	0.720
Nondeposit sources				
Fed funds and repos	4,000	0.04	8.20	0.328
Other borrowed money	5,000	0.04	8.30	0.332
Notes and debentures	2,000	0.02	8.50	0.170
Equity	10,000	0.09	20.00	1.800
Total	$110,000	1.00	Marginal cost = 8.79%	

* Marginal cost is based on total financial and operating costs per dollar of funds available for investment. Marginal costs of funds vary according to the risk(s) of these funds.

† The marginal cost of equity is on a before-tax basis in order to compare it with debt forms of funding. The marginal tax rate of the bank is assumed to be 0.34, such that the required rate of return by shareholders is 13.20%.

Finally, the marginal cost of funds may not be appropriate in making long-run investment decisions. For such decisions a weighted-average of the marginal cost of long-term funds can be used to calculate what is known as the marginal cost of capital. The marginal cost of capital can serve as a hurdle rate in capital budgeting decisions involving the purchase of nonfinancial assets, such as bank office buildings, equipment, and furniture, as well as long-term financial assets, such as corporate and municipal bonds. In general, long-term funds have maturities greater than one year and, therefore, are acquired from the capital market rather than the money market. Capital funding sources for banks are notes, debentures, and equity, including capital stock and retained earnings. Because bank assets are primarily short term or have yields that can be adjusted more than once a year, the marginal cost of funds is relatively more important than the marginal cost of capital in financial decision making.[5]

SUMMARY

Sources of bank funds have changed substantially over time because of changes in inflation, rising competition, and deregulation of deposit rates and financial services. In recent years banks have increased their usage of deposit funding and decreased nondeposit funding. In this regard, brokered deposits have been symptomatic of increasing risk in the banking industry, in addition to the national-level competition for deposit funds. The wide variety of retail deposit accounts that have been introduced—such as NOWs, ATSs, MMDAs, and retail CDs—have transformed the liability side of banks' balance sheets. Low interest rates in the 2000s have continued to alter liability management, as banks have been aggressively offering electronic deposit services, sweep accounts, IRAs, credit cards, and investment services to retain deposit customers seeking higher yields.

The pricing committee is responsible primarily for the management of bank liabilities and is composed of employees throughout the bank. The task of formulating pricing policy involves deposit pricing, bank profitability, loan policies, customer relations, and various marketing elements. The large number of different types of deposit accounts offered to customers today makes pricing a challenging task that requires balancing funds needs of the bank, profitability, and customer relations.

Regarding the profit dimension of liability management, estimating the costs of bank funds is the crucial factor. These costs can be estimated using both average costs and marginal costs; however, the latter is definitely superior to the former. A weighted-average cost of funds can be calculated to analyze problems and opportunities in funds acquisition. Also, a marginal cost of funds can be calculated to serve as a cutoff rate in bank investment decisions.

Key Terms

Automatic transfer service (ATS)
Average costs
Banker's acceptance
Brokered deposits
Capital notes and debentures
Commercial paper
Core deposits
Cost/revenue analysis
Demand deposits
Discount window advance
Eurodollar deposit
Explicit pricing
Federal funds
Implicit pricing
IRA
Keogh plans
Large time deposits
Marginal costs
MMDAs
MMMFs
Negotiable certificate of deposit
Net interest margins
Nondeposit funds
NOW accounts
Pricing policy
Pricing strategy
Product differentiation
Promotional pricing
Purchased deposits
Regulation Q
Relationship banking
Repurchase agreement (RP)
Retail CD
Savings certificate
Super NOW (SNOW) accounts
Sweep accounts
Time and savings deposits
Wholesale cost of funds

QUESTIONS

13.1 Define core deposits of a bank. Also define purchased deposits.

13.2 Why are purchased deposits generally considered to be more risky than core deposits?

13.3 What does the Glass-Steagall Act have to do with deposit rate regulation? What is the rationale for this regulation?

13.4 Are commercial accounts still subject to Regulation Q? Would a corporate client prefer compensating balances or service fees on a loan, all else the same?

13.5 Historically low interest rates after the 2008-2009 financial crisis have challenged banks to retain deposit customers. How have banks sought to keep deposit customers seeking higher yields?

13.6 How has the mix of deposit and nondeposit funds changed in banks after the 2008-2009 financial crisis? What could explain these trends?

13.7 What are explicit and implicit deposit costs?

13.8 What advantage does a MMDA possibly have over a money market mutual fund (MMMF) account?

13.9 What is a negotiable certificate of deposit?

13.10 Why is there a tiered CD market?

13.11 Is a dollar held in a bank office in Hong Kong a Eurodollar deposit? Are such deposits eligible for FDIC insurance?

13.12 What are brokered deposits? Do all banks have access to brokered deposits?

13.13 What are "managed liabilities"? List three differences between deposit funds and managed liabilities (or purchased funds). What are sweep programs?

13.14 List and briefly discuss four sources of nondeposit liabilities.

13.15 How do the deposit compositions of small and large banks differ?

13.16 Pricing deposit accounts is a complex process. Give at least four factors affecting the pricing of consumer deposits.

13.17 Is there an optimal level of bank deposits in the sense of maximizing bank profitability? Use a graph to illustrate your answer and discuss your graph.

13.18 How does the Financial Service Modernization Act of 1999 affect the management of bank sources of funds?

13.19 Go to the Federal Reserve's Uniform Bank Performance Report (UBPR) website (www.ffiec.gov/ubpr.htm). Click the link for individual bank UBPR reports. Print out the UBPR reports for a specific individual bank. What do these reports indicate with respect to bank liabilities?

13.20 Go to the Federal Reserve Bank of Chicago's website (www.chicagofed.org). Search on the keywords "discount window" to obtain materials on discount window rules and activities of banks. Write a one-page summary of recent or proposed changes to discount window rules.

13.21 Go to the Federal Reserve Board's Commercial Bank Examination Manual (http://www.federalreserve.gov/boarddocs/supmanual/supervision_cbem.htm). Select the "Liabilities and Capital" PDF document link. Write a short report on the Examination Objectives of supervisory staff and bank examiners outlined in this document.

PROBLEMS

13.1 (a) Given the data in Exhibit 13-1 (next page) showing the amounts and costs of funds for ABC Bank, calculate its weighted average cost of funds.

(b) Which sources of funds had average costs that exceeded the weighted average cost of funds?

(c) Does it appear that some sources of funds are relatively costly considering their risk?

13.2 (a) Given the data in Exhibit 13-2 (next page), calculate the marginal weighted average cost of funds for ABC Bank.

(b) For what purpose can bank management use the marginal cost result in part (a)?

(c) Why do various costs of funds differ? Under what conditions would they be equal?

EXHIBIT 13-1 AVERAGE COSTS OF FUNDS FOR ABC BANK IN 200X

Source of Funds	Average Amount Available for investment ($ millions)	Average Cost (%)
Deposits		
Demand deposits	$15	5.00%
Interest-bearing checking	30	7.00
Passbook savings	10	8.00
Small CDs	20	9.00
Large CDs	30	10.00
Eurodollar CDs	5	10.40
Nondeposits		
Fed funds	6	8.00
Repos	10	8.50
Discount window advances	4	7.50
Other liabilities	12	10.00
Stockholders equity	12	15.00

EXHIBIT 13-2 MARGINAL COSTS OF FUNDS FOR ABC BANK IN 200X

Source of Funds	Funds Acquired ($ millions)	Marginal Cost (%)
Deposits		
Demand deposits	$18.0	6.00%
Interest-bearing checking	33.0	7.25
Passbook savings	11.0	8.30
Small CDs	20.0	9.15
Large CDs	32.0	10.15
Eurodollar CDs	5.5	10.55
Nondeposits		
Fed funds	6.0	8.40
Repos	10.0	8.80
Discount window advances	4.0	7.90
Other liabilities	12.0	10.50
Stockholders equity	12.0	15.00

(d) If 10 percent of funds raised must be placed in nonearning assets, what would be the effective marginal cost of funds?

13.3 (a) Go to the Federal Reserve's Uniform Bank Performance Report (UBPR) website at www.ffiec.gov/UBPR.

(b) Under Report, Select "Call/TFR." Select a specific individual bank in the peer group report. Select a single date that is three months prior to the current data. Now click the Search button.

(c) Download the Call Report in a PDF file format.

(d) Go through the Call Report to see the balance sheet and income statement data that banks report to regulator and tax authorities.

CASE: Hometown Bank and Trust

Over the last decade Hometown Bank and Trust has continually adjusted its interest rates and service features of its different interest-bearing sources of funds. Considerable decreases in interest rates in the last year, to 20-year historic lows, have caused the bank to lose some of its deposit customers to higher-interest-rate products such as money market mutual fund (MMMF) accounts and various money market securities sold through security brokers. Ben Bridge, the bank's president and CEO, was privately beginning to worry that, if a large number of the bank's most interest-sensitive customers pulled out of Hometown, the bank would have difficulty meeting the credit needs in the community. Based on this apprehension, Ben called a meeting of top management to discuss the problem. The meeting culminated with a unanimous vote to set up a Task Force on Bank Liabilities comprised of middle managers close to deposit holders and other sources of bank funds. The Task Force was charged with the responsibility to examine the bank's sources of funds over the past five years and make recommendations to top management.

Jennifer Jones had worked for Hometown for four years after graduating from college with a finance degree. She had passed through the one-year training program credit analyst without any problems and had been assigned to various aspects of managing the bank's different deposit accounts. While still motivated by her work, Jennifer was getting anxious for a chance to demonstrate her leadership abilities. She often imagined that a "big break" would propel her forward from the middle-management ranks and onto a path to a top management position in the bank. That afternoon her immediate supervisor, Jason Jacobs, called her into his office to ask if she would head up the Task Force on Bank Liabilities, with five other middle managers serving in the group also. It was a great opportunity -- to either succeed or fail.

To get things going, Jennifer immediately sent a memo to all Task Force members to notify them of an initial meeting at the beginning of the next week. At this first meeting, she informed the members of their mission, namely, to evaluate historical data on bank liabilities and make recommendations for a top management decision concerning the bank's sources of funds. Their task was *not* to make the final decisions concerning pricing policy. Next, she asked the group to list alternative approaches to achieving their mission. Three-person teams were assigned to collect the necessary bank data for the past five years and present it at the next meeting. Jennifer felt the group was off to a good start. The members were quite diverse with different viewpoints, which allowed open interaction and the potential for sharing of skills with one another in their joint effort.

At the next meeting the data in Exhibits 13-3 and 13-4 were presented. After all questions were answered on the details of collecting the data, and everyone was satisfied with the accuracy of the numbers, Jennifer asked each member of the Task Force to write an independent report. Each report was to have three sections: (1) Trends in Bank Liabilities, (2) Implications of Current Low Interest Rate Market Conditions to Bank Liabilities, and (3) Strategies to Offset Current and Potential Deposit Losses. As a member of the Task Force, follow these guidelines to write your report.

EXHIBIT 13-3 **COMPOSITION OF LIABILITIES OVER TIME: HOMETOWN BANK AND TRUST**

	Percentage of Total Assets				
Liability Item	**2016**	**2015**	**2014**	**2013**	**2012**
Demand deposits	10.92	10.85	10.91	11.42	11.98
NOW and ATS accounts	12.02	10.83	11.02	10.48	10.42
MMDAs	10.06	9.20	9.27	9.11	9.82
Other savings deposits	8.37	6.93	7.06	6.76	7.01
Retail time deposits	35.07	37.80	37.60	37.25	35.51
Core deposits	80.95	79.74	79.94	79.09	79.00
Time deposits ≥ $100,000	7.18	8.57	8.40	9.24	9.26
Deposits in foreign offices	3.62	3.98	3.92	3.92	4.11
Total deposits	89.20	89.36	89.36	89.36	89.27
Federal funds purchased and RPs	0.22	0.18	0.20	0.15	0.18
Other borrowings	0.04	0.03	0.04	0.04	0.05
Acceptances and other liabilities	0.81	0.96	0.94	1.03	1.04
Total liabilities	91.41	91.63	91.62	91.65	91.64

EXHIBIT 13-4

INTEREST COST OF BANK SOURCES OF FUNDS OVER TIME: HOMETOWN BANK AND TRUST (Includes implicit and explicit costs)

Liability Item	2016	2015	2014	2013	2012
Total interest-bearing deposits	4.61	6.28	6.13	6.93	7.02
NOW and ATS accounts	3.32	4.75	4.65	5.00	5.04
MMDAs	3.69	5.31	5.18	5.79	5.87
Other savings deposits	3.73	5.04	4.97	5.20	5.20
Large CDs	5.05	7.08	6.91	7.81	7.94
Deposits in foreign offices	4.02	6.34	6.11	8.21	9.08
Federal funds purchased and RPs	3.69	5.80	5.60	7.67	8.74
Other borrowings	2.78	4.41	4.32	5.05	6.35
Acceptances and other liabilities	3.80	5.90	5.70	7.75	8.85

ENDNOTES

1. Immediately available funds can be defined as those bank funds that can be withdrawn or used for payment by the public on any given business day. They consist of the collected liabilities of commercial banks plus the deposit liabilities of Federal Reserve banks.
2. This is known as a time draft, as opposed to a sight draft, which is payable to the exporter upon its presentation to the bank.
3. Interest costs and allocated operating costs of various sources of funds, in addition to cost breakdowns of various asset categories, are available through the Federal Reserve System's Functional Cost Analysis (FCA) service. Banks can voluntarily participate in this program by providing necessary data. Alternatively, many banks have implemented in-house cost accounting systems to collect data.
4. In the CAPM the cost of equity equals the riskless rate of interest plus a risk premium, where the risk premium is calculated as the firm's beta multiplied by the yield spread between the market rate of return and the riskless rate of interest. For example, if the Treasury bill rate is three percent, beta for the bank's stock is estimated to be 0.8, and the rate of return on the Standard & Poor's 500 Index is 10 percent, the cost of equity is $3\% + (0.8 \times 7\%) = 8.6\%$. Readers should refer to a standard managerial finance textbook for further discussion and methods of obtaining beta estimates.
5. By contrast, because nonfinancial, private business firms have substantial long-term investments, the marginal cost of capital is emphasized in investment decisions.

Chapter 14

Off-Balance-Sheet Activities

After reading this chapter, you will be able to:

- Define off-balance-sheet activities that banks are expanding rapidly to meet market demands.
- Describe the different types of contingent claims offered by banks.
- Discuss the growing derivatives securities activities of banks, which is challenging regulators to control potential risks inherent in this growth market.
- Compare the risk implications of different off-balance-sheet activities.
- Identify other off-balance-sheet services t hat do not involve contingent claims or derivative securities.

The 1980s witnessed wild gyrations in market rates of interest, economic booms and busts, and inflation and deflation. The 1990s experienced low and stable interest rates with little or no inflation ending in the dot.com technology stock market crash in 2000. Over this time period, price volatility in the United States and other industrialized countries' stock markets exceeded historical experience. Also, emerging market countries suffered periodic bouts of extreme financial market turmoil that at times spilled over into developed countries (such as the economic and financial crises in Russia, southeast Asia, and Latin America). The 2008-2009 financial crisis brought stock and bond price volatility to the United States and Europe, as a bubble in the mortgage market collapsed that led to the Great Recession as well as global financial turmoil. The net impact of this global volatility has been increased variability of profits and, therefore, risk of doing business in financial markets.

In response to increased risk as well as the need to satisfy customers' demands, generate stable fee income, and increase their capital to asset ratios, banks have developed new financial services that do not appear on their balance sheets as assets or liabilities -- so called ***off-balance-sheet activities***. Generally speaking, most off-balance-sheet activities are commitments based on contingent claims. A ***contingent claim*** is an obligation by a bank to provide funds (i.e., lend funds or buy securities) if a contingency is realized. In other words, the bank has underwritten an obligation of a third party and currently stands behind the risk. Default by the party on whose behalf the obligation was written may trigger an immediate loss or may result in the bank acquiring a substandard claim. Importantly, the claims do not appear on the balance sheet until they are exercised, when the loan is made, or the securities are purchased.

Two broad groups of off-balance-sheet activities are presented in this chapter—namely, financial guarantees and derivative instruments. For the sake of completeness, we also discuss some other types of off-balance-sheet activities, including trade finance, cash management services, and networking (or strategic alliances). Together, these rapidly growing areas of off-balance-sheet activities generate fee income for banks.

These new financial products are transforming the banking business from being deposit/lending institutions to being risk management institutions. Indeed, large banks have become the key players in managing various financial market risks. While risk management services clearly are needed in today's more volatile financial marketplace, and banks' off-balance-sheet activities have exploded over the last two decades in response to these needs, there are serious concerns about these new products. How much total risk are banks taking in off-balance-sheet activities? What are the different kinds of risk involved? To what extent should these activities be regulated? Should reporting requirements for regulators and the public be increased? As we shall see, while these new financial products help manage financial market risks, these benefits are not achieved without some costs, including greater complexity of financial transactions and new potential risks.

FIGURE 14-1 SCHEDULE RC-L CONTAINED IN THE REPORT OF CONDITION: DERIVATIVES AND OFF-BALANCE-SHEET ITEMS

1. Unused commitments
   a. Revolving, open-end lines secured by 1–4 family residential properties
   b. Credit card lines
   c. Commercial real estate, construction, and land development
      (1) Commitments to fund loans secured by real estate
      (2) Commitments to fund loans not secured by real estate
   d. Securities underwriting
   e. Other unused commitments
2. Financial standby letters of credit and foreign office guarantees
3. Performance standby letters of credit and foreign office guarantees
4. Commercial and similar letters of credit
5. Participations in acceptances conveyed to others by the reporting bank
6. Securities lent
7. Credit derivatives
   a. Notional amount of credit derivatives on which the reporting bank is the guarantor
      (1) Gross positive fair value
      (2) Gross negative fair value
   b. Notional amount of credit derivatives on which the reporting bank is the beneficiary
      (1) Gross positive fair value
      (2) Gross negative fair value
8. Spot foreign exchange contracts
9. All other off-balance-sheet liabilities (excluding derivatives)
10. All other off-balance-sheet assets (excluding derivatives)
11. Year-to-date merchant credit card sales volume
    a. Sales for which the reporting bank is the acquiring bank
    b. Sales for which the reporting bank is the agent bank with risk
12. Gross amounts (e.g., notional amounts)
    a. Futures contracts
    b. Forward contracts
       (1) Written options
       (2) Purchased options
    c. Exchange-traded options contracts
       (1) Written options
       (2) Purchased options
    d. Over-the-counter option contracts
       (1) Written options
       (2) Purchased options
    e. Swaps

Source: Federal Financial Institutions Examination Commission.

FINANCIAL GUARANTEES

Figure 14-1 shows Schedule RC-L of the Report of Condition for banks entitled "Commitments and Contingencies." Most of the items shown there are based on financial guarantees of banks. A financial guarantee is an undertaking by a bank (the guarantor) to stand behind the current obligation of a third party, and to carry out that obligation if the third party fails to do so. For example, a bank can make a loan guarantee whereby it guarantees the repayment of a loan made from party A to party B. The guarantor assumes that it is a more effective credit analyst than other capital market participants because the ultimate liability of the debt is shifted from the borrower to the guarantor. Assuming the guarantor's credit is better than that of the borrower, the rate of return required by the market on the borrower's debt obligations is reduced. From the bank's perspective, fees ranging from 10 to 150 basis points are charged, depending on the reduction in the borrower's debt costs and risk exposure of the bank.

STANDBY LETTERS OF CREDIT

Standby letters of credit (SLCs) obligate the bank to pay the beneficiary if the ***account party*** defaults on a financial obligation or performance contract. A fee of about one percent of the guarantee is charged by the issuing bank. Most SLCs never become a bank liability; however, if bank payment is required, it usually means that a problem loan is acquired by the bank. There are two types of SLCs. A *financial SLC* is related to a financial commitment, such as repayment of commercial paper. A performance SLC is nonfinancial in nature, such as a commitment to complete a construction project or deliver certain merchandise. Although national banks and most state banks are prohibited from issuing guarantees, SLCs serve the same function and do not violate the law. Banks earn not only fee income on SLCs but also interest income in the event credit must be extended to the account party to cover a payment of funds to the beneficiary. SLCs are comparable to an over-the-counter put option written by the bank (i.e., the firm defaulting "puts" the credit obligation back to the bank). Table 14-1 reports outstanding standby letters of credit held by U.S. commercial banks as of the third quarter of 2015. As shown there, financial standby letters of credit account for about 80 percent of total SLCs. Also, it should be recognized that billion dollar banks dominated smaller banks by holding about 98 percent of total SLCs.

TABLE 14-1 **STANDBY LETTERS OF CREDIT ISSUED BY U.S. COMMERCIAL BANKS (Billions of Dollars)**

	2011	2012	2013	2014	2015, Q3
Letters of credit	694.4	649.4	749.9	738.9	664.9
Financial SLCs	589.5	552.7	633.1	609.9	543.1
All other SLCs	104.9	96.8	116.8	129.0	121.8

Source: Board of Governors of the Federal Reserve System, *EFA Project -- Depository Institutions: Off-Balance Sheet Items.*

Uses of Standby Letters of Credit

Standby letters of credit are commonly used in connection with the issuance of debt obligations (i.e., bonds, notes, and commercial paper) as backup lines of credit. For example, the city of Burlington, Kansas, issued $106.5 million bonds with a seven-year maturity to fund pollution control and improvements. The bonds are to be repaid by payments received by the city from project users. If the payments are not sufficient to cover the interest and principal, the bonds are backed by irrevocable letters of credit from Westpac Banking Corporation (an Australian bank holding company) and the Long-Term Credit Bank of Japan, Limited. In essence, these banking organizations supported the city's ability to borrow funds without the banks raising deposits or making loans.

Another common use of SLCs is in connection with building contractors' obligations to complete a construction project. For example, a contractor (the account party) promises a beneficiary that a hydroelectric plant will be completed on or before a stated date. If the project is not completed before that date, the bank is required to pay the beneficiary. The reason the project was not completed is not relevant. The only thing that is important is that the account party failed to perform (defaulted) on the obligation to the beneficiary. In this case, the SLC is a substitute for a surety bond. Surety bonds are sold by insurance companies to insure against loss, damage, or default. They are a special type of insurance policy and should not be confused with the debt obligations that are likewise called bonds.

SLCs are also used to ensure the delivery of merchandise, to ensure the performance of options or futures contracts, to back other loans, and even to guarantee alimony and child support payments. A fundamental aspect of SLCs is that they are dependent on a bank's credit rating. If the bank's safety and soundness deteriorates, the value of its SLCs would seriously decline, as well as its ability to issue new SLCs.

Risk

Many banks evaluate account parties that want standby letters of credit in the same way that they evaluate commercial loans. SLCs are considered loans for the purpose of calculating legal lending limits. Because bankers accept only those credits that they believe are least likely to default and be taken down (loans made), they consider their credit risk minimal. Even so, risk is inherent to the business of lending. Unexpected economic and financial events can reduce the ability of many emerging market countries to repay their debts, which forced U.S. banks to write off many of these loans and reschedule the payments on other loans in the 1980s and 1990s.

To further reduce the risk to banks, many SLCs are backed by deposits or collateral. Nevertheless, the long-term nature of some of the commitments can cause risks to change over time. Consequently, some banks require periodic renegotiation of SLC terms. If and when a SLC is taken down, the bank might book the unreimbursed balance as a commercial loan.

Banks can manage their risk by limiting the donor amount of standby letters of credit they issue, diversifying their portfolio of such letters, and increasing capital.[1]

Even so, SLCs subject banks to both liquidity risk -- also known as funding risk in this context --and capital risk, because losses can rapidly accumulate due to, for example, an economic downturn that can cause more than one borrower to default at the same time. Also, interest rate risk is present in SLCs, either from possible changes in their duration gap or the increased (decreased) likelihood of default as interest rate levels increase (decrease).

Finally, SLCs expose banks to an ill-defined legal risk. Most SLCs contain a ***material adverse change (MAC) clause*** that enables a bank to withdraw its commitment under certain conditions (such as, the financial condition of the firm has seriously declined). From the borrower's viewpoint, payment of the SLC fee is intended to cover the bank for the risk that its ability to pay the debt will deteriorate. Such a clause would seem to unnecessarily favor the bank, therefore. However, from the bank's viewpoint, the clause is needed to deter the firm from taking excessive risks and exploiting the bank's guarantee.

Pricing

Standby letters of credit might have upfront and annual fees. For example, the upfront fee might be one percent of the outstanding and unused guarantee, and the annual fees might range from 25 to 150 basis points lower than the bank would charge for loans of equivalent maturity and risk. The annual fees on standby letters of credit are lower than loan fees, in part because of the lower administrative cost and other expenses associated with them and because normally no funding is required. Of course, if the bank does loan funds, the interest rate must be priced according to standard methods of evaluating loan risk.

BANK LOAN COMMITMENTS

In general terms, a ***loan commitment*** represents a bank's promise to a customer to make a future loan(s) or a guarantee under certain conditions. The agreement between the bank and the customer can be informal or formal; however, *some* agreements are not legally binding on the bank or the potential borrower. The major benefits of loan commitments are the assurance of funds to the borrower and fees or compensating balances of equivalent value to the bank. The major drawback is that the bank is acquiring a credit exposure in the future because it may have to make a loan or a guarantee. Nevertheless, loan commitments increased from $1 trillion in 1990 to about $9 trillion just before the 2008-2009 financial crisis. After the crisis, commitments have decreased to about $7 trillion due to credit lines that were either cut by banks or drawn down by business firms. About half of unused commitments are credit card lines.

Line of Credit

As explained in Chapter 9, a ***line of credit*** is an agreement between a bank and a customer that the bank will entertain a request for a loan from that customer. In most cases the bank will make the loans even though it is not obligated to do so. Lines are frequently informal agreements, and banks do not collect a fee for the service. Accordingly, a line of credit is not a "firm" commitment by the bank to lend funds.

Revolving Loan Commitments

In contrast, a ***revolving loan commitment*** is a formal agreement between the bank and a customer, which obligates the bank to lend funds according to the terms of the contract. The contract specifies the terms under which loans will be made, including the maximum amounts to be loaned, interest rate, maturities, and the customer pays the bank a commitment fee, which is also called a ***facility fee***, for the privilege of being able to borrow funds at a future date. The fee, for example, may be 0.5 percent per year of the unused balance. As in the case of SLCs, some revolving loan commitments contain (MAC) clauses that release the bank from its obligation to make a loan if there has been a substantial change in the customer's financial condition.

Revolving loan commitments protect the borrower from both availability risk and markup risk. Markup risk is associated with the premium added on the reference rate (e.g., prime rate) to compensate the bank for credit risk. Revolving commitments fix the premium, in contrast to a confirmed credit line that sets the rate at the time funds are taken down. Thus, revolving loan commitments are tantamount to options contracts, wherein the bank must offer a loan at the agreed-upon price. Because revolving commitments expose the bank to interest rate risk, the commitment fee is priced to capture this bank risk. Confirmed credit lines generally do not require commitment fees.

Table 14-2 shows loan commitments made by U.S. commercial banks in one week in November, 2015. Here we see that over 85 percent of all commercial and industrial loans were based on earlier commitments by banks. In this regard, we should note that large (small) banks have commitments of about 95 (80) percent of total business loans.

TABLE 14-2 **COMMERCIAL AND INDUSTRIAL LOAN COMMITMENTS BY U.S. COMMERCIAL BANKS IN NOVEMBER 2-6, 2015**

Type of business loans	Total loans ($ millions)	Secured by collateral (%)	Prime based (%)	SBA based (%)	Syndicate based (%)	Commitment based (%)
All C&I loans	116,369	61.9	14.5	0.8	55.5	87.4
Minimal risk	2,593	49.3	11.2	0	41.8	84.4
Low risk	33,208	41.2	7.6	0.6	45	86.8
Moderate risk	33,797	58.1	18.3	1.2	48.4	82.3
Other	22,268	68.2	27.1	1	41.2	83.4

Source: Board of Governors of the Federal Reserve System, *Survey of Business Lending, Schedule E2.*

Funding Risk

The major risk facing a bank with loan commitments is that a large number of borrowers will take down their loan simultaneously, and the bank may not have sufficient funds to make the loans. This funding or liquidity risk (also referred to as quantity risk) is most likely to occur during periods of tight credit. Because the bank is obligated to make the loans, it may have to raise additional funds; honoring such commitments can be difficult at such times.

If the bank does not honor the commitment, a customer with a legally binding commitment could bring legal action against the bank. Such an action could damage the bank's reputation, which could impair its future growth and profitability.

Certain types of commitments are considered irrevocable (unconditional and binding). According to the Bank for International Settlements, these include the following:

- ***Asset sale and repurchase agreements***. An arrangement whereby a bank sells a loan, security, or fixed asset to a third party with a commitment to repurchase the asset after a certain time, or in the event of a certain contingency.
- ***Outright forward purchases***. A commitment to purchase a loan, security, or other asset at a specified future date, typically on prearranged terms.
- An ***irrevocable revolving line of credit.***
- ***Note issuance facilities***, which will be explained shortly.

Similarly, certain types of commitments are considered revocable. These include credit lines and undrawn overdraft facilities.

Initially, interest rate volatility was the motivation for the growth of loan commitments. However, deregulation is another important trend that has become a key factor in explaining their continued growth even when interest rates are at historically low levels, as in the 1990s and 2000s. Interest rate deregulation allowed banks to explicitly price deposit accounts and loans – implicit pricing, an informal style of bank commitments, was prominent under interest rate regulation. Subsequent to this deregulation, borrowers began demanding formal commitments with explicit prices. Since loan commitments naturally fit into this pricing framework, they have become increasingly important in recent years, regardless of the volatility of interest rates.

NOTE ISSUANCE FACILITIES

Euronotes

Note issuance facility (NIF) is one of several terms used to describe medium-term (two to seven years) agreements whereby banks guarantee the sale of a borrower's short-term, negotiable promissory notes at or below predetermined interest rates. If a borrower cannot readily obtain short-term funds in a timely fashion for one reason or another, the bank will step in and buy the securities. Other terms for similar financial guarantees are revolving underwriting facilities (RUFs) and standby note issuance facilities (SNIFs). For bank borrowers the short-term securities are usually certificates of deposit (sometimes called a Roly-Poly CD Facility). For non-bank borrowers the short-term debt securities are called ***Euronotes.*** Euronotes are denominated in U.S. dollars and usually have a face value of $500,000 or more. They are held mainly by governments and institutional investors. As the term *Euronotes* implies, most of the activity in this market involves international banking. Euronotes are not registered with the Securities and Exchange Commission and cannot be sold in the United States. The major nonbank sovereign borrowers in the Euronote market are the United States, Austria, and Great Britain. The main buyers of Euronotes are European and Japanese banks. However, similar standby arrangements are used for the sale of commercial paper in the United States. Various other terms used for these types of agreements are *RUFs, transferable RUFs (TRUFs), SNIFs, note purchase facility, multiple component facilities, and Euronote facilities.*

ARRANGERS AND TENDER PANELS

One contingent risk to banks in these arrangements arises from their roles as underwriters or arrangers. The NIF can be organized or underwritten by a single bank (the arranger) or by a group of 15 or more banks and financial institutions (the tender panel) that have the right to bid for the short-term notes issued under the facility. The advantage of a tender panel is the broader competitive market offered by many institutions bidding for the securities, rather than having one bidder. The tender panel also provides a means to place larger dollar amounts of securities than might be possible for a single arranger.

The arranger or tender panel assures the borrower access to short-term funds (e.g., 90 days) over the five to seven years covered by the agreement. This process is known as maturity transformation. Maturity transformation results in increased credit risk for the arranger or tender panel, which may have to lend the borrower funds if the borrower is unable to sell the short-term securities at the interest rates (or prices) agreed upon. The NIFs also increase the funding risk of the underwriting banks if they are called upon to make the loans.

DERIVATIVES

In this section we supplement material presented in Chapter 6 by overviewing different kinds of derivative securities: swaps, options, futures, forward contracts, and securitized assets. Derivatives are financial instruments that are derived from underlying securities. It is therefore necessary to understand not only the risks of the underlying security but the transactions involved in the derivative and their associated risks (see Management of Risk: Counting the Risks in Derivatives for a summary of relevant risks). Interestingly, while derivatives are generally spoken of as off-balance-sheet activities, most (but not all) derivatives are reported on the balance sheet.

The Federal Reserve, Comptroller of the Currency, and FDIC have cited seven key categories of risk associated with derivatives.

Counterparty credit risk is the risk that a counterparty in a financial transaction will default, resulting in a financial loss to the other party. Credit exposure is measured not by the notational amount of the contract but by the cost of replacing its cash flows in the market. In an interest rate swap, for example, the present value of expected cash flows on the underlying instruments would need to be calculated.

Price risk, or ***market risk***, is the risk that the market price of the derivative security will change. This risk is closely related to the price risk of the underlying instrument. Most banks break overall price risk into components, including interest rate risk, exchange rate risk, commodity price risk, and others.

Settlement risk occurs when one party in a financial transaction pays out funds to the other party before it receives its own cash or assets. Thus, settlement risk is linked to credit risk.

Liquidity risk is the risk that a counterparty will default and a liquidity shortfall will occur due to losses.

Operating risk is an often-overlooked area of commercial bank risk that can arise due to:

- *Inadequate internal controls.* The complexity of some derivatives, human error, and fraud are all sources of risk that demand internal monitoring and control by management.
- *Valuation risk.* The valuations of many derivatives rely on fairly sophisticated mathematical models that are highly dependent on assumptions about market conditions, which together can make valuation a difficult task.
- *Regulatory risk.* As already mentioned, regulators are scrutinizing OTC derivatives due to their explosive growth, and this attention could draw changes in accounting procedures, capital adequacy, restrictions on activities, and other banking practices.

Legal risk: The OTC market for derivatives is private in nature, fast developing, and innovative in security design, all of which means that disputes within this new market will require a period of legal cases to clearly establish the rights and obligations of all participants. The International Swap Dealers Association has established some rules in cooperation with most large industrialized countries, but the differences in national bankruptcy laws raise legal concerns about the risks in international deals.

Aggregation risk comes about from the complex interconnections that can occur in derivatives deals that involve a number of markets and instruments. It becomes difficult to assess the risks to individual parties or groups of parties in such transactions.

The largest banks and securities firms are best able to manage these risks due to the operational demands of capital and expertise. However, large regional banks also are attempting to enter the derivatives market, either on their own or in cooperation with money center banks seeking to expand their reach in the derivatives market. Are derivatives too risky for banks? Should there be greater regulatory control of OTC derivatives? These questions have no simple answers and will be the focus of much academic and regulatory study in the years ahead.

The importance of derivatives markets stems from their magnitude. As shown in Figure 14-2 (next page), the notional amount of OTC derivatives grew to approximately $700 trillion in 2013, but declined to about $550 trillion in 2015. Interest rate contracts, including forward, swap, and option contracts, dominate the OTC derivatives market with over 80 percent of the total outstanding. The second largest volume of contracts is foreign exchange (FX), including forward, currency swap, and option contracts. The gross market value of OTC derivatives peaked in 2008 at about

$35 trillion but sharply decreased after the 2008-2009 financial crisis to about $15 trillion by 2015. Here we see that the crisis severely affected the OTC market around the world as banks experienced derivatives losses and cut back on their activities.

FIGURE 14-2 GLOBAL OTC DERIVATIVES MARKETS: 2007-2015

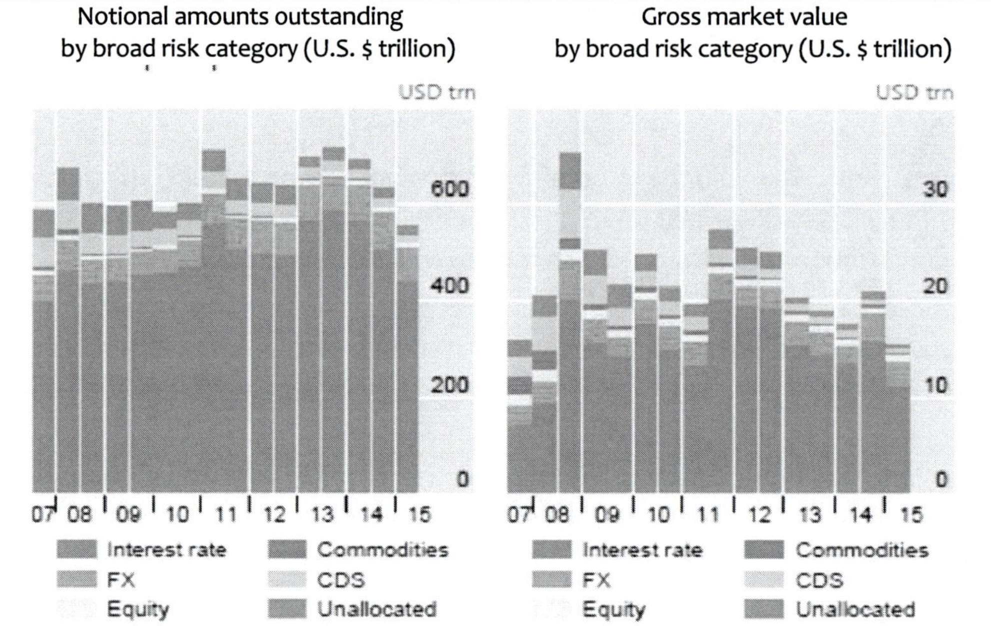

Source: Bank for International Settlements (BIS), *Statistical Release: OTC Derivatives Statistics at End-June 2015*, Monetary and Economic Department (November 2015).

There are two derivatives markets: (1) the privately traded over-the-counter (OTC) market dominated by money center banks and large securities firms that custom design products for users, and (2) the organized exchanges that offer standardized contracts and a clearinghouse for handling transactions—for example, the Chicago Board of Trade (CBOT), which is the largest, in addition to the CME Group, Chicago Board Options Exchange (CBOE) and CBOE Futures Exchange (CFE) (both owned by CBOE Holdings, Inc.), ICE Futures Europe (owned by IntercontinentalExchange group), Eurex Exchange, Euronext Paris, Tokyo Financial Exchange (TFE), and other regional exchanges. In the OTC market swaps account for most of the activity in the "Derivatives Department" within commercial banks. The top 100 banks in the United States account for about 99 percent of OTC derivatives in terms of notional volume, and the top four banks hold about 90 percent of the total. It is clear from these numbers that derivatives activities are concentrated in the largest banks. Today, the OTC market exceeds the exchange-traded market in dollar terms.

The magnitude of the market and potential for unknown risks due to their unprecedented growth has attracted regulators' attention, including the Commodity Futures Trading Commission (CFTC), SEC, Federal Reserve System (FRS), Office of the Comptroller of the Currency (OCC), and FDIC. Regulators worry that, while most participants at present are large and reputable financial institutions, the market may well attract inexperienced or fraudulent participants. Such participants would introduce new risks for all players. Also, competition in the derivatives securities markets could drive some large banks to precarious positions and expose them to sudden liquidity risks.[2] This potential is made more real by the fact that there were historically few regulatory barriers in the OTC market, compared with the relatively formal regulatory oversight of exchanged-traded products by the CFTC. The Dodd-Frank Act of 2010 mandates that regulators increase transparency and reduce systemic risk in the derivatives market.

Standardized contracts should be traded on organized exchanges. OTC products are subject to higher margin requirements than traded contracts. Also, higher capital requirements have been implemented to help offset risk exposures associated with bank derivatives.

CURRENCY AND INTEREST RATE SWAPS

A *swap* is an agreement between two counterparties to exchange cash flows and is based upon some notional principal amount of money, maturity, and interest rates. The counterparties are financial institutions, business concerns, government agencies, and international agencies. In the classic "plain vanilla" interest rate swap, counterparties literally swap their interest payments, where one party has fixed interest payments and the other has variable interest payments. There is no transfer of principal between the counterparties, which is why the term *notional principal amount* is used. Swaps in essence are two forward agreements to exchange cash flows between two counterparties.

The International Swaps and Derivatives Association, or ISDA (www.isda.org), is a global trade association that represents leading participants in the privately negotiated derivatives industry, a business that includes interest rate, currency, commodity and equity swaps as well as related products such as caps, collars, floors and swaptions. ISDA was chartered in 1985, and members include most of the world's major institutions who deal in and are leading end-users of privately negotiated derivatives.

TYPES OF SWAPS

Currency swaps and *interest rate swaps* are the two principal types of swap arrangements involving exchanges of interest payments between two or more parties. The generic or plain vanilla interest rate swap is especially useful for managing interest rate gap problems for banks and nonbank firms. A currency swap includes not only the exchange of interest payments (in different currencies) but also the exchange of the initial and final principal amounts at the beginning and end of the swap. Currency swaps are used to hedge not only an interest rate gap but also cash flow risks (for example, a U.S. company with long-term fixed receivables in Euros may hedge the exposure with a currency swap).

As noted earlier, an interest rate swap involves the exchange of a stream of interest payments over time. The three main types of interest rate swaps are:

1. ***Coupon swaps***, where interest payments are based on fixed rates (e.g., 11 percent) and floating rates of interest (e.g., six-month LIBOR, or London interbank offered rate).
2. ***Basis swaps***, where interest payments are based on two different floating rates of interest (e.g., six-month LIBOR and U.S. prime commercial paper rates, or two variable-rate contracts with different maturities).
3. ***Cross-currency interest rate swaps*** (simply termed currency swaps), which involve three counterparties (A, B, and C) and, for example, the interest payments between A and B are based on fixed rate flows in one currency and interest rate, and the interest payments between A and C are based on floating-rate flows in another currency and interest rate. A plain deal currency swap is between two counterparties with equal interest payments in different currencies.

Figure 14-3 shows the growth of OTC interest rate forward rate agreements (FRAs), swaps, and options. The graph shows that these derivatives expanded rapidly from 1995 to more than $2.5 trillion in 2013. The middle panel documents that interest rate swaps are the most heavily traded contracts. Most trading has been between a small number of derivatives dealers (i.e., large banks and securities firms) but a diverse group of other financial institutions have been increasing in importance since 2001.

FIGURE 14-3 **OTC INTEREST RATE DERIVATIVES OVER TIME (billion $)**

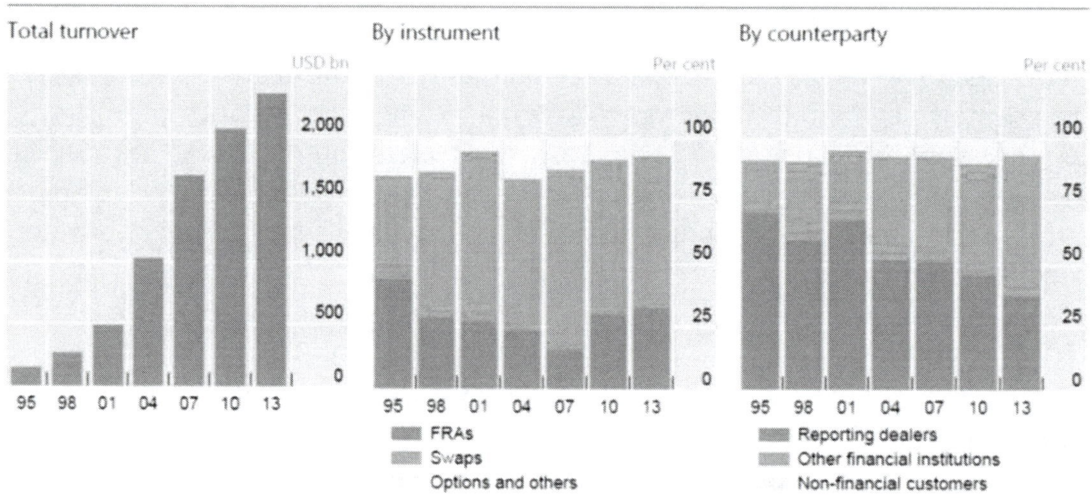

Source: Triennial Central Bank Survey, Bank of International Settlements (BIS). Jacob Gyntelberg and Christian Upper, "The OTC Interest Rate Derivatives Market in 2013," *BIS Quarterly Review* (December 2013), pp. 69-82

EXAMPLE OF A SWAP

Figure 14-4 (next page) illustrates a coupon interest rate swap based on a notional amount of $10 million. The swap agreement has a maturity of seven years, and the payment frequency is semiannually. This is a classic plain vanilla swap between two banks.

Bank A is the *fixed rate* counterparty—the one that pays the fixed rate of interest. Bank B is the *floating rate* counterparty—the one that pays the floating rate of interest. The figure shows that Bank A has fixed-rate assets and floating-rate liabilities that are mismatched, which is not a good combination if market interest rates increase. Bank B has mismatched floating-rate assets and fixed-rate liabilities, which is not a good combination if market interest rates fall. To match their respective balance sheets, both banks exchange streams of interest payments. The fixed-rate payer (Bank A) pays Bank B 12 percent on the notional amount so that Bank B will earn a positive spread between its fixed-rate liabilities and its assets. Similarly, the floating-rate payer (Bank B) pays Bank A's cost of its floating-rate liabilities.

FIGURE 14-4 COUPON INTEREST RATE SWAP

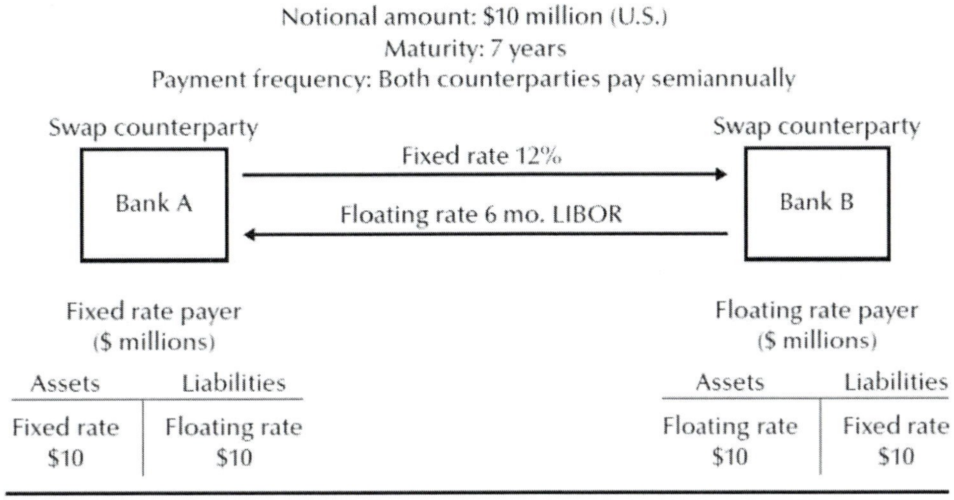

Let's examine the impact of this transaction on Bank A for the first six months. The relevant interest rates that we will use in our simplified calculation are:

6-month LIBOR	10.0%
Bank A's fixed-rate payment	12.0
Bank A's variable-rate liabilities	9.0

Based on these rates, we can determine the net fixed-rate cost of funds to Bank A in the following manner.

Fixed-rate payments made by Bank A	12.0%
minus	
Floating-rate payment received	
plus	–10.0
Interest paid on floating-rate liabilities	+9.0
Net fixed cost	11.0%

In terms of dollar amounts, Bank A will make the first semiannual fixed-rate payment of \$600,000 (\$10 million × 0.12/2) to Bank B, pay \$450,000 (\$10 million × 0.09/2) on its floating-rate liabilities, and receive a floating-rate payment of \$506,778 from Bank B. The floating-rate payment is based on 181 days and a 360-day year.

First interest period	(1/1 to 6/30)
Number of days	181
6-month LIBOR	10.0%
Principal amount	\$10 million

$$\text{Payment} = \frac{\text{Principal} \times \text{LIBOR} \times \text{Number of days}}{\text{Days in year}}$$

$$= \frac{\$10 \text{ million} \times 0.10 \times 181}{360}$$

$$= \$506{,}777.78$$

Bank A's net fixed cost for the first six months expressed in dollar terms is:

Fixed-rate payment	\$600,000
plus	
Floating-rate liabilities	+450,000
minus	
Floating-rate payment received	–507,778
	\$542,222

Because the above generic swap is not suitable for all needs, such as debt call features, deferred payments and resetting interest rates have evolved. In addition, a secondary market in swaps has developed so that they can be sold or terminated by one of the counterparties. Innovation in the swap market is creating many new financial products. The derivatives at work example below gives an interesting example of how swaps can be used to repackage risks and returns among different participants in the swap market.

DERIVATIVES AT WORK

Derivatives can be used to manage both risks and returns. The following example is based on an article in the *Wall Street Journal*.[3] It demonstrates how different players in the financial markets can interact in a derivatives deal. While individual components of the deal are simple, the entire package requires an understanding of a variety of contracts and their relationships to one another.

To begin, a money management firm (MF) is assisting a pension fund (PF) in its investment portfolio management. MF puts together a derivatives deal as follows:

1. \$30 million from PF is invested in high-quality, short-term notes paying 3.8 percent.
2. MF contacts a large foreign bank (BANK) to arrange a swap of these notes for the S&P 500 stock index.

3. BANK buys the S&P 500 stock index futures at a financing cost of 3.30 percent off-balance-sheet.
4. Results:
   - BANK earns a small spread of 0.04 percent.
   - PF earns the S&P 500 stock index plus 0.46% (= 3.80% – 3.34%).

Notice that the PF has "beaten the market" by earning 0.46 percent more than the market index. If the market return is negative, PF will lose 0.46 percent less than the market. The risk to PF of this derivatives strategy is that the notes could default and PF must then continue to pay BANK its part of the swap. Also, if BANK is closed by regulators, PF will have to contend with BANK's creditors to obtain its S&P return. However, these risks are quite low due to the high quality of the notes and money center status of most banks participating in such deals.

MF would earn a fee for these investment and swap services from PF, thereby lowering its increment over the S&P return to less than 0.46 percent. In sum, all parties benefit from the derivative deal. BANK benefits least of the parties involved but is partially motivated by the desire to develop and maintain market contracts that could be valuable in other derivatives deals or traditional business services.

RISKS ASSOCIATED WITH SWAPS

The volume of swap contracts outstanding at money center banks can be quite large compared with total assets on the balance sheet. It is not uncommon for such banks to have swap levels equal to ten times their on-balance-sheet total assets. Until the late 1980s, organized exchanges served as the swap counterparties. Over time banks and other financial institutions developed a dealer market for swaps. However, due to regulatory changes after the 2008 financial crisis, exchanges are increasing their role as a clearinghouse for trading swaps. Relevant to bank risk management, counterparties in swap agreements face credit risk and price (or market) risk. Credit risk is the risk that one of the parties to the swap arrangement will default, which will result in a liability to the bank. To reduce this credit risk, standby letters of credit to guarantee payments can be used.

Price risk is the risk that interest rates or exchange rates may change and have an adverse effect on one or more of the participants in the swap agreement. Consider the case of a savings and loan association that seeks to lock in mortgage loan rates of eight percent and borrowing rates of six percent. The thrift institution entered into swap agreements as a floating-rate payer -- receiving six percent interest and paying the floating rate. Now suppose that interest rates decline after making the swap agreement. Falling interest rates would motivate homeowners to refinance their higher-cost mortgages at lower rates, thereby lowering mortgage portfolio rates of return below eight percent. Additionally, even though deposits rates may have declined to, say, four percent, they are stuck with the six percent cost from the swap agreement. One method of controlling this price risk is to enter into an offsetting swap. Another method is to sell the swap in the secondary market, if a buyer can be found.

Another complication of swaps is the difficulty in finding sufficient interest on both sides of a swap. It may be necessary to use more than two assets or parties to get approximate matches of interest rate or currency needs. In some cases, there simply may not be enough counterparty interest to make a swap feasible. If there is residual risk to the institution after doing a swap, financial futures can be used. Of course, covering unhedged balance sheet risk in this way complicates the risk manager's job to some extent.

Banks and securities firms established the International Swaps Dealers Association (ISDA) in 1985 to promote standardization and sound business practices in the swap market. This self-regulation helps to reduce risk. In the early 1990s ISDA introduced "an informal and non-legalistic market practice advisory service" that arbitrates disputes between member firms. An operational code of conduct was developed, and ISDA now serves as an intermediary with regulators to address their concerns and provide information as needed. Regarding reporting requirements, beginning in June, 1999 new accounting rules by the Financial Accounting Standards Board (FASB) require all derivatives, including swaps, to be stated at fair market value. Hence, paper gains and losses, even if they have not yet been realized, must be reported in the accounting statements. This accounting change forces many banks and firms to factor in the potential impact of a swap (or other derivative instrument) on their financial position when using these contracts to hedge various risks.

OVER-THE-COUNTER OPTIONS, FUTURES, AND FORWARDS

OVER-THE-COUNTER OPTIONS

In Chapter 6 it was explained that from the option buyer's (or seller's) point of view, puts are options to sell (or buy) assets and calls are options to buy (or sell) them. Put and call options traded on organized stock exchanges are standardized contracts. In other words, the terms of the options contracts (striking price, maturity, etc.) are standardized to facilitate trading. Such standardized contracts, however, do not satisfy the needs of all participants in the market, and an over-the-counter (OTC) market developed for nonstandardized options by banks and other financial institutions (i.e., dealers that act as market makers). ***Over-the-counter options*** are usually written on Treasury securities and currencies that are not traded on exchanges. With no clearinghouse to act as a safety net, one party has an option to exercise a contract, while the other party has an obligation.

FLOOR-CEILING AGREEMENTS

The concept of options is useful in analyzing some of the off-balance-sheet products and services offered by banks to manage interest costs (known as ***interest rate options***). Consider the case of ***ceiling agreements*** (also called ***caps***). A ceiling agreement between a bank and its customer specifies the maximum lending rate on a loan and, therefore, protects the customer from interest rate risk. For example, a corporation obtains a three-year loan, with interest rates based on Treasury bills at eight percent and quarterly payments. The corporation is willing to pay the bank an upfront fee of three percent to guarantee that it will not have to pay more than 10 percent over the life of the loan. If the interest rate goes above 10 percent, the bank will compensate the corporation. For example, if the rate goes to 11 percent, the corporation will receive one quarter (quarterly settlements) of one percent of the loan. On a $50 million loan, the corporation would receive $125,000. In this case, the bank selling the ceiling agreement analogously is the writer of an out-of-the-money call option. The call option is out-of-the-money because the current level of interest rates is below the strike interest rate of the call option. The corporation is the buyer of the call option, and benefits if interest rates rise above the strike interest rate. It should be noted, as mentioned in Chapter 6, that buying a call option in interest rates is equivalent to buying a put option in prices (i.e., prices and interest rates move in opposite directions). We use interest rates rather than prices to describe the option contract for ease of exposition and understanding.

Floor agreements specify the minimum rate of interest on a loan and, therefore, protect the bank from interest rate risk. If interest rates go below the floor, the customer pays the bank the difference between the actual rate and the floor rate. Here the bank is buyer of an out-of-the-money put option. The option is out-of-the-money because the current level of interest rates is above the strike interest rate. Do not be confused by the term out-of-the-money. It means simply that the strike interest rate for the call (put) option is above (below) the current level of interest rates. Therefore it cannot be exercised for a profit at the present time. An "in-the-money" put option is one in which interest rates have fallen below the strike interest rate. The bank could lower its loan fee to purchase this put option on the loan.

Figure 14-5 provides diagrams that show the gains and losses on caps and floors from the perspective of the buyer of these options as interest rates change. Again, notice that we have expressed the option buyer's gains and losses on caps and floors in terms of interest rates, but they could be easily converted to prices (e.g., falling interest rates in a floor are hedged by buying a call option in prices which is in the money as prices increase above the strike price).

FIGURE 14-5 **CAPS AND FLOORS ON LOAN RATES**

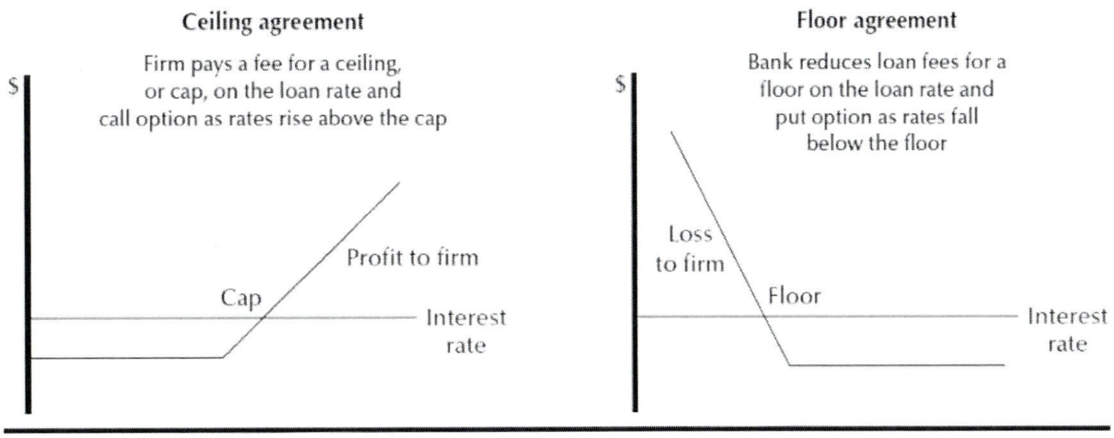

An OTC option that combines ceiling and floor mechanics is the ***interest rate collar.*** A put-option premium is paid to create an interest rate cap, and this premium cost is offset in whole or part by a call option that establishes an interest rate floor. A variable-rate debt holder could therefore set upper and lower limits on their interest costs.

Finally, innovation in OTC options is extending their use from interest rate risk management to credit risk management. The main idea here is to set a lower limit on credit risk. As an example, banks can design an OTC option called a *credit risk derivative.* If an investor held (say) AAA-rated bonds and was concerned that the rating agencies might downgrade the bonds to AA, causing the yield to rise and price to fall, the investor could purchase an option that would pay the amount of the lost capital value of the bonds if downgraded. In this way, investors can insure the credit risk of their bond portfolios. Of course, writers of these options would profit to the extent that credit risk does not increase in the future. This so-called ***credit option*** is essentially an insurance contract.

Another common type of credit derivative is a ***credit swap*** in which two banks simply exchange interest and principal payments on portions of their loan portfolios. This swap enables the participating banks to diversify their credit risk to a greater extent than previously possible. A twist on the credit swap is a ***total return swap***, wherein (for example) Bank A swaps payments received on a risky loan portfolio for a cash flow stream from Bank B comprised of a benchmark rate of interest (e.g., LIBOR) plus some negotiated compensation for the credit risk premium that it has given up. This swap transfers the credit risk from Bank A to Bank B, even though Bank B did not make the loan. In general, a key advantage of credit derivatives is that they transfer credit risk without any sale of the underlying debt contract. For example, a bank can retain its relationship with a customer by providing credit and retaining the loan on its balance sheet but subsequently transfer the associated risk into the financial markets. This advantage is valuable in cases in which a bank holds a large concentration of loans in a particular industry (for example, high holdings of energy loans and commercial real estate loans have been problematic in the past for many banks). Credit derivatives allow the bank to reduce its exposure to concentrated credit risks and thereby better diversify its loan portfolio.

FORWARD RATE AGREEMENTS

A *forward rate agreement (FRA)* is essentially an over-the-counter interest rate futures contract for bonds or some other financial asset. The buyer and seller agree on some interest rate to be paid on some notional amount at a specified time in the future. The major advantages of FRAs over exchange traded futures contracts is that they can be tailored to meet the needs of the parties involved, and there are no margin requirements.

Buying a FRA (or futures contract) is analogous to buying a call and selling a put, where the forward price is equal to the exercise price of the options. To understand this analogy, keep in mind that the buyer of the FRA is obligated to buy the bond -- it is mandatory. Suppose that a bank buys a FRA on a bond at 100 for delivery in three months. If the bond is selling at 90 three months from now, the bank can buy the bond (i.e., it is put to the bank) at 100 and then sell it at a loss or keep it in its portfolio at the lower value. On the other hand, if the bond is selling at 110 at that time, the bank will buy the bond (i.e., like a call) and sell it at a profit. Thus, the price of the FRA (or purchased futures) that the bank bought was determined as though it was a purchased call and sold put option. Conversely, the sale of forward contract is analogous to buying a put and selling a call.

SYNTHETIC LOANS

Interest rate futures contracts and options can be used to create synthetic loans and securities. To illustrate how this is done, suppose that a construction company, believing that interest rates would decline, wanted to borrow $30 million for 120 days, on a floating-rate basis, repricing the loan every 30 days at the CD rate plus four percentage points. The current rate of interest on CDs was 10.5 percent, and the initial cost of the loan was 14.5 percent. The bank, however, wanted to make the loan at a fixed rate. To accommodate the customer, the bank resolved the dilemma by using the interest rate futures market to "convert" the floating-rate loan into a fixed-rate loan, thereby creating a **synthetic loan**. To accomplish this, the bank bought T-bill futures. If interest rates decrease, the market value of the securities represented by the futures contract will increase and the contracts can be sold at a profit. The profit is used to offset the lower interest from the floating interest rate loan. The details of the transaction are presented in Table 14-5 (next page).

The top part of the table shows the cost of the loan at floating rates of interest. The interest on the loan from the September 1 to October 1 period was $362,500 ([$30 million × 14.5%]/12 months). Using the interest rates shown, the total interest earned by the bank for the term of the loan was $1,310,000.

On September 1, the bank bought three 90-day futures contracts for T-bills. Each contract is for ten T-bills, and each T-bill has a face value of $1 million. The price of each bill is calculated as follows. There are four 90-day T-bill issues each year. Therefore, the annual interest rate of 11.5 percent is equal to 0.02875 for 90 days, or $28,750 interest per $1 million of T-bills. The price of a T-bill is the face amount less the interest, or $1 million – $28,750 = $971,250. Because there are ten bills in each contract, a contract would be worth $9,712,500. The bank is required to put up a small margin deposit to buy the contracts. The margin and the commissions are not included in this example. On October 1, the bank sold one of the T-bill futures contracts at the current market price. Because interest rates declined, the market value of the futures contracts increased and the bank earned $362,500, the same amount of interest they would have paid on a fixed-rate loan.

Similarly, the total gains from the futures market ($140,000) plus the total interest expense on the variable-rate loan ($1,131,000) are equivalent to the amount of interest that would have been received on a fixed-rate loan ($1,450,000).

The purpose of using the interest rate futures market was to convert the floating-rate loan into a fixed-rate loan in terms of the interest received by the bank.

By using this technique, the bank received the equivalent of a fixed-rate loan and the customer received a floating loan.

If interest rates had increased, instead of declined, losses from the futures contracts would have offset higher interest payments from the floating-rate loan and the bank would still earn the equivalent of a fixed-rate loan.

TABLE 14-5 DATA FOR SYNTHETIC LOAN

	Dates				
	9/1–10/1	10/1–10/30	10/30–11/30	11/30–12/30	Totals
			Loan at Floating Rate		
Loan $30 million					
floating interest rate	14.5%	13.2%	12.6%	12.1%	
Interest	$362,500	$330,000	$315,000	$302,500	$1,310,000
			Futures Contracts		
	Buy 3 (9/1)	Sell 1 (10/1)	Sell 1 (10/30)	Sell 1 (11/30)	
Yield	11.5%	10.2%	9.6%	9.1%	
Contract value*	$9,712,500	$9,745,000	$9,760,000	$9,772,500	
Profit or (loss)		$32,500	$47,500	$60,000	140,000
					$1,450,000
			Loan at Fixed Rate		
Fixed interest rate	14.5%	14.5%	14.5%	14.5%	
Interest	$362,500	$362,500	$362,500	$362,500	$1,450,000

* Contracts are for 10 Treasury bills. Each bill has a face value of $1 million.

This example illustrates a synthetic loan. Similarly, banks and others can use futures contracts to convert fixed-rate deposits into floating-rate deposits, and vice versa.

Unlike forward contracts, futures contracts expose the bank to liquidity risk due to the fact that their value is marked-to-market daily. Gains or losses on futures contracts must be settled daily against margin positions, thereby opening up the possibility of cash demands. Moreover, futures contracts, like any hedging method, in most cases cannot eliminate all price risk. On the plus side, futures exchanges act as clearinghouses and guarantee performance of contracts, eliminating default risk.

SECURITIZATION

As explained in earlier chapters, ***securitization*** involves the packaging of loans into large pools and issuance of securities to investors that earn returns based on the payments on the loans. The rapid growth of loan securitization has changed the nature of the banking business. Instead of making loans and bearing all of their associated risks and returns, banks make loans, securitize them, and sell the securities into the financial marketplace. In the process they change their risk exposures to loans and increase service revenues. In regard to service revenues, banks can serve multiple roles in the securitization process, including loan originator, loan packager, and loan service company.

Asset-backed securitization in the United States began in 1985 and has rapidly grown to become common practice in most areas of bank lending. Typical assets used in the securitization process are automobiles, trucks, equipment, recreational vehicles, home equity loans, and credit cards. Other more exotic asset-backed deals include computer leases, consumer loans, trade receivables, time shares, and small business loans. In the 1990s several large banks began to package large commercial and industrial loans as well as commercial real estate into so-called *collateralized loan obligations (CLOs)* and *commercial mortgage-backed securities (CMBSs)*.

Securitized assets are counted as off-balance-sheet items *only* if the assets have been transferred with recourse. "With recourse" in this case means that the bank has moved the asset off its balance sheet but is still exposed to part or all of the risk associated with the asset. Residential mortgages are the most securitized asset in the financial market (e.g., over 80 percent of new home loans in the United States are now financed by this means), but they are not off-balance-sheet assets. The originating bank sells the loan to one of the federal housing agencies and many times services the loan payments for a fee. However, the bank is not liable for default on mortgage payments. On the other hand, credit card loans that are securitized expose the bank to credit risk. If credit payment flows fall to a predetermined level, the originating bank must repurchase the remaining securitized loans.

In order for an asset category to be securitized, it must offer a steady income stream for investors. By pooling assets from across the country and taking advantage of geographic diversification, the variance of income streams can be reduced and made amenable for securitization. A key benefit for banks, whether the securitized asset is an on- or off-balance-sheet item, is increased service revenues. If the asset can be moved off the balance sheet, the return on assets can be boosted by reducing the denominator of the profit ratio. And, if the asset is still on the balance sheet, the risk has been transferred from the bank to the financial market.

Commercial banks compete with investment banks and other securities firms for asset-backed financing business, not to mention foreign institutional entrants. Also, large automobile manufacturers with captive finance companies are large issuers of asset-backed securities. The presence of a variety of large institutions and firms in asset-backed securities markets suggests that this market is highly competitive. Some studies have shown that securitization of the residential mortgage market has reduced home loan interest rates by as much as 30 to 40 basis points. Thus, borrowers directly benefit from competitive asset-backed pricing due to lower borrowing costs.

An excellent example of how securitization solves risk management problems is the case of savings and loan associations. Today, many savings institutions are owned by bank holding companies, as federal income tax incentives make it worthwhile to operate them as separate entities within the bank holding company structure. Nonetheless, they may well be controlled for all practical purposes by a lead bank in a bank holding company. Because savings and loans employ short-term retail deposits and make long-term mortgage loans, they have a severely negative dollar gap that makes them extremely sensitive to interest rate movements. Interest rates do not have to increase very much before interest costs rise above mortgage portfolio yields and produce losses that wipe out equity capital. By securitizing home loans and then purchasing mortgage-backed securities with much shorter terms to maturity, their gap problem can be substantially reduced. Also, mortgage loans tend to be highly geographically concentrated. By securitizing these loans and purchasing the related securities, a geographically diversified asset portfolio can be achieved. Thus, interest rate risk and credit risk are normally reduced, and stable, low-risk service revenues are received.

OTHER OFF-BALANCE-SHEET ACTIVITIES

LOAN SALES

Banks can sell loans to a third party as a source of funds. Such loans are normally purchased by large banks and nonbank financial institutions. For a fee the selling bank often continues to service the loan payment, enforce debt covenants, and monitor the borrower's creditworthiness. Loan sales can be made with or without recourse. Sales with recourse mean that even though the loan was sold by *assignment* (i.e., the buyer owns the loan), the selling bank retains some credit risk (in whole or part) for loan losses. Loan sales enable banks to increase diversification, lower capital requirements, and eliminate low-earning assets from their portfolio. It is not known whether loan sales decrease or increase credit risk as whole for banks. While selling off loans that are not replaced would clearly reduces credit risk, it is possible that a bank could sell off high-quality, highly marketable loans and eventually end up with lower quality loans on their balance sheet. Some interesting implications of loan sales are that they enable banks to (1) make loans without relying on deposits as a source of funds and (2) convert traditional lending into a quasi-securities business. Moreover, by purchasing loans, other nonbank financial institutions are becoming more like banks. In turn, distinctions between banks, securities firms, and other financial institutions are gradually being blurred as the volume of loan sales increases.

TRADE FINANCE

Most trade finance is on-balance-sheet. However, there are some international aspects of trade finance that are off-balance-sheet commitments by banks.

Commercial Letters of Credit

Trade finance includes commercial letters of credit and acceptance participations, both of which are used to finance international trade. Letters of credit, which are further explained in Chapter 18, have been used by banks for many years. A ***letter of credit (LOC)*** involves a bank (the issuer) that guarantees the bank's customer (the account party) to pay a contractual debt to a third party (the beneficiary). Letters of credit are contingent liabilities because payment does not take place until the proper documents (i.e., title, invoices, etc.) are presented to the bank. Payment is dependent on the bank's creditworthiness, not the buyer's financial strength. LOCs are specific to the period of time involved in the shipment and storage of goods, result in fee income for banks from the buyer, and require the buyer to reimburse the bank for payment of goods.

LOCs expose banks to credit risk and documentary risk. Credit risk in this case differs from a typical loan that is carefully evaluated by a loan officer. Instead, because LOCs are essentially working capital loans with a fast turnaround and are offered to otherwise creditworthy buyers, little credit risk evaluation is made in common practice. Of course, to the extent that credit review standards are lowered, there is some degree of credit risk, as some proportion of even sound buyers can experience a deterioration in their ability to pay at times. Documentary risk is associated with the complexity of international commerce, which can become tangled by different countries' legal systems and international legal rules. It is possible for conflicts between sellers and buyers to spill over to banks involved in their transactions.

Acceptance Participations

A ***banker's acceptance*** (also discussed in Chapter 13) is created when a bank accepts a time draft (a bill of exchange) and agrees to pay it at face value on maturity. The draft normally covers the sale of goods, particularly with respect to international trade. The banker's acceptance is booked as an asset. Some banks sell participations (called ***acceptance participations***) for all or part of the time draft, which reduces the dollar amount shown on their books. However, the accepting bank is still obligated to pay the face amount of the acceptance at maturity. Banks that buy acceptance participations have a contingent liability that does not appear on their balance sheets.

FOREIGN EXCHANGE

Most large banks operate foreign exchange trading desks for the purposes of brokerage and dealing, speculating, and providing forward contracts in currencies. Regarding the latter, a typical foreign exchange service is to hedge currency risks for firms engaged in international trade. For example, if a U.S. firm bought some goods from Europe but was allowed 30 days trade credit before paying, a forward contract in Euros could be purchased to lock in the dollar cost at the time of purchase (e.g., one million Euros are purchased at an agreed dollar price now for future delivery in 30 days). In the 1990s some large banks speculated in currencies and suffered tremendous losses, which prompted greater regulatory oversight and reporting requirements. Like securities activities, today most foreign exchange trading is reported in financial statements and, therefore, is not off-balance-sheet.

SERVICES FOR FEES

A fairly riskless source of bank income is advisory and management fees. Such services do not involve commitments or contingencies on assets listed either on or off the balance sheet. Traditional fiduciary services, including trust funds and portfolio management, remain significant sources of fee income, as banks are one of the largest institutional managers of capital funds in the United States. Two growth areas in the banking industry are cash management and networking.

Cash Management

Cash management systems for business concerns are one of the most popular off-balance-sheet service areas offered by banks. Cash management systems are used to help business concerns collect remittances and use their bank balances efficiently. Lock boxes are an important part of cash management systems. Lock boxes are post office boxes where customers' remittances are sent by mail and then collected by bankers who deposit them in a business concern's account (see Chapter 16 for further discussion). Banks receive fees for collection and processing the funds. With the exception of the computers used to process the funds and an increase in cash (from the collected funds), no other specific items on their balance sheets are directly attributable to cash management systems. Treasury services seek to better manage cash for bank customers by means of speeding up cash inflow and slowing down cash outflows with the business. Today, business cards, electronic payments, and other technology is evolving to manage cash.

Networking

Networking refers to linkages among different companies that seek to exploit comparative advantages in the production and delivery of a product. Another popular term for such joint arrangements is strategic alliance. As an example, a bank might contract with a discount broker to execute securities transactions for its customers for a fee, part of which goes to the bank. Similarly, many banks have contractual relationships with mutual funds to provide investment services. Another way to network is the placement of branch offices in supermarkets and other high-traffic retail stores by banks. This symbiotic relationship seeks to increase customer convenience for both the retailer and bank.

Banks also use networks to sell insurance, data processing, and other services. Networks permit banks to expand certain specialized services without a major investment on their part. Chapters 15 and 16 further discuss new banking services that banks are developing through networking, particularly investment and insurance services.

INTERNATIONAL EXPANSION OF DERIVATIVES

Financial derivatives opened trading on organized exchanges in the United States in the 1970s. The Chicago Board Options Exchange (CBOE) and CME Group account for over 60 percent of worldwide derivative trading on exchanges. In the

1980s international exchanges began to appear that patterned themselves after the U.S. exchanges. For example, in 1987 the Tokyo Stock Exchange began trading government bond futures, and the Tokyo International Financial Futures Exchange (TIFFE) was founded in 1989 to expand the growing derivatives activity. By 1990, about 13 percent of total global derivatives trading took place in Japan, and the Nikkei 225 stock index futures contract became the most actively traded derivatives contract in the world. Other Pacific Rim financial derivative exchanges are located in Australia, Hong Kong, Malaysia, New Zealand, the Philippines, and Singapore.

In Europe, the London International Financial Futures and Options Exchange (LIFFE, now part of IntercontinentalExchange group) is the oldest marketplace for financial derivatives. Trading the greatest volume of contracts in Europe, and third in the world behind the United States and Japan, LIFFE has an international scope, with contracts from the European Community (EC) at large, Japan, and the United States. France and Germany also have fairly large derivatives exchanges -- the Marché à Terme International de France (MATIF, now part of Euronext Paris) since 1986 and Deutsche Terminbörse (DTB) since 1990 which merged with the Swiss Options and Financial Futures (SOFFEX) to become Eurex Exchange (part of Eurex Group). Other European financial derivatives exchanges are found in Austria, Belgium, Denmark, Finland, Holland, Ireland, Italy, Luxembourg, the Netherlands, Norway, Spain, Sweden, Switzerland, and the U.K.

Exchange-traded financial derivatives are relatively new compared with OTC trading. The growing number and volume of trading at organized exchanges is transforming the derivatives marketplace. OTC markets are adopting some of the clearinghouse features of organized exchanges to reduce counterparty credit risk (i.e., this is relevant only for lower-quality counterparties). Also, organized exchanges are clearing and trading OTC derivative contracts. Consequently, the evolving financial derivatives market is very competitive -- a prerequisite for not only efficient pricing but also financial innovation. It can be inferred that financial derivatives will continue to expand their role in the financial marketplace in the years to come.

SUMMARY

Over the past two decades, a dramatic shift occurred in the way banks do business. In response to increases in financial markets' volatility in the 1980s and 1990s, banks adapted by expanding beyond making traditional loans and gathering deposits to fee-generating activities that do not appear on their balance sheets. These activities include a variety of commitments and contingent claims that business firms are increasingly demanding, including financial guarantees, SLCs, loan commitments, and NIFs. In addition, banks are offering various derivative securities services, such as swaps, options, futures and forward contracts, as well as asset securitization, to assist customers in coping with the greater volatility that exists in today's financial marketplace.

While off-balance-sheet activities provide fee income and can be used to manage banks' risk exposures, they also introduce new risks. Indeed, large off-balance-sheet exposures of money center banks, many times exceeding booked assets, is increasing regulatory attention to these new risks. The challenge for bankers is to provide the off-balance-sheet services that customers demand and, at the same time, control the risk implications of these services.

KEY TERMS AND CONCEPTS

- Acceptance participation
- Account party
- Aggregation risk
- Banker's acceptance
- Basis risk
- Cash management
- Ceiling agreement (cap)
- Contingent claim
- Counterparty credit risk
- Coupon swap
- Credit option
- Credit swap
- Cross-currency interest rate swap
- Currency swap
- Euronotes
- Facility fee
- Financial guarantee
- Floor agreement
- Forward rate agreement
- Interest rate collar
- Interest rate options
- Interest rate swap
- Legal risk
- Letters of credit (LOC)
- Line of credit
- Liquidity risk
- Loan commitment
- Loan guarantee
- Market risk
- Material adverse change (MAC) clause
- Networking
- Off-balance-sheet activity
- Operating risk
- Over-the-counter option
- Price risk
- Revolving loan commitment
- Securitization
- Settlement risk
- Standby letter of credit (SLC)
- Swap
- Synthetic loan
- Total return swap

QUESTIONS

14.1 Why did banks substantially increase off-balance-sheet activities over the past two decades?

14.2 Briefly describe two broad groups of off-balance-sheet activities.

14.3 List and define four kinds of risk inherent in banking.

14.4 Distinguish between the issuer, account party, and beneficiary of a letter of credit.

14.5 Define the following terms: (a) acceptance participation, (b) loan guarantee, (c) standby letter of credit, (d) surety bond, and (e) loan commitment.

14.6 What is the difference between a line of credit and a revolving loan commitment? Regarding the latter, what is a MAC clause?

14.7 What is funding risk? What is the potential long-run pitfall of this kind of risk for a bank?

14.8 What are NIFs, RUFs, and SNIFs? Euronotes?

14.9 Who are arrangers and tender panels in NIFs?

14.10 Define the term *securitization.* What does "with recourse" mean regarding securitized loan portfolios?

14.11 Define a swap. What are two principal types of swaps? What other kinds of interest rate swaps are there?

14.12 Why has the OTC option market evolved?

14.13 Briefly define the following terms: (a) floor agreement, (b) ceiling agreement, (c) forward rate agreement, (d) synthetic loan, and (e) lock box.

14.14 What is a credit risk derivative? Give two examples of how can they help to control credit risk.

14.15 Browse on a search engine to fine the Quarterly Report on Bank Derivatives Activities published by the Office of the Comptroller of the Currency. Using the most recent publication of this report, summarize some of the findings in the report.

14.16 Visit the website for the International Swaps and Derivatives Association (ISDA) at www.isda.org. Under the tab "Asset Classes," select a contract type, read one of the reports, and summarize its contents.

14.17 The CME Group website is at http://www.cmegroup.com/. Click the "About" tab and write a summary of this organization.

PROBLEMS

14.1 Corporation XYZ obtains a ceiling agreement from a bank for a five-year loan of $20 million at a rate of seven percent (tied to LIBOR). An upfront fee of two percent is paid by XYZ for the guarantee that rates will not exceed 10 percent.

(a) If LIBOR goes to 12 percent, calculate the quarterly compensation the bank must pay XYZ.

(b) What kind of option is this for the bank? XYZ? When is it "in-the-money?"

14.2 A forward rate agreement (FRA) on bonds is purchased by a bank at 90 for delivery in three months.

(a) If the price of the bonds is 100 on the delivery date, what is the profit (loss) of the bank? What type of option is analogous to this example?

(b) If the price of the bonds falls to 80 three months from now, what is the profit (loss) of the bank? What type of option is analogous to this example?

(c) From parts (a) and (b), what can we conclude regarding FRAs and their relationship to options?

14.3 A bank makes a three-month floating-rate loan of $60 million at 15.0 percent. The loan is repriced every 30 days. To hedge against declining interest rates the bank creates a synthetic loan by purchasing and then selling a 90-day T-bill futures contract yielding 12.0 percent every 30 days (i.e., this is done three times). Each contract is for ten T-bills at $1 million face value for each T-bill. The following interest rate assumptions are made by the bank:

Days =	30	60	90	120
Floating rate on loan	15.0%	14.0%	13.0%	12.0%
T-bill futures yield	12.0	11.6	11.2	10.8

Show that the bank has converted the floating-rate loan to a fixed-rate 15 percent loan by calculating the cash inflows on the floating-rate loan and the long position in a T-bill futures and comparing their total to the total cash inflows from a 15 percent fixed-rate loan.

14.4 A large U.S. bank is working with an insurance company to put together an equity swap. The insurance company wishes to invest $20 million in equities. A large German bank has indicated interest as the counterparty in the swap if it can earn LIBOR plus 0.4 percent. Explain how the U.S. bank could structure a derivatives deal that would satisfy these diverse demands, in addition to the risks and returns to each party.

CASE: ISWAP/USWAP

ISWAP is a nonfinancial firm with a weak financial condition. Local banking institutions are willing to offer ISWAP only variable-rate loans. A fixed-rate loan would be more desirable, in light of a long-term investment in a new product that it is contemplating. USWAP is a large, strongly capitalized bank in a nearby city that would benefit from variable-rate funding for its short-term asset portfolio. The opportunities to borrow funds for the two parties is as follows:

	Variable Rate	Fixed Rate
ISWAP(firm)	LIBOR + 1%	14%
USWAP(bank)	LIBOR + 0.5%	12%

From this information, it is clear that ISWAP pays a two percent premium for fixed-rate funds but only a 0.5 percent premium for variable-rate funds.

Assume that an intermediary is contacted to handle the details of the swap. ISWAP takes out a variable-rate loan at LIBOR + one percent but swaps this loan's payments with USWAP, who issues seven-year notes at 12 percent. ISWAP pays USWAPs interest bill plus 0.1 percent fee to the intermediating bank. USWAP pays the LIBOR component of ISWAP's variable-rate loan and leaves the fixed one percent to be paid by ISWAP.

First, draw a diagram that shows all parties, including arrows showing the flow of funds in the swap, as well as the interest rates paid by ISWAP and USWAP through the intermediary. Second, make a table showing ISWAP's costs, ISWAP's savings from the swap, USWAP's costs, USWAP's savings from the swap, the intermediary's fees, and the receipts and payments between ISWAP and USWAP. After completing this work, write a final statement on the feasibility of the swap.

Source: This problem is based on J. Gregg Whittaker, "Interest Rate Swaps: Risk and Regulation," *Economic Review*, Federal Reserve Bank of Kansas City, March 1987, pp. 3–13.

ENDNOTES

1. Empirical research has revealed that large money center and superregional banks.

2. An historical example of potential liquidity problems in derivatives market is the 2008-2009 financial crisis. At that time portfolio insurance strategies based on financial derivatives (such as credit default swaps, or CDSs) to protect investors in mortgage-related securities broke down, causing large securities losses for many market participants. For example, global insurance company American International Group (AIG) had about $500 billion of CDS contracts outstanding in 2008. Losses of $30 billion on these contracts, $21 billion of losses on securities lending activities, and other losses led to a $85 billion loan from the Federal Reserve to prevent the firm from failure.

3. *Source:* Craig Torres, "How a Simple Deal Using Derivatives Works, Step by Step," *Wall Street Journal*, August 17, 1993, p. A8.

4. For those interested in further information about credit derivatives, an excellent overview and references to relevant literature can be found in James T. Moser, "Credit Derivatives: Just In-Time Provisioning for Loan Losses," *Economic Perspectives*, Federal Reserve Bank of Chicago, Fourth Quarter 1988, pp. 2–11.

PART 5

DOMESTIC AND INTERNATIONAL FINANCIAL SERVICES

Chapter 15

Securities, Investment & Insurance Services

After reading this chapter, you will be able to:

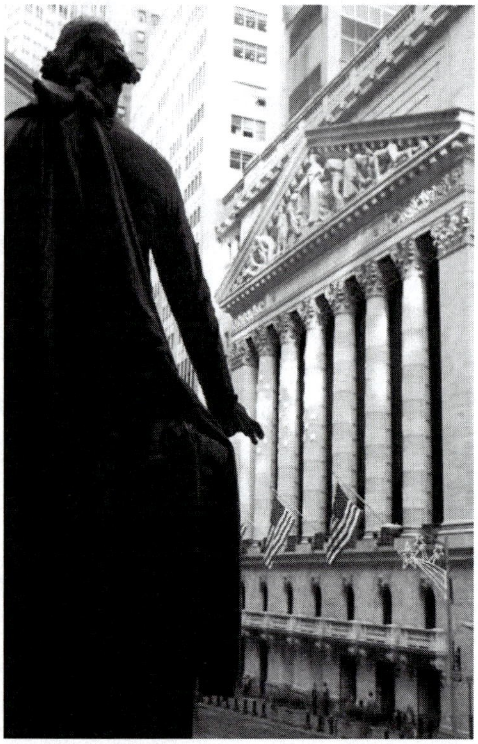

- Understand the significance of consolidation and convergence of financial services
- Explain the concept and benefits of financial intermediation
- Describe the major types of insurance companies and how they differ
- Explain the differences between securities brokers or dealers, and investment banks
- Understand why banks like mutual funds

Two trends in financial services are consolidation and convergence. Simply stated, this means that banks, securities firms, insurance companies and other types of financial intermediaries are combining their resources to create financial supermarkets. This chapter examines the concept of financial intermediaries and shows how they are similar, and, at the same time, different.

CONSOLIDATION AND CONVERGENCE OF FINANCIAL SERVICES

CONSOLIDATION

The term *"consolidation,"* as used here, refers to the concentration of assets due to mergers and acquisitions. Consolidation is a natural consequence of economic growth in an industry. In one sense, it is a variant of Darwin's survival of the fittest. But in this case it refers to firms and not species. By way of illustration, both the automotive and airline industries began with a large number of firms entering the industry but, over the years, only the fittest firms survived to dominate the industry. In the early phases of their development, a large number of firms entered the automobile and airline industries. Today, only a small number of large firms in the United States dominate the automobile industry (e.g. Chrysler, Ford, General Motors) and airline industry (e.g. Delta Airlines, United Airlines, Southwest Airlines, American Airlines).

Similarly, the number of banks in the United States increased from 11,474 in 1896 to 30,456 in 1921.[1] In the following years, the number of commercial banks declined due to mergers, acquisitions and failures to 5,472 in the Second Quarter, 2015.[2] Of that total number of commercial banks, 94 large commercial banks with assets greater than $10 billion controlled 83 percent of total bank assets which were $14.7 trillion.[3]

A *Bank Holding Company* is a company that owns and or controls one or more U.S. banks or one that owns, or has controlling interest in, one or more banks or another bank holding company. The four largest bank holding companies In the United States, shown in Table 15-1, had $8.1 trillion in assets, accounting for 55.1 percent of total commercial bank assets.

TABLE 15-1 FOUR LARGEST U.S. BANK HOLDING COMPANIES

Name	Location	Total Assets
JPMorgan Chase & Co.	New York, NY	$2.4 trillion
Bank of America Corporation	Charlotte, NC	$2.2 trillion
Citigroup Inc.	New York, NY	$1.8 trillion
Wells Fargo & Co.	San Francisco	$1.7 trillion
Total		$8.1 trillion

Source: Federal Financial Institutions Examination Council (FFEIC), National Information Center, "Holding Companies with Assets Greater Than $10 Billion," June, 2015

Although JPMorgan Chase is the largest banking organization in the United States, it was the sixth largest bank in the world in 2015.[4] The largest bank was the Industrial and Commercial Bank of China with total assets of $3.6 trillion, followed by three more banks in China and HSBC Holdings in the United Kingdom. HSBC North America Holdings Inc. is the thirteenth largest bank holding company in the United States.[5]

To put JPMorgan Chase & Company in perspective, it is headquartered in New York City and has operations in more than 45 countries. It offers asset management, card services, commercial banking, investment banking, retail financial services, and treasury and securities services.[6] It is considered to be a ***"Large, Complex, Financial, Institution (LCFI)."***

Large asset size gives companies the advantages of economies of scale and economies of scope. ***Economies of scale*** are when businesses can increase their revenue and spread their fixed costs over a wide variety of products and services. That cause the average cost of producing something to fall as the volume of its output increases. Economies of scope occur where it is cheaper to produce a range of products rather than specialize in a handful of products. JP Morgan Chase is an example of an LCFI.

CONVERGENCE

Convergence is another concept that is important. Convergence refers to different types of financial institutions (such as banks, insurance, securities brokers) merging their various lines of business into one organization. Convergence of financial institutions has been going on in Europe, but was prohibited in the United States because of the 1933 Glass-Steagall Act, until the passage of the Gramm-Leach-Bliley Act of 1999, which removed the prohibitions. It allowed banks to form financial holding companies (FHC) to acquire securities and insurance companies. Consequently, today, the biggest banking organizations, JPMorgan Chase, Bank of America, Citigroup, Wells Fargo, and others, provide various types of insurance, annuities, asset management and retirement funds, securities and investment banking, and other financial services.

FINANCIAL INTERMEDIARIES

William J. McDonough, former President of the Federal Reserve Bank of New York, said that "Understanding how financial firms beyond banks and securities firms operate has become imperative, because the largest insurance companies, mutual funds, hedge funds, and finance companies increasingly rival banks and securities firms not only in their asset size but also in their ability to reshape financial activity."[7] The fact is that they are all financial intermediaries, but banks, insurance companies, and securities firms do different jobs and they have different time horizons.

Financial intermediaries are economic units whose principal function is managing the financial assets of other economic units -- business concerns and individuals.

They bring savers and borrowers together by selling securities to savers for money and lending that money to borrowers. The term financial intermediary can be applied to a variety of institutions, some of which are listed below.

Commercial banks	Mutual funds
Mutual savings banks	Stockbrokers and stock dealers
Credit unions	Finance companies
Insurance companies	Leasing companies
On-line lenders (e.g. Lending Tree, Lending Club)[8]	Trust companies
	Pension funds

Given this definition of financial intermediaries -- economic units whose principal business is managing financial assets -- some business concerns could be considered quasi-financial intermediaries. For example, the American Express Company is a bank holding company and "... a global services company with four reportable operating segments: U.S. Card Services (USCS), International Card Services (ICS), Global Commercial Services (GCS) and Global Network and Merchant Services (GNMS). We provide our customers with access to products, insights and experiences that enrich lives and build business success. Our principal products and services are charge and credit payment card products and travel-related services offered to consumers and businesses around the world."[9]

INTERMEDIATION

Financial intermediation is the process that takes place when business concerns and individuals invest funds in financial intermediaries such as banks. The businesses and individuals receive claims (secondary securities) with stable market values and high liquidity, such as demand deposits (checking accounts) and time and savings accounts. In turn, the financial intermediaries invest the funds in various kinds of bonds, mortgages, commercial loans (primary securities) that have unstable or fluctuating market values and in some cases low liquidity. In essence, financial intermediaries change risky primary securities (assets) into less risky secondary securities (liabilities).

BENEFITS OF INTERMEDIATION

Intermediation enables individuals to invest their funds safely and business firms to borrow funds, so that the borrowing-lending process in our economic system functions smoothly. Imagine what would happen if General Electric wanted to borrow $100 million and had to seek out individuals who would lend them that amount. Or, assume that you had $500 in surplus funds to lend. How would you as an individual find a borrower who wanted that exact amount? Fortunately, neither General Electric nor you must face that problem because financial institutions serve as intermediaries, pooling the funds of individual savers and lending them to borrowers.

There are other benefits of the intermediation process. Pooling of funds provides certain administrative economies of scale, since it is less costly to administer one $10 million loan than it is to administer ten $1 million loans. Equally important, pooling of independent funds reduces an individual's per-dollar risk with respect to loan default, since many types of secondary securities are insured, thereby reducing investors' risk in holding secondary deposits (for example, the Federal Deposit Insurance Corporation insures bank deposits).

On the other side of the balance sheet, laws and regulatory authorities set guidelines concerning capital requirements to protect insured deposits. In addition, the financial institutions that specialize in selected types of financing can lower costs to the borrowers. For example, some life insurance companies have particular expertise in large real estate developments. Real estate developers can reasonably expect to borrow at a slightly lower cost from these insurance companies than from institutions that specialize in other types of investments.

BUSINESS CONCERNS

Nonfinancial business concerns are one of the principal "customers" of financial intermediaries. They produce goods and services for profit. Most business concerns can be classified as sole proprietorships, partnerships, or corporations.[10] In order to understand how a business concern is distinguished from a financial intermediary, it is helpful to examine a hypothetical corporate balance sheet, as shown in Table 15-2.

TABLE 15-2 BALANCE SHEET FOR NONFINANCIAL BUSINESS CONCERNS

Assets	Liabilities	
Financial assets (cash, accts. receivable)	Trade credit	Primary securities
Real assets (plant, equipment, inventories)	Bonds & notes	Primary securities
	Mortgages	Primary securities
	Bank loans	Primary securities
	Net worth	Primary securities
	Stocks	Primary securities
	Retained earnings	

Primary securities are claims (total liabilities and equity securities) against business concerns and individuals. In the case of business concerns, bonds, notes, bank loans, mortgages, and stocks are examples of claims or primary securities. In the case of individuals, they are home mortgages and consumer installment debt.

Some financial *intermediaries* specialize in dealing in particular types of primary securities. For example, mutual funds specialize in stocks and bonds. In contrast, commercial banks invest in mortgages, commercial and industrial loans, consumer loans, and other types of loans.

Some types of primary securities are considered risky by investors for two reasons. First, the market value of primary securities can change dramatically. For example, during the financial crises, the Dow Jones Industrial average of stock prices plunged from 13,170 in 2007 to 8,876 in 2009.[11] Also, in recent years the market values of outstanding bonds and mortgages have varied widely.

In the case of bonds and mortgages, the market price varies inversely as interest rates change. If interest rates increase, the price of these debt instruments declines. Market rates of interest were at record low levels in 2015.

INDIVIDUALS

The term ***individual*** is used in the broad sense of the word, and refers to "persons" in contrast to "business." One difference between individuals and business is that individuals acquire real assets for the services they provide rather than for use as a capital good. Their real assets are houses, automobiles, and other consumer durables (see Table 15-3).

Individuals' liabilities consist of home mortgage debt and consumer debt. This statement serves to re-emphasize that individuals acquire real assets for the services they provide instead of financing capital goods. Home mortgage debt is used to finance a place for individuals to live. Similarly, consumer credit is used to finance automobiles, television sets, and other consumer goods. In contrast, a business concern uses mortgage debt to finance a factory or warehouse that is used in the production of other goods.

Another difference between individuals and businesses is that, generally speaking, individuals are considered risk averters. An example of a risk averter is someone who buys fire insurance on his house, accepting a certain small loss (the insurance premium) in preference to the small chance of a large loss (the value of the house). Individuals' aversion to risk is relative. They do not borrow large sums for risky capital investments, but they do borrow to finance mortgages, car loans, and other consumer pur-chases. In contrast, business firms are willing to take more risks than individuals and invest in risky projects. The final point is that since individuals are mortal, and many business concerns are thought of as perpetual, their investment goals are different.

Within the context of the economic system, individuals are net savers and put their surplus funds in secondary securities. If the investment return on primary securities is significantly higher than the return on secondary securities, they may invest some of their funds in primary securities, but more often they provide funds to financial intermediaries, who in turn acquire primary securities. Their liabilities and net worth are considered primary securities.

TABLE 15-3 BALANCE SHEET FOR INDIVIDUALS

Assets	Liabilities
Secondary securities	Home mortgage debt
Primary securities	Consumer credit
Stocks	
Bonds	
Real assets	
Houses	
Automobiles	
Consumer durables	Net worth

FINANCIAL INTERMEDIARIES

The assets of financial intermediaries consist of primary securities and real assets, while their liabilities consist of secondary securities. Just as business concerns sell primary securities to obtain funds, financial intermediaries sell secondary securities to obtain funds to finance their activities (See Table 15-4). Real assets include the land, buildings, and equipment that financial institutions need to carry on their business.

Secondary securities are claims against financial intermediaries. These secondary securities may take the form of demand deposits (checking accounts), savings accounts, certificates of deposit, life insurance policies, and, in some cases, bonds and other types of securities of secondary securities. They are liabilities of financial intermediaries.

TABLE 15-4 HYPOTHETICAL BALANCE SHEET FOR FINANCIAL INTERMEDIARIES

Assets	Liabilities	
Primary securities	Demand deposits	Secondary securities
Real assets	Time and savings deposits	Secondary securities
	Insurance and pension fund reserves	Secondary securities
	Mutual fund shares	Secondary securities
	Stocks	Secondary securities
	Net worth	Secondary securities
	Retained earnings	Secondary securities

Table 15-5 illustrates the entire process of financial intermediation -- how intermediaries obtain funds from individuals and invest in business concerns. Thus, the liabilities of business concerns and individuals (primary securities) become and assets of financial intermediaries; and liabilities of the intermediaries (secondary securities) become the assets of individual investors and businesses.

TABLE 15-5 PRIMARY AND SECONDARY SECURITIES

Business Concerns			Financial Intermediaries			Individuals	
Assets	Liabilities		Assets	Liabilities		Assets	Liabilities
Secondary securities	Primary securities	→	Primary securities	Secondary securities	→	Secondary securities	Primary securities

In summary, banks, insurance companies, investment companies, and stock brokerage firms are all financial intermediaries. Next we will discuss how they differ from each other in the composition of their primary and secondary securities. Because of the extensive coverage of banks throughout this text, they are not addressed here.

INSURANCE COMPANIES

The insurance industry can be divided into two groups, life insurance and nonlife, which consists of every type of insurance other than life insurance. Property and casualty insurance, health insurance and reinsurance (insurance on insurance to reduce the original issuers' risk) are examples of other types of insurance. In the United States, life insurance accounted for about 42 percent of total insurance premiums paid, and property and casualty for the remaining 58 percent in 2013. Worldwide, life insurance accounts for about 56 percent of total insurance premiums.[12]

According to the Insurance Information Institute, "***Insurance*** is a product that transfers risk from an individual or business to an insurance company. It differs from most products in that insurers must price and sell their policies before the full cost of coverage is known. In property and casualty insurance, claims may be more frequent and costly than anticipated and investment income may not fully offset the shortfall. In life insurance, expected returns from investments may not be sufficient to fund annuity contracts, especially fixed dollar annuities. If there is a downturn in the economy, policyholders may cancel life insurance policies before the company can recoup its selling expenses. They may also cash in policies that are based on stock market returns if the stock market falls."[13]

The McCarran-Ferguson Act of 1945 delegated the regulation of insurance companies to the states. The National Association of Insurance Commissioners (NAIC) has developed model rules and laws for the states, and an accreditation program. The NAIC dates back to 1871, when it was organized to coordinate the multistate regulation of insurance companies. Today it includes insurance regulators from the 50 states, the District of Columbia, and the four U.S. territories (American Samoa, Guam, Puerto Rico, and the Virgin Islands).[14]

LIFE INSURANCE

Life insurance is a type of insurance policy that pays a benefit if the person who is insured by the contract dies while the insurance is in force.[15] There are two basic types of life insurance policies, term and whole life. However, there are many combinations and variations of them. Only the basic policies are described here.

Today, the primary business of many life insurance companies is underwriting ***annuities*** -- a financial contract between an insurer and a customer under which the insurer promises to make a series of periodic benefit payments to a named individual -- the payee -- in exchange for the contract owner's payment of a premium or series of premiums to the insurer.[16] Life insurers also offer asset management and retirement funds.

Term insurance provides limited protection for a given amount of time, such as one year, five years, or ten years. The face amount of the policy is payable to a beneficiary at the death of the insured if it occurs within a specified period. Some term policies are convertible into whole life or endowment policies. Two important types of term insurance are decreasing term and credit life insurance. ***Decreasing term insurance*** provides for large amounts of protection in the early years of the policy, and then the amount declines each year and stabilizes at some lower level. ***Credit Life insurance*** is issued by a lender or an insurance company to cover the payment of a loan or obligation in the case of death.

Whole life insurance, sometime called straight life or ordinary life, gives permanent protection. The face amount of the policy is paid upon the death of the insured regardless of when it occurs. The premiums for whole life insurance can be paid for life or compressed into a shorter time span. The insured can borrow the cash value of the policy in the form of a policy loan, use the accumulated cash to buy additional insurance, or surrender the policy and withdraw the entire amount. Thus, the total value of a whole life policy can be thought of as a combination of declining term plus savings.

In summary, life insurance policies can provide a combination of insurance protection and savings (cash values). Term policy consists of insurance protection and no savings. In contrast, whole life policy consists principally of term protection with some savings. Equally important, the focus of insurance companies has shifted toward providing annuities and other financial services. In 2013, annuities accounted for 48 percent of total net premiums, health insurance accounted for 30 percent, and life insurance accounted for 22 percent of the total.[17]

LIFE INSURANCE COMPANIES

To put the size of life insurance companies in perspective, their total assets were $6.2 trillion in 2013, compared to bank assets of $14.4 trillion in the same year.[18] Most life insurance companies in the United States are ***legal reserve life insurance companies***. This means that they operate under state insurance laws that specify the minimum reserves that insurance companies must maintain on the policies that they issue. As shown in Table 15- 6, policy reserves, also known as legal reserves, are the major liability of life insurance companies. Policy reserves represent funds set aside to meet the insurer's obligations to policyholders and beneficiaries -- the recipients of the policy proceeds.

Policyholders can borrow (take out policy loans) on part of their accumulated life insurance policy reserves without forfeiting their policies; or they can cancel the policies and recoup a substantial part of their policy reserves or savings (*cash surrender value*). Thus, in a limited sense, life insurance policy reserves are a liquid asset for some policyholders.

Policy reserves account for about 85 percent of U.S. life insurance companies' total obligations and surplus funds.[19] Using the terminology developed earlier in this chapter, policy reserves are secondary securities, or liabilities of life insurance companies.

TABLE 15-6 PRINCIPAL ASSETS AND LIABILITIES OF LIFE INSURANCE COMPANIES

Assets	Obligations and Surplus Funds
Bonds (government and corporate)	Policy reserves
Stocks	Other liabilities
Mortgages (commercial real estate)	Net worth

Some insurers, such as fraternal groups that provide insurance for their members, do not qualify as legal reserve life insurance companies.

Life insurance ***premiums*** are paid in advance of the contract period. In addition, most life insurance policies use *level premium plans* whereby the premiums paid remain unchanged during the premium paying period. This produces a positive cash flow, which the life insurance companies can invest in earning assets. Since the risk of death is lower in the early years of life insurance contracts than in the later years, premiums and investment income accumulate to meet the rising level of death claims as the policies approach maturity.

The long-term nature of life insurance obligations (liabilities) permits life insurance companies to invest heavily in assets with long-term maturities. About 49 percent of life insurance companies' assets are invested in long-term bonds and mortgage-backed securities, 33 percent in stocks, and remainder in short-term investments, and other invested assets.[20] Equity capital and surplus account for about 5.6 percent of total assets.

PROPERTY AND CASUALTY INSURANCE

Property insurance provides financial protection against the loss of, or damage to, the insured's property as the result of the occurrence of specified risks, such as fire, theft, or accidents described in the policy. ***Casualty insurance***, also known as ***liability insurance***, provides financial protection against legal liabilities resulting from injury to other persons or damage to their property.

Property and casualty insurance companies differ significantly from life insurance companies in their behavior as financial intermediaries. Life insurance companies tend to match long-term claims with long-term investments. In contrast, claims against property and casualty companies are primarily short-term and are less predictable and more volatile because of the nature of the perils they insure. For example, it is not known where the next tornado will strike, how much damage an earthquake or hurricane will cause, or if there will be another terrorist attack similar to the 9/11/01 attack on the World Trade Center. In addition, the costs of claims of automobile repairs have increased over the years. Accordingly, property and casualty insurance companies tend to match their short-term claims with more liquid assets of similar terms to maturity. These assets include U.S. government securities, municipal securities, and corporate and foreign bonds. Their largest liabilities are reserves against anticipated claims.

Property and casualty insurance companies, as well as life insurance companies, frequently suffer net losses from underwriting. This means that the premiums they receive are less than their insured losses and expenses, resulting in net underwriting losses. However, their gains from investment income have more than offset the underwriting losses, resulting in positive operating earnings. For example, net underwriting losses for property and casualty insurance companies during the financial crises in 2008 were $19.6 billion, but net investment income was $53.1 billion.[21]

In terms of insurance premiums paid, automobile insurance is the largest single line of business, almost four times greater than the next line of business, homeowner's insurance and almost six time greater than worker's compensation premiums.

Although property and casualty insurance companies tend to specialize in commercial or personal insurance lines, some companies offer a wide range of insurance lines and financial services.

SECURITIES BROKERS/DEALERS AND INVESTMENT BANKING

The term ***broker*** refers to one who receives a commission for bringing buyers and sellers together. Brokers earn a commission for their services. Stockbrokers earn commissions for helping their customers buy and sell securities. The term dealer refers to one who buys or sells for his or own account. Securities dealers profit from buying securities at low prices and selling them at higher prices. Therefore it is riskier to be a securities dealer than a broker.

The term ***stockbrokerage firm*** is widely used to describe firms that buy and sell stock, bonds, and other investments. They frequently act as both brokers and dealers, but not in the same transaction. Such firms have expanded their activities to include wealth management, management or pension and retirement plans, and other financial services that they hope will be profitable. Some also function as ***investment bankers*** who bring together business concerns and government that need funds with investors who have funds to invest. The firms can operate individually or as part of a ***syndicate***, a group of investment banking firms. Basically, investment bankers ***underwrite*** primary securities – stocks and bonds. They buy the securities from the issuing firm at one price and then sell them to investors at a higher price. In doing so, they help to allocate capital efficiently and help the economy to grow.

Investment banking is the "wholesale" side of the stockbrokerage business. Most investment bankers have a retail distribution network that can be part of the same firm or a syndicate. The "full service" stockbrokerage firms also provide other financial services, such as money market accounts, credit cards, wealth management, mutual funds, and so on.

In the past, traditional full-service stockbrokerage firms depended on local offices to serve their customers. However, the growth of discount brokers/dealers online has prompted full-service stockbrokerage firms, such as Merrill Lynch, to provide both local offices and online services for their customers.[22] Conversely, Charles Schwab, which started out as an online discount broker, has expanded its services and opened offices around the country to serve its customers. Today it is a full-service brokerage firm.

Investment banks also serve institutional investors such as banks and insurance companies. Part of that service includes dealing in ***asset-backed securities (ABS),*** which are bonds that represent pools of similar types loans, such as federally-backed mortgages (collateral mortgage obligations – CMOs), uninsured mortgages, credit cards, business loans.

Some investment bankers deal extensively in ***derivative securities*** – privately and exchange-traded contracts that derive their value from the underlying assets such as stocks, interest rates, or foreign exchange rates. Derivative securities include futures, options, swaps, structured debt obligations, caps, collars, floors, and combinations thereof. According to the International Swaps and Derivatives Association (ISDA), in the first three quarters of 2015, the notional amount (nominal amount or face value) of all interest rate and currency swaps outstanding was $546 trillion.[23] To put this number in perspective, the total assets of all commercial banks in United States in Second Quarter 2015 was $14.7 trillion. Stated otherwise, the total notional amount of interest rate and currency derivatives were about 37 times the asset size of banks!

MUTUAL FUNDS

A ***mutual fund*** is an investment company that buys a portfolio of securities selected by investment advisors to meet specified investment objectives, such as growth, income, or matching the performance of a particular stock market index. Mutual funds are willing to buy back (redeem) their shares at their net asset value (equation 15-1).

Net asset value = (market value of asset – liabilities)/number of shares outstanding (15-1)

Sales charges and redemption fees may apply in certain cases.

Mutual funds are organized either as a corporation or as a business trust. Investors buy shares of the fund, and those funds are then invested in securities. Most mutual funds are ***"open-end" investment companies***, meaning that they continuously offer new shares to investors. In addition, there are "closed-end" funds with a limited number of shares, ***unit investment trusts (UITs)*** that have generally fixed portfolio of securities, and ***exchange traded funds (ETFs)*** whose shares are traded on stock exchanges.

The shareholders of mutual funds that are organized as corporations have the voting rights to elect the directors, approve material changes in the fund's contracts with its investment advisers, and vote on other important issues.

The fund's sponsor or organizer hires a third party investment administrator or adviser who manages the fund for a fee in accordance with the investment objectives and policies described in the fund's prospectus. The fee is generally based on the fund's average asset size.

At the end of 2013 there were 15,018 mutual funds, up from 3,079 in 1990.[24] Of that total, 279 were closed-end funds, 1,675 were ETFs, and 87 were UITs. There are a variety of investments offered by mutual funds. ***Money market funds*** invest in short-term, high-grade securities. They may be taxable or tax exempt. ***Equity funds*** invest primarily in stocks, and they may specialize in terms of growth or income, or invest in particular industries or geographic regions (such as emerging markets). ***Index funds*** invest in a variety of ***stock and bond market indexes.*** *Hybrid funds* invest in a mix of debt, equity, and derivative securities. ***Bond funds*** invest primarily in bonds and may specialize in particular types of bonds (such as tax exempt, high yield), or in certain geographic areas (global, Asia).

The total net assets of U.S. investment companies in 2013 was $17.1 trillion, and they were held by 96.2 million people, accounting for 46 percent of U.S. households. [25] Financial institutions find mutual funds attractive for the following reasons. First, it gives them access to 46 percent of U.S. households that own mutual funds as investments and retirement vehicles. Second, it provides fee income. Third, it requires little or no capital investment.

By way of illustration of convergence in general and mutual funds in particular, consider that as of September 30, 2015, BNY Mellon had $28.5 trillion in assets under custody or administration, and $1.63 trillion in assets under management. BNY Mellon, i.e., the corporate brand of The Bank of New York Mellon Corporation, owns Dreyfus Corporation, which manages approximately $286 billion in mutual funds and separately managed accounts.[26]

Other banks offer nonproprietary funds by having arrangements with independent mutual fund operators, such a Putnam, Oppenheimer, and Fidelity, to provide mutual funds access for their customers. Retail bank customers and small businesses usually buy mutual fund shares in connection with banks' brokerage services and in connection with retirement plans. The retirement plans are referred to by the various sections in the tax law. For example, 401(k) plans are employer-sponsored plans that enable employees to make tax-deferred contributions from their salaries to the plans. Similarly, 403(b) plans are sponsored by universities, public schools, and non-profit organizations; and 457 plans are sponsored by state and local governments.

Operational risk is the downside of banks owning mutual funds. Operational risk refers to losses resulting from inadequate or failed internal processes, people and systems, or from external events. It includes, but is not limited to, the risk of inadequate or failed internal systems, such as computer failures or fraud, compliance issues, as well as external events including lawsuits.[27] In 2003, New York Attorney General Eliot Spitzer was the driving force in the mutual fund inquiries that uncovered civil and criminal acts as well as other activities that were wrong but not illegal. Charging some retail mutual fund customers substantially higher fees than say, hedge funds, is one example.[28] Subsequently, civil or criminal charges were brought against Alliance Capital Management Holding LP, Canary Capital Partners (a hedge fund), Prudential Securities, Putnam Investments, Strong Capital Management, and others.[29] As previously noted, Prudential Securities is owned by Wachovia Corporation – a bank holding company. Thus, banks that own mutual funds can be adversely affected by the improper actions of their divisions or subsidiaries.

The charges against the mutual funds involved "market timing," "late trading," and other fraud and civil charges. ***Market timing*** refers to short-term buying and selling of mutual fund shares in order to take advantage of inefficiencies in mutual fund pricing. ***Late trading*** refers to placing orders to trade mutual fund shares at the closing price (net asset value, NAV) after the financial markets closed at 4 p.m. Eastern Standard Time, and it is illegal. Employees at Prudential's Boston and New York offices allowed hedge-fund clients to do late trading. According to Attorney General Spitzer, late trading is "like allowing betting on a horse race after the horses have crossed the finish line."[30]

SUMMARY

Following the passage of the Gramm-Leach-Bliley Act in 1999, it was widely assumed that there would be convergence between banks, securities brokers/dealers, insurance firms, and investment banking in the U.S. In Europe such firms were already combined in "universal banks." The process of melding various types of financial intermediaries in the U.S has begun, but it is not widespread.

In this chapter, we examined the concepts of financial intermediation, as well as selected types of financial intermediaries: insurance companies, securities brokers, dealers, investment banking, and mutual funds. Some of our large, complex, financial organizations, such as JP Morgan Chase and Bank of America, are involved in all of these activities. Similarly, in the insurance industry, Prudential Financial, Inc., State Farm Mutual Automobile Insurance Company (i.e., State Farm) and other insurance companies offer a wide range of financial services in addition to their basic insurance products. Basically, all financial intermediaries bring together savers and borrowers -- those who have funds to invest with those who need them. However, the intermediaries differ in terms of types of lenders and borrowers they deal with. Thus, the assets and liabilities of banks differ from those of mutual funds.

In the short run, the most likely outcome of the consolidation and convergence in our financial intermediaries will be limited to the largest firms. In turn, smaller financial intermediaries can join in the process by taking advantage of strategic alliances with the larger firms, or among themselves.

KEY TERMS AND CONCEPTS

Annuities
Asset-backed securities (ABS)
Bank Holding Company
Bond funds (mutual funds)
Broker
Cash surrender value
Casualty insurance
Closed-end mutual fund
Consolidation
Convergence
Conversion
Credit derivatives
Credit life insurance
Dealer
Decreasing term insurance
Derivative securities
Economies of Scale
Economies of Scope
Equity funds (mutual funds)
Exchange traded funds (ETF)
Financial intermediaries
Hybrid funds (mutual funds)
Index funds
Insurance
Intermediation
Investment banking
Large Complex Financial Institutions (LCFIs)
Late trading
Legal reserve life insurance companies
Liability insurance
Life insurance
Market timing
Money market funds
Mutual funds
Net asset value (mutual funds)
Open-end investment company
Operational risk
Premium (life insurance)
Primary securities
Property insurance
Secondary securities
Stockbrokerage firms
Syndicate
Term insurance
Underwrite (securities)
Unit investment trusts (UIT)
Whole life insurance

QUESTIONS

15.1 How does consolidation in our financial system affect competition for financial services?

15.2 Is convergence in our financial system good or bad for competition?

15.3 What are the benefits of financial intermediation?

15.4 Explain what is meant buy primary and secondary securities.

15.6 What type of secondary securities would be held by banks, insurance companies, and mutual funds?

15.7 How does life insurance differ from casualty insurance?

15.8 Describe the key differences between whole life and term insurance policies.

15.9 If property/casualty insurance companies consistently lose money on underwriting new policies, how can they survive?

15.10 What is property insurance?

15.11 How are stockbrokers and dealers compensated?

15.12. Investment bankers underwrite securities. What does that mean?

15.13 What are derivative securities? Give several examples.

15.14 Describe the major types of mutual funds.

15.15 Is the term "net asset value" the same as "book value per share?"

15.16 What is an ETF?

15.17 Are money market funds safer than bond funds? Why?

15.18 What financial services are offered by:

a) Citigroup? http://www.citigroup.com

b) Merrill Lynch? http://www.ml.com

c) American International Group? http://www.aig.com

15.19 According to the *Mutual Fund Fact Book*, http://www.ici.org what is the total dollar value of money market funds?

15.20 How does the value of money market funds compare to the value of deposits at commercial banks? (See http://www.fdic.gov and look for the Quarterly Banking Profile for the answer), or the Board of Governors of the Federal Reserve System (http://www.federalreserve.gov).

ENDNOTES

1. Board of Governors of the Federal Reserve System, *All Bank Statistics: United States, 1896-1955*. Table A-1a, p. 37.

2. FDIC Quarterly Banking Profile, Second Quarter 2015, Table III-A. Data are for FDIC-insured commercial banks.

3. Ibid.

4. "Top Banks in the World 2015," Banks around World, http://www.relbanks.com/

5. Federal Financial Institutions Examination Council (FFEIC), National Information Center, "Holding Companies with Assets Greater Than $10 Billion," 6/30/15.

6. JPMorgan Chase & Co., *The History of JPMorgan Chase & Co.* 2008, https://www.jpmorganchase.com/corporate/About-JPMC/document/shorthistory.pdf

7. "Report from the President," *2002 Annual Report*, Federal Reserve Bank of New York, p. 5.

8. See www.lendingtree.com, www.lendingclub.com. Google "on line loans."

9. 2014 American Express Company, Annual Report, pp. 18, 19.

10. For legal purposes, a *sole proprietor* is one who has the legal right or exclusive title to a business; a *partnership* is a voluntary contract between two or more people who agree to carry on a business together on terms of mutual participation in its profits and losses; a *corporation* is an artificial person or legal entity with rights, privileges, and liabilities separate from those of its owners.

11. Economic Indicators, "Common Stock Prices and Yields," United States Government Publishing Office, September, 2015.

12. *International Insurance Fact Book 2015*, Insurance Information Institute, 2015, p.3.

13. *The Financial Services Fact Book 2003*, New York, Insurance Information Institute and The Financial Services Roundtable, 2003, 31.

14. To learn more about the insurance industry and ratings, see the following websites: National Association of Insurance Commissioners: http://www.naic.org; A..M. Best Insurance Information Centers: /

http://www.ambest.com/insurance/; J.D. Power, http://www.jdpower.com/ratings/industry/insurance

15. For a glossary/definitions of insurance terms see The Insurance Information Institute, http://www.iii.org/media/glossary/; and The Baltimore Life Companies Glossary of Insurance Terms: http://www.baltimorelife.com/site/i_glossary_AD.html

16. Ibid.

17. *Life Insurers Fact Book*, "Distribution of Life Insurers' Net Premium Receipts, 2013," Figure 4.1,

18. Ibid. Figure 2.1; FDIC Quarterly Banking Profile, First Quarter 2014, Table II-A.

19. *Statistical Abstract of the United States: 2000*, Washington, D.C., U.S. Census Bureau, 2002, No. 1200; and *The Financial Services Fact Book 2003*, New York, Insurance Information Institute and The Financial Services Roundtable, 2003.

20. *Life Insurers Fact Book*, "Distribution of Life Insurers' Assets, by Account Type, 2013," Table 2.1.

21. *Statistical Abstract of the United States: 2012*, Washington, D.C., U.S. Census Bureau, 2011, No. 1222.

22. For additional details about investing online, see Benton E. Gup, *Investing Online*, Malden MA., Blackwell Publishing, 2003. Also see Merrill Lynch: http://www.ml.com, and Charles Schwab: http://schwab.com.

23. ISDA SwapsInfo Third Quarter 2015 Review, November 23, 2015, http://www2.isda.org/functional-areas/research/research-notes/ For more information about derivatives – see the International Swap Dealers Association website: http://www.isda.org/index.html; For a global perspective see Bank for International Settlements, Statistical release OTC derivatives statistics at end-June 2015 Monetary and Economic Department November 2015, https://www.bis.org/publ/otc_hy1511.pdf

24. *2014 Investment Company Fact Book*, Investment Company Institute, 2015, *Mutual Fund Fact Book 2003*, New York, Investment Company Institute, 2003. For further information, see the Investment Company Institute web site: http://www.ici.org

25. Ibid.

26. https://www.dreyfus.com/ BNY MELLON Dreyfus; https://public.dreyfus.com/about-dreyfus/About-Dreyfus.html

27. This definition of operational risk is used in connection with the Basel II capital requirements.

28. Deborah Solomon, "It's Spitzer vs. SEC on Mutual Funds' Fees," *The Wall Street Journal*, December 19, 2003, C1, C17.

29. See Harvey J. Goldschmidt, SEC Commissioner, "Mutual Fund Regulation: A Time for Healing and Reform," ICI Securities Law Developments Conference, Washington, D.C., December 4, 2003, http://www.sec.gov/news/speech/spch120403hjg.htm; U. S. Securities and Exchange Commission Press Release 2003-143, "SEC Announces Fraud Charges Against Former Portfolio Manager of Lipper Convertible Hedge Funds," October 29, 2003, http://www.sec.gov/news/press/2003-143.htm; ; U. S. Securities and Exchange Commission Press Release 2003-142, "SEC Brings Enforcement Actions Against Putnam Investment Management LLC and Two Putnam Managing Directors For Self-Dealing in Putnam Funds," October 28, 2003.

30. Leiff Carbraser Heimann & Bernstein LLP, "Mutual Fund Industry Fraud Litigation," http://www.lieffcabraser.com/mf_main.htm (visited 12/27/03). Leiff Carbraser Heimann & Bernstein LLP, is a law firm with offices in New York, San Francisco, and Washington, D.C.

Chapter 16

Other Financial Services

After reading this chapter, you will be able to:

- Understand the range of services offered by banks
- Explain why banks provide cash management and data processing services to business
- Determine FDIC insurance coverage for bank accounts
- Describe how banks can offer investment products
- Understand the widespread uses of trusts

This chapter is about selected wholesale and retail financial services offered by banks that have not been covered in previous chapters, or that require further explanation. Wholesale services are those offered primarily to business concerns, and retail services are those offered to individuals. The term *bank*, as explained in Chapter 1, has a variety of meanings. The legal definition of a "bank" is determined by laws and bank regulators. There are different types of banks: commercial banks, limited purpose banks, and savings banks are a few examples. In addition to banks, there are ***bank holding companies*** -- companies that own or control one or more banks, Bank holding companies can engage in a range of activities that "are closely related to banking," and that are approved by the Federal Reserve Board. For example, bank holding companies can engage in data processing; they can lease personal or real property; they can make, acquire, or service loans or other extensions of credit; and they can provide other approved activities. [1]

Finally, bank holding companies might elect to become ***financial holding companies*** -- companies that can engage in underwriting and selling insurance and securities, commercial and merchant banking, investing in and developing real estate, and "complementary activities." Simply stated, banking is a very complex business. While most of this book has focused on traditional banking activities, this chapter is intended to reveal the diverse nature of the financial services that they offer.

CASH MANAGEMENT SERVICES

Banks provide cash management services for their business customers to earn fee income, to cross-sell their products, and to increase relationships with their customers. ***Cash management*** is the process of combining banking services, data collection, and communications systems to enhance the collection, control and utilization of cash for business concerns. Cash management services help businesses collect their receivables faster and to make their payments more efficiently. Faster collections reduce a firm's float. *Float* is the dollar amount of checks that been received by a firm that are in the process of collection, but have not yet been converted into cash. Firms typically want to reduce the float when collecting funds owed to them. Conversely, they want to take advantage of float when making payments to others.

As will be explained in the next chapter, the ***Check 21 Act*** will go a long way toward reducing float. The act permits institutions to make digital images of checks, truncate the original paper check, and process the payment information electronically. Thus, customers will send their checks to, say American Express, who will make a digital image of it, and then digitally process the payment. The original check will not be returned to the customer.

CASH CONCENTRATION FOR COLLECTION OF FUNDS

Many business concerns, such as grocery store chains, receive retail payments and make relatively small daily deposits in the various cities where the stores are located. Cash concentration brings all of the deposits together in one account so that the firm's corporate headquarters can use those funds efficiently.

CONTROLLED DISBURSEMENT

Banks can help business concerns make better use of their cash resources by helping control disbursements (such as payments). A *zero balance account* is one technique. This is a bank account that has a zero dollar balance, most of the time. When a check drawn against a business is presented to its bank for collection, the bank notifies the business, which then deposits the appropriate amount to cover the check. By using a zero balance account, businesses minimize the amount of funds deposited in non-interest earning bank accounts.

LOCK BOXES FOR COLLECTIONS

A **lock box** is a post office box of a business concern that is used to receive payments for goods and services that it sold to customers. For example, bill payments made to retail stores and utilities are sent to a post office box in a city that minimizes the mail time in transit. Instead of the retailer sending payments to the company headquarters in Seattle, for example, the payments from customers located in the Southeastrn part of the United States are sent to a post office box in Atlanta, which reduces mailing time from three days to one day. A bank in Atlanta will empty the post office box several times each day, deposit the checks, and notify the receiving company of its collections. The company can then invest those funds or reduce its debts. Companies may have lock boxes located in various cities, depending on the size and scope of their operations.

One of the problems a company faces is to determine the optimal number of lock boxes to maximize profits. To demonstrate the basic calculations, consider a bank that attempting to design a lock box system for a small corporate customer. Based on their past experiences, the bank assumes that 10 lock boxes are used, and, given information on mail delivery speeds in places where the boxes are located, the following information is assembled:

1) Average number of daily payments to the lock boxes	= 300
2) Average amount of payment	= $2,000
3 Daily rate of interest	= 0.01%
4) Decrease in mailing time	= 0.9 days
5 Decrease in processing time	= 0.5 days

These data enable the calculation of the amount by which the cash is increased for the firm, or

300 payments/day x $2,000/payment x (0.09 +0.5) days = $840,000

This increase in cash balances, if invested at 0.01 percent per day, would yield $84 per day for the firm. If the bank charges $0.16 to process each check (or 300 x $0.16 = $45), then the net gain to the bank after fees is $39 per day, or $1,170 per month (30 days x $45 = $1,170).

Lock box systems are an excellent example of how banks and firms can work together for their mutual advantage. However, because digital payments are becoming widespread, the number of payments made by paper check is declining.

FDIC INSURED DEPOSITS

One thing that differentiates banks from other types of financial institutions that offer competing products and services is that bank deposits are insured by the Federal Deposit Insurance Corporation (FDIC). The standard insurance for each depositor amount is $250,000 in an FDIC-insured bank or savings association, for each account ownership category, due to failure of the institution. "FDIC insurance covers all types of deposits received at an insured bank, including deposits in a checking account, negotiable order of withdrawal (NOW) account, savings account, money market deposit account (MMDA), time deposit such as a certificate of deposit (CD), or an official item issued by a bank, such as a cashier's check or money order."[2] It does NOT cover stock investments, bond investments, mutual funds, life insurance policies, annuities, U.S. Treasury or municipal securities, and safe deposit boxes or their contents.

INVESTMENT PRODUCTS

As noted in Chapter 15, the 1999 Gramm-Leach-Bliley Act ended the 1933 Glass-Steagal Act's prohibitions on commercial banks directly participating in investment banking and insurance. Basically, it endorsed the formation of Citigroup that was formed by the merger of Citicorp (a banking organization) and Travelers Group (an insurance organization) in 1998, and the formation of hundreds of other financial holding companies.[3] However, following the September 11, 2001 terrorist attacks on the World Trade Center in New York City, Citigroup spun off the Travelers Property and Casualty insurance underwriting business in 2002 due to large losses both from the attack and natural disasters. Citigroup sold the life insurance and annuities underwriting business to MetLife in 2005. Today, Citicorp "sells" all forms of insurance but does not "underwrite" the policies.[4]

Citigroup is a *large, complex financial organization* (LCFO) that brings together banking, insurance, and investments. As an LCFO, it had total assets in excess of $1.8 trillion in June, 2015, making it the third largest bank holding company in the U.S. after JP Morgan Chase and Co., with assets of $2.4 trillion. and Bank of America Corporation, with assets of $2.2 trillion.[5] Citigroup "has approximately 200 million customer accounts and does business in more than 160 countries and jurisdictions. Citi provides consumers, corporations, governments and institutions with a broad range of financial products and services, including consumer banking and credit, corporate and investment banking, securities brokerage, transaction services, and wealth management."

ANNUITIES

Some banking organizations and their affiliates offer annuities to their customers. An ***annuity*** refers to a schedule of payments at fixed intervals for a stated number of years, or for the duration of the life of the person receiving the payments (the annuitant), or the lives of two or more persons. In addition, an annuity with a *life income with installment certain option* allows income to continue to be paid for a specified period (such as16 years) if the principal beneficiary dies early. Finally, in cash refund annuities, the insurer subtracts from the present value of the annuity at its starting date the total of all payments made to the annuitant at the time of death. Any difference is paid to the beneficiary.

The payout of annuity proceeds can be fixed, providing for a constant stream of income, or variable, where the income can change over time. Another payout option is a lump sum payment instead of an annuity.

Annuities are used to provide tax-deferred income for retirees and for other investment purposes. They are investment products that are subject to investment risks, and they are not guaranteed by the bank offering them, nor are they insured by the FDIC.

SWEEP ACCOUNTS

Sweep accounts are used for the temporary transfer of funds from non-interest bearing transaction accounts into an investment account where the funds earn interest. Usually there is a minimum amount, such as $5,000, in the account, before the funds are swept into the investment account. Funds are returned to the transaction account when they are needed to cover payments. Thus, a small-business customer or wealthy individual who has $100,000 in a demand deposit account each business day might earn $3,000 or more annually if the funds are in an investment account. Large corporations actively manage their own transaction accounts.

Some banks give their customers a choice of having the funds in the sweep account invested in an FDIC-insured savings account or in a various money market funds. Banks receive fee income from the mutual fund providers. As noted previously, funds invested in mutual funds are not covered by FDIC insurance.

SYNDICATED/SHARED NATIONAL CREDITS (SNCs)

Commercial banks have learned from investment banks that syndication can be profitable. When underwriting new securities issues, a group of investment banking firms, called a ***syndicate***, buy stocks and bonds from the corporation or governments issuing the new securities, and then sells them to the public. The originating investment bank is the syndicate manager. Each firm in the syndicate agrees to buy a stipulated amount of the new issue, and their profit is the difference between the price paid the issuer of the security and the price at which it is sold to investors. Commercial banks have applied that same strategy to underwrite large commercial loans and loan commitments that they either hold or sell to other financial institutions, such as small banks that buy parts of syndicated loans to diversify their portfolios. "A ***shared national credit*** (SNC) is any loan or formal loan commitment, and any asset such as real estate, stocks, notes, bonds, and debentures taken as debts previously contracted, extended to borrowers by a federally supervised institution, its subsidiaries, and affiliates, that aggregates to $20 million or more and is shared by three or more unaffiliated federally supervised institutions, or a portion of which is sold to two or more unaffiliated federally supervised institutions." [7]

In 1977, the Board of Governors of the Federal Reserve System, the Federal Deposit Insurance Corporation, and the Office of the Comptroller of the Currency established a "Program" to review and classify SNCs made by U.S. banks, foreign banking organizations (FBOs), and nonbank institutions. In 2015, the total volume of outstanding SNCs was $1.9 trillion. U.S. banks accounted for 43 percent of the commitments, foreign banking organizations accounted for 34 percent, and nonbanks for 23 percent.[8]

TABLE 16-1 **SNC COMMITMENTS**

Share of Total Commitments	2015
U.S. Banks	43%
FBOs	34%
Nonbanks	23%

Source: "Shared National Credits Program, 2015 Review," Board of Governors of the Federal Reserve System, FDIC, OCC, November, 2015, Table 1.

PRIVATE WEALTH MANAGEMENT

Wealth management refers to custom tailored services provided to high net worth individuals to help manage their assets and estates. Because it is only available to high net worth individuals, it is also called private banking by some banks. For example, "As a client of Wells Fargo Private Bank, you can expect: Unmatched personal attention from one of the nation's leading providers of financial services and wealth management for high-net-worth individuals and families."[9] BNY Mellon says that, "For more than two centuries, we have provided private banking services for the nation's wealthiest individuals and families. From checking and savings programs to sophisticated financing structures, we have responded to the evolving needs of our clients with innovative solutions and unmatched personal service."[10]

Deutsche Bank (Germany) and others use the term "Wealth Management."[11] Deutsche Bank states that "Your personal client advisor understands your investment preferences and family environment in order to meet your expectations and deliver what we stand for: lasting value for our clients."

Similarly, UBS bank of Switzerland "offers high net worth and affluent individuals around the world a complete range of tailored advice and investment services ... UBS Investment Bank provides corporate, institutional, and wealth management clients with expert advice, innovative financial solutions, outstanding execution and comprehensive access to the world's capital markets."

Needless to say, banks providing private banking services for high net worth individuals earn substantial fee income.

Caveat Emptor (let the buyer beware). Investment, insurance, and annuity products are not FDIC insured, or guaranteed by any Federal Government Agency, and they may go down in value.[13]

TRUST SERVICES

Trusts were created during the crusades. When English knights went in search of the Holy Grail, someone had to manage their land and property. Women had no legal standing at that time, so the knight's property was put in trust for someone else to manage. Over the years, common law recognized trusts. Today a trust is a legal entity that can hold and manage assets for one of more beneficiaries for as long as the trust exists. All trusts have the same general structure. A trust is established by a "grantor" (the creator of the trust) who transfers assets to a trust that is managed by the "trustee" for the benefit of the "beneficiaries" in accordance with the terms of the trust agreement. The trustee may be an individual, a trust institution such as a ***trust company*** or trust department, or both could be co-trustees. The trustee receives fee income for managing the trust. The amount of fee income depends on the market value of the trust and the services provided, and there is no capital requirement for trust departments.

Most of the fee income comes from investment management, administration and custody services, and benefits consulting.

Trust institutions also act as "agents" for trustees. For example, the trustee for a corporate employee benefit program hires a trust institution as an agent to invest and manage the funds. The trustee will tell the agent how the funds are to be managed, and the agent carries out the orders for a fee. However, the agent does not have the same fiduciary responsibility as a trustee when managing the funds. For example, if the trustee tells the agent to invest all of the funds in one volatile stock, the agent will do so. If the trust institution was the trustee for those funds, it would have to invest the funds prudently, taking into account risk, diversification, and other factors.

Trust institutions usually are organized into two or three lines of business. One line of business deals with employee benefit programs, another with personal trusts and estates, and the third with corporate trusts. Personal trusts manage assets for individuals and their beneficiaries. Corporate trusts, for example, act as trustees for bond issues, and they are responsible for dispensing interest payments to bondholders, maintaining escrow accounts, and other related tasks.

The employee benefit line of business deals with deferred compensation plans. The three principal types of deferred compensation are 1) profit sharing plans, 2) defined benefit plans, and 3) defined contribution plans such as the popular 401(k) plans. The funds from defined contribution plans can be invested in mutual funds and other investments.

Trusts are not limited to financial institutions. The federal government is the trustee for funds that have been established by law. The federal old-age, survivors and disability insurance fund, Medicare, and federal supplemental insurance are the largest funds they manage.

Table 16-2 shows the largest institutions by trust assets as of 3Q 2015:

TABLE 16-2 LARGEST INSTITUTIONS BY TRUST ASSETS ($ BILLIONS)

1.	State Street Bank and Trust Company	$6,722
2.	The Bank of New York Mellon	$1,842
3.	The Northern Trust Company	$1,497
4.	Wells Fargo Bank, National Association	$1,037
5.	JPMorgan Chase Bank, National Association	$1,003

Source: FDIC Data, American Bankers Association, https://www.aba.com/Tools/Research/Documents/Top25InstitutionsbyTrustAssets.pdf

TYPES OF TRUSTS

Business

Trusts can be created for any purpose that is legal. Trusts are used for business, investment, and estate management. In terms of historical development, trusts were a widely used form of corporate organization by which several corporations engaged in the same line of business formed a trust to conduct their business without having to merge. In the 1870s and 1880s, the "trusts" were business monopolies in oil, coal, tobacco, and other industries. These monopolies, and their anti-competitive behavior, gave rise to the passage the Sherman Antitrust Act of 1890. This was the first of a series of acts that dealt with antitrust activities. Others acts include the Clayton Act and the Federal Trade Commission Act of 1914, the Robinson-Patman Act of 1936, and the Celler Antimerger Act of 1950. Section 7 of the Clayton Act prohibited one firm from acquiring the stock of a competitor when the effect was to lesson competition. The Celler Act strengthened Section 7 of the Clayton Act by prohibiting one firm from acquiring the assets of competitors when the effect is to reduce competition. Bank and other types of mergers involve both stock and asset acquisitions, and bank mergers are subject to antitrust scrutiny before they are approved.

Today, holding companies and consortiums have replaced trusts as common forms of business organization. For example, bank holding companies control most of the bank assets in the United States. A consortium is any association or partnership. Consortium also is defined as an association of financial institutions for effecting a venture requiring extensive financial resources, especially in international finance.

A consortium of some of the largest banks in the world and a technology vendor established Global Trust Enterprise in 1999 for the purpose of providing businesses with a single electronic identity that they can use in electronic commerce. Global Trust then formed a legal entity called "IdenTrust" that vouches for the identity of trading parties -- business customers of banks -- doing business on the internet.-The banks involved in IdenTrust include ABN Amro, Bank of America, Bankers Trust, Barclays Bank, CIBC, Chase Manhattan, Citigroup, Deutsche Bank, Hypo Vereinsbank, and Sanwa Bank.

Real Estate Investment Trusts (REITS)

The ***Real Estate Investment Trust (REIT)*** is a financial device used by investors to buy shares in a trust that owns and may operate income-producing real estate.[14] They are required to distribute at least 90 percent of their taxable income to shareholders annually in the form of dividends to their shareholders, who pay the income taxes on the dividends. There are three different types of REITS. Equity REITS own and operate income-producing real estate. Mortgage REITS lend funds to the owners and operators of income-producing real estate. Hybrid REITS both own income-producing real estate and lend money to real estate owners and operators. Some REITS specialize in particular types of properties, such as shopping centers, office buildings, or multi-family residential properties (apartments). A number of REITs are actively traded on major stock exchanges. There are about 224 public and privately held REITS in the U.S.

Trust Company

A *trust company* is a corporation formed for the purpose of taking, accepting, and executing all lawful trusts committed to it, and acting as trustee, executor, guardian, fiscal agent, transfer agent for stocks and bonds, wealth management, and the like. The U.S. Trust Company of New York was the nation's first trust company, and it was established in 1853.[15] It is a wealth management company providing investment management, fiduciary and private banking services to affluent individuals, families and institutions nationwide through its offices in California, Connecticut, Delaware, Florida, Minnesota, New Jersey, North Carolina, Oregon, Pennsylvania, Texas, Virginia, and Washington, D.C.

In 2000, U.S. Trust Corporation was acquired by The Charles Schwab Corporation -- a company that is known primarily for its investment services. Subsequently, it was sold to Bank of America in 2007. Bank of America also owns Merrill Lynch, which provides wealth management and investment services.

Bank of America's Global Wealth and Investment Management (GWIM) "... consists of two primary businesses: Merrill Lynch Global Wealth Management (MLGWM) and U.S. Trust, Bank of America Private Wealth Management (U.S. Trust). MLGWM's advisory business provides a high-touch client experience through a network of financial advisors focused on clients with over $250,000 in total investable assets. MLGWM provides tailored solutions to meet our clients' needs through a full set of brokerage, banking and retirement products. U.S. Trust, together with MLGWM's Private Banking & Investments Group, provides comprehensive wealth management solutions targeted to high net worth and ultra high net worth clients, as well as customized solutions to meet clients' wealth structuring, investment management, trust and banking needs, including specialty asset management services."[16] Collectively, they produced $18 billion in revenue for Bank of America in 2014.[17] Bank of America Corporation had $2.1 trillion in assets in 2014.[18]

Many banks have established trust departments within their banks in order to provide additional services to their customers, such as estate planning. Trusts are used by individuals for estate planning in order to distribute their assets and to reduce their estate taxes.[19] [20]

Several types of widely used trusts are listed below.

Revocable Living Trust

A revocable living trust (also known as "living trust," or "inter vivos" trust) allows the grantor to retain control over the assets during his or her lifetime. All trust assets are included in the estate for tax purposes.

Credit Shelter Trust

A credit shelter trust is designed to take full advantage of estate tax credits for individuals. The maximum estate tax exclusion amount was $5.43 million in 2015.

Marital Trust

A marital trust shelters from the estate tax any amount that is transferred to the surviving spouse in trust for their benefit if the trust qualifies for the marital deduction.

Irrevocable Trust

Trust assets in an irrevocable trust may be excluded from estate tax by the estate tax exclusion amount. In addition, irrevocable trusts are used to own life insurance policies to avoid estate taxes and to protect trust assets from creditors.

Other Types of Trusts

Several other types of trusts are listed here to illustrate other uses. This listing of trusts in not complete.

Charitable Trust: These are trusts that are designed to benefit particular charities, educational institutions, or religions.

Trust Deposit: Money or property is deposited with a bank, but not commingled with other property or deposits of the bank. The money or property is to be returned in kind to the depositor, or for some special purpose such as payment of a particular debt obligation of the depositor.

Unit Investment Trusts: Unit investment trusts are used for investment purposes. A unit investment trust (UIT) is a registered investment company that buys and holds a relatively fixed portfolio of stocks, bonds, and other securities until the trust's termination date. When the trust is dissolved, the proceeds are paid to the shareholders. The fact that UITs have relatively fixed portfolios makes them different from mutual funds that have portfolios that are actively traded.

The reason for the relatively fixed portfolio is that stock UITs are structured to replicate the performance of a particular stock index, and they hold only the stocks in that index. From time to time, stocks in the index may change, and then the portfolio is changed accordingly. For example, SPDRs (pronounced "Spiders") which stands for Standard & Poor's Depository Receipts, is linked to the S&P 500 stock index. SPDRs are Exchange Traded Funds (ETFs) that are traded on the American Stock Exchange under the ticker symbol "SPY." **Exchange Traded Funds, (ETFs)** are a type of exchange-traded investment product that must register with the SEC under the 1940 Act as either an open-end investment company (generally known as "funds") or a unit investment trust.[21]

SPDRs are designed to provide investment results that correspond to the price and yield performance of the S&P 500 stock Index. SPDRs compete with index mutual funds, such as the Vanguard Index 500 fund, that also tries to match the performance of the Standard and Poor's 500 Stock Index. SPDRs and other UITs are generally used by active traders, while index mutual funds tend to be used by passive investors.

Similarly, Diamonds Trust Series 1 is an index-based product that mirrors the Dow Jones Industrial Average and trades on the American Stock Exchange, and there are UITs that mirror the technology sector, the energy sector, and so on.

SUMMARY

The range of financial services offered by banking organizations extends far beyond taking deposits and making loans. This chapter examined a few of the many services offered to both wholesale and retail customers. On the wholesale side of the business, banks provide cash management, data processing, loan syndications, sweep accounts, and selected trust services to business concerns and financial institutions. On the retail side of the business, they provide FDIC- insured deposits, annuities, mutual funds, sweep accounts, and selected trust services. This listing of services is not complete. But it is sufficient to demonstrate that banks, viewed collectively, are financial supermarkets and that they are becoming increasingly dependent on fee income. As electronic banking becomes more pervasive, banks will continue to expand both their wholesale and retail services.

KEY TERMS

annuities
bank holding company
cash management
Check 21 Act
controlled disbursement
Exchange Traded Funds (EFTs)
FDIC insured deposits
financial holding company
large, complex financial organization (LCFO)
late trading
lock box
market timing
private banking
Real Estate Investment Trusts (REITS)
shared national credits (SNCs)
Standard & Poor's Depository Receipts (SPDR)
syndicate (loans/securities)
sweep accounts
trade finance
trust company
trust services
types of trusts:
- *revocable living trust*
- *credit shelter trust*
- *marital trust*
- *irrevocable trust*
- *charitable trust*
- *trust deposit*
- *unit investment trust (UIT)*

wealth management
zero balance account

QUESTIONS

16. 1 Can bank holding companies engage in any financial service that is closely related and incident to banking?

16-2. In cash management services, what is meant by "cash concentration?"

16-3. What is "controlled disbursement?"

16-4. Explain the use of lock boxes.

16-5. What type of data processing services can bank holding companies provide?

16-6. What bank products and services are FDIC insured?

16-7. What does the Glass-Steagal Act of 1933 have to say about commercial banks and investment banking?

16-8. Some banks are selling annuities for insurance companies. What is an annuity, and why are they doing it.

16.9. Are Money Market Mutual Funds as safe as bank deposits? Explain your position.

16-10. What is a sweep account?

16-11. What is loan syndication?

16-12. What is the general structure of a "trust?"

16.13. Explain why trusts are used in estate planning.

CASE: INFORMATION, PLEASE

Jeremy Lincoln called the bank's board of directors meeting to order. The first item on the agenda concerned the wealth of information that the bank had about its customers, especially those that made extensive use of their credit and debit cards. Jeremy gave each of the board members a copy of the Consumer Data (Table 16-3) listing some examples of the type of information that the bank has or can obtain for each of its customers.

"Ladies and gentlemen," he said. "What do you think is the best way to use this information? First, I know that we can use the information internally to improve the marketing of our services and to open new market opportunities for us. There is no controversy about that. However, there is some controversy about our second option. We can sell the information to various types of vendors who can use it for their own marketing purposes, providing that our customers give us permission to do so. As you know, the Gramm-Leach-Bliley Act gives consumers of financial institutions the right to "opt out" of sharing some of their personal financial information with unrelated third parties. But if they don't opt out, we are entitled to sell their data, and this would bring in a lot of money over the years to come, which would make our stockholders very happy. After all, we are a publicly held company, and one of our key objectives is to maximize shareholder wealth. On the other, selling such information might irritate our customers, especially those who have a strong belief in the right of privacy. I know that there are a lot of our customers who believe that what they buy and do with their money is their thing and they want to keep it private. Those are the issues that we must consider. What should we do with all this information – protect it or sell it? Are there other alternatives? Tell me what you think."

TABLE 16-2 Consumer Data

Descriptive data	Name, address, phone number
	Income and debts, and payments history
Transactions	Amounts spent, purchase dates, vendors, category of goods acquired
Trigger events	Birthdays, relocation, birth of child

ENDNOTES

1. For more information, see Federal Reserve Regulation Y. 12 CFR 225. It regulates the acquisition and control of banks and bank holding companies by companies and individuals, defines and regulates the nonbanking activities in which bank holding companies (including financial holding companies) and foreign banking organizations with United States operations may engage, and establishes the minimum ratios of capital to assets that bank holding companies must maintain.

2. FDIC, "Accounts Covered by the FDIC," "https://www.fdic.gov/deposit/covered/insured.html; For additional information, see; FDIC, "Understanding Deposit Insurance," https://www.fdic.gov/deposit/deposits/

3. For a listing of Financial Holding Companies, see the Board of Governors of the Federal Reserve System, Financial Holding Companies: http://www.federalreserve.gov/generalinfo/fhc/.

4. "Citigroup," From Wikipedia, https://en.wikipedia.org/wiki/Citigroup

5. "Holding Companies with Assets Greater Than $10 Billion," National Information Center, http://www.ffiec.gov/nicpubweb/nicweb/HCSGreaterThan10B.aspx

6. "Citi at a Glance," http://www.citigroup.com/citi/about/citi_at_a_glance.html

7. "Shared National Credits Program, 2015 Review," Board of Governors of the Federal Reserve System, FDIC, OCC, November, 2015.

8. Ibid.

9. Wells Fargo: The Private Bank, https://www.wellsfargo.com/jump/the-private-bank/conversations.

10. BNY Mellon: "We're the oldest private bank in the U.S. Why would you want your money anywhere else?" http://www.bnymellonwealthmanagement.com/

11. For details, see: https://deutscheawm.com/Our-Businesses/Wealth

12. For details see: https://www.ubs.com/us/en.html

13. Private Wealth Management, Regions, https://www.regions.com/personal_banking/investment_management_consulting_services.rf

14. For additional information, see the National Association of Real Estate Investment Trusts, NAREIT, at http://www.nareit.org/home.cfm

15. For additional information, see U.S. Trust, http://www.ustrust.com

16. Bank of America Corporation, 2014 Annual Report, p.39.

17. Ibid.

18. Federal Financial Institutions Examination Council, National Information Center, "Holding Companies with Assets Greater Than $10 Billion Dollars," 12/31/14, http://www.ffiec.gov/nicpubweb/nicweb/HCSGreaterThan10B.aspx

19. For additional information about estate taxes, see: IRS Estate Tax, and Form 706; https://www.irs.gov/Businesses/Small-Businesses-&-Self-Employed/Estate-Tax.

'For decedents who died in 2015, Form 706 must be filed by the executor of the estate of every U.S. citizen or resident:

a. Whose gross estate, plus adjusted taxable gifts and specific exemption, is more than $5,430,000; or,

b. Whose executor elects to transfer the *Deceased Spousal Unused Exclusion* (DSUE) amount to the surviving spouse, regardless of the size of the decedent's gross estate.

20. For information about FDIC deposit insurance coverage for all types of accounts, including trust accounts, see: FDIC, "Your Insured Deposits," https://www.fdic.gov/deposit/deposits/brochures/your_insured_deposits-english.html#RTA

21. For more information about ETFs, see: Securities and Exchange Commission, "Investor Bulletin: Exchange-Traded-Funds (ETFs)," http://www.sec.gov/investor/alerts/etfs.pdf

22. FDIC Consumer News, "Test Your Deposit Insurance IQ," Winter 2013/2014, https://www.fdic.gov/consumers/consumer/news/cnwin1314/insurancequiz.html

APPENDIX A: FDIC INSURANCE COVERAGE

What does FDIC insurance coverage mean? Is it $250,000 per account? Or does it mean $250,000 per person? Or does it mean $250,000 in one bank or in all of the banks where an individual has deposits? The rules covering FDIC- insured deposits are extensive and confusing. A complete listing of the rules and discussion of them is beyond the scope of this book. Nevertheless, the following true or false statements and answers provide some insight into FDIC deposit insurance coverage

Do you think you know how FDIC insurance works? Take this quiz and find out.

1. If your FDIC-insured bank or savings association fails, the $250,000 federal insurance coverage would include both the money you've deposited and the interest you've earned.

True. If your insured institution fails, FDIC insurance will cover your deposit accounts, including principal and any accrued interest, up to the insurance limit.

2. Historically, insured funds are available to depositors shortly after the closing of an insured bank.

True. The FDIC protects insured depositors by arranging an immediate sale to a healthy bank or paying depositors by check within a few days after a bank closing. And remember that since the start of the FDIC in 1933, no depositor has ever lost a penny of insured deposits. Note: Certificates of deposit (CDs) purchased or arranged through a broker may take longer to be paid because the FDIC may need to obtain the broker's records to determine insurance coverage.

3. FDIC insurance protects more than just deposits. If you purchase stocks, bonds, mutual funds or annuities at an FDIC-insured bank, the FDIC also will protect those investments against loss. True or False?

False. The FDIC does not insure the money you invest in stocks, bonds, mutual funds, life insurance policies, annuities or municipal securities, even if you purchased these products from an insured bank. The FDIC also does not insure U.S. Treasury bills, bonds or notes, although those investments are backed by the full faith and credit of the United States government.

4.The basic insurance limit is $250,000 per depositor per bank but it is possible to qualify for more coverage under the FDIC's rules. True or False?

True. You may qualify for more than $250,000 in coverage at one insured institution if you own deposit accounts in different ownership categories as defined by the FDIC. The most common ownership categories are single, retirement, joint, and revocable trust accounts (accounts in which the owner retains full control over the money during his or her lifetime). Your deposits in each of those categories are separately insured to $250,000. If certain conditions are met, your revocable trust accounts are insured up to $250,000 for each beneficiary. For more details, consult the FDIC publication "Your Insured Deposits".

5. You're thinking about taking a $300,000 lump-sum, eligible rollover distribution from your employer's qualified pension plan and depositing it into two different IRAs at your bank. That's safe to do because each IRA would be separately insured to $250,000. True or False?

False. All of your self-directed retirement accounts (you decide where the money is deposited) at the same insured bank are added together and the total is insured up to $250,000. Opening multiple IRAs or adding beneficiaries will not increase insurance coverage

6. You want to open a "payable-on-death" account naming your two children as the beneficiaries. Under the FDIC's insurance rules, this account qualifies for $500,000 of insurance — $250,000 for each eligible beneficiary — not $250,000 in total. True or False?

True. In general, the owner of payable-on-death (POD) accounts and other revocable trust accounts at a bank is insured up to $250,000 for each "eligible beneficiary." To be eligible, a beneficiary must be a living person, a charity or a nonprofit organization (the latter two must be valid under IRS rules). If the owner names five or fewer beneficiaries, he or she will qualify for $250,000 of coverage for each different beneficiary named. Different rules apply, though, if there are six or more beneficiaries. Using our example, and assuming this is the only POD account you have at this bank, if you establish a POD account naming your two children as beneficiaries it would be insured up to $500,000.

7. You have three different joint accounts at the same bank -- one for $250,000 with your spouse, another for $250,000 with your sister, and a third for $250,000 with your brother. Because you own each account with a different person, each account qualifies for $250,000 of insurance. True or False?

False. For each $250,000 joint account, your ownership interest would be $125,000, because the interests of the co-owners are presumed equal. This means your interest in all three joint accounts would be $375,000. But under the FDIC's rules, each person's interest in all joint accounts at the same institution is insured up to a combined total of $250,000. In this example, you'd be uninsured in the amount of $125,000.

Chapter 17

Electronic Banking

After reading this chapter, you will be able to:

- Evaluate the role of electronic banking in the retail (small dollar) payments systems
- Understand the wide variety of financial services provided by electronic banking
- Describe the role of electronic banking in the wholesale (large dollar) payments system
- Compare the different types of settlement systems for financial transactions
- Identify payment systems risks
- Explain why paper checks and dollars will be around for a long time

PAYMENT SYSTEMS AND FINANCIAL SERVICES

ELECTRONIC BANKING

Electronic banking is any banking activity accessed by electronic means such as the internet, payment systems, and credit cards. Both commercial banks and non-bank financial institutions offer electronic banking services such as accessing accounts, paying bills, transferring funds, money market accounts, transacting business, obtaining information, and so on. Banks might provide these services in-house, or contract with outside providers.[1] CheckFreePay and Intuit QuickBooks, for example, are outside providers of payment services that contract with banks.[2]

Large traditional "brick and mortar" banks, such as Bank of America, Citibank, and Wells Fargo, have their own web pages, and they offer the same on-line services as internet banks, plus other products and services that require a physical presence, such as ATMs and safety deposit boxes. Most of the banks focus on retail business to consumer (b2c) banking services, and an increasing number are developing business-to-business (b2b) banking services. Along this line, some have formed strategic alliances with technology companies to develop b2b exchanges and market places.[3]

Another important aspect of electronic banking is that customers can shop for banking services and compare rates online at Bankrate (http://wwwbankrate.com) and Lendingtree (http://lendingtree.com).

Most people believe that electronic banking began with the development of computers and the internet. That is not the case. The first use of electronic banking in the United States was in the 1870s when Western Union telegraphs were used to transfer funds from one part of the country to another.

Another form of electronic banking is the ***automated teller machine (ATM)*** that came into use in 1960s. Since then the use of ATMs in the U.S. and globally has become widespread. More will said about ATMs shortly.

In 1995, Security First Network Bank (SFNB) became the first fully transactional internet bank. In 1998, it became part of the Royal Bank Financial Group (Canada), with assets of $180 billion and 9.5 million customers.[4] Since then, the number of banks offering internet services has grown rapidly. Today, the use of internet banking has become widespread, and includes not only domestic banks but also credit unions.[5]

The growth of digital banking and transfers of funds and mobile payments used for banking has reduced the need for cash and branch banks in: a) *retail and wholesale payments and services* made by individuals and businesses, b) *wholesale*, or *large-dollar transfers* made mostly by banks, businesses, and governments, and c) *other services*.

"A recent survey by the Federal Reserve Board concluded that, as of December, 2014, about 81 percent of U.S. banks offered *mobile banking services* to their customers and that one-third of their customers used these services. The overwhelming percentage of banks offering mobile banking is driven, in part, by the 87 percent of U.S. adults who own a mobile phone, of which 71 percent are smartphones."[6] The term "mobile banking" includes smart phones, cell phones, and other mobile communications devices. The "Internet, mobile, and contactless payments can be used alone or together to facilitate electronic transactions, further reducing the use of paper checks. The use of currency is expected to retain some appeal because of its anonymity; however, the substitution of electronic payment vehicles for cash micro payments (transactions under $5.00) is expected to increase."[7]

Fifty-two percent of smartphone owners with a bank account have used their phones to check account balances, transfer funds, and deposit checks.[8]

And in 2015, more bank customers used their mobile banking on a weekly basis than visited their branch banks.[9]

One consequence of the increased use of mobile and electronic access to banks is that many branch banks are underperforming. A typical U.S. branch bank requires at least 5,000 transactions per month to cover the cost of operations. A recent study estimated that about one-third of typical regional banks fall below that level.[10] A 2014 study revealed a decline in the number of branches as banks try to trim costs as a result of the increased use of mobile and electronic banking.[11] However, as shown in Table 17-1, while some large banks trimmed the number of branches, others increased them. Branch banks provide bankers with valuable information about borrowers and local economic conditions; therefore, they "are not likely to be done away with any time soon." [12]

TABLE 17-1 TOP 10 BANKS RANKED BY NUMBER OF BRANCH LOCATIONS

Bank Name	Number of Branches June 30, 2012	Number of Branches June 30, 2015
1. Wells Fargo Bank	6,325	6,252
2. JPMorgan Chase Bank	5,701	5,580
3. Bank of America	5,693	4,889
4. U.S. Bank	3,124	3,220
5. PNC Bank	3,062	2,797
6. Branch Banking and Trust	1,888	2,180
7. Regions Bank	1,731	1,643
8. SunTrust Bank	1,692	1,474
9. Fifth Third Bank	1,374	1,344
10. TD Bank	1,312	1,318

Source: US Bank Locations, Banks Ranked by Number of Branches, http://www.usbanklocations.com/bank-rank/number-of-branches.html

Most of retail payments and transfers in the United States are processed by banks that then become large-value transactions between banks.[13] The two primary domestic payments systems for interbank large dollar transfers between banks are the *Fedwire Funds Transfer (Fedwire®)* which is operated by Federal Reserve Banks, and the *Clearing House for Interbank Payments (CHIPS)* which is a privately operated real-time payments system associated with bank transfers of funds and securities transactions. It also plays a large role in payments related to international transactions. *SWIFT* is a private international communications link that provides a messaging infrastructure between banks making payments. It is not a payments system. *Informal Value Transfer Systems (IVTS)* (such as *hawalas*) refers to currency or value transfer systems that operate informally to transfer money as a business. They may legally operate as a Money Service Business subject to applicable state and federal laws. Persons living in the United States may use them to transfer funds to their home countries and to places that are not served by formal banks. Because IVTS do not have the same record keeping and identification requirements as banks, they have raised concerns about money laundering and financing terrorism.

Digital payments made to many small and mid-sized businesses require the use of *Third-Party-Payment-Processers and Senders (TPPPs)* to provide electronic payment services that do not have access to such services.[14] However, lack of regulatory scrutiny over TPPPs makes them vulnerable to money laundering, identity theft, and fraud, requiring greater monitoring by financial institutions.

Some transactions require a digital signature. *"The Electronic Signatures in Global and National Commerce Act (E-Sign Act)* signed into law on June 30, 2000, provides a general rule of validity for electronic records and signatures for transactions in or affecting interstate or foreign commerce.[15] The term "electronic" means "technology having electrical, digital, magnetic, wireless, optical, electromagnetic, or similar capabilities... Oral communications shall not qualify as an electronic record." [16]

Another important trend is that credit and debit card use has grown significantly, while the number of check payments has declined.[17] Nevertheless, checks still remain a significant portion of noncash payments. The processing and clearing of most checks is done by electronic image exchange, or they are converted to *Automated Clearing House (ACH)* payments. The Automated Clearing House (ACH) is the primary system that agencies use for *electronic funds transfer (EFT)* where payments are made electronically, without having to use paper checks.[18] Each year, the ACH moves more than $40 trillion and nearly 23 billion electronic financial transactions, and it supports more than 90 percent of the total value of all electronic payments in the U.S.[19]

Blockchains are the latest technology in payments systems. In a blockchain network of computers, data about financial transactions is stored on many computers (run by individuals called "miners"). Every computer is in contact (a "node") with all of the other computers in the network, so that everyone shares the same information about payments being paid and received in near real time -- when it happens. Thus, participants can see when payments have been made and received. The information in the blockchain is secured by digital signatures. Blockchains are being examined by some of the World's leading banks, such as JP Morgan, Citibank, Royal Bank of Scotland (RBS), Goldman Sachs, Barclays, and others.[20]

ELECTRONIC BANKING SERVICES

RETAIL SERVICES

Electronic banking provides a wide variety of services to both retail and wholesale customers (see Table 17-2). *Retail customers* refers to individuals and wholesale to businesses of all sizes. First, electronic banking is convenient because consumers are no longer bound by geography or traditional 9 A.M. to 4 P.M. banking hours to obtain financial services. They can use the internet and cell phones or other electronic devices 24/7 (24 hours a day, seven days a week) from any location to obtain financial services. In addition, they have privacy and security. However, there are some privacy of information issues as well as security issues concerning fraud and cybercrimes.[21] These issues are not limited to electronic payments. The channels of delivery include automatic teller machines (ATMs), smartphone phone banking, and other forms of computer-based banking. To increase their security, some banks are offering biometric measures to authenticate customers.[22] For example, Citibank offers voice authentication that starts with a brief sample of the customer's voice; then that voice is matched to more than 100 different characteristics on prerecorded data.

Account aggregation is another convenience of electronic banking. ***Account aggregation*** refers to gathering information from various websites or accounts (i.e., bank, brokerage, credit card) and presenting that information to customers in a consolidated format.

TABLE 17-2 COMMON ELECTRONIC BANKING SERVICES

Retail Services	Wholesale Services
Account management	Account management
Bill payment and presentment	Cash management
Opening new accounts	Small business loan applications, approvals, and advances
Consumer wire transfers	Commercial wire transfers
Investment/brokerage services	Business-to-business payments
Loan applications and approval	Employee benefits/pension administration
Account aggregation	

Source: E-Banking, IT Examination Handbook, Federal Financial Institutions Examination Council, August, 2003, Table 1. For more information, including presentations, see: http://ithandbook.ffiec.gov/presentations.aspx

Last, but not least, the finality of electronic payments such as credit cards is generally better than for checks. ***Payment finality*** is a legal concept that specifies the circumstances under which one type of financial claim extinguishes another.[23] Cash payments for goods and services are final. The debt is cleared upon the payment of cash. Checks are different. Suppose that Joe Smith (the payor) sends a check to the phone company (the payee) to pay his phone bill. Joe assumes that when the check is cashed, the debt is extinguished as long as there are sufficient funds in the account. The payment is final. However, if there are not sufficient funds in his account, or it contains an invalid account number, the check is returned and the payment is not final. The rules for credit card payments are such that the payee must go through more steps to collect the funds. For example, the payee must have a merchant account with the credit card company, verify the customer's identity, obtain authorization for the payment, and other procedures. Collectively, the procedures tend to increase the chances of payment finality of credit card transactions.

WHOLESALE SERVICES

Selected electronic banking products and services for the wholesale market are listed in Table 17-2. Other services include derivatives trading, foreign exchange, and global treasury services on-line for corporate customers, letters of credit and other wholesale banking services including securities and cash-transaction reporting, and more.

Although small business may be considered "retail," the point here is that banks are offering an expanding range of electronic-based services to all of their customers. For example, electronic check conversion allows a business to accept a paper check at the point of sale or elsewhere, and convert it into an electronic payment. The customer signs a receipt authorizing the merchant to present the check to the customer's bank electronically, and deposit the funds in the merchant's account. Thus, the check is used as a source of information (check number, account number, and bank's number), and that information is used to process the electronic payment. The *Check Clearing for the 21st Century Act* (PL 108-100), commonly called the *Check 21 Act*, permits depository institutions to make digital images of checks, truncate the original paper check, and process the payment information electronically. Check payments can also be made through a smartphones.

AUTOMATED TELLER MACHINES (ATMs)

There are three types of ATM systems in use. 1. The first ATMs were *proprietary systems* that were operated by the institutions that purchased or leased the equipment. Today they are less prevalent as 2. *shared/regional systems* and 3. *national/international systems* have become increasingly popular.[24]

The shared/regional and national/international systems have network externalities. *Network externalities* means that the benefit one person gets from using the system depends on how many others are using it. The internet is a good example. The usefulness of the internet increases as more people use it. The networks make it possible to use ATMs anywhere in the world for cash advances that can be obtained by using ATM cards, debit cards, and credit cards. Many ATM cards can be used as debit cards.

Customers using ATMs are generally required to have a *personal identification number (PIN)* to access the machines. PIN numbers are four-digit numbers that can be used on ATM machines and point-of-sale (POS) terminals. Merchants with POS terminals prefer debit cards with PIN numbers to those that require signatures because it costs less to process. For example, a $40 PIN debt transaction has an interchange of $0.18 compared to a charge of $0.60 for a signature transaction.[25] The ***interchange rates*** are paid to the card issuers for clearing the transactions. MasterCard and Visa credit cards may change their interchange rates twice per year.[26] The fees vary depending where the cards are used, whether the card is present, and other factors.

Regulations for debit card interchange and routing fees are regulated by the Federal Reserve. "Regulation II (Debit Card Interchange Fees and Routing) establishes standards for assessing whether a debit card interchange fee received by a debit card issuer for an electronic debit transaction is reasonable and proportional to the costs incurred by the issuer with respect to the transaction. The standards allow for a fraud-prevention adjustment to an issuer's debit card interchange fee if the issuer develops and implements policies and procedures reasonably designed to achieve the fraud-prevention standards set out in the rule. Certain small debit card issuers, government-administered payment programs and reloadable general-use prepaid cards are exempt from the interchange fee limitations." [27]

There are different types of ATM machines. Full-service ATM machines perform multiple banking and payments functions as well as dispense cash. At the other end of the spectrum are ATM machines that are exclusively cash dispensers that are being used in supermarkets, gas stations, and elsewhere.

Banks often charge noncustomers fees for using their ATMs. For example, Bank of America customers might be charged for using a non-Bank of America ATM – "Withdrawals, transfers, and balance inquiries from ATMs at other financial institutions in the United States may be assessed a fee. You may also be charged a fee by the ATM operator or any network used. You may be charged a fee for a balance inquiry even if you do not complete a funds transfer. Other account fees may apply to the transaction such as an Excess Withdrawal fee for savings." [28]

Customers using credit cards to obtain cash advances from ATMs are subject to an additional cash advance transaction fee as well as a finance charge and interest on the funds withdrawn. For example, the credit card issuers might charge a cash advance transaction fee of the greater of $3 or 3 percent of each balance transferred. Some credit cards have a maximum cash transaction fee (such as $25) specified for each transaction, while others have no maximum amount. If the cash advance is in a foreign currency, there may be additional costs, such as increasing the exchange rate by one percent.

Consider the following example from the author's monthly billing statement for a \$300 cash advance using a Citibank Gold AAdvantage credit card. [29] There was a finance charge of 3 percent of the amount withdrawn (\$9). The interest rate charged on cash advances (19.99 percent) is substantially higher than the interest rate on purchases (17.15 percent), and the interest charges begin the day the cash is withdrawn. The interest for the billing period was \$3.97. The Annual Percentage Rate (APR) on the cash advance for this billing period was 51.880 percent! The bank computed the APR in the following manner:

$$\text{APR} = \frac{(\text{finance charge} + \text{interest}) \times 12 \text{ months}}{\text{Amount of cash advance}} \qquad (17.1)$$

$$= \frac{(\$9.00 + \$3.97) \times 12}{\$300} = 51.88\%$$

The interest rate on the cash advance accrues daily from the date of the advance until payment is made in full. Therefore, the minimum payment due on the cash advance exceed the amount of interest shown in the monthly statement. The monthly statement listed the finance charge and interest as \$12.97, but the minimum payment required on the cash advance portion of the billing statement was \$16.48. Banks encourage their customers to use cash advances because such transactions yield high returns. Caveat Emptor -- Let the buyer beware.

ELECTRONIC BILL PRESENTATION AND PAYMENT (EBPP)

"Electronic bill presentment and payment (EBPP) - An electronic alternative to traditional bill payment, EBPP allows a merchant or utility to present its customers with an electronic bill and the payer to pay the bill electronically. EBPP systems usually fall within two models: direct and consolidation-aggregation. In the direct model, the merchant or utility generates an electronic version of the consumer's billing information and notifies the consumer of a pending bill, generally via e-mail. The consumer can initiate payment of the electronically presented bill using a variety of payment mechanisms, typically a credit card. In the consolidation-aggregation model, the consumer's bills are consolidated by a consolidator acting on behalf of merchants and utilities (or aggregated on behalf of the consumer), combining data from multiple bills and presenting a single source for the consumer to initiate payment. Some consolidators present bills at their own websites. Typically, most support the aggregation of bills by consumer service providers such an internet portals, financial institutions, and brokerage web sites." [30]

The electronic format is expected to reduce billing costs for billers and to be more convenient for customers. It costs billers about \$0.90 to print and mail bills and to process customer's checks and remittance information.[31] This cost does not include the Federal Reserve's costs of operating the payments system or the other costs associated with clearing small-dollar payments. It is estimated that electronic billing will reduce billers' costs to about \$0.32 per transaction.

EBPP billing requires the billing firm to hire a system operator to present the bill to the customer. The system operator can be a bank or a technology company such as First Data or Microsoft. The operator can post the bills on a website or on an internet portal. This allows the household to view the bills at one convenient internet location. The household must arrange with their bank, the biller's bank, or the system operator for funds to be transferred. After reviewing the bills, the household can direct the payments to be made immediately or at some later date.

Table 17-3 shows a comparison of paper and EBPP payment systems. The electronic system eliminates the use of paper bills, checks, and mail, and it reduces the time and cost incurred presenting bills and collecting payments. Note that the electronic-based system still utilizes the Federal Reserve and clearing houses in the payment process. Many of the clearing houses belong to the Automated Clearinghouse (ACH) network that was established in the 1970s to provide an electronic alternative to the traditional paper-based check clearing systems.[32] Clearing is the process of transmitting and reconciling payment or transfer instructions, confirming payment orders, or the security of instructions prior to settlement.[33] Settlement is the discharge of obligations with respect to the transfer of funds or securities between two or more parties.

TABLE 17-3 COMPARISON OF PAPER AND EBPP SYSTEMS

Step		Paper-based System	Electronic-based System
1	Statement preparation	Printed statement	Electronic file
2	Delivery to customer	Mail	Web site
3	Payment initiation	Customer writes check/mails it to biller	Customer reviews bill, authorizes payment on net
4	Return delivery to biller	Post office delivers check to biller	System operator sends biller a file
5	Updating customer account	open mail, record payment, deposit check	file updated electronically
6	Presentment at the Federal Reserve	Checks delivered to Fed.	Operator forwards payment to clearinghouse
7	Presentment at paying bank	Fed presents check to paying bank	Through clearing house, Fed notifies bank of debit
8	Interbank settlement	Fed debits reserve acct. of customer's bank and credit's biller's bank	Fed debits reserve acct. of customer's bank and credit's biller's bank
9	Debiting and crediting bank accounts	Customer debited and biller credited according to information on paper check	Customer debited and biller credited according to information in electronic file

Source: Based on Lawrence J. Radecki and John Wenniger, "Paying Electronic Bills Electronically," *Current Issues in Economics and Finance*, Federal Reserve Bank of New York, January, 1999.

The conversion from our current paper-based system to an EBPP system faces some obstacles in the United States. Unlike Europe where EBPP is the norm because only two or three institutions dominate each country, there are more than 8,000 financial service providers and hundreds of thousands of billers in the United States, most of whom may not have the technology to provide a seamless network.

From the consumer's point of view, studies have shown that unless consumers are able to receive and pay bills from multiple billers, they will not change their payment habits. Moreover, it is not clear who will be responsible for and have the liability for the integrity of the EBPP system. Thus, a study by the Federal Reserve Bank of New York stated that the "EBPP systems face a chicken and egg problem. If a biller or a customer believes that most other billers and customers will not adopt new EBPP solutions, it will not adopt them either. The spread of EBPP systems thus depends largely on a coordinated response between billers and customers."[34] Other hurdles to using EBPP include: [35]

- Approximately 20 percent of all payments are one-time payments, which are unlikely candidates for on-line billing.
- Who "owns" the customer and how payment discrepancies are resolved is a major issue especially where third-party processors are involved.
- When a customer inquiries about a bill, the company customer service representative does not view the same version of the billing information.
- Writing a small number of checks still takes less time than going online and clicking on websites.

Banks reduce their costs of dealing with paper transactions, and can increase their fee income when customers pay their bills on line. Some, but not all banks charge $5-17 per month for viewing and paying bills on line.[36]

ELECTRONIC FUNDS TRANSFER (ETF)

In order to reduce the cost of dealing in paper checks, most large companies and government organizations use electronic funds transfer (ETF) to pay their employees, and pay retirement benefits.

EFT takes a variety of forms. These include ATMs, direct deposit, pay-by-phone, personal computer banking, point of sale transfers, and electronic check conversion.[37]

The Electronic Funds Transfer Act of 1978 (EFT Act), and the resulting *Federal Reserve Regulation E* requires financial institutions using electronic funds transfer to provide: [38]

- written receipts for transactions;
- procedures for stopping preauthorized payments;
- adequate information about how to deal with billing errors, unauthorized, lost, or stolen debit cards, and
- limits on the amount that may be deducted if there is an unauthorized transactions.

The EFT Act does not included stored value cards, such as those issued by merchants, prepaid telephone cards, mass transit passes, and gift cards.

Although an increasing number of payments are being made using EFT, the 2013 FDIC National Survey of Unbanked and Underbanked Households revealed that only 67 percent of households were *fully banked* using all of the banking services, and 20.0 percent were *underbanked*, using prepaid cards, money orders, and other financial services. But 7.7 percent of households in the United States were *unbanked* in 2013. "Unbanked" means they do not have an account at an insured institution. The primary reasons for not having a bank account were that: 1) they did not have enough money; 2) they did not like or trust banks; and 3) the account fees were too high. The FDIC study also noted that 20.0 percent of U.S. households (24.8 million) were *underbanked* in 2013, meaning that they had a bank account but also used alternative financial services (AFS) outside of the banking system.[39] *Alternative financial systems* include, but are not limited to, money orders, check cashing, remittances, payday loans, refund anticipation loans, rent-to-own services, pawn shops loans, or auto title loans.

ELECTRONIC MONEY

Abraham Lincoln said in 1839 that no duty is more imperative on government than the duty it owes its people to furnish them with a sound and uniform currency.[40] Yet today we are talking about and using electronic money, which means different things to different people. ***"Money"*** is a term of art that is generally described by its functions. The primary function of money is that it is generally accepted as a means of exchange in terms of a defined unit of account. Until now, there have been four major innovations in how people pay for things with money: metallic coins, checks, paper money, and payment cards. Now we can add electronic money to that list. Another function is that money is a store of value. A wide variety of things have been used as money including gold, silver, checks, and credit cards. Congress and the courts grant some forms of money the special status of being legal tender, which creditors must accept as payment for debts. United States coins and currency are legal tender. The phrase "This note is ***legal tender*** for all debts public and private" appears on Federal Reserve notes. Creditors are not required by law to accept other forms of payment.[41] However, some vendors post signs, which are conditional sales contracts, stating that they will not accept currency larger than $20.

In the broadest sense, *electronic money* refers to the variety of ways that electronic and other payments systems can be used as a means of exchange. Electronic money takes many different forms. One form of electronic money is funds held in on-line accounts that can be transferred over the internet.[42] Another form of electronic money is a stored value card that contains a magnetic strip recording the dollar value of the card. Most stored value cards are part of a "closed system" that can only be used at specific locations, such as a subway or toll road. A "smart card" contains a computer chip carrying $100 or more of electronic money that can be debited by a merchant at the point of sale or elsewhere. One type of smart card is called an "electronic purse." The purse is commonly referred to as an "open system" because it can be used at multiple locations. Both stored value cards and smart cards may be "reloaded" -- having additional amounts of value added. Yet another form is digital money that takes the form of bits on someone's hard drive. Credit cards are also considered electronic money. Electronic Data Capture (EDC) is a point-of-sale terminal that captures the information provided by the credit card, and it electronically authorizes the transaction.[43] In addition, by using a cryptographic standard known as secured electronic transactions (SET) and other means, credit cards can be used for secure transactions over the internet.[44] Because the electronic-based systems involves the clearing process, a credit (or debit) card transaction may take several days before it is debited or credited to the user's account. Thus, retail electronic payments systems are not instantaneous, but they are faster than paper-based systems.

Finally, there are *cryptocurrencies* – such as Bitcoin, Amazon Coins, Ripple, OpenCoin, MintChip, Linden Dollars, and others.[45] They allow users to trade directly, without going through a bank. Although they are legally used for some but not all transactions, they are not money for the following reasons: 1) they are not a generally accepted means of exchange; 2) they are not legal tender; 3) they have no intrinsic value; and 4) finally, because Bitcoins are an electronic "commodity," its price is very volatile, as shown in Figure 17-1.

FIGURE 17-1 BITCOIN PRICE AND VOLATILITY

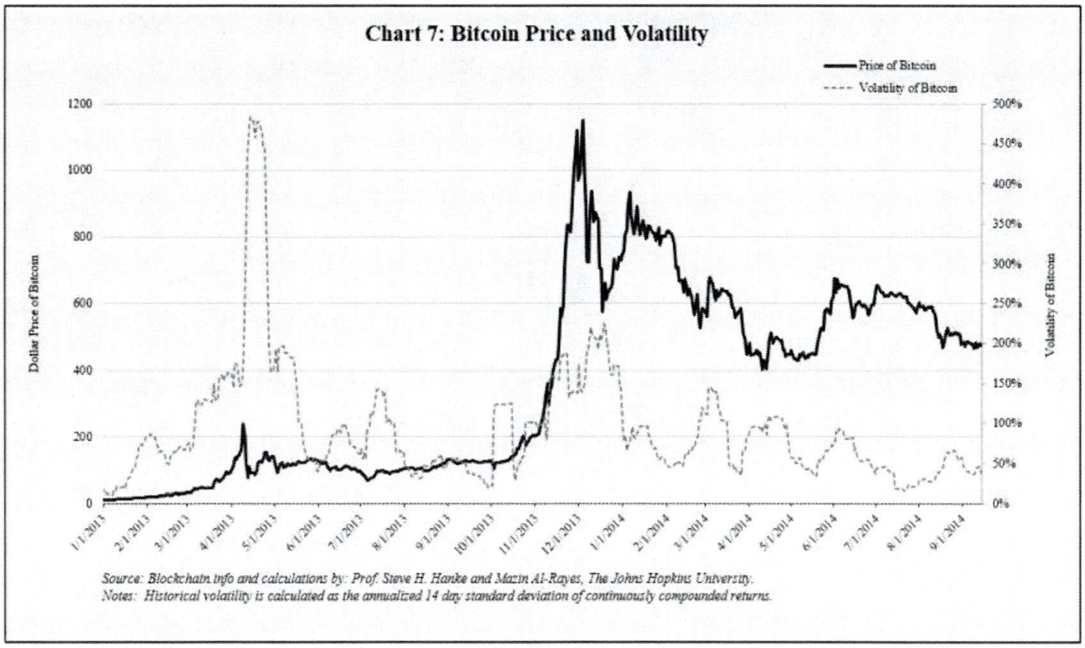

Source: Steve H. Hanke, "Bitcoin Charts, Finally," Posted 9/18/14; Huff Post Business, January 17, 2016. http://www.huffingtonpost.com/steve-h-hanke/bitcoin-charts_b_5838132.html

Advantages and Disadvantages

The advantages of electronic money are that it can be used in ordinary stores and over the internet to deal in electronic commerce and in precise amounts.[46] It is fast and convenient. Some forms of electronic payment, such as credit cards payments made by computers and smart phones, leave a record of transactions, whereas other forms of electronic money (e.g., prepaid and stored-value cards) are untraceable. Safety is a different issue. There is always the issue of loss due to theft, cyber crime, and the possibility that issuer is unwilling or unable to honor payments made with its electronic liabilities. [47]

While there are advantages to using electronic money, there are also some disadvantages. Electronic payment innovations that involve non-banks and new business models pose new oversight and regulatory challenges as well as legal, security, and law-enforcement concerns. The cross-border nature of some e-money schemes requires international coordination and co-operation.[48]

Security and privacy are two obvious disadvantages of various forms of electronic money. Another is that electronic money is not legal tender. Cash, on the other hand, is legal tender; and it protects the user's privacy. Moreover, cash is uniform and it can be redeemed at full par value. Therefore, it is treated the same by all merchants and banks. Finally, there is no need to verify the counterparty's credibility when using cash.

The development of electronic money raises a number of interesting policy issues that will be resolved by Congress and the courts over time. What is the proper role of government with respect to electronic money?

A U.S. Department of Treasury study said that the central issue is who can "coin" digitized money, whether it is stored virtually or on plastic.[49] Should electronic money be covered by deposit insurance? "The public has looked to government to set and enforce basic rules that provide a foundation for, among other things, consumer rights and responsibilities (in such areas as protections against loss and invasions of privacy); law enforcement tools and techniques to combat financial crimes; the issuance of legal tender; and the management of the money supply and the payments system." [50]

Seigniorage

Seigniorage is an issue involved with electronic money. The original definition of this term was the difference between the monetary value of a coin or currency and the cost of production. However, seigniorage income derived from Federal Reserve notes is interest payments on Treasury securities held to collateralize Federal Reserve notes.[51]

The word "seigniorage" is a French word that refers to the fee that merchants paid the King to have their bullion made into coins. An additional fee, called brassage, was charged to coin the bullion, thereby standardizing it. Similarly, if the U.S. Treasury issued a new quarter, (par value of $0.25) that cost $0.09 to produce, the seigniorge would be $0.16.

Today in the U.S., seigniorage is considered the interest saved by the Treasury from having currency, which is non-interest bearing debt, circulating as a medium of exchange. It can be thought of a profit for the Treasury, where the profit is the difference between the interest earned on assets financed by issuing currency and the cost of issuing and redeeming it.[52] In 2014, the United States Mint returned

$250 million in circulating seigniorage to the Treasury. However, it lost money producing one-cent and five-cent coins.[53] The production cost of producing the one-cent coin (penny) was $0.0166 and the five-cent coin (nickel) was ($0.809). It only cost $0.0391 to produce a dime and $0.0895 to produce a quarter.

As previously noted, there are private money systems that compete with the Treasury. The use of private money is not a recent development. It dates back to colonial times. Private money is not backed or issued by the government, but it may have the characteristics of money. It is generally accepted as a means of exchange, a store of value, and a unit of account. The new electronic forms of payments can be thought of as the latest version of private money. As electronic means of payment and credit become more widespread, the Treasury's profits from seigniorage will diminish. A 1977 study by the Congressional Budget Office estimated that if electronic money replaces 10 percent of the coin and currency in denominations of $10 and under, the government will lose about $370 million per year.[55] The more electronic money is used, the more the Treasury will lose.

Home Mortgage Loans Over the Internet

It used to be that residential mortgage lending was a local business. The internet changed that. Today, it is an important part of electronic banking as an increasing number of financial institutions are offering online mortgage services. This includes both traditional banks as well as nonbank online lenders such as SoFi and Quicken Loans.[56] This has increased the availability of mortgage credit and made mortgage rates and terms competitive. Loans can be approved in minutes, but the approval may be conditional, requiring that a long list of conditions must be met.

The institutions offering mortgage loans over the internet fall into four general categories.[57] First, some of them are direct lenders that underwrite the mortgages themselves. Second, some are brokers that find the best deal for their customers and they handle the paperwork. The third type are referral services that find loans for borrowers, but they do not do the paperwork. Finally, there are mortgage auction sites that solicit bids from lenders based on the profiles of the customers and loans.

Obtaining a mortgage online is not necessarily easier nor less costly than going through a traditional lender. Most internet sites charge a fee, based on the value of the loan, when a borrower applies, which may be rebated at the time of the closing. Although the internet can be used to handle much of the paperwork, there is still some contact with humans. At closings, documents need to be signed and notarized.

LARGE-DOLLAR TRANSFERS

In the United States, *large-dollar transfers*, or wholesale payments as they are commonly called, are used by banks, businesses and governments. The large-dollar transfers are made over the Fedwire or by using the Clearing House Interbank Payments System (CHIPS). International payments also involve Society for Worldwide Interbank Financial Telecommunications (S.W.I.F.T.).

FEDWIRE

Domestic interbank payments are transferred over the ***Fedwire***, an electronic funds transfer system that is operated by the Federal Reserve. When a financial transaction occurs, financial market utilities (FMUs) are responsible for finalizing the transaction by clearing transactions and settling the exchange of payment and securities between financial institutions.[58] It is a real-time gross settlements (RTGS) system. RTGS means that the system settles transactions individually as they occur, rather then processing them in a batch. It operates 18 hrs per day, from 12:30 A.M. Eastern Time until 6:30 P.M. to facilitate international funds transfers. "In 2014, the Service processed on average $1.1 trillion of securities transfers against payment (measured by cash value, not par amount) every business day... All securities transfers made over the Fedwire Securities Service against payment are settled on the books of the Reserve Banks and, therefore, in central bank money." [59]

Because the Federal Reserve grants payment finality, the payments are final and irrevocable. Stated otherwise, the Federal Reserve assumes the credit risk associated with the transfer of funds. This credit risk is commonly referred to as a daylight overdraft. If the funds involved in the transfer are not repaid at the end of the day, they become unsecured overnight overdrafts. The Federal Reserve discourages overdrafts by imposing monetary penalties and taking administrative actions against those institutions that repeatedly have daylight and overnight overdrafts. To reduce their risk, the Federal Reserve imposes limits (debt caps) on the amount of daylight overdrafts for each depository institution based on the institution's risk-based capital.

NACHA AND THE ACH NETWORK

NACHA (The Electronic Payments Association) and the Automated Clearing House Association (ACH) Network are at the center of American commerce, moving more than $40 trillion each year.[60] That's consisted of almost 23 billion electronic financial transactions, including Direct Deposit via ACH, Social Security and government benefits, electronic bill payments such as utility and mortgage payments, and person-to-person (P2P) and business-to-business (B2B) payments. The ACH Network supports more than 20 percent of all electronic payments in the U.S.

CHIPS

International funds transfers use CHIPS *(Clearing House Interbank Payments System)* operated by the New York Clearing House Association (NYCHA). It began operating in 1970 as an electronic replacement for paper checks for international dollar payments. Today CHIPS is the largest private-sector U.S.-dollar funds-transfer system in the world, clearing and settling an average of $1.5 trillion in cross-border and domestic payments daily. CHIPS serves 49 foreign and domestic banks, representing 215 countries, through a network of sending and receiving devices, which range from microcomputers to large-scale mainframe computers. CHIPS combines two types of payments systems: the liquidity efficiency of a netting system and the intraday finality of a Real Time Gross Settlements.[61] On an average day, CHIPS transmits and settles over 400,000 "payment messages." A "payment message" is an electronic message that, when released by CHIPS to the receiving participant, instructs the receiving bank to pay or cause another bank to pay a fixed amount of money to a beneficiary. Suppose that a French firm bought $3 million in parts from a U.S. manufacturing firm. The French firm instructed its bank in Paris to debit its account in francs for the dollar equivalent of $3 million, and then to pay the U.S. supplier's bank in New York. The French bank has a branch in New York, and it makes the $3 million payment to the U.S. bank.

As the funds are transferred throughout the day, CHIPS calculates each participant's single net position vis-à-vis all of the other participants. Each of the CHIPS participants has a bilateral agreement and credit limit with the other CHIPS participants. In other words, CHIPS nets or offsets mutual obligations to reduce the number of obligations that the participants must deal with. This system of settlement is called multilateral netting. When all of the positions are settled at the end of the day (same-day settlement), those banks with a net credit position receive a Fedwire funds transfer from the NYCHA, and the CHIPS account at the Federal Reserve Bank of New York has a zero position. Now the transaction between the French and U.S. bank is final.

Because CHIPS is the largest privately operated payments system, there is concern about payment and settlement risk.[63] *Settlement risk* involves a) *credit risk* (due to the failure of one party to deliver a promised payment), b) *unwinding risk* (payment instructions to receivers of funds may be reversed), and c) *liquidity risk* (payment instructions cannot be settled due to lack of liquidity). The Federal Reserve requires CHIPS and other private wholesale transfer systems to ensure settlement in the event of default by a major participant. CHIPS has a procedure for dealing with the failure of its two largest participants.[64] Despite the risks involved with international settlements, CHIPS has never failed to settle.

SWIFT

The Society for Worldwide Interbank Financial Telecommunications (SWIFT), incorporated in Belgium, is a cooperative owned by banks throughout the world to facilitate payments and financial messages among its members.[65] SWIFT is used primarily for communications; the actual transfers of funds are done by the CHIPS and the Fedwire. SWIFT's messaging services are used by more than 11,000 financial institutions in more than 200 countries and territories around the world. Over 6.1 billion secure messages were sent in 2015, which is equal to a traffic volume of 24.22 million messages per day.[66]

FOREIGN EXCHANGE

Foreign exchange transactions arise from international trade and investments as well as from hedging and speculation in foreign currencies. The settlement transactions result in U.S. dollars being exchanged for another currency such as the French franc. There are two settlements in such transactions: dollars being settled in the United States, and the foreign currency being settled in the other country's payment system.

There are both bilateral and multilateral netting systems for foreign exchange transactions. In a *bilateral netting system*, two banks that may have multiple contract to settle in a foreign currency, such as German marks, can replace them with a single contract for the net amount to be sent through the Deutsche Bundesbank is actively involved in processing payments German payments system for clearing. Other international payment processors include, but are not limited to SWIFT, and LCH.Clearnet. (Exchange Clearing House, London), to find about 100 acquirers and processors around the world. [67]

SUMMARY

Electronic/digital banking has developed in three distinct areas, one dealing with retail, small-dollar transactions, the second with wholesale, large-dollar transactions, and the third with how payments are made. On the retail side, about 88% of all households used some form of electronic payments (ATM, debit cards, direct deposit, automatic bill paying, and smart cards).[68] The 2013 Federal Reserve Payments Study revealed the "card use may have replaced check use for certain payments, but the increase in the number of card payments has far exceeded the decline in the number of check payments from 2009 to 2012." [69]

Nevertheless, checks are still an important part of retail payments. The reasons why this is so is that they are convenient to use and were widely accepted; the legal foundations of check collection were well-established; and the check writers like the float. Finally, the legal framework that establishes the rights and liabilities of the participants using various forms of digital payments is evolving, and not as well-understood as the current paper-based system.

Digital payments dominate the wholesale side of payments, and will continue to do so.

KEY TERMS AND CONCEPTS

Account aggregation
Automated Clearing House (ACH)
Automated teller machines (ATMs)
Bilateral netting
Blockchains
Check 21 Act (Check Clearing for the 21st Century Act (PL 108-100))
CHIPS (Clearing House Interbank Payments System)
Clearing
Credit risk
Cross currency settlement risk
Cyber crimes
Cryptocurrencies
Electronic bill presentment and payment (EBPP)
Electronic banking
Electronic check conversion
Electronic funds transfer (EFT)
Electronic Funds Transfer Act of 1978 (EFT Act)
Electronic money
Federal Reserve Regulation E
Fedwire®
Fedwire Funds Transfer
Finality (payments)
Foreign exchange
Herstatt risk
Informal Value Transfer Systems (IVTS) (e.g. hawalas)
Interchange rates
Large-dollar transfers
Legal tender
Liquidity risk
Money
Multilateral netting
NACHA, The Electronics, Payment Association
Personal identification number (PIN)
Real-time gross settlements
Same-day settlement
Seigniorage
Settlement
Settlement risk
Substitute check
SWIFT (Society for Worldwide Interbank Financial Telecommunications)
Third-Party-Payment-Processers and Senders (TPPPs)
Unbanked (people)
Unwinding risk

QUESTIONS

17.1 What is electronic banking?
17.2 Electronic banking has developed in several distinct directions. Explain its development.
17.3 What are the principal retail electronic banking products?
17.4 How does "network externalities" affect electronic banking?
17.5 How do banks earn fee income from ATMs?
17.6 What are the advantages of electronic bill presentment and payment systems?
17.7 What is Federal Reserve "Regulation E?"

17.8 What is electronic money?
17.9 What is the difference between seigniorage and brassage?
17.10. What is the difference between real-time gross settlements and multilateral netting? What are the Fedwire, CHIPS, and SWIFT?

CASE: TROLLING THE NET

Julia Chan is the Vice President in charge of Coastal Bank and Trust's (CBT) Private Banking Department. CBT is a $4 billion regional bank, and the Private Banking Department caters to the financial needs of individuals with high net worth (more than $1 million). She wants to develop better ways to build strong customer relationships with them and to attract new business by improving their internet financial services. The first step in her quest is to benchmark the internet financial services offered by other institutions. To do this, she began trolling the net at the following sites:

Banks	**Websites**
Bank of America:	http://www.bankamerica.com
Chase Manhattan Bank	http://www.chase.com
Citibank	http://citibank.com
Security First Network Bank	http://www.sfnb.com
Telebank	http://www.telebank.com
Wells Fargo	http://www.wellsfargo.com
Wingspan Bank	http://www.wingspan.com
Other Institutions	
American Express Financial Direct	http://americanexpress.com/direct
Charles Schwab	http://schwab.com
Fidelity	http://fidelity.com

1. Make a list of the financial services that would be most attractive to high net worth individuals.
2. Select one of these services, and develop a brief scenario of how to market this service to clients that are female, married, and over 35 years old.
3. How would you market that service to individuals of your age?

ENDNOTES

1. Not all institutions that advertise themselves as "banks" are FDIC-insured. Moreover, FDIC-insured institutions offer products, such as mutual funds, that are not covered by deposit insurance.
2. For additional information, see; https://www.checkfreepay.com/info/payinperson, and Intuit QuickBooks: http://quickbooks.intuit.com/payments/?xcid=seq_intuit_pay_click_prod_cat
3. "Electronic Banking Group Initiatives and White Papers," Basel Committee on Banking Supervision, Basel Switzerland, October, 2000.
4. Rebecca Sausner, "Royal Bank's Aim: Become a Personal Web Channel," *FutureBanker*, April 1999, 48.
5. For a listing of best online/internet banks, see: http://online-only-banks-review.toptenreviews.com/
6. FDIC Consumer News, "Mobile Banking and Payments: New Uses for Phones...and Even Watches," Summer, 2015.
7. FFIEC IT Examination Handbook InfoBase - Emerging Retail Payment Technologies, 2015
8. Consumers and Mobile Financial Services, 2015, Board of Governors of the Federal Reserve System, March 2015.
9. "Report: Mobile Banking Users Outpace Branch Customers in 2015," *ABA BANKING JOURNAL*, January 12, 2016.

10. Richard Fleming and Mark Schofield, "Four Ways to Save the Dying Bank Branch," *American Banker*, January 14, 2016.

11. Saabira Chaudhuri, "U.S. Banks Prune More Branches," *The Wall Street Journal*, January 27, 2014.

12. Kristle Romero Cortés, "The Role of Bank Branches Play in a Mobile Age," Economic Commentary, Federal Reserve Bank of Cleveland, November 16, 2015.

13. "Funds Transfer – Overview," Bank Secrecy Act, Anti-Money Laundering Examination Manual, Board of Governors of the Federal Reserve System: http://www.ffiec.gov/%5C/bsa_aml_infobase/pages_manual/OLM_057.htm

14. Jodie Ruby, "Managing TPPPS and TPSs in the Current Regulatory Environment," G2 Web Services, www.g2webservices.com, American Banker White Paper, 2015. FFEIC BSA/AML Examination Manual, p 236.

15. Public Law 106-229, June 30, 2000.

16. FDIC, Compliance Examination Manual, "The Electronic Signatures in Global and National Commerce Act (E-Sign Act)," January 2014, X-3.1-X-3.3; https://www.fdic.gov/regulations/compliance/manual/10/X-3.1.pdf

17. "Strategies for Improving the U.S. Payment System," Federal Reserve System, January 26, 2015

18. For additional information see: "The Bureau of the Fiscal Service (Fiscal Service)," U.S. Department of Treasury, https://www.fiscal.treasury.gov/fsindex.htm; Also see NACHA, The Electronic Payments Association, https://www.nacha.org/

19. NACHA, ibid.

20. Barry Glick, "Why blockchain heralds a rethink of the entire banking industry," *ComputerWeekly*, October 15, 2015, www.coputerweekly.com.

21. For information about cybercrimes, see the FBI website: Cyber Crime, https://www.fbi.gov/about-us/investigate/cyber. For the latest information about cyber security, see "the cyberwire," http://www.thecyberwire.com/

22. Brian Yurcan, "Banks Embrace Biometrics, But Will Customers?" *American Banker*, January 15, 2016.

23. Charles M. Kahn and William Roberds, "The Economics of Payment Finality," Economic Review, Federal Reserve Bank of Atlanta, Second Quarter, 2002, 1-12. This article provides an overview of payment finality in various models of payments systems. Also see Kenneth N. Kuttner and James J. McAndrews, "Personal On-Line Payments," FRBNY Economic Policy Review, Federal Reserve Bank of New York, December, 2001, 35-50.

24. John D. Hueter and Ben R. Craig, "Global ATM Banking: Casting the Net," Federal Reserve Bank of Cleveland, August 15, 1998.

25. Robert M. Hunt, "Antitrust Issues in Payment Card Networks: Can They Do That? Should We Let Them?" Business Review, Federal Reserve Bank of Philadelphia, Second Quarter, 2003, 14-23.

26. For Visa fees, see "Visa Interchange Reimbursement Feed, April 2015," For MasterCard, see "MasterCard 2015–2016 Effective April 17, 2015 U.S. Region Interchange Programs and Rates."

27. Board of Governors of the Federal Reserve System, "Regulation II (Debit Card Interchange Fees and Routing)" http://www.federalreserve.gov/paymentsystems/regii-about.htm

28. Bank of America, FAQs ATMs and ATM Fees, https://www.bankofamerica.com/deposits/manage/faq-atm-fees.go

29. This example is from the author's monthly billing statement from June, 1999.

30. Federal Financial Institutions Examination Council, IT Examination HandBook InfoBase, Glossary, http://ithandbook.ffiec.gov/glossary.aspx

31. Lawrence J. Radecki and John Wenniger, "Paying Electronic Bills Electronically," Current Issues in Economics and Finance, Federal Reserve Bank of New York, January 1999.

32. For additional details about the ACH network, see Weber, Margaret, "Understanding and Managing ACH Credit Risk," *The Journal of Lending & Credit Risk Management*, May 1999, 66-71.

33. The definitions of clearing and settlement are from "The Future of Retail Electronic Payment Systems: Industry Interviews and Analysis," Board of Governors of the Federal Reserve System, Staff Study

175, December 2002, and from "A Glossary of Terms Used in Payments and Settlement Systems," Committee on Payment and Settlement Systems, Bank for International Settlements, Basel Switzerland, January 2001.
34. Chris Stefanadis, "Why Hasn't Electronic Bill Presentment and Payment Taken Off?" Current Issues in Economics and Finance, Federal Reserve Bank of New York, July/August 2002.
35. "Electronic Bill Presentment & Payment Models," Treasury Resources@ PhoenixHect.com. http://www.phoenixhecht.com/TreasuryResources/EBPP.html
36. Michelle Higgins, "Honest, the Check Is in the E-Mail," *The Wall Street Journal*," September 4, 2002, D1, D4.
37. For further information, see "Electronic Banking," *Facts for Consumers*, Federal Trade Commission, 2002, www.ftc.gov.
38. Tim Schilling and Keith Feiler, *Electronic Money*, Federal Reserve Bank of Chicago, July, 1998, 11.
39. FDIC, "2013 FDIC National Survey of Unbanked and Underbanked Households, October, 2014.
40. Federal Reserve Bank of Cleveland 1995 Annual Report, Federal Reserve Bank of Cleveland, 1996.
41. For a more detailed discussion of legal tender, see Benton E. Gup, "The Changing Role of Legal Tender: An Historical Perspective," appears in *Marketing Exchange Relationships, Transactions, and Their Media*, Frank Houston, ed., Westport CT, Quorum Books, 1994, 239-246.
42. Elijah Brewer and Douglas D. Evanoff, "Payments Systems – Getting Ready for the 21st Century, *Chicago Fed Letter*, Federal Reserve Bank of Chicago, Special Issue No. 174a, 1998.
43. Electronic Data Capture (EDC) is part of Electronic Data Interchange (EDI) which is the exchange of information electronically between business applications in a structured format. Many corporations use EDI for purchase and sale orders. Bank clearing houses also use EDI. (Diane B. Glossman, and Carole S. Berger, "On-Demand Banking: Power to the People," Salomon Brothers, September 1995).
44. James J. McAndrews, "Making Payments on the Internet," Federal Reserve Bank of Philadelphia, *Business Review*, January/February 1997, 3-14.
45. For additional information, see Benton E. Gup, "What Is Money? From Commodities to Virtual Currencies/ Bitcoin," *Alternative Investment Analyst Review*, Q3, 2014, 52-59.
46. Yasushi Nakayma, et. al., "An Electronic Money Scheme," Bank of Japan, Institute of Monetary and Economic Studies, Discussion Paper No. 97-E-4, June 1997. Note that there is usually a small charge for processing a credit card transaction. Therefore, they are not used for very small amounts - micro payments - such as $0.25.
47. "Electronic Money: Consumer Protection, Law Enforcement, Supervisory and Cross Border Issues," Group of Ten Report of the Working Party on Electronic Money," April, 1997. For more information about Cyber Crime, see FBI – Cyber Crime: https://www.fbi.gov/about-us/investigate/cyber
48. Ben Fung, Miguel Molico, and Gerald Stuber, "Electronic Money and Payments: Recent Developments and Issues" Bank of Canada Discussion Paper 2014-2 April, 2014.
49. Robert E. Litan and Jonathan Rauch, *American Finance for the 21st Century*, U.S. Department of Treasury, November 17, 1997.
50. David G. Hayes, James F. E. Gillespie, Peter H. Daly, Gary Grippo, Pamela J. Johnson, "An Introduction to Electronic Money Issues - Toward Electronic Money and Banking: The Role of Government," U.S. Department of the Treasury, September 19-20, 1996. http://www.occ.treas.gov/topics/bank-operations/bit/intro-to-electronic-money-issues.pdf
51. Michael Lambert, Shaun Ferrari, and Brian Wajert, "Costs and Benefits of Replacing the $1 Federal Reserve Note with a $1 Coin, Staff Working Paper, Federal Reserve Board, December 2013. The key findings of this study were that we should not replace the $1 Federal Reserve Note with a $1 U.S. Coin.
52. William P. Osterberg and James B. Thompson, "Bank Notes and Stored Value Card: Stepping Lightly into the Past," Federal Reserve Bank of Cleveland, Economic Commentary, September 1, 1998. The author is also indebted to Philip Bartholomew, Chief Economist Democratic Staff, Committee on Banking and Financial Services, U.S. House of Representatives, for his help with defining these terms.
53. United States Mint, 2014 Annual Report, p. 10.
54. 2014 Biennial Report To Congress, United States Mint, December 2014
55. Litan and Rauch, op. cit.,

56. For additional information see: https://www.sofi.com/, and http://www.quicken.com/
57. Karen Hube, "E-Mortgage World: Data-Packed, Tricky," *The Wall Street Journal*, April 28, 1999, C1, C24.
58. Financial market utilities (FMUs) are multilateral systems that provide the infrastructure for transferring, clearing, and settling payments, securities, and other financial transactions among financial institutions or between financial institutions and the system. They are responsible for finalizing the transaction by clearing transactions and settling the exchange of payment and securities between financial institutions. 12 U.S.C. § 5461 (Dodd-Frank Act § 802). Also see "Designated Financial Market Utilities," Board of Governors of the Federal Reserve System, paymentsystems/designated_fmu_about.htm
59. "Fedwire® Securities Service Disclosure," Board of Governors of the Federal Reserve System Date of this disclosure: December 14, 2015, p. 10.
60. For additional information, see: "ACH Network: How it Works," https://www.nacha.org/ach-network
61. The Clearing House, Payments: https://www.theclearinghouse.org/payments/chips
62. Clearing House Interbank Payment System ("CHIPS®") Self-Assessment Of Compliance With Core Principles For Systemically Important Payment Systems, 2014, CHIPS%20Core%20Principles%20Self%20Assessment%202014%20(1).pdf
63. For additional discussion of CHIPS, see Norman R. Nelson, "Private Sector Clearing and Payment Systems," appears in Proceedings, Payments Systems in the Global Economy: Risks and Opportunities, Federal Reserve Bank of Chicago, May 1998, 22 – 26.
64. Elijah Brewer and Douglas D. Evanoff, op. cit.
65. U.S. General Accounting Office, Payments, Clearance, and Settlement, op. cit. For additional information about S.W.I.F.T., see their website: https://www.swift.com/
66. website: https://www.swift.com/
67. For additional information, see "Global Connections & Methods of Payment Map," showing acquirers and processors in over 190 countries; Cybersource®, http://www.cybersource.com/products/global_map/
68. Loretta Mester, "Changes in the Use of Electronic Means of Payments: 1995-2001," Business Review, Federal Reserve Bank of Philadelphia, Third Quarter, 2003, 18-20.
69. "The 2013 Federal Reserve Payments Study," December 19, 2013, The Federal Reserve System. https://www.frbservices.org/files/communications/pdf/research/2013_payments_study_summary.pdf. The Federal Reserve Announced that the Sixth Triennial Study to Examine U.S. Payments is expected to be published in December 2016. "Federal Reserve Announces Sixth Triennial Study to Examine U.S. Payments Usage," Federal Reserve System, November 15, 2015, https://www.frbservices.org/files/communications/pdf/press/110515_2016_frps_news.pdf

Chapter 18

Global Financial Services

After reading this chapter, you will be able to:

- Understand why and how U.S. banks engage in international banking, and how foreign banks operate here
- Explain how international lending by banks differs from domestic lending
- Understand the basics of understanding foreign exchange rates
- Evaluate the risks of dealing in foreign exchange
- Explain why business concerns use letters of credit supplied by banks
- Define the meaning of direct and indirect foreign exchange rates

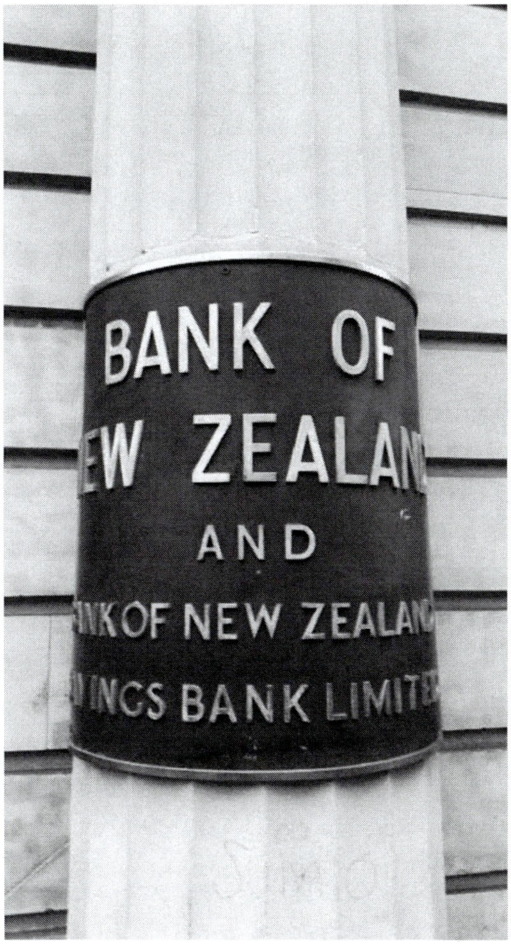

WHY AND HOW U.S. BANKS ENGAGE IN INTERNATIONAL BANKING

WHY ENGAGE IN INTERNATIONAL BANKING?

Banks engage in international banking for several reasons. The first, and most important, reason is to serve the needs of their customers. We live in a global economy where we buy and sell goods around the world. Banks have customers that both import and export goods and services, and they need banking services to facilitate trade. In this regard, some banks that have domestic customers with foreign operations follow them abroad to provide services. Similarly, banks with overseas foreign customers may want to be closer to them in order provide better service. Obviously, it is hoped that serving the needs of customers will generate profits.

The profit motive is the second reason for international banking. International banking opens new markets, some of which may have greater profit potential than is available in domestic markets. High expected returns are consistent with high risks. Following decades of making large profits in foreign markets, many international banks experienced large losses in 1998 on loans to countries such as Indonesia, Russia, South Korea, and Thailand.

Prestige is another reason for global expansion. It adds to a bank's prestige to advertise that it has offices in London, Tokyo, Rio de Janeiro and other international financial centers. This, in turn, gives them access to multinational firms that operate in those markets. Thus, they can serve their customers' needs in those markets and attract new customers.

Based on these and other factors, the biggest U.S. chartered bank holding companies in the United States are global financial institutions. JPMorgan Chase operates in more than 60 countries, Bank of America has operations in more than 35 countries, and Citi's Global Consumer Bank serves clients in 35 countries.[1] Similarly, large foreign-owned bank holding companies with assets greater than $50 billion operate in the United States. They are: HSBC North America Holdings Inc. (England), TD Group US Holdings LLC (Canada), Santander Holdings USA, Inc. (Spain), BMO Financial Corp. (Canada), MUFG America Holdings Corp. (Japan), BBVA Compass Bancshares, Inc. (Spain), and Deutsche Bank Trust Corp. (Germany).[2] Smaller foreign-owned bank holding companies also operate in the U.S. The point is that global markets require global banking operations from both domestic and foreign-owned banks.

The remainder of this section presents the principal methods used by U.S. banking organizations to participate in international banking. The extent to which banks use these methods depends on whether international banking is an occasional or full-time activity.

CORRESPONDENT BANKING

The vast majority of banks do not engage in international banking on a regular basis. On those occasions when a customer requires international banking services, banks use a correspondent bank that provides such services. ***Correspondent***

banks are large banks that provide the gamut of banking products and services to other banks in exchange for fees or deposits. Typically, correspondent banks providing international banking services are money center banks (large banks located in New York and other money centers), large regional banks, and foreign banks located in the United States. Some correspondent banks maintain deposits in foreign banks that can be used to facilitate trade by making or receiving payments, which is commonly referred to as ***trade finance***. Other services can include foreign exchange of currencies, letters of credit and introduction, and credit information on overseas firms. In addition to the services mentioned, correspondent banks make international loans and sell "participations" in those loans to other banks. They also deal in swaps and provide investment and other services.

Banks that deal extensively in international trade also use correspondent banks on a regular basis. For example, a U.S. bank might use the Bank of Tokyo-Mitsubishi Ltd. as its principal correspondent in Japan if it does a lot of business in Japan. Accordingly, payments to or collections from other banks in Japan will be routed through the Bank of Tokyo-Mitsubishi UFJ.[3] Likewise, the U.S. bank maintains correspondent relationships in other money centers of the world. Such networks provide the channels that facilitate the efficient flow of funds in the capital markets throughout the world.

FOREIGN BANKS AND BRANCHES

Subpart B of the Federal Reserve's Regulation K defines a foreign bank as "an organization that is organized under the laws of a foreign country and that engages directly in the business of banking outside the U.S.," and a foreign banking organization (FBO) as any such foreign bank, or "any company of which the foreign bank is a subsidiary" [4]

Banks have foreign branches in the same fashion that they have domestic branches. That is, a branch represents the parent firm at some distant location. Some branches are full-service branches offering a full range of banking services to their customers, while other branches only offer limited services. The full range of services includes taking deposits, making loans, and investments, for example.

Under provisions of the Federal Reserve Act, banks that are members of the Federal Reserve System may establish foreign branches with the approval of the Federal Reserve Board.

REPRESENTATIVE OFFICES

A representative office is a quasi sales office. Representative offices cannot book loans or take deposits, but they can develop business for the head office and arrange for these things to happen elsewhere. They also establish a bank's presence in an area where the business is not sufficient to justify the cost of establishing a branch, or where new branch offices are not permitted by local regulations.

FOREIGN AFFILIATES

Domestic commercial banks and bank holding companies sometimes acquire an equity interest in foreign financial organizations such as banks, finance companies and leasing companies. They might own all or part of the stock. The affiliates might be subsidiaries or joint ventures. One advantage of foreign affiliates is that the affiliate is not "foreign" in its own country. This can have tax, political, and marketing advantages. On the other side of the coin, a bank with minority ownership is subject to the same problems as any minority stockholder. Minority stockholders might have little influence in the operating policies of a corporation.

EDGE ACT OFFICES

The ***Edge Act of 1919*** (an amendment to the Federal Reserve Act by Senator Walter Edge) permits national banking organizations to have subsidiary corporations that have offices throughout the United States to provide a means of financing international trade, especially exports. The Federal Reserve's 2014 Annual Report states that "Edge Act corporations are international banking organizations chartered by the Board to provide all segments of the U.S. economy with a means of financing international business, especially exports. ***Agreement corporations*** are similar organizations, state or federally chartered, that enter into agreements with the Board to refrain from exercising any power that is not permissible for an Edge Act corporation. Sections 25 and 25A of the Federal Reserve Act grant Edge Act and agreement corporations permission to engage in international banking and foreign financial transactions. These corporations, most of which are subsidiaries of member banks, may (1) conduct a deposit and loan business in states other than that of the parent, provided that the business is strictly related to international transactions and (2) make foreign investments that are broader than those permissible for member banks. At year-end 2014, out of 44 banking organizations chartered as Edge Act or agreement corporations, three operated seven Edge Act and agreement branches. Foreign banks continue to be significant participants in the U.S. banking system. As of year-end 2014, 163 foreign banks from 49 countries operated 187 state-licensed branches and agencies, of which six were insured by the Federal Deposit Insurance Corporation (FDIC), and 48 OCC-licensed branches and agencies, of which four were insured by the FDIC. These foreign banks also owned 10 Edge Act and agreement corporations and one commercial lending company. In addition, they held a controlling interest in 47 U.S. commercial banks. Altogether, the U.S. offices of these foreign banks controlled approximately 21 percent of U.S. commercial banking assets. These 163 foreign banks also operated 89 representative offices; an additional 34 foreign banks operated in the United States through a representative office. [5]

Some Edge Act offices are located overseas. The Edge Act offices may engage in banking practices that are permitted in foreign countries but that are denied to other types of U.S. banking organizations.

The International Banking Act of 1978 amended the Edge Act to permit domestic banks to acquire foreign financial organizations. To establish reciprocity, foreign financial organizations were permitted to acquire domestic banks. It also permitted foreign banks to establish Edge Act banking offices.

INTERNATIONAL BANKING FACILITIES

In the 1960s and 1970s, offshore banking increased as a means of avoiding reserve requirements, limitations on interest rates placed on time and savings deposits, and other regulations. So called ***shell banks*** were opened in the Bahamas and Cayman Islands. They were nothing more than "name plates" that were used to book transactions "offshore" that actually took place in the United States.

Beginning in 1981, the Federal Reserve Board permitted domestic and foreign banks to establish ***international banking facilities (IBFs)*** to take deposits and make loans to nonresidents, and serve as record-keeping facilities.

International banking facilities enable depository institutions in the United States to offer deposit and loan services to foreign residents and institutions free of Federal Reserve System reserve requirements, as well as some state and local taxes on income.

IBFs permit U.S. banks to use their domestic U.S. offices to offer foreign customers deposit and loan services that formerly could be provided competitively only from foreign offices.

Among depository institutions that may establish an IBF are U.S. commercial banks, Edge Act corporations, foreign commercial banks through branches and agencies in the U.S., savings and loan associations, and mutual savings banks.

Despite the use of terms such as "international banking facilities," "international banking zones," "international banking branches," and the "Yankee dollar market," which convey a meaning of special offices in separate locations, activities of IBFs can be conducted by institutions from existing quarters. However, IBFs' transactions must be maintained on separate books or ledgers of the institution. IBFs enable institutions operating in the U.S. to compete more effectively for foreign-source deposit and loan business in the Eurocurrency markets abroad.'[6]

In reality, an IBF is a set of accounts in a domestic bank that is segregated from the other accounts of that organization. In other words, an IBF is not a bank, per se, but an accounting system. IBF accounts do not have the same reserve requirements as domestic banks, and they are granted special tax status by some states. The tax breaks are inducements by the states to encourage the development of international financial centers.

IBFs are subject to some restrictions that do not apply to foreign branches of U.S. banks. For example, they are not permitted to accept deposits or make loans to U.S. residents. They may not issue negotiable instruments, because they might fall into the hands of U.S. residents. Nonbank customers' deposits have a minimum maturity of two days so they cannot act as substitutes for domestic demand deposits. The minimum denomination of deposits for nonbank customers is $100,000. Because of the minimum size of the deposits, they are not covered by the FDIC deposit insurance.

FOREIGN BANKS IN THE UNITED STATES

The Bank of Montreal was the first foreign bank to establish operations in the United States. Today, it is a bank holding company operating under the name BMO Financial Corp., and it was the 26th largest holding company in the United States with total assets of $125 billion.[7] There are about 330 foreign branches and agencies doing business in the United States with offices scattered throughout the country in major cities such as New York and Atlanta.[8]

The International Banking Act of 1978 codified the federal regulation of foreign banking activities in the U.S. The regulation and supervision are carried out primarily by the Federal Reserve. However, the Comptroller of the Currency, the FDIC and state banking authorities may also be involved in their regulation. According to the Act, foreign banks can operate agencies, branches, investment companies, commercial bank subsidiaries, and Edge Act offices in the United States. The Act does not require reciprocity for U.S. banks operating in foreign countries.

AGENCY

According the International Banking Act of 1978, an *agency* is any office or any place of business of a foreign bank located in any state of the United States or District of Columbia at which credit balances are maintained, checks are paid, or money lent, but deposits may not be accepted for a citizen or resident of the United States. Agencies are used primarily to facilitate international trade between the U.S. and the foreign bank's native land.

BRANCH

The definition for a branch is similar to that of an agency, except a branch "may accept deposits that are incidental to, or for the purpose of carrying out transactions in foreign countries." The branch can do almost anything that the parent bank can do, in exactly the same way domestic branch banks operate.

The foreign parent bank must decide in which state the branch will be located. The parent bank can apply for a state-chartered branch, in which case it must operate under the banking laws of that state. Alternately, it might apply for a federal charter from the Comptroller of the Currency, in which case it will be treated as a member bank of the Federal Reserve System (like all national banks) and be covered by FDIC insurance. U.S. branches of foreign banks are required to have FDIC insurance.

A limited branch is an Edge Act office set up outside the home state, or some other facility that does not have all of the powers of the branch bank. ***Representative offices*** established by a foreign bank are similar to those described for domestic banks.

INVESTMENT COMPANY

Investment companies owned by foreign financial organizations are similar to state chartered commercial banks with the following exceptions. They can deal in securities such as common stock, while banks are not permitted to invest in stocks. In addition, an investment company can lend more than 10 percent of its capital and surplus to one customer, while banks have limitations relative to capital on the amount they can lend. Finally, an investment company cannot accept deposits.

Do not confuse foreign investment companies with domestic investment companies (i.e. mutual funds). Although both are called investment companies, they are different types of financial organizations. Domestic investment companies, commonly called mutual funds, pool investors' funds and invest them in securities to obtain capital gains, income, or some other financial objective. Foreign investment companies make loans and equity investments on the behalf of their owners.

SUBSIDIARY

Foreign banks can own U.S. banks, in whole or in part. The U.S. offices of foreign banking organizations consist of:

- U.S. branches and agencies of foreign banks.
- Bank subsidiaries of foreign banking organizations are U.S. commercial banks of which more than 25 percent is owned by a foreign banking organization, or where the relationship is reported as being a controlling relationship by the foreign bank. It also includes ownership of Edge Act and agreement corporations, and U.S. representative offices of foreign banks, and New York State investment companies owned by foreign banking organizations.[9]

The banks that they own are subject to the same rules and regulations as any other domestic banks. Several examples of large foreign-bank owned U.S. banks or their holding companies:

- Union Bank of California (The bank's holding company is UnionBanCalCorporation, which is owned by The Bank of Tokyo-Mitsubishi, Ltd.),
- Marine Midland Bank, Buffalo, New York was acquired by HSBC Holdings PLC (Formerly known as Hong Kong & Shanghai Banking Corp.) and changed its name to HSBC Bank USA in 1999.
- Republic National Bank of New York merged with HSBC Bank USA in 1999.
- BMO Harris Bank, N.A. based in Chicago is wholly owned by BMO Financial Group, one of Canada's largest full-service investment firms. BMO Financial Group is an outgrowth of the Bank of Montreal that was Canada's first bank founded in 1817.
- Deutsche Bank Trust Company Americas, formerly known as Bankers Trust Company, was acquired by Deutsche Bank AG, Frankfurt, Germany.

This partial listing of foreign-owned subsidiaries suggests that foreign banks play an important role in our financial system.

FINANCE COMPANIES

Foreign financial organizations may own or operate finance companies – nonbank firms that make loans. For example, Fuji Bank Ltd., Tokyo bought Heller Financial, Inc., Chicago. Because of financial difficulties, Fuji became a subsidiary of Mizuho Holdings Inc., and subsequently sold Heller to GE Capital.

Some of the names of these entities are so familiar to those engaged in banking that it is easy to forget that they are owned by foreign banks.

FINANCIAL HOLDING COMPANIES

Perhaps the best way to appreciate the extent to which foreign banks and their subsidiaries are operating in the U.S. is to review the list of foreign-owned financial holding companies shown in Table 18-1. Notice that most of them are located in the New York Federal Reserve District. The Financial Services Modernization Act of 1999 allowed financial holding companies (FHCs) to own banks, securities firms, and insurance companies (i.e., financial services firms as approved by the Federal Reserve).

TABLE 18-1 SELECTED FOREIGN-OWNED FINANCIAL HOLDING COMPANIES IN THE U.S., JANUARY 14, 2016

Financial Holding Company	Location	Regulatory Federal Reserve District
Abbey National plc	London, United Kingdom	New York
Australia & New Zealand BKG GR	Docklands Australia	New York
Banco Bradesco SA	Osasco-Sao Paulo, Brazil	New York
Banco Santander S.A.	Boadilla Del Monte Madrid, Spain	Boston
Bank of Montreal	Montreal, Canada	Chicago
Bank of Nova Scotia	Toronto, Canada	New York
Bank of Tokyo-Mitsubishi UFJ	Tokyo, Japan	San Francisco
Barclays PLC	London, England	New York
BNP Paribas	Paris, France	San Francisco
Caixa de Aforros de Vigo, Ourense e Pontevedra	Vigo, Spain	Atlanta
Caja de Ahorros y Monte de Piedad de Madrid	Madrid, Spain	Atlanta
Canadian Imperial Bank of Commerce	Toronto, Canada	New York
Credit Agricole SA	Montrouge Cedex,, France	New York
Credit Suisse Group	Zurich, Switzerland	New York
Deutsche Bank AG	Frankfurt, Germany	New York
DNB ASA	Oslo, Norwary	New York
Governor & Co of BK of Ireland	Dublin, Ireland	New York
HBOS PLC	Edinburgh, Scotland	New York
KB FNCL GRP	Seoul, South Korea	New York
KBC BK NV	Brussels, Belgium	New York
Norinchukin BK	Tokyo, Japan	New York
Rabobank Intl. Hold BV	Utrecht, Netherlands	New York
Unicredit BK AG	Munich, Germany	New York
Unicredit SPA	Milan, Italy	New York

Source: Federal Reserve Board, "Financial Holding Companies," January 14, 2016. http://www.federalreserve.gov/bankinforeg/fhc.htm

INTERNATIONAL LENDING

Some features of international lending are different from domestic lending. There are some similar practices, also. This section examines only those lending practices that are typically associated with international lending.

SYNDICATED LOANS

Both domestic and foreign loans can be syndicated. Syndication is presented here because it permits banks of different sizes to participate in international lending.

The ***syndication*** of large loans has advantages for both the borrower and the lender. From the borrower's point of view, syndication provides for a larger amount of funds than might be available from any single lender. In addition, the credit terms may be better than for a large number of smaller loans. From the lender's point of view, syndication provides a means of diversifying some of the risks of foreign lending that were discussed previously. Another advantage of syndication is that it provides the lead bank with off-balance-sheet income for that portion of the loan that is sold to other participants. The lead bank and other banks that co-manage the loan receive fee income for their management services. Typically the management fee is paid by the borrower at the time the loan is made. Such fees range from 0.5 percent to more than two percent of the total amount of the loan. Finally, syndication can enhance relations with foreign governments because it is a means of financing their domestic economic activity.

THE SYNDICATION PROCESS

There are two types of syndicated bank loans. The first occurs when there is an agreement between the borrower and each lender. The second is a participation loan, which is a cross between traditional bank lending and underwriting. In this form of participation, there are three levels of banks in the syndicate: lead banks, managing banks, and participating banks. The lead banks negotiate with the borrower on the terms of the loan and assemble the management group that will underwrite it. They are also responsible for all documentation of the loan (notes, security agreements, legal opinions, and so on). Moreover, they are expected to underwrite a share of the loans themselves, at least as large as that of the other lenders. After the underwriting group has been established, information will be sent to other banks that might be interested in participating. For example, the initial telex cables advise the name of the borrower, maturity of the loan, and interest rates. If a bank is interested in participating, it advises a member of the underwriting group and receives additional information that permits it to analyze the credit. Although the loan may be attractive, some banks could reject it because they have already reached their lending limits in that country or region. Finally, syndication does not relieve each participating bank from doing its own credit analysis and assessment of risks.

LOAN PRICING

LIBOR (London Interbank Offer Rate) is the rate at which banks lend to other banks that are operating in the wholesale money market in London. It is also a financial index that is used in the United States that is used for loan pricing, but more commonly used in the United Kingdom and elsewhere.

Although LIBOR changes on a day-to-day basis, the interest rates on the loans are usually adjusted every three or six months. Additional loan costs include commitment fees, underwriting fees, and other charges. Commitment fees are based on the unused portion of the credit that is available to the firm under the terms of the agreement. For example, the fee might be 0.5 percent annually of that amount.

Unlike domestic loans, there may be an underwriting fee, which is a one-time front-end cost. Such fees are divided among the lead banks and the other banks in proportion to their participation.

Finally, the loans might also have clauses dealing with foreign taxes and reserve requirements, so that the lenders receive all the payments that are necessary to pay for the principal and interest on the loans.

LETTERS OF CREDIT

Financing international trade is related to, but different from, dealing in foreign exchange and international lending. International sellers want to be paid for the goods and services they are selling to foreign buyers whom they may not know or trust. However, the buyers do not want to pay until they have received the goods that were ordered. Differences between national laws, currencies, and customs frustrate the payment process. Nevertheless, payments can be made to the satisfaction of both the seller and the buyer by using commercial letters of credit.

IMPORT LETTERS OF CREDIT

Commercial *letters of credit* issued by a domestic bank in favor of a beneficiary in a foreign country are referred to as *import letters of credit*. By way of illustration, we will examine an import letter of credit for Sabra Photos. The mechanics of *export letters of credit* are the same as the illustration, except that the letter of credit is issued by a foreign bank in favor of a beneficiary in this country.

Sabra Photos of Los Angeles wants to import cameras from Shogun Distributors in Japan, but neither has done business with the other before. The manager of Sabra Photos does not want to pay for the goods until they are shipped, and the manager of Shogun Distributors does not want to wait for the goods to arrive before being paid. One solution to this problem is to include in the purchase contract for the cameras that the payment will be paid by a commercial letter of credit if certain conditions are met. The importer's commercial bank is called the issuing bank. The *issuing bank* issues a letter of credit, which is a document agreeing to make payment, from its own account, to the exporter when the conditions of the letter credit are met. In other words, the bank is substituting its own credit for that of the importer. Before issuing the letter of credit, the importer and the bank agree on the terms and conditions under which the bank will make payment to the exporter. These terms and conditions should agree with those in the purchase contract between Sabra Photos and Shogun Distributors. But the bank is bound only by the provisions of the letter of credit.

The issuing bank forwards the letter of credit to the seller's *advising bank* overseas. Depending on the terms of the letter of credit, the advising bank negotiates the documents, and if they are in order, sends them to the issuing bank for payments to be made. The issuer may then pay the seller through the advising (paying) bank. If the advising bank "confirms" the letter of credit, it becomes an obligation of that bank to make payments if the terms of the letter of credit are met. Otherwise, it is acting only as an intermediary between the buyer and seller and will only pay if sufficient funds are available.

Terms that are commonly found in letters of credit include:

- The issuing bank will have title to the merchandise.
- The bank is not responsible for the validity, genuineness, or sufficiency of the documents representing title to the merchandise.
- The importer assumes all the risks from legal actions brought by the exporter or those who use the letter ofcredit.
- The bank is not responsible for quality, condition, or value of the merchandise represented by the documents, unless stated otherwise.
- The importer agrees to pay the bank a fee for its services.
- An itemized list of the documents that are to be delivered to the bank (or its correspondent) by the exporter is included.

If the importer agrees to these and other terms, the bank will issue a letter of credit. The terms and definitions used in connection with letters of credit are published by the International Chamber of Commerce (ICC) in Paris, France, in the *Uniform Customs and Practices for Documentary Credits,* that has been adopted my many of the world's leading trading countries.[10] The purpose of this document to provide a common understanding and interpretation of the technical aspects of letters of credit. It includes information on shipping documents, expiration dates, partial shipments, transfers, installment shipments, and other items.

A letter of credit is considered a contingent liability of the issuing bank because the actual payment of the credit is not made until the exporter presents the proper documents. Note that the bank is not interested in the merchandise per se. It is interested in the documents.

Bill of Lading

The *bill of lading*, represents the title to the merchandise that was shipped. When the exporter, Shogun Distributors, delivers the cameras to a shipper who will transport the goods, the shipper acknowledges receipt of the goods and details of the shipment with a bill of lading. It also states who is to receive the merchandise and the title to it. Of course, if the goods are damaged and the documents are not in order, the bank will not pay under the terms of the credit agreement.

Other Documents

Other documents that could be required by the bank include the following:

1. An *invoice* describing the items that have been sold, the price, and other information.

2. A *certificate of origin* stating the country where the goods were manufactured or grown.

3. An *inspection certificate*, which is usually issued by an independent third party, stating that the merchandise is what is called for in the purchase agreement.

4. A ***draft***, or ***bill of exchange***, drawn by the exporter (Shogun Distributors) on the importer's (Sabra Photos) bank for the amount due as stated in the letter of credit. The draft can be drawn so that it is payable at sight or at some predetermined time (a time draft) after sight. Most drafts are drawn so that they are payable a certain number of days after sight. In such cases, if all the documents are presented to the issuing bank and everything is in order, the bank can accept the draft by stamping the word ***ACCEPTED*** on its face and sign it. The time draft then becomes a ***banker's acceptance***, an irrevocable obligation of the bank, and it can be sold by the exporter at a discount in order to obtain the funds due before the date of maturity. The maturity is usually less than nine months.

To illustrate the use of a banker's acceptance, suppose that the face amount of a time draft is $1 million and that it matures in six months. The bank's acceptance charge (commission plus discount rate) is six percent per annum. The amount of money to received by the maker of the draft is $970,000

a) 6% x $1 million x 6/12 = $30,000 acceptance charges

b) $1 million - $30,000 = $970,000 amount received

The acceptance charge is the gross income to the bank. It does not take into account reserve, the cost of funds, or handling costs.

The acceptance is a negotiable instrument and can be sold by the bank for the account of the payee. Since the acceptance is an obligation of the bank as well as the payee, it is considered a safe investment by investors. Some banker's acceptances are "eligible" for rediscounting with the Federal Reserve System. There are no reserve requirements on eligible acceptances, but there are reserve requirements on ineligible acceptances.

CONFIRMED LETTERS OF CREDIT

In some cases, the exporter of goods may not be satisfied by the financial strength of the importer's advising bank that issued the letter of credit. In this case, the exporter may have his bank confirm the letter by adding its guarantee that the funds will be paid in accordance with the terms of the credit.

The failure of Penn Square bank underscores the importance of confirmed letters of credit. Penn Square Bank, N.A., was located in Oklahoma City, Oklahoma. The bank was known as an originator and servicer of energy (oil) loans. It failed in 1982. Before it failed, Penn Square issued irrevocable letters of credit (some are revocable) worth $1.6 million to SGI Holland Inc. and SGI International Holdings.[11] These letters of credit were not issued in connection with international trade, but served as security for a $1.1 million promissory note made by a local oilman. When the note came due, the oilman did not pay it. The FDIC, which had taken over the bank, refused to honor the letters of credit. The point is that the quality of a letter of credit is only as secure as the quality of the issuer. The failure of Penn Square bank should serve as a warning that banks fail, too. Having the endorsement of a second bank reduces the risk. Confirmed letters of credit of this type are also known as standby letters of credit. In this case, the confirming bank pays only in the event of default of the issuing bank.

COLLECTION

The term ***collection*** refers to the process of presenting an item, such as a check, to the maker for payment. In the United States, most items for collection are handled by local clearinghouses or by the Federal Reserve System. However, no similar system exists for collection of international negotiable instruments. Therefore, banks located in one country use correspondent banks or their foreign branches to facilitate the clearing process.

CLEAN COLLECTIONS

Collections are divided into two categories, clean and documentary. ***Clean collections*** means that there are no documents attached. Traveler's checks and money orders are examples of clean collections. For example, suppose that you were on vacation in Europe and cashed a traveler's check that was drawn on a U.S. bank. The foreign bank where the traveler's check was deposited would collect on that item by sending it to a correspondent bank in the United States (or its overseas branch) to be credited to the foreign bank's account. The correspondent presents the traveler's check to the issuing bank for payment. When the payment is received, it is credited to the foreign bank's account. In some cases, the correspondent bank credits the foreign bank's account before the item is collected.

If a check drawn on a foreign bank was deposited in the United States, the reverse process would occur. Because the length of time necessary to clear the collection item, credit may not be given until the U.S. bank has received the funds or had them credited to its account. Therefore, there may be a substantial difference between the ledger balance of the account and the amount of funds that are available for use.

DOCUMENTARY COLLECTIONS

Drafts, or bills of exchange, were discussed previously in connection with letters of credit. Now consider the case of an exporter that wants to use the ***collection method*** instead of a letter of credit. In this example, the U.S. exporter has an order to sell auto parts to a South American firm. The parts are shipped, and the exporter takes a copy of the bill of lading, the draft, and other documents to her bank for collection. She tells the banker to present the draft and documents to the importer for collection. The U. S. bank will use a South American correspondent to accomplish this. The correspondent works with the importer's bank, and collects the funds and presents the bill of lading and other documents to the importer. This collection method is called documents against payment. The bank receives a fee for acting as the exporter's agent in the collection process.

Banks that are actively engaged in such collections may have form letters that give explicit instructions as to how the payments are to be made, the documents that are involved, and other pertinent information.

Banks are also involved in collections with imports. The U. S. banks present the exporter's draft and documents to the importer for payment. Collections may also be in the form of U.S. dollars or a foreign currency.

The basic difference between the collection method and a letter of credit is that an irrevocable letter of credit is an obligation of the issuing bank, whereas an exporter's draft is drawn on the importer. The collection method is less costly than a letter of credit and is frequently used when the risks to the exporter are relatively small.

FOREIGN EXCHANGE MARKETS

This remainder of this chapter deals with technical aspects of international banking, some of which are confusing and difficult to comprehend. Nevertheless, they are an integral part of international finance and lending; understanding them will give you an appreciation of the complexities.

FOREIGN EXCHANGE

Foreign exchange (FX) refers to exchanging one country's currency for a foreign currency. Thus, the U.S. dollar can be exchanged for the Japanese yen or the Mexican peso. The need to exchange currencies arises from *international flows* of goods and services and from capital flows. For example, suppose that you were going to vacation in England, where the domestic currency is the British Pound. In order to pay cash for the goods and services you acquire there, you must pay in pounds. Similarly, suppose that a company is buying electronic components from a Japanese manufacturing firm. The Japanese firm wants to be paid in yen. And European firms want to be paid in Euros. To handle these and other financial needs, some commercial banks have developed expertise in dealing with FX.

Most FX transactions in the United States are handled by a small group of money center banks headquartered in New York, Chicago, San Francisco, and other major cities. These banks have affiliates in London, Frankfort, Tokyo, and elsewhere throughout the world. Conversely, as noted previously, major foreign banks have operations located in the United States. This network of banks forms what is called the **interbank market** where foreign currencies can be bought and sold. The FX market is the largest financial market in the world!

In addition to the interbank market, there are *foreign exchange brokers* that facilitate the efficient operations of the FX market. They deal with banks, business concerns, and governments. Even banks that are part of the interbank market make use of FX brokers for certain types of transactions.

EXCHANGE RATES

The FX market operates 24 hours per day because of time differences throughout the world. When it is 5 A.M. in Chicago, it is 11 A.M. in London, and 8 P.M. of the same day in Tokyo. Changes in the values of currencies affect governments, corporations with international operations, traders and speculators throughout the world. Therefore, an **exchange rate**, the price of one currency in terms of another, can change at any time.

In theory, any two currencies can be exchanged in an FX transaction. For example, Swiss francs can be sold for Japanese yen. Such transactions typically are between banks and their customers. In practice, most transactions in the interbank market involve the purchase or sale of U.S. dollars for a foreign currency. The reasons for this are that the dollar is the principal currency used in international transactions and investment; and the dollar market for each currency may be more active than the market between Swiss francs and Japanese yen. Let's examine exchange rates first, and then how different currencies are exchanged in terms of dollars.

Direct and Indirect Exchange Rates

The exchange rate between two currencies may be stated in terms of either currency, on a direct or an indirect basis. The direct exchange rate for home country is the number of the home currency units that can be exchanged for one unit of a foreign currency. For example, as shown in Table 18-2 (next page), the exchange rate between the U.S. dollar (home currency) and the Canadian dollar (foreign currency) on a direct basis may be stated as:

$$\text{Direct rate for U.S.} = \$0.6996 \ \$/\text{CD} \qquad (18\text{-}1)$$

CD/$ is used to designate the number of Canadian dollars. Stated otherwise, $0.6996 may be exchanged for one Canadian dollar.

The indirect exchange rate is the number of foreign currency units exchanged for one unit of the home currency. For example, Table 18-1 shows that 1,4294 Canadian dollars can be exchanged for one U.S. dollar.

$$\text{Indirect rate for U.S.} = 1{,}4294 \ \text{CD}/\$ \qquad (18\text{-}2)$$

TABLE 18-2 **SELECTED FOREIGN EXCHANGE RATES**

Country and Monetary Unit	Direct Rate	Indirect Rate
	Foreign Currency/$	$/Foreign Currency
Canadian dollar	$0.6996	1.4294
United Kingdom pound	$1.4249	0.7018
Japanese yen	$0.008453	118.30
Switzerland franc	$ .9873	1.10129

Source: *The Wall Street Journal*, Markets Digest, Currencies, January 26, 2016.

Similarly, the direct and indirect rates for the United Kingdom pound may be stated as:

Direct rate for U.S.: = $1.4249 $/UK pound

Indirect rate for U.S.: = 0.7018 UK pounds/$

The direct and indirect exchange rates are reciprocals of the other; therefore when rates change, they move in opposite directions. For example, if the direct rate for the U.S. dollar increased, and was

$1.6000 $/UK pound,

The indirect rate for the U.S. dollar would be:

0.62500 UK pounds/$

Next, suppose that the indirect exchange rate for the UK pound decreased from 0.62500 UK pounds/$ to 0.62000 UK pounds/dollar. In the case of the indirect exchange rate, the value of dollars *depreciated* against the UK pound because fewer UK pounds were received per dollar. The opposite is true in the case of the direct exchange rate. The direct rate increased from $1.6000 $/UK pound to 1.6129 $/UK pound. Therefore, the UK pound *appreciated* against the dollar because more dollars are received per UK pound.

Cross-Rate

Suppose that a bank wants to exchange Japanese yen for euros. As mentioned previously, most foreign exchange transactions involve dollars. The rate at which yen and euros can be exchanged using dollars is called the cross-rate. Stated otherwise, the cross-rate is the exchange rate between two currencies in terms of a third currency. It is determined by dividing the direct exchange rates of the euro by the direct exchange rate of the yen.

Cross-rate Euro (EUR)/Japanese yen (JPY)

= (EUR)/$) / (JPY)/$) (18-3)

= 1.0853/0.0084= 129.2024 EUR/JPY

Table 18-3 shows the cross rates for selected currencies.

TABLE 18-3 SELECTED CROSS RATES

	USD	EUR	JPY	GPB
USD (USA)	-	1.0853	0.0084	1.4352
EUR (Euro)	0.9214	-	0.0078	1.3224
JPY (Japan)	118.48	128.566	-	170.043
GBP (UK)	0.6968	0.7562	0.0059	-
AUD (Australia)	1.4263	1.548	0.012	2.0471

Source: Bloomberg Business/Markets (1/26/16) http://www.bloomberg.com/markets/currencies/cross-rates

FOREIGN EXCHANGE TRANSACTIONS

In a FX transaction, the buyer and seller agree to pay each other on a predetermined date called the ***value date***. The value date may be the same day as the transaction or at a later date.

Spot Market

Most FX transactions take place in the ***spot market*** where the value date is usually two business days after the transaction originated. For example, on September 8, U.S. bank A buys one million Australian dollars (AUD) from Australian bank B at a cross rate of 1.4263 for value on September 15. On the value date, Australian bank B credits bank A's account in Australian with one million Australian dollars; and bank A credits bank B's account in the United States with $701,114.77 (1 million AUD/1.4263). These transactions consist mostly of bank deposits. Except for tourists, currency rarely leaves the country of origin.

Forward Markets

Some of the following information duplicates information in other chapters. It is presented here to facilitate your understanding of FX transactions, which can be very complex.

There are differences between the spot market, the forward interbank market, and the futures market for foreign currencies. The ***spot*** or ***cash market*** is where an actual physical commodity is bought or sold as distinguished from a *futures market* where futures contracts are traded. In the futures market, standardized transferable legal agreements to make or take delivery of a certain commodity at a known price and time are traded on organized futures exchanges.[12] In the ***forward market***, contracts are not standardized, nor are they traded on organized exchanges. A ***forward contract*** is "A cash transaction common in many industries, including commodity merchandising, in which a commercial buyer and seller agree upon delivery of a specified quality and quantity of goods at a specified future date. Terms may be more "personalized" than is the case with standardized futures contracts (i.e., delivery time and amount are as determined between seller and buyer). A price may be agreed upon in advance, or there may be agreement that the price will be determined at the time of delivery." [13]

Forward contracts are widely used in day-to-day cash transactions involving loans, leases, real estate, and certain currencies. The forward rates provide useful information. By way of illustration, consider the following hypothetical example. Suppose that you have the opportunity to invest $1,000 for six months in a Singapore based investment paying 10 percent per annum (five percent for six months). Using the forward rates for price information, what is the expected return on this investment?

Using the direct spot rate, we determine that $1,000 will buy SD793.7428 ($1,000/$0.1726). The five percent return plus the principal amounts to SD6,083.4299 at the end of six months (SD5,793.7428 x 1.05). Converting that amount back into dollars using the six-month forward rate reveals that the investment is worth $1,009.72 (SD5, 793.7428 x $0.1742). The six-month return on the investment is expected to be $9.72 ($1,009.72 - $1,000), or 1.94 percent per year (($9.72 x 2)/$1,000). The annual return on the investment is low because the dollar appreciated against the SD.

The important lesson to be learned from this example is that investing in an asset denominated in a foreign currency involves the risk of adverse changes in foreign exchange rates.

Method of Transaction

In the spot and forward interbank market, most trading is conducted by electronic means between banks, FX brokers, and corporations who negotiate the terms of the transaction with each other. In order to reduce the risk of default on such transactions, participants in the FX market usually have information about the creditworthiness of each other.

Contracts

Contracts in the forward market are privately negotiated bilateral agreements that are tailored to meet the needs of the parties involved. They can be any size and in any currency. But some currencies are subject to exchange controls that can limit forward trading.

Maturity

Maturities of futures and forward contracts can range from days to many months or longer. Once again, consider the exchange rates for the Singapore dollar (SD):

	Direct Rate $/SD
Spot rate	$0.1726
1 month forward	0.1729
3 months forward	0.1735
6 months forward	0.1742

If the forward rates for a currency exceed the spot rate, the currency is trading at a premium in the forward market. The premium may reflect expected price changes or the present value of funds to be received in the future. If the forward rates are less than the spot rate, it is trading at a discount. The direct forward rates shown above are at a premium.

In forward transactions, the exchange rate is fixed when the transaction occurs, but no funds exchange hands until the maturity date. Because exchange rates can change between the time the contract is initiated and the time it matures, there are risks involved in forward transactions.

Forward rates are frequently quoted as a percentage deviation from the spot rate on an annual basis. For simplicity, we use a 365 day year. The annual forward direct rate, expressed as a premium or a discount, can be determined by using the following equation.

$$\text{Annual forward rate (as a premium or a discount)} = \frac{(F-S) \times 100}{S} \times \frac{365}{n} \quad (18\text{-}4)$$

where

F = forward rate

S = spot rate

n = number of days to maturity

To illustrate the use of this equation, the forward direct rate on the 90-day Singapore dollar ($/SD) is

$$\frac{(0.1735 - 0.1726) \times 100}{0.1729} \times \frac{365}{90} = 2.11\% \text{ (premium)}$$

FOREIGN EXCHANGE RISKS

Dealing in foreign exchange exposes banks to four principal types of risk: exchange rate risk, interest rate risk, credit risk, and country risk.

EXCHANGE RATE RISK

When a bank buys more currency than it sells it has a ***long position***. Conversely, if a bank sells more than it buys it has a ***short position***. The bank is said to be in a ***net covered position*** when it buys and sells an equivalent amount in the same currency. When banks have either open or short positions, a change in exchange rates can cause a profit or a loss when the positions are closed out. The change in profit or loss due to changing exchange rates is called *exchange rate risk*. Even if a bank's open position in one currency is offset by its short position in another currency, it can still be exposed to adverse rate movements. Although these comments refer to currency positions, a bank must consider all assets and liabilities denominated in foreign currencies when assessing its total foreign currency exposure.

A bank can limit its trading exposure in foreign currencies by using hedging techniques, by imposing dollar limits on positions in a currency, by imposing dollar limits on regions of the world, and by imposing dollar limits on particular customers. Hedging techniques in the currency market are similar to those discussed in connection with interest rate futures.

INTEREST RATE RISK

Mismatches in the maturity structure of a bank's foreign exchange position give rise to ***interest rate risk***. For example, assume that bank E sells one million Brazilian Real (BRL1 million) on September 15 for value on September 17 to customer X and simultaneously buys BRL 1 million for value on September 27 from customer Y. Assume that the direct exchange rate is $1 = BRL 2.4. Thus, BRL 1 million is worth $418,667 to the bank. Nevertheless, the bank charges customer X more than the exchange rate for BRL 1 million ($418,767) and makes $100 profit on this transaction. Likewise, the bank pays customer Y ($418,567) less than the exchange rate and makes an additional $100 profit.

The bank has a covered position, but on September 17, it must pay BRL 1 million to customer X and it will not receive the equivalent amount from customer Y until September 27 -- a mismatch of maturities. To eliminate the risk of adverse interest rate movements during the maturity gap, bank E can arrange for a swap with bank F. Bank E will sell BRL 1 million spot and buy the same amount for value on September 27. These transactions are summarized below.

Exchange rates: $1 = BRL 2.4

Bank E	**Bank F**
September 17 Value date	
Pays BRL 1 million to customer X	Receives BRL 1 million from Bank E
Receives $418,767 from customer X	Pays $418,667 to Bank E
Profit (418,767 - $418,667 = $100)	
September 27 Value date	
Receives BRL 1 million from customer Y	Pays BRL 1 million to Bank E
Pays $418,567 to customer Y	Receives $418,667 from Bank E
Profit (418,667 - $418,567) = $100	
Total profit = $200	

To simplify this example, it was assumed that there was no cost or profit on the swap itself and that the profit was made by selling and buying BRL from customers X and Y. In reality, there are costs to the swap, but that is an unnecessary complication at this point. The illustration demonstrated that the bank could establish a gross profit of $200 on the transactions with customers X and Y, and eliminate exchange risk and interest rate risk. In practice, banks deal with hundreds of customers, and they take advantage of interest rate differentials between countries to borrow, lend, or arbitrage to their advantage. Therefore, the process of swapping for the entire bank is much more complex than was presented here.

ARBITRAGE

Arbitrage refers to the purchase of securities (assets) in one market for the *immediate* resale in another market in order to profit from price differences in the two markets. Arbitrage also may occur if there are price differences between like securities. For example, convertible bonds may be overvalued with respect to the common stocks into which they are convertible. Arbitrageurs, like speculators in the commodities markets, provide depth to market and help to keep the market efficient.

To illustrate arbitrage between different markets, suppose that the three-month secondary rate on domestic certificates of deposits (CDs) is 10.00 percent and the three-month offer rate on Eurodollar deposits is 10.10 percent. At first glance, it appears that Eurodollar rates are higher than CD rates, but all the relevant costs have not been taken into account. The FDIC insurance premium is $0.28 per $100 per year on assessable domestic deposits. In addition, the reserve requirements on the CDs is three percent. There is no reserve requirement on Eurocurrency liabilities. Using these figures the effective cost of the CDs is

$$\frac{10.0\% + 0.28\%}{(1 - 0.03)} = 10.60\%$$

The cost of the Eurodollar deposits is 10.10%.

Spread = 10.60% - 10.1=% = 0.50%

Although the nominal cost of the Eurodollars is higher than the nominal cost of the CDs, the effective cost of the Eurodollars is 50 basis points lower. Therefore, domestic banks will borrow Eurodollars instead of borrowing by using CDs. The type of arbitrage that was just described is called an *inward arbitrage* because the funds are flowing into the United States. The inward arbitrage will continue until upward pressure on the Eurodollar rates and downward pressure on CD rates equalize the effective cost of funds.

An *outward arbitrage* occurs when the effective cost of CDs is less than the effective cost of Eurodollars. Then United States banks will find it less costly to borrow in the United States than in Europe. The increased demand for CDs will bid up the yield until the effective cost of CDs and Eurodollars is equal.

Under normal market conditions, investors should not be able to make arbitrage profits because the premiums or discounts in the various currencies should be exactly offset by the adjusted interest rate differentials. For example, if the short-term interest rates were higher in London than in the United States by one percentage point per year (0.5 percentage points for six months), the six-month forward rate for pounds in terms of dollars would be about a 0.5 percentage point discount from the spot rate. This relationship is known as covered interest arbitrage or ***interest rate parity.*** However, since the market imperfections do exist, there are opportunities for arbitrage profits.

The conditions under which there is no incentive for covered interest arbitrage can be determined by using the following equations.

Where

S = spot rate (dollars per pound in our example)

F = forward rate (six-month forward exchange rate in dollars per pound in our example)

$p = \frac{F - S}{S}$ = premium or discount on the forward pound expressed in decimal form where - is the discount and + is the premium

N = short-term interest rate in the United States (per six months, expressed in decimal form)

L = short-term interest rate in London (per six months, expressed in decimal form)

Then

$$1 + N = \frac{1}{S}(1 + L)F \qquad (18\text{-}5)$$

In English, this equation means that there is no incentive for covered interest arbitrage when one dollar plus the six-month rate of interest in the United States is equal to one dollar's worth of spot pounds plus the six-month interest rate in the EU reconverted into dollars at the forward rate. It follows from the definition of p that F/S = 1 + p, and that the equilibrium condition becomes

$$p = N - L - pL$$

Therefore, the precise interest rate parity can be determined by solving

$$P = \frac{(N - L)}{(1 + L)} \qquad (18\text{-}6)$$

However, since p and L are usually small, an approximation of the interest rate parity condition is

$$p = N - L \qquad (18\text{-}7)$$

Because of adjustments for FDIC insurance, reserves, and other factors, p is actually a band, sometime called an arbitrage tunnel, within which there is no incentive for arbitrage.

CREDIT RISK

There is ***credit risk*** in foreign exchange transactions because of the possibility that the counterparty (the other bank or broker) in the transaction may be unwilling or unable to meet its contractual obligations. The credit risk associated with foreign exchange risk is not included in the definition of risk for establishing legal lending limits. The only real control on credit risk associated with foreign exchange forward exposure is self imposed. For example, in 1974, the Bankhouse I.D. Herstatt failed in Germany. Because of differences in time zones, some U.S. banks and others had paid marks to Herstatt early in the day, but Herstatt failed later in the day before completing the other side of the foreign exchange transactions -- the U.S. banks did not receive the dollars that were due to them. This particular form of credit risk is called ***settlement risk***.

Also consider the case of a bank that buys £1 million [£ = U.K. pounds] for a customer on January 5 at a rate of $2.0 ($2 million) for value on March 13. In late February, the customer declares bankruptcy and the court-appointed trustee informs the bank that it will not honor the contract. During this time, the price of sterling increased to $2.10, and the bank has to cover its unexpected short position of £1 million at the higher price, resulting in an increased cost of $100,000 to the bank. Of course, the bank can dispute its contract and loss in court, but that is a costly process and the outcome is not clear.

The point of these examples is that although the intention of dealing in foreign exchange is not to extend credit per se, there are credit risks in dealing in foreign exchange.

COUNTRY RISK

Country risk is a whole spectrum of risks arising from economic, social, and political environments of a given foreign country, having potentially favorable or adverse consequences for the profitability or recovery of debt or equity investments made in that country. Such risks include but are not limited to branching restrictions confiscation, restrictions on earnings remittances, and war. In addition, country risk includes investments in foreign subsidiaries as well as outsourcing with foreign providers. Finally, it also includes domestic counterparties where they may be adversely affected by events in a foreign country.[14]

Country risk is frequently separated into two broad categories, sovereign risk and transfer risk. ***Sovereign risk*** occurs when a national government defaults on debts, or refuses to permit loans to be repaid or seizes bank assets without adequate compensation.[15] In 1998, for example, Russia defaulted on some of its short-term debts. ***Transfer risk*** occurs when foreign borrowers have problems converting domestic currency into foreign exchange because of foreign exchange controls or for other reasons. Sometimes this results in a *currency crisis.* "A currency crisis can be defined as a speculative attack on the foreign exchange value of a currency, resulting in a sharp depreciation or forcing the authorities to sell foreign exchange reserves and raise domestic interest rates. The Latin American Tequila Crisis following Mexico's peso devaluation in 1994-95, the financial crisis that swept through Asia in 1997-98 and, more recently, the global financial crisis in 2008-09 that forced sharp depreciations in many advanced as well as developing economies are examples of currency crises."[16] Crises are often associated with banking crises. Commercial banks must assess both types of risk. Although cases of expropriation or outright repudiation on loans are rare in the post-World War II period (Cuba and Chile are two examples), cases of debt rescheduling have been commonplace, such as Russia in 1998. The restructuring or refinancing are usually preceded by a foreign exchange crisis. *Restructuring debt* usually involves stretching principal and interest payments, whereas *refinancing* usually involves new loans. As one humorist said, refinancing and restructuring loans is good because "a rolling loan gathers no losses."

International lenders use statistical indicators to help gauge country risk. The data for the indicators is published by the World Bank. Unfortunately, the data are often out of date by the time they are available, so the indicators are of limited value. Equally important, these data may not accurately predict a crisis. The World Bank, for example, praised Indonesia for its macroeconomic performance shortly before its financial crisis began in 1997.[17]

The extent of country risk exposure can be limited by placing dollar limits on investments in foreign countries or regions of the world. In addition, some foreign banks and central governments will guarantee both the principal and interest on certain risks. Sometimes, however, governments renege on their financial obligations. Russia in 1998 and Argentina in 2001 are two examples.

Summary

Although there are many similarities between domestic bank operations and international banking operations, there are also many differences. In fact, it is sometimes said that the international banking part of a bank is a bank within a bank because it makes loans, takes payments, makes payments, and performs most of the services of a bank. This chapter focused on several aspects of banking that are uniquely international. These included why banks deal in international markets, foreign exchange operations, international lending, and collections. Dealing in foreign exchange entails certain risks. To some extent, the exchange rate risk and interest rate risk can be reduced by hedging, swaps, and arbitrage. Credit risk and country risk exposure can be reduced by other means, including diversification of portfolios, lending limits, and government guarantees and insurance.

Many large-scale international loans are syndicated, which is a hybrid of investment banking and traditional participation loans. Such loans can be beneficial to both the borrower and the lenders if everything goes as planned.

Letters of credit are widely used in international trade to facilitate the payment process; the other side of the coin is the collection process. Both are important aspects of international banking.

KEY TERMS AND CONCEPTS

Agency (foreign bank)
Agreement corporations
Arbitrage
Banker's acceptance
Bill of exchange (draft)
Bill of lading
Cash market (spot market)
Certificate of origin
Clean collection
Collection
Collection method
Commitment fees
Confirmed letter of credit
Correspondent banking
Country risk
Covered interest arbitrage
Credit risk (FX)
Cross-rate
Currency crisis
Draft (bill of exchange)
Edge Act
Exchange rate (direct, indirect, cross-rate, risk)
Euro
Exchange rate, direct, indirect
Finance companies
Financial holding companies
Foreign exchange (FX)
Foreign investment companies
Forward market

Forward contract
Inspection certificate
Interest rate parity
Interbank market
Interest rate parity
Interest rate risk
Invoice
International banking facilities (IBFs)
Letter of credit (commercial, import, export)
LIBOR
Long position
Net covered position
Participation loan
Refinancing
Representative offices
Restructuring debt
Settlement risk
Shell banks
Short position
SIBOR
Spot market (cash market)
Sovereign risk
Standby letter of credit
Syndication (loans)
Trade finance
Transfer risk
Value date

Questions

18.1. What distinguishes domestic from international banking?

18-2. The Edge Act permits banks to operate Edge Act offices in any state or overseas. True or false. Explain your position.

18-3. Are foreign commercial banks operating in the United States subject to the same rules and regulations as domestic banks?

18-4. Define the term foreign exchange. Give an example.

18-5. What is meant by direct and indirect exchange rates for U.S. dollars?

18-6. What is the relationship between direct and indirect exchange rates? How
can they be used to calculate the cross-rate between the Swiss franc and the Euro?

18.7. Suppose that the indirect rate for the South African Rand changed from 5.5000 to 5.0000. Did the value of U.S. dollars appreciate or depreciate? Why?

18.8. Define the following terms:

- value date
- spot market
- futures market
- forward market

18.9. Distinguish between margins for stocks and margins for futures contracts.

18.10. Briefly describe the risks in a forward transaction.

18.11. Briefly discuss the four risks associated with foreign exchange.

18.12. Distinguish between inward and outward arbitrage.

18.13. What is meant by interest rate parity?

18-14. Briefly describe two kinds of country risk.

18.15. What is a letter of credit in foreign exchange?

PROBLEMS

18-1. Calculate the annual forward direct rate on 30-day U.K. pounds with a forward rate of $2.20 and a spot rate of $2.00.

18.2 Calculate the cross-rate for pounds and marks, given the indirect rate for pounds is 0.5 and the direct rate for marks is $2.40.

18-3. Bank A has a maturity mismatch in its foreign exchange position. It has sold 5 million Swiss francs on November 13 for value on November 15 to bank X for $2,501,000 and bought 5 million francs for value on November 25 from bank Z for $2,499,000. The exchange rate is $1 = 2 francs on 1
franc = $.50. To eliminate possible interest rate risk during the maturity gap, it arranges a swap with bank B. Write out the transactions of bank A and B on these value dates. What are the profits to bank A of the swap?

18-4. Assuming FDIC insurance costs 0.40 percent per year on domestic deposits, and the reserve requirements is 3 percent on all deposits, what is the effective cost of three-month CDs paying 9 percent and three-month Eurodollars offering 9.20 percent? Which will banks prefer to borrow? What kind of arbitrage is this?

18-5. Given the following information:

spot rate = $2/pound

six-month forward rate = $2.20/pound

six-month interest rate in U.S. = .05

six-month interest rate in London = .04

Is there an opportunity for covered interest arbitrage?

ENDNOTES

1. JPMorgan Chase & Co., *About Us*, https://www.jpmorganchase.com/corporate/About-JPMC/about-us.htm Our Story, "Where We Are," Delivering for our clients worldwide," Bank of America, http://about.bankofamerica.com/en-us/our-story/where-we-are.html#fbid=79rcOxmhXEx; ; "Global Consumer Banking," 2014 Annual Report, Citi®, https://www.citigroup.com/citi/investor/quarterly/2015/annual-report/. For the risk exposure for the U.S. banks operating overseas, see: "Country Exposure Lending Survey, Federal Financial Institutions Examination Council Statistical Release E.16 (126) Period: September 30, 2015, http://www.ffiec.gov/pdf/e16/E16_201509.pdf

2. "Holding Companies with Assets Greater Than $10 Billion," National Information Center, 9/30/15. http://www.ffiec.gov/nicpubweb/nicweb/OrgHierarchySearchForm.aspx?parID_RSSD=3232316&parDT_END=99991231

3. For additional information, see the website for the Bank of Tokyo-Mitsubishi UFJ; http://www.bk.mufg.jp/global/

4. William Goulding and Daniel E. Nolle,"Foreign Banks in the U.S.: A primer," Board of Governors of the Federal Reserve System International Finance Discussion Papers Number 1064 November 2012, http://www.federalreserve.gov/pubs/ifdp/2012/1064/ifdp1064.pdf. For further information about "Structure Data for U.S. Banking Offices of Foreign Entities," see the Federal Reserve Board: http://www.federalreserve.gov/releases/iba/201509/default.htm\

5. Board of Governors of the Federal Reserve, "Banking Supervision and Regulation Annual Report, 2014." http://www.federalreserve.gov/publications/annual-report/2014-supervision-and-regulation.htm

6. "International Banking Facilities," Federal Reserve Bank of New York, April, 2007, https://www.newyorkfed.org/aboutthefed/fedpoint/fed34.html

7. "Holding Companies with Assets Greater Than $10 Billion," National Information Center, 9/30/15. Op. cit. For detailed data, see: "Holding Companies with Assets Greater Than $10 Billion," National Information Center, 9/30/15. http://www.ffiec.gov/nicpubweb/nicweb/OrgHierarchySearchForm.aspx?parID_RSSD=3232316&parDT_END=99991231

8. Manta Media Inc., http://www.manta.com/mb_34_A1051_000/branches_and_agencies_of_foreign_banks?pg=1

9. Structure and Share Data for U.S. Offices of Foreign Banks, (About), Board of Governors of the Federal Reserve System. http://www.federalreserve.gov/releases/iba/201509/default.htm

10. For more information about the ICC, see http://www.iccwbo.org/index.asp

11. "2 Firms, Investors File Penn Square Suits," *Tulsa World*," October 3, 1982, p. B-5.

12. Definitions used here are based on those of the CME Group, which includes - CME, CBOT, NYMEX and COMEX.

13. CME Group, Glossary of Terms, http://www.advantagefutures.com/education/glossary-of-futures-terms/

14. "Country Risk," *OCC Bulletin*, OCC 2002-10, March 11, 2002. For additional information about coun-

try risk, see: Country Risk Management October, 2001. http://www.occ.gov/publications/publications-by-type/comptrollers-handbook/_paginated/countryriskmanagement/default.htm

15. For current sovereign ratings, see Moody's: www.moodys.com

16. Reuven Glick and Michael Hutchinson, "Country Crises, Federal Reserve Bank of San Francisco", Working Paper 2011-22. http://www.frbsf.org/economic-research/files/wp11-22bk.pdf

17. Salomon, Jay, "World Bank Says It Was Wrong on Indonesia," *The Wall Street Journal*, February 5, 1998, A17.

GLOSSARY

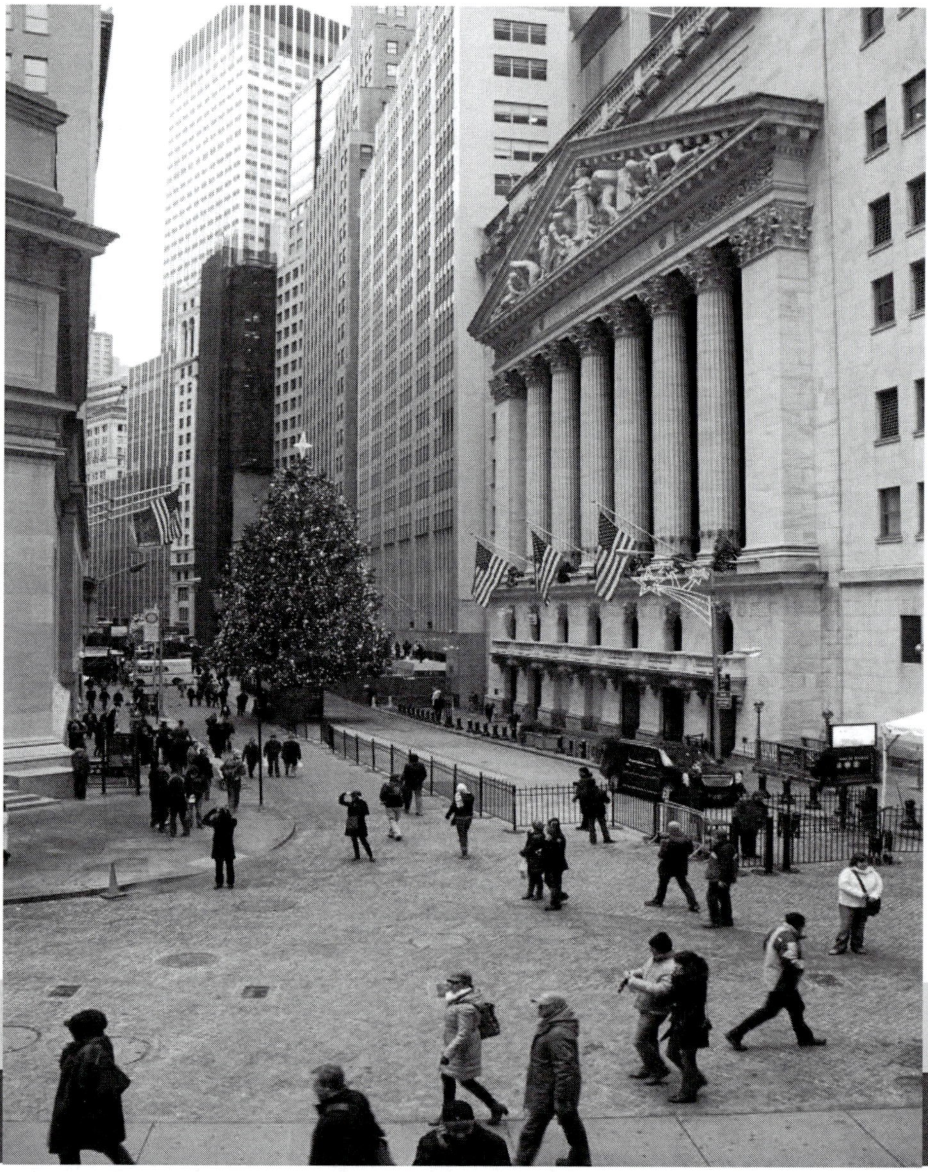

Acceptance participation: This marketable money market instrument is created when a bank accepts a time draft (a bill of exchange) and agrees to pay it at face value on maturity. The draft normally covers the sale of goods, particularly with respect to international trade.

Account party: One of the participants in a financial obligation or performance contract.

Acquisition: The purchase of a target firm by a bidder firm in which the target. In a bank acquisition the target bank retains its bank charter, CEO, and board of directors. It becomes an affiliate member of the bank holding company (BHC) in which the buying bank belongs.

Adjustable Rate Mortgages: An adjustable rate mortgage is one in which the interest rate changes over the life of the loan. These changes can alter monthly payments, the term of the loan, and/or the principal amount.

Adverse selection: Adverse selection means that high-risk borrowers try to get loans from banks because they are willing to pay the average rate of interest which is less than they would have to pay if their true condition were known to the bank.

Agency: According the International Banking Act of 1978, an agency is "any office or any place of business of a foreign bank located in any state of the United States or District of Columbia at which credit balances are maintained, checks are paid, or money lent, but deposits may not be accepted for a citizen or resident of the United States."

Agency cost: The loss in shareholder wealth due to self-serving actions by managers, who seek to maximize their own salary, fringe benefits, job security, etc. at the expense of shareholders.

Agency securities: Many federal agencies issue securities that are not direct obligations of the U.S. Treasury but nonetheless are federally sponsored or guaranteed. Some examples of federal agencies are the Government National Mortgage Association (GNMA or Ginnie Mae), Federal Home Loan Mortgage Corporation (FHLMC or Freddie Mac), Federal Housing Administration (FHA), Veterans Administration (VA), Farm Credit Administration (FCA), Federal Land Banks (FLB), and Small Business Administration (SBA).

Aggregation risk: This risk comes about from the complex interconnections that can occur in derivatives deals which involve a number of markets and instruments. It becomes difficult to assess the risks to individual parties or groups of parties in such transactions.

Aggressive/defensive asset liability management: The goal of defensive asset/liability management is to insulate the net interest income from changes in interest rates; that is, to prevent interest rate changes from decreasing or increasing the net interest income. In contrast, aggressive asset/liability management focuses on increasing the net interest income through altering the portfolio of the institution.

Aggressive investment strategies: These strategies do require active management and so are more complex and costly approaches than passive strategies. Some examples of these strategies are playing the yield curve, riding the yield curve, and various kinds of bond swaps.

Aggressive liquidity approach: An approach to liquidity management that seeks to take advantage of yield curve relationships to buy and sell securities and make potential earnings gains.

Annual percentage rate: The annual percentage rate (APR) is the percentage cost of credit on an annual basis.

Annuity: An annuity refers to a schedule of payments at fixed intervals for a stated number of years, or for the duration of the life of the person receiving the payments (the annuitant), or the lives of two or more persons.

Arbitrage: Arbitrage refers to the purchase of securities (assets) in one market for the immediate resale in another market in order to profit from price differences in the two markets.

Asset-based lending: The major distinctions between asset-based loans and other secured loans is that much greater weight is given to the market value of the collateral in asset based lending than in regular commerical and industrial loans. In addition, asset based lenders place greater emphasis on monitoring than do traditional bank lenders.

Asset/liability management (ALM): The process of making decisions about the composition of assets and liabilities and their risk assessment is known as asset/liability management.

Asset liquidity: The sale of money market instruments to meet cash demands for loans, securities investments, etc.

Asset management: This type of liquidity management refers to meeting liquidity needs by using near-cash assets, including net funds sold to other banks and money market securities.

Asset utilization: This financial ratio represents the ability of management to employ assets effectively to generate revenues. It is calculated as operating revenue to total assets.

Asymmetric information: Asymmetric information means that the borrowers have more information about themselves than is available to the bank.

Automatic transfer service accounts: ATS accounts allow small depositors to minimize transactions balances by automatically transferring funds from their interest-bearing savings account to their checking account as overdrafts occur.

Average costs: The cost of funds calculated by dividing dollar costs of funds by the dollar amount of funds.

Balance sheet: This accounting statement contains the record of assets, liabilities, and equity at the end of a period.

Balloon Mortgage: Balloon mortgage loans are relatively short-term loans, such as five years. At the end of that period, the entire amount of the loan comes due and a new loan is negotiated.

Bancassurance: A conglomerate financial services firm that combines banking and insurance activities.

Bank: A bank is an organization that makes loans, has FDIC insured deposits, and has been granted banking powers either by the state or the federal government.

Bank capital: The sum of equity (i.e., common stock, preferred stock, surplus, and undivided profits) plus long-term debt plus reserves that are set aside to meet anticipated bank operating losses from loans, leases, and securities.

Bankers' acceptance: These are short-term time drafts used in international trade that are "accepted" by a large bank to arrange financing the shipment of goods. The bank may discount the acceptance in the money market to finance the transaction.

Bank holding company: A corporation that holds stock in one or more banks and other financial service organizations.

Banking Act of 1933: This act was also known as the Glass-Steagall Act. It separated commercial banking from investment banking, established the Federal Deposit Insurance Corporation (FDIC), permitted the Federal Reserve to regulate the interest paid on time deposits, and prohibited the payment of interest on demand deposits, and raised the minimum capital requirements for national banks.

Banking Act of 1935: This act was primarily intended to strengthen the Federal Reserve System and its monetary management power. The act gave the Federal Reserve Board expanded reserve requirement authority, it could regulate discount rates of the District Banks, and it had the power to regulate the rate of interest paid by member banks on time and savings deposits .

Bank risk management: Banks must manage their operations in terms of their risk/return characteristics with the goal of maximizing shareholder wealth. There are different types of risk (credit risk, interest rate risk, liquidity risk, price risk, foreign exchange risk, operational risk, compliance risk, strategic risk, and reputation risk) that impact on the total risk of the organization.

Bank runs: Runs occur when depositors or other creditors fear for the safety or availability of their funds, and large numbers of depositors try to withdraw their funds at the same time.

Basis risk: The difference between the cash price and futures price used in futures and options hedging.

Basis swaps: A swap involving the exchange of interest payments on two different floating rates of interest (e.g., 6-month LIBOR and U.S. prime commercial paper rates or two variable-rate contracts with different maturities).

Basle Agreement: This landmark international banking agreement was signed in June 1988 by 12 industrialized nations under the auspices of the Bank for International Settlements (BIS). By year-end 1992 all U.S. banks were required to comply with the new rules.

Bidder: This is the buyer in a merger or acquisition involving two firms.

Bilateral netting: In a bilateral netting system, two banks that may have multiple contracts to settle in a foreign currency, such as German marks, can replace them with a single contract for the net amount to be sent through the German payments system for clearing.

Board of directors written loan policy: The Board of Directors has the ultimate responsibility for all of the loans made by their bank. Because the Board delegates the task of making loans to others, it must have a written loan policy that establishes the guidelines and principles for the bank's lending activities.

Book value of equity: This equity account on the balance sheet equals the sum of common stock, preferred stock, surplus, and undivided profits.

Bridge loan: Bridge loans "bridge a gap" in a borrower's financing until some specific event occurs. For example, a firm wants to acquire a new warehouse facility, but needs funds to finance the transaction until the old warehouse can be sold. A bridge loan can be used to fill the gap.

Brokered deposits: Small and large time deposits obtained by banks from middlemen seeking insured deposit accounts on behalf of their customers.

Call option: This option contract gives the buyer the right (but not the obligation) to buy an underlying instrument (such as a T-bill futures contract) at a specified price (called the exercise or strike price) and the seller the comparable right to sell the underlying instrument at the same price.

Call risk: The risk of an issuing firm refinancing a bond during a period of low interest rates, which forces bondholders to reinvest their funds in bonds bearing lower interest yields.

CAMELS: This acronym stands for: Capital adequacy; Asset quality; Management; Earnings; Liquidity; and Sensitivity to market risk (interest rates, foreign exchange) and the ability of the bank to manage that risk. The composite score given by bank examiners ranges from 1 (good) to 5 (unsafe).

Cap: An interest rate cap is a contract that reduces the exposure of a floating rate borrower to increases in interest rates by setting the maximum or ceiling on the interest rate. A firm can implement a cap by purchasing an interest rate call option contract.

Capital adequacy: This term is most frequently used in the context of regulatory policy, which seeks to require banks to maintain sufficient capital levels to ensure safety and soundness in the banking industry while at the same time encouraging bank efficiency and competitiveness.

Capital gain: The change in value or price of an asset between two points in time.

Capital impairment: This occurs when a bank has insufficient capital to absorb losses, which generally triggers regulators to close the bank.

Capital market risk: The liabilities management problem that low interest rate levels will motivate investors to transfer deposit funds to the capital market in an attempt to earn higher rates of return.

Capital notes and debentures: These long-term debt instruments are senior debt capital sources of external funds.

Capital reserves: Reserves that are counted as capital on the balance sheet of banks and that can be used to absorb unexpected losses. These reserves are employed by regulators in measures of capital adequacy.

Carry trade strategy: This strategy is implemented by borrowing short-term funds (e.g., fed funds) and investing in longer-term securities (e.g., one- and two-year Treasury securities). As long as interest rates do not increase, the carry trade can earn a positive yield spread.

Cash management: These services for business concerns are one of the most popular off-balance sheet activities offered by banks. Cash management systems are used to help business concerns collect remittances and use their bank balances efficiently. Lock boxes are an important part of cash management systems.

Ceiling agreement: Also called a cap, this agreement between a bank and its customer specifies the maximum lending rate on a loan and, therefore, protects the customer from interest rate risk.

Charged-off (loan): A loan is charged-off, which means that it is removed from the balance sheet, when it is no longer of sufficient value to be considered creditworthy.

CHIPS: International funds transfers use CHIPS (Clearing House Interbank Payments System) operated by the New York Clearing House Association (NYCHA).

Collateral: Collateral refers to an asset pledged against the performance of an obligation. If a borrower defaults on a loan, the bank takes the collateral and sells it.

Commercial mortgages: These include loans for land, construction and real estate development, and loans on commercial properties such as shopping centers, office buildings or warehouses.

Commercial paper: These are short-term, unsecured promissory notes issued by major U.S. corporations with strong credit ratings. Banks can use their holding companies to issue commercial paper and use funds to acquire loans and investments.

Commitment: See loan commitment.

Common stock: This equity account on the balance sheet equals the number of common shares outstanding multiplied by their par value per share. Common stock represents ownership rights to residual earnings of the firm, as well as voting power on important decisions affecting the firm.

Community Reinvestment Act: The Community Reinvestment Act is directed at federally regulated lenders that take deposits and extend credit. The intent of the legislation is to facilitate the availability of mortgage loans and other types of loans to all qualified applicants, without regard to their race, nationality, or sex.

Comprehensive contingency funding plans: These plans outline courses of action to various liquidity problems and define coincident management responsibilities to deal with such problems.

Confirmed letter of credit: A bank guarantee to pay a letter of credit.

Commercial and industrial loans: C&I loans are loans made for business purposes, such as financing working capital and equipment.

Consumer credit: Consumer credit consists of loans to individuals for personal, household, or family consumption.

Contemporaneous reserve requirement accounting: The computation and maintenance periods overlap for the most part in reserve requirement management. This method was used from 1984 to 1994 in the U.S. among depository institutions.

Contingent claim: An obligation by a bank to provide funds (i.e., lend funds or buy securities) if a contingency is realized. In other words, the bank has underwritten an obligation of a third party and currently stands behind the risk.

Conventional mortgage loans: Conventional mortgage loans are those that are not insured by the Federal Housing Administration (FHA) or guaranteed by the Veterans Administration (VA).

Core deposits: These deposits are typically made by regular bank customers, including business firms, government units, and households. Core deposits provide a stable, long-term source of funds. They are not sensitive to changes in interest rates.

Corporate bond: These are long-term debt securities issued by a private corporation.

Corporate control: This term applies to the control of management and, in turn, bank operations, by shareholders. More concentrated ownership in the hands of fewer shareholders tends to enhance management control. In closely-held banks, because the owners are often the executive officers, minimal conflicts of self-interest arise. In banks that are not closely held, however, it is possible that managers and shareholders have different objectives with resultant agency costs.

Correspondent balances: These are excess funds deposited by smaller banks in their larger correspondent banks.

Correspondent banks: Banks that provide the gamut of banking products and services to other banks in exchange for fees and/or deposits.

Cost/revenue analysis: An approach to managing liabilities wherein the goal of bank management should be to maximize deposit revenues and minimize deposit costs in an effort to maximize bank profitability.

Counterparty credit risk: This is the risk that a counterparty in a financial transaction will default, resulting in a financial loss to the other party over time.

Country risk: Country risk refers to the whole spectrum of risks arising from economic, social, and political environments of a given foreign country having potentially favorable or adverse consequences for the profitability and/or recovery of debt or equity investments made in that country.

Coupon swaps: A swap wherein the exchange of interest payments is based on fixed rates (e.g., 11 percent) and floating rates of interest (e.g., LIBOR or London interbank offered rate).

Credit card: A credit card is any card or device that may be used from time to time and over and over again to borrow money, or buy goods and services on credit.

Credit option: Essentially an insurance credit derivative contract, this option would pay the amount of lost capital value in the event bonds held by the investor are downgraded.

Credit risk: Credit risk is the risk to earnings and capital that an obligor will fail to meet the terms of any contract with the bank, or otherwise fail to perform as agreed. It is usually associated with loans and investments, but it can also arise in connection with derivatives, foreign exchange, and other extensions of bank credit.

Credit risk capital requirements: Under risk-based capital requirements, bank assets are weighted to force banks to hold more capital against higher credit risk assets (e.g., zero default risk items have a 0 percent weight, mortgaged-backed bonds issued by U.S. government and U.S. government sponsored agencies and general obligation municipal bonds have a 20 percent weight, home loans, revenue bonds, and some other mortgage-backed securities carry a 50 percent weight, and all other assets have a 100 percent weight).

Credit scoring: Credit scoring is the use of statistical models to determine the likelihood that a prospective borrower will default on a loan. Credit scoring models are widely used to evaluate business, real estate, and consumer loans.

Credit swap: A credit derivative in which two banks simply exchange interest and principal payments on portions of their loan portfolios. This swap enables the participating banks to diversify their credit risk to a greater extent than previously possible.

Crisis liquidity: Liquidity problems that threaten the solvency of a bank, which can arise either from problems specific to the institution or problems that affect all institutions.

Cross-currency interest rate swaps: An interest rate swap that is based on interest payments in different currencies.

Cumulative gap: The cumulative gap measures the difference between rate-sensitive assets and liabilities over an extended periods or maturity buckets. The cumulative gap is the sum of the incremental gaps.

Currency swaps: This swap involves not only the exchange of interest payments (in different currencies) but also the exchange of the initial and final principal amounts at the beginning and end of the swap.

Debit card: A debit card is any card or device that may be used to buy goods and services by withdrawing funds from the holders account. No credit is extended.

Deposit Insurance: The Banking Act of 1933 (Glass-Steagall Act) established the Federal Deposit Insurance Corporation to protect small depositors to reduce the incidence of bank runs by insuring their bank deposits up to a predetermined amount.

Depository Institutions Deregulation and Monetary Control Act (DIDMCA, 1980): Uniform reserve requirements were extended to all depository institutions; Federal Reserve services were offered to all depository institutions; Regulation Q phased out interest rate ceilings on deposit accounts at all depository institutions; and, savings and loan's lending powers were broadened.

Deregulation: Deregulation in banking has three separate although closely related dimensions: price (e.g., deposit rate) deregulation, product deregulation, and geographic deregulation. Price deregulation refers to the lifting of legal restrictions on the interest rates that depository institutions may pay to obtain funds. Product deregulation refers to the removal of the restrictions placed on banks and other depository institutions regarding the types of services offered, such as investment banking services or insurance underwriting. Geographic deregulation refers to the removal of limitations on the geographic extent over which banks (and other depository institutions) may operate deposit-taking facilities.

Demand deposits: These deposits are checking accounts that pay no interest by law.

DINB: A Deposit Insurance National Bank (or so-called bridge bank) can be chartered by the FDIC to take over operations of a troubled bank until it is either closed or acquired by another bank.

Discount window: Operated by the Federal Reserve, this source of funds is employed by banks to meet unexpected shortfalls of cash, especially to meet reserve requirements on deposit accounts.

Discount window advance: Banks can borrow funds from the 12 regional Federal Reserve banks by this means (subject to the provisions of Regulation A). Advances can be used by banks to meet unanticipated reserve deficiencies or to meet more persistent outflows of funds that are transitory in nature (e.g., an unexpected loss of deposits, surge in credit demands, or natural disaster).

Dividend yield/return: This financial ratio is calculated as cash dividends to the current stock price of the firm.

Dollar gap: The dollar gap (also referred to as the funding gap or the maturity gap), is the difference between the dollar amount of interest rate-sensitive assets and the dollar amount of interest rate-sensitive liabilities.

Dollar gap ratio: This ratio measures the sensitivity of a bank's net interest margin to a change in interest rates. It is calculated as interest rate sensitive assets minus interest sensitive liabilities divided by total assets.

Dual banking system: Banks can be chartered by the Office of the Comptroller of the Currency for a national charter, or they can receive a state charter.

Duration: A measure of interest rate sensitivity of a financial instrument. The weighted average time to receive all cash flows from a financial instrument.

Duration drift: The change in the duration of a financial instrument over time.

Duration gap: The duration gap is the difference between the duration of a banks assets and liabilities. It is a measure of interest rate sensitivity that helps to explain how changes in interest rates affect the market value of a bank's assets and liabilities, and, in turn, its net worth.

Earning assets: Loans, investment securities, and short-term investments that generate interest and yield related fee income.

Economic value added (EVA): This measure is calculated as adjusted earnings minus the opportunity cost of capital. It is used to evaluate the economic profitability of loans, projects, product lines, etc. in order to evaluate whether the investment will increase shareholder wealth. It is generally employed for the purpose of internal performance evaluations.

Economies of scale and scope: Economies of scale usually refer to a situation where a firm that has high volume of a commodity can produce it a low costs per unit. Economies of scope exist when two different products can be produced more cheaply at one firm than at two separate firms.

Edge Act: The Edge Act of 1919 permits National banking organizations to have subsidiary corporations which may have offices throughout the United States to provide a means of financing international trade, especially exports.

Electronic banking: Electronic banking refers to any banking activity accessed by electronic means such as ATMs, automated call centers, personal computers, screen telephones, and so on. These can be used to pay bills, transfer funds, apply for loans, buy mutual fund shares, and to provide other financial services.

Electronic bill presentment and payment (EBPP: Electronic bill presentment and payment (EBPP) is a substitute for the current paper-based systems for recurring bill presentment and paying processes, and for preauthorized debits to checking accounts.

Electronic money: In the broadest sense, electronic money refers to the variety of ways that electronic and other payments systems can be used as a means of exchange.

EPS: Earnings per share is calculated as earnings available for shareholders divided by the number of outstanding shares of stock.

Equity multiplier: The ratio of total assets to total equity, which a measure of financial leverage.

Euro: The Euro is the unified European currency issued by the European Central Bank. It began trading in January 1999.

Eurocurrency liabilities: Used mainly by large banks as a source of funds, these funds represent net borrowings from unrelated foreign depository institutions, loans to U.S. residents made by overseas branches of domestic depository institutions, and sales of assets by U.S. depository institutions by their overseas offices.

Eurodollar: U. S. dollar denominated deposits in foreign banks are called Eurodollar deposits.

Eurodollar deposit: This is a dollar-denominated deposit in a bank office outside of the United States. Originally dominated by European-based bank offices, the term still applies to out-of-country dollar deposits in general. Eurodollar deposits have grown with international business expansion, as firms maintain dollar deposits in foreign countries.

Euronotes: These debt securities are denominated in U.S. dollars and usually have a face value of $500,000 or more. Most of the activity in this market involves international banking. Euronotes are not registered with the Securities and Exchange Commission and cannot be sold in the United States. The major nonbank sovereign borrowers in the Euronote market are the United States, Austria, and Great Britain. Banks guarantee the sale of a borrower's short-term, negotiable promissory notes at or below predetermined interest rates. If a borrower cannot obtain short-term funds readily, the bank guarantor stands ready to do so.

Exchange clearinghouse: An organized exchange, such as the Chicago Board of Trade, Chicago Board Options Exchange, and Chicago Mercantile Exchange, that guarantees payments on futures and options contract and thereby eliminates default risk for counterparties in these financial contracts.

Exchange rate: An exchange rate is the price of one currency in terms of another, such as the dollar value of the Japanese yen.

Expectations theory: A theory of the yield curve that assumes that investors do not distinguish between short-term and long-term securities in terms of risk, such that the rate of return is inferred to be the same regardless of the investor's holding period (e.g., a two-year bond will earn the same amount as a two one - year bonds).

Explicit pricing: The interest rate associated with a deposit account, as opposed to implicit pricing that relates to noninterest expenses.

FABC: In the 1950's, the Federal Reserve Board began using the Form for Analyzing Bank Capital to classify assets into six different risk categories. Banks were required to hold a different percentage of capital against each asset category (e.g., 0.4% capital against U.S. Treasury bills and 10% capital against business loans). Also, smaller banks had higher capital requirements because of the perception that their portfolio diversification was less than larger banks.

FDIC: The Federal Deposit Insurance Corporation insures deposits held by approximately 98% of all U.S. commercial banks. Banks are required to pay premiums to insure deposit accounts up to $100,000. The FDIC regulates insured banks, with particular responsibility for state chartered independent banks (as opposed to national chartered banks and bank holding companies).

FDIC Improvement Act: The Savings and Loan Insurance Fund was dissolved and replaced with the Savings Associations Insurance Funds (SAIF). Also, healthy banks in a multibank holding company (MBHC) are liable to the FDIC for the losses of failed member banks. And, federal banking agencies are empowered to apply prompt corrective action (PCA) to undercapitalized institutions that are increasingly restrictive as an institution's capital declines.

FDIC insured deposits: The Federal Deposit Insurance Corporation (FDIC). The FDIC insures certain deposits for amounts up to $100,000 from losses due to the failure of a bank.

FRB: The Federal Reserve Board is the policy making body of the Federal Reserve System.

Facility fee: The commitment fee paid by a customer to the bank for the privilege of being able to borrow funds at a future date under a revolving line of credit. The fee, for example, may be 1/2 percent per year of the unused balance.

Federal agency securities: These securities are issued by various government agencies (e.g., the Federal Home Loan Banks, Federal National Mortgage Association, Federal Home Loan Mortgage Association, etc.) that are sponsored or owned by the federal government and, therefore, have little or no default risk. Funds are allocated to sectors of the economy that the government wishes to support in terms of financing.

Federal funds sold/purchased: These are short-term, unsecured transfers of immediately available funds (excess cash balances) between depository institutions for use in one business day (i.e., overnight loans).

Federal Home Loan Bank: The Federal Home Loan Bank system is a government sponsored enterprise (GSE) whose function is to enhance the availability of residential mortgage credit by making low-cost funds available to member institutions. Banks that are members of the system can borrow funds from regional Federal Home Loan Banks.

Fedwire: Domestic interbank payments are transferred over the Fedwire, an electronic funds transfer system that is operated by the Federal Reserve.

Fee income: Banks charge fees for services that they provide to customers, such as loan commitment fees, ATM fees, etc.

Finance charge: The finance charge is the total dollar amount paid for the use of credit. It is the difference between the amount repaid and the amount borrowed. It includes interest, service charges, and other fees that are charged the borrower as a condition of or incident to the extension of credit.

Financial guarantee: This off-balance sheet activity occurs when a bank (the guarantor) stands behind the current obligation of a third party, and will carry out that obligation if the third party fails to do so.

Financial Institutions Reform, Recovery, and Enforcement Act (FIRREA) (1989): The Federal Home Loan Bank Board (FHLBB) was closed and ceased to be the regulator for thrifts. The Office of Thrift Supervision (OTS) was established to replace it. The Federal Housing Finance Board was established.

Financial intermediation: Financial intermediaries are economic units whose principal function is obtaining funds from depositors and others, and then lending them to borrowers.

Financial leverage: The use of debt, as opposed to equity, finance. As financial leverage increases, the percentage change, or variability, of EPS increases.

Financial repression: Financial repression implies that the government intervenes heavily in the economy and in the financial markets. Most often found in developing countries.

Financial Services Modernization Act of 1999: This act, also known as the Gramm-Leach-Bliley Act, was signed into law in November 14, 1999. It marked the end of both the 1933 Glass-Steagall prohibitions concerning the separation of banks from investment banking and the 1956 Bank Holding Company Act's prohibitions on insurance underwriting.

Fixed rate mortgages: Mortgages that have level payments over time consisting of a combination of interest and principal, with higher interest payments in the early years of the mortgage and higher principal payments in later years.

Floor (or floor agreement): An interest rate floor is a contract that limits the exposure of the borrower to downward movements in interest rates by setting a minimum interest rate. A firm can implement a floor by purchasing an interest rate put option contract.

Foreign Exchange: Foreign exchange (FX) refers to exchanging one country's currency for a foreign currency.

Forward contract: The purchase or sale of an asset now for future delivery in the over-the-counter (OTC) market.

Forward market: In the forward market, contracts are not standardized, nor are they traded on organized exchanges. A forward contract is a cash market transaction in which delivery of the commodity (e.g., currency) is deferred until after the contract (a bilateral agreement between buyer and seller) has been made. Exchange rates for currencies are quoted for 30-day (1 month) forward, 90-day (3 months) forward, and 180-day (6 months) forward.

Forward rate agreement: This agreement is essentially

an over-the-counter interest rate futures contract for bonds or some other financial asset. The buyer and seller agree on the interest rate to be paid on some notional amount at a specified time in the future. The major advantages of FRAs over exchange traded futures contracts are that they can be tailored to meet the needs of the parties involved and that there are no margin requirements.

Funding-liquidity risk: The risk that insufficient cash will be available to meet the securities investment objectives of the bank.

Funds management: This liquidity management approach compares total liquidity needs to total liquidity sources.

Futures contract: A standardized agreement to buy or sell a specified quantity of a financial instrument on a specified date at a set price.

Futures option contract: an option on a futures contract that enables the buyer to only execute the futures contract in the event it is profitable, thereby avoiding daily trading losses on the futures position due to marked-to-market practices and related liquidity needs.

Garn-St Germain Depository Institutions Act of 1982: This act provided FDIC/FSLIC assistance for floundering and failing institutions; net worth certificates - an exchange of debt (called net worth certificates) between depository institutions and the regulatory agencies; additional thrift institution restructuring; and, money market deposit accounts for banks.

General market risk: Under the new market risk capital requirements for banks adopted in 1998 as an amendment to the 1988 Basle Agreement, this risk is associated with the financial market as a whole. The calculation of market-risk equivalent assets is determined by individual banks using their own internal risk model. Such a model estimates the daily value-at-risk (VAR) for the trading account assets.

Globalization: Globalization refers to the extent to which each country's economy and financial markets becomes increasingly integrated resulting in development toward a single world market.

Government backed mortgages: Mortgage loans that are insured by the Federal Housing Administration (FHA) or guaranteed by the Veterans Administration (VA) are called government backed or insured mortgages.

Graduated Payment Mortgage: A type of fixed-rate mortgage loan where the monthly payments are low at first and then rise over a period of years.

Growth stock: A stock with a high P/E (price/earnings) ratio.

Harmonization: This refers to uniform international banking regulations. It also refers to stemming the divergent standards that are applied to similar activities of different financial institutions.

Herstatt risk: Herstatt risk refers to the risk of cross currency (foreign exchange) settlements associated with differences in time zones and operating hours of banks throughout the world. Banks with different operating hours did not settle a transaction instantaneously, and some banks suffered losses when the Herstatt bank in Germany failed and did not honor its part of foreign exchange transactions.

Home equity loan: A home equity loan can be a traditional second mortgage, or a revolving line of credit in which case the line of credit has a second mortgage status, but would be the first lien if the borrower has no mortgage debt outstanding when the credit line was established.

Home Mortgage Disclosure Act: The HMDA was intended to make available to the public information concerning the extent to which financial institutions are serving the housing credit needs of their communities.

Hostile takeover: If a bank's shares are undervalued, other well-managed banks might seek to purchase a controlling interest in the bank and remove existing management.

Hubris hypothesis: The notion that the managers of the buying firm in a merger or acquisition believe that they can better manage the target firm than its current management, thereby increasing its share valuation.

IRA: Individual retirement accounts are personal pension plans that individuals may use to defer federal income taxes on contributions and subsequent investment earnings. Individuals can set aside earnings for retirement up to an allowable maximum per year. IRS rules determine how much of these contributions can be deducted for income (if any). This personal retirement account is subject to a 10-percent tax penalty if withdrawn before age 59½.

Income statement: This accounting statement contains the record of revenues, expenses, and profits during a period of time.

Inflation risk: This risk is associated with investor concern that the general price level will increase more than expected in the future. Unanticipated increases in inflation lower the purchasing power of earnings on securities. An unexpected surge in inflation can cause interest rates on bonds to suddenly increase with potentially large price declines.

Immunization: Immunization or isolation of the market value of equity to interest rate changes will be effective only if interest rates for all maturity securities shift up or down by exactly the same amount (i.e., only if the yield curve moves upward or downward by a constant percentage amount).

Implicit pricing: Noninterest expenses associated with deposit accounts, such as free checking services, which are payments in kind.

Interest-bearing liabilities: These are deposits and borrowed funds on which interest is paid.

Interest rate collar: The use of interest rate put and call options to establish both a floor and a ceiling interest rate on variable rate financial instruments. The floor benefits variable rate lenders and the ceiling benefits variable rate borrowers.

Interest rate futures contract: An interest rate futures contract is an agreement between two parties to buy (or sell) a commodity for a fixed price at a specified time in the future. Various financial instruments, such as Treasury bonds and Eurodollars, are packaged as interest rate commodities and are actively traded.

Interest rate options: Option contracts in interest bearing bonds that can be used to manage interest rate risk, including the use of interest rate caps, floors, and collars.

Interest rate parity: Under normal market conditions, investors should not be able to make arbitrage profits because the premiums or discounts in the various currencies should be exactly offset by the adjusted interest rate differentials.

Interest rate risk: Interest rate risk is the risk to earnings and capital associated with changes in market rates of interest. This risk arises from differences in timing of rate changes and the timing of cash flows (repricing risk), from changes in the shape of the yield curve (yield curve risk), and from option values embedded in bank products (options risk).

Interest rate spread: The difference between the average rate earned on earning assets on a taxable equivalent basis and the average rate paid for interest-bearing liabilities.

Interest rate swap: The exchange of obligations to pay or receive interest between two parties. It is important to note that the payments are swapped and not the underlying principal balances.

Interest rate swap: An interest rate swap is a contract in which a bank and another party (referred to as a counterparty) trade payment streams but not principal amounts. For example, a bank with a long-term fixed rate mortgage portfolio could agree to receive a floating rate payment stream and to pay the counterparty an equivalent fixed rate payment stream.

Interest-sensitive assets/liabilities: Earning assets and interest-bearing liabilities that can be repriced or will mature within a relatively short period of time.

Interest sensitivity gap: A measure of the exposure of a bank to changes in market rates of interest, its vulnerability to such changes, and the associated effect on net interest income.

Internal capital generation rate (ICR): The rate at which a bank can internally expand its assets and still maintain its capital ratio.

International banking facilities: Beginning in 1981, the Federal Reserve Board permitted domestic and foreign banks to establish international banking facilities (IBFs) to take deposits and make loans to nonresidents, and serve as a record keeping facility. In other words, an IBF is not a bank, per se, it is an accounting system.

International Lending Supervision Act: This 1983 Act gave regulators legal authority to establish minimum capital requirements and enforce them. Regulators require violating banks to submit a plan to correct a capital shortfall, which is now enforceable in the courts.

Investment banking: Underwriting original issues of stocks and bonds.

Leasing: Long-term and short term leases are used to finance tangible assets such as airliners, cars, computers, and trucks.

Investment grade: These bonds have one of four top quality ratings and have a lower probability of default than lower rated junk bonds.

Investment policy: Consistent with the overall goals of the organization, this policy seeks to maximize the return per unit risk on the investment portfolio of securities, with attention to regulatory requirements, lending needs, tax laws, liquidity sources, and other constraints on profit maximization.

Junk bonds: Corporate bonds rated below the four rating investment grade categories, which have a higher probability of default than higher rated bonds.

Keogh plans: Personal pension plans that individuals may use to defer federal income taxes on contributions and subsequent investment earnings. Keogh plans have been available to self-employed individuals since 1962. They allow up to 25 percent of earned, nonsalaried income but not greater than $30,000 to be deposited in a tax-deferred account. These personal retirement accounts are subject to a 10-percent tax penalty if withdrawn before age 59½.

Lagged reserve requirement accounting: The current method of managing reserve requirements under Federal Reserve Regulation D applicable to depository institutions, wherein a 14-day computation period begins 30 days before the 14-day maintenance period begins.

Large time deposits: These time deposits are issued in denominations of $100,000 or more and are also known as negotiable certificates of deposit (NCDs or simply CDs). Large, or "jumbo," CDs are marketable securities with maturities ranging from 14 days to 18 months.

Legal risk: As applied to over-the-counter derivatives contracts, the OTC market is private in nature, fast developing, and innovative in security design, all of which means that disputes within this new market will require a period of legal cases to clearly establish the rights and obligations of all participants.

Lender liability: Lender liability means that the lender may be sued by borrowers or others for losses and damages.

Letter of credit (LOC): This off-balance sheet activity involves a bank (the issuer) that guarantees the bank's customer (the account party) to pay a contractual debt to a third party (the beneficiary). Letters of credit are contingent liabilities because payment does not take place until the proper documents (i.e., title, invoices, etc.) are presented to the bank. Payment is dependent on the bank's creditworthiness, not the buyer's financial strength. LOCs are specific to the period of time involved in the shipment and storage of goods, result in fee income for banks from the buyer, and require the buyer to reimburse the bank for payment of goods.

Letters of credit: Commercial banks issue letters of

credit to facilitate international trade. Commercial letters of credit issued by a domestic bank in favor of a beneficiary in a foreign country are referred to as import letters of credit.

Liability management: This type of liquidity management refers to meeting liquidity needs by using outside sources of discretionary funds (e.g., Fed funds, discount window borrowings, repurchase agreements, certificates of deposit, and other borrowings).

LIBOR: LIBOR is the London interbank offered rate, the rate at which banks lend funds to other banks in the Euromarket.

Line of credit: An agreement between a bank and a customer that the bank will entertain a request for a loan from that customer and in most cases will make the loan even though not obligated to do so.

Line of credit: A line of credit is an agreement between a customer and the bank, to approve requests from the customer for a loan up to a predetermined amount. The line of credit is established when the bank gives a letter to the customer stating the dollar amount of the line, the time it is in effect (e.g., 1 year), and other conditions or provisions, such as the relationship the customer must maintain with the bank and the customer's financial condition.

Liquidity: The ability of an entity to meet its cash flow requirements. For a bank it is measured by the ability to convert assets into cash quickly with minimal exposure to interest rate risk, by the size and stability of the core funding base, and by additional borrowing capacity within the money markets.

Liquidity premium: The added return, or premium, that risk-averse lenders demand for lending funds for a longer period of time compared to a shorter period of time.

Liquidity risk: In the context of liquidity management, the risk that liquidity sources will fall short of liquidity needs. As applied to derivatives contracts, the risk that a counterparty will default and a liquidity shortfall will occur due to losses.

Liquidity Risk: Liquidity risk is the risk to earnings or capital arising from a bank's ability to meet the needs of depositors and borrowers by turning assets into cash quickly with minimal loss, being unable to borrow funds when needed, or falling short of funds to execute profitable securities trading activities.

Loan commitment: A loan commitment is an agreement between a bank and a firm to lend funds under terms that are agreed upon in writing. Loan commitments specify the amount of the commitment fee, the amount of funds to be borrowed, but the cost of borrowing depends on the prevailing rates at the time the loan is made.

Loan commitment: A bank's promise to a customer to make a future loan(s) or a guarantee under certain conditions. The agreement between the bank and the customer may be informal or formal.

Loan guarantee: A bank guarantees the repayment of a loan made from party A to party B. The guarantors assume that they are more effective credit analysts than other capital market participants because the ultimate liability of the debt is shifted from the borrower to the guarantor.

Loan loss reserves: Bank earnings that are set aside in anticipation of future loan losses. When a loan defaults, the loss does not necessarily reduce current earnings because it can be deducted from the reserve account.

Lock box: A lock box is a post office box of a business concern that is used to receive payments for goods and services sold to customers. See cash management.

Long hedge: This term applies to a long position in a financial futures contract.

Long position: The buyer in a futures contract that will benefit if the price of contract rises. This term is also used in purchasing spot market assets, such as stocks, bonds, real estate etc., with the belief that the price will rise in the future. Finally, a buyer in an options contract is said to hold a long position regardless of expected future price movements.

MMDA: A money market deposit account has no rate restrictions and allows consumers to make up to six transfers (three by check) per month. Authorized under the Garn-St Germain Act of 1982, MMDAs were designed to compete with money market mutual funds (MMMFs). Unlike MMMFs, FDIC insurance is applicable to MMDAs.

MMMF: A money market mutual fund is a mutual fund that specializes in purchasing money market instruments. Investors receive unit shares of own **Macro hedge**: Hedges that are intended to protect against the price risks associated with an entire portfolio or balance sheet.

Management information systems: Computer-based methods that measure and respond to liquidity needs by collecting both on- and off-balance sheet information and by using forecasting techniques in a simulation setting.

Mandatory convertible debt: This type of debt must be converted into equity within a stated period of time by a firm.

Margin: A performance bond that is posted with the exchange clearinghouse that guarantees the buyer or seller of the contract will fulfill the commitment. It normally is a small fraction of total value of the underlying financial instrument in futures and options contracts.

Marginal costs: The cost of funds represented by the incremental costs of acquiring an additional dollar of funds.

Marked-to-market: Gains or losses on futures and options positions are reckoned up at the end of each trading day by the exchange clearinghouse. Market participants' margin accounts are credited or debited to reflect changes in daily earnings (losses).

Market share: This measure reflects the extent of bank assets in a market (e.g., a county or metropolitan statistical area) held by one banking organization.

Marketability risk: The risk that some amount of value will be lost due to selling an asset quickly (as opposed to more slowly) in the financial market.

Market discipline: Market discipline is defined here as the mechanisms that signal the behavior of firms to holders of debt and equity who, in turn, affect the franchise value of the firm and influence its future behavior.

Market-liquidity risk: Temporary illiquidity for a bank caused by financial market turmoil that widens the bid/ask spreads of financial assets.

Market power: The ability of a bank (or other firm) to reach sufficient size to maintain its competitive position in the market.

Market risk: This risk is associated with changes in financial market conditions, including price volatility, general economic and business trends, and interest rate changes.

Market risk capital requirements: Fully implemented in January 1998, these amended rules to risk-based capital requirements under the 1988 Basle Agreement supplement the credit risk capital requirements by invoking market value rules to the risk-based capital ratio. Insured state member banks and bank holding companies with significant trading activity are exposed to the new market risk rules. Two types of market risk adjustments are necessary: (1) general market risk associated with the financial market as a whole, and (2) specific risk due to other risk factors (including credit risk of the securities issuer).

Market value accounting: These rules require banks to classify securities as "assets held for sale" (or trading) and "assets held for maturity," where the former must be valued at book value or market value, whichever is lower, and the latter is valued at book value.

Market value of equity: The market price of common stock times the number of outstanding shares. Market values reflect not only the past, such as the historical book value of equity, but also the expected future cash flows of the firm and their associated risks. Preferred stock may also be included.

Material adverse change (MAC) clause: This clause enables the bank to withdraw its standby letter of commitment (SLC) under certain conditions (e.g., the financial condition of the firm has seriously declined).

Maturity buckets: The time periods (e.g., 90 days, 180 days) used in asset/liability management are referred to as maturity buckets or planning horizons.

Megabank: Large banking institution with global operations that span a wide variety of financial services.

Merger: The purchase of a target firm by a bidder firm. The target bank is absorbed into the bidding or buying bank. As such, the target loses its bank charter, does not need a CEO and board of directors anymore, and is converted to a branch office of the buying bank.

Micro hedge: Hedges that are intended to protect against the price risks associated with a specific asset (i.e., cash or spot market asset).

Money market approach: An approach to asset management of liquidity wherein the matches the maturities of assets with specific future liquidity needs.

Moral hazard: Moral hazard is the risk that the borrower (managers) might use the borrowed funds (assets) to engage in higher risk activities in expectation of earning higher returns.

Moral hazard problem: A situation in which there are incentives for one party to take excessive risks or otherwise act irresponsibly at the expense of another party. For example, deposit insurance at fixed rates or premiums creates incentives for bank managers and shareholders to take excessive risks, as losses are paid by the insuring agency (e.g., the FDIC).

Mortgage: The term mortgage is used in connection with real estate lending. In general terms, a mortgage is a written conveyance of title to real property. It provides the lender with a security interest in the property, if the mortgage is properly recorded in the county courthouse.

Multilateral netting: As the international funds are transferred throughout the day, CHIPS calculates each participants single net position vis-à-vis all of the other participants. This system of settlement is called multilateral netting.

Municipal bonds: These debt securities are issued by state and local governments to finance various public works, such as roads, schools, fire departments, parks, and so on. Interest on these securities is not subject to federal income taxes.

Mutual Funds: A mutual fund is an investment company that pools its shareholders' funds and invests them in a portfolio of securities.

NOW: Negotiable order of withdrawal accounts were authorized nationwide in January 1981 under DIDMCA of 1980. They are interest-bearing demand deposits or checking accounts.

National bank charter: Banks chartered by the Office of the Comptroller of the Currency are national banks, having the word "national" or N.A. (National Association) in their name.

Negotiable certificates of deposit: These large time deposits are issued in denominations of $100,000 or more and are also known as NCDs or simply CDs. Large, or "jumbo," CDs are marketable securities with maturities ranging from 14 days to 18 months.

Net charge-offs: The amount of loans written off as uncollectible less recoveries of loans previouslyl written off.

Net interest margins: This financial ratio is calculated as the difference between total interest revenue and total interest expenses divided by total assets.

Networking: This refers to linkages among different companies that take advantage of comparative advantages in the production and delivery of a product. Another popular term for such joint arrangements is strategic alliance.

Nondeposit funds: As opposed to demand, savings, and

time deposits, these sources of funds include federal funds, repurchase agreements, discount window advance, Federal Home Loan Bank borrowings, bankers' acceptances, commercial paper, and notes and debentures. Generally speaking, they are money market liabilities that are purchased for relatively short periods of time to adjust liquidity demands. Because they are typically used in liability management, they are often referred to as managed liabilities.

Nonperforming assets: Loans on which interest income is not being accrued, restructured loans on which interest rates or terms of repayment have been materially revised and real properties acquired through foreclosure.

Nonpersonal time deposits: These deposits are time deposits, including savings deposits, that are not transactions accounts and that in general are not held by an individual, with the exception of money market deposit accounts (MMDAs).

Non-rate sensitive assets/liabilities: Those assets and liabilities whose interest return or cost do not vary with interest rate movements over the same time horizon are referred to as nonrate-sensitive (NRS).

OCC: The Office of the Comptroller of the Currency is the federal regulator of nationally chartered banks, which are generally the largest banks in the U.S.

Off-balance sheet activities: Financial services that do not appear on their balance sheets as assets or liabilities. Generally speaking, most off-balance sheet activities are commitments based on contingent claims, including financial guarantees and derivative instruments. A contingent claim is an obligation by a bank to provide funds (i.e., lend funds or buy securities) if a contingency is realized. In other words, the bank has underwritten an obligation of a third party and currently stands behind the risk.

Omnibus Budget Reconciliation Act of 1993: This act provided that insured depositors of failed banks have a priority of claims over noninsured depo **Operating risk:** Generally speaking, everyday risk inherent in banking practice. As applied to derivatives contracts, risks that arise due to inadequate internal controls, valuation risk, and regulatory risk.

Operational liquidity: Liquidity practice in normal everyday operations that evaluates liquidity needs and liquidity sources.

Optimum liquidity: Balancing risks and returns in liquidity management. For example, liquidity needs to sufficient to meet unexpected changes in liquidity needs and sources, but at the same time liquidity should not be so high that there is excessive opportunity costs of investing in low earning assets.

sitors/creditors claims.

Overdraft: An overdraft occurs when a customer writes a check on uncollected funds, or when there are insufficient funds in the account to cover the withdrawal.

Over-the-counter option: These options are usually written on Treasury securities and currencies that are not traded on exchanges. With no clearinghouse to act as a safety net, one party has an option to exercise a contract, while the other party has an obligation.

Participations: Banks buy parts of loans, called participations, from other banks. The buying acquiring banks have pro rata shares of the credit risk.

Passive investment strategies: These strategies do not require active management and so are simple and less cost approaches. The spaced-maturity, or ladder, approach and split-maturity, or barbell, approach are two well-known examples of these strategies.

Payments system: The payments refers to the means by which financial transactions are settled including checking accounts, coin and currency, credit cards, electronic payments, and wire transfers.

Portfolio risk: This risk considers the effects of a loan, security, or other asset on the overall risk of the bank's asset portfolio. By investing in assets with different patterns of returns over time, a bank can reduce the risk of its asset portfolio.

Preferred habitat: This theory of the yield curve takes into account all three explanations for the yield curve, including expectations, liquidity, and segmented markets theories.

Preferred stock: This type of equity pays fixed dividends that are paid before common stock dividends. However, unlike common stock, voting privileges are not normally allowed.

Prepayment risk: The risk that low interest rates will prompt increased prepayments of home loans by borrowers seeking lower mortgage rates, which causes the rate of return on mortgage-backed securities to fall as higher earning loans are replaced by lower earning loans in the agency pool of home loans.

Price-book ratio: This financial ratio is calculated as the current stock price as determined in the financial market to book value of equity as reported on the balance sheet.

Price-earnings multiple or ratio: This measure summarizes the outlook for the future of the bank--the amount of its earnings and dividends, the timing of earnings and dividends, and the risk of those earnings and dividends. It is calculated by dividing the current market price by earnings per share.

Price risk: This risk refers to the inverse relationship between changes in the level of interest rates and the price of securities.

Price, or market, risk (derivatives): This is the risk that the market price of the derivative security will change, which is closely related to the price risk of the underlying instrument. Most banks break overall price risk into components, including interest rate risk, exchange rate risk, commodity price risk, and others.

Pricing policy: A written document that contains the pricing details of deposit services, it addresses a number of key areas, including service fees versus minimum balance requirements, deposit costs and volumes and their relationship to profits, credit availability and compensating balances, customer relationship pricing, promotional pricing of new products, and other relevant factors.

Pricing strategy: Banks attempt to price deposits to take into account a combination of convenience (e.g., ATMs, or automated teller machines), service charges, minimum balances to avoid service charges or earn interest (or both), and other unique characteristics of the particular account. In general, these pricing features are traded off against one another in the pricing mix.

Primary capital: This measures of equity capital was used by federal regulars in measuring capital adequacy in the 1980s. Primary capital was defined as common stock, perpetual preferred stock, capital surplus, undivided profits, capital reserves, and other nondebt instruments.

Primary reserve: Cash held in a bank's vault and on deposit at a Federal Reserve district bank for the purpose of meeting reserve requirements and other cash needs of the bank.

Prime rate: The prime rate on business loans is a reference interest rate used by banks to price their loans.

Private banking: Private banking refers to custom tailored services provided to high net worth individuals.

Product differentiation: This liabilities management strategy seeks to design products and services to meet the needs of specific market segments.

Profit margin: This financial ratio provides information about the ability of management to control expenses, including taxes, given a particular level of operating income. It is calculated as net income to operating revenue.

Promotional pricing: This liabilities management strategy is used to introduce new products by pricing below cost to attract market attention. More frequently, promotional pricing is used to support or rejuvenate demand for existing products.

Provision for loan losses (PLL): This expense item on the income statement represents fund set aside in the next accounting period to absorb anticipated loan losses.

Prudential regulation: Prudential regulation of banks deals with their safety and soundness.

Purchased deposits: These funds are acquired on an impersonal basis from the financial market by offering competitive interest rates and serve as a liquidity reserve.

Put option: This options contract gives the buyer the right (although not the obligation) to sell a specified underlying security at a price stipulated in the contract and the seller the obligation to buy the underlying security at that price.

Quality spread: The difference in interest rates on underlying assets (or liabilities) in a swap involving the exchange of payments or receipts between a firm with higher quality assets (liabilities) and another firm with lower quality assets (liabilities).

RAROC: The Risk-Adjusted Return on Capital allocated equity capital depending on risk of loss, calculates a required rate of return on equity, and then uses this information in pricing loans to make sure that they are profitably to the bank. It is generally employed for the purpose of internal performance evaluations.

Rate of return: This measure of what an investor obtains from holding a share of stock for a year or some other period is composed of two parts: (1) the dividend return (D_t) and (2) the capital gain in the value of the stock ($P_t - P_{t-1}$).

Rate-sensitive assets/liabilities: Those assets and liabilities whose interest return or costs vary with interest rate changes over some given time horizon are referred to as rate-sensitive assets (RSAs) or rate-sensitive liabilities (RSLs).

Real Estate Settlement Procedures Act: The intent of RESPA is to provide buyers and sellers with information about the settlement process. RESPA covers most residential real estate loans including lots for houses or mobile homes.

Real-time gross settlements (RTGS) system. RTGS means that the system (such as the Federal Reserve) settles each payments transaction individually as they occur, rather then processing them in a batch.

Regulation Q: This regulation placed a ceiling on interest rates payable by banks on deposit accounts. In the 1980s it was deregulated for the most part.

Relationship banking: This approach to bank management encompasses the total financial needs of the public rather than just specific needs. It also includes fulfilling long-term needs, as opposed to immediate needs, such as cashing a check. This can be done by cross-selling a variety of services that tends to lower user costs and increase convenience compared to selling each service separately. Also, patrons are viewed as clients, as opposed to customers, according to this viewpoint.

Relative gap ratio: The relative gap ratio expresses the dollar amount of the gap (dollar RSAs – dollar RSLs) as a percentage of total assets.

Report of Condition: This accounting statement is the balance sheet.

Report of Income: This accounting statement is the income statement.

Repurchase agreements: RPs or repos are securities purchased (sold) under agreement to resell (repurchase) with a securities dealer. An overnight RP can be defined as a secured, one-day loan in which claim to the collateral is transferred. Multiple-day RPs can be arranged for a fixed term ("term RPs") or on a continuing basis. The repurchase price is typically the initial sale price plus a negotiated rate of interest.

Reserve for loan losses: This account is reported on the asset side to the balance sheet and is also known as the allowance for loan losses. It is calculated as the cumulative PLL minus net loan charge-offs. Since this reserve is subtracted from total loans to get net loans, it is a contra-asset account. Part of the reserve for loan losses is counted as capital reserves on the right-hand-side of the balance sheet.

Residential mortgage loans: These are loans used to finance 1-4 family home mortgage loans.

Retail CDs: This is a small time deposit of less than $100,000.

Return on average assets (ROA): A measure that indicates how effectively an entity uses its total resources. It is calculated by dividing the net income by average assets.

Return on equity (ROE): A measure of how productively an entity's equity has been employed. It is calculated by dividing annual net income by total equity.

Reverse annuity mortgage: Owners borrower against the equity in their homes, and the loan is repaid at the borrower's demise.

Revolving consumer loans: Revolving consumer loans, or open-end credit, are those where the borrower has a line of credit up to a certain amount, and may payoff the loans and credit charges over an indefinite period of time. Revolving loans have no definite maturity.

Revolving commercial loans: A revolving commercial loan is an agreement between a customer and the bank, to borrow a predetermined amount of funds. Revolving loans are to finance borrowers' temporary and seasonal working capital needs. The bank is obligated to make the loans up to the maximum amount of the loan, if the borrower is in compliance with the terms of the agreement.

Revolving loan commitment: A formal agreement between the bank and a customer obligating the bank to lend funds per the terms of the contract.

Riegle-Neal Interstate Banking and Branching Efficiency Act of 1994: The act opened the door for interstate banking by allowing bank holding companies to acquire banks in any state, subject to certain conditions. Beginning in 1997, the Act eased most restrictions on interstate branching.

Risk-adjusted assets: Used in calculating risk-based capital requirements under the 1988 Basle Agreement, this dollar amount is a weighted sum of different categories of bank assets.

Risk-based capital rules: International capital rules for banking institutions under the 1988 Basle Agreement that establish standardized requirements based on credit risk and market risk. Off-balance sheet activities are included in the calculations.

Risk-based deposit insurance: Adopted by the FDIC in 1994, the strongest institutions pay 0 cents per each $100 of domestic deposits, while the weakest pay 27 cents. Premiums can vary within this range for institutions depending on capital levels and supervisory ratings.

Savings certificate: This is a small time deposit of less than $100,000.

Secondary reserve: Near-money financial instruments that have no formal regulatory requirements and provide an additional reserve of liquid assets above primary reserves to meet cash needs.

Securitization: Securitization is the issuance of a debt instrument in which the promised payments are derived from revenues generated by a defined pool of loans. The pools include mortgage loans, credit card loans, car loans, and loans to businesses.

Segmented markets: A theory of the yield curve that argues that the financial market is divided into a money market and a capital market, with different supply and demand forces in these two separate markets.

Seigniorage: Seigniorage is considered the interest saved by the Treasury from having currency, which is non-interest bearing debt, circulation as a medium of exchange.

Settlement risk: A type of credit risk where financial transactions may not settle: See Herstatt risk.

Settlement risk: This occurs when one party in a financial transaction pays out funds to the other party before it receives its own cash or assets. Thus, settlement risk is linked to credit risk.

Shared national credit: Participations by three or more unaffiliated banks in loans or formal loan commitments in excess of $20 million are called shared national credits.

Short position: The seller in a futures contract that will benefit if the price of contract falls. This term is also used in borrowing spot market assets (such as stocks and bonds) from a brokerage firm, selling them into the financial market, and then repurchasing them later and returning the assets to the brokerage firm under the belief that the repurchase price will be less than the selling price due to fall in pricesl over time. Finally, a seller in an options contract is said to hold a short position regardless of expected future price movements.

SIBOR: SIBOR is the Singapore intermarket offered rate on loans.

Simulated asset/liability models: Simulations are used to evaluate the dollar gap, duration gap, and other asset/liability measures to changes in interest rates and various balance sheet strategies.

Sources and uses of funds method: A method of estimating future liquidity needs of a bank by evaluating potential future changes in its individual asset and liability accounts.

Sovereign risk: Sovereign risk occurs when a national government defaults on debts, or refuses to permit loans to be repaid or seizes bank assets without adequate compensation.

Specific risk: Under the new market risk capital requirements for banks adopted in 1998 as an amendment to the 1988 Basle Agreement, this risk is associated with other risk factors (including credit risk of the securities issuer) not covered by general market risk. It can be calculated either using standardized measurement methods or using the bank's individual internal model.

Standby letter of credit: A letter of credit that is only payable in the event of a default, such as bond issuer failing to make interest payments.

Standby letters of credit (SLCs): These off-balance sheet guarantees obligate the bank to pay the beneficiary if the account party defaults on a financial obligation or performance contract.

Stress testing: This refers to testing the "worst case" scenarios in simulated asset/liability models.

Structure-of-deposits method: This method of evaluating future liquidity needs lists the different types of deposits of a bank and then assigns a probability of withdrawal to each type of deposit with a specific planning horizon.

Subordinated notes and debentures: These sources of long-term debt is second in priority to depositor claims in the event of bank failure.

Super-NOW accounts: Established by DIDMCA of 1980, these accounts were similar to NOW accounts at that time but had no interest rate ceiling. Effective January, 1983, later deregulation of interest rates in 1986 eliminated the distinction between NOWs and Super NOWS.

Surplus: This is the amount of paid-in capital in excess of par value realized by a bank upon the initial sale of stock.

Swap: An agreement between two counterparties to exchange cash flows based upon some notional principal amount of money, maturity, and interest rates.

Swaption: This contract represents an option on a swap. The buyer has the right (but not the obligation) to enter into an interest rate swap at terms specified in the contract.

Sweep Accounts: Sweep accounts are used for the temporary transfer of funds from non-interest bearing transaction accounts into an investment account where the funds earn interest.

Sweep programs: This retail deposit service moves funds from transactions accounts (e.g., NOW accounts) with reserve requirements to savings accounts with no reserve requirements. In many cases the deposits over a designated level are upstreamed from the bank to the parent bank holding company or another affiliate bank for reinvestment in commercial paper and other money market instruments. As such, these programs offer better average yields to depositors than transactions accounts alone and enable the bank to free up some reserves for investment in loans and other assets.

S.W.I.F.T: The Society for Worldwide Interbank Financial Telecommunications is a cooperative owned by banks throughout the world to facilitate payments and financial messages among its members. S.W.I.F.T is used primarily for communications and the actual transfers of funds are done by the CHIPS and the Fedwire: Domestic interbank payments are transferred over the Fedwire, an electronic funds transfer system that is operated by the Federal Reserve.

Syndication: When underwriting new securities issues, a group of investment banking firms, called the syndicate, buy stocks and bonds from the corporation or governments issuing the new securities, and then sells them to the public. Loans can be syndicated as well, and sold to other banks and investors.

Synergy: Economies of scale and scope associated with mergers and acquisitions that drive down operating costs per unit output of financial services.

Synthetic loan: When a bank uses an interest rate futures contract (or other derivative contract) to "convert" a floating rate loan into a fixed rate loan.

Target: This is the seller in a merger or acquisition involving two firms.

Taxable equivalent income: Income that has been adjusted by increasing tax exempt income to a level that is comparable to taxable income before any taxes are applied.

Tax-equivalent yield: The before-tax yield on a taxable bond (such as a corporate and government bond) that is comparable to the yield on a municipal security of similar risk which is partially taxable.

Temporary investments ratio: This ratio is a measure of bank liquidity and is calculated by adding Federal funds sold plus securities with maturities of one year or less plus cash due from banks divided by total assets.

Term loan: A term loan is usually a single loan for a stated period of time, or a series of loans on specified dates. They are used for a specific purpose, such as acquiring machinery, renovating a building, refinancing debt, and so forth.

Tier 1 capital: This so-called "core" capital under risk-based capital requirements is equal to the sum of tangible equity, including common stock, surplus, retained earnings, and perpetual preferred stock.

Tier 2 capital: This so-called "supplemental" capital under risk-based capital requirements is comprised of loan loss reserves, subordinated debt, intermediate-term preferred stock, and other items counted previously as primary capital (e.g., mandatory convertible debt and cumulative perpetual preferred stock with unpaid dividends).

Time and savings deposits: Small deposits of less than $100,000 may be acquired through time deposits (otherwise known as savings certificates, or retail CDs) and savings deposits. Small time deposits can be offered with denominations as low as $1,000. These deposits have fixed maturities and yields that approximate those of Treasury securities of equal maturity. A slight premium is normally required by depositors over the Treasury yield, however, because these deposit instruments are nonnegotiable and have early withdrawal penalties attached to them.

Too-Big-To Fail doctrine: The TBTF policy has been applied by governments when they believe that some event will result in severe economic distress. In the United States, the government has intervened on behalf of large banks, railroads (Reconstruction Finance

Corporation), troubled government sponsored enterprises (The Farm Credit System), Chrysler Corporation, and labor strikes.

Total capital: In banks this total is comprised of equity, long-term debt, and capital reserves (otherwise known as the allowance for loan losses).

Total return swap: A twist on the credit swap, wherein bank A (for example) swaps payments received on a risky loan portfolio for a cash flow stream from bank B comprised of a benchmark rate of interest (e.g., LIBOR) plus some negotiated compensation for the credit risk premium that it has given up. This swap tranfers the credit risk from bank A to bank B, even though bank B did not make the loan.

Trade finance: Banks providing services to facilitate payments in international trade is commonly referred to as trade finance.

Transactions accounts: All deposits on which the account holder is permitted to make withdrawals by various means to make payments to third parties or others, including demand deposits, NOW accounts, and share draft accounts (offered by credit unions).

Treasury bills: These are direct obligations of the U.S. government that have an original maturity of one year or less.

Treasury notes and bonds: These are direct obligations of the U.S. government that have an original maturity exceeding one year. Notes generally have maturities in the 1 to 5 year range, while bonds have maturities greater than 5 years.

Trust: A trust is established by a "grantor" (the creator of the trust) who transfers assets to a trust that is managed by the "trustee" for the benefit of the beneficiaries in accordance with the terms of the trust agreement.

Truth in Lending: The purpose of the Truth in Lending Act is for creditors to disclose to individual consumers who are borrowers the amount of the finance charge and the annual interest rate (APR) they are paying to facilitate the comparison of finance charges from different sources of credit.

Undivided profits: This equity account equals retained earnings, which are the cumulative net profits of the bank not paid out in the form of dividends to shareholders.

Uniform Bank Performance Report (UBPR): This report is published by the Federal Financial Institutions Examination Council (FFIEC) and contains various financial ratio reports for individual banks.

Value-at-risk (VAR): This risk measure considers the maximum amount that could be lost in investment and lending activities in a specified period of time. More specifically, given a certain probability and holding period, VAR gives the amount by which the investment or loan portfolio will decline in value.

Value stock: A stock with a low P/E (price/earnings) ratio.

Volatile liability dependency: This ratio is a measure of bank liquidity and is calculated by subtracting temporary investments from volatile liabilities (i.e., brokered deposits, jumbo CDs, deposits in foreign offices, Federal funds purchased, and other borrowings) and dividing by net loans and leases.

Wholesale cost of funds: The interest costs of large CDs and other large deposit and nondeposit funds.

Yield curve: A plot of yields of Treasury securities with different maturities. Plots for other types of bonds are possible, assuming all risks except those related to the time to maturity are held constant.

Yield spread: The difference in yields between low- and high-quality bonds.

INDEX

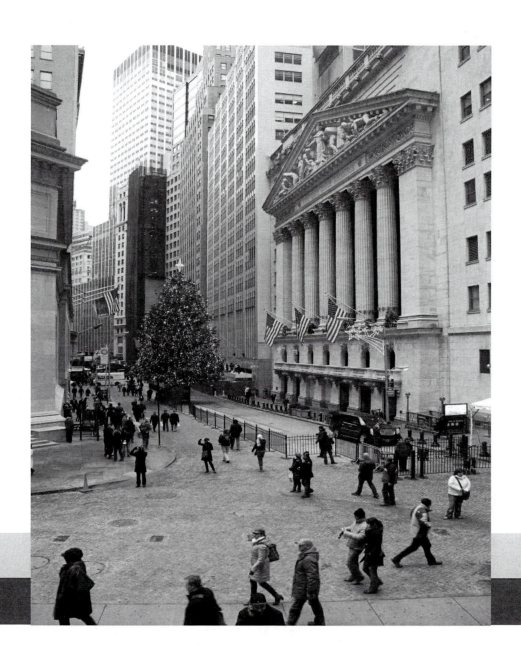

F

H

I

M

Z